The publisher gratefully acknowledges the generous contribution to this book provided by the following individuals and organizations:

JOHN M. AND JOLA ANDERSON

FRANK A. CAMPINI FOUNDATION

ELDORADO FOUNDATION

DAVID B. GOLD FOUNDATION

WILLIAM AND FLORA HEWLETT FOUNDATION

PATRICIA S. DINNER

and by the General Endowment Fund of the University of California Press.

The Advent Project

Nave showing the schola cantorum, San Clemente (12th century, with earlier materials), Rome.

The Advent Project
The Later-Seventh-Century Creation of the Roman Mass Proper

JAMES McKINNON

University of California Press

BERKELEY   LOS ANGELES   LONDON

University of California Press
Berkeley and Los Angeles, California

University of California Press, Ltd.
London, England

© 2000 by the Regents of the University of California

Library of Congress Cataloging-in-Publication Data

McKinnon, James W., 1932–.
The Advent project : the later-seventh-century creation of the Roman Mass proper /
    James McKinnon.
        p.   cm.
    Includes bibliographical references and index.
    ISBN 0-520-22198-2 (alk. paper)
    1. Mass (Music)—500–1400.   2. Propers (Music)—500–1400— History and criticism.   3. Chants (Plain, Gregorian, etc.)—History and criticism.   4. Church music—Catholic Church—500–1400.   I. Title.
ML3088.M35   2000
782.32'35'094563209021—dc21   99-056492
                                                              CIP
                                                              MN

Manufactured in the United States of America

09 08 07 06 05 04 03 02 01 00

10 9 8 7 6 5 4 3 2 1

The paper used in this publication is both acid-free and totally chlorine-free (TCF). The paper used in this publication meets the minimum requirements of ANSI/NISO Z39.48-1992 (R 1997) (*Permanence of Paper*). ∞

This novice's volume is dedicated to Helmut Hucke, Michel Huglo, David Hughes and Kenneth Levy, giants on whose shoulders I presume to stand.

Contents

		List of Tables	ix
		Acknowledgments	xi
		Introduction	1
I:	THE PREHISTORY		
	1.	The First Centuries	19
	2.	The Later Fourth Century	35
	3.	Centuries of Silence: Gaul	60
	4.	Centuries of Silence: Rome and England	77
II:	THE SEVENTH-CENTURY ROMAN BACKGROUND		
	5.	Sacramentary, Lectionary and Antiphoner	101
	6.	Dating the Mass Proper I: Advent and the Thursdays in Lent	125
	7.	Dating the Mass Proper II: The Sanctorale	154
III:	THE ADVENT PROJECT		
	8.	The Introit	195
	9.	The Gradual	222
	10.	The Alleluia	249
	11.	The Tract	280
	12.	The Offertory	298
	13.	The Communion	326
	14.	The Creation of the Roman Mass Proper	356
		Epilogue: The Central Question of Gregorian Chant	375
		Notes	405
		Works Cited	445
		Index	455

Tables

1. Gregorian and PI-type gospels compared — 114
2. Roman and Frankish Lenten introits — 126
3. Roman and Frankish Advent-Christmas introits — 130
4. Lenten Thursday communions — 134
5. Roman Advent-Christmas communions — 138
6. Roman Ember Day introits and communions — 143
7. Roman Ember Day graduals and offertories — 145
8. Advent in seventh-century Roman liturgical books — 148
9. Advent Sunday stations in chant books — 152
10. Roman Paschaltime sanctorale (comparison of liturgical books) — 159
11. The Roman sanctorale — 160
12. Unique sanctoral chants in Vat lat 5319 — 174
13. The four seventh-century Marian feasts — 182
14. Melodic formulas in Roman Paschaltime introits — 203
15. Roman Advent-Christmas introits — 209
16. Roman temporal Paschaltime introits — 211
17. Post-Pentecostal introits, Roman and Gregorian — 212
18. Roman Advent-Christmas graduals — 232
19. The gradual responds of the Psalter of St-Germain-des-Prés — 237
20. Post-Pentecostal graduals — 242

21. Roman alleluia repertory (with Byzantine textual concordances) — 255
22. Roman Easter week vesper alleluias — 258
23. Roman and Frankish Christmastime alleluias — 262
24. Roman and Frankish Paschaltime alleluias — 264
25. Post-Pentecostal alleluias—melodic continuity with Gregorian — 268
26. Roman tracts — 284
27. Roman temporal G-8 tracts — 290
28. Roman sanctoral tracts — 292
29. The text of the offertory verse *Ego autem* — 304
30. Roman Christmastime offertories—textual adjustment — 310
31. Roman Paschaltime offertories — 317
32. Roman post-Pentecostal offertories — 319
33. Roman Advent-Christmas communions — 330
34. Lenten weekday communions — 332
35. Roman Paschaltime communions — 340
36. Roman post-Pentecostal communions — 344
37. The assignments of *Domine quinque talenta* — 350

Acknowledgments

When I was diagnosed with cancer in April 1998, I had fortunately just finished a carefully wrought draft of the entire book. Up to that point my work had been a solitary effort of sorts. What I mean by this is that I had not sought a publisher, had not shared the reading of chapters with colleagues, had not asked their advice on certain issues or sought out their advice on various controversial matters. I certainly let my friends know what I was up to, but I did everything pretty much on my own.

This is not to say that I did not feel an immense sense of gratitude to others, namely, to the community of chant scholars as a whole, who provided the context without which an endeavor such as mine would lack all meaning. I felt this with particular keenness, perhaps, because I came to chant studies late in my career but was warmly welcomed nonetheless by those who had devoted their lives to the discipline. I have in mind, for example, being invited to become a regular participant in the magnificent series of *Cantus Planus* meetings promoted by László Dobszay and his Hungarian colleagues. I was able also to look on in admiration at the tireless efforts of Ruth Steiner to maintain her CANTUS project, which has doubtless done more than any comparable endeavor to encourage young scholars from virtually every country in the western world to take up chant studies as their academic specialty. And then there is an individual, David Hiley, who amounts in effect to an institution, seemingly omnipresent in his efforts to aid any project or any person involved in chant, and ever inspiring by the sheer quality of his own scholarship.

I have benefited in a more individual way by conversations on music in seventh- and eighth-century Rome with that small cadre of scholars particularly qualified to engage in such a rarified pastime. I have in mind especially Joseph Dyer, Edward Nowacki, Peter Jeffery and John Boe; the last named scholar, especially, never ceased to astonish me with the uncannily pertinent questions with which he was able to challenge my not always carefully thought out hypotheses. It is one of my regrets that I did not have the time to submit whole chapters to his critical eye. There have, to be sure, been valuable conversations on chant with more than the select group of Romanisti just mentioned. Here I surely offend by omissions, but I must at least record the pleasure and profit I have experienced in discussing chant more broadly with Charles Atkinson, Calvin Bower, Alejandro Planchart, James Borders and Claire Maître. Again I speak here of that rich general context of chant scholarship without which I might not have thought it worthwhile to pursue my project.

I have, moreover, received a special kind of encouragement about the book from at least two individuals. Thomas Kelly has allowed no occasion to pass without urging me on to its completion and has even requested that publishers goad me to do so as well. Richard Crocker has performed a similar function with his series of penetrating and witty letters in reaction to the various minor publications I have sent him over the past several years. He has gone so far as to claim that he would have these put together in book form on his own if I did not get on soon to the long awaited publication phase myself. Crocker, by the way, is the scholar who has to my mind put forth the wisest overview of both Roman and Frankish chant, particularly in the masterful survey that appears in *The New Oxford History of Music*.

The book is dedicated to Helmut Hucke, Michel Huglo, David Hughes and Kenneth Levy, not just because they are among the greatest chant scholars of our time, figures without whom my work would be impossible, but because all four were particularly warm and generous to me personally as I made my first tentative efforts in the early 1990s at speaking and writing within their domain.

If work on the book had been something of a solitary affair up to the time of the April diagnosis, this stopped abruptly at that point. Offers of help in every form flowed in from one colleague after another, but the most tangible and practical source of such help was to come from my friends here in Chapel Hill. Severine Neff set the tone as she was about to embark upon a year's Fulbright fellowship in Moscow; she said, in words to this effect: "Be rude, Jim, don't waste time socializing; tell them you have a book to finish." Since then I have tried hard not to be rude, but I have been single-mindedly in attempting to revise my manuscript. Help has been lavish. Letitia Glozer, my teaching assistant in the last difficult days of that spring semester, took over much of my nonpersonal correspondence and eventually reworked the entire footnote and abbreviation apparatus of the manuscript into *Chicago* style. Colleagues such as James Haar, Sean Gallagher and John Nádas not only helped by their constant encouragement but did, moreover, every sort of specific help that was called for. John Nádas, for example, saw to it that all the computers involved were operating with the same software and in the end translated the entire document from my own preferred language to another more acceptable to the publisher. James Haar was particularly helpful in securing the best possible publisher. I had had conversations myself for several years about the book with Bruce Phillips of Oxford University Press and regret that it became impossible to follow through with him. On his suggestion, however, we turned to Lynne Withey at the University of California Press, with altogether happy results.

But it was my young colleague Brad Maiani who did the most. When, in early June 1998, I was able to resume work, I penciled and inked in revisions at a rate that surprised us all. Brad typed everything in, but it was the typing of an experienced chant scholar and one, moreover, thoroughly acquainted with my peculiar approach to the subject, and also with my rabbit warren of a study with its labyrinthian filing system. He tracked down dozens of elusive references and questioned my inconsistencies and above all reviewed my musical analysis. He made numerous suggestions, some of which were accepted and some of which were not, probably to the detriment of the final product. The final product is, by the way, totally mine, down to every last word and punctuation mark of the prose; I had at my beck and call scholars of superb editorial ability, figures such as Haar, Nádas and Gallagher, but I stubbornly insisted that no one but me would bear any responsibility for whatever infelicities of thought or presentation that the book may hold. Brad, finally, provided all the musical examples with his unique ability to produce elegant neumatic notation on the computer. In short, I simply could not have finished the book without him.

Nor could I have finished the book without the support of my family. My beloved wife, Sally, tolerated my neglect of much else, and above all sustained me physically and spiritually during a period that had to be immeasurably more trying for her than for me. My five children—Rita, James, Mary, Neil and Paula—surpassed one another in their constant care; at no time, in hospital or in home, was there not at least one of them (along with Sally) by my side. Nor were their spouses—Natalie, Dawn, Philippe and Timothy—to be outdone in their own display of consideration. Finally I must mention my six adored grandchildren—Joel, Sarah, Sophia, Aurianna, Jimmy and Christine—who gave me joy beyond what any man deserves.

Editorial Note

James McKinnon died on February 23, 1999. He lived long enough to see and greet a number of distinguished scholars, all of them personal friends, who gathered in Chapel Hill to honor him at a symposium on topics in early chant history. Since his death several of his departmental colleagues have taken on the task of seeing this book through to publication. Among those deserving of thanks is Harrison O'Dell Williams, who compiled the list of works cited. In our task we have been greatly helped by the sympathetic cooperation of Lynne Withey, senior editor at the University of California Press, and by the editorial acumen of Edith Gladstone, who copyedited the manuscript, and of Rachel Berchten of the Press's editorial staff. Our sincere thanks go to them and to all at the Press who have helped make this book an achievement we are proud of and something the author, at once the kindest of human beings and the most demanding of scholars, might, we hope, give his seal of approval.

Chapel Hill
November 1999

Introduction

The creation of the Roman Mass Proper must have been something like constructing a house while living in it. The Roman cantors did not have the luxury of waiting for its completion before having to sing Mass each day. They might have concentrated on graduals one year and on introits another, while every year they had to deal with the complication of a temporal cycle and a sanctoral cycle that were intermeshed from day to day. They labored more systematically on the temporal cycle than the sanctoral dates, and they found the shorter genres of introit and communion more manageable than the longer graduals and offertories—not to speak of alleluias and tracts. They appear at a certain point to have stopped work on the project (sometime in the later seventh century) without having finished it according to plan. The result was an impressive if imperfect edifice: the Advent-Christmas season (to pursue the figure to the end) presented a splendid facade, admirable in every detail; Lent and Paschaltime provided a substantially complete interior, although the latter showed signs of hasty improvisation; and the post-Pentecostal season stood at the rear as little more than an unroofed frame.

Such a view of the Mass Proper implies that it was the product of a plan, something undertaken and executed within a limited period of time (what I call the "Advent Project," for reasons to be made clear later in this introduction). The notion that the Mass Proper is more the result of a concerted short-term effort than of a centuries-long process of incremental change is not unique to me; something similar to it has recommended itself to other scholars, particularly those who have attempted to account for the entire body of the chant rather than to focus on some limited aspect of it. I have in mind especially the eminent Peter Wagner and his admirable contemporaries, the earlier twentieth-century monks of Solesmes.[1] They knew chant either from a lifetime of study or from singing it every day in choir, and they observed, particularly in the Mass Proper as it unfolded throughout the liturgical year, numerous signs of planning and design. But they saw the hand of Gregory the Great (590–604) in it all; they viewed him as personally supervising a systematic revision of the chant by his *schola cantorum*.[2] I, on the other hand, look upon the first Gregory as a pope who was much too occupied with other matters—no less, for example, than the physical survival of Rome and its inhabitants—to take much interest in liturgy and chant. I see a revision of the chant (if "revision" is the correct word) as taking place considerably later; at one time I was even inclined to see a role in it for Gregory II (715–31), the pope that François-Auguste Gevaert already in 1890 proposed as *the* authentic Gregory,[3] although in the course of writing the present volume I came to think that it was Sergius I (687–701) who presided over the conclusion of the process.

Wagner and the Solesmes scholars devoted their efforts more or less equally to Mass and Office. I lack the capacity to do so and find that I must limit myself in the present study to the Mass Proper, omitting even the Mass Ordinary. And some might consider an attempt to treat the approximately six hundred chants of the Mass Proper within a single volume an overly ambitious enterprise, indeed one smacking of hubris. Be that as it may, I will endeavor to provide a balanced survey of the entire Mass Proper, hoping that others will step in and remedy what are certain to be lapses in my coverage. As for exclusion of the Office, this is done not only in the hope of making my task somewhat more manageable, but also because I have come to see the development of Mass and Office as histories that differ in kind. The two experienced their periods of maximum growth at different times, in response to different circumstances and at the hands of different ecclesiastical constituencies. Still, the Office chants cannot be ignored altogether in a study of Mass chants; neither body of music can be understood in complete isolation from the other, and I will try in these pages to summarize how the chants of the Roman Office might have influenced those of the Mass. Primarily the responsibility of monastic rather than clerical singers, the Office chants appear to have experienced considerable development earlier than those of the Mass, although the latter—in the burst of creative activity that is the subject of this book—moved to a state of relative completion that was matched by the music of the Office only much later, if at all.

I differ from my distinguished betters, too, in that I attempt to tell what took place in seventh-century Rome rather than to rest content with the study of what we call Gregorian chant. It is, of course, the Gregorian chant

—that dominant branch of western ecclesiastical song that came about from the eighth- and ninth-century Frankish absorption and transformation of the Roman chant—that I, along with most other students of western chant, know and love best. I was privileged to sing it on a daily basis throughout my adolescence and early adult years, even if I cannot claim anything like the intimate relationship with it that some Benedictine monks continue to enjoy even today. It is, as much as anything else, the sheer beauty of this incomparable music that drives me to inquire into its origins. But I find myself perplexed by the tendency of some to discuss questions of chant origins while using only Gregorian evidence. Not infrequently, for example, we witness an attempt to define the earliest chants of a particular genre by analyzing the Gregorian version of their melodies and placing them in the context of Frankish liturgy—this, while the chants in question are clearly part of the core repertory transmitted from Rome to the Carolingian realm in the eighth century.

THE PREHISTORY

If I speak repeatedly here of seventh- and eighth-century Rome, I do not mean to say that nothing of significance took place before then. It is simply that I have come to look upon this period as the most crucial in the formation of Roman chant; I date the so-called Advent Project, my name for the ambitious plan that brought about the final revision of the Roman Mass Proper, to the later decades of the seventh century. But I aim in this volume, nevertheless, to trace the formation of the Mass Proper from its early Christian beginnings.

Indeed my career as a scholar began with a study of early Christianity, my 1966 Columbia University dissertation, "The Church Fathers and Musical Instruments." The topic seemed to me at the time a comparatively unproblematic one from a conceptual point of view. It does so still. The Church Fathers, sharp-tongued polemicists such as Augustine, Jerome, Basil and John Chrysostom, left little doubt as to their attitude toward the uses of musical instruments in the pagan culture of their day. But what these authors had to say about the liturgical song of their time was more elusive in character; their remarks, though numerous, struck me as isolated, fragmentary and oblique. It was not until two decades later, when I attempted to assemble in my *Music in Early Christian Literature*[4] virtually all such patristic references to early Christian chant and to place them in chronological and regional order, that I began to reconstruct a reasonably clear outline of the subject's history. I speak, of course, not of musical style and substance, but of matters such as the origins of a particular genre of chant, its liturgical placement and the singers who performed it.

The most dramatic developments of that history took place in the later fourth and earlier fifth centuries, during a period when the Church flourished after its emancipation under Emperor Constantine in 313. Coincidental with this era of ecclesiastical prosperity was the golden age of patristic literary production, allowing us to chart with a considerable degree of confidence the achievements of the time in liturgy and chant. I would estimate that there exist somewhere between two and three hundred references to church song from this period; I have counted well more than one hundred and fifty from the sermons of St. Augustine alone.[5] This rich flow of patristic writing, however, was not to continue; it came to a halt almost overnight—the flow slowing to a trickle—as the Roman Empire was overrun by waves of invading Germanic tribes. Emblematic of the close of an era was the death of Augustine in 430, at the very moment the Vandals laid siege to his episcopal seat of Hippo.

For the two or three following centuries the historiographic approach taken in this volume must radically shift—from an attempt to define a liturgical and musical norm from relatively abundant evidence to a search for any sort of a coherent pattern from extremely sparse and scattered remarks about sacred song in contemporary documents. Making the task more difficult is the circumstance that this material, scarce as it is, is better represented in Gallican and English sources than in Roman ones. In aid of speculation about the Roman situation, however, is the immensely valuable *Ordo romanus I*, which provides us with a detailed description of the papal Mass in about 700. We have, then, a fairly clear view of the early-fifth-century Mass and a remarkably full one of the late-seventh-century Mass, presenting us with the task of filling in the gap, so to speak. Here we have more to go on for some items of the Mass Proper than for others. The existence of the gradual psalm, for example, is not only well established by the end of the fourth century but is cited occasionally during these "centuries of silence" (as they will be called here in the titles of chapters three and four). The introit and offertory psalms, on the other hand, are not cited in either patristic sources or in those of the interim period but are clearly referred to in *Ordo romanus I*. Speaking of their origins, then, is in one sense a matter of pure guessing, but still there are, it is hoped, enough indications in the later evidence to render the exercise of peering backward into the darkness a historically responsible one.

SEVENTH-CENTURY ROME: MUSICAL ARCHEOLOGY

There is much of such peering backward in this book, and when it reaches its goal of seventh-century Rome, one form of that exercise simply replaces another. Here it amounts to a sort of musical archeology. We have no musical sources from seventh-century Rome, whether notated or unnotated, so that we are required to study the later collections of Mass chants, both Roman and Frankish, for indications of how the annual cycles might have developed. A roughly similar process has long since been employed by liturgical historians in their attempt to reconstruct the annual cycles of orations and readings for seventh-century Rome. These scholars, too, had to work without benefit of seventh-century Roman manuscripts yet managed, by a study of eighth- and ninth-century Frankish documents, to establish with near certainty the Roman evangeliary of about 645, for example, and the papal sacramentary of about 680.[6]

That no one has heretofore attempted anything of the sort with the Roman Mass chants reflects the nature of the task, seemingly analogous to that undertaken for orations and readings but in fact more complex and less likely to yield precisely certain results. Still the outcome, I hope to show, is one of sufficient historical plausibility to justify the effort.

FALL 1989: THE ANNUAL COMMUNION CYCLE

I was encouraged to think so with what I consider to be the first "breakthrough" in the matter; it happened in the course of a graduate seminar on the communion that took place at Chapel Hill in the fall of 1989. I had been much impressed by the description of a seminar conducted at Harvard by David Hughes in which the students transcribed just two alleluias from some two hundred sources.[7] The one alleluia, *Dies sanctificatus,* an earlier chant, manifested remarkable melodic stability; the other, *Non vos relinquam,* a later chant, displayed considerable variation from source to source. This result prompted me, in my naïveté, to reverse the Hughes approach and to have the students transcribe a great number of chants, actually an entire liturgical genre, from a small group of representative sources. My hope was to uncover layers of comparative stability and instability within the genre, and thus to establish a chronology for its composition. I chose communions for the simple reason that they are short, and we were able to work our way through the entire temporale of some one hundred chants, and to get a good start on the remaining fifty or so chants of the sanctorale.

My more experienced colleagues could have told me that the results would be disappointing. Virtually all the communions would turn out to be melodically stable, with only obvious exceptions such as the five much-discussed Lenten gospel communions. What I did not realize at the time was that the distinction between an "early" and a "late" chant like the alleluias *Dies sanctificatus* and *Non vos relinquam* was not between earlier and later chants of the core Franco-Roman repertory, but between chants of the core repertory and those added to it in various regions after the eighth- and ninth-century period of Carolingian unity.

The breakthrough referred to above came from an unexpected quarter — the texts. As the students in the seminar occupied themselves with transcribing the melodies, I took it as my responsibility to give them an overview of the texts as they are assigned throughout the liturgical year.[8] The results were little short of astonishing: the entire communion temporale, once every text is laid out in liturgical sequence, displays the most obvious evidence of compositional planning. The well-known numerical ordering of the Lenten weekday communions (with their texts derived in succession from Psalms 1 through 26) is perhaps the least remarkable instance of this. The ten communions of Advent and Christmas day form a homogeneous group of short, lyrical texts of prophetic content from the Old Testament. The ten that complete the Christmas cycle, from the feast of St. Stephen to the third Sunday after the Epiphany, create a sharp contrast; they are all derived from the New Testament, in most cases from the gospel of the day, and include several examples of colorful narratives and vivid dialogues of considerable length.[9]

The series of twenty-six numerically ordered weekday Lenten communions, mentioned above, extends from Ash Wednesday to the Friday before Palm Sunday. Against this homogeneous background the communions of Holy Week, the Lenten Sundays and the five interpolated gospel communions offer the contrast of a strikingly heterogeneous group, including instances of nonpsalmic narratives and dialogues, greatly suggestive of a later chronological layer.

The texts for the first forty days of Paschaltime, from Easter Sunday to Ascension Thursday, maintain the festal style of the post-Christmas chants; most of them draw on the gospel of the day although a number of them feature the innovation of texts taken from the epistles. The last ten communion texts of Paschaltime, from the Sunday after the Ascension to the Saturday after Pentecost, appear at first to continue in the same vein. They are all gospel texts and yet — as closer examination shows — not a single one is derived from the gospel of the day, as had been the case for virtually every gospel text from the preceding portions of the liturgical cycle. One who is faced with this abrupt change in practice cannot but entertain the thought that those responsible for the composition of the communion cycle came to suffer from an exhaustion of creative energy as they neared the end of their work on the festal portions of the church year. That there is more than whimsy in such a notion will be seen presently when a number of musical considerations are added to this survey of communion texts.

The texts of the post-Pentecostal sequence, finally, display evidence of a unique kind of structuring. One discerns here an original core of some sixteen communions united by a rich theme of harvest, sacrifice and eucharist. At a later point in its history it appears that the group was added to (chiefly with borrowings from Lent) in order to bring its number to the Roman liturgical requirement of twenty-two, and that the entire cycle was rearranged in the numerical order of the psalms from which the texts were derived.

Once this overview of the texts was completed, musical considerations fell readily into place. Observations about musical style that might have seemed vague and tenuous in isolation, or that might have been missed altogether, took on a certain concreteness when viewed against the background of the textual program. Layers of melodic stability and instability, to be sure, were not much in evidence, but other equally significant musical phenomena did emerge. For example, no less than seven of the ten short prophetic texts of the Advent-Christmas day group are set in a sweet lyric style, one that is characterized by a tonal foundation on the interval *re-fa*, with an intensifying movement to upper *ut* once in the brief existence of each chant. The thought that a sort of concerted musical effort goes hand in hand with that of the texts here is supported by the circumstance that there are only a scattering of similar melodies in the entire remainder of the communion repertory.

Conversely, many of the dramatic gospel-derived texts are given musical settings of striking originality. There is, for example, from the post-Christmas season the extraordinary *Dicit dominus* of the second Sunday after the Epiphany, in which Jesus, the chief steward and the narrator create a dramatic enactment of the miracle at the wedding feast of Cana. And *Video caelos* too, in which one virtually sees the heavens open as the dying protomartyr Stephen, his voice elevated into a higher tessitura, cries, "Lord Jesus, take thou my soul." From Paschaltime there is the arresting beginning of *Factus est repente*, where its quick syllabic texture and its abruptly rebounding leap of a fifth unmistakably suggest the sudden rush of wind that signifies the Holy Spirit, the *spiritus vehementis*. From Holy Week itself there is the scene of Jesus washing the feet of his disciples in *Dominus Jesus* of Holy Thursday, a somberly beautiful D-mode chant that moves in a limited range until the ascending scalar passage introduces the question of Jesus: "Do you know what it is I do to you, I your lord and master?"

A large proportion of the communions from festal segments of the church year with gospel-derived texts are like those just described. Significantly, a comparably large proportion of communions from these same segments of the annual cycle employ the less extravagant musical means of the typical communion with psalmic texts. In observing the mixture of the two contrasting musical types against the background of the homogeneously designed gospel textual sequences, one cannot but suspect that the creators of the chants were consciously choosing between a traditional musical style and a more fashionable one.

The ten communions of the Sunday after the Ascension to the Saturday after Pentecost were singled out above as something of an anomaly; all their texts are gospel-derived but yet are not taken from the gospel of the day. This circumstance gave rise to the seemingly flippant suggestion that the creators of the communion cycle were losing their creative edge as they neared completion of their work. And it turns out, in fact, that an examination of the musical sources shows all ten chants to have been borrowed from the offices of Ascension and Pentecost; three are antiphons and seven are responsories. It would appear, then, that the festal sequence of communions that was begun with great care for Advent and Christmas ends in haste and compromise at the close of the Easter season.

There is a latent methodology in what we learned about communions that fall. First the texts of a particular genre are laid out in liturgical sequence in the hope of discovering patterns that reveal programmatic planning. Next the music is examined to see if there are analogous, if less readily discernible and less rigorously applied, patterns of musical design. Then the whole is studied for chronological implications: for example, apparently later sequences of gospel chants in contrast to supposedly earlier series of psalmic communions.

If, nevertheless, it were possible from such observations to construct a chronology, it would be only an internal or relative chronology, one lacking in actual dates. These could be obtained only by tying certain features of the relative chronology to external historical events. Precious few of such events are documented in the history of Roman liturgy before the mid-eighth-century transmission of the *cantus romanus* to the Franks; the best known is the establishment by Gregory II of the Lenten Thursdays as liturgical. By an examination of the borrowings that took place to provide chants for these days, it can be seen that at least the psalmic communions predate Gregory's action. We thought we were able, that fall, to detect certain lesser chronological indications—datable changes, for example, in the assignment of gospels—that suggest surprisingly late dates for at least certain gospel communions. Our overall conclusion was that an "early" communion might be from the later decades of the seventh century, and a "late" one, from the earlier decades of the eighth. As indicated already in this introduction, however, I am more inclined now to date the completion of the Roman Mass Proper to the time of Sergius I.

FALL 1993: ADVENT

The methodology just described was developed exclusively from a study of the annual communion cycle. Still, there seemed no reason why it should not work with other chant genres. One had only to apply the three steps: to lay out the texts of any genre in liturgical sequence and thus to reveal compositional design; to examine the music for matching traits; and, finally, to tie in any indications of internal chronological layering with datable events in liturgical history. After long experience with using this approach I am convinced that it remains the most rewarding way to study any chant genre, but one must not expect such obvious results as those yielded by communions. It turns out that communions—selected as the subject of the 1989 seminar, it will be remembered, because they are short—were an altogether fortuitous choice. Communions are unique among items of the Mass Proper for the extent to which they are characterized by compositional planning in their texts and for the stylistic heterogeneity of their music, the very traits that make the application of the method work so well for the genre. But take introits, for example: their annual cycle frustrates because of its seeming perfection. The introit temporale consists of about one hundred chants of apparently homogeneous musical style, each of which is uniquely assigned to a date in the liturgical year; the cycle can be likened to a seamless garment in contrast to the patchwork quilt of the communion cycle. The only chronological indication that emerges, at least from reflection upon a superficial initial investigation, is that the introit cycle might be the product of a single unified effort rather than one, like the communion temporale, that is chronologically layered.

But if introits and communions appear to differ in this respect, they take on the aspect of a closely allied pair within the context of the Mass Proper as a whole. By the summer of 1993 I had made a study of the entire Mass Proper (still much more cursory than what was to follow), endeavoring to apply the method learned from studying the communion. The results of the survey were summarized in an unpublished paper presented at the Royaumont Foundation in September of that year. The central finding was that only two cycles were completed: the annual cycles of the introit and communion. Those of the gradual, offertory and alleluia (not to speak of the tract) were not. Stated thus baldly, this observation should come as no surprise. One might suspect it simply from the numbers involved: nearly one hundred and fifty introits and communions each in the core repertory, but only slightly more than a hundred graduals, fewer than a hundred offertories, about fifty alleluias and fewer than twenty tracts.

More significant than total numbers is the distribution of the chants in each genre throughout the liturgical year (we are now, finally, approaching the promised explanation for the meaning of the phrase "the Advent Project"). An application of the above-discussed method shows that the graduals and offertories of the Advent-Christmas segment of the church year, and even the alleluias to a lesser extent, give the same care and attention to detail as do the introits and communions of the season. Every date of the period has uniquely assigned chants in each genre, chants, moreover, that are thematically appropriate to the liturgical occasion (one recalls here the splendid facade of the great house described in the figure that opened this introduction).

The shorter, and presumably more manageable, introits and communions maintain these traits for the entire annual cycle, but graduals, offertories and especially alleluias manifest something akin to a breakdown, particularly in the closing weeks of Paschaltime and throughout the entire post-Pentecostal season. They no longer enjoy sequences of unique chants, specifically designed for particular dates; rather chants are freely borrowed to fill out the cycles, occasionally with minimum regard for liturgical appropriateness. The Mass Proper as a whole, then, leaves the distinct impression of an ambitiously conceived project undertaken to provide a set of Proper chants for every day of the church year—a task that was simply too large for perfect realization, and that was brought to an end with a number of compromises. This purported project clearly began with Advent. Hence the title of the present book.

That such a project would commence with Advent might not strike some as particularly noteworthy. Advent, after all, is known to be the beginning of the liturgical year. But in point of fact, Advent was not looked upon as the beginning of the liturgical year in seventh-century Rome; the vigil of Christmas was. Every Roman liturgical book of the time—sacramentaries, epistolaries, evangeliaries and homiliaries—begins the year with Christmas Eve, while the season of Advent figures as no more than a group of Sundays that completes the sequence of post-Pentecost Sundays. Advent appears at the head of the church year only in chant books, where it takes on the aspect of a lyric prophetic prelude to the mystery of Christmas. It can be said that this compelling conception, which would eventually come to be universally accepted in the Latin churches, is the creation of the Roman schola cantorum.

At what time might the Roman singers have accomplished this? I will attempt to show in these pages—from an analysis of Advent's history as it appears in the liturgical books—that the placement of the season at the beginning of the church year and the inception of the Advent Project occurred well into the second half of the seventh century. Thus the commencement of the Advent Project at this time might be something of a terminus a quo for the creation of the Roman Mass Proper, just as Gregory II's bringing of the Lenten Thursdays into the church year several decades later has traditionally served as a terminus ad quem. But, again, I believe that we must move its terminus ad quem forward to the reign of Sergius I.

SPRING 1997: THE SANCTORALE

That last conclusion—that the completion of the Advent Project should be dated to the later seventh century rather than the earlier eighth—did not force itself upon me until I was actually engaged (early in 1997) in the writing of chapter seven, "Dating the Mass Proper II: The Sanctorale." There is a measure of irony involved here. Initially, reflection upon the sanctorale (at a very superficial level, to be sure) had compelled me to adopt a singularly late date for the composition of the Mass Proper, and now a more thorough study of the sanctorale requires me to move the date several decades forward.

The key sanctoral date in question is that of the 13 May Dedication of the church of Sancta Maria ad Martyres, the former Roman Pantheon. The *Liber pontificalis* tells us that this dedication was carried out by Pope Boniface IV (608–15),[10] while chant scholars have observed that the Proper for this date (beginning with the introit *Terribilis est locus iste*) is the last set of chants to have been composed for an individual feast as opposed to having been borrowed from previously existing chants. The traditional conclusion from this pair of circumstances is the eminently plausible one that the creative phase of chant production, which was supervised by Gregory I, was brought to a close under Boniface, who died just a decade later.

The difficulty with this argument is that the dedication of the Pantheon as the church of Sancta Maria ad Martyres does not necessarily imply the celebration of the event subsequently with an annual festival, complete with Proper chants, prayers and readings. Indeed the festival appears to be absent from a number of seventh-century liturgical books. I was, it turns out, on the right track in making this observation but took matters entirely too far by concluding that the establishment of the feast dated to the time of Gregory III (731–41), who, as the *Liber pontificalis* informs us, carried out extensive repairs on the church in question.[11]

The chapter on the sanctorale is the longest and most complex in this volume. Prior to writing it I had neglected the sanctorale in favor of the temporale, which, with its obvious liturgical structuring, was a more appropriate context for employing the methodology developed in the communion seminar. Writing it, however, forced me to work with the sanctorale systematically, that is, to trace the seventh-century development of the Roman sanctoral calendar (and the place of the Sancta Maria ad Martyres festival within it) in all of the available liturgical books before turning to the sanctoral chants themselves. It is difficult for me to exaggerate the sense of excited discovery I experienced while at work on this chapter; I found myself virtually sputtering as I sought to explain my findings to any friend and colleague tolerant enough to hear me out.

In a word, I concluded that there was a "Sanctoral Project" undertaken to create sanctoral Mass Propers, much like the Advent Project to create temporal chants. The Sanctoral Project differs most obviously from the Advent Project in that the Roman singers never imagined that they could create a unique set of Proper chants for every sanctoral date in the calendar but settled instead for providing a representative number of such chants for each date, apportioning them more or less according to a feast's importance. The project was begun, probably, somewhat later than the Advent Project and was completed at about the same time. Both liturgical and musical evidence places the completion of the Sanctoral Project in the reign of Sergius I. Because the textual and musical traits of the most recent sanctoral chants are identical to those of the most recent temporal chants, it would appear that the Advent Project, too, was completed in the time of Sergius.

FURTHER OBSERVATIONS

If my experience with the sanctorale amounts to a third breakthrough in the present study—a quasi-datable event, that is, like those involving the communion cycle and the season of Advent—there are any number of more general findings that have emerged during the period. The most fundamental of these, perhaps, is the confirmation of something noticed already by Peter Wagner: that the Mass Proper appears to be structured genre by genre —vertically, so to speak—rather than horizontally, that is, festival by festival.[12] There are, of course, exceptions to this: several of the chants of a particular occasion might be drawn from the same psalm or suggested by the day's stational church. Still, one generally observes the Roman singers working their way systematically through a single genre, whether it be introit, gradual or whatever item of the Mass Proper.

But not throughout the entire liturgical year! Instead they do so for one at a time of its four segments: Advent-Christmas, Lent, Paschaltime or the post-Pentecostal period. This quadripartite structure of the church year may be something that we take for granted now, but it was not always present. Some of its dividing points existed virtually from the beginning, at least implicitly, but the finished product is the work of those same seventh-century Roman singers who placed Advent at the beginning of the year and fashioned coherent sequences of chants extending from the first Sunday of Advent to the third Sunday after the Epiphany. They did something of the sort for the entire temporale, creating a "four-movement" opus, so to speak, which is only vaguely prefigured in the more "through-composed" annual cycles of orations and readings.

The distinction between psalmic and nonpsalmic chants—those with texts derived from the Psalms rather than other books of the Bible—comes into play constantly throughout this volume. The conventional assumption that psalmic chants are generally (not always) earlier than nonpsalmic ones will be confirmed, and the relative placement of these two categories of chant within the different portions of the church year will tell us much about the compositional strategies of the Roman singers.

Related to the distinction between psalmic and nonpsalmic chants is the distinction between chants that use an unaltered segment of Scripture for their texts and those that freely adjust the biblical original. The phenomenon of freely paraphrased nonpsalmic offertory texts has been given full treatment in the literature,[13] but it has not been observed that precisely the same expedient has been widely employed throughout the entire Mass Proper, particularly in the introit and communion. Two important findings stem from a survey of the practice (dealt with here under the rubric of "textual adjustment"). First is the more general conclusion: if a chant text is a carefully crafted composition, it is more likely to be something prepared at one time as a vehicle for a unique musical creation, rather than for some sort of sung liturgical entity that mysteriously evolves over the centuries. And second is the use that can be made of the distinction between integral and adjusted texts in examining sequences of chants in search of compositional strategies. Just as nonpsalmic chants are generally later than psalmic chants, it will be seen here that chants with adjusted texts are often later than chants with integral texts. The two distinctions, used hand in hand, will reveal much about the relative chronology of various segments of the Mass Proper.

Finally—if it can be established that an Advent Project (and concomitant Sanctoral Project) was in fact realized in the later seventh century—it must be asked what came before the Advent Project. I was taken aback by this very question put to me by Ruth Steiner after I read a paper entitled "The Advent Project" at the 1995 New York meeting of the American Musicological Society. I could do no more at the time than respond with the vague generalization that there must have been lists of psalmic introits, graduals and so forth for general usage, and that many of these chants would eventually find a permanent place in the Lenten and post-Pentecostal chant sequences of the Advent Project.

That generalization, it turns out, has served well as a starting point for speculation on what did in fact precede the Advent Project, precede it immediately, that is, in the decades just after the mid-seventh-century founding of the Roman schola cantorum. Those quasi-professional singers, it will be argued here, must have established the mature form of the various items of the Mass Proper. At first they would have generated a repertory of chants for general usage (psalmic chants for the most part), but they must also have created a number of uniquely assigned chants for the more important festivals (here including nonpsalmic chants as well). This activity, carried out over a number of years, led all but inevitably to the idea of doing the job right by composing unique Proper chants for the entire annual cycle—our Advent Project. In the course of preparing the chapters of this volume that treat the individual items of the Mass Proper, I could occasionally determine with some degree of probability specific chants that predated the Advent Project.

THE CENTRAL QUESTION OF GREGORIAN CHANT

What does it mean precisely to say that the later seventh-century Roman singers created the Mass Proper? We know that they produced the texts and assigned them to an annual cycle, and we know that they sang these texts. But what was the nature of the melodies that they chanted? We have two extant versions of them as they came to be notated after their respective periods of oral transmission: the so-called Gregorian and the so-called Old

Roman. Which of the two more closely resembles the original Roman? This question (what I will call the "central question" in paraphrase of Willi Apel's "central problem")[14] lurks below the surface of everything written in the later stages of this volume and occasionally breaks through when the music of one item or the other of the Mass Proper is under discussion. It will be directly addressed in an epilogue entitled "The Central Question of Gregorian Chant."

To pose the question somewhat more fully: was it the Roman singers who were responsible for the Gregorian chant, characterized as it is by sharply defined modality and highly individualized melodies with their graceful contours and strategically placed intervals? Or was it the Franks, musicians of genius working under Chrodegang of Metz (d.766) and his successor Angilram (d.791)? In favor of the former possibility is the chronology proposed in this book, which places the creation of the Roman Mass Proper not much more than a half-century before the pivotal event in the transmission of the Roman chant to the north—Pope Stephen's momentous visit, accompanied in all probability by the schola cantorum, with King Pépin III at St-Denis in 754. Against such a proposition is considerable evidence that the Franks experienced difficulty in mastering the Roman chant, for example, the famous anecdotes recounted by John the Deacon and Nokter of St. Gall.

Against it also stands the Roman melodic style as represented in the Old Roman manuscripts. Is this style—less tonally defined than the Gregorian, and less melodically sculptured with its tendency toward conjunct motion and uniform surface ornamentation—closer to the seventh-century Roman original? Or did it in the course of its more than three centuries of oral transmission (it was not notated until the eleventh century) suffer some kind of gradual melodic impoverishment? Or, just as likely, did it have to be reconstituted after a period of disruption, some time in the troubled history of early medieval Rome when the schola cantorum might have been silenced for a number of years?

I

THE PREHISTORY

CHAPTER 1

The First Centuries

Could it be said that the Proper of the Mass had its beginnings at the very first celebration of the Eucharist—the Last Supper? The gospels of Matthew (26.30) and Mark (14.26) conclude their descriptions of the occasion with the identical verse: "And while singing a hymn (ὑμνήσαντες) they went out to the Mount of Olives." If, as the three Synoptic gospels indicate, the Last Supper took place on the first evening of the Passover (John has it on the preceding day), the hymn would in all likelihood have been the Hallel (Psalms 113–18),[1] which was customarily sung by Jewish families at the evening meal on this day.

PRECONDITIONS FOR A LITURGICAL PROPER

But it is only in a poetic or spiritual sense that the singing of the Hallel at the Last Supper could be spoken of as the beginning of the Mass Proper. In the sense of descriptive liturgical history the idea is obviously anachronistic. Two broad conditions are necessary before even the most elementary liturgical Proper can come into existence. The first requirement is the development of stable orders of worship; in the case of the Eucharist or Mass,[2] this would involve especially the establishment of a pre-eucharistic service of readings and discourse, in which the singing of a responsorial psalm would be a discrete and prescribed event. The second requirement is the development of an annual round of festal commemorations comprising the Paschaltime cycle, the Christmas or Epiphany cycle and the dates on which particularly revered martyrs enjoyed their *dies natalis*. It would be about three centuries after the Last Supper before these conditions would be met, not until well into the fourth century.

And even when such conditions come to be in place, one should not assume that a complete annual cycle of permanently assigned chants follows immediately thereafter. It is true that there is a universally observed tendency in the Christian churches, East and West, to develop liturgical Propers; they do so with respect to prayers, readings and chants. It is to be expected that certain readings and certain psalms are so obviously appropriate to certain liturgical occasions that they become associated with these festivals at an early date. Thus it is virtually inevitable that the account of the first Pentecost in the Acts of the Apostles (2.1–42) would come to be read each year on that day, just as Psalm 41, *Sicut cervus* ("As the hart longs for the springs of water"), would come to be sung in connection with the baptismal ceremonies of the Easter Vigil. Such instances, however, are better thought of as associations rather than assignments; they are elements of an oral tradition rather than items in an organized plan that requires, because of its sheer extent, recording in writing—at first in the margins of biblical books and eventually in separate liturgical books. And we shall see that in the earlier centuries such associations are the exception rather than the rule; they exist in a liturgical context where either the celebrant selects readings and psalms on a daily basis, or where readings are regulated according to the system of *lectio currens*, that is, the reading of a book of the Bible (including the Psalter) from the point where one had left off the previous day.

To speak at all of a Mass Proper, then, in this first chapter is premature. The development of a Proper is the last stage in a general process of liturgical stabilization, a process that involves on the one hand a profound conflict between the tendency toward spiritual freedom and evangelical enthusiasm, and, on the other, the desire for order, predictability and control. It is a conflict that is usually settled eventually in favor of the latter impulses. The first broad liturgical category to become stabilized (granted the existence of an annual cycle of festivals) is that of the succession of events or format of a service—in Dom Gregory Dix's felicitous phrase, "the shape of the liturgy." In the case of the Eucharist or Mass, there is the bipartite structure of a preliminary service of reading and instruction succeeded by the eucharistic rite as such. Following next in time are Ordinary items, such as a prescribed eucharistic prayer, or the Sanctus and the Lord's Prayer, although it must be said that the establishment of certain of these Ordinary items within a liturgical order is part of the establishment of the order itself. Lastly come the items that vary from day to day, those that will eventually be fixed in a liturgical Proper.

This final phase of the process of liturgical stabilization, what I have referred to elsewhere by the admittedly ungainly term "properization," is itself greatly complex.[3] It proceeds at a different pace and according to different principles in different regions and does so even in different aspects of the liturgy of a particular center. But to describe it now in even the most general terms would take us too far from the subject matter of the present chapter, the beginnings of Christianity, when it is the first sort of liturgical stabilization defined above—that of service format—which is chiefly at issue. We start by returning to the Last Supper.

SONG AT COMMON EVENING MEALS

What is particularly significant about the singing at the Last Supper is not so much that it involves the proto-Eucharist, but the plain circumstance that it took place at a supper. An examination of all the extant references to ritual song from the first three centuries of Christian literature reveals that the most detailed and explicit of these passages describe singing at common evening meals, whether eucharistic celebrations or not.[4]

Tertullian of Carthage (d.c.225) describes the liturgical practices of his community in his *Apologeticum;* among these are the agape, or love feast, an evening ritual meal at which singing plays a prominent part:

> Our meal reveals its meaning in its very name; it is called that which signifies love among Greeks. . . . One does not recline at table without first savoring a prayer to God; and then one eats what the hungry would take and drinks what would serve the needs of the temperate. They thus satisfy themselves as those who remember that God is to be worshipped even at night, and they converse as do those who know that God listens. After the washing of hands and the lighting of lamps, each is urged to come into the middle and sing to God, either from the sacred scriptures or from his own invention (*de proprio ingenio*). In this way is the manner of his drinking tested. Similarly the banquet is brought to a close with prayer.[5]

The sentence "In this way is the manner of his drinking tested," while not especially relevant to present purposes, will inevitably catch the eye of the modern reader and hence requires brief comment. Tertullian was a notoriously rigorous ecclesiastic, and we must not indulge the thought that he had in mind anything like the notion of being able "to hold one's liquor." In view of what he said earlier in the passage about temperance in food and drink, it is clear he meant that a successful display of singing would prove the singer's moderation in drinking. The point of the passage that is more relevant is the obvious one that singing is mentioned prominently in a description of the agape. To be noted also is that the song chosen is either from Scripture, from the Book of Psalms, for example, or of one's own composition, whether prepared in advance or improvised on the spot.

Tertullian's Alexandrian contemporary Clement (d.c.215) devotes an entire chapter of his *Paedagogus* to the subject of "How to conduct oneself at banquets."[6] Clement does not use the term "agape" in describing these banquets even if he does develop the theme of charity: "For if you love the Lord your God and then your neighbor, you should be genial first to God in thanksgiving and psalmody and secondly to your neighbor in dignified friendship." Like Tertullian he emphasizes both sobriety—"let carousing be absent from our rational enjoyment, and also foolish vigils which revel in drunkenness"—and the essential element of pious song: "Just as it is appropriate for us to praise the creator of all before partaking of food, so too is it proper while drinking to sing to him as the beneficiaries of his creation. For a psalm is a harmonious and reasonable blessing, and the Apostle calls a psalm a spiritual song."

A third contemporary, the Roman presbyter Hippolytus (d.c.236), reflects upon the liturgy of his city in his *Apostolic Tradition*; singing is mentioned only once in this work, in the closing portion of its description of the agape:

> And let them arise therefore after supper and pray; let the boys sing psalms, the virgins also. And afterwards let the deacon, as he takes the mingled chalice of oblation, say a psalm from those in which Alleluia is written. And afterwards, if the presbyter so orders, again from these psalms. And after the bishop has offered the chalice, let him say a psalm from those appropriate to the chalice—always one with Alleluia, which all say. When they recite the psalms, let all say Alleluia, which means, "We praise him who is God; glory and praise to him who created the entire world through his work alone." And when the psalm is finished let him bless the chalice and give of its fragments to all the faithful.[7]

The passage, while contributing to the theme of song at ritual meals, raises questions about terminology that must be taken up here in a brief digression. Two pairs of words are involved: those that are translated "say" and "sing," and those translated "psalm" and "hymn." Words meaning "to say" in the most general sense, like the Latin *dicere* and the Greek λέγειν, are used in patristic literature to cover a great variety of liturgical utterance from simple recitation to tuneful song. The modern observer can only try to determine what is intended from the context. Words meaning "to sing," on the other hand, like the Latin *cantare* and the Greek ᾄδειν, must surely be taken to specify some manner of performance that is decidedly closer to the fully melodious pole of textual delivery. In the first sentence of the present passage, then, there should be no doubt that genuine singing on the part of the young men and women is intended. As for the psalms that the deacon and bishop "say," one can only guess how melodious their recitation might have been. Individual ability and inclination would no doubt count as factors, as might the text of the psalm involved, whether it was more lyric in character, for example, or more didactic.

The terms that one transliterates "psalm" and "hymn" from their Latin and Greek cognates are completely interchangeable in patristic usage, and we must always rely upon context to determine the intended meaning. The phrase "a hymn of David," for example, would surely refer to a biblical psalm, while "a psalm of one's own making" would refer to a nonbiblical hymn. (In my own text, as opposed to patristic passages, I will of course follow the modern convention of using the terms "psalm" and "psalmody" to refer to biblical psalms and "hymns" and "hymnody" to refer to newly composed hymns.) In the passage from the *Apostolic Tradition* there appears to be no hint as to whether the "psalms" sung by the young men and women were biblical psalms, newly composed hymns or—as was indicated in Tertullian's description of the agape—a free mixture of both. The "psalms" of the deacon and bishop, however, were in all probability biblical psalms, drawn from those twenty that have "alleluia" superscribed in the Book of Psalms.[8] Perhaps one might wish to see a link between the singing of alleluia-psalms at the Roman agape and the singing at the Last Supper of the Hallel, which forms a continuous set of six from the twenty.

To return to the theme of singing at Christian evening meals, the last passage to be quoted, from Cyprian of Carthage (d.258), appears to describe a meal that is less liturgically defined than the agape. Cyprian, in any case, displays a uniquely warm approbation of sacred song in requesting his guest Donatus to favor the company with a "psalm":

> And since this is a restful holiday and a time of leisure, now as the sun is sinking toward evening, let us spend what remains of the day in gladness and not allow the hour of repast to go untouched by heavenly grace. Let a psalm be heard at the sober banquet, and since your memory is sure and your voice pleasant (*vox canora*), undertake this task as is your custom. You will better nurture your friends, if you provide a spiritual recital (*spiritalis auditio*) for us and beguile our ears with sweet religious strains (*religiosa mulcedo*).[9]

That singing at common evening meals figures so prominently in early Christian references to sacred song should occasion no surprise. Musical diversion of some sort at meals where friends and associates gather, whether at court or in some more modest venue, is a nearly universally observed phenomenon in ancient cultures. The Greek symposium comes readily to mind, as do, with greater relevance, Jewish ceremonial meals, even if the latter tend to be more restricted to family than their early Christian counterparts, which often involve the larger community.[10] The question that must be asked at this point, however, is what bearing this custom of singing at Christian evening meals might have upon singing at the Eucharist.

The Eucharist of apostolic times continued the tradition of the Last Supper in that it was celebrated in conjunction with a common evening meal. The phrase "the breaking of bread" that appears several times in the Acts of the Apostles is widely assumed to refer to eucharistic meals, at least upon occasion if not always. In his first epistle to the Corinthians (11.20–34) Paul reproaches this notoriously irrepressible congregation for their excesses in eating and drinking at the "Lord's Supper." It is presumably because of such abuses that the Eucharist came to be separated from an evening meal and to be celebrated instead in the early morning hours. The early agape, by the way, is generally identified with the eucharistic feast of apostolic times, so that one speaks of the separation of the Eucharist from the agape and the continuation into later centuries of the agape as a noneucharistic evening gathering, frequently involving charity to the poorer faithful.

THE MORNING EUCHARIST

No sources allow us to determine precisely when the celebration of the Eucharist was transferred to the morning, but we do possess from Justin Martyr's (d.c.165) *Apology* a superbly explicit description of Sunday morning Eucharist in mid-second-century Rome:

> And on the day named for the sun there is an assembly in one place for all who live in the towns and in the country; and the memoirs of the Apostles and the writings of the Prophets are read as long as time permits. Then, when the reader has finished, he who presides speaks, giving admonishment and exhortation to imitate those noble deeds. Then we all stand together and offer prayers. And when, as we said above, we are finished with the prayers, bread is brought, and wine and water, and he who presides likewise offers prayers and thanksgiving, according to his ability, and the people give their assent by exclaiming Amen. And there takes place the distribution to each and the partaking of that over which thanksgiving has been said, and it is brought to those not present by the deacon.[11]

This marvelous passage reveals that by the mid-second century virtually all the essential elements of the mature Eucharist or Mass are in place; missing only is the formal separation of the first part of the ceremony, what will come to be called the Fore-Mass or Mass of the Catechumens, from the Eucharist proper, the later Mass of the Faithful.[12] (This division is a function of the conversion in the fourth century of entire populations, when it was not thought proper to reveal the mystery of the Eucharist to those not yet baptized.) The first part of Justin's service is made up of readings, exhortation (the homily) and common prayer; in the second part, bread, wine and water are brought in (the offertory), the presiding official provides an extended eucharistic prayer to which the congregation responds "Amen," and the eucharistic elements are distributed to those present.

The service—when viewed as an example of the process of liturgical stabilization described at the beginning of this chapter—shows that the first category of stabilization, that involving liturgical orders or formats, is well advanced. There is no evidence, however, of the second category, that of Ordinary items; the one possibility, the eucharistic prayer, is offered by the presiding official "according to his ability." But by the later fourth century the Latin eucharistic prayer appears to be relatively fixed; Ambrose of Milan quotes a prayer in his *De Sacramentis* that is very close to the medieval Canon of the Mass.[13] As for Proper items, these also are absent from Justin's service; "the memoirs of the Apostles and the writings of the Prophets are read as long as time permits."

PSALMODY AT THE MORNING EUCHARIST?

But what of psalmody, Proper or otherwise? Justin makes no mention of it, an omission that is particularly disquieting in view of the widely held assumption of an indispensable link between the readings and psalmody of the Fore-Mass.[14] Are we to conclude from Justin's silence on the matter that there was no singing in the early-morning Eucharist of his time—that the custom was no longer considered appropriate when the ceremony was separated from the evening meal? An attempt to answer the question follows below but must await a review of any other pertinent evidence that may be available.

There is only one other surviving description of an orthodox pre-eucharistic service from before the later fourth century; it appears in the *Apologeticum* of Tertullian, the same work quoted above in connection with the agape. The passage is given here with only Tertullian's description of the essential elements of the service (and without his commentary on each item):

> I myself shall now set down the practices of the Christian community. ... We come together in an assembly and congregation to surround God with prayer. ... We gather together to consider the divine Scrip-

tures.... And at the same time there is encouragement, correction and holy censure.[15]

The same three elements of Justin's pre-eucharistic service are present here—reading, discourse and prayer—but psalmody is not mentioned. There is, however, a second passage from Tertullian that might be taken to supply the missing element. In his *De anima* Tertullian describes how a charismatic woman finds inspiration for her visions in the content of the pre-eucharistic service, which apparently includes psalmody:

> There is among us today a sister favored with gifts of revelation which she experiences through an ecstasy of the spirit during the Sunday liturgy. She converses with angels, at one time even with the Lord; she sees and hears mysteries, reads the hearts of people and applies remedies to those who need them. The material for her visions is supplied as the scriptures are read, psalms are sung (*psalmi canuntur*), the homily delivered and prayers are offered.[16]

On first reading the passage seems clear enough: Tertullian gives the four conventionally cited elements of the early Christian pre-eucharistic service in their proper order—reading, psalmody, homily and prayer. There are, however, two major difficulties with this interpretation. The first is that *De anima* is a late work, from the time after Tertullian had become an adherent of the Montanists, an heretical group characterized, most notably, by an excessive regard for individual spiritual gifts. Thus he describes not an orthodox Christian service in this passage, but a presumably more animated Montanist gathering. The second difficulty has to do with the above discussed ambiguity of the term "psalms." In view of the premium placed by the Montanists upon personal inspiration, could not the "psalms" of this service be thought of as individual creations rather than biblical psalms?

Some light might be thrown on the question by returning to Paul's first epistle to the Corinthians. Paul found it necessary to rebuke the Corinthians not only for their lack of restraint in eating and drinking at the Lord's Supper, but also for their overreliance upon individual spiritual gifts, a trait that likens them to the later Montanists. In the course of a long passage on the subject Paul provides a brief description of a Corinthian gathering (whether eucharistic or not is beside the point): "What then brethren? When you come together each one has a psalm, has a teaching, has a revelation, has a tongue, has an interpretation" (1 Cor 14.26). The larger context of the brief passage, and indeed the passage itself, creates the overwhelming impression that the utterance each individual typically shares with the Corinthian congregation is personal in nature, whether it be a tongue, a revelation or, indeed, a "psalm."[17] A "psalm" of this sort would not necessarily exclude, say, a few memorized verses from a favorite biblical psalm, but it would just as likely be something else, for example, the declamation of pious verses improvised on the spot or the singing of a hymn recalled from a previous occasion.[18] The possibilities are manifold but seem confined, nonetheless, to individual expressions of a free and personal nature. What does appear to be beyond the realm of such possibilities is a set liturgical event, like the required biblical psalm of the day.

The example of the Corinthian "psalm" lends plausibility to the possibility that the Montanist "psalms" cited by Tertullian might be similarly personal creations, and plausibility approaches probability when one considers an additional passage from Tertullian. In the *Adversus Marcionem*, another work from his Montanist period, Tertullian challenges Marcion, the leader of a rival heretical sect, to produce the fruits of genuine divine inspiration, including a "psalm":

> So let Marcion display the gifts of his god—some prophets, who have spoken not from human understanding but from the spirit of God, who have both foretold the future and revealed the secrets of the heart. Let him produce a psalm, a vision, a prayer; only let it be of the spirit, while in ecstasy, that is, a state beyond reason, when some interpretation of tongues has come upon him. Let him also show me a woman of his group who has prophesied . . .[19]

Clearly the "psalm" of this passage is a personal creation rather than a biblical psalm, and the similarity of context with the passage from *De anima* (both texts focus upon the workings of divine inspiration and cite a woman of purported prophetic gifts) lends further credence to the likelihood that the "psalms" of the Montanist pre-eucharistic service might also be newly created songs. One cannot be certain of this, but neither can one be confident at all of the alternative view, that is, that the quotation from *De anima* is conclusive evidence for the existence of a third-century pre-eucharistic service of readings in which biblical psalmody is a formally observed event.

What we are to conclude, however, from the totality of the second- and third-century evidence presented thus far must await a rather extended series of more general reflections about the period.

THE "DIRECTNESS" OF THE FIRST CHRISTIAN CENTURIES

The Christian church of the time prior to its emancipation under the emperor Constantine the Great in 313 was not the triumphant institution that developed after that event. The contrasting condition of the pre- and post-Constantinian church is best grasped by reference to its architecture. With the creation of the Christian basilica the fourth century witnessed what it is no exaggeration to call an architectural revolution.[20] Constantine (d.337) himself was personally involved in sponsoring several of the grander examples of the type in Rome, Bethlehem and Jerusalem, while in the course of the century virtually every city and town of the empire saw the erection of impressive stone edifices, capable of accommodating the large throngs that resulted from the conversion of entire populations.

The pre-Constantinian church was more modestly housed. It is true that it was not, as the Romantic nineteenth-century notion would have it, a "church of the catacombs." The catacombs were mostly confined to Rome, where they served as the burial place not only for the faithful but for other groups of Roman citizens as well. The cramped chambers that occasionally intersected the long subterranean corridors of the catacombs could hardly accommodate a gathering of even modest size. Christian congregations of the first centuries met not in the catacombs but in their homes; thus early Christian architecture was not ecclesiastical architecture but domestic architecture. A large room in the home of a prominent member of a community was the typical meeting place, whether a room in a Roman tenement or a graceful peristyle villa, as in the famous house-church at Dura-Europos. Such a home could be altered to meet the congregation's needs. At Dura-Europos the assembly took place in a room of about seventeen by forty-three feet that had a raised platform at one end for the altar table; adjoining the larger room was a smaller one with a stone baptismal basin constructed at one end.[21]

The Christians of the first centuries could be said to make use of what was at hand for their liturgical needs. They employed their homes as churches, their tableware as eucharistic vessels and their contemporary garments as vestments. There were no candles at their services except those needed to light the room and no bells to signal key points in the ceremony; a table served as the eucharistic altar. This was not a case of self-conscious puritanism, particularly in the very earliest stages of Christianity, but more a matter-of-fact focus upon essential goals, what Dom Gregory Dix called "directness."[22] It must have been something of the same sort with liturgical song. Just as there was no ecclesiastical architecture in the proper sense, there was no ecclesiastical music as such, that is, no sharply defined ecclesiastical genres and styles, no carefully drilled musical organizations and no exclusively Christian tonal system. We have seen already that as often as not members of the congregation supplied the song, even if we might presume that those of special aptitude and more extroverted inclination were the ones who generally did so. Eventually designated lectors would assume the role of psalmodist, at least in the cathedrals of important ecclesiastical centers, but even these individuals were not what we would call professional singers. The earlier singers might have sung a biblical psalm, a portion thereof or, more likely, perhaps—an issue to be taken up below—a newly created hymn or song. In doing so, for all we know, Jewish-Christians might have used tunes remembered from the psalmody of the Temple of Jerusalem, and Gentile-Christians might have improvised melodies that represented the everyday tonal environment of their native region. Some might even—before the heated patristic polemic against musical instruments of the third and especially fourth centuries—have accompanied themselves on the lyre or harp.[23] Such song might have been restrained and simple, but it might also upon occasion have been attractively melodious and even rhapsodic. We are speaking here of a diverse population existing over two or three centuries; the possibilities are manifold.

In any event early Christians did in fact sing; at least most congregations must have done so. There is a warm fostering of song in the New Testament, and no calls are heard in the subsequent literature of the patristic period for a suppression of song until issued by a disgruntled (and unsuccessful) minority in the later fourth century.[24] The New Testament references —whether it be Paul exhorting the Ephesians to "be filled with the spirit, speaking to one another in psalms and hymns and spiritual songs, singing and making melody in your hearts to the Lord" (Eph 5.19), or James urging Christians at large: "Is anyone cheerful? Let him sing" (Jas 5.13)—set the tone. It is frequently difficult to place New Testament references to song into any sort of situational context, liturgical or otherwise; indeed it is sometimes difficult to say if certain references (including that just quoted from Paul) are not more to metaphorical or spiritual singing rather than to the physical variety. But what is unmistakable is their generally positive character, a trait that matches the evangelical impulse of early Christianity, its enthusiasm for the "good news." This attitude maintains itself throughout the following centuries, as when Justin Martyr, speaking of Christians in the second century, avows that "in gratitude to him we offer solemn prayers and hymns for his creation,"[25] and when Clement of Alexandria asserts in the third, "we plough the fields while giving praise, we sail the sea while singing hymns."[26] In the fourth, even the severe Athanasius concedes that God "ordained that the canticles be sung with melody and the psalms read with song."[27]

HYMNS OR PSALMS?

Thus song, in general, is characteristic of early Christianity. But no discussion of the subject is complete without mention of a view widely held at present among liturgical historians: that newly composed hymnody was considerably more cherished in the earliest centuries than biblical psalmody. This way of thinking, especially associated with Balthasar Fischer, can be summarized as follows.[28] It is true that the Psalter was the favorite book of the Old Testament among early Christians; it was by far the most frequently quoted book in the New Testament and came to be looked upon as a treasury of Christian typology—Jesus (the new David) was seen to pray, suffer and rejoice in virtually every verse of the Psalms. But in the earliest centuries the Psalter was in fact a book to be read, not a book to be sung from, as it would become only later. And in the Jewish tradition too, the Psalter was clearly a book for reading, one of the prophetic books in the threefold categorization of the Law, the Prophets and the Sacred Writings. Newly composed hymns were especially cultivated as the lyric expression of early Christians. The New Testament is rich in fragments of such hymns, which stand out against the prevailing prose texture of its pages, and a collection such as the early-second-century *Songs of Solomon* bears witness to a continuation of the hymnic tradition. The Book of Psalms (still according to this view) came finally in the fourth century to be used as a Christian hymnal chiefly because of a newly developed prejudice against hymnody. The prejudice had its roots in the third century, when heretics like Bardaisan and Valentinus exploited hymns as a tool of proselytization. Orthodox Christians, then, began to foster the biblical psalms as a counterweight to the popular heretical hymns. Thus Tertullian (a polemicist, it would seem, who delights in contesting any side of an issue) asserts: "The Psalms come to our aid on this point, not the psalms of that apostate, heretic and Platonist, Valentinus, but those of the most holy and illustrious prophet David."[29]

The position of Fischer and his followers has much to recommend it, but it must be balanced by a number of qualifying considerations. It is an oversimplification, for one, to say that among the ancient Jews the Book of Psalms was a book for reading rather than for singing. A better oversimplification is the proposition that the Psalter was a book for reading in the synagogue but a book for singing in the temple. The Mishnah testifies to the singing of at least two groups of psalms in the temple: the seven that were sung, one each, on the seven days of the week during the morning sacrifice;[30] and the six psalms of the Hallel that were sung during the sacrifice of the Paschal lambs.³¹ In addition to these explicit Mishnaic references, John A. Smith has argued convincingly from other categories of evidence that well over half of the 150 Psalms must have been sung in the temple liturgy.³²

And surely it defies credibility that the temple's use of the Psalter as a quasi hymnal would have been entirely without influence upon other areas of life within Palestinian Judaism. There is a hint, at least, of such influence in a passage from the Mishnaic tractate *Sukkah* that describes the joyous festivities of the first night of the Feast of Tabernacles:

> And the Levites on harps, and on lyres, and with cymbals, and with trumpets and with other instruments of music without number upon the fifteen steps leading down from the court of the Israelites to the Women's Court, corresponding to The Fifteen Songs of Ascent in the Psalms; upon them the Levites used to stand with musical instruments and sing hymns.³³

A strict reading of the passage might lead to the conclusion that only the Levites sang and that they confined their singing to the fifteen gradual psalms (Psalms 120–34), but the context of the passage suggests otherwise. Singing and dancing by both men and women continued in the Women's Court all night to the light of bonfires, and one well imagines that psalms other than the gradual psalms would have been sung by the Levites, and that they might have been joined in this by the people for at least certain better-known psalms. This is a kind of participation, moreover, that could have been extended to various circumstances beyond the visit of the people to the temple at this particular time of pilgrimage.

I have argued elsewhere that there was a genuine inhibition in ancient Judaism to duplicating the psalmodic practices of the temple in overtly liturgical situations outside its sacred precincts.³⁴ But such an inhibition need not apply in less formal situations, whether it be family meals or other circumstances. As for early Christians, they would have no reason to share even the liturgical inhibition, once they had ceased to look upon the temple as the center of their worship, nor would there be any reason for them not to sing particularly appropriate psalms when they gathered for worship.

For another point, there is that frequently heard claim that the New Testament is shot through with hymnic fragments. One of the more credible examples appears in Paul's first epistle to Timothy (3.16):

> And great certainly is the mystery of our religion:
> Who was manifested in the flesh
> was vindicated in the spirit

> seen by angels
> preached among the nations
> believed in the world
> taken up in glory.

I share the recently expressed skepticism that this and other (less likely) passages are fragments of liturgical hymns.[35] They are at least as plausibly interpreted as passages of rhetorical prose, couched in precisely the sort of elevated language one might expect to encounter in sermons or in pastoral letters that are intended to be read to a congregation. And a more basic objection is that the advocates of the hymnic assumption fail to define the liturgical context in which these purported hymns might have been sung.[36]

Finally, there is the contention that the Psalter came to be looked upon as a Christian hymnal only because of a reaction against popular heretical hymns. On the contrary, heretical hymns could just as well spur the composition of orthodox hymns; it is well known that the incomparable hymns of Ephraem Syrus (d.373) were explicitly created as a counterforce to those of Bardaisan. Certainly the status of the Davidic psalms as part of the biblical canon was an essential element in their eventual acceptance as a sort of Christian hymnal, but it was more a precondition than an active causal factor in the unprecedented popularity that the singing of psalms would achieve in the later decades of the fourth century. We shall see in the following chapter that this dramatic development—what I call the "psalmodic movement"—was owing to factors other than the simple fact of biblical canonicity.

To summarize this question of the comparative popularity of hymns and psalms in the first Christian centuries, it is true that the Psalter was looked upon as a book for reading, and it is true that personally created hymns were much cultivated. Yet it defies credibility to claim that therefore the Davidic psalms were not sung or that they were sung only rarely. As for which category of song was heard more frequently, this is something we can hardly determine with any certainty.

THE FIRST CENTURIES: AN OVERVIEW

It is only in a very remote sense that we can say the Proper of the Mass began with the singing of Jesus and his disciples at the Last Supper, even if we knew for certain it was the Hallel that they sang. The most basic preconditions for the creation of a liturgical Proper—an annual cycle of festivals and fixed positions for chants within stable liturgical orders—would not be present until the second half of the fourth century, and even then the Mass

Proper would be slow to develop. What is especially significant about the singing of the Last Supper, however, is that it took place at a common evening meal. Subsequently our fullest and most vivid descriptions of Christian singing (before, that is, the great expansion of liturgical song in the fourth century) are also of singing at meals. It is true that the texts in question are all from the earlier third century, but any number of factors, such as the virtually universal character of musical diversion at ceremonial meals and the generally warm endorsement of sacred song by early Christianity, lead us to assume that it was a typical feature of common Christian meals in the first and second centuries as well. We are confirmed in this assumption also by the circumstance that among these third-century texts are the two fullest descriptions of the agape that we possess from any period (those of Tertullian and Hippolytus), and that they give a prominent role to singing. The agape is generally accepted to be the product of primitive Christianity, and we have no reason to believe that it acquired its customary singing only in the third century.

The early Eucharist was celebrated at such meals, and we can thus suppose that psalmody and hymnody were a typical if not obligatory feature of the early Eucharist. And at some time between Paul's mid-first-century criticism of abuses at Corinthian eucharistic meals and Justin Martyr's mid-second-century description of Sunday morning Eucharist at Rome, the rite had made this radical change in its setting. It had acquired, too, its classic bipartite shape of a service of readings, discourse and prayer followed by the Eucharist in the stricter sense. Justin, however, makes no mention of psalmody in the pre-eucharistic service, nor does Tertullian in his description of a similar orthodox ceremony, even if he does mention "psalms" in his description of a Montanist pre-eucharistic service. What are we to conclude from this admittedly meager evidence?

I would propose that singing was essential not to the Eucharist as such but to the evening meal, and that it should come as no surprise that singing was not as typical of the morning celebration of the Eucharist as it had been of its earlier setting. What was essential to the morning pre-eucharistic service was reading—in Justin's words: "and the memoirs of the Apostles and the writings of the Prophets are read as long as time permits." This is not to say that psalms (as opposed to hymns) would never be chanted in this service. Readings from the Book of Psalms would certainly figure upon occasion as selections from "the writings of the Prophets," and we can well imagine that "readings" from the Psalter might vary widely in their mode of execution from something indistinguishable from the reading of any other biblical passage to something that responds with full musicality to the latent lyricism of the Psalms. This would depend upon the aptitude of the lector and liturgical personality of the congregation, so that Tertullian's charismatic Montanist congregation might be more than typically animated in the rendering of its "psalms," whether personal or biblical.

But the central point is that the recitation of psalms in the pre-eucharistic service of the second and third centuries was essentially a biblical reading rather than a discrete and independent act of liturgical song. And whatever singing of psalms might have taken place was probably occasional rather than regular; certainly it was not a defined event that one could rightly refer to as *the* psalmody of the Fore-Mass. This hypothesis will be borne out, I believe, by the evidence of the later fourth century, which will reveal to us the development of a legitimate category of pre-eucharistic psalmody.

These speculations have focused on the pre-eucharistic service for the good reason that virtually all the documentary evidence we possess concerns that portion of the eucharistic rite. We can close now, however, with brief mention of another event in the celebration of the Eucharist that might very well have been particularly hospitable to psalmody. This is the distribution of communion. We will see that the singing of a psalm at communion time became a regular event in the Eucharist of the later fourth century. It seems quite possible that such psalmody might also have taken place with some frequency in at least certain congregations of the second and third centuries. Continuity between the custom of singing at earlier eucharistic meals and of singing at the morning distribution of communion is an entirely plausible sequence of events. Such psalmody would, by the way, be psalmody as such rather than psalmody as reading; and it might even lay a claim of its own to represent the origins of the Mass Proper.

CHAPTER 2

The Later Fourth Century

The closing decades of the fourth century saw one of the richest and most productive periods in the history of Christian liturgy, East and West. It was, for one thing, the time that the church year achieved recognizable shape.[1] Easter and Pentecost had been celebrated from apostolic times (even if it took more than a century of controversy before the original Thursday Passover observance was fixed on Easter Sunday). But the full Easter cycle—comprising a Lenten quadragesima (forty days) culminating in the baptism of the catechumens at the Easter vigil and followed by the Paschal quinquagesima (fifty days), punctuated on its fortieth day by the newly established feast of Ascension Thursday—did not come into place until the second half of the fourth century. New, too, were the festivals commemorating the birth of Christ: Epiphany (6 January) in the East and Christmas (25 December) in the West. The two would begin to sort out their complementary identities by the end of the century (with Christmas seen as the birthdate and Epiphany as the date of the birth's manifestation to the world). Advent, the period of preparation for the Christmas mystery that would eventually be looked upon as a symmetrical calendric counterpart to Lent, consisted in no more than an irregularly observed three-day fast. The beginnings of what we call the sanctoral cycle also date to this period. The Philocalian Calendar of 354 includes a sort of proto-martyrology; it lists some twenty-three martyrs whose date of death was honored annually at Rome.[2]

The later fourth century is also the time that both Office and Eucharist (hereafter Mass) achieved an outline essentially the same as that of the Middle Ages. The "cathedral offices" of lauds and vespers began to be observed publicly soon after the emancipation of the Church in 313 but took definite shape only later in the century. The "monastic office" made its contribution at the same time with the predawn service of matins (called vigils then) and the daytime hours of tierce, sext and none. Only prime and compline remained to be permanently established by century's end. The Mass clarified its bipartite structure in the course of the century by marking the division of its two segments with a ritualized dismissal of the catechumens before the Mass of the Faithful commenced. And, finally, the psalmody of the Fore-Mass (generally a single psalm, as we shall see) became a regular liturgical event during the second half of the century, as did the psalm accompanying the distribution of communion.

All this is well documented in the prodigious outpouring of ecclesiastical literature that issues from the pens of the great later fourth-century and earlier fifth-century Church Fathers, both those writing in Greek, such as Athanasius (d.373), Basil (d.379) and John Chrysostom (d.407), and those writing in Latin, such as Ambrose (d.397), Jerome (d.420) and Augustine (d.430). One might object that we tend to attribute to this period the liturgical accomplishments outlined above simply because they happen to be contemporary with the writing that describes them. Should we not be more cautious in assuming the lack of such developments during earlier periods of comparative silence? We shall see, in fact, that the texts of the period in question reveal most of these developments not to be already fixed but to be in the process of becoming so. Indeed I believe it is fair to say that the abundant Christian literature of the later fourth century is itself a product of the same historical forces, those set loose by the emancipation of the Church, that helped to bring about the liturgical progress of the time.

The liturgical developments that the present chapter will focus on are the psalmody of the Fore-Mass and that of communion time. That these two liturgical events, however, come to be all but universally observed in the Church can be understood only against the background of what I call "the later fourth-century psalmodic movement." We must digress, then, with a review of this extraordinary phenomenon.[3]

THE LATER FOURTH-CENTURY PSALMODIC MOVEMENT

The story begins with the unlikely figure of the hermit Antony (d.356) and in the unlikely place of the Lower Egyptian desert. Antony had left Alexandria for the nearby desert in about 285 in order to pursue a life of ascetic deprivation and solitude. He was followed in the course of time by numerous stalwart souls seeking to escape the temptations of fourth-century urban existence and to restore the purity of primitive Christian life. They established what we refer to as the eremetic mode of monasticism, living alone in their huts, but in close proximity to charismatic leaders like Antony, around whom they gathered periodically for guidance and encouragement. Meanwhile, to the south in the deserts of Upper Egypt, the cenobitic, or common, mode of monasticism developed, as men and women formed communities devoted to the ascetic life, under the leadership of figures such as the much revered Pachomius (d.346).

Enormous numbers of monks and nuns were involved, "making of the desert a city," in the famous phrase of Antony's biographer Athanasius. They became an inspiration to Christianity at large, as many of the outstanding figures of the fourth-century Church visited the famous Egyptian communities and stayed for extended periods of time in order to imbibe the monastic spirit. In the course of the century the monastic movement spread to the cities; monasteries were established in close proximity to the cathedrals of the principal ecclesiastical centers. It is particularly significant that virtually all the outstanding ecclesiastical leaders of the later fourth century lived as monks at some point in their careers. Included are no less than Augustine, Jerome, Basil, John Chrysostom and Gregory of Nyssa; virtually the only notable exception is Ambrose, who nevertheless fostered monasticism in his diocese of Milan.

And what might all this have to do with psalmody? The central ideal of the first desert monks was to put into literal practice the Pauline maxim "to pray without ceasing" (1 Thes 5.17), and the peculiar device they happened upon to realize this was the recitation of the Psalter. It was not a matter of selecting particularly cherished or appropriate psalms, but an entirely new practice—psalmody "in course," or continuous psalmody, the saying at one time of extended portions of the Psalter in numerical order. The desert monks did so especially in solitary nighttime vigils, when they might recite the entire Book of Psalms by heart, and they did so also at appointed morning and evening office hours, whether in solitude or in common.

Their psalmody in common must not be thought of as a splendid display of choral praise like that of, say, eleventh-century Cluny, but rather a mantra-like inducement to meditation. The monks sat on the floor in silence, weaving linen or plaiting rope, while a single one of their number chanted a series of psalms, interspersed with prayer. If this psalmody was not self-consciously musical, neither was it self-consciously nonmusical. Certainly the stark ascetic context would suggest that a relatively subdued mode of declamation was typical, but there might very well have been a certain beauty to the chanting of at least some individuals. In any event later fourth-century descriptive references to monasticism generally make prominent mention of psalmody, and many of these references have a warm aesthetic resonance. John Chrysostom, for example, says: "As soon as they are up, they stand and sing the prophetic hymns with great harmony, and well ordered melody. Neither cithara, nor syrinx, nor any other musical instrument emits such sound as is to be heard in the deep silence and solitude of these holy men as they sing."[4] And then there is that stirring paean to Davidic psalmody attributed to John, which concludes: "In the deserts men crucified to this world hold converse with God, and David is first and middle and last. And at night all men are dominated by physical sleep and drawn into the depths, and David alone stands by, arousing all the servants of God to angelic vigils, turning earth into heaven and making angels of men."[5]

Monastic psalmody had a specific (and well-documented) influence on two liturgical developments of the later fourth century: the daily ecclesiastical Office and the popular psalmodic vigil. As remarked above, morning and evening offices, the forerunners of western lauds and vespers, came to be observed in the principal ecclesiastical centers after the emancipation of the Church in 313. Liturgical historians since Baumstark refer to this pair of services as the "cathedral office." The services consisted in a combination of ceremony (the *lucernarium*, or lamp lighting, for example, at vespers), prayer, psalmody and a concluding episcopal blessing. The psalmody was "selective" rather than "continuous"; thus Psalm 62, "O God my God, I rise before thee at the break of day," was sung in most churches at lauds, and at vespers Psalm 140, with its appropriate second verse, "Let my prayer be directed to thee as incense, and the lifting up of my hands as an evening sacrifice."

In the second half of the century the Office was radically transformed by the participation of urban monastic communities. Remarkably the "cathedral" core remained intact; it was, however, enveloped by services that consisted almost entirely of continuous monastic psalmody with its customary interspersed prayer. Thus a long monastic vigil service (what we call matins) preceded lauds, and three shorter daytime services of monastic psalmody (tierce, sext and none) were added to the horarium. Vespers itself was begun with a prelude of monastic psalmody. All this is best observed in Egeria's description of the Jerusalem liturgy, where the monastic and cathedral portions of the daily office are clearly distinguished by the respective absence or presence of the bishop. At vespers, for example, the bishop delays his entrance into the church until the conclusion of the monastic psalmody.

Monastic psalmody is equally central to the development of what I call the "popular psalmodic vigil." This was an informal gathering of the faithful in the early hours of the morning before Saturday and Sunday Mass, during which psalms were sung (interspersed with prayer and less often readings) for hours on end, in some cases for the entire night. The sources show a prominent monastic involvement in such meetings, as their popularity spread from East to West in the final quarter of the fourth century. In Egeria's Jerusalem, in fact, we see that the daily matins of the resident monks and nuns (*monazontes* and *parthenae* in her terminology) was omitted on Sunday, and in its place the laity held a vigil that duplicated it in minute detail.

However one might assess the role of monasticism in the phenomenon, it cannot be denied that the closing decades of the fourth century were a time of unprecedented popularity for the singing of biblical psalms. There is no evidence that anything so pervasive and intense existed before this time, nor that anything quite like it would be witnessed again in the history of Christianity. Its literary manifestation was an extraordinary series of extended encomiums of psalmody from the pen of authors including Athanasius, Basil, John Chrysostom, Ambrose and Niceta of Remesiana. Among the various themes prominent in these texts is the explicit endorsement of the role that musical pleasure plays in the efficacy of psalmody. Thus Niceta, for example, tells us that "a psalm is sweet to the ear when sung, it penetrates the soul while it gives pleasure, it is easily remembered when sung often, and what the harshness of the Law cannot force from the minds of man it excludes by the suavity of song," [6] and John Chrysostom writes: "For nothing so arouses the soul, gives it wing, sets it free from the earth, releases it from the prison of the body . . . as concordant melody and sacred song composed in rhythm." [7]

This digression on the general popularity of psalmody in the later fourth century provides the necessary background to understand better the establishment of psalmody in the contemporary Mass. The psalmody of the Mass was limited, confined typically to a single psalm in the Fore-Mass and another at communion time, but these were overtly musical events that were accepted as such in the principal ecclesiastical centers of the time. The Mass psalmody of the period was thus a liturgical innovation—not in the sense, as we saw in the previous chapter, that psalms had never been chanted in the Mass before but in the sense that psalmody now had the privileged position of a formal liturgical act. For centuries to come the celebration of Mass without the singing of psalms would be somehow incomplete. It is this new status of psalmody in the later fourth-century Mass that I would argue is not entirely comprehensible outside the context of the contemporary psalmodic movement.

THE LATER FOURTH-CENTURY MASS

My claim here that the psalmody of the later fourth-century Mass was confined typically to a single psalm in the Fore-Mass and another at communion time is best understood within an overview of the contemporary Mass. The ceremony began immediately with the readings after a brief greeting from the celebrant. In the abundant references, East and West, to the Fore-Mass of the time we have no mention of the preliminary prayers that come to characterize the medieval Mass and certainly no mention of an entrance chant. There is in fact a passage from Augustine's *De civitate Dei* that explicitly describes the abrupt beginning of the Fore-Mass, on no less a festivity than Easter. A miracle had taken place in the church just before Mass, and Augustine entered the church while the ensuing din still reigned. "I entered among the people," he tells us; "the church was full and rang with their joyful voices: 'Thanks be to God, God be praised!' Not a one was silent throughout the clamoring throng. I greeted the people, and again they cried out with still more fervent voice. Finally when all had become silent there was the accustomed reading of the divine scriptures."[8]

The readings of the time were sharply defined, as opposed to the freely expansive practice suggested by Justin's "the memoirs of the Apostles and the writings of the Prophets are read as long as time permits." Not untypical is Augustine's summary: "We heard the Apostle [epistle], we heard the Psalm, we heard the Gospel; all the divine readings (*divinae lectiones*) sound together."[9] The limited number of readings and psalms in the Fore-Mass[10] is an issue that must be dealt with later in this chapter; liturgical and musical historians alike have tended to ignore the explicit patristic testimony on the point. It is also of great importance that Augustine refers to all three items in the passage as readings; that the psalm of the Fore-Mass was still spoken of as a reading in his time—and clearly looked upon also as a chant—reveals much, as we shall see, about its history.

The Mass of the Faithful is not nearly as well described in the fourth-century literature as the Fore-Mass. We know at least, however, of the separation of the two portions of the eucharistic rite and the dismissal of the catechumens after the first of the two, an act that took place in Egeria's Jerusalem "according to the custom as it is observed everywhere."[11] As for offertory psalmody, we have no unequivocal evidence of its existence in the literature of the time. We cannot claim absolutely that psalms were never sung in any region at this point in the service, but the numerous contemporary references to psalmody in the Fore-Mass and at the distribution of communion lend support to the argument from silence on the point. There is, to be sure, a frequently quoted text from Augustine that some would see as a reference to offertory psalmody; it appears in his *Liber retractationem,* a late work in which he discusses his literary output, in this case a lost tract entitled *Contra Hilarem:*

> Meanwhile a certain Hilary, a lay Catholic of tribune rank, angered I know not why against the ministers of God, as often happens, attacked the custom which had begun then in Carthage—in abusive censorious terms, whenever possible, asserting it ought not to be—of singing (*dicerentur*) at the altar hymns from the Book of Psalms both before the oblation and while what had been offered was distributed to the people. I responded to him at the urging of the brethren, and the book was called *Against Hilary.*[12]

It is unfortunate that we do not possess this work, and its presumably more detailed information on the point at issue, but what we do have in the text from the *Retractationes* is by no means insignificant. Augustine mentions psalmody at two times: "before the oblation and while what had been offered was distributed to the people." There is, of course, no doubt that the second reference is to psalmody during the distribution of communion; it is the identity of the first that one might question—what is meant by psalmody "before the oblation (*ante oblationem*)"? The more obvious meaning, surely, is psalmody during the Fore-Mass. We have numerous contemporary references to psalmody at two places in the Mass and only two, the Fore-Mass and communion, whereas there are no references (other than this purported one) to offertory psalmody from the period, indeed none until some three centuries later in *Ordo romanus I.* Certainly, then, the word "oblation" should be taken in the broad sense of the eucharistic sacrifice as a whole, that is, the Mass of the Faithful as opposed to the preceding Mass of the Catechumens. This would seem to me to be the most plausible reading of the term even in the absence of what we know otherwise about the psalmody of the contemporary Mass. Thus psalmody "before the oblation" must refer to psalmody during the Fore-Mass.

But there is another possible interpretation, a more complex one, which is not entirely lacking in plausibility. It is that "before the oblation" refers to the time when the gifts are brought in, whereas the "oblation" itself takes place during the recitation of the eucharistic prayer over the gifts. Therefore Hilary objects to psalmody at what we would call the offertory and the communion. But why no mention of psalmody during the Fore-Mass? Because, presumably, Hilary objects only to psalmody during the hallowed time of the eucharistic service as such, not the more public service of instruction that precedes it.

This is, I think, a fair summary of the basic case for each position. There is more to be said for both, and the issue will be pursued below in the chapter devoted to the offertory. For present purposes the issue is exhausted since there exist no other putative references to a western offertory chant until the turn of the eighth century. We must simply admit the possibility, however remote, that this single passage refers to offertory psalmody and go on to study the rich fund of material on psalmody in the Fore-Mass and during Communion. It should be noted, moreover, that the psalmody at issue was considered an innovation by Augustine, a point to be considered below.

Within our survey of the later fourth-century Mass, the presence of the Sanctus in most, if not all, of the eucharistic prayers of the time is worthy of mention. Typically it took the form of a lyric congregational interjection, as described in the *Apostolic Constitutions,* where "all the people say with them [the angels] 'Holy, holy, holy, Lord of Sabaoth, heaven and earth are full of his glory; blessed be he for ever; Amen.'"[13] The Sanctus, of course, is an Ordinary rather than a Proper item, but no discussion of early Christian music is complete without at least passing reference to Kenneth Levy's marvelous revelation that the simple melody of the Sanctus, which we know from the early western sources (and in fact the tones of the entire accompanying eucharistic dialogue between celebrant and people), is very likely the same as that sung in the fourth century.[14]

To bring this overview of the ancient Mass to an end, there is, of course, the psalmody of communion time, which we will deal with now in some detail before taking up the more complex subject of Fore-Mass psalmody.

COMMUNION PSALMODY

Our earliest reference to communion psalmody may be from the *Mystagogical Catechesis* attributed to Cyril of Jerusalem (d.388), where we read: "After these things, listen to the singer (ψάλλοντος), who invites us with a sacred melody to communion in the holy mysteries, and says: 'Taste and see that the Lord is good'" (Ps 33.9).[15] Cyril was appointed bishop of Jerusalem in 349 and delivered a series of Lenten lectures, his *Catechesis* of 350, to the catechumens about to be baptized at the Easter Vigil. The *Mystagogical Catechesis,* a more advanced series of lectures for the newly baptized, was traditionally thought to have been written by Cyril not long after the *Catechesis.* Recently, however, the authenticity of the *Mystagogical Catechesis* has been questioned by some, who have attributed it to Cyril's successor John, bishop of Jerusalem from 387 to 417.[16] It is not certain, then, whether the reference to the communion from the work dates to the mid-fourth century or several decades later.

One notes, in any event, that the passage cites the well-known verse 9 of Psalm 33: "Taste and see that the Lord is good." The singling out of a particular verse in this manner gives reason to imagine that the entire psalm was sung with "Taste and see" as response. The assumption is given support from other roughly contemporary references to communion psalmody. The *Apostolic Constitutions* tell us that the entire psalm was sung: "Let the thirty-third psalm be sung while all the rest receive,"[17] and Jerome, addressing his monastic community at Bethlehem, suggests that "Taste and see" is sung by all: "Each day filled with the heavenly bread we say: 'Taste and see how sweet is the Lord.'"[18] Canon 97 of the so-called *Canons of Basil*, while not citing Psalm 33 in its reference to communion psalmody, is insistent on the point of congregational response: "The congregation shall respond with vigor after every psalm."[19]

The phrase "after every psalm" in this last quoted reference raises the distinct possibility that more than one psalm might be sung during communion. Thus psalms other than Psalm 33 could be sung, a possibility lent further support by John Chrysostom in his commentary on Psalm 144: "It is worth paying special attention to this psalm. For this is the psalm containing the words that initiate one into the mysteries and that are sung continually in response: 'The eyes of all look to thee, and thou givest them their food in due season'" (Ps 144.15).[20] Chrysostom's phrase "initiate one into the mysteries," along with the psalm's reference to "food in due season," is enough to confirm that this is a communion reference, if there is any doubt on that score. The passage has a certain interest in that it dates from John's Antioch period, 381–98, while the above-quoted *Apostolic Constitutions*, which specify the singing of Psalm 33 at communion, are generally thought to describe the liturgy of Antioch in about 380. John's phrase "sung continually in response" raises another, more general, point, one about the precise nature of responsorial psalmody during the patristic period. Although we have abundant references to congregational psalmodic response from the period, I know of no text that tells us just how often the response verse is sung. This could vary, theoretically, anywhere from a single response at the end of the psalm to one after every verse. John's "sung continually in response" could be taken to mean something closer to the latter possibility.

The final extant patristic reference to communion psalmody, and our sole western text on the subject, is that quoted above in connection with Augustine's lost *Contra Hilarem*. It cites "hymns from the Book of Psalms both before the oblation and while what had been offered was distributed to the people." The plural "hymns" has numerous syntactically valid meanings: it could mean a single psalm at each of the two places in the service or it could mean multiple psalms at each place; and it could just as well mean multiple psalms over the course of the year as opposed to multiple psalms on a single day. There seems little point in insisting upon one or the other of these possibilities; we must be content to add the questions raised here to those raised already by our five eastern texts. Before attempting to fashion a hypothesis from all six, we should note only that Augustine, in referring to communion psalmody as a "custom which had begun then in Carthage," obviously considered it to be an innovation in his time, at least in Carthage.

There is surely enough evidence in this modest assemblage of sources to conclude that Psalm 33 was the communion psalm of choice in the later fourth-century East, even if not in the West. This is confirmed by the special status of Γεύσασθε καὶ ἴδετε (Ps 33.9) among the Byzantine koinonica; the chant gives the appearance of having been the proto-communion by its exclusive use in the Mass of the Pre-Sanctified, which was said in the Byzantine liturgy on all those ordinary occasions of the year, the weekdays of Lent, for example, that do not have later, more Proper, liturgical formularies.[21] There is surely enough evidence, too, to conclude that the typical manner of performance for Psalm 33 was responsorial, with "Taste and see" as the response verse. Other psalms, such as Psalm 144, with its own appropriate verse 15, "and thou givest them their food in due season," were also heard occasionally, and more than one psalm might have been sung in some locations, depending, one assumes, upon the number of communicants.

There is no firm evidence that a communion psalm was sung before the late fourth century (indeed one must admit that the weight of evidence supports John of Jerusalem's authorship of the *Mystagogical Catechesis* over the traditional claim for his predecessor Cyril). I would continue to think, however, that the occasional singing of an appropriate psalm at communion, particularly in the East, was a distinct possibility as early as the third century, and that such singing became a prescribed event in the later decades of the fourth century during the above-described period of great popularity for the singing of psalms. As for the circumstance that the practice appears to have been an innovation in Augustine's Carthage, I have argued elsewhere that the "psalmodic movement" can be seen to move from East to West in the 370s and 380s and would suggest now that a similar progress of the custom of prescribed communion psalmody is a good possibility.

Finally, can the special status of Psalm 33 be looked upon as the first step in the establishment of the communion chant as Mass Proper? In a sense, yes, at least in the East, although, paradoxically, its regular usage in the later fourth century, corroborated as it is by the comparable usage of the medieval Byzantine Γεύσασθε καὶ ἴδετε, might lead one to refer to it as an Ordinary rather than a Proper item. Still, its position of parentage—as genuinely Proper Byzantine koinonika came to be created in later centuries for various festivals—allows us to speak of it as the proto-communion chant of the Byzantine Proper. As for the West, we do not know if the same claim is valid. There are no fourth-century western references to the singing of "Taste and see," and there are no traces of a special status for its Latin equivalent in the medieval Roman Mass Proper, where the communion *Gustate et videte* figures as no more than a single undifferentiated item in the post-Pentecostal series.

THE SINGLE FORE-MASS PSALM

The psalmody of the Fore-Mass is a more complex subject than communion psalmody. The many patristic texts that refer to it raise questions on at least four issues of basic importance: (1) the number of psalms that were typically sung at each service; (2) the nature of the historical shift from psalm as reading to psalm as chant; (3) the typical manner of Fore-Mass psalmody; was it responsorial or direct? and (4) the degree of continuity or discontinuity between the psalmody of the ancient Fore-Mass and the chants of the early medieval Roman Mass Proper.

The question of the number of psalms in the later fourth-century Fore-Mass is inseparable from that of the number of readings. Not long ago I addressed both in a lengthy review of Aimé Georges Martimort's *Les lectures liturgiques et leurs livres*.[22] I expressed total agreement with Monsignor Martimort's position on the number of readings and went on to spell out the corollary position on the number of psalms. Here, I will offer only a brief summary of what I wrote there; I would hope that the truth of the matter is obvious enough to allow for considerable abbreviation.

From a historiographic point of view Martimort simply showed that certain widely held assumptions about the number of readings in the ancient Fore-Mass are flatly contradicted by the witness of the patristic sources. The classic assumption about the structure of the ancient Fore-Mass, formulated by Louis Duchesne in his *Origines du culte chrétien* of 1899[23]— and subsequently embraced by liturgiologists and musicologists alike—is that the readings and chants followed a neatly symmetrical fivefold sequence: (1) Old Testament reading, (2) psalm, (3) New Testament reading, (4) psalm and (5) gospel. One of the readings was eventually dropped at

Rome, resulting in the early medieval pattern of (1) epistle (from either Old or New Testament), (2) gradual (except during Paschaltime), (3) alleluia or tract and (4) gospel. An essential element of the Duchesne position, and one adopted with special fervor by music historians, is that the ancient psalms did not function as independent liturgical items but rather as responses to the readings that preceded them. Following this logic, then, the two chants of the medieval Fore-Mass, following a single reading as they do, are evidence for a missing reading.

It is hardly an exaggeration to say that Duchesne's scheme collapses entirely in the face of a single Augustinian text like the following from Sermon 176: "First you heard the reading from the Apostle . . . then you sang a psalm . . . after this the evangelical reading."[24] We have here not a fivefold but a threefold pattern: epistle, psalm and gospel. And as for the notion that the psalm is merely a lyric response to the preceding reading, one need only recall the Augustinian reference quoted earlier: "You heard the Apostle, you heard the psalm, you heard the gospel. All the divine readings sound together." The psalm is an equal partner in a series of readings.

In quoting passages such as these, Martimort's intention is not to set up a rival scheme to those of earlier liturgical historians like Duchesne. His point is simply to show that no such scheme was universally observed in the early Church; rather there was a great variety of practice from region to region and indeed from day to day within the same ecclesiastical center. At the same time, he observes that more often than not the sources show only a single reading before the gospel (aside from the psalm), either from the Old Testament or more often from the New, as opposed to the purportedly obligatory readings from both.

My own purposes diverge slightly from those of Martimort's in view of my obvious involvement with psalmody. While I agree entirely with his overall position on the variety of Fore-Mass patterns, I must insist, as I did in the review, upon the more particular point that a single psalm is typical, whatever the number of readings. Take the following passage from John Chrysostom as an example:

> Just as there are various flowers in the meadow and, since all in a row are exceedingly lovely, each draws the eye of the beholder to look upon them, so too can one view the Holy Scriptures. For blessed David attracts our understanding to himself, so too the apostolic passage concerning Timothy which was read, and further the bold Isaiah philosophizing on human nature, and their Lord Jesus, speaking to the disciples and saying, "The harvest is plentiful, but the laborers are few" (Mt 9.37).[25]

John speaks of four "flowers" from the Holy Scriptures, one each from the Psalms, the epistle to Timothy, Isaiah and the gospel of Matthew. Similarly Basil of Caesarea, in a homily directed to those about to be baptized, cites, in turn, a verse from Isaiah, Psalm 33, Acts and Matthew; each of the four verses is clearly relevant to baptism and Basil concludes by saying, "all this in the reading of today works toward the same end."[26] It is true that John and Basil both mention an Old and New Testament reading, but still only a single psalm, itself in each case spoken of as a reading.

It is not my intention to claim that a single psalm was the absolute rule in the Fore-Mass of the later fourth century. Indeed I discussed two texts in my review—one from Chrysostom's Antiochene period and another from the Antiochene *Apostolic Constitutions*—that opened up the possibility of multiple psalms upon occasion at one or the other ecclesiastical center. What the sources overwhelmingly indicate is that a single psalm was the *norm*, both in the East and, more especially, the West. One might claim also that the patristic tendency to think of the Fore-Mass psalm as a reading adds further probability to this conclusion; it seems unlikely that two readings would be chosen from the same book of the Bible at the same Fore-Mass.

THE ORIGINS OF THE FORE-MASS PSALM

Thus to invoke the conception of Fore-Mass psalmody as reading, in any event, leads naturally to a consideration of the second in the series of four questions posed above: how to describe the historical shift from the psalm as reading to the psalm as chant. In the previous chapter I observed that psalms must have figured occasionally among the Old Testament readings of the Fore-Mass in the second and third centuries, and I speculated that the inherent lyric character of the psalms might have inspired certain lectors in certain congregations to declaim them in a more musical fashion than they would the other readings. I speculated further, at the beginning of the present chapter, that the great enthusiasm for the singing of psalms that characterized the closing decades of the fourth century motivated the ecclesiastical leaders of the time to include a psalm regularly among the readings of the Fore-Mass rather than occasionally and, moreover, to encourage an overtly musical performance of the psalm. This was, after all, the period in which a bishop such as Niceta of Remesiana was only echoing the sentiments of his contemporaries when he said: "A psalm is sweet to the ear when sung, it penetrates the soul while it gives pleasure."[27]

These speculations are supported by the duality of the later fourth-century texts that refer to the psalm of the Fore-Mass. Several texts that characterize this psalm as a reading have been quoted here already,[28] but there are just as many that speak of it as something that is sung. Augustine, for example, says of Psalm 119: "The psalm which we have just now heard sung and responded to in singing, is short and highly beneficial."[29] One notes, moreover, the reference to responsorial psalmody, a sure indication of musical rendition. John Chrysostom, to choose an example from an eastern author, cites, in commenting on Psalm 117, the congregational singing of the verse that one recognizes as the *Haec dies* of the Easter gradual: "The passage of the psalm which the people are accustomed to sing in response is this: 'This is the day the Lord has made, let us rejoice in it and be glad'" (Ps 117.24).[30] And, again, in a homily preached on Palm Sunday he exhorts his congregation: "Let us also go out, and displaying in place of palm branches good intentions, let us cry out as we sang today in response: 'Praise the Lord, O my soul! I will praise the Lord as long as I live!'" (Ps 145.2).[31] Augustine reveals that such congregational responses could be memorably tuneful; in speaking of the opening verse of Psalm 132, *Ecce quam bonum*, he says: "So sweet is that sound that even they who are ignorant of the Psalter sing that verse . . . this sweet sound, this lovely melody (*suavis melodia*)."[32]

To state the historical process, then, that is implicit in all this: the occasional appearance in earlier centuries of a psalm among the readings of the Fore-Mass becomes a regular liturgical event in the later fourth century, one that is unapologetically musical in character, even while it retains its formal status as a reading.

RESPONSORIAL OR DIRECT PSALMODY?

The third question in the presently considered series calls for a more specific definition of this Fore-Mass psalm: was it generally executed in the responsorial manner, and can it be looked upon as the ancestor of the medieval gradual? I advocated this view more than a decade ago but have since been chided by Philippe Bernard: "McKinnon nous semble oublier totalement le trait."[33] I acknowledge a measure of justice in the criticism. In focusing upon the numerous passages of the later fourth century that single out congregational responses, I failed to recognize the possibility that the psalm of the Fore-Mass might also have been sung without responses, that is, *in directum*, or "directly," to cite the standard terminology. My lapse stems from a circumstance of language. If a psalm verse is singled out, we know that responsorial psalmody is involved—as, for example, when Ambrose says, "Hence what was sung today as a response to the psalm (*psalmi responsorio decantatum est*): 'With expectation I have waited for the Lord, and he was attentive to me'" (Ps 39.2). His remark reinforces our point.[34] But on many occasions an author will simply mention that a certain psalm had been sung without citing a particular verse; thus Jerome, in his homily on Psalm 9, tells his monastic community: "The ninth psalm, which was sung by you to the Lord, is grand in its poetry and grand in its mysteries."[35]

We know from this text only that Psalm 9 was sung; its language does not reveal whether it was sung with responses or not. We must, then, admit the possibility, indeed I would say the probability, that at least certain of such passages refer to direct psalmody. But we need not go so far as Bernard, Olivier Cullin and other French scholars, who claim that the psalmody of the Fore-Mass (consisting, incidentally, always in two psalms) was exclusively direct before the fourth century, when it was altered to become responsorial in character, and who go on from there to make the extraordinary claim that the gradual of the Mass evolved from the tract.[36] I prefer to postpone discussion of this issue to my chapter on the tract and now simply express positively what I imagine to be the more likely sequence of events.

It may very well be that the psalms that figured occasionally among the readings of the earlier Fore-Mass were more often than not recited without refrains. This would appear to be only natural in those venues and on those occasions when the psalm was performed in a manner not unlike that employed for the other readings. But we cannot rule out the possibility that responses were sometimes included. Responsorial singing is hardly an invention of the later fourth century. The periodic response of a group with easily memorized refrains to a longer text recited by a song leader is a widely, perhaps even universally, observed musical phenomenon. It was certainly one well known to the ancient Jews and Christians: responsorial psalmody was a feature of temple worship;[37] it was practiced by the Jewish *Therapeutai* described by Philo of Alexandria (d.c.50);[38] and Tertullian (d.c.225) appears to have it in mind when he says: "The more exacting in their prayer are accustomed to add to their prayers an alleluia and that sort of psalm in which those present respond with the closing verses (*clausulis respondeant*)."[39] Who can deny that the practice might from time to time have been applied to a psalm read during the early Fore-Mass, particularly on a more festive occasion or when the psalm was one with a traditionally cherished response verse?

The operative distinction, I believe, is not one of chronology but one of a psalm's musical quotient, so to speak. To the extent that a psalm functions merely as a reading, it seems more likely that it would be rendered directly, but to the extent that it is looked upon as a musical event, it would more likely be sung with responses. Thus rather than a simple chronological movement from direct to responsorial psalmody in the ancient Fore-Mass, we should assume a parallel movement of the two types, with the latter becoming considerably more common in the heightened musical climate of the later fourth century.

I may seem to beg the question on this latter point, that is, that the psalm of the later fourth-century Fore-Mass was in fact sung typically with responses, in spite of the existence of many passages like that quoted above from Jerome's homily on Psalm 9, which do not specify this type of singing. Anyone who works for a long period of time with the patristic sources is susceptible to the overwhelming impression created by the numerous references to responsorial psalmody, but the reader of this volume needs something more objective than this. Some half dozen texts describing responsorial psalmody have been quoted already in the immediately preceding paragraphs, texts from Augustine, Ambrose and John Chrysostom; these could be multiplied almost indefinitely, but still one asks if there is some sort of quantitative standard that could be applied to them against those that are silent on the subject of responses. I have, in fact, sought to collect every reference of Augustine to liturgical psalmody from his more than 700 extant sermons.[40] I find that there are about 150 explicit references to the singing of a psalm in the service prior to the sermon in question and that slightly more than 100 of these cite a specific verse that had been sung, as often as not indicating in some way that the verse figured as a response. Surely one would conclude from this that also a large proportion, perhaps even a majority, of the fewer texts that do not explicitly cite response verses also refer to psalms that had been sung responsorially.

Another sort of argument for the prevalence of responsorial performance would be a contemporary service order that specified it. In point of fact we have only one service order from the period, the *Apostolic Constitutions*. It tells us: "After two readings let someone else sing the hymns of David, and let the people respond with verses (ἀκροστίχια)."[41] This is, incidentally, one of the two passages referred to above, but not quoted, that might be construed to indicate the singing of more than one psalm in the Fore-Mass. The passage is ambiguous on that point—the plural "hymns of David" can be taken to refer not only to singing at a single service but to the singing of psalms throughout the year—but it is clear on the responsorial manner of the psalmody. By coincidence the other passage in question also specifies responsorial psalmody; it is from a homily of John Chrysostom on the gospel of Matthew: "When you are dismissed, after singing the response to two or three psalms and saying the accustomed prayers superficially and in an indifferent manner, you consider this to be enough for your salvation."[42] There is good reason to think that this passage is addressed to catechumens in a homily preached during the Fore-Mass: the subject of the homily is a gospel (always a good indication of a eucharistic service), the reference to salvation conveys a sense that the service is an obligatory one and the mention of dismissal reminds one that catechumens are dismissed at the conclusion of the Fore-Mass.[43] If this interpretation is correct, the reference to multiple psalms is not ambiguous, as was the case with the passage from the *Apostolic Constitutions*. But, to return to the point presently at issue, the reference to responsorial psalmody is equally unambiguous.

One might add also that the generally responsorial character of communion psalmody at this time, as described earlier in this chapter, would seem to suggest a similar performance of Fore-Mass psalmody. And, finally, it will be seen in the next chapter that the sources of the immediately succeeding centuries (admittedly sparse) speak exclusively of responsorial psalmody in the Fore-Mass.

If it can be accepted, then, that the psalm of the Fore-Mass was typically sung with responses, there remains the likelihood that it was sometimes sung, or at least recited, directly. Thus if one usually thinks of it as a sort of proto-gradual, one must consider that it was upon occasion a kind of proto-tract. I would, by the way, think that this situation applies more to the West than to the East—if for no other reason than the presence of the medieval Roman tract and the absence of a comparable Byzantine chant. The typical responsorial psalm of antiquity, in any event, and the exceptional direct psalm are nicely matched by the early medieval situation where the gradual was sung throughout most of the year and the tract only with comparative rarity. Might we also assume that direct psalmody tended to be employed typically on penitential occasions, as was the medieval tract, and responsorial psalmody on festive occasions, in keeping with its more overtly musical character? I believe that this remains an eminently reasonable hypothesis, even if we have no positive evidence for it, and even if we cannot make absolute claims for it in the face of a passage from Augustine like the following: "The voice of the penitent is recognized in the words with which we respond to the singer: 'Hide thy face from my sin, and blot out all my iniquities'" (Ps 50.11).[44]

If the prevalence of proto-gradual over proto-tract is clear, there remains the question of proto-alleluia. This is a subject to which I have devoted much attention in the past and that I will take up again in the chapter on the alleluia; here I will say only what is absolutely essential to the present exposition. It is true that the exclamation "Alleluia" figures at times as the response to the psalm of the Fore-Mass; in his commentary on Psalm 113, Augustine mentions "this psalm to which we just now responded by pronouncing and singing alleluia (*nunc alleluia pronuntiato cantatoque respondimus*)."[45] I find at least five other examples in the sermons of Augustine where he refers to the singing of alleluia in connection with a psalm. Not all of them are quite so explicit about the function of the alleluia as response, but it is a fair assumption: the five psalms involved (Psalms 104, 110, 117, 148 and 149) are, like Psalm 113, from those twenty that have "alleluia" superscribed in the Bible. I think it probable, then, that alleluia was the generally employed response for such psalms, although Psalm 117 was an exception in that Augustine, while citing alleluia as the response in one homily, quotes the familiar *Haec dies* (verse 24) in no less than three.[46]

I think it an obvious assumption, too, that the liturgical season during which these alleluia psalms would have been sung in the Fore-Mass was Paschaltime; in his commentary on Psalm 110 Augustine contrasts the fifty joyful days of the Easter season with the preceding forty of Lent: "The days have come for us to sing alleluia. . . . For as these days, with grateful gladness regularly follow the preceding days of Quadragesima each year, by which is signified the sorrow of this life before the resurrection of the Lord's body . . . and signified by the number forty. . . . But signified by the number fifty after the resurrection of the Lord, when we sing alleluia . . ."[47] Still we cannot assume that an alleluia-psalm with alleluia response was sung on every day of Paschaltime. We have indications that Psalm 140 (not an alleluia-psalm) was sung in Augustine's church on the vigil of Pentecost and that Psalm 44 (likewise not an alleluia-psalm) was sung on Pentecost day.[48] Moreover, the three homilies, mentioned above, that cite *Haec dies* as a response for the alleluia-psalm Psalm 117 were preached, respectively, on the day of Easter, during Easter week and on the octave of Easter (assignments that have a remarkable resemblance to the liturgical placement of the early medieval gradual *Haec dies*, a point to be pursued presently).

Should we think, then, of the occasional appearance of an alleluia-psalm with alleluia response during Paschaltime as the proto-alleluia? Perhaps it is better to say that the gradual psalm of Augustine's church was on occasion, particularly during Paschaltime, an alleluia-psalm. The circumstance that legitimizes such language is the existence of a single psalm at this time in the Fore-Mass, a psalm whose placement, moreover, and whose form and very name manifest historical continuity with the early medieval *responsum* or *responsum graduale*. A genuine proto-alleluia would require the regular appearance of two psalms in the Fore-Mass, the second of which is always sung with alleluia as response. It happens that precisely that pattern does appear in relatively ancient times, but only in Jerusalem, and not until the second or third decade of the fifth century, too late, apparently, to influence the West.[49] By that time the inroads of the Germanic tribes had already begun to bring about the isolation of the western ecclesiastical centers that would result in the various Latin liturgies we refer to as the Mozarabic, Milanese, Gallican, Roman and Beneventan. But this is a subject to be taken up in the following chapter; for now we note the typical existence of a single psalm in the Fore-Mass, one generally sung responsorially, even if with alleluia as response on a number of dates in Paschaltime, and even if, in the West at least, sung directly on some less festive occasions.

REPERTORIAL CONTINUITY
BETWEEN FOURTH AND SEVENTH CENTURIES?

The fourth and final question concerning the psalmody of the ancient Fore-Mass has to do with the extent to which we can see the beginnings of the early medieval Roman Mass Proper in the psalmody of the ancient Fore-Mass. At issue here is not an attempt to define the origins of certain Mass Proper items, a task just performed, but rather to see whether the specific psalmic assignments for various ancient festivals manifest historical continuity with the texts of medieval Roman chants. Before taking up this inquiry, however, one must first acknowledge a difficulty that besets any attempt to link the liturgical history of the fourth century with that of medieval Rome: we are forced to rely heavily upon the sermons of Augustine, which, of course, were preached not at Rome but at Hippo and Carthage. There is a lesser fund of relevant material from Ambrose's Milan, but virtually nothing from Rome itself.[50] The generally acknowledged close liturgical relationship between the churches of Milan, Rome and North Africa is surely of some relevance to our subject, but I would think that it does little more than assure us that the overall structure of the Fore-Mass was by and large homogeneous in these different locations. The assignments of specific psalms, the issue under present consideration, is an entirely different matter. Indeed, far from claiming that these psalms are generally the same from city to city within the Milanese to North African liturgical axis, I would argue that the notion of stable year-to-year psalmic assignments even within the same church is an anachronism at the turn of the fifth century. This crucially important phenomenon, what I call "discontinuity of liturgical assignment," would, I hope, render moot the difficulty involved in having to invoke the testimony of Augustine of Hippo so frequently in a book devoted to the history of the Roman Mass Proper.

If discontinuity of liturgical assignment is the rule, there are nonetheless exceptions, and each of them must be cherished as a historical treasure. The Easter response "This is the day the Lord has made" (Ps 117.24) is an obvious example. We have seen already that both Augustine in the West and John Chrysostom in the East cite it, and it reappears as the response verse not only of the Roman Easter gradual *Haec dies,* but also of the Byzantine prokeimenon Αὕτη ἡ ἡμέρα.

One can ask, however, whether this identical assignment is a matter of genuine shared tradition between East and West or simply a coincidence. The latter possibility cannot be dismissed out of hand; there are some psalm texts so obviously appropriate to certain occasions that we can well imagine different liturgical centers using them independently of one another. This would appear to be the case, for example, with *Ascendit deus in jubilatione* (Ps 46.4) and the feast of the Ascension; we have no early Christian evidence of its liturgical use, and when it appears in medieval Rome and Byzantium, it does so in different liturgical placements, as communion in the former and *alleluiarion* (alleluia verse) in the latter. In the case of *Haec dies,* however, I would assume that its ancient appearance as well as its virtual ubiquity in the medieval Fore-Mass of Easter (that of Jerusalem, Toledo and Milan in addition to Rome and Byzantium) speaks for a shared tradition of great antiquity.

It was mentioned above that Augustine cites the singing of *Haec dies* throughout Easter week. This is truly remarkable in view of the seeming anomaly that *Haec dies* appears in the Roman liturgy as gradual response throughout Easter week, whereas the gradual is not sung for the rest of Paschaltime. The first of two alleluias appears instead, reminding us of the use of alleluia as psalm response during Paschaltime in the early Church. Surely there is a historical connection underlying this striking set of circumstances, one that merits renewed attention in our chapter on the Roman alleluia.

Bearing some resemblance to the case of *Haec dies* is that of *In omnem terram exivit sonus eorum,* "Their sound has gone forth in all the earth" (Ps 18.5). It is a text particularly appropriate to an apostle, one who broadcasts the "sound" of the gospel "in all the earth." A variation of the idea is a commonplace in patristic psalm commentaries, where its expression is occasioned by the appearance of the word "trumpet" in a psalm. Athanasius of Alexandria, for example, in his commentary on the verse "Blow a trumpet at the new moon" (Ps 80.4), says: "Just as Israel in ancient times took sensible trumpets and blew upon them at the new moon . . . so too the new people, using the gospel trumpet, whose 'sound has gone forth in all the earth'" (Ps 18.5).[51] Augustine cites the singing of the verse *In omnem terram* on the feast of SS. Peter and Paul (19 June at that time),[52] while the Roman Mass Proper has the gradual *In omnem terram* on three apostolic feasts: the octave of SS. Peter and Paul, the feast of SS. Simon and Jude and the vigil of St. Andrew. The Greek counterpart, Εἰς πασαν τὴν γῆν, is the Common prokeimenon for feasts of the apostles. We have no example of the verse's use as a response in the eastern patristic sources, but this is no surprise in view of the comparatively small total of references to specific psalm responses in these sources. I would imagine that the source of the widespread use of *In omnem terram* on apostolic liturgical occasions is the exegetical commonplace of the gospel trumpet mentioned above. It is found already in the writings of Clement of Alexandria (d.c.215), who says: "The trumpet of Christ is his gospel: he has blown it and we have heard."[53]

Martyrs, like apostles, were heroes of early Christianity and thus constitute another category with which we might expect to have some appropriate response associated. Augustine, in fact, cites the response *Pretiosa in conspectu domini mors sanctorum ejus*, "Precious in the sight of the Lord is the death of his saints" (Ps 115.15), in two different sermons preached on the anniversary of martyrs' deaths;[54] and the Roman Proper has the text for the gradual of St. Sebastian, a martyr venerable enough to be mentioned in the Philocalian Calendar. The text, however, is not found in the repertory of the Byzantine prokeimenon.

A final pair of examples comes not from the responsorial psalm of the Fore-Mass, but from the canticles of the Easter Vigil: Augustine mentions two of these, the canticle of Moses, *Cantemus domino*, and the baptismal psalm *Sicut cervus*.[55] There are no less than six extant sermons preached by Augustine at the Easter Vigil, and in one of them he says: "We sang to the Lord, 'For he is gloriously magnified . . . he cast Moses and the riders into the sea'" (Ex 15.1).[56] And in his enarration to Psalm 41 he writes: "'As the hart longs for the springs of water so my soul longs for Thee, O God' [Ps 41.1]. And indeed the voice [that utters these words] is well understood as the cry of those who, since they are still catechumens, are hastening to the grace of the holy bath. And thus this psalm is customarily chanted that they may long for the fountain of the remission of sins."[57] These words may not have been preached on the Easter Vigil, but Augustine's clear reference to the customary singing of *Sicut cervus* at the baptism of the catechumens leaves little doubt what he has in mind on that occasion, the universally observed time for baptism in the later fourth century. If, incidentally, his quoting of a single verse in both the case of *Cantemus domino* and *Sicut cervus* suggests responsorial singing, as opposed to the direct psalmody of the medieval Easter Vigil chants, this should occasion no surprise. The rubrics of the Armenian Lectionary make it clear that *Cantemus domino* was sung in fifth-century Jerusalem with its first verse as a response,[58] and at least one early medieval source refers to the Easter Vigil's *Sicut cervus* as *responsoriu[m] psalmi d[aui]d*.[59] The medieval custom of singing the Easter Vigil canticles directly, using the mode-8 tract melody, as we shall see in chapter 11, is a Frankish adaptation of the original Roman canticles, which were still declaimed by the lector in the seventh century.

The group of texts just discussed are perhaps the most likely examples of a continuous tradition of association between early Christian psalm responses and Roman Proper chants. A sixth verse, what we might call a "near miss," is *Dominus dixit ad me: Filius meus es tu, ego hodie genui*, "The Lord said to me: Thou art my son, this day I have begotten Thee" (Ps 2.7), which we recognize as the Roman introit antiphon for the first Mass of Christmas. A fourth-century Arian sermon cites this verse from the "just now sung psalm" (*in presenti decantato psalmo*), an apparent reference to the psalm sung in the Fore-Mass before the homily was preached.[60] Philippe Bernard, even while acknowledging that the reference is to the psalmody of the Fore-Mass rather than to an entrance psalm, makes the extraordinary claim that there is proof in these sermons that the chants preserved in the ninth-century manuscripts go back to the fourth century.[61] Surely the more likely view of the passage is that a certain fourth-century Arian bishop found Psalm 2, because of the verse in question, a good choice to be sung on a particular Christmas (there are three more Christmas sermons in the collection, but these do not cite Psalm 2), just as the early medieval Roman singers, quite independently in all probability, thought Psalm 2 a good choice for an introit psalm and *Dominus dixit* a good choice for its antiphon. The Byzantine prokeimenon response, it is true, uses the same verse, and it is conceivable, even if not likely, that there is some sort of historical connection between the Latin Arian usage and the medieval Byzantine; it is not entirely out of the question that both come from some unknown ancient eastern tradition. But even if this were so, Augustine is unaware of it; he passes over the verse in his lengthy enarration to Psalm 2 without so much as a mention of Christmas. The verse that he does associate with Christmas, in no less than four extant sermons, is *Veritas de terra orta est*, "Truth is sprung out of the earth" (Ps 84.12).[62] This text, in turn, appears nowhere in the Roman Mass Proper for Christmas, and for that matter nowhere in any Latin Christmas Proper, not the Milanese, the Beneventan nor the Mozarabic. And to reverse our perspective, and take the psalm that is most prominent in the Roman Mass Proper for Christmas, Psalm 97, which furnishes the *Viderunt omnes* of the gradual and communion as well as the introit psalm, Augustine, again, fails to associate it with Christmas in his enarration on the psalm.

What we have in this cluster of Christmas psalms is a clear example of discontinuity of assignment—discontinuity from ancient times to the early Middle Ages, and even discontinuity from region to region in ancient times. Such discontinuity would appear to be the norm, while the handful of examples like *Haec dies, In omnem terram* and *Sicut cervus*, precious though they be, are the exception. The norm is represented by numerous examples like the following: John Chrysostom's testimony to the singing of the response "Praise the Lord, O my soul" (Ps 145.2) on Palm Sunday,[63] which is not matched by the Byzantine prokeimenon for the day; and Augustine's testimony to singing of "Save us, O Lord" (Ps 105.47) on New Year's Day,[64] which is not matched by any chant from a Latin medieval Fore-Mass.[65] And, again, one can look backward from the medieval Proper to the fourth century and witness the same sort of discontinuity. Many of the most obviously appropriate texts of the medieval Mass Proper are not similarly associated in the patristic sources: in addition to Christmas's *Viderunt omnes*, mentioned above, there are, for example, the Epiphany's *Reges Tharsis* (Ps 71.10), the Ascension's *Ascendit deus in jubilatione* (Ps 46.4) and Pentecost's *Emitte spiritum tuum* (Ps 103.30).

Such discontinuity of assignment should come as no surprise. Indeed the very term "assignment" is an anachronism when applied to the fourth century, implying as it does a systematic allotment of psalms to every date in the calendar, and the reuse of them each year; this is a process that would require a written record of some sort, even if only marginal notations within a psalter. There exists, it is true, a book that answers at least partially to this description, the so-called Psalter of St-Germain-des-Prés, but it dates from the later sixth century and it simply places an *R* in the margin to identify likely response verses, without indicating liturgical assignments in any way.[66] The exceptional responses like *Haec dies*, then, are not part of a system of assignments, but rather strikingly appropriate verses that are widely associated with certain festivals. They were surely players within an oral liturgical tradition long before they became recorded in liturgical books.

The normal manner of choosing psalms for most occasions of the ancient church year was simply that the celebrant picked them for reasons that he deemed appropriate at the time. Thus Augustine tells his congregation, "We had prepared for ourselves a short psalm, which we had ordered to be sung by the reader; but as it seems, when the time came he was confused and read a different one rather than the other."[67] Augustine goes on to say that he recognized the will of God in the lector's mistake and thus preached on the psalm that was actually sung rather than the one he had anticipated. He speaks of a similar event in another sermon: "We did not order the lector to sing this psalm, but he from his boyish heart ordered what he thought would be useful for you to hear."[68] Apparently, even a young lector might take it upon himself to choose the psalm. A less commonly employed means of selection is what liturgical historians call *lectio currens*, that is, proceeding from day to day through a book of the Bible in order. Jerome appears to have done this at the Sunday Eucharist in his monastery at Bethlehem. In his homily on Psalm 7 he says: "Last Sunday the sixth psalm was read . . . now however the seventh psalm is read,"[69] and preaching on Psalm 14 he says: "Appropriately, the fourteenth psalm was read; and it occurs thus in sequence (*secundum ordinem*) and so seems read almost by design. The psalm is read in sequence—I believe this happens by a dispensation of God, that what might be of benefit to you was recited today in the normal order of exposition."[70] In this second example he points out that the appearance of Psalm 14 in numerical sequence is providential; he finds some point in its content that is particular relevant to what he wishes to say on the day in question.

The manner of choosing psalms is quite similar to that of choosing readings, which is as it should be in view of the related history of the two liturgical genres. Augustine tells us that the people objected to his decision to have all four Passion narratives read one year on Good Friday because they had become accustomed to the exclusive reading of the Matthew Passion.[71] This would seem to be a matter of traditional association, just like the singing of *Haec dies;* Augustine decides to exercise his normal prerogative of choice but is overruled by what his congregation remembers from previous years. There is a historiographic sequence of events concerning the Augustinian readings for Paschaltime that some might find amusing. Successive scholars have sought to analyze the many extant sermons preached from year to year during the season and to reconstruct Augustine's Paschaltime evangeliary. The highly conflicting "assignments," however, led them to develop ever more complex chronological layers of newly established gospel assignments. Finally, Anton Zwinggi, taking a sensible view of the matter, concluded simply that Augustine chose his readings on a year-to-year basis.[72] As for *lectio currens*, the same Zwinggi demonstrates that this approach was considerably less common in Augustine's church than some liturgical historians have supposed.[73]

THE FOURTH-CENTURY FULFILLMENT

Against the later fourth-century background of unprecedented enthusiasm for the singing of psalms, two musical events become established in the Mass: the singing of a psalm during the distribution of communion and another during the readings of the Fore-Mass. The psalm generally heard at communion time, at least in the East, is Psalm 33, and it is usually sung responsorially with verse 9, "Taste and see that the Lord is good," serving as congregational refrain.

The psalm of the Fore-Mass exists in historical continuity with the occasional declamation in earlier centuries of a psalm as an Old Testament reading. We know this because ecclesiastical authors of the later fourth century—John Chrysostom, Basil, Ambrose and Augustine—still speak of this psalm as a biblical reading. At the same time, however, their language reveals that they also look upon it as a distinctly musical event. A single psalm is the norm, although there are isolated texts suggesting that more than one might be sung at times in certain eastern locations. The usual manner of singing the psalm is with one of its verses serving as congregational response. During Paschaltime alleluia-psalms might be sung with the superscribed "alleluia" as response, and during Lent, in the West at least, the psalm might sometimes be sung without responses. Yet the evidence as a whole suggests that this single, typically responsorial, psalm is the direct ancestor of the Roman *responsum graduale* and the Byzantine prokeimenon. Such historical continuity, however, is primarily a matter of the liturgical placement of the item, and its musical form; its textual content is an entirely different matter. Only a handful of traditional associations, like that of *Haec dies* with Easter, survive from antiquity to the Middle Ages; discontinuity of psalmic assignment, indeed the absence of fixed assignment, is by far the norm.

CHAPTER 3

Centuries of Silence: Gaul

Augustine lay dying in 430 as the Vandals held his episcopal see of Hippo under siege. It must have seemed like the end of civilization to him. Already two decades before, in the year 410, when the Visigoth king Alaric had looted Rome, the bishop was prompted to set down his musings on the evanescent nature of temporal power in his monumental *De civitate Dei*. But this later assault was altogether more final and devastating than the events of 410. The Vandals had left their native region in the Oder Valley in the fourth century and swept west through France and Spain, finally entering North Africa in 429 and moving east to subdue most of the southern Mediterranean coast. Their ruthlessness matched the popular conception of the ravages wrought by the barbarian tribes who brought about the collapse of the Roman Empire, and of the unrelieved degradation that was to follow in the centuries that we call the Dark Ages.

The historical reality, needless to say, is much more complex than that. There was in the East, of course, the survival of fortress Byzantium for more than a millennium until its final surrender to the Turks in 1453. Its frontiers were harassed, it is true, by successive waves of barbarians, Persians and Moslems, but the great city itself remained intact, as did its splendid imperial court, not to speak of its correspondingly grand ecclesiastical cadres. And if we cannot fail to note the sharp decline in the vigor and originality of its intellectual life, we must remain in awe of an architectural accomplishment such as the building of Hagia Sophia during the reign of Justinian I (527–65).

The situation in the West was essentially different. In the East barbarians were at the gates; in the West they ruled from within. Indeed, the last Roman emperor, the boy Romulus Augustulus, was deposed virtually unnoticed in 476 by the German warrior Odoacer. But certain of the new sovereigns were capable of enlightened and benevolent governance; they admired many features of Roman civilization and sought to preserve them. Italy saw a kind of twilight of Roman culture under the Ostrogoth Theodoric the Great (d.526); it was in his court at Ravenna that Boethius composed his digests of classical learning (even if he was eventually executed for allegedly siding with the renewed imperial ambitions of Justinian against Theodoric). In Gaul at this time, many members of the aristocracy retreated to the guarded confines of their country estates, but some cities retained a semblance of Roman urban life under the leadership of stalwart bishops like Caesarius of Arles (d.542) and Gregory of Tours (d.594). Spain developed a vigorous ecclesiastical life under the Visigoths at cities such as Toledo and produced the Iberian counterpart to Boethius in Isidore of Seville (d.636).

The entire era in the West is better characterized as one of gradual decline from Roman civilization rather than one of abrupt cessation—and a decline, moreover, that saw intervals of relative tranquillity and even partial restoration. Ironically, the most disastrous time for Rome was brought about by Justinian's plan to restore imperial rule in the West. The army of his general Belisarius reconquered North Africa within a matter of months but met with fierce and persistent resistance from the Ostrogoths in Italy. The so-called Gothic Wars were fought for some twenty years (535–54), leaving the peninsula utterly devastated. Then, not much more than a decade later, it was easy prey for the Lombards who invaded in 568 and took possession of virtually all but its southernmost regions. At Rome, the ravages of siege and pillage were joined by the natural disasters of plague, flood and famine, leaving it in the most piteous condition at the time of Gregory the Great's accession to the papacy in 590. One gains some insight into the city's plight by considering that its population, which was about 800,000 at the end of the fourth century, had plummeted to about 30,000 by the middle of the sixth, and if it grew to about 90,000 in Gregory's time, this was only because of the influx of refugees from the ruined countryside.[1]

WESTERN LITERARY OUTPUT

However one wishes to characterize the general condition of the West during this period, there can be no doubt about the sharp decline in its literary output, including the kinds of ecclesiastical writing that might furnish us with evidence about the state of contemporary liturgy and chant. The notable exception is monastic rules: from Gaul we have ones from Caesarius of Arles and Aurelian of Arles (d.551), and from contemporary Italy the Rule of the Master and the incomparable Rule of St. Benedict (d.c.550). Unfortunately these works, while giving detailed descriptions of the Office, have virtually nothing to say about the contemporary Mass. The sermons of Caesarius of Arles and the historical works of Gregory of Tours furnish many scattered remarks about ecclesiastical song in Gaul; the majority of these also are more relevant to the Office, but there are a number of valuable references to the Mass. There is, of course, the intriguing description of a Gallican Mass in the *Expositio brevis antiquae liturgiae gallicanae* of Pseudo-Germanus of Paris. From Gaul also, and from Spain, there are the proceedings of several church councils that occasionally provide information on the Mass chants of the fifth and sixth centuries. For the following century in England, the Venerable Bede's (d.735) great *Historia ecclesiastica* furnishes us with several fascinating anecdotes about the activities of church musicians there, and the proceedings of the eighth-century councils add a few highly pertinent texts.

Unfortunately we have no more information from Rome before the eighth century than we do from the other regions, perhaps even less. There are not much more than a handful of relevant remarks that one can glean from the sermons of Pope Leo the Great (440–61), the *Liber pontificalis,* the pseudo-correspondence of Jerome and Damasus and the letter of the Roman presbyter Senarius. The greatest disappointment is Gregory the Great himself (590–604), a prolific author on matters ecclesiastical but remarkably silent on liturgy and chant, the subjects supposedly of greatest concern to him.

The main task of the present chapter, devoted to Gaul, and the next, devoted to Rome and England, is to sift through this material, taking note of virtually every relevant scrap of evidence, in an effort to find some meaningful pattern.

LECTOR CHANT AND SCHOLA CHANT

There is a conceptual tool that I believe can greatly facilitate this task, that of the essential difference between "lector chant" and "schola chant," a distinction first made by Dom Jean Claire.[2] Later fourth-century Mass psalmody, certainly, is lector chant, whereas the Roman Mass Proper of the seventh and eighth centuries is schola chant. In any attempt to date the creation of the Roman Mass Proper, then, it is fundamentally important to determine the period when Roman ecclesiastical song passed from the state of lector chant to schola chant. But first a summary definition of the terms.

We have seen enough evidence in the preceding chapter to have formed already some idea of the nature of lector chant, at least as it was employed in the responsorial psalmody of the ancient Mass. The lector declaims a psalm and the congregation responds, in some pattern or another, with the response verse. The lector might sing the psalm from memory or he might use a kind of psalter, while the people, surely, sing the brief response to a well-known tune without the aid of a written text. Augustine, as we saw, speaks of the lector's "boyish heart," but we need not suppose that he is just any youth chosen from the congregation at random. Already at this time a lector holds a minor clerical office, which for some individuals will lead eventually to the priesthood. And a lector selected to sing the psalm could be so chosen because of his musical aptitude; Ambrose tells us: "One is considered better qualified to enunciate a reading, another more pleasing with a psalm."[3] In the contemporary East, in fact, the term *psaltes* (cantor) appears occasionally; the *Apostolic Constitutions* speak of the clergy receiving communion in hierarchical order: "Let the bishop receive, then the priests, and the deacons, and the subdeacons, and the lectors and the cantors (ψάλται)."[4] The office of clerical cantor fails to become so clearly distinguished in the ancient West, however, so the usage "lector chant" seems preferable in present circumstances to the not entirely inappropriate "cantor chant." The reader of this volume will note, incidentally, interesting parallels between the history of the terms *lector* and *psaltes* and developments described in the previous chapter. That it is a lector who sings psalms comes as no surprise, for example, in a liturgical culture where a sung psalm is called a reading, and that the East develops a separate term for the clerical singer before the West does is in keeping with the general eastern leadership in early Christian psalmody.

While schola chant is essentially different from lector chant, the difference is not necessarily one of musical quality. Congregational responses, as we saw in the case of *Ecce quam bonum* (Ps 132.1), could be memorably tuneful, and a particular lector could be gifted with a lovely voice and a talent for melodic improvisation. The essential difference is twofold: repertorial and organizational. Schola chant involves the creation of a large body of chant and its maintenance from year to year, related tasks that can be accomplished only by an established group of quasi-professional musicians. Lector chant, on the other hand, is both more individual and more ephemeral, some might say more free, relating it to the charisma and spontaneity of early Christian worship, as opposed to the quest for order and uniformity that characterizes medieval liturgy.

Be that as it may, a body of ecclesiastical song like the Roman Mass Proper, consisting in some 600 discrete items, could scarcely be created and maintained without a group like the Roman schola cantorum. The task of creation alone would have been enormous, whether it conformed to the model of the Advent Project described in the introduction to this volume or was carried out in stages over many generations. It would seem to require the undivided attention of a cadre of talented singers who were free from all other responsibilities so that they could devote themselves for years on end to their work. And the task of maintaining the repertory from year to year would also require the existence of such an organization. The texts of the Roman Mass Proper were no doubt recorded in writing, but the preservation of the melodies—whether reproduced precisely from year to year or only approximately—would require the shared memory of a like-minded community. Practice time would be necessary for choral chants such as the introit and communion antiphons; at these sessions some members, particularly those originally responsible for the creation of certain segments of the repertory, could prod the memories of their colleagues. This same sort of interplay between individual and common memory might also aid in the maintenance of solo chants; different individuals, for example, might be assigned the year-to-year responsibility for certain long chants like the tracts *Qui habitat* and *Deus deus meus,* or certain series of similar chants like the graduals on A-final.

It is hard to imagine all this taking place outside the confines of a resident group, and we know for a fact that the Roman schola had quarters at the Lateran Palace and eventually at St. Peter's basilica also.[5] A substantial commitment of personnel and funding is called for: a valuable segment of the Roman clergy must be relieved of other duties and suitably housed, clothed and fed. The Roman schola is not altogether unlike the *chapelle* or *cappella* of a prosperous Renaissance court and requires the pope to assume, along with his other responsibilities, the role of musical patron.

If supporting an organization like the Roman schola from year to year calls for a measure of both ecclesiastical prosperity and commitment to the development of church music, its initial founding requires even more. The ecclesiastical culture of the time must be one characterized by a sense of optimism and expansion, indeed a certain kind of pride. There must be felt the need for a liturgy that corresponds in splendor to the self-image of a great ecclesiastical center. The members of the musical organization, in turn, must be driven by the prodigious creative and spiritual urge to fashion something of extraordinary scope and beauty. The maintenance of the organization through the years, or even its restoration after a period of disruption, would seem to call for less of such qualities; it is its original founding that would appear to require special historical circumstances.

This distinction between lector and schola chant is not the only consideration to have in mind when we review the meager literary evidence of the fifth through seventh centuries, but it is perhaps the single most important.

THE TESTIMONY OF GAUL

The testimony of the Gallican sources offers us the opportunity to reflect analogously on what might have been taking place in contemporary Rome. Gennadius (fl.470) provides a particularly informative passage about the priest Musaeus of Marseilles in his *De viris illustribus:*

> Musaeus, priest of the church of Marseilles, a man learned in the Divine Scripture and refined by the most subtle exercise of its interpretation, schooled, also in the language, selected, at the urging of the holy bishop Venerius, readings from the Holy Writings appropriate to the feast days of the entire year and responsorial psalms (*responsoria psalmorum capitula*) appropriate to the season and to the readings. This most necessary task is ratified by the lectors.[6]

The passage refers, in all probability, to the Mass; it mentions readings, responsorial psalms and the lector, whereas the typical contemporary reference to the Office reads much differently, generally speaking of the numbers of psalms to be sung by the resident monks at the various hours, and describing them in antiphonal and responsorial groupings. Of special interest in this text is that readings and psalms "appropriate to the feast days of the entire year" are planned at one time by a single individual, as opposed to being chosen by the celebrant on each occasion. This is clearly an example of a Mass Proper, apparently recorded in writing. It is one, however, that is confined to the church of a single city, Marseilles, and one that might very well be limited to only the more important festivals of the year, omitting, for example, ordinary Sundays. We must not suppose, moreover, that it continued in use for centuries after its creation as did the later Roman Mass Proper. As for the particularly musical aspects of the passage, it clearly refers to lector chant: entire psalms are sung (a *capitulum* of the Book of Psalms is a psalm) and they are sung responsorially, apparently by lectors.

The Armenian Lectionary, mentioned in the previous chapter, provides an eastern counterpart to the lectionary of Musaeus. It is somewhat earlier (reproducing the liturgy of Jerusalem before 439, whereas Musaeus flourished around 450), and probably more extensive, providing the responsorial and alleluia psalms for some fifty dates from the Epiphany (6 January) to the feast of James and John (29 December). What its liturgy shares with that of Musaeus is the responsorial manner of singing the psalms; this is

66 / The Prehistory

explicitly indicated for the Fore-Mass of the Armenian Lectionary, thus bearing out the impression in this regard conveyed in the previous chapter. It similarly bears witness to the historical discontinuity that is characteristic of ancient psalmic assignments. Even though its response verses are recorded in writing, only a small minority of them appear with the same liturgical placement in the eighth-century Fore-Mass of Jerusalem as represented by the Georgian Lectionary.[7] One finds among these exceptions, not surprisingly, the response verses *Haec dies* (Ps 117.24) for Easter and *Ascendit deus* (Ps 46.4) for the Ascension.

CAESARIUS OF ARLES

The writings of Caesarius of Arles tell us considerably more about the Office of his time than the Mass, but there are at least three passages from his sermons that merit quotation here. In Sermon 20 he says, "The lector sounds forth (*lector sonat*), the priest preaches, the deacon proclaims the 'silentium.'"[8] This is clearly a reference to the Mass (with the deacon enjoining the people to silence before the readings); the lector's role is defined by the verb *sonare*, which very frequently conveys musical connotation, in this case seeming to suggest the lector's dual role of reader and psalmist.

In Sermon 204, preached on Easter, Caesarius refers to the traditional psalm response *Haec dies* when he says: "'This,' therefore, 'is the day,' dearly beloved, 'which the Lord has made' [Ps 117.24], as you heard."[9] If this sermon provides an instance of continuity of psalmic assignment, the same cannot be said for Sermon 211, preached one year on the feast of Pentecost. Caesarius tells which readings were heard that day at Mass:

> Today, dear brethren, all that was read to us is appropriate to the festival. There is the psalm: "Restore to me," it says, "the joy of thy salvation, and strengthen me with a perfect spirit" [Ps 50.14]; there is the gospel, which says: "The spirit of truth cometh" [Jn 16.13]; and the writings of the Apostolic Acts: "All are filled with the Holy Spirit" [Acts 2.4]. Therefore all is completed and perfected: the psalm asks for the coming of the Holy Spirit; the gospel promises that he is to come; and the Acts of the Apostles recalls that he has already come. Thus there is nothing lacking from the order of divine things in the readings: because in prophecy there is petition, in the gospel promise, and in Acts the fulfillment.[10]

The sermon could have been preached a century earlier by Augustine; it speaks of three "readings": the psalm, the gospel and the epistle. They are not cited in proper order, but this is because of Caesarius's homiletic trope of petition, promise and fulfillment. The psalm verse quoted (Ps 50.14) is not described explicitly as a response verse, even if we might suspect that it is one because of the general tendency in antiquity to single out the response verse in sermons. Psalm 50, in any event, is not cited by Augustine as a psalm sung at Pentecost, nor is it used in the Roman Mass Proper at Pentecost. Neither is chapter 16 of John's gospel, although the obviously appropriate chapter 2 of Acts, which tells the story of the first Pentecost Sunday, is the Roman epistle. One might note, finally, the absence of any reference to an alleluia psalm, even though Pentecost is the final day of the Paschal quinquagesima.

GREGORY OF TOURS

There are two passages from Gregory of Tours that bear directly on the psalmody of the Fore-Mass. In one, from his *Historia Francorum*, Gregory narrates an incident that took place at the table of King Gunthram in the year 585:

> When the meal was more than half way over, the king bade me to order my deacon, who had sung the responsorial psalm (*psalmum responsorium*) at Mass yesterday, to sing. While the deacon was singing, the king gave me a second command: that I call upon every priest present to have a cleric belonging to his church sing before the king. I told them the king's wish, and each cleric sang a responsorial psalm before the king to the best of his ability.[11]

In Gregory's time, apparently, it was no longer a lector, but a deacon, who sang the responsorial psalm at Mass, and at least some deacons sang in a manner sufficiently elaborate to afford entertainment for the king at a common meal. Still, the passage speaks of an individual singing an entire psalm rather than a single verse with choral response like the later Roman gradual.

The second passage, from Gregory's *Vitae patrum*, describes an incident involving his uncle, the saintly bishop Gallus of Clermont. It tells of a deacon, Valentinus, who accompanies Gallus to attend Mass in the church of a fellow bishop. The prideful deacon, in spite of Gallus's command to maintain silence, takes it upon himself to sing:

> He sang so disagreeably (*deformiter*) that he was laughed at by all. On a subsequent Sunday, however, as our bishop was saying Mass, he ordered the deacon to come out: "Now," he said, "in the name of the Lord accomplish what you wish." Which he did, in a voice rendered so splendid that he was praised by all.[12]

Gregory's point is that the disobedient deacon sings poorly, whereas the same man, when heeding the orders of his bishop, sings beautifully. For present purposes we note, again, that it is a deacon who sings at Mass, and that there is a considerable aesthetic dimension involved in his singing. I think, too, that there is an air of arbitrariness and happenstance about the entire anecdote that is incompatible with the sort of order and predictability we might expect in the context of schola chant.

THE PSALTER OF ST-GERMAIN-DES-PRÉS

What might this deacon have been singing? It seems not unlikely that he, as was the case with Gregory's deacon at King Gunthram's banquet, was chanting the responsorial psalm. And, by a happy accident of manuscript preservation, it turns out that we have an example of the sort of book he might have consulted for his singing—the so-called Psalter of St-Germain-des-Prés that was mentioned in the previous chapter.[13] The book, copied in the sixth century, is an elegant manuscript of considerable size; it comprises 291 parchment folios, measuring about 272 by 175 mm, with its text written in silver uncials. The feature of greatest interest to music historians is that the letter *R* is inscribed in gold leaf in the margin opposite verses that are to serve as responses. Bernard Lowe thinks the book is too sophisticated an artifact to have been produced anywhere but Italy,[14] yet its preservation in Paris and the variants of its text speak for a Gallican origin. Gallican or Italian, the manuscript is contemporary with Gregory of Tours's singing deacons and would appear to represent a sort of proto-cantatorium. Given its size and precious character, it may not have been actually handled by a singer at Mass; perhaps it was consulted by him before the service, or perhaps it was simply a gift book belonging to some wealthy ecclesiastical figure. Whatever the case may be, it provides a record of the psalm verses that served as responses at a particular ecclesiastical center of the sixth century, and it strongly suggests that entire psalms were still sung there rather than chants like the medieval gradual.

Which verses were singled out as responses, and what bearing might this choice have on the question of continuity or discontinuity of assignment? Seventy verses are so indicated, and it happens that a considerable number of these figure as gradual responses in the Roman Mass Proper, twenty-one in all, including, not surprisingly, *Haec dies* (Ps 117.24).[15] But certainly one must not ignore the forty-nine response verses that do not appear as Roman graduals. And, again, as in the comparison of Augustine's response verses with those of the Roman gradual, the Psalter of St-Germain fails to include among its response verses certain of the most appropriate medieval graduals such as Advent's *Prope est dominus* (Ps 144.18) and Christmas's *Benedictus qui venit* (Ps 117.26–27) and *Viderunt omnes* (Ps 97.3). Discontinuity of assignment, then, is more characteristic than continuity in this sixth-century psalter's choice of response verses.[16] But even more important is the fact that no liturgical assignments are indicated for these verses, as we might expect if psalms were in fact given fixed assignments at the time and place of the manuscript's copying. This could easily have been done with either marginal markings or a list at the end of the book, devices common in roughly contemporary biblical books used as lectionaries.

Thus, if one accepts, as I do, the conventional view that the Psalter of St-Germain's *R*s indicate response verses of the Fore-Mass, then one must conclude the following: at the time and place of its copying—sixth-century Italy or Gaul—an entire psalm was still sung in the Fore-Mass; the psalm was sung responsorially; certain verses were singled out to serve as response verses; and, while some psalms and response verses were no doubt traditionally associated with particular festivals, there was not yet a written record of annual psalmic assignments.

THE *EXPOSITIO* OF PSEUDO-GERMANUS

The final item of Gallican evidence is the famous *Expositio brevis antiquae liturgiae gallicanae*, the first portion of which is a full description of a Gallican Mass, interlaced with allegorical interpretation of each item.[17] The *Expositio* was formerly attributed to Saint Germanus of Paris, bishop from 555 to 576 and the same saint after whom the just discussed psalter is named. The time and place of the document's composition have been controversial in recent years, with the majority of scholars following André Wilmart, who dates it to about 700 and places it somewhere in southern France, perhaps Autun, where the unique eighth-century copy of the manuscript was preserved throughout the Middle Ages.[18] Very recently, however, Anders Ekenberg has argued for the authorship of an unknown writer, closer in time to Germanus, who cites him as an authority for the liturgy he describes, a liturgy not unlike that practiced in Paris toward the close of the sixth century.[19] I find Ekenberg's position convincing and should like to add a comment of my own. Among the frequently heard arguments for the date of around 700 is that the liturgy described in the *Expositio* is too elaborate for so early a date as the later sixth century. But surely the state of church and society in general was altogether more healthy in sixth-century Gaul than it was in the later seventh and earlier eighth centuries, the darkest period, as we shall see, in the entire medieval history of the region.

Whether Autun around 700 or Paris around 600, the conclusions I would derive from the text are the same. Particularly relevant to our present purposes is the single brief reference to Fore-Mass psalmody:

> And for this reason the Church maintains an order of service in which no collect is inserted between the Hymn of the Three Youths (*Benedictio*) and the gospel, but only the response (*responsurium*), which is sung by children (*paruolis*) as a representation of those Innocents whose deaths as companions of Christ in birth, are narrated in the gospel [see Mt 2.16], or of those children who cried out to the Lord in the temple, "Hosanna to the Son of David" as he drew near to his Passion—as the psalmist declares, "Out of the mouth of infants and of sucklings you have perfected praise."[20]

To set the passage in context, the *Expositio* has a paragraph devoted to the readings (both Old and New Testament, as we would expect in a Gallican document), then a paragraph devoted to the canticle of the three youths in the fiery furnace (Dn 3.52–90, a common feature, apparently, of Gallican liturgies),[21] and then, finally, the passage quoted above. The author is at pains, as Edward Ratcliff explains, to speak against the common practice of inserting a collect at this point in the service and hence insists that only the *responsurium* intervenes between the canticle and the gospel.[22] The *responsurium*, unfortunately, is not defined, although everything we have seen up to this point suggests that it is a responsorial psalm rather than, say, a responsory, like the later Office responsory. Note, too, the linguistic proximity of *responsurium* with Gregory of Tours's *psalmum responsorium*. In any event, one observes that the chant is not tied to the readings in the purportedly obligatory reading-psalm scheme and that it stands alone without an additional alleluia-psalm or chant.

It is sung in this description by *paruolis* (little ones, or children) rather than a deacon, perhaps a peculiarity of the particular church in question, or of some occasion of special solemnity. Or, more likely still, the word might simply refer, in a sort of reverse hyperbole, to the youth of lectors—one recalls here Augustine's mention of a lector's "boyish heart." Strictly speaking the Latin *parvulus* includes not only the very young but also what we would call adolescents, and if the term is still nonetheless misleading in this passage, its use is apparently motivated by the author's wish to indulge in his series of scriptural citations of singing children. We cannot exclude the possibility that the responsorial psalm was still sung by lectors at some locations during the late sixth century simply because Gregory of Tours attributes this duty to deacons in the two passages quoted above. The same Gregory tells us of St. Nicetius of Lyons (d.573):

> He strove above all for this: that he would teach reading and imbue with psalms all the boys who were born in his house, as soon as they put aside the wailing of infancy and began to speak.[23]

That these boys were born in Nicetius's house I find puzzling (if not scandalous), but the custom of introducing boys slated for the clerical life into the home of a priest or bishop, where they would exist in a kind of seminary, was a common one in late antiquity. And it is safe to assume, I would imagine, that at least some of the boys who were taught psalms in the home of Nicetius would come to serve as lectors. Earlier in the century, in 529, at the Council of Vaison, presided over by Caesarius of Arles, it was decreed:

> That all priests who are established in parishes, according to the custom which we know to be well enough maintained through all of Italy, take into their homes all their young lectors who are unmarried . . . and that they strive, as good fathers providing spiritual nurture, to have them prepare psalms (*psalmos parare*), be steadfast in sacred reading and learn the law of the Lord.[24]

Given the totality of evidence from the time and region, it seems far more plausible that the *Expositio*'s *responsurium quod a paruolis canitur* was a responsorial psalm sung by an adolescent lector (different lectors singing on different occasions to account for the plural) than a Proper schola gradual response sung by a choir of children.

THE OTHER CHANTS OF THE *EXPOSITIO*

The elaborate Mass described in the *Expositio* mentions several other chants besides the *responsurium* of the Fore-Mass. Of particular interest are two antiphons that appear to be borrowed from the Byzantine Eucharist, the Cheroubikon and the Trisagion. The Cheroubikon (the cherubic hymn) is the Ordinary antiphon sung during the Great Entrance, the offertory procession of the Byzantine Mass.[25] The sacred elements of bread and wine are brought to the altar at the beginning of the sacrificial rite, the bread in a tower-shaped vessel and the wine in a chalice. The Cheroubikon, which begins with the words "We who mystically represent the cherubim," was sung during the procession as early as the mid-sixth century and made obligatory under Justin II around 573. There is good reason to believe, as Johannes Quasten maintains, that the "Sonum," the offertory chant described in the

Expositio, is the Cheroubikon.[26] The text is not given, but the Sonum is spoken of as an "angelic song, which has a first, second and third alleluia." The Cheroubikon is clearly an angelic song and, in the version that begins "Let all mortal flesh be silent," terminates with three alleluias. If these indications appear somewhat tenuous, more concrete is the circumstance that, in the words of the *Expositio,* "The body of the Lord is carried within towers," precisely as in the Byzantine Great Entrance. Gregory of Tours, moreover, narrates a story of a certain deacon who, when "the time to offer the sacrifice had arrived, and having accepted the tower in which the mystery of the Lord's body is contained. . . ."[27] The point of Gregory's anecdote is that the deacon, an adulterer, is unworthy to hold the vessel, which takes flight and deposits itself on the altar, but its significance for us is additional Gallican testimony to the use of the distinctively Byzantine *turris* in the offertory procession. It lends credence to the view that the Byzantine offertory rite as a whole, including its characteristic chant, the Cheroubikon, was adopted in certain Gallican centers.

There can be no doubt that the singing of the Trisagion was so adopted. This hymn (a *tersanctus,* but not to be confused with the *tersanctus* that concludes the preface of the eucharistic prayer) was introduced as an entrance chant into the Byzantine Eucharist toward the end of the fifth century.[28] It is sung no less than three times in the rite described in the *Expositio:* in Greek immediately after the deacon proclaims the *silentium* before the readings; in Greek before the gospel and in Latin after the gospel. It is worth noting, incidentally, that on one of these occasions the *Expositio* is explicit about who sings the Trisagion: before the gospel it is sung by a single cleric (*clerus*).

That the Trisagion, and probably the Cheroubikon, was borrowed from the Byzantine rite raises the question of when such Byzantine influence upon the Gallican rite might have been exercised. The most appropriate time would seem to be the later sixth century, particularly if the *Expositio's* newly proposed dating to that period is sound. Ruling out an earlier date for the adoption of the Cheroubikon is the simple fact that it was not introduced into the Byzantine liturgy itself, as we have seen, until about 573. As for the Trisagion, there is no Gallican reference to its presence before the *Expositio;* in fact there is a passage from a letter of Avitus of Vienne (d.518) in which he praises the singing of the Trisagion in the East in such a way as to imply its absence in the West.[29]

The general historical background also favors the later sixth century. The eastern empire was well established then in its exarchate at Ravenna and in the southernmost reaches of Italy. From the latter in particular it had ready access by sea to the Mediterranean coasts of Gaul and Spain;[30] there is evidence, in fact, of Greek-speaking colonies in the Rhône Valley during the sixth century. It is remarkable that there was no comparable Byzantine influence on the Roman Mass of the time (such influence, it will be maintained in subsequent chapters, appears only about a century later). The Cheroubikon never found its way into the Roman rite, and the Trisagion was sung only at the adoration of the Cross on Good Friday, and not until centuries after it was adopted for that occasion by the ninth-century Franks, presumably from the indigenous Gallican rites.[31] Rome, as we shall see, manifested a distinct preference for variable psalmody in its Mass rather than Ordinary antiphons like the Cheroubikon and Trisagion.

There is at least one other chant cited in the *Expositio* that merits attention here. The very first item mentioned is the *antiphona ad praelegendum*, the "antiphon before the readings"; it was sung by clerics (*psallentibus clericis*) as the priest moved in procession from the sacristy. The text offers no further hint as to its character. It was not the Trisagion, which served as the contemporary Byzantine entrance antiphon; the Trisagion was heard moments later in the service, after the deacon proclaimed the pre-lectionary *silentium*. And if it were some other distinctive Ordinary antiphon like the Trisagion, we should expect it to be specified in the text. I would imagine it was an antiphonal psalm, that is, a psalm with antiphon;[32] the term *antiphona* is used consistently in monastic rules from the fourth to the sixth centuries to indicate such antiphonal psalms. The phrase *psallentibus clericis*, moreover, would seem to suggest psalmody of some sort, even if strictly speaking the verb *psallere* can mean simply "to sing," whether psalms, canticles or whatever. We know that clerics and monks are enjoined to memorize psalms from their earliest years, and there are phrases similar to *psallentibus clericis* in the contemporary literature that strongly suggest the singing of psalms. We read, for example, in Gregory of Tours's narrative of the funeral of his namesake, St. Gregory of Langres: "In the morning, with choirs of psalm-singers (*cum choris psallentium*), they took the sarcophagus that was before the altar and moved it into the apse built by the blessed bishop Tertritus."[33] The plural form of such phrases (whether "choirs" are cited or not) would seem also to imply some sort of choral involvement, whether the unison singing of a memorized psalm or of a familiar antiphon. If, then, the *antiphona ad praelegendum* can be taken as an entrance psalm with antiphon, it is contemporary with the Roman introit psalm or, quite possibly, earlier than it. The antiphons, then, may constitute a sort of primitive Proper, perhaps a fund of short antiphons, not unlike those of the Roman ferial Office, that are retained in memory and sung to a limited set of tunes. It is hard to imagine, however, in view of everything that has gone before in this chapter (the R markings of the Psalter of St-Germain, for example), that such antiphons could amount to a fully articulated example of schola chant, that is, a large repertory of antiphons, committed to writing and permanently assigned throughout the church year.

At communion time, finally, the *Expositio* cites the singing of the "Trecanum." The text offers no more than the suggestion that it is a Trinitarian hymn of some sort; efforts to identify it have been inconclusive.[34] The failure of the *Expositio* to mention psalmody during the distribution of communion is somewhat surprising. Perhaps it is the result of a defect in the text; editors do suspect a gap after the paragraph on the Trecanum.[35] But there is, to my knowledge, only one brief reference to communion psalmody preserved in Gallican sources: Aurelian of Arles says in his monastic rule that "all communicate with psalmody" (*psallendo omnes communicent*).[36] Again, the verb *psallere* can mean simply "to sing," even if "to sing psalms" might seem the more likely meaning here. Still the evidence remains inconclusive; we are not certain whether or not the singing of a psalm was a typical occurrence during the distribution of communion in Gallican churches of the fifth and sixth centuries.

THE DECLINE OF THE GALLICAN CHURCHES

If the evidence from fifth- and sixth-century Gaul for the chants of the Mass is fragmentary, it is all but nonexistent in the century or more to follow (unless one wishes to date the *Expositio* to the turn of the eighth century). The true "Dark Ages" of Gaul fall in this time between the Gallo-Roman period of the fifth and sixth centuries and the Carolingian revival of the mid-eighth century. Not, certainly, that the earlier period was one of continuous tranquillity and prosperity: Caesarius's Arles, for example, suffered grievously during the long siege of 507–508, and there was nearly continual internecine warfare among the Frankish princes during the time of Gregory of Tours. Still, we know that urban ecclesiastical life enjoyed at least a comparatively healthy existence during the period from the very literary output of figures like Caesarius and Gregory, as well as from contemporary reports of church councils. But by the second half of the seventh century the Merovingian dynasty was in disarray, its retreat to its refuges deep in the northern forests signaling its desertion of the deteriorating cities. There are virtually no extant ecclesiastical writings from the period, and even councils ceased to meet by mid-century. One gains a sense of the chaos in the life of the Church by reading the existing council edicts of the earlier seventh century with their strictures against the crudest manifestations of clerical immorality and superstition. Even so we would expect monasteries to fare better than cathedrals in such circumstances, and while many monasteries simply vanished from the historical record of the time, a number of important northern abbeys—Corbie, Chelles, Fleury, Laon and St-Martin of Tours—managed to preserve something of Christian culture within their walls.

When the Carolingian ecclesiastical revival took place under St. Boniface (d.754) and the ubiquitous Chrodegang of Metz (d.766), men and women versed in the ways of the Church were found in these monastic institutions (and it is my own guess that it was there also that the remnants of Gallican chant were preserved). But some idea of the more general condition of the times is gained from Boniface's letter of 742 to Pope Zachary, in which he writes: "The Franks have not held a council for more than eighty years,[37] nor have they ordained an archbishop, nor established or restored the canon law of any church . . . episcopal sees in the cities are in the hands of greedy laymen . . . certain bishops, although they deny they are fornicators and adulterers, are drunkards and shiftless men, given to hunting, and to fighting in the army like soldiers."[38]

CHRODEGANG'S SCHOLA CANTORUM

In summary, urban ecclesiastical life in the time of Caesarius and Gregory might have been sufficiently vigorous to support an organization like the Roman schola cantorum at some city like Arles, Tours or Paris, but we have no evidence that anything of the sort existed. On the contrary, what references we do have to chant at Mass suggest a continuation of the lector chant of Christian antiquity. They do not preclude ecclesiastical song of some elaboration at certain times and places. Deacons might have sung prolix responsorial psalms; clerics might have sung antiphons like the Cheroubikon and Trisagion with their Byzantine melodies; and certainly monks and clerics alike were capable of a variety of psalmodic executions, antiphonal and responsorial, solo and choral. And there might have been, in certain cathedrals, congregations who knew a repertory of psalm verses set to traditional tunes, as was the case in Augustine's church. But it seems highly unlikely that there was anything like a Proper of the Mass, consisting in hundreds of different chants, permanently assigned within the ecclesiastical calendar, their texts preserved in writing and their melodies reproduced each year with some measure of constancy by a resident cadre of dedicated musician clerics.

If such a set of circumstances is unlikely for any ecclesiastical center of the Gallo-Roman period, it is all but inconceivable for the grim times of the later seventh and earlier eighth centuries. The environment for this sort of development, however, dramatically improved in the mid-eighth-century, and in fact a celebrated schola cantorum developed under Chrodegang of Metz (742–66) and his successor, Angilram (768–91). Chrodegang established discipline within his clergy early in his tenure as bishop, writing a rule for them that was greatly influenced by Benedict's monastic rule, and thus setting a standard for cathedral clergy—henceforth to be called "canons"—for the rest of the Middle Ages.[39] Visiting Rome in 753 in order to accompany Pope Stephen II (752–57) on his journey north to sojourn with King Pépin (d.768) at St-Denis, Chrodegang had the opportunity to observe the Roman schola at close hand for several months and subsequently revised his rule to conform more closely to the Roman model.[40] His clerics were able, apparently, to accomplish the enormous task of absorbing the Roman Mass Proper. We do not know precisely how they managed this—even if Roman cantors in extended periods of residence must have been a factor—nor do we know precisely how much the Roman melodic style was transformed in the process—this, after all, is the so-called central question of Gregorian chant. But we do know that Chrodegang's and Angilram's canons count among their number the first firmly documented representatives of schola chant in four centuries of Gallican ecclesiastical history; indeed Angilram refers to his chief singer as *primus scole*.[41]

CHAPTER 4

Centuries of Silence: Rome and England

It is unfortunate that we have no outstanding ecclesiastical figure writing in Rome toward the end of the fourth century. Milan has Ambrose, Hippo and Carthage have Augustine, Caesarea has Basil, Alexandria has Athanasius, Antioch and Constantinople have John Chrysostom and Jerusalem has Egeria; but for Rome the silence that characterizes the so-called Dark Ages begins at least a century earlier than in the other important Christian centers. We have no direct witness, then, to psalmody in the Roman Mass at the turn of the fifth century. We have seen that psalms with alleluia refrain were sung in the Roman agape already in the time of Hippolytus (d.c.236), and one easily assumes that psalmody in general—in the form, for example, of the popular psalmodic vigil—would have flourished in the late-fourth-century Roman church, just as it did in Milan, North Africa and even in Niceta's church of Remesiana in remote Dacia. And if such was the case, surely there would be both a responsorial psalm in the Fore-Mass and a communion psalm would have been sung at least occasionally in Rome at the time, if not a few decades later.

LEO THE GREAT

The assumption seems not unwarranted, even if we lack contemporary evidence for it, and even if the later evidence is only marginally supportive. Leo the Great, pope from 440 to 461, provides us with nearly 100 sermons, preached, it would appear, at Mass during his pontificate. In Sermon 3, delivered on the third anniversary of his installation to the papacy, he says:

> Wherefore we sang with harmonious voice (*consona voce cantavimus*), dearly beloved, the Davidic psalm, not for our own exaltation but for the glory of Christ our Lord. For it was he of whom it was written in

prophecy: "Thou art a priest for ever according to the order of Melchisedech" [Ps 109.4].¹

And again he tells us on a later (undetermined) anniversary of the same occasion:

> The most exalted Pontifex [Christ] is not absent from the congregation of his priests, and rightly is there sung to him from the mouth of the entire Church and all his priests: "The Lord swore and denied it not: 'Thou art a priest for ever according to the order of Melchisedech'" [Ps 109.4].²

Thus verse 4 of Psalm 109 was sung on at least two anniversaries of Leo's accession to the papacy, presumably as the refrain verse to the responsorial singing of Psalm 109 in the Fore-Mass preceding his homily. But if this presumption is correct, it does not necessarily follow that the singing of a responsorial psalm was a regular event in the Roman Fore-Mass of Leo's time. The anniversary in question was a special occasion, and one attended by a great number of priests, who would certainly have been familiar with the psalm and verse in question.

It happens, too, that this pair of texts constitutes the sum total of explicit references to the singing of psalms in Leo's sermons. One additional passage, however, comes close to inclusion in such a category; in a sermon preached on the Epiphany Leo declares:

> This day David sang in the psalms, saying: "All the nations that thou hast made shall come and adore before thee, O Lord, and they shall glorify thy name" [Ps 85.9]. And this: "The Lord has made known his salvation; he has revealed his justice in the sight of the gentiles" [Ps 97.2].³

He does not use the sort of locutions we are accustomed to from Augustine's sermons—*modo cantavimus* (we just now sang), for example, or *modo cantastis* (you just now sang)—rather he says that David sings, but perhaps he means that David's singing is to be taken as the actual singing of the lector and congregation. Yet, that verses from two different psalms are cited gives pause; perhaps they were sung before Mass at some earlier service, matins or a popular psalmodic vigil.

In a sermon preached on Christmas Leo cites the verse *Veritas de terra orta est* (Ps 84.12),⁴ the same verse Augustine frequently mentions in connection with Christmas. Leo, however, simply quotes the verse without so much as a hint of its having been sung, whereas Augustine on one occasion said, "If Mary is the earth, let us recognize what it is that we sing: 'Truth is sprung out of the earth.'"⁵

CELESTINE I

Leo's admittedly meager testimony to psalmody in the Roman Mass of the mid-fifth century must be viewed in the light of the most frequently discussed of all references to early Roman chant, the following passage from the *Liber pontificalis* biography of Pope Celestine I (422–32):

> He decreed that the 150 psalms of David be sung before the sacrifice [antiphonally from all (*antephonatim ex omnibus*)], which was not done before; only the epistle of blessed Paul was recited and the holy gospel.[6]

As Louis Duchesne established in his standard edition, the bulk of the passage is from an earlier version of the *Liber pontificalis*, compiled during the time of Pope Hormisdas (514–23), whereas the phrase in brackets, *antephonatim ex omnibus*, is an interpolation of a somewhat later version, from the time of Pope Vigilius (537–55).[7] The troublesome addition will be treated presently; the original text is our central concern.

Traditionally the text has been taken to refer to the introit of the Mass, but surely Peter Jeffery is correct in maintaining that it refers to the responsorial psalm of the Fore-Mass.[8] This psalmody was heard "before the sacrifice" (*ante sacrificium*), and Jeffery points out that the phrase must be taken to mean before the eucharistic portion of the Mass rather than before the entire ceremony.[9] The earlier portions of the *Liber pontificalis* consistently use the term *missa* to refer to the Mass as a whole (thus conforming, in fact, to contemporary usage) but generally restrict *sacrificium* to mean the sacrificial rite as such. One might recall here the similar conclusion reached above in chapter two regarding Augustine's use of the phrase *ante oblationem* in his passage from the *Retractationes*' passage dealing with *Contra Hilarem*.

Jeffery notes further that the passage places the psalms on the same footing as the epistle and gospel, just as patristic sermons had treated the three items equally as scriptural readings.[10] It was this point, in fact—the obvious contiguity of the three in the text—that prompted me also to conclude that the passage referred to the gradual psalm rather than the introit psalm.[11] And surely the reader of this volume, after encountering passages like Augustine's "We heard the Apostle, we heard the Psalm, we heard the Gospel," must come to the same conclusion.

Jeffery made still another valuable observation in his analysis of the quotation from the *Liber pontificalis*; the point involves a closely contemporary Roman text, from the pseudo-correspondence of St. Jerome and Pope

Damasus. In it pseudo-Damasus laments the lack of psalmody in the Roman Mass:

> There is evidence of such crudity that on Sunday only one epistle of the Apostle is recited, and one chapter of the gospel is said, while no voice resounds in psalmody (*nec psallendo vox ululatur*) and the hymnodist [David] is unknown to our lips.[12]

Scholars have long since noted the remarkable similarity of the text to the passage from the *Liber pontificalis*, most of them assuming that the latter is dependent upon the former. Jeffery, however, in a series of telling arguments, shows that the reverse must be true—the text of the pseudo-correspondence depends upon that of the *Liber pontificalis*.[13]

For present purposes it is enough to note that of two Roman documents from the earlier sixth century, one laments that no psalm was sung in the Fore-Mass at the time of Pope Damasus I (366–84), and the other claims that the practice was established a few decades later by Pope Celestine. Some might be reluctant to accept so precise a chronology, but there can be little doubt that the custom of Fore-Mass psalmody was firmly established in Rome by the earlier sixth century, such that its introduction was attributed to a pope who lived a full century earlier. On the other hand these texts also suggest a certain tenuousness about the status of the practice (the memory of its absence was still alive in the sixth century); one cannot but recall the less than overwhelmingly positive testimony of Leo the Great on the subject. I would conclude that Fore-Mass psalmody achieved the status of a fixed liturgical event in Rome somewhat later than in Augustine's North Africa. Still I do not wish to exaggerate the difference in time. One must remember that Augustine became bishop of Hippo only in about 395 and that he lived until 430; thus his sermons citing Fore-Mass psalmody were preached just a few decades before the time of Leo. And one must remember also that Augustine refers in his *Contra Hilarem* to the Fore-Mass and communion psalmody of the church of Carthage as "a custom which had begun then," that is, only at the time of Hilary's complaint.

Reference was made above to the "troublesome" phrase *antephonatim ex omnibus*. It is troublesome for two reasons: (1) the term *antephonatim* seems inappropriate in reference to the responsorial psalm of the Fore-Mass, and (2) the preposition *ex* means "from" or "out of," whereas translators usually take the easy way out and render the phrase *ex omnibus* as "by all," that is to say, by everybody.[14] Jeffery offers a solution that is both grammatically correct and thoroughly ingenious.[15] He takes the phrase to mean "antiphonally from all [of the 150 psalms]," that is, that antiphons and other such excerpted portions of the psalms are sung rather than entire psalms, in effect, chants not unlike the Proper chants of later centuries. Thus the earlier version of the text refers to Celestine's introduction of responsorial psalmody into the Fore-Mass and the later version to the subsequent development of genuine Mass Proper chants. I have no better alternative to Jeffery's interpretation, but I am unable to embrace his fully. For a smaller point, the text of the later version still refers only to the Fore-Mass (*ante sacrificium*), so that if *antephonatim* refers to chants based on excerpted texts, it must refer only to the chants of that portion of the service, chants that would, of course, be responsorial rather than antiphonal chants, a distinction presumably known to sixth-century authors. But the larger point is that this brief ungainly phrase—*antephonatim ex omnibus*—is simply an insufficient foundation upon which to base so crucial a step in the history of the Roman Mass Proper; for me, at least, its meaning must remain a mystery.[16]

DAMASUS

There is one additional text from earlier sixth-century Rome that merits discussion; the *Liber pontificalis* biography of Pope Damasus says of him:

> He decreed that the psalms be sung day and night (*psalmos die noctuque canerentur*) in all the churches, ordering this of priests, bishops and monasteries.[17]

It is Jeffery, once again, who reminds us that the passage is an interpolation appearing only in the second edition of the *Liber pontificalis*.[18] This circumstance is central to his argument for the chronological priority of the original version of the *Liber pontificalis* over the pseudo-correspondence of Damasus and Jerome. The original version has nothing to say on the subject of Damasus and chant, but the second version has him actively involved; the pseudo-correspondence, then, in which Damasus shows keen interest in chant, probably became known at Rome sometime between the redaction of the two.

I would add an additional point to those adduced by Jeffery. It is that both the pseudo-correspondence and the passage just quoted from the biography of Damasus have more to do with the psalmody of the Office than that of the Mass. The bulk of the pseudo-correspondence (not quoted here) is concerned with the question of whether *Gloria patri* and *alleluia* ought to be added to psalms sung in the Office,[19] and the phrase *die noctuque*, as will be seen presently, is standard shorthand in the *Liber pontificalis* to cover the eight Office hours of the daily cursus. If the author of the Damasus interpolation had not been thinking almost exclusively of the Office, and had kept Fore-Mass psalmody in mind also, he would have placed himself in obvious contradiction with the passage that attributed the introduction of Fore-Mass psalmody to Celestine I, who reigned several decades after Damasus.

THE ROMAN MONASTERIES

Be that as it may, my primary reason for including the passage from the Damasus biography is to serve as a reminder of the presence of Office psalmody in Rome. It is a presence that is ancient and pervasive, and a presence that involves monasticism. We know, thanks especially to Guy Ferrari's classic monograph, *Early Roman Monasteries*,[20] that these institutions were attached to all the principal Roman basilicas and that their chief task was the daily performance of the sung Office.

In chapter two we saw the spread of the monastic ideal during the second half of the fourth century from the deserts of Egypt to the chief cities, East and West, and we saw that psalmody was the hallmark of the monastic life. Rome was not immune to this trend; Augustine and especially Jerome bear witness to pious men and women of Rome who lived an ascetic life based on the observance of the monastic horarium. We see Jerome, for example, advocating the monastic way of life even for the child Laeta, daughter of Paula:

> Let an elderly virgin of good faith, morals and modesty be placed in charge of her, who will instruct her and familiarize her by example to rise at night for prayer and psalms, to sing hymns at dawn, to stand in the ranks as a warrior for Christ at the third, sixth and ninth hours, and to proffer an evening sacrifice at the lighting of the lamp.[21]

We do not know precisely when the informal observance of the monastic ideal coalesced into the foundation at fixed locations of cenobitic monasteries and convents, but it could not have been long after the time of Augustine and Jerome. The first reference we have to such institutions appears in the *Liber pontificalis* biography of Pope Sixtus III (432–40): "He built a monastery at the Catacombs [basilica of St. Sebastian]."[22] Sixtus's successor Leo the Great "established a monastery at St. Peter's";[23] and Leo's successor Hilarius (461–68) "built a monastery at St. Lawrence's" and again "in Rome a monastery, Ad Lunam."[24] There must have been many monasteries attached to basilicas by the time that the second edition of the *Liber pontificalis* cites them in the biography of Damasus, and their responsibility for performing the Office *die noctuque* must have been long since established, even if it did not extend quite to the time of Damasus.

Two and a half centuries later, in the *Liber pontificalis* biography of Leo III (795–816) we are given a list of no less than forty-nine Roman monasteries.[25] They are mostly attached to the four principal basilicas—St. Peter's, the Lateran, St. Mary Major and St. Paul's, each of which has three or four affiliated monasteries that share the task of singing the Office. The eighth-century references to monasteries in the *Liber pontificalis* are more discursive than the earlier ones and are more explicit about the purpose of the institutions. Of particular interest is a variant in the text of Gregory II's (715–31) biography. One version has him restoring a monastery at St. Mary Major (the monastery of SS. Cosmas and Damian) and decreeing that "each day of the week they [the monks] perform terce, sext, none and matins in the same church of the holy Mother of God," while the variant has him ordering the monks to sing praise to God "every day and night (*singulis diebus atque noctibus*),"[26] thus providing a nice demonstration of how the phrase for "day and night" serves as shorthand for naming the specific services of the horarium. A final point of some interest about the Office of the basilican monasteries is that, while we might expect the monasteries attached to the pope's own Lateran basilica to exercise a kind of liturgical leadership in Rome, this role appears to fall to the monasteries at St. Peter's. We read in the biography of Gregory III (731–41) that he restored the monastery of St. John the Evangelist alongside the basilica of Our Savior at the Lateran, and that he "established an abbot and congregation of monks there to perform the holy offices of divine praise each day in the basilica of the Savior, our Lord Jesus Christ, called the Constantinian, close to the Lateran, as ordained for day and night, according to the model of the services of Blessed Peter the Apostle."[27]

This digression on the basilican Office, occasioned by the notice on Damasus in the *Liber pontificalis*, is essential to an understanding of how the Roman Mass Proper must have developed. We have no positive knowledge of the Office's influence upon the chants of the Mass, that is, no texts that actually speak of it. But it is hardly an exaggeration to say that the musical context in which the Roman Mass Proper came into being was the daily Office psalmody of the monks attached to the principal basilicas. Resident monastic choirs were active for more than a century before the schola cantorum came into existence; their "continuous" psalmody was heard for hours each day in the churches, frequently in the presence of pope and clergy. We will have occasion to speculate on what effect this psalmody might have had upon the individual chants of the Mass as they are taken up later in this volume.

GREGORY THE GREAT

By the mid-sixth century Rome had plunged into the terrible period of the Gothic Wars and the Lombard invasion described in the previous chapter. We hear nothing of ecclesiastical song again until the time of Gregory the Great (590–604). Our first reference comes from a Gallican source, Gregory of Tours's *Historia Francorum*. Gregory of Tours's deacon Agiulf had visited Rome in 589 and remained there for Gregory I's installation the following year. Agiulf reported vividly on the disastrous flood of 589 and the resulting plague that still raged as Gregory assumed office. He recorded Gregory's inaugural sermon, in the course of which the pope himself expanded on the horrors of the plague, and then Agiulf described the famous supplicatory procession that followed the service:

> After these words Gregory ordered the assembled groups of churchmen (*congregatis clericorum catervis*) to sing psalms (*psallere*) for three days. At the third hour all the choirs (*chori psallentium*) came to the church, crying *Kyrie eleison* through the streets of the city . . . while the people were making supplication to the Lord, eighty of them fell dead to the ground.[28]

This storied event (used to illustrate the Litany in fifteenth-century books of hours) certainly included the chanting of the Litany (*Kyrie eleison*), and in all probability certain psalms as well. The passage is useful—in addition to giving us some feeling for the historical circumstances of Gregory's installation—for affording a glimpse of the Roman ecclesiastical musical forces at the end of the sixth century. The portion of the text quoted here mentions only *clericorum catervis* and *chori psallentium,* but in his sermon Gregory had specified in considerable detail the various bodies of monks, nuns, clergy and laity who were to leave from particular churches and come together at St. Mary Major. Monks would probably have outnumbered priests and been more organized and practiced in their singing; we know that most churches of Rome at the time were served by only a single presbyter, whereas the typical number had been two or three a few generations before.[29]

A Gregorian passage with more direct bearing on the chants of the Mass is the frequently quoted order of 595 that deacons be forbidden to serve as cantors:

> Recently the exceedingly reprehensible custom has arisen that certain singers (*cantores*) have been chosen for the service of the holy altar, and, when ordained members of the order of deacon, they serve by the musicality (*modulationi*) of their voice, thus making them unavailable for the office of preaching and the collection of alms. Whence it happens frequently that while a pleasant voice (*blanda vox*) is sought for the sacred ministry, the pursuit of a proper life is neglected. So a cantorial minister (*cantor minister*) irritates God with his morals while he delights the people with his voice. Wherefore I order in the present decree that in this diocese the holy ministers of the altar ought not to sing, and ought to perform only the office of reading the gospel at the solemnities of the Mass; the psalms and the other readings I wish to be presented by the subdeacons, or, if necessity demands, by those in minor orders.[30]

The central intent of Gregory's decree is spelled out clearly enough: he wishes to put an end to deacons serving as cantors at Mass. That they had been doing so in Rome had at least two undesirable consequences: they were chosen for the office of deacon because of their pleasant voices rather than their virtue, and they were rendered unavailable for more essentially diaconal tasks such as preaching and collecting alms. Deacons were clerics of considerable distinction in the Roman church, and Gregory insisted that the duties of a mere cantor were better left to those of lesser clerical rank—subdeacons and presumably lectors.

More relevant to the present study is what the passage suggests about the state of Mass Proper chants in Gregory's time. I offer the following hypothesis: Gregory had in mind especially the singing by deacons of the responsorial psalm of the Fore-Mass, the same practice we observe in contemporary Gaul. He appears to place the singing of the deacons in just this context when he says that they ought not to serve as cantors but only to read the gospel, while the psalms and other readings should be the responsibility of lesser clerics. Present are the same three elements of the Fore-Mass (reading, psalmody and gospel) that we are familiar with from patristic references, from the description by Caesarius of a Pentecost Fore-Mass and from the *Liber pontificalis* biography of Pope Celestine. Gregory speaks, moreover, of "psalms and other readings," thus maintaining the patristic conception of the psalm as a reading. The plural of "psalms and other readings," incidentally, presents no difficulty. We have seen already several instances where the plural is used in similar passages to refer to the psalms and readings performed in the course of a year rather than on a single day. We know for a fact that there was only one reading other than the gospel in the Roman Fore-Mass, and similarly the passage can be read to refer to a liturgy in which only one psalm was regularly sung. I do not mean, by the way, to insist that the singing of only one psalm was the absolute rule in the Fore-Mass of Gregory's time, even if I believe that it was the more typical practice; I mean only to show that Gregory's language could very well refer to Fore-Mass "readings" consisting in an epistle, one responsorial psalm and a gospel.

At the same time, even if Gregory was particularly intent upon the responsorial psalm of the Fore-Mass (the key musical event of the Mass, one must remember, where a vain deacon might be especially tempted to display his vocal prowess), this would not exclude the possibility that Gregory might also have had communion psalmody in mind. But he probably would not have been thinking of other Mass chants, for example, the introit psalm, if in fact it existed at this time. Presumably a reference to such a chant would not speak of a single vainglorious cantor but of clerical groups, like the *chori psallentium* who sang in the procession at the time of Gregory's installation and *psallentibus clericis* who sang the *antiphona ad praelegendum* during the entrance procession of the priest in the Mass of the Gallican *Expositio*.

THE ROMAN SCHOLA CANTORUM

In sum, I believe this passage is most plausibly interpreted as belonging within the context of early Christian lector chant rather than that of medieval schola chant. Curiously some have read it as evidence that Gregory founded the schola cantorum. Because, the argument goes, he forbade deacons to sing at Mass, it was necessary that he establish a school of singers to take their place. Surely this is not a legitimate inference; Gregory simply insists that subdeacons and those in still lesser orders be responsible for the psalms and readings other than the gospel, and he says nothing to suggest that these individuals were inadequate to the task. In point of fact the obvious inference to be drawn from the passage is that the schola cantorum was not yet in existence at the time this decree was issued; if it had been there would have been no need to speak of other clergy performing functions that would have been the responsibility of the schola.

Joseph Dyer, in his definitive study of the schola's early history, draws similar conclusions from Gregory's edict, and he goes on to note another passage from Gregory's writings suggesting that the organization did not yet exist in his time.[31] In his much discussed letter of 598 to Bishop John of Syracuse (to be treated here in connection with the alleluia) he says of the Kyrie of the Roman Mass that "among us it is said by the clergy (*a clericis dicitur*) and responded to by the people," whereas about a century later *Ordo romanus I* reads: "The schola begins the *Kyrie eleison*, and the prior of the schola (*prior scholae*) watches the pope should he wish to nod to him in order to cut short the invocations of the litany (*mutare numerum litaniae*)."[32] In Gregory's time the ordinary clergy and the congregation perform the Kyrie, but a century later the schola does.

The schola figures prominently in *Ordo romanus I*. It is represented as performing most of the chants of the Mass, and more than that it is shown to have a formal organization with traditional rituals. Not only the *prior scholae* is mentioned but the *secundus, tertius, quartus* (or *archiparaphonista*), the *paraphonistae* (men singers) and *infantes*.[33] Before Mass the regional subdeacons must tell the pope which member of the schola will serve as cantor, and should the *archiparaphonista* change this assignment, he is subject to excommunication.[34] By the time of *Ordo romanus I*, then, the schola is a well-established institution. We do not know the exact date of *Ordo I*'s composition, but it is generally thought to be not long after the reign of Pope Sergius I (687–701); the *Liber pontificalis* tells us that Sergius introduced the *Agnus dei* into the Roman Mass,[35] and the *Agnus dei* is mentioned in *Ordo I*.[36] It happens that it is the same *Liber pontificalis* biography of Sergius from which we have our earliest unequivocal reference to the schola; it says of the young Sergius, who came to Rome from his native Sicily during the reign of Pope Adeodatus II (672–76), that "because he was studious and competent in the ministry of song, he was given over to the prior of the singers (*priori cantorum*) for teaching."[37] A "prior of singers," in all probability, who is responsible for educating young clerics is to be identified with the *prior scholae*, so that we can safely assume the organization to be well established by about 675.

There are musical references to two seventh-century predecessors of Sergius in the *Liber pontificalis* that are sometimes taken as evidence for the existence of the schola: Leo II (682–83) was said to be "distinguished for his singing and psalmody (*cantilena ac psalmodia praecipuus*),"[38] and Benedict II (684–85) is said to have displayed a proficiency worthy of his name (he who is blessed) "in chant from his boyhood (*cantilena a puerili etate*)."[39] Neither reference, however, says anything, explicitly or by implication, about training in an institution like the schola cantorum. It would seem, then, in view of Gregory's silence on the schola (he was, it should be noted, a prolific author who had much to say otherwise on the makeup of the Roman church), and in view of the passages from his writings quoted above that imply the nonexistence of the organization in his time, that we can only say it was established sometime after his reign and before that of Adeodatus.

If we will never know just when within that span of some seventy years the schola was founded, reflection on the general historical background at least helps us to imagine some of the factors involved.[40] In the last chapter I spoke of the conditions necessary for the creation of an organization like the schola: domestic tranquillity, ecclesiastical prosperity and a certain churchly pride. These were hardly qualities that characterized Rome at the time of Gregory's accession to the papacy. It is part of his genuine greatness, however, that he strove mightily, in spite of his poor health, to rescue Rome, city and church, from its piteous state. He saw to the reestablishment of civic government, he took responsibility for the care of the sick and the feeding of the poor, he had one of the city's aqueducts rebuilt and he even became personally involved in the preparation of defenses against the ever threatening Lombards. In view of such enormous demands on his time and energy, it should come as no surprise that he failed to show more than ordinary interest in the niceties of liturgy and chant. It could be said, however, that by setting the seventh-century restoration of Rome on course he, ultimately, did make possible the dramatic liturgical and musical developments of the time. As that century progressed, the circumstances developed that would provide an appropriate context for the founding of the schola: relative freedom from siege, plague and famine; expanding wealth for the church as thousands of pilgrims visited the city each year; and a growing sense of self-esteem as Rome asserted itself theologically against Byzantium and the Italian population asserted itself politically and militarily.

There is one other background factor to be taken into consideration: Gregory's well-known tendency to favor monks over clergy in matters of ecclesiastical preferment.[41] He lived, one recalls, as a monk himself and converted his own home into a monastery. Throughout his reign, moreover, he arrogated to monks privileges and functions traditionally associated with the clergy: he turned churches over to the care of monks, for example, and involved them in administrative matters at the Lateran and in the care of the papal estates in Sicily. His motives were no doubt unimpeachable; he felt, apparently, that the more spiritually inclined monks were better suited to these tasks than were the secular clergy. In the decades immediately following Gregory's reign one notes a fluctuation in the papal tendency in this respect; a pope like Boniface IV (608–15) would "make his own house into a monastery,"[42] while a pope like Deusdedit (615–18) "greatly loved the clergy; he restored the priests and clergy to their original place."[43] Honorius (625–38) was also a pope of strong monastic sympathies, but after his time the clerical party was generally in the ascendancy. The schola cantorum, of course, was a characteristically clerical institution, manifesting the frequently noted tendency of the Roman clergy to form groups and to articulate them with internal hierarchies. It was an institution, moreover, that assumed a significant role in Roman liturgy and chant, an area formerly dominated by monks. That it came into being in a period of Roman clerical ascendency would seem more probable. And if we do not know just when this happened, at least some decades after the reign of Gregory would seem a probable time, that is, a period when both Rome and its clergy flourished. By the same token its founding would seem to have taken place some years, or even decades, before the reign of Adeodatus, when the organization was already well established. Perhaps, then, one might narrow down the time of the schola's founding to the second third of the seventh century; for the sake of presentational economy in what follows, I will say simply "the mid-seventh century."

THE MISSION TO ENGLAND

Another of Gregory's genuine accomplishments was his initiative to evangelize England. "The holy Gregory," we read in his brief *Liber pontificalis* biography, "sent the servants of God Mellitus, Augustine and John, and many other god-fearing monks; he sent them to preach to the people of England so that they might be converted to our Lord Jesus Christ."[44] This is, of course, the famous mission of St. Augustine of Canterbury, former prior of St. Andrew's monastery, the one that Gregory had established in his home. Augustine and his group of some forty monks arrived in Kent in the summer of 597; their efforts would prove eventually to be blessed with singular success, a story of which we are well informed thanks to the masterful narration of the Venerable Bede's *Ecclesiastical History of the English People*. Part of the story involves the strivings of various cantors to establish ecclesiastical song in England. Most of these figures have Roman connections, and Bede's description of their work casts some light on what might have been the state of church music not only in England but in Rome itself.

VENERABLE BEDE'S SINGERS

The first of the singers mentioned by Bede is a certain James the Deacon who taught chant for many years at York. Bishop Paulinus, a member of a reinforcing group Gregory sent to England in 601, left James at York in 633 when he moved south to become bishop of Rochester.

> Paulinus had left in his church at York the deacon James, a churchman, certainly, and a holy man, who remained for a long time thereafter.... Because he was highly skilled at singing in church, he began — after

peace had been restored in the province and the number of the faithful increased—also to serve many as a master of ecclesiastical song according to the custom of the Roman and Kentish people.⁴⁵

It is difficult to say what was the nature of James' teaching. Did he work alone or did he train others? Did he use any sort of written texts beyond a psalter? Was he in residence at one time in Augustine's monastic foundation of SS. Peter and Paul at Canterbury, where he would have participated in the Roman Office as transmitted to England by the Roman monks at the turn of the century? What sort of Mass psalmody would these monks have brought from Rome? Should we presume that James would have been more likely to teach something of this sort to the people of York, rather than the monastic Office?

The second cantor mentioned by Bede is Stephen, or Aeddi; he was invited north from Kent by Wilfred (d.709), the first native English bishop; Wilfred's invitation to Stephen came in the wake of the ecclesiastical revival stirred by the efforts of Theodore, who arrived in England in 669 to assume the archbishopric of Canterbury.

> But from this time they began to teach in all the churches of England the ecclesiastical song (*sonos cantandi in ecclesias*), which up to then was known only in Kent. The first singing master of the Northumbrian churches was Stephen, surnamed Aeddi (except for James of whom we spoke above); he was invited from Kent by the greatly revered Wilfred.⁴⁶

Once again Kent is mentioned; apparently the ecclesiastical centers of Kent, such as Canterbury and Rochester, maintained a tradition of church singing, the reputation of which continued into Bede's time. One presumes, as suggested above, that this tradition owes much to the Roman monastic practice as transmitted by the members of Augustine's mission. It must also have experienced periodic renewal from Rome. Certainly the activity of Bishop Theodore must be looked upon as an episode of such renewal. St. Theodore of Canterbury, archbishop of that see from 669 to his death in 690, was born in Tarsus but ordained in Rome. He is one of the most important figures in the ecclesiastical history of England; he traveled widely throughout the country and in 673 at the synod of Hertford he organized the hitherto chaotic diocesan system, placing it under direct control of Canterbury. He was a monk and as such must have participated in singing the Office at one of the Roman basilicas, and we can assume that he was acquainted with the singing of the schola cantorum at stational Masses. That he was at least partially responsible for the spread of singing in English churches, narrated above by Bede, is clear from the context of the quoted passage. And we can assume that there is some measure of Roman influence in what was taught, but we have no way of telling how far it rose above the level of primitivity suggested by the circumstance that Stephen was only the second teacher of church song in northern England up to his time.

The third of Bede's named singers is John, the celebrated archicantor of St. Peter's in the Vatican; he was brought to England by one of the more interesting figures in the early ecclesiastical history of England, St. Benedict Bishop (d.c.689). Benedict, the patron saint of English Benedictines and a mentor of Bede himself, was a scion of a noble Northumberland family. He manifested a lifelong ambition to improve the church of his native country in every respect and saw conformity with Rome as the chief means to this end; he visited the city no less than five times, an extraordinary record of travel for his day. His concern with the basic organizational needs of the English church is exemplified in his having accompanied Theodore on his journey from Rome to Canterbury, but he is especially famous for his interest in the amenities of worship. He brought paintings, relics and manuscripts back from Rome and is said to have been inspired by the architecture of the city to introduce the building of stone churches in England and their illumination with stained glass. Nor did he neglect chant; on the return from his final visit to Rome, in 678, he brought with him the singer John.

John was no less than the abbot of St. Martin's, a monastery attached to St. Peter's in the Vatican, and the archicantor of that centrally important basilica. Benedict brought him north to his monastery at Wearmouth, as Bede narrates:

> Benedict obtained also [permission from Pope Agatho] to bring the aforementioned abbot John so that he could teach in his monastery the annual cycle of chant (*cursum canendi annuum*) as it was practiced at St. Peter's in Rome. And abbot John undertook the commission of the pope, that is to say, he taught the singers of this monastery the order and ritual of singing and reading orally (*viva voce*) and he also committed to writing those things that were necessary for the celebration of festival dates for the entire annual cycle (*totius anni circulus*). These [writings] were hitherto preserved in this same monastery, and by now have been copied by many all about. Not only did this same John instruct the brothers of this monastery, but those who were adept at singing flocked together from almost all the monasteries of the province to hear him; many, moreover, took care to invite him to come to places where he might himself teach.[47]

This remarkable passage, while still leaving us guessing about much, provides a wealth of information upon which to base our speculations. We read that John's teaching was twofold: he taught "the order and ritual of singing and reading orally (*viva voce*)" and also committed to writing what was "necessary for the celebration of festival dates for the entire annual cycle." The phrase *viva voce* could be taken in either of two ways: it could mean that he taught the material involved "orally" or he taught the manner of singing and reading "aloud." The difference is unimportant; however, the essential point is that he taught "the order and ritual" of singing and reading, that is, in all probability, the daily and festal routines of psalms and readings. This stands in contrast to the second phase of his teaching, which is of much more interest to us—that which "was necessary for the celebration of festival dates for the entire annual cycle" and which was required to be recorded in writing. Here rather than simply the order of worship, John teaches its content. This would seem to involve a genuine Proper; the passage, in fact, gives us our first use in any Latin document of telling phrases like *cursus annuus* and *circulum anni*. But what was the precise nature of this Proper? John appears not to have brought written exemplars of Roman Office and Mass chant books; the passage has him doing the writing. Did he, perhaps, provide a mixture of his own creation and of what he remembered of Roman antiphons and responses, adapting it to the needs and abilities of the monks at Wearmouth?

The monastic context must also be kept in mind. John is from a Roman basilican monastery, not the schola cantorum; he teaches the singers of the monastery at Wearmouth, and monks come eventually from other monasteries to learn from him and he, in turn, visits other monasteries to teach. Similarly, his written collection of chant texts is both preserved at Wearmouth and copied by monks from other northern monasteries. As far as his written contribution is concerned, then, John would seem to have provided the monks of the English north with a modified version of what would be used in a Roman monastery of about 678. We can only guess at what these Roman written materials might have been like, something that I will allow myself to do in the following chapter. Suffice it to say for now that they would probably take the physical form not of bound codexes but of pamphlet-like *libelli*. Separate *libelli* would more likely exist for the two basic genres of antiphon and responsory than for the Mass and Office, and the bulk of the chants might be organized numerically according to the order of the Psalter with brief supplements of selected texts for principal festivals.

The fourth and last of Bede's singers is Maban.[48] He was invited to come north to Hexham from Kent by Acca, who succeeded Wilfred as bishop of Hexham in 709.

Acca, with great diligence, collected histories of [the apostles' and martyrs'] passions, along with other ecclesiastical books, creating a large and worthy library; and with great ardor he provided sacred vessels, lamps and other such objects for the adornment of the house of God. He also invited a distinguished singer, Maban by name, who had been taught the chant (*cantandi sonos*) at Kent by the successors of the disciples of blessed Gregory, to instruct him and his [monks and clergy]; and he retained him for twelve years so that he could teach the ecclesiastical chants (*carmina*) which they did not know and restore anew by his teaching those which, while known at one time, had begun to be corrupted by long use or neglect.[49]

Hexham, founded as an abbey by Wilfred in 674, was quite possibly one of those Northumberland monasteries that had profited from John's teaching in the previous generation. Perhaps they retained tattered copies of *libelli* with the texts of John's chants but only an imperfect memory of the original melodies. And at Kent, where Maban had been trained as a singer, did they sing the same melodies, or at least melodies similar to those that John had taught in the north, and, if so, did they remember them better there in the cradle of English Christianity than in the more primitive north? It is difficult even to speculate responsibly about that. But it seems safe to conclude from this passage that there were new chants being sung in Kent at the time of Maban's departure (those "which they did not know"), chants that were either developed there or transmitted from Rome. On the question of whether Maban's teaching was entirely oral or whether it involved the use of written chant texts, Bede is silent, although as suggested above, Hexham might have retained *libelli* from John's teaching, and it is possible that the "other ecclesiastical books" collected by Maban included chant manuscripts of some sort from either Canterbury or Rome.

Bede mentions Gregory in this passage. Maban represents the third generation of the mission that Gregory dispatched to England—he was taught chant at Kent "by the successors of the disciples of blessed Gregory." I think the text provides no grounds for saying that Bede implies a liturgical or musical role for Gregory. He simply says that Maban was instructed in chant at Kent by the generation of ecclesiastics who succeeded the original members of the Augustinian mission, and he had already singled out Kent as a center of chant while failing to mention Gregory. He would seem thus to connect Gregory only with the mission in general, not with chant in particular. We shall see presently, nonetheless, that Bede's grateful memory of Gregory's missionary initiative is not without significance for our subject.

AFTER BEDE

The extant English sources are silent on the subject of chant for several decades after the time of Maban. The next reference comes from the edicts of the Council of Clovesho, summoned by the archbishop of Canterbury in 747 to deal with ecclesiastical abuses in his province. The thirteenth decree of the council has something quite explicit to say about written Roman sources.

> It is determined by the thirteenth decree: That the holy festivals of the Lord's incarnation be conducted in one and the same manner; and that in all things which duly pertain to them, that is, in the office of baptism, in the celebration of Mass, and in the manner of singing (*in cantilenae modo*), they be celebrated according to the written exemplar (*exemplar . . . scriptum*) we have from the church of Rome. And that through the cycle of the entire year (*gyrum totius anni*) the "birthdays" of the saints be honored on one and the same date, according to the martyrology of the same Roman church, with the psalmody and chant (*psalmodio seu cantilena*) appropriate to that day.[50]

The decree speaks of a Roman liturgical book, the earliest preserved reference of the sort from England. The manuscript, with its inclusion of material for baptism, would seem to encompass a wide range of ritual material, yet the decree appears to emphasize the Mass and, more than that, to give special attention to the chants of that service. It nicely defines, moreover, the liturgical year, speaking first of the feasts of the Lord's incarnation, what we would call the *temporale*, and then the feasts of the saints, our *sanctorale*. Surely, then, the document must contain, among other things, the text of the Roman Mass Proper, or at least significant portions of it, as it existed sometime prior to 747.

If this is in fact the case, can we assume that a transmission of Roman chant, not unlike that which was to begin in the Carolingian realm a few years later with Pope Stephen's visit of 754 to King Pépin, took place as a result of this decree? Surely it need not be argued here that the full implementation of such a program at this stage in England's ecclesiastical history defies all plausibility. No doubt some sort of transmission did take place, a continuation and development of the musical bonds that we know existed already between Rome and Canterbury. But the successful transmission of an entire Mass Proper—just like its creation and maintenance within a musical schola—is something that requires very special circumstances. The Roman schola cantorum itself spent months on Frankish soil, singing the daily liturgy in the presence of pope, Roman curia and Frankish king and clergy. Chrodegang, presumably, was present also; he had accompanied

Pope Stephen north and subsequently reorganized his cathedral canons at Metz after the model of the Roman schola. Still it was no easy task for the Frankish singers, even those at Metz, to absorb the Roman chant. Charlemagne issued not just one decree that this be done, as did the Council of Clovesho, but a long series of them. We read, too, of numerous incidents in the history of the transmission, pleas for additional manuscripts from Rome, exchanges of singers, complaints that the Franks were unable to sing in the Roman manner, and testimony that the Mass chants were more successfully assimilated than the less manageable Office chants. And, finally, we witness the testimony of the Frankish manuscripts themselves, at first unnotated and later notated, reproducing the Roman repertory, its texts intact and its melodies preserved in essence if altered considerably in their surface elaboration.

That sort of transmission will take place in England not in the eighth century but in the closing decades of the tenth, as England recovers from the terrible years of the Scandinavian incursions.[51] The great figures of the later tenth-century monastic revival such as Dunstan, Oswald and Ethelwold will play a key role, and the transmission will come not from Rome but from continental monasteries like those of Ghent, Fleury and Corbie. But this is a story that takes us far beyond the scope of the present volume. Indeed my purpose in quoting a series of seventh- and eighth-century references to ecclesiastical song in England was not so much to trace the history of chant in England itself, but to see what light these documents might reflect upon the development of chant in Rome at the time. They turn out to complement nicely what we might imagine to be taking place in Rome. The English testimony, to put it in the broadest terms, can be said to mirror a threefold Roman development. The first and most obvious of these is a movement from the oral to written transmission of chant texts; there is no mention of writing in connection with the singers James and Stephen, while the archicantor John commits to writing what he remembers of Roman chant, and the Council of Clovesho cites the presence of an actual Roman document. There is a movement, too, toward a more explicit and detailed description of a chant Proper; Bede's passages about James and Stephen speak of church song in only the most general way, but John is said to have taught chants for the festivals of the entire year and the Council of Clovesho goes so far as to spell out the distinction between the temporale and sanctorale. Finally there is, at least between the narrative of John and the decree of Clovesho, a shift away from a nearly exclusive monastic focus to a broader ecclesiastical concern. Hand in hand with this last change, perhaps, we should assume a move toward more emphasis upon Mass chants (without, necessarily, a diminishment of concern with the Office). In a word the English documents reflect progress in the contemporary development of a written, albeit unnotated, Roman Mass Proper.

ENGLAND AND THE GREGORIAN MYTH

Reflected also in the seventh- and eighth-century English documents is a very special affection for Gregory the Great, an affection that, I have argued elsewhere, plays a key role in the development of the myth of Gregory's musical involvement.[52] Gregory is mentioned in only one of the passages quoted here, where Bede had the singer Maban instructed at Kent by the successors to the members of the mission Gregory sent to England. But he is mentioned frequently elsewhere in Bede's work; indeed the *Ecclesiastical History* is interrupted at one point by the insertion of a chapter-length biography of Gregory. The first independent biography of Gregory, moreover, was penned by an English contemporary of Bede, the anonymous monk of Whitby, writing between 706 and 714.[53] The reason for the enthusiasm of the English for Gregory, of course, stems from his central role in the conversion of their country; it has nothing to do with Gregory's purported interest in chant, and both Bede's biography and that of the monk of Whitby are entirely silent on the subject of Gregory and liturgical music.

Meanwhile in Rome Gregory is all but forgotten as the seventh century progresses; his biography in the *Liber pontificalis* is startlingly brief, and he is virtually never mentioned in seventh- and eighth-century sources.[54] Indeed, it might be said that his memory was deliberately repressed owing to clerical resentment over his arrogation of clerical privileges and functions to monks.[55] How, then, did he come to be championed as the central figure in the creation of the chant that bears his name? Simplistic as it seems, I believe it was a case of mistaken identity, a confusion with his later namesake Gregory II that was resolved in favor of the first Gregory by English scholars in residence at the court of Charlemagne.[56]

The crux of the matter lies in the short prefaces at the beginning of the earliest graduals; they vary in length and wording but all have the essential words *Gregorius presul composuit hunc libellum musicae artis scholae cantorum per circulum anni* (Gregory, the prelate, compiled this little book of musical art for the schola cantorum [to be used] over the annual cycle). Bruno Stäblein collected these prefaces and subjected the variations in their texts to a careful analysis.[57] Most of them are Frankish in origin, but the earliest (and longest) is Italian, that of the Lucca codex, copied in the 780s. The text sings the praises of its Gregory for some thirty-two lines but omits all mention of the one achievement for which Gregory the Great was universally admired, his authorship of books of moral theology. By contrast two of the later northern prefaces appear to allude to such writings: that of the Fleury gradual has the line *hic vitam scribens hominum moresque bonorum* (writing on the life and virtues of good men), almost certainly an allusion to Gregory's hagiographic *Dialogues*, and that of the St-Denis gradual has *numerosa volumina sacra, quae pius afflatu finxit dictante superno* (numerous sacred books, which this holy man wrote by inspiration of the most high spirit), surely an allusion to the famous scene of the Holy Spirit, sitting on Gregory's shoulder in the form of a dove, inspiring him to compose works like the *Moralia in Job*. Stäblein concludes, rightly I think, that the original Italian versions of this preface referred not to Gregory the Great, but to Gregory II, while the Franks took the unspecified Gregory to be Gregory I.

There is good reason for both the Roman and the Frankish attributions. If Gregory I was all but forgotten in Italy by the presumed date of the preface's composition, the middle to later eighth century, Gregory II was a towering figure. He was, among other things, the pope who defied Constantinople by refusing to pay taxes on the Sicilian papal estates that fed Rome, and the pope who refused to accept the Byzantine position on iconoclasm.[58] Moreover, he reigned at the very time that the Roman Mass Proper was taking its final form. Indeed, it must be added that Gregory II's successor, Gregory III, was also a commanding figure, and one with documented liturgical involvement as well.[59] It is just possible that there was a measure of Gregorian conflation taking place in the mind of the preface's Italian author. As for the Franks, they would have altogether dimmer notions of earlier eighth-century popes; for them the Gregory of the preface could be any Gregory, and it is here that the special English predilection for Gregory the Great comes into play. English scholars such as Alcuin of York were influential in the overall intellectual life of the Carolingian court and particularly involved in its liturgical program;[60] they would naturally assume that Gregory the Great was the pope who "compiled this little book of musical art . . . for the annual cycle," that is to say, the Roman Mass Proper.

Thereafter the legend could flourish, especially in the Carolingian court and in monastic circles, where the writings of Gregory were prized for their contribution to the ascetic life. The monk Walafrid Strabo, abbot of Reichenau (d.849), expanded the legend in his *De exordiis*.[61] John Hymonides ("John the Deacon," d.c.880), who penned the classic form of the Gregorian legend, explicitly attributing to him the founding of the schola and the composition of the antiphonary, was a Roman cleric; but he was also at one time a monk of Monte Cassino and, more significantly, a visitor to the court of Charlemagne's grandson, Charles the Bald (d.877).[62] It was there, apparently, that he learned much of his Gregorian lore. The famous anecdote of the Roman cantors on Carolingian soil, narrated by him in a pro-Roman version and by Nokter of St. Gall in a pro-Frankish version, exists in a little-noticed earlier version from the monastery of Lorsch, near Worms, a foundation with connections to Chrodegang and the Carolingian court.[63] Finally the Gregorian legend is complete when the topos of the Holy Spirit dictating Gregory's theological works is transferred to Gregory's composition of the antiphoner; its earliest preserved instance is the miniature that serves as frontispiece to the Hartker antiphoner, copied in St. Gall around the year 1000.[64]

II

THE SEVENTH-CENTURY
ROMAN BACKGROUND

CHAPTER 5

Sacramentary, Lectionary and Antiphoner

This set of three chapters sets the seventh-century Roman stage for the Advent Project. The first treats the development of the sacramentary and lectionary in the hope that recounting the histories of these books will shed light on that of the more illusive Mass antiphoner. The second and the third attempt in differing ways to date the composition of that antiphoner, this being synonymous with dating the Advent Project itself. I introduce the three by invoking a fundamentally important distinction that Willi Apel makes in discussing the origins of Proper chants.

APEL'S THREEFOLD DISTINCTION

Apel maintains that we must take care to separate three different aspects in the development of chant formularies—the institution of a feast, the assignment of chant texts to it and the composition of its chant melodies. In his own words:

> It seems advisable to divide the whole field of investigation into three areas: the first concerning the cycle of feasts throughout the year; the second, dealing with the texts of the chants for the Masses and Offices of these feasts; and the third, with the melodies for these chants. The failure to distinguish clearly between these three aspects of the development has caused numerous erroneous conclusions on the part of the scholars, or, at least, erroneous impressions among their readers.[1]

Apel goes on to a detailed examination of the three areas in turn, seeking to demonstrate that they amount in historical reality to three chronological stages. To put it in the simplest of terms, a particular feast day might have been instituted in the fifth century, while the texts of its chants might date to the time of Gregory I's reform and its melodies might be the work of ninth-century Frankish cantors. There is much in Apel's extended discussion of the three stages that is perceptive and still valuable, even if many chant scholars today would differ with it in certain respects. My purpose, however, in citing Apel's scheme is neither to agree nor disagree with his reflections on it but to offer my own.

FESTIVAL VERSUS CHANT FORMULARY

Apel's threefold distinction can be broken down into a pair of twofold distinctions. What of the first of these, that between the establishment of a feast day and the creation of its chant formulary? Is there a necessary chronological gap between the two? Certainly most would agree that there is a gap of many centuries between the origins of an ancient festival like Easter Sunday and the assignment of its Proper chants but could well imagine that preparations for the first solemn observance of a thirteenth-century feast like Corpus Christi might involve chants for use on that date. The difference between the two examples is obvious: the first is from a period before liturgical genres like the introit, gradual and offertory had come into existence, and the second from a period when Mass could hardly have been celebrated publicly without a full complement of such chants. We should expect, then, that the assignment of chants to a festival would be approximately contemporary to its institution, once we had entered upon that period in the history of ecclesiastical song when it was customary to have a set of permanently assigned chants for each date in the calendar. Just when that might have been, it is hoped, will be somewhat clearer at the conclusion of these three chapters.

TEXT VERSUS MELODY

The second twofold distinction is that between a chant's text and its melody —should we expect a chronological gap to exist between these? The answer, I should think, is very similar to that involving festival and chant formulary. Once we are within that period of music history when chants are assigned to a new festival contemporary to its institution, we should expect the selection of a text and the creation of its melody to be approximately contemporaneous. Or to put it in terms friendly to the thesis of the present book, once within the era of the Advent Project the text and melody of a particular chant come into being at more or less the same time. I do not mean to say, of course, that the melody in question undergoes no change once fashioned; a Roman melody of the seventh century has a dual history of oral transmission resulting eventually in its Gregorian and Old Roman versions. I mean to say only that, whatever the ultimate shape of a particular melody, it probably originated as part of the same creative enterprise that produced its text.

There is compelling evidence for this proposition in the nature of the texts. Most of them are derived from Scripture, especially the Psalter, and one might be led to think, then, that they had somehow always been there, waiting to be set to music eventually. But a comparison of the chant texts with the original scriptural texts shows that in a great number of cases—as much as half of the chants of the Mass Proper—the original is altered in order to provide a suitable chant text. This is the phenomenon referred to in the introduction to this volume under the rubric "textual adjustment."[2] The verbal discrepancies involved are not just a matter of conflicting versions of the biblical text but are clearly deliberate adaptations on the part of those fashioning the chant texts.

The changes range from some that transform an entire text to others involving a single word or two. The most frequently encountered major change is the omission of a substantial segment of the original; in an extreme example, in the introit *Dicit dominus,* derived from Jeremiah 29.11–14, there are four such omissions, resulting in a text stitched together from the five remaining clauses and phrases. Occasionally a text is a fusion of material from different biblical books. The gradual response *Hodie scietis,* for example, is made up of a single sentence, the opening portion of which is derived from Exodus 16.6–7 and the closing portion from Isaiah 35.4; the material from the two sources is, moreover, paraphrased freely. The device of free paraphrase—used less often than that of stitching together integral sections of the biblical original—can reach such extremes, as in the introit *Populus sion,* purportedly derived from Isaiah 30.19–20, that one might suspect the result to be a quasi-original composition created by the author from remembered biblical fragments, rather than a conscious adaptation of a specific scriptural passage.

In addition to such radical transformations of the biblical original, there are frequently encountered minor changes. The most common of these is the insertion of some form of the word *dominus* in order to make the chant text function better as an independent unit after removal from its biblical context. Thus passages that are addressed to the Lord will regularly have the vocative *domine* inserted at an appropriate place, and passages that quote the Lord will be prefaced by *dixit dominus.* Conversely, conjunctions like *autem* and *etenim,* which might serve some connective or logical purpose in the original, are routinely omitted in the self-contained, and more lyrically intended, chant text. Occasionally a small change is made to clarify the meaning of a chant text. The communion *Beatus servus* (Mt 24.46–47) has the word *vigilantem* (keeping watch) in place of the original *sic facientem* (acting thus); this is done because the context of the passage involves keeping watch (verse 42 begins *Vigilate ergo*), and the derived chant text would lose all significance if it read *Beatus servus quem cum venerit dominus invenerit sic facientem* ("Blessed that servant whom the Lord, when he comes, finds acting thus").

So it might be said, then, that those responsible for the texts of the Mass Proper select a verse or two from Scripture for each chant and alter it, if necessary, to provide a suitable "libretto," or retain it in its original form if it is already deemed to be suitable. What this suggests, I think, is that the act of fashioning an appropriate chant text and setting it to music are part of the same process, carried out, perhaps, by two members of the schola cantorum working closely together, or maybe by a single individual. The alternate scenario is hardly plausible, that is, that at one time texts for the entire Mass Proper were meticulously fashioned, compiled in writing and allowed to remain thus for generations until set to music.

These brief reflections on the comparative chronology of festival, text and melody suggest that all three might be approximately contemporaneous—once, that is, the period of the Roman Mass Proper's final revision (this volume's Advent Project) has been entered into. The task of this set of three chapters, as stated above, is to try and define this period, after first searching out the development of the seventh-century Roman sacramentary and lectionary in the hope of shedding light on the contemporary antiphoner.

THE SACRAMENTARY

Chants make up just one element in the developing Roman Mass Proper; there are also prayers and readings. The prayers, that is, the variable orations read by the celebrant such as the collect, secret and post-communion, are contained, along with other material for sacerdotal use like Proper prefaces and the Ordinary of the Mass, in liturgical books called sacramentaries. The Roman Mass readings, namely the epistle which is read by a subdeacon and the gospel which is read by a deacon, are recorded in lectionaries, usually separately in epistolaries and evangeliaries. There are no extant seventh- or eighth-century Roman manuscripts of sacramentaries or lectionaries, but liturgical historians are able to reconstruct them with considerable accuracy from a rich fund of eighth- and ninth-century Frankish manuscripts.

To begin with the sacramentary, its historiography distinguishes three types: the Leonine, Gelasian and Gregorian. Each was named in the seventeenth century for a pope supposedly involved in its composition—Leo I (440–61), Gelasius I (492–96) and Gregory I (590–604)—attributions, needless to say, that are no longer generally accepted. The first of these, the so-called Leonine sacramentary, is in fact not a type as such but a book represented by a single manuscript copied in the early seventh century, probably in Verona, hence its preferred sobriquet, the Veronensis.[3] Nor is it actually a sacramentary in the formal sense of a liturgical book that provides prayer sets and prefaces for each date in the liturgical calendar. Rather it is a kind of pre-sacramentary, compiled from separate *libelli*, each of which has groups of prayer sets—for individual feasts or for short portions of the church year. The *libelli* are arranged according to the calendric rather than liturgical year, that is, by the month, although January, February, March and the beginning of April are missing.

The prayer sets are Roman in origin, indeed probably papal, dating to the fifth and sixth centuries and appearing to have been assembled sometime between 558 and 590. The most striking feature of the formularies is that there is a variety of them for each occasion, five for St. Cecilia, for example, and no less than twelve for St. Lawrence. That they are written down suggests that the age of improvised prayers by the celebrant at Mass is coming to an end in the sixth century, but that there is such a variety suggests that the age of a fixed Proper of Mass prayers has not yet arrived. Clearly the presence of multiple formularies for each festival leads us to think that the Roman prelate of the time was free to exercise choice in the matter. The implications of this for ecclesiastical chant are obvious; one recalls the contemporary Psalter of St-Germain, which indicates suitable response verses without indicating specific liturgical occasions. Choice rather than fixed assignment is the common trait of the two books, even if the Veronensis represents a step beyond the Psalter of St-Germain in that it offers a choice within a group of possibilities designed for a specific occasion.

The second type of Roman sacramentary is the so-called Gelasian. Here one must distinguish between the unique "Old Gelasian" and the "Eighth-Century," or "Frankish," Gelasians. The latter is a type represented by several Frankish manuscripts that are derived from a lost Frankish monastic original, which was a carefully worked-out synthesis of material from the Old Gelasian and the Gregorian, with a generous admixture of indigenous Frankish elements. It is not this type that concerns us here, but the more purely Roman Old Gelasian. It exists in a single manuscript, probably copied around 750 in the convent of Chelles, near Paris.[4] Its material is basically

Roman, with a number of clearly separable Frankish additions such as the Sundays of Advent and a handful of sanctoral dates not celebrated at Rome. The Roman liturgy represented is thought to be that of the *tituli* (the parish churches, so to speak, of Rome), rather than the papal liturgy of the Lateran. It appears to incorporate some older *libelli* with sixth-century prayer sets, but the makeup of the overall book is clearly later. It has the four Marian feasts that were introduced sometime in the seventh century and the feast of the Exaltation of the Holy Cross, which could hardly have been instituted before the recovery of the True Cross from the Persians by Emperor Heraclius in 628. It does not have the Thursdays in Lent, which were pronounced liturgical by Gregory II in about 720, so that one must conclude it dates to sometime between 628 and 720 (certainly closer to the earlier date). Its most striking overall feature is its separation of the temporale from the sanctorale.

Of relevance to the present study is that unlike the Veronensis it is a genuine sacramentary, that is, a liturgical book with fixed prayer sets for more or less the entire church year. It begins, in fact, with the words *Incipit liber sacramentorum romanae aecclesiae ordinis anni circuli.* From this we can see that the concept of a Mass Proper is thoroughly established in seventh-century Rome. But there remain gaps in its complete realization, most notably with the ordinary Sundays of the year. Prayer sets are assigned for the Sundays after Easter, but not for the Sundays after Epiphany or after Pentecost. Prayers are to be selected for these dates, one presumes, from the group of sixteen that are given at the beginning of the book's third major division, under the rubric ORACIONES ET PRAECES CUM CANONE PER DOMINICIS DIEBUS (orations and prayers with canon [preface] for Sundays). These are "generic" formularies, each of which is introduced by the rubric ITEM. They are obviously appropriate for selection by the celebrant on an ad hoc basis for Sundays after Epiphany and Pentecost, and one can imagine him supplementing them as well from a personal *libellus* or even improvising them on occasion. Music historians will recognize a trace of such provisionalism in the final form of the post-Pentecostal chant formularies (most obviously in the alleluia lists), and they will be asked later in this chapter to exercise their imaginations over similar possibilities in the manner Mass chants were chosen during the years before the final revision of the Mass Proper.

The third and final type of Roman sacramentary is the so-called Gregorian. The term is used to refer to the papal sacramentary in use at the Lateran and for the stational liturgy; it coexisted throughout the seventh and eighth centuries with the Gelasian of the Roman *tituli.* It is preserved in numerous ninth-century, chiefly Frankish, manuscripts, the substantial variations among which reveal a complex history that appears to begin with a first redaction during the pontificate of Honorius I (625–38). The best-known stage in that history involves the "Hadrianum" version of the Gregorian, sent by Pope Hadrian I (772–95) to Charlemagne shortly before 790 in fulfillment of the latter's request for an "authentic" Gregorian sacramentary. The Frankish scholars, as is well known, were disappointed by the obvious gaps in the Hadrianum—its lack of ordinary Sundays, for example, which Benedict of Aniane remedied with his famous *Hucusque* supplement. It is not the Hadrianum, however, which is immediately relevant to our discussion, but two redactions of the Gregorian from the second half of the seventh century, the "Paduensis" and "Trent," so called from the ninth-century manuscripts from which they are reconstructed.

PADUENSIS AND TRENT

The Paduensis was adapted from its Lateran original for presbyteral use at St. Peter's basilica sometime between 650 and 680, perhaps around 663.[5] It omits certain papal items, such as prayers for baptisms and ordinations, and adds others, most notably prayers for the ordinary Sundays; these include five sets for Sundays after Epiphany, five for Sundays after Easter and twenty-three for Sundays after Pentecost, the last group arranged in the Roman manner with four after Pentecost, five after the feast of Peter and Paul (29 June), five after St. Lawrence (10 August) and nine after the Dedication of St. Michael the Archangel (29 September). The Paduensis, unlike the original Roman Old Gelasian, does have a group of Advent Sundays, a point that will be of considerable interest to us in the following chapter. Crucial to the dating of the Paduensis is the absence of a pair of sanctoral festivals that were added to the Roman calendar in the 680s, the dedication anniversaries of St. George the Martyr in Velabro (23 April) and St. Peter in Chains (1 August). That they do not appear in the Paduensis is strong evidence for the above-cited terminus ad quem of 680. More complex is the situation with the four Marian feasts. The Presentation ("Hypopanti," 2 February), which may have been introduced into the Roman liturgy as early as the pontificate of Theodore I (642–49), is represented with the same prayer sets as will appear in the Hadrianum; this tells us that the important date was well established in the papal liturgy before 680. The Annunciation (25 March), the Assumption (15 August) and the Nativity of Mary (8 September), however, while present in the Paduensis, do not have the same prayer sets as in the Hadrianum. Those of the Hadrianum are generally considered to be the work of Sergius I (687–701), a circumstance that raises the possibility that the three feasts themselves may not have been introduced until his reign. Finally, the Thursdays in Lent are represented, but with prayer sets that are clearly Frankish additions; they are clumsily adapted from Gelasian formularies, are applied to the wrong weeks and—inconceivable for a Roman redactor—are given the wrong stations.

If it appears that the Roman prototype of the Paduensis was compiled sometime between 650 and 680, perhaps between 663 and 680, the dating for the prototype of the Trent Gregorian can be more precisely determined.[6] Represented by a single manuscript copied in the vicinity of Salzburg, perhaps as early as 825, it stems from a sacramentary compiled at the Lateran between 680 and the liturgical innovations of Sergius I; it has the two abovementioned festivals introduced in the 680s that are absent from the Paduensis (the dedications of St. George and St. Peter in Chains) but lacks Sergius I's prayers for the Annunciation, the Assumption and the Nativity of Mary. (It lacks, moreover, the *Agnus dei* in its Mass Ordinary, a well-known innovation of Sergius.) Trent's provision of the ordinary Sundays is interesting. One recalls that the Paduensis had to add them to the material derived from its Lateran original and entered the post-Pentecost Sundays in the typical Roman manner, that is, with groups of masses after Pentecost, the feasts of SS. Peter and Paul, of St. Lawrence and of St. Michael. Trent adds fully worked out series of Sundays after Epiphany, Easter and Pentecost, numbered in the Frankish manner, and does so in a supplement just as Benedict of Aniane had done a few years earlier in his supplement to the Hadrianum. Curiously an additional set of fifty-nine undifferentiated collects, to be used ad libitum presumably, is included (in the section containing the *Ordo missae*); thus the book provides both the oldest and newest way of furnishing prayer sets for the ordinary Sundays.

The discrepancies among specific sanctoral occasions in the different redactions of the Gregorian sacramentary will be taken up again in chapter seven, where they will aid in our attempt to reconstruct the history of the Roman sanctorale. The lesson that has a more direct bearing on the present chapter is that of the striking lack of stability and uniformity that prevails among seventh-century sacramentaries. By their very nature—as compilations of *libelli* stemming from different individuals and different times—the sacramentaries seem bound to display a certain lack of coherence and unity. These circumstances are further complicated at Rome by the varying needs and histories of the presbyteral and papal liturgies. The result is the contrasting formats of Roman sacramentaries and their differing content. Matters are further complicated in the Frankish north, where imported Gelasian and Gregorian sacramentaries need to be reconciled with both themselves and indigenous liturgical needs. The struggle, only partially successful, of Carolingian liturgical scholars to achieve uniformity from this welter of material makes for a fascinating story that cannot be retold here; suffice it to say that Gerald Ellard's magisterial chapter on the subject is entitled "Liturgical Anarchy."[7]

SACRAMENTARY VERSUS ANTIPHONER

The instability of the sacramentary stands in sharp contrast to the uniformity of the antiphoner. I use, by the way, the early Roman term "antiphoner" in this chapter, or more fully "Mass antiphoner" or "antiphoner of the Mass," rather than "gradual," which is the standard term for later manifestations of the type. The two are essentially the same book. Just as we speak of a seventh-century Roman sacramentary reconstructed from later Frankish manuscripts, I intend to speak of a seventh-century Roman antiphoner of the Mass reconstructed from ninth-century Frankish graduals—and, in fact, from the much later Old Roman graduals. That the Old Roman manuscripts play a part in this reconstruction may come as a surprise to some, but they most assuredly do. This is a point to be pursued at length in the following chapter, where it will be seen that the Mass Proper of the Roman graduals and that of the earliest Frankish graduals are virtually identical from book to book; the only exceptions of any consequence (aside from the alleluia repertory) are to be found in festivals added either in Rome or in the Carolingian realm after the mid-eighth-century transmission of the *cantus romanus* to the north. For now I will assume this uniformity of the Mass Proper tradition and attempt to explain why it is so much at variance with the instability of the sacramentary.

One reason might be that prayer sets are by their very nature more malleable than chants, that is, chants of the carefully crafted type referred to in this work as schola chants. One can readily imagine clerics adapting earlier prayers to contemporary taste and new liturgical occasions, but a Roman schola chant, on the other hand, appears to display a more overtly concrete presence than a celebrant's prayer—it stands out almost as a sculptured object, with heft and physiognomy. Call to mind an introit like the first Sunday of Advent's *Ad te levavi*. We tend to identify the entire Mass of the day with it; in later centuries, in fact, Sundays came to be named after their introits, "Laetare Sunday," for example, and "Da pacem Sunday." Such quasi landmarks of liturgy are not so easily changed; there is nothing quite so proper, one might say, as a Mass Proper chant. Early medieval singers came to know the entire Mass Proper by heart. Can we imagine the same for a priest and the annual cycle of Mass prayer sets?

But more fundamental to this question of diversity and uniformity in sacramentaries and graduals are the contrasting historical circumstances surrounding the creation of the two liturgical genres: the sacramentaries are the product of different individuals and groups working at different times and in different places, the gradual the product of a single community working for a limited period. The history of the sacramentaries involves fifth-, sixth- and seventh-century *libelli* compiled at various times for use in the diverse Roman churches and at the Lateran. The history of the antiphoner as a written book would appear to be much more limited before its final compilation by the schola cantorum at the Lateran in the later seventh century. The transmission of the two liturgical genres to the Carolingian north is similarly contrasting. Sacramentaries filtered into Frankish Gaul in different redactions over a period of nearly two centuries, there to be combined with all manner of indigenous material. The antiphoner of the Mass came as a unified book, brought by Pope Stephen and his retinue at a particular historical event. It was copied faithfully by the Carolingian cantors—again, as I plan to show in the following chapter—who added only a small number of Frankish feasts and liturgical practices, expanded the insufficient alleluia repertory and changed the way in which the post-Pentecost Sundays are numbered. The continuity between the Roman and Frankish repertories is remarkable, indeed baffling to those scholars (as I gather in conversation with them) who work amid the great diversity of sacramentaries.

It is necessary when comparing sacramentaries and the antiphoner to speak of Carolingians for the obvious reason that most of the relevant manuscripts are Frankish, but it is the strictly Roman history of these books that is relevant here at present, and the point that I wish to make is that everything being said here suggests a relatively late date for the compilation of the Mass antiphoner (and a correspondingly late date for the Mass Proper chants therein). There is a great variety of eighth- and ninth-century Frankish sacramentary manuscripts from which we can reconstruct the complex seventh-century history of the Roman sacramentaries, but nothing remotely comparable for the gradual. It would seem that if written graduals had existed at Rome in various states of completion throughout the entire seventh century, there would be, as is the case with sacramentaries, eighth- and ninth-century Frankish manuscript evidence of this. Instead we have only ninth-century Frankish graduals (the *Sextuplex* manuscripts), which reveal a unified Roman model. There is a curious reversal here of Walter

Howard Frere's famous maxim, "fixity means antiquity."[8] The fixity of the gradual appears to be attributable to the circumstances that it was compiled at a time when the chants of the Roman Mass Proper were set, and that it was compiled within a relatively short period, leaving no manuscript evidence of its evolution.

Clearly its fixity has to do also with the circumstance that it is the product of a single community, the schola cantorum in residence at the Lateran, rather than of various Roman ecclesiastical bodies, as was the case with the sacramentaries. This throws light on an entirely different issue, one not yet alluded to in this volume—the "two-chant" hypothesis advocated at one time by scholars such as Stephen van Dijk and Bruno Stäblein, that is, the view that there existed in seventh- and eighth-century Rome a separate urban or presbyteral chant and a papal or Lateran chant.[9] The hypothesis is prompted both by the analogy of separate presbyteral and papal sacramentaries at Rome and by the differing melodic traits of the Roman and Gregorian (Frankish-Roman) chants. There are many reasons speaking against the validity of two-chant theories, and these will be recounted in the epilogue to this book, but for now it is appropriate to point out that the virtual liturgical identity of all extant Roman and Frankish graduals argues against two separate Roman chants. As for the differing melodic surfaces of the Roman and Gregorian chants, they are best explained, as most chant scholars would agree today, as the result of differing histories of oral transmission experienced by the same body of chant in two different regions.

In summary, the Roman sacramentary and the Roman gradual have sharply contrasting histories. The former involves centuries of different versions from different locations, the latter the relatively late appearance of a single unified type.

THE LECTIONARY

The history of the Roman Mass lectionaries (epistolaries and evangeliaries) has at least one trait in common with that of the sacramentaries; it illustrates the general tendency to move from the ad hoc selection of liturgical materials to the eventual establishment of a fixed Proper, a point to be pursued here presently. As for differences between the two, the most fundamental one stems from the differing sources of their content. The material for the readings of the Mass, one might say, comes ready-made; it derives from the Bible and has only to be selected, while Mass prayers must be composed. There are other differences as well, all of which point to the comparatively less complex task of achieving a fixed Proper of readings. The Roman

Mass has only two readings, while there are several prayers. It is true that by the time of the Gregorian sacramentary there are only three, the classic formulary of collect, secret and post-communion, but the Old Gelasian has varying numbers for each occasion, most frequently five (an extra collect and an *oratio ad populum* in addition to the other three). And then, as we have seen, the *libelli* of the Veronensis has multiple prayer sets for each occasion. Surely sorting out such a proliferation of possibilities would work to retard the stabilization of the sacramentary. This is not to say that the stabilization of the Roman lectionary, that is, the eventual elimination of choice in readings, was not a formidable accomplishment itself, but only that it was a less formidable one than stabilizing the sacramentary, and that we should not be surprised to see it accomplished at a somewhat earlier date.

Obviously readings were not yet fixed at the time of our earliest preserved reference to them at Mass, that from Justin Martyr's above-quoted description of Sunday Eucharist at mid-second-century Rome; we are told there that "the memoirs of the Apostles and the writings of the Prophets are read as long as time permits." We saw in chapter two that significant progress toward an annual cycle of readings had taken place already by the time of Augustine—it was not yet so much a matter of fixed readings for certain dates as the association of particular books of Scripture with whole seasons. Thus the Paschaltime gospels were derived chiefly from John and the Paschaltime epistles from the Acts of the Apostles.[10] It is possible in this context, too, that a single specific reading would have come to be associated with a particular feast in cases where the relationship was especially appropriate. Thus, as we saw above, the Pentecost narration from chapter two of Acts was read on Pentecost in the time of Caesarius of Arles and was also the medieval Roman epistle for the date. It seems safe to assume that Augustine as well would have chosen this same portion of Acts for reading each Pentecost, even if we have no sermon that documents it.

Our first references to the drawing up of an annual list of readings come from later fifth-century Gaul. Musaeus of Marseilles (d.c.460), quoted above in chapter three, is said to have "selected . . . readings from the Holy Writings appropriate to the feast days of the entire year,"[11] and Claudianus Mamertus of Vienne (d.c.474) is said "to have prepared for the annual solemnities that which when read is appropriate to the time."[12] A written record of some sort must have been utilized by both Musaeus and Claudianus, in short a kind of lectionary.

There are three possible ways to compile a lectionary.[13] The most primitive is simply to supply marginal indications of some sort in a biblical text

—by an *X*, for example, or by the name of the feast day involved. Surviving examples of this type are much more consistent about indicating the beginning of the pericope than the end, which one presumes was left to the memory or discretion of the reader. The second possibility is the listing of incipits and explicits at the front or back of the scriptural book, or in a separate *libellus*. The third is to write out the pericopes in full, the type of lectionary to which one generally applies the term *comes* (companion) or *liber comitis*.

The three types might appear at first as chronological stages in the history of the lectionary, and one can in fact imagine a rough chronological procession of the sort in the early, undocumented, history of the genre, but the extant manuscripts show the coexistence of the three for nearly a millennium. Indeed the earliest preserved lectionary is of the third type, a manuscript copied in southern Gaul about 500, which some, without strong justification, would like to identify with the above-mentioned work of Musaeus or of Claudianus.[14] This remarkable document, a palimpsest representing about half of the original, is not only the oldest extant lectionary but our first liturgical book of any sort (not surprisingly, in view of the above-stated claim that readings are more likely to become fixed at an earlier date than prayer formularies). This is not to say, however, that the particular readings given in this book became in fact part of a permanent lectionary; they fail to correspond with the readings of other early Gallican books, not to speak of the medieval Roman readings.

Another factor accounting for the chronological confusion among the three types of lectionary is the circumstance that there existed no method in earlier centuries for indicating the chapters and verses of biblical books other than the four gospels. The system in present use for the entire Bible is very late, sixteenth-century, but Eusebius of Caesarea had worked out a scheme for the gospels already in the fourth century, his so-called *canones* or *sectiones;* these were numbered sense units, each the equivalent of several verses of the later system. Thus it was practical to use the second type of lectionary, the list of incipits and explicits, for evangeliaries but not for epistolaries. This type of evangeliary came to be called a capitulary, because typically it would give—along with the name of the feast day and the incipit and explicit of the gospel—the number of its Eusebian section or chapter preceded by the abbreviation *cap*. In the absence of such a system for the readings from the Old Testament and the Epistles, one would need almost total recall of the Bible to find the epistle of the day from no more than the name of the book in addition to the incipit and explicit of the pericope.

Table 1. Gregorian and PI-type Gospels Compared

	Greg Gospel	*PI Gospel*
Temporale		
Christmas Night	Lk 2.1–14	—
Epiphany	Mt 2.1–12	—
Septuagesima	Mt 20.1–16	—
Sexagesima	Lk 8.4–15	—
Quinquagesima	Lk 18.31–44	—
Quadragesima	Mt 4.1–11	—
Quadragesima V	Jn 8.45–69	—
Easter	Mk 16.1–7	—
Easter Monday	Lk 24.13–35	—
Easter Wednesday	Jn 21.1–14	—
Easter Thursday	Jn 20.11–18	—
Easter Saturday	Jn 20.1–9	Jn 20.19–33
Easter Octave	Jn 20.19–31	Jn 20.24–31
Easter II	Jn 10.11–16	—
Ascension	Mk 16.14–20	—
Pentecost	Jn 14.23–31	—
Pent I	Lk 14.16–24	[Lk 15.1–10]
Pent II	Lk 16.19–31	[—]
Pent III	Lk 15.1–10	[Lk 14.16–24]
September Ember Friday	Lk 7.36–50	Lk 5.17–26
Sept Ember Saturday	Lk 13.6–13	Lk 13.10–17
III Sunday before Xmas	Lk 21.25–42	Mt 21.1–9
II Sunday before Xmas	Mt 11.2–10	Lk 21.25–33
I Sunday before Xmas	Jn 1.19–28	Mt 11.2–10
December Ember Saturday	Lk 3.1–11	Lk 3.1–6
Sanctorale		
Agnes I	Mt 25.1–13	—
Agnes II	Mt 13.44–52	—
Sebastian	Lk 14.25–33	Lk 6.17–23
Pancratius	Jn 15.12–16	Jn 18.17–25
Nereus & Achilles	Jn 4.46–53	Mt 19.3–11
Processus & Martinianus	Lk 9.23–27	Mt 24.3–13
Felicitas	Mt 12.46–50	—

(*continued*)

Table 1. (continued)

	Greg Gospel	PI Gospel
Mennas	Lk 21.9–19	Lk 9.23–27
Felix	Lk 12.35–40	Lk 10.16–20
Clement	Mt 22.1–13	Mt 22.1–13
Andrew	Mt 4.18–22	—
Sylvester	Mt 25.14–30	Mt 24.42–47

Our earliest evidence for Roman readings comes from the sermons of Gregory I. We have some forty sermons of his that indicate both the liturgical occasion on which they were preached and the gospel on which they were based. From this one can reconstruct a Gregorian evangeliary for about a quarter of the liturgical year, including especially the more important dates, occasions like Christmas, Epiphany, Quadragesima Sunday, Easter, Ascension and Pentecost. More important, one can compare Gregory's gospels with those of the earliest type of complete Roman evangeliary, Theodor Klauser's PI-type of about 645.[15] Table 1 compares the two within the temporale and sanctorale. The first column gives the festival on which Gregory's homily was preached, the second the gospel on which the homily was based and the third the gospel of the PI-type evangeliary for the same date. If the two gospels correspond, there is a dash in the PI-type column; if not, the differing gospel is given there.

What is one to conclude from the comparison? First it must be said that the PI-type list is substantially the same as all subsequent Roman lists (the same indeed as that of the Tridentine *Missale romanum*) and hence represents a firmly fixed Roman gospel Proper at the relatively early date of about 645. Gregory's list shows that much of the temporale, at least its more important dates, from Christmas to Pentecost, was fixed in his day, but that most of the sanctorale was not. One might ask whether the Gregorian gospels that appear to be fixed are actually recorded in a list of some sort or whether they are simply traditional associations maintained in memory. For the latter possibility one might argue that a gospel like Christmas night's Luke 2.1–14, the nucleus of the Lucan Christmas story, is an unavoidable choice for the occasion, and all the more easily remembered from year to year because it, like the other Gregorian choices, represents a single Eusebian section. But certainly the maintenance from year to year of assignments like those for the three ferial dates of Easter week demonstrates that in Gregory's time, as opposed to that of Augustine, there must have been a written gospel list. It was a list, however, that either was incomplete or changed considerably during the early decades of the seventh century. My own guess would lean more toward the former alternative; I would imagine that many dates, most of the sanctorale, for example, and the ordinary Sundays, did not yet have permanent gospels assigned in Gregory's time. But the entire annual cycle is in place by 645 at the latest, a comparatively early date in view of the instability of the contemporary sacramentary.

We do not have the sort of precise chronology for the Roman epistolary as we do for the evangeliary.[16] There are a number of reasons for this. For one there is no partial epistle list from Gregory's time similar to the gospel list reconstructed from his homilies. And then there are only a handful of early Frankish manuscripts with epistle lists, in contrast to the great number of gospel lists that permitted Klauser to consolidate his chronology. The reason for so few extant epistolaries, no doubt, is the above-mentioned difficulty of providing an epistle list in the absence of a chapter and verse system. The earliest extant Roman epistle list, in fact, that of the eighth-century Würzburg manuscript, appears to consist of incipits and explicits extracted from an earlier manuscript with completely written-out pericopes.[17] As for the date of the original Roman list reproduced in the Würzburg manuscript, certain archaic features of the list inclined scholars at one time to place it as early as the later sixth century, but the more recent view is that, while undoubtedly containing some early material, it represents the Roman liturgy of the second half of the seventh century.[18] A noteworthy peculiarity of the list is the presence of multiple epistles for several occasions, particularly in the earlier stages of the liturgical year. This was formerly taken as evidence for the now discredited view that the ancient Roman Fore-Mass regularly had two readings before the gospel, one each from the Old and New Testaments. But for various reasons—among them that the dual readings of the Würzburg list are frequently from the same Testament—it is now thought that they represent a fusion of two different lists.

Another peculiarity of the Würzburg list is the very small number of sanctoral dates that it provides, only some ten festivals of special importance, such as those of St. John the Baptist and St. Lawrence. One recalls the analogous lag between the temporale and sanctorale of the evangeliary and concludes that epistles might not have been permanently assigned to most sanctoral dates before the mid-seventh century, and that a kind of de facto Common of the Saints was in effect. Finally, while the majority of epistle assignments appearing in the Würzburg list are the same as those of later lists (if one is allowed, that is, to choose among the dual listings of Würzburg), there is a somewhat greater number of discrepancies than there is between the PI-type evangeliary and its followers. All in all the Roman epistolary appears to have become fixed at a somewhat later date than the evangeliary, even if still earlier than the sacramentary.

The overall lesson to be learned from the lectionaries, both evangeliaries and epistolaries, is that while their early Roman histories may not be as many layered as that of the sacramentaries, they still exceed the antiphoner greatly in this respect. Thus they confirm the impression created by the sacramentary of a comparatively shorter life span for the development of the antiphoner. Another lesson to be learned is that Mass readings as well as prayers tend to develop from a state in which there is great freedom in their choice to one in which there are strictly prescribed daily formularies. This is a principle to be observed in our speculations on the creation of the Mass antiphoner.

THE FIRST CHANT BOOKS

There was no need for a chant book in the time of Augustine. If one did exist, it would surely have taken the form of a *libellus* that simply listed the particular verses traditionally selected as responses for each psalm. But certainly the more practical way to record such information would be by marginal markings in a psalter, as is the case with the Psalter of St-Germain and its gold-leaf Rs. Still, we have the passage about Musaeus of Marseilles, who not only compiled a lectionary but also selected "responsorial psalms (*responsoria psalmorum capitula*) appropriate to the season and to the readings." If, as we think, he recorded in writing the readings for the more important dates in the calendar, he probably did the same for the psalms and their response verses. The responsorial psalm of the day, after all, was still looked upon as a reading in the time of Musaeus, and its inclusion within an ancient lectionary should not be surprising. One recalls the example of the Armenian Lectionary of early-fifth-century Jerusalem with its listing of two responsorial psalms in the Fore-Mass along with the other readings. So this model of Musaeus may, for all we know, have been fairly common in both East and West during the fifth and sixth centuries. Perhaps it was used in conjunction with a psalter like that of St-Germain. The two together could be considered a perfectly adequate proto-gradual, or at least cantatorium; one would have in the *libellus* the assigned gradual psalm for Mass each day of the year, and in the psalter the text of the psalm and the designation of its response verse.

But everything we have observed up to now in this volume under the rubric of "discontinuity of psalmic assignment" cautions us against assuming too much in this respect. We have, it will be recalled, evidence for only a handful of ancient psalmic associations with a particular festival, such as Easter's *Haec dies,* that are retained in medieval chant. If various churches drew up lists of annual psalmic assignments, it seems likely that their application was only regional and that they were subject to change and disuse with shifts in historical circumstances. Such lists, moreover, probably would not include every date in the temporal and sanctoral cycles but rather would leave many of the less important occasions open to choice.

There is another cautionary point to bear in mind. We saw in the introduction to this chapter that a chant text of the type employed in the Roman Mass Proper is not just a segment of a psalm or other biblical text, but a quasi libretto. The psalmic assignments of Musaeus, then, and the designated response verses of the Psalter of St-Germain represent something different in kind from the gradual texts of the Roman Mass antiphonary; they are aids to the lector, not a compilation of the schola cantorum's repertory. It may be worth noting in this respect that the sentence in the text following the reference to Musaeus's assignment of readings and psalms begins, "This most necessary task is ratified by the lectors . . ."

THE IMMEDIATE ROMAN BACKGROUND

Our subject might best be pursued by developing the following oversimplification. In the mid-seventh century the newly established Roman schola cantorum began the compilation of a Mass antiphoner by bringing together two kinds of material—lists of antiphons modeled after Office chants and lists of gradual psalm responses utilized already by Roman subdeacons and lectors at Mass.

To appreciate the first of these purported lists involves some understanding of the part monasticism must have played in the development and maintenance of ecclesiastical song during the fifth through the seventh centuries. In the troubled times between the collapse of classical civilization and the dawn of the Middle Ages, the monasteries were best suited for this task. As cities deteriorated and urban ecclesiastical establishments were increasingly characterized by ignorance and corruption, a substantial number of monasteries were able to preserve a goodly measure of Christian culture within their walls. We have seen, for example, that this was the case with the Gallican monastic establishments such as Bobbio, Lorsch and St-Denis during the dark years of the later seventh and earlier eighth centuries, and we must assume that something similar was true also for certain of the Roman basilican monasteries during the disastrous decades of the middle and later sixth century.

A monastery of the sixth century, even if it did not devote eight or more hours a day to the singing of the Office in the manner of a tenth- or eleventh-century institution, did spend at least three or four hours in that activity. All one hundred and fifty psalms were chanted in the course of the week, and numerous responsories and antiphons were sung as well. We know that this was so from sixth-century monastic rules like those of Caesarius of Arles, of Benedict and of the anonymous Italian "Master," and we have no reason to believe that the Roman basilican monasteries were an exception. This is not to say, however, that the antiphons and responsories that were sung in the sixth century were the identical chants that we know from the medieval Office antiphoners, an extravagant claim one hears from time to time. That Benedict's little band of unlettered recruits, for example, living in the primitive conditions of earlier sixth-century Monte Cassino, were singing the same vast repertory of responsories and antiphons that were sung at Monte Cassino in the age of Desiderius (1058–87) defies all historical plausibility.

The situation with the Roman basilican monasteries must have differed by degree. We should not expect that they were singing the same repertory of responsories and antiphons in the sixth century as they were in the eighth, but there is a lesser span of time involved here than in the example of Monte Cassino, and a history of greater institutional stability—Monte Cassino, after all, was destroyed by the Lombards in 580, to remain deserted for more than a century. Not that all Roman monasteries remained unscathed during the ravages of the sixth century; perhaps even the majority suffered grievously. The most common type of seventh- and eighth-century reference to the basilican monasteries is that a particular pope *restored* a certain monastery so that the Office could be celebrated fittingly day and night. Still, several Roman monasteries must have continued with their essential functions throughout the troubled times of the sixth century; monastic choirs, we recall, were available to sing in procession on the day of Gregory I's installation in 590.

These monasteries must have sung responsories of some sort in conjunction with the readings of matins, and antiphons in conjunction with the psalmody throughout the day. It is the latter that are of particular interest here. I have suggested in these pages already that such monastic antiphons inspired the antiphonal psalmody of the Roman introit and communion (although I will confine my present remarks to the introit for the sake of presentational convenience). One assumes that the majority of these antiphons were psalmic and that they were sung in association with the continuous psalmody of matins, vespers and the day hours. But at the same time, if some monastery responsible for singing the Office at one of the great basilicas—a monastery with a relatively stable history and a cadre of particularly resourceful singers—maintained a large repertory of numerically ordered psalmic antiphons, we can well imagine that at least some Proper antiphons with nonpsalmic texts would come to be devised for at least the more important festivals of the Christmas and Easter seasons. At some point in the accumulation of such repertory, it would in all probability become necessary to record it in *libelli*, perhaps after the model of the sacramentary, that is, separate *libelli* for the psalmic antiphons and for festal groupings, say Christmas day or the post-Christmas sanctoral series, Easter week or the Ascension-Pentecost fortnight.

As for the melodies of these early Office antiphons, it is entirely possible that they were close in style to the simple syllabic antiphons that are so characteristic of the two preserved twelfth-century Roman antiphoners.[19] Indeed it is not out of the question that there might be at least some degree of continuity in melodic substance between certain sixth-century antiphons and the more common melody types of the mature chants. I think it a plausible proposition that frequently employed syllabic tunes tend to be more stable in oral transmission than elaborate individual ones. Our concern here, however, is not with continuity between early and late Roman Office antiphons, but with the relationship between Roman Office antiphons and the introit of the Mass.

It remains an altogether likely proposition that the introit of the Mass is somehow modeled on monastic Office psalmody. It is in fact so likely that one readily, indeed eagerly, compares the two repertories looking for concordances, both textual and melodic. The results, however, are singularly disappointing. It is not just that the introit is longer and more florid than its counterpart (which could be explained as a matter of expansion and development), but what is more to the point, there is only a negligible degree of textual concordance between the incipits of the two repertories, and virtually no evidence of melodic relationship in those instances where the same text is used.[20] This negative conclusion about repertories aside, I will attempt to summarize what remains positive in the relationship between Office antiphons and the Mass antiphoner after turning to the second of our two potential sources for the origins of the Roman Mass antiphon—the gradual psalm responses of the clerical cantors and lectors.

THE CLERICAL RESPONSORIAL PSALM

What might one say about the responsorial psalm of the Fore-Mass in the period immediately preceding the first redactions of the Mass antiphoner by the schola cantorum, that is, at about the time Gregory found it necessary to forbid deacons to sing the chant?

Perhaps the most fundamental factor to take into account is the perennial question of the "truncated psalm." How can one explain the difference between the responsorial psalm of antiquity and the gradual of the medieval Mass Proper—the difference between a psalm chanted in its entirety by a lector with congregational responses and a single melismatic verse sung by a cantor with a choral response of comparable elaboration? I have already said much in these pages against the notion of a responsorial psalm that grows more elaborate with each generation until it is finally necessary to curtail its length by lopping off all its verses but one. The primary objection to such a model is our frequently mentioned "discontinuity of psalmic assignment," which would seem to rule out evolution of that sort. So too do certain characteristics of the gradual's text: responses that are nonpsalmic or of the textually adjusted type and verses that are chosen from the interior of the psalm rather than the beginning.

Still the difference between an entire psalm with response and a chant with a single verse must be accounted for, and the notion of an impracticably long and elaborate responsorial psalm remains an eminently plausible factor in any attempt to reconstruct the prehistory of the gradual. We have before us, moreover, in both Gregory of Tours's Gaul and Gregory I's Rome, the example of late-sixth-century deacons who sang the responsorial psalm in a manner that served to entertain the listeners. The objection to the unsatisfactory model given above is not to the idea of an overly long and elaborate responsorial psalm that required shortening, but to an evolution in its history that is gradual and uninterrupted. For one thing a development that is steadily incremental is surely less plausible in any musical context than one that is subject to more abrupt changes dependent upon particular historical circumstances—we can imagine periods of relative stylistic stability for the responsorial psalm, periods when it all but fell into disuse and periods of rapidly blossoming elaboration. And for another, the evidence cited above, particularly that of repertorial discontinuity, clearly calls for a disruption in the history of the responsorial psalm and a new beginning. We will never know what happened from century to century and from decade to decade, but a good possibility, I think, is a period of expansion and elaboration in the way the clergy sang the responsorial psalm around the time of Gregory and then a sort of disruption in the process when the schola cantorum in mid-century assumed responsibility for the chant and transformed it into the gradual. Indeed it is possible that the lectors and subdeacons before them could already have been limiting the number of verses sung; one recalls in this regard the practice described in the *ordines romani* where the pope nods to the schola when he wishes them to bring the introit and offertory psalms to a close—he very well could have done the same for the gradual psalm at one time.

When we speak, by the way, of the different roles played by the schola and the Roman subdeacons and lectors in this process, we are forced to think about the relationship of these clerical groups in the earlier seventh century. Does it not seem likely, for one thing, that the very increase in the elaboration of clerical psalmody at the time would be one of the factors creating the need for a more musically focused group like the schola, and for another, that its early membership must have included some of the more outstanding lector and subdeacon singers?

And what of the contemporary monastic singers; what might their relationship with the schola be? As monks they, unlike the subdeacons and lectors, could not become members of a clerical group like the schola; indeed we know that there was a measure of antagonism between monks and clergy in the earlier seventh century over issues of ecclesiastical preferment. And we know that monks and clergy had quite separate liturgical responsibilities in the seventh and eighth centuries, with the former tending to the singing of the Office in the basilicas and the latter to the singing of the papal Mass. But they were, nonetheless, coreligionists performing similar duties in the same churches, and we have no reason to believe that the tensions of the earlier seventh century were entirely characteristic of the century as a whole. It is not at all fanciful to imagine friendly musical competition between the two groups—each heard the other singing, after all, on a daily basis—and to imagine even a systematic exchange of new musical developments. We know, in fact, that there were similar musical advances taking place in Office and Mass later in the century; we have hard evidence of this in the hybrid forms of responsory-communion and antiphon-communion.

THE PREHISTORY OF THE ROMAN ANTIPHONER

I was at great pains earlier in this chapter to claim that the Roman antiphoner of the Mass did not have a prehistory similar to that of the Roman sacramentary and lectionary, that is, a series of redactions demonstrating a long and complex development. But what can we say positively about its prehistory beyond our oversimplification that it involved collections of Mass antiphons inspired by similar collections of monastic Office antiphons, and clerical lists of Mass responsorial psalms?

One imagines that the schola in the first years of its existence would still be using a variety of short *libelli* to record the texts of chants. These *libelli* would simply be jotted down as aide-mémoires, because the melodic aspect of the schola's singing was at first very much a matter of oral transmission. They would early on, however, have sorted out the styles in use for the various chant genres, a more melismatic style for the gradual, for example, in contrast to a consistently neumatic style for the introit antiphon. Similarly they tended to record the texts of their chants in separate *libelli* for responses and antiphons.[21] At least, that is, for the chants of ferias and ordinary Sundays. For a few important festivals, like Christmas, Easter and Pentecost, they might have used separate *libelli* with all the chants of each feast, and for the lesser sanctoral dates they might have recorded a few sets of chants for different categories of saints, a kind of proto-Common. At first well less than half the eventual repertory was represented; it was nearly entirely psalmic, with only a relatively small number of nonpsalmic texts on certain major feasts.

The middle to later seventh century, however, was a period of intense liturgical and musical activity for the members of the schola. While defining still more precisely the musical styles of the differing genres they continued to expand the repertory, especially its festal portions with their larger numbers of nonpsalmic chants. In doing so they developed the habit of fashioning and carefully crafting texts, adapting the original biblical passages to suit their lyric purposes. Their art was still primarily a vocal one, but this practice of composing quasi librettos added a literary element to it that required closer attention to the way the repertory was recorded.

The period in question is like living in a house while still constructing it, and it must have come to be experienced as inadequate, discomforting even, leading to the decision to provide appropriate sets of chants for every date in the calendar—in a word, the Advent Project.

The physical object representing this formidable undertaking, the antiphoner, would not itself be all that impressive. Even so it was carefully wrought, bearing very little trace of the disparate *libelli* that preceded it; these were nicely integrated into a work remarkable for its consistency, uniformity and state of completion. It was not remotely equaled in this respect by any other contemporary liturgical document. Still it was a slight manuscript of no more than a few dozen folios, bound together perhaps with a papal sacramentary—it is after all still referred to as a *libellus* by the eighth-century Roman cleric who wrote, *Gregorius presul composuit hunc libellum musicae artis scholae cantorum.* Small as it was in physical stature, however, it was conversely mighty in liturgical and cultural significance, surpassed in this respect for centuries to come by precious few medieval products of the pen.

CHAPTER 6

Dating the Mass Proper I
Advent and the Thursdays in Lent

The previous chapter closes with an effort to visualize what the Roman Mass antiphoner might have been like in the decades immediately preceding its final revision. Throughout that exercise the unspoken assumption was maintained that we know the content of that final revision. But do we? It would seem all but essential to give a positive answer to that question before turning to the attempt in this and the following chapter to attach a date to it.

THE OLD ROMAN GRADUALS:
WITNESS TO THE EIGHTH-CENTURY ROMAN REPERTORY

The content of the final revision—a project that took place in the later decades of the seventh century, as I will argue in due course—is there to be seen in the three so-called Old Roman graduals, even if these manuscripts were not copied until centuries later. To expand upon this claim, I find Vat lat 5319 to be particularly representative of the group, and to be nearly identical in content to the manuscript (or manuscripts) that Pope Stephen's singers must have brought with them in their momentous visit with King Pépin III in 754. When I say "content," I refer, of course, to the texts of the chants and their liturgical assignments. The earliest Frankish manuscripts, as is well known, lack musical notation, and we all assume that the Roman exemplars from which they were copied did so also. The Roman melodies were transmitted orally by the Roman singers to their Frankish counterparts and must have undergone at least some measure of change in the process. But melodies are not our present concern; texts and liturgical assignments are, and these of course were transmitted in writing.

By repertory, then, I mean texts and liturgical assignments, and it is my

Table 2. Roman and Frankish Lenten Introits

	Vat lat 5319	Bod 74	SPtr F22	Rhei- nau	Blan- din	Com- piègne	Cor- bie	Sen- lis
Septg	Circumdederunt	—	—	—	—	—	—	—
Sexg	Exsurge quare	—	—	—	—	—	—	—
Quing	Esto mihi	—	—	—	—	—	—	—
Ash Wednesday	Misereris omnium	—	—	…	—	—	—	—
Thursday	Dum clamarem	—	—	…	—	—	—	—
Friday	Audivit dominus	—	—	…	—	—	—	—
Quad	Invocabis me	—	—	—	—	—	—	—
Monday	Sicut oculi	—	—	—	—	—	—	—
Tuesday	Domine refugium	—	—	—	—	—	—	—
Wednesday	Reminiscere	—	—	…	—	—	—	—
Thursday	Confessio et pul	—	—	…	—	—	—	—
Friday	De necessitatibus	—	—	…	—	—	—	—
Saturday	Intret oratio	—	—	—	—	—	—	—
Monday	Redime me domine	—	—	…	—	—	—	—
Tuesday	Tibi dixit	—	—	…	—	—	—	—
Wednesday	Ne derelinquas	—	—	—	—	—	—	—
Thursday	Deus in adjutor	—	—	—	—	—	—	—
Friday	Ego autem cum	—	—	…	—	—	—	—
Saturday	Lex domini	—	—	…	—	—	—	—
Quad III	Oculi mei	—	—	—	—	—	—	—
Monday	In deo laudabo	—	—	…	—	—	—	—
Tuesday	Ego clamavi	—	—	…	—	—	—	—
Wednesday	Ego autem in domino	—	—	—	—	—	—	—
Thursday	Salus populi	—	—	…	—	—	—	—
Friday	Fac mecum domine	—	—	—	—	—	—	—
Saturday	Verba mea	—	—	—	—	—	—	—
Quad IV	Laetare Hierusalem	—	—	—	—	—	—	—
Monday	Deus in nomine	—	—	…	—	—	—	—
Tuesday	Exaudi deus	—	—	…	—	—	—	—
Wednesday	Dum sanctificatus	—	—	—	—	—	—	—
Thursday	Laetetur cor	—	—	…	—	—	—	—
Friday	Meditatio cordis	—	—	—	—	—	—	—

(continued)

Table 2. (continued)

		Bod 74	SPtr F22	Rhei- nau	Blan- din	Com- piègne	Cor- bie	Sen- lis
Saturday	Sitientes venite	—	—	—	—	—	—	—
Quad V	Judica me deus	—	—	—	—	—	—	—
Monday	Misere, conculcavit	—	—	…	—	—	—	—
Tuesday	Expecta dominum	—	—	…	—	—	—	—
Wednesday	Liberator meus	—	—	—	—	—	—	—
Thursday	Omnium que fec	—	—	—	—	—	—	—
Friday	Miserere, tribulor	—	—	…	—	—	—	—
Palm Sunday	Domine ne longe	—	—	—	—	—	—	—
Monday	Judica domine	—	—	—	—	—	—	—
Tuesday	Nos autem	—	—	—	—	—	—	—
Wednesday	In nomine domini	—	—	—	—	—	—	—
Thursday	Nos autem	—	—	—	—	—	—	—

immediate task to make explicit and to defend the assumption that the textual and liturgical content of the extant Roman graduals is basically the same as that of the Roman Mass antiphoner of the earlier eighth century.[1] I use the term "assumption" advisedly. I believe that many chant scholars, perhaps the majority, have simply taken the substantial identity of the later and earlier repertories for granted, but in recent years there have been doubts expressed about it,[2] and hence the need to provide explicit defense of it. This is, I think, not so much a matter of logic and argument as one of simple demonstration, and I begin with an illustration from the introits of Lent (table 2), confining, for the moment, the demonstration to introits for the sake of presentational economy.

The table gives the Roman and Frankish introits for the forty-four dates from Septuagesima Sunday to Thursday in Holy Week. The chant incipits are taken from Vat lat 5319; dashes in subsequent columns mean that the indicated manuscript has the same introit as Vat lat 5319. The next two columns are for the other two Roman graduals, Bodmer 74 and San Pietro F22; the dashes in their columns demonstrate absolute stability of assignment within the three Roman manuscripts.[3] The remaining five columns are for the relevant five Frankish manuscripts edited in René-Jean Hesbert's *Sextuplex:* Rheinau, Blandin, Compiègne, Corbie and Senlis. (Monza is omitted, of course, because as a cantatorium it has no introits.) An ellipsis in the Rheinau column simply indicates that that notoriously eccentric manuscript omits the liturgical date entirely; whenever it includes the occasion, the introit is the same as that of the other manuscripts. Thus, there is absolute stability of assignment within the early Frankish graduals and, more to the point, absolute continuity with the Roman graduals.

While this example of the Lenten introits shows total identity of content between the Roman and Frankish graduals, I spoke above of "nearly identical" content. Unlike this remarkable display from the Lenten introits, there are exceptions to be met with in other areas of the Mass Proper. I believe that the exceptions themselves do much to bolster the proposition in question, and I will turn to them after a consideration of what we should conclude from the case of the Lenten introits.

What we are dealing with, as I said above, is not so much a matter of argument and logic as one of simple demonstration. We extract from the three extant Roman graduals, late as they are, the repertory that we *see* adapted in the Frankish graduals. The earliest of the latter, Rheinau and Blandin, date to about 800, and they stand before us with the repertory that was transmitted to them from Rome in the second half of the eighth century. The only other logical explanation for what we witness in table 2 would be to reverse the direction of transmission—to have it move not from Rome to Francia, but from Francia to Rome. This is logically conceivable but historically untenable; it directly contradicts an overwhelming mass of indisputable evidence.[4] There are the numerous Carolingian decrees calling for the adoption of the *cantus romanus,* the many reports of the efforts to obtain additional Roman manuscripts and Roman cantorial assistance, and the various anecdotes that narrate the difficulty of the Frankish singers in absorbing the Roman melodic style. Above all, there are the thousands of folios of Frankish liturgical manuscripts that document in great detail the Carolingian program to master the Roman liturgy.

Among these manuscript pages are the early unnotated graduals of table 2, and I think that their rubrics provide a vivid illustration of the direction of transmission. They are clearly Roman rubrics, copied from Roman manuscripts. The Frankish scribes recorded, for one thing, the geographically irrelevant Roman stational indications. They appended, moreover, different versions of the celebrated *Gregorius presul* preface to their graduals, always retaining the central part of it claiming that it was Gregory, a Roman pope, who *composuit hunc libellum musicae artis scholae cantorum.*[5] One of the rubrics they regularly copied is regionally inappropriate to the point of hilarity: for the Saturday before Palm Sunday we read SABBATO

VACAT QUANDO DOMNUS PAPA ELEMOSYNAM DAT.[6] There are only two possible explanations for this rubric: either it was copied from Roman graduals or the pope was accustomed to spending the Saturday before Palm Sunday going about the Carolingian realm distributing alms.

The most telling rubric, however, was *not* copied from the Roman exemplars. It appears in the Blandin manuscript at the head of the seventh Sunday after Pentecost, a date that was added by the Franks to the Roman post-Pentecostal series of twenty-two Sundays to bring its number to the more practical twenty-three.[7] The rubric reads, ISTA HEBDOMATA NON EST IN ANTEFONARIOS ROMANOS,[8] a vivid reminder from the scribe of the Blandin gradual that this Sunday is an exception to the bulk of the material in his manuscript, copied as it all is from Roman books. It is clearly an exception in the mind of this Frankish scribe, and it is an exception also of the sort that I referred to above, that is, a classic case of an exception proving the rule. This, because the seventh Sunday after Pentecost, with its introit *Omnes gentes*, is absent not only from the eighth-century Roman Mass antiphoners that this Carolingian scribe has seen but also from the late Roman graduals in our possession today. These manuscripts, then, if the *Omnes gentes* Sunday is any indication, would seem to preserve the eighth-century Roman repertory without any Frankish additions.

But is the case of *Omnes gentes* typical? To find out we must broaden our survey of the introit repertory to a segment of the church year where the continuity between Rome and Francia is not quite as pure as it is during Lent, the Advent-Christmas season (table 3). Certainly there is at least substantial continuity here. This is clear from the predominance of dashes, particularly if one discounts the ellipses, which, again, simply indicate the absence of the liturgical occasions in question from a manuscript (the first three festivals are missing from the Compiègne gradual [C], for example, because of a missing folio).[9] There are four genuine exceptions, appearing at the fourth Sunday of Advent, the feast of St. Sylvester and the first and second Sundays after the Epiphany.

The case of the fourth Sunday of Advent is particularly instructive. The date was a DOMINICA VACAT in Rome, one of those Sundays when the pope failed to celebrate Mass because of the lengthy ordination ceremonies of the preceding Ember Saturday vigil. Some of the Frankish centers, however, add the date to their calendars (even if the Compiègne copyist, for one, retains the contradictory Roman rubric DOMINICA VACAT). Without Roman assignments to guide them, the Franks either borrow their introits from one feast or another (as in the case of Rheinau's *Veni et ostende* from Rome's Ember Saturday and Senlis's *Rorate caeli desuper* from Rome's Ember

Table 3. Roman and Frankish Advent-Christmas Introits

	Vat lat 5319	Bod 74	SPtr F22	Rhei-nau	Blan-din	Com-piègne	Corbie	Senlis
Advent I	Ad te lev	—	—	—	—	...	—	—
Advent II	Populus	—	—	—	—	...	—	—
Lucy	Dilexisti	—	—	—	—	...	—	—
Advent III	Gaudete	—	—	—	—	—	—	—
Ember Wednesday	Rorate caeli	—	—	—	—	—	—	—
Ember Friday	Prope esto	—	—	...	—	—	—	—
Ember Saturday	Veni et ostende	—	—	—	—	—	—	—
Advent IV	[DOM VACAT]	—	—	Veni	...	Memento	...	Rorate
Vigil Xmas	Hodie scietis	—	—	—	—	—	—	—
Xmas I	Dominus	—	—	—	—	—	—	—
Xmas II	Lux fulg	—	—	—	—	—	—	—
Xmas III	Puer natus	—	—	—	—	—	—	—
Stephen	Etenim sed	—	—	...	—	—	—	—
Vigil John	Ego autem	—	—	—	—	—	—	—
John	In medio	—	—	—	—	—	—	—
Innocents	Ex ore	—	—	—	—	—	—	—
Sylvester	Sac eius	—	—	...	S tui	S tui	S tui	S tui
Sunday	Dum medium	—	...	—	—	—	—	—
Epiphany	Ecce adv	—	—	—	—	—	—	—
Eph I	Omnis terra	—	—	In excelso	In ex	In ex	In ex	In ex
Eph II	In excelso	—	—	Omnis terra	Omnis	Omnis	Omnis	
Eph III	Adorate	—	—	—	—	—	—	—

Wednesday) or, as does Compiègne, they use the new Frankish introit, *Memento nostri domine,* which eventually becomes the standard assignment for the date. *Memento,* like the seventh Sunday after Pentecost's *Omnes gentes,* fails to appear in the Roman manuscripts, similarly attesting to their freedom from early Frankish taint.

The remaining three exceptions are not so significant; as a group they appear to be the sort of minor lapses that might easily have taken place in the initial Frankish copying of the Roman *libelli* used in the transmission. *Sacerdotes tui* is substituted for the Roman *Sacerdotes eius*, while *Omnis terra* and *In excelso*, the Roman introits for the first and second Sundays after the Epiphany, are simply reversed in the Frankish graduals.

The introits of the Advent-Christmas season thus add to the picture provided by those of Lent a confirmation of overwhelming continuity between the eighth-century Roman Mass antiphoner, as known from the later Roman graduals, and the gradual of the eighth- and ninth-century Franks; and, more than that, they add the leaven of occasional exceptions to this continuity that serve only to confirm the overall impression. If one continues the process of illustration begun here throughout the remainder of the introit repertory, the following results. There is a core repertory of 145 introits common to the Roman and Frankish manuscripts. The Franks add just six to this fund—four more in addition to *Omnes gentes* and *Memento nostri*—while the Romans add four of their own, a factor not yet referred to here. Virtually all of these ten exceptional chants fall clearly into the category of chants added to either repertory after the transmission of the Roman chant to the Franks, usually to serve in new festivals. Of the six new Frankish introits, three beyond *Omnes gentes* and *Memento nostri* are instances of this: *Benedicta sit* for the new Carolingian feast of Trinity Sunday; *Probasti domine* for the added Frankish celebration of the octave of St. Lawrence; and *Narrabo nomen tuum* for the similarly added vigil of the Ascension. The remaining one of the six, *Sicut fui*, the introit for the feast of a pope in the later ninth-century Senlis gradual, falls into a peculiar category of its own, to be taken up immediately below.

As for the introits appearing in the Roman manuscripts but not the Frankish, the situation is analogous to that of the added Frankish chants. Two of these, *Uxor tua* and *Rogamus te domine,* the introits for the Roman nuptial mass and the mass for the dead, respectively, are clearly for occasions added to the Roman liturgy after the mid-eighth-century transmission to the north. The other two, *Benedicet te hodie* for the "ordination" of a bishop and *Elegit te dominus* for the "ordination" of a pope, fall into that same curious category as the Frankish chant *Sicut fui*, mentioned at the close of the previous paragraph. For reasons not known to me, all chants, not just introits, having to do with the consecration of popes and bishops, display this same lack of continuity between Rome and Francia.

To summarize what we have seen here with introits, we observe the earlier eighth-century Roman repertory as it is adopted in Frankish manuscripts, the earliest of which are dated to about 800. The two repertories and their liturgical assignments (Roman and Frankish) are virtually identical, but it is the exceptions that are the most revealing. The Frankish additions do not appear in the Roman manuscripts, and the Roman additions do not appear in the Frankish manuscripts. The introit of Trinity Sunday, for example, *Benedicta sit,* does not appear in the Roman manuscripts, and that of the Roman funeral mass, *Rogamus te domine,* does not appear in the Frankish manuscripts. What this tells us is that in the century or two immediately following the eighth-century transmission of the Roman chant to the north, the two repertories maintain their mutual integrity. Most importantly, there is no seepage from eighth- and ninth-century Frankish chant back to Rome.[10] This is true also of the items of the Mass Proper other than the introit—including the offertory, for which the claim has been made that Gallican offertories are "entrenched . . . firmly within the liturgy of Urban Rome."[11] There are no less than twelve offertories added to the Roman repertory in the *Sextuplex* manuscripts (*Audi Israel, Benedictus est deus, Domine ad adiuvandum, Elegerunt, Exultabunt, Factus est, Ingressus est, In omnem terram, Posuisti, Sicut in holocausto, Stetit angelus* and *Viri Galilei*); not one of these chants appears in the Roman graduals. Individual offertories among them, moreover, comport themselves precisely in the same manner as similarly situated introits. *Benedictus est deus,* for example, the offertory for the newly instituted Frankish feast of the Trinity, is absent from the Roman graduals, just as is its counterpart introit, *Benedicta sit.* And, again, we have the scribe of the Blandin manuscript inserting the rubric telling us that the Frankish EBDOMATA VII [POST OCTABAS PENTECOSTEN]—including its offertory *Sicut in holocausto*—NON EST IN ANTEFONARIOS ROMANOS. Thus we can define the Roman repertory (that is, its texts and liturgical assignments that were transmitted north in the eighth century) by taking the repertory of the three late Roman graduals and by subtracting both the Roman and Frankish chants added to it after the transmission to the north.

And we must, of course (if it need even be mentioned) subtract also the obvious Gregorian additions of the eleventh century: the Christmas introit tropes, the sequences and Gregorian and Beneventan alleluias of Bodmer 74, for example; and the sequences, Gregorian alleluias and Easter vigil canticle-tracts of Vat lat 5319. These stand out like oil from water in their Roman context because of their Gregorian melodies. I do not think that any chant scholar would claim them to be anything but the result of the overwhelming northern ecclesiastical influence on the church of Rome in the tenth and eleventh centuries. What we fail to find in the Roman manuscripts are examples of ninth-century Frankish chants added to the Roman repertory at a period early enough to be absorbed into the Roman melodic ductus.

I would hope, then, to have shown (at the risk of seeming to prove the circle is round) that we can extract with near precision the eighth-century Roman Mass antiphoner from the late Roman graduals. That being the case I am ready to begin my attempt to date the final revision of the Mass Proper that makes up the contents of that book. The first phase of the effort, and the subject of the present chapter, involves the temporale; it makes use of a dated liturgical event already well known to scholars, the establishment of the Thursdays in Lent as liturgical under Pope Gregory II (715–31) and introduces another of my own invention, the creation of the Advent chants by the Roman schola cantorum. I see the former as a kind of terminus ad quem for the final revision of the Mass Proper, and the latter as a kind of terminus a quo. First to the better known of these boundaries.

THE THURSDAYS IN LENT

The *Liber pontificalis* tells us that Gregory II "decreed that there be a celebration of Mass on the Thursdays of Lent, which had not been done before."[12] Prior to Gregory's time there had been a stational Mass for every day of the week in Lent except Thursday. Even without this report of the *Liber pontificalis*, we would know that the Thursdays were a late addition to the Lenten liturgy because the readings and chants for every other date of the season are uniquely assigned, whereas those of the Thursdays are borrowed from other dates. The numerical series of Lenten weekday psalmic communions, for example, has a gap at each Thursday. Now the special contribution of the notice in the *Liber pontificalis* is that it provides a date for the event in question, perhaps the only such explicit chronological indication we have for the entire ancient Roman liturgy. The date, in fact, can be given with even more precision than the sixteen-year span of Gregory's reign. The first recension of his *Liber pontificalis* biography was already in the process of composition during his lifetime and appears to follow a chronological organization.[13] The passage about the Lenten Thursdays comes immediately after one telling of a particularly memorable victory of the Franks over the Moors in 721; I will use the date "about 720" (in preference to "about 722") in what follows.

We have a quaint explanation for the absence of stational liturgy on Lenten Thursdays in the so-called *Hucusque* preface to the Hadrianum sacramentary. The author of the preface, probably Benedict of Aniane, liturgical advisor to Louis the Pious, writing in about 815, tells us: "As we have often heard it related, the pope holds no station at all on these days because, wearied by the stational observances on the other days of the week, he frees

Table 4. Lenten Thursday Communions

Thursday after Ash Wednesday	*Acceptabis*	Ps 50.21	Apostles V
Thursday after Lent I	*Panis quem ego*	Jn 6.52	Lawrence IV
Thursday after Lent II	*Qui manducat*	Jn 6.57	Lawrence V
Thursday after Lent III	*Tu mandasti domine*	Ps 118.4–5	Angel III
Thursday after Lent IV	*Domine memorabor*	Ps 70.16–18	Lawrence VI
Thursday after Lent V	*Memento verbi*	Ps 118.49–50	Angel IV

himself for rest on these, so that without the tumultuous crowds of people he can more easily distribute alms to the poor and attend to administrative matters."[14] Curiously, Benedict explains the traditional absence of stational celebration on Lenten Thursdays but not why Gregory II, surely as busy a pope as any, chose eventually to make them liturgical. Gregory's action is perhaps best looked upon as simply the completion of a long process. Roman liturgical observance of Lenten Wednesdays and Fridays goes back at least as far as the mid-fifth century.[15] Mondays, Tuesdays and Saturdays were added by the early sixth century, leaving the Thursday hiatus for well more than a century prior to Gregory's time. Now liturgy abhors a vacuum, and it comes as no surprise that a liturgically active pontiff like Gregory II would see to the filling in of this particularly prominent example of one.

In any event the Lenten Thursdays are established as liturgical in about 720 and consequently require Mass Propers. They borrow these from previously existing chants; this is the consensus among liturgical and musical historians, and my own review of the evidence simply confirms it. The significance of the conclusion is that the Mass Proper must have been by and large complete by the time in question, about 720, and possibly considerably earlier.

The conclusion, however, rests on the assumption that Lenten Thursdays borrow previously existing chants; the validity of the assumption should be put to some kind of test. Consider the Thursday communions of Lent (table 4). There are six Thursdays involved, beginning with the Thursday after Ash Wednesday and ending with that of the fifth week in Lent. Thursday in Holy Week, of course, a liturgical occasion of some antiquity, is not part of the series.[16] The six Thursday communions are also found assigned to Roman post-Pentecost Sundays. The Sundays in question are given in the column at the right, where they are indicated in the Roman manner of reckoning post-Pentecost Sundays: "Apostles V" is the fifth Sunday after the feast of SS. Peter and Paul (29 June); "Lawrence IV" is the fourth Sunday after the feast of St. Lawrence (10 August); "Angel III" is the third Sunday after the feast of St. Michael the Archangel (29 September) and so forth.

Each of the six chants occurs only in the two places given here, a Thursday in Lent and a Sunday after Pentecost. In which direction did the borrowing take place? Given no more information than that which table 4 provides, one could say that we cannot tell. Why then the universal assumption that the Lenten Thursdays are the borrowers, and not the opposite? It has to do with looking at the two groups of chants in context—Lenten Thursday communions within the entire Lenten weekday cycle, and the six post-Pentecostal communions within their cycle—and comparing the plausibility of borrowing scenarios.

The Lenten six are, to start with, obvious additions to a previously arranged series; they fill in gaps in the numerical series of twenty-six psalmic communions that extends from Ash Wednesday to the Friday before Palm Sunday. Thus, whereas Ash Wednesday's communion *Exaudi nos* is taken from Psalm 1, and the following Friday's *Audivit dominus* from Psalm 2, Thursday's *Acceptabis* (Ps 50.21) clearly breaks the series, therefore appearing to be borrowed from the fifth Sunday after the feast of the apostles. A glance at the scriptural derivations of the remaining Thursday chants and their presumably original post-Pentecostal assignments confirms the impression—when it came time to provide communions for the Lenten Thursdays, they were borrowed from preexistent chants. The obvious place for the Roman singers to look for these was among the less seasonally specific chants of the post-Pentecostal period rather than those of Christmastime or Paschaltime, and they chose accordingly. This is a perfectly plausible sequence of events, but now consider the alternative.

At some time after the year 720, the Roman singers grow dissatisfied with their post-Pentecostal series of only sixteen chants and decide to extend it to a total of twenty-two. They look to Lent and, ignoring all other Lenten communions, choose only those of the six Thursdays. And then they do not assign these chants as a group, say, at the end of the series, but insert them singly at various points in the sequence with no apparent pattern.

Most would agree that the first of the two scenarios is considerably more plausible, but some might see merit in the second, particularly if the composition of the six new Lenten Thursday communions was still fresh in the memory of the Roman singers and they therefore looked upon them as the most obvious candidates to complete their inadequate post-Pentecostal cycles. This involves, however, the assumption that each genre of chant, not just the communions, consists in a series of sixteen post-Pentecostal chants requiring the borrowing of six Lenten Thursday chants to achieve the necessary twenty-two. In fact the assumption does not hold true beyond the communions; there are several instances among the other genres where the borrowing does not involve one-to-one relationships between Lenten Thursdays and Pentecost Sundays. There are, moreover, specific examples of such borrowing that would seem to invalidate the second scenario. Take just introits, where there are two instances of the sort. The sharing of *Laetetur cor* (Ps 104.3–4) is not between a Lenten Thursday and a post-Pentecost Sunday, but rather between a Lenten Thursday (the fourth week) and the Friday of the September Ember Days. Does it not seem quite improbable that one, and only one, of the three September Ember Days would be in need of an introit in 720? The other example—*Confessio et pulchritudo* (Ps 95.6), shared by the Thursday after Quadragesima Sunday and no less than the feast of St. Lawrence—is still more telling. It is difficult to imagine that the introit for this feast, one of the most important in the Roman sanctorale, was not yet in place by 720. But there is more to it than that. The offertory for the feast of St. Lawrence also uses the text *Confessio et pulchritudo*, and the offertory, unlike the introit, is not shared by any other liturgical date. From this we must conclude that the text had special associations with St. Lawrence for the early Roman liturgists, and if the offertory was exclusively assigned to his feast, so too must the introit have been originally. Any borrowing taking place in around 720 would have to have been by the Lenten Thursday from the venerable sanctoral date. But why would the Romans borrow this properly Lawrentian chant for a seemingly nondescript Thursday in Lent? It happens that the stational church assigned to the Thursday is that of San Lorenzo in Panisperna, and what could be more fitting than to borrow one of that saint's chants for the Mass of the day?[17]

In sum, there is no reason to question the conventional wisdom on the subject, namely, that when Gregory II established the Lenten Thursdays as liturgical in about 720, the Roman singers borrowed chants for these days primarily, but not exclusively, from the Sundays after Pentecost. We can conclude from this that at the very least the chants of Lent and the post-Pentecostal season were already in place at the time. More than that, the apparent borrowing of a chant from the feast of St. Lawrence allows us to think that the sanctorale—the last portion of the Mass Proper to be completed, it will be argued in the following chapter—was also in existence. One can easily accept, then, 720 as a terminus ad quem for the final revision of the Roman Mass Proper or, to put it in other terms, that the creative period of Roman Mass composition was at an end by that date. How much earlier than 720 is a question I intend to address in the remainder of this chapter and particularly in the next.

ADVENT: THE PROJECT DESCRIBED

If the establishment of the Lenten Thursdays as liturgical occasions points to the end of creative work on the Roman Mass Proper, the development of Advent within the Roman liturgy has much to do with the beginning of that work or, more precisely, with the beginning of the Mass Proper's final revision. I spoke of this in the introduction to this volume at some length, referring to the ambitious enterprise involved as the Advent Project, my title for the volume, and claiming that the project can be dated by a reexamination of the liturgical history of Advent. In what immediately follows, I will expand somewhat on my introductory remarks about the phenomenon of the Advent Project, leaving still more detailed discussion for the chapters on individual chant genres. I will close the present chapter with an attempt to date the project.

The Advent-Christmas season occupies a special place in the Roman Mass Proper; its chants display a level of compositional planning and perfection of execution not met with elsewhere in the annual cycle. There are three factors that go into pronouncing such a judgment. First of all, we expect Proper chants to be "unique," that is, to be uniquely assigned to one festival rather than being shared by two or more. Second, we expect them to be liturgically appropriate, to have texts that manifest some kind of thematic link with the occasion to which they are assigned. These two traits are essential; the third is an enhancing characteristic, encountered only occasionally in a liturgical Proper—the arrangement of a series of chants in a coherent sequence. Such arrangements can be either horizontal, so to speak, or vertical: the former when the chants of a particular festival display some unifying feature, for example, their derivation from the same psalm; the latter when the chants of a specific genre pursue some pattern over a series of dates, for example, the use of the same mode or melody type for a segment of the church year. The first two of these traits are maintained with near perfection throughout the Advent-Christmas chants, and the third to a considerably greater extent than elsewhere in the church year.

The Advent-Christmas communions (briefly described already in the introduction to this volume) can serve as an illustration (table 5). They fall into two distinct groups, the ten chants of Advent and Christmas day, and the nine post-Christmas chants. All nineteen are unique and all nineteen

Table 5. Roman Advent-Christmas Communions

			Mode Roman	Mode Gregorian
Advent-Xmas				
Advent I	*Dominus dabit*	Ps 84.13	D	1
Advent II	*Hierusalem surge*	Bar 5.5, 4, 36	D	2
Advent III	*Dicite pusillanimis*	Is 35.4	G	7
Ember Wednesday	*Ecce virgo concipiet*	Is 7.14	D	1
Ember Friday	*Ecce dominus veniet*	Zec 14.5–7	F	6
Ember Saturday	*Exultavit ut gigas*	Ps 18.6–7	F	6
Vigil Xmas	*Revelabitur gloria*	Is 40.5	D	1
Xmas I	*In splendoribus*	Ps 109.3	C	6
Xmas II	*Exulta satis filia sion*	Zec 9.9	E	4
Xmas III	*Viderunt omnes*	Ps 97.3	D	1
Post-Christmas Communions				
Stephen	*Video caelos apertos*	Acts 7.56–60	G	8
John Evangelist	*Exiit sermo*	Jn 21.22–23	A	2
Innocents	*Vox in rama*	Mt 2.18	E	7
Sylvester	*Beatus servus*	Mt 24.46–47	E	3
Sunday	*Tolle puerum*	Mt 2.20	G	7
Epiphany	*Vidimus stellam*	Mt 2.2	B	4
Eph I	*Fili quid fecisti*	Lk 2.48–49	D	1
Eph II	*Dicit dominus implete*	Jn 2.7–11	C	6
Eph III	*Puer Jesus*[a]	Lk 2.52	G	—

[a] The Frankish sources have *Mirabantur* (Lk 4.22).

are thematically appropriate to their assigned dates; all, in a word, are carefully designed to fit just one liturgical occasion.[18] There is, moreover, an overall compositional plan of the vertical type described above. The ten chants of the Advent–Christmas Day set all have short prophetic texts, six of them from the Prophets as such and four from David, who ranks in the medieval mind along with Isaiah as the prophet par excellence of Christ's coming. The texts of the nine post-Christmas chants form a sharply contrasting group; they are all derived from the New Testament and have in each case a vivid narrative quality as opposed to the meditative or lyric quality of the prophetic set. They signal a new departure, moreover, in chant creation; nearly all of them are derived not only from the gospels, but from the gospel of the day. St. Stephen's *Video caelos* (Acts 7.56–60) is only an apparent exception; in maintaining the narrative character of the entire group, it derives its text from the epistle of the day—from the narration of Stephen's martyrdom in the Acts of the Apostles, the book that continues the gospel story.

Perhaps it is not fanciful to see a kind of *Vita Christi* in the post-Christmas group, once one removes the sanctoral dates from consideration. These chants form a series of colorful vignettes that depict the principal events in the life of the youthful Jesus, ranging from his early childhood to his first miracle at the wedding feast of Cana, so vividly narrated in the second Sunday after the Epiphany's *Dicit dominus* (Jn 2.7–11). But the last chant in the group, the third Sunday after the Epiphany's *Puer Jesus* (Lk 2.52), breaks the chronological pattern. It returns to the period of childhood, and it ignores, moreover, the gospel of the day, Matthew 8.1–13. That gospel, however, was ignored with good reason; it was assigned to the date long before the schola cantorum embarked upon its provisioning of these dates with communions (before 645, that is) and happens to narrate an event from well into the public life of Jesus, the healing of the centurion's servant. The Franks recognized the incongruity of both communion and gospel to the narrative sequence and stepped in themselves to remedy the defect. They brought the sequence to an elegant conclusion by replacing the gospel with Luke 4.14–22, which tells the story of Jesus' first proclamation of his Messianic mission in the synagogue of his native Nazareth, and by replacing the communion with the gospel-derived *Mirabantur omnes* (Lk 4.22).

Once the examination of the texts has established the objective framework just described—the group of ten prophetic utterances and the group of nine New Testament narratives—observations about musical style and other aesthetic considerations that might otherwise have seemed vague and subjective take on an air of concreteness and credibility. All ten of the prophetic chants are short lyric pieces, and no less than seven of them are composed in the same engaging manner, well illustrated by the first Mass of Christmas' *In splendoribus*. These chants have a clearly marked tonality that uses the interval D-F as a kind of fundament in which F is the magnetic force. At one point in the brief existence of each chant there is an intensifying gesture upward to c before the final resting place on F or D (it matters little which). That the proximity of these seven chants is no accident is strongly suggested by the circumstance that there exist only a handful of similar chants in the entire remainder of the communion repertory.[19] Allowing myself a moment of whimsy, I have referred to the composer of the seven as "the Master of the *Re-Fa* Advent Lyrics."[20]

The nine post-Christmas New Testament chants are not as musically homogeneous as the ten prophetic ones. There are one or the other brief, self-contained pieces like the Epiphany's *Vidimus stellam,* but there are several examples of a lengthy flamboyant type in which dialogue plays an essential role. *Dicit dominus* is the pièce de résistance of the type. The text, which is stitched together from paraphrased segments of the gospel original, tells the story of Jesus' turning water into wine at the marriage feast of Cana. It does not take an excess of imagination to sense the person of Jesus in the deep tones of *implete hydrias aqua,* to picture the excited chief steward as he cries on high, *servasti vinum bonum usque adhuc,* and to recognize the matter-of-fact style of the narrator in the syllabic conclusion, *hoc signum fecit Jesus.* The same sort of dramatic personification is apparent in St. Stephen's *Video caelos,* as the dying martyr proclaims his heavenly vision, leaping a fifth upward to exclaim ecstatically, *Domine Jesu, accipe spiritum meum;* and it is present also in the first Sunday after Epiphany's *Fili, quid fecisti nobis sic,* as the sorrowing Mary addresses those plaintive opening words in low minor-like tones to her recently lost son.[21]

If these two groups of communions are minor masterpieces of liturgical compositional planning, I do not mean to claim that anything quite so extraordinary is to be found in the other chant genres. Still, the same general care to provide an ideal Mass Proper is evident in all the chants of the Advent-Christmas season. Only the graduals and alleluias share with the communions a vertical compositional plan, the graduals with their series of Advent A-mode chants followed by the more festive Christmas series in F-mode, and the alleluias with a series of Christmas through Epiphany chants set in the *Dies sanctificatus* melody type. But the two essential traits of unique assignment and explicit liturgical appropriateness are displayed from the first Sunday of Advent to the feast of Epiphany in a nearly absolute degree by introits, graduals and offertories, and to a lesser extent by alleluias.

The Advent-Christmas season is marked also by a high proportion of what was referred to above as horizontal compositional planning, that is, the maintenance of some common theme throughout the Proper of a particular festival. This is a rare phenomenon in the Mass Proper; there are only a handful of examples in the entire liturgical year, and two of them are found in this season. The first Sunday of Advent derives its introit, gradual and offertory from the same psalm, Psalm 24,[22] and the second Sunday of Advent, with its station at the church of Santa Croce in Gerusalemme, has a distinct Holy City theme in its chants; there is its introit *Populus sion*, its gradual *Ex sion* and its communion *Hierusalem surge*. The Franks, by the way, appreciated this theme and added their own alleluia *Laetatus sum* to the mix, derived as it is from Psalm 121, which celebrates Jerusalem from start to finish.

It was mentioned above that alleluias participate to a noticeable degree in the careful planning of the Advent-Christmas chants. This should come as something of a surprise to those familiar with the behavior throughout the liturgical year as a whole of this quasi stepchild among chant genres. Chant scholars since Peter Wagner have remarked upon the chaotic state of alleluia assignment, noting especially the complete absence of fixed assignment in the post-Pentecostal period—when cantors chose their alleluias each Sunday from lists—and even considerable instability during Paschaltime, when the supposedly more ancient alleluias should manifest some degree of fixity.[23] Recently I have shown that this instability is even more extreme than hitherto thought, and that nearly half of the total number of fixed alleluia assignments at Rome (seven of fifteen) are to be found in the series of alleluias extending from Christmas to the Epiphany.[24] This is, moreover, the only segment of the church year where fixed alleluia assignments run in a continuous liturgical sequence.[25]

The alleluia, then, displays in the opening portion of the church year a fair measure of the kind of careful liturgical planning under discussion here, but little of the sort in the remaining season. Is this characteristic of the Mass Proper as a whole? Clearly I cannot survey the entire Mass Proper in the present chapter, but I can give a brief summary of what will be seen in subsequent chapters and also offer, after that summary, a representative illustration of my findings by using the four annual sets of Ember Days chants.

THE UNIQUENESS OF INTROITS AND COMMUNIONS

An examination of the entire temporale leads to a single conclusion as clear and indisputable as it is broad and significant: introits and communions consistently maintain the two essential traits of uniqueness and liturgical appropriateness throughout the entire church year, while graduals, offertories and, as we have already seen, alleluias do not. Virtually every introit and communion of the entire temporale (some 100 dates) is uniquely assigned, and virtually every one of these chants, during the seasons when explicit liturgical appropriateness is possible (Advent-Christmas and Paschaltime as opposed to Lent and post-Pentecost), displays this characteristic as well.

Communions, moreover, as outlined in the introduction, maintain the special characteristic of vertical compositional planning throughout the entire annual cycle. Graduals, alleluias and offertories, on the other hand, once the Advent-Christmas season is at an end, cease to manifest with any consistency the traits of unique assignment and liturgical appropriateness, let alone vertical planning. Instead there is frequent sharing of graduals and offertories among various liturgical occasions with a resultant lack of explicit relevance to the feasts in question. And alleluias not only lack unique liturgical assignments but, as noted above, generally lack fixed assignments altogether and are chosen, one presumes, on an ad hoc basis.

The simple statistic of the number of chants in each genre casts considerable light on the conclusion just stated. There are 145 introits in the core repertory of the Mass Proper and 140 communions, but only 105 graduals and 93 offertories;[26] obviously the gradual and offertory repertories were never expanded sufficiently to cover the church year adequately. For alleluias it is difficult to give precise numbers, but there are certainly not many more than 50 of them in the original Roman repertory, a number so wanting that the Franks had nearly to double it within a century of their reception of the Roman chant.[27] What all this strongly suggests is that at some point the members of the schola cantorum decided to produce a full and complete Proper of the Mass for every date in the church year. They began with Advent and achieved their aims with near perfection for the Advent-Christmas season[28] but, for the rest of the year, were able to maintain their high standards only with the more manageable introits and communions. They were forced to make large-scale compromises with the more lengthy graduals and offertories, while with the alleluias, latecomers to the Mass Proper, they were barely able to get started before their great burst of creativity came to a close.

THE EMBER DAYS

I promised an illustration of all this in the four annual sets of Ember Days. They can serve this purpose because they appear in each of the four major portions of the church year: Advent-Christmas, Lent, Paschaltime and post-Pentecost. This is a matter of happy coincidence, because they came into existence before the church year was so clearly defined. Known in Latin as the *quattuor tempora* (the English "Ember Days" is a corruption of the German *Quatember*), their origin is obscure; the theory of Morin that they were adaptations of pagan agricultural festivals is no longer maintained.[29] They were in any event observed at Rome as an annual set of three-day fasts—

Table 6. Roman Ember Day Introits and Communions

	Introits		Communions	
		Advent		
Wednesday	Rorate caeli	Is 45.8	<u>Ecce virgo concipiet</u>	Is 7.14
Friday	Prope esto	Ps 118.151	Ecce dominus veniet	Zec 14.5–7
Saturday	Veni et ostende	Ps 79.4	Exultavit ut gigas	Ps 18.6–8
		Lent		
Wednesday	Reminiscere	Ps 24.6	Intellege	Ps 5.2–4
Friday	De necessitatibus	Ps 24.17–18	Erubescant	Ps 6.11
Saturday	Intret oratio	Ps 87.3	Domine deus	Ps 7.2
		Pentecost week		
Wednesday	Deus dum egred	Ps 67.8–9	Pacem meam	Jn 14.27
Friday	Repleatur	Ps 70.8	<u>Spiritus ubi</u>	Jn 3.8
Saturday	Karitas dei	Rom 5.10–11	Non vos relinquam	Jn 14.18
		September		
Wednesday	Exultate deo	Ps 80.2–5	Comedite pinguia	Neh 8.10
Friday	Laetetur cor	Ps 104.3–4	Aufer a me	Ps 118.22–24
Saturday	Venite adoremus	Ps 94.6–7	Mense septimo	Lv 23.41–43

Wednesday, Friday and Saturday—at least as early as the time of Leo I (440–61), who left a series of sermons on them. By the early Middle Ages they had come to be the occasion of ordinations, with the culminating event celebrated during the long Saturday vigil, a ceremony that is of special interest to chant scholars because of its multiple graduals and alleluias. Their symmetrical distribution throughout the four major portions of the church year, in any event, provides us with a convenient microcosm of the entire temporale.

Table 6 gives the Ember Day introits and communions (shared chants are underlined). Only one introit is shared, Friday in September's (the month of the post-Pentecostal set) *Laetetur cor* (Ps 104.3–4). The chant, however, was clearly unique at the time of its origin; it is one of those introits borrowed for the Thursdays in Lent. There are two shared communions. The history of one of them, Pentecost Friday's *Spiritus ubi*, is like that of the introit *Laetetur cor*. It is, with its allusion to the Holy Spirit, obviously a chant designed for Pentecost week, and the two dates with which it is shared, the festivals of the Finding and Exaltation of the Cross, are late additions to the Roman calendar. The Advent communion *Ecce virgo concipiet* may not be quite so open and shut a case. It is shared with the feast of Annunciation, a late addition to the Roman sanctorale, and on the surface would appear to be borrowed from the presumably earlier temporal Mass Proper. But I am not sure just how late the establishment of the feast of the Annunciation is in relation to the composition of the Advent communions. That the two are nearly contemporaneous is a possibility that I will explore in the following chapter. But the overall score, in any case, for the uniqueness of Ember Day introits and communions throughout the entire year is very high.

Whether or not *Ecce virgo concipiet* can be classified as a chant that was originally unique to Wednesday in Advent's Ember week, there can be no doubt of its liturgical appropriateness to the day. And one need do no more than glance at the introit and communion incipits of the Advent and Pentecost week groups to see that this is the case for all of these chants. Such could hardly be possible, of course, for Lenten chants, and one might have thought the same for the September group, but there is a delightful surprise with a number of these chants. The communions *Comedite pinguia et bibite mulsum* ("Eat fat meats and drink sweet wine" [Neh 8.10]) and *Mense septimo festa celebratis* ("Celebrate a festival on the seventh month" [Lv 23.41–43]) are both references to the Old Testament feast of Sukkoth ("booths" or "tabernacles"). The connection of Sukkoth to the Ember Days would have been clear to a learned early medieval ecclesiastic: Sukkoth was celebrated on the seventh month of the Hebrew calendar, Tishri, and the September Ember Days were frequently referred to in the Middle Ages as the *jejunium mensis septimi*, after the ancient custom of considering March the first month of the liturgical year. The introit *Exultate deo* (Ps 80.2–5) was no doubt meant to share in the allusion; Psalm 80.4, "Blow a trumpet at the new moon," has clear reference to the pilgrimage festivals, although it is perhaps more obviously relevant to Passover than to Sukkoth.

The graduals and offertories of the Advent Ember Days participate fully in the aims of the Advent Project (table 7). Every one of the graduals is unique and only one offertory, *Ad te levavi*, is borrowed. The borrowing of the chant is from the first Sunday of Advent, thus preserving the quality of liturgical appropriateness, a trait that is admirably exemplified in every gradual and offertory of the season. To cite just one example, Isaiah prophesies in Wednesday's offertory *Confortamini, deus noster . . . veniet et salvos*

Table 7. Roman Ember Day Graduals and Offertories

	Graduals (Alleluias)		Offertories	
Advent				
Wednesday	Tollite portas	Ps 23.1	Confortamini	Is 35.4
	Prope est dominus	Ps 144.18		
Friday	Ostende nobis domine	Ps 84.8	Ad te domine	Ps 24.1–3
Saturday	A summo caelo	Ps 18.7	Exulta satis	Zec 9.9
	In sole posuit	Ps 18.6		
	Domine deus virtutum	Ps 79.20		
	Excita domine	Ps 79.3		
Lent				
Wednesday	Tribulationes	Ps 24.17	Meditabar	Ps 118.47
Friday	Salvum fac serv	Ps 85.2	Benedic anima	Ps 102.2
Saturday	Propitius esto	Ps 78.9	Domine deus	Ps 87.2
	Dirigatur	Ps 140.2		
	Convertere	Ps 89.13		
	Protector noster	Ps 83.10		
	Salvum fac	Ps 27.9		
Pentecost week				
Wednesday	All Qui confidunt	Ps 124.1–2	Meditabar	Ps 118.47
	All Lauda anima	Ps 145.2		
Friday	All Te decet	Ps 64.2	Populum humilem	Ps 17.28
Saturday	All Emitte spiritum	nonbibl	Domine deus	Ps 87.2
	All Spiritus domini	Wis 1.7		
	All Lauda anima	Ps 145.2		
	All Lauda Hierusalem	Ps 147.12		
	All Laudate pueri	Ps 112.1		
September				
Wednesday	Protector noster	Ps 83.10	Meditabar	Ps 118.47
	Custodi me domine	Ps 16.8		
Friday	Dirigatur	Ps 140.2	Benedicam dnm	Ps 15.7–8
Saturday	Propitius esto	Ps 78.9	Domine deus	Ps 87.2
	Protector noster	Ps 83.10		
	Convertere	Ps 98.13		
	Dirigatur	Ps 140.2		

nos faciet (Is 35.4). The graduals, finally, display vertical compositional planning with every chant except *Prope est,* set in the A-mode melody type.

For the rest of the year, however, the Ember Day graduals, alleluias and offertories manifest a virtual breakdown in the liturgical programming of Advent. The underlining of incipits in the table shows that there are only two unique chants in the entire group, the gradual *Tribulationes* and the offertory *Benedic anima mea.* Offertories use virtually the same set of three chants for Lent, Pentecost week and September, and graduals more or less the same chants for Lent and September. A small measure of liturgical appropriateness is salvaged for the alleluias of Pentecost Saturday by borrowing the two Pentecostal chants *Emitte spiritum* and *Spiritus domini,* but generally liturgical appropriateness is impossible to achieve in the face of such indiscriminate borrowing. The Frankish reaction to this is instructive; the early northern sources as often as not simply provide rubrics of the QUALE VOLUERIS type (that is, any chant will do) in place of specific graduals and alleluias for the Lenten, Pentecostal and September Ember Days.

If, then, the Ember Days are at all representative of the temporale as a whole (and they are, as will be seen in subsequent chapters), we appear to be in the presence of an ambitious effort to provide fitting Proper chants for the entire annual cycle. What was accomplished was monumental: the high standards set for the Advent-Christmas season were met throughout the entire church year for introits and communions, even if it was too much to expect that the same could be achieved for the lengthy graduals and offertories, let alone for alleluias.

ADVENT: ITS EARLY HISTORY

The point of all this that is of immediate relevance (and is, indeed, the central point of the present book) is that the project begins with Advent. But where else would one expect it to begin? Is not Advent the beginning of the liturgical year? Not so, it might surprise some to learn, in seventh-century Rome. The Roman church year began with the vigil of Christmas. The placement of Advent at the head of the church year as a kind of lyric prelude to Christmas, the conception that is so familiar to us today, was the work of the Roman schola cantorum. All Roman liturgical books, except for the chant books, begin with the vigil of Christmas. Advent as we know it today, apparently, was the creation of the Roman singers and, more than that, must have come into existence as part of the Advent Project. The creation of Advent and the beginning of the Advent Project are in fact one and the same event, and I believe that it can be assigned an approximate date as a result of reviewing the season's history.

Advent came late to the Roman liturgical year. In the beginning it had little resemblance to the season we know from the early medieval graduals.[30] Christmas and Epiphany themselves, we must remember, are fairly late entries to the early Christian calendar, making their appearance in the West only in the fourth century. Accordingly, the prehistory of Advent begins at about this same time, but the evidence is fragmentary and scattered; suffice it to say that the very first indications refer to a three-day fast before the Epiphany, observed not at Rome but in Spain and Gaul. We are on firmer ground in sixth-century Gaul, from where we have a number of references to the so-called St. Martin's Fast, a quadragesima (forty-day period) observed in analogy with Lent, beginning just after the festival of St. Martin, on 11 November. In contemporary Rome, however, indications are still lacking. The December Ember Days were observed there, but without reference to the approach of Christmas; the sermons preached on these days by Leo the Great have no Advent content, nor do the December prayer sets of the sixth-century Veronensis.

Evidence appears finally for the Roman observance of Advent in two liturgical books: the Old Gelasian sacramentary and the Würzburg epistle list (table 8). These books, as observed in the previous chapter, probably transmit certain material from the Roman liturgy of the later sixth century and thus attest to the introduction of Advent during that period. But the extant manuscripts, a single one for each book, appear to be copied from mid-seventh-century Roman prototypes and as such would seem to provide us with the state of Roman liturgy in the first half of the seventh century. This is the key consideration for present purposes—not when Advent was introduced into the Roman liturgy, but what shape it maintained in the seventh century.

Both books, the Old Gelasian and the Würzburg epistolary, provide Proper items for the three Advent Ember Days, indicating each day in the expected way: *Feria IV, Feria VI* and *Sabbato*. There is no such explicit designation of Sundays, however; instead, the sacramentary simply has a group of five sets of *Orationes de adventum* [sic] *domini*, curiously placed at the end of the sanctorale, and the epistolary a series of five epistles *De adventu domini* at the end of the post-Pentecostal cycle. Five prayer sets and epistles, for a season of presumably four Sundays, might appear to be puzzling, but I think the explanation lies in the circumstance that these are two common sets to be used on an ad hoc basis for Advent Sundays and perhaps for ferias

Table 8. Advent in Seventh-Century Roman Liturgical Books

Old Gelasian Sacramentary
  70. Orationes de adventum domini
  71. Item alia missa
  72. Item alia missa
  73. Item alia missa
  74. Item alia missa

Würzburg Epistle List
  170. De adventu dni. *Scientes quia* (Rom 13.11–14)
  171. De adventu dni. *Ecce dies ueniet* (Jer 23.5–8)
  172. De adventu dni. *Quaecumque scripta* (Rom 15.4–13)
  173. De adventu dni. *Sic nos exist* (1 Cor 4.1–5)
  174. De adventu dni. *Gaudete in domino* (Phil 4.4–7)

PI-type Evangeliary
  238. Ebdomada IIII ante natale dni. *Cum adprop* (Mt 21.1–9)
  239. Ebdomada III ante natale dni. *Erunt signa* (Lk 21.25–33)
  240. Ebdomada II ante natale dni. *Cum audisset* (Mt 11.2–10)
  241. Ebdomada I ante natale dni. *Miserunt Jud* (Jn 1.19–28)

Hadrianum Sacramentary
  185. Mense Decembri ort. de adventu dominica prima
  186. Dominica secunda
  187. Nat. s. luciae
  188. Dominica tertia ad s. petrum
  189. Feria IIII ad s. mariam
  190. Feria VI ad apostolos
  191. Sabb. ad s. petrum XII lectiones
  192. [Die] dom vacat
  193. Aliae orationes de adventu

also. This is precisely the way prayer sets are designated in the Old Gelasian for the ordinary Sundays of the year; there is, as we have seen, a group of sixteen *Orationes et praeces . . . per dominicis diebus,* to be used at the discretion of the celebrant for the Sundays not explicitly provided for in the sacramentary, namely, the Sundays after Epiphany and the Sundays after Pentecost. Thus, neither the Old Gelasian nor the Würzburg epistolary assigns Proper items to the Sundays of Advent in the same way that they do for the Advent Ember Days. They leave open, moreover, the question of how many Advent Sundays are celebrated in earlier seventh-century Rome, suggesting the possibility that the number is not yet fixed.

The evangeliary of 645 (Klauser's PI-type) might appear to provide gospels for the conventionally conceived Advent: it numbers the Sundays (EBDOMADA IIII ANTE NATALE DOMINI, etc.) and confines the number to four. Still, it places them awkwardly: not only do they come at the end of the church year rather than at the beginning, but they appear between the 13 December feast of St. Lucy and the December Ember Days.[31] The later seventh-century Gregorian sacramentaries, the Paduensis and the Hadrianum, continue the practice of placing their Advent material at the end of the church year, but they present a more calendrically rational order of the material: the first two Sundays, the feast of St. Lucy, the third Sunday, the three Ember Days and the fourth Sunday. They add, however, a seemingly redundant *Aliae orationes de adventu,* and more significantly they preface the prayer sets for the first Sunday with the following rubric: MENSE DECEMBRI INCIPIUNT ORATIONES DE ADVENTU DOMINICA PRIMA.[32]

The phrase MENSE DECEMBRI calls for an Advent that is confined to the month of December, whereas the season as we know it can begin anywhere from 28 November to 3 December, depending upon the number of days intervening between the fourth Sunday of Advent and Christmas day, 25 December. In the course of the years the first Sunday of Advent falls in the month of November about as often as it does in December. That being the case, the rubrics of the Gregorian sacramentaries, confining Advent to the month of December, suggest that Advent had just three Sundays as often as it had four. The four gospels of the 645 evangeliary, then, and the four (in fact five) prayer sets of the Gregorian sacramentaries would provide for the possibility of a four-Sunday Advent, although in practice the number appears to have been variable.

CALENDRIC VERSUS FESTAL CHURCH YEAR

But how much weight should we attach to this particular rubric that appears to confine Advent to December? Very much, I would say, because a division of the church year by months rather than by variable festivals is an ancient and enduring tradition in Rome, still in the process of being altered during the very seventh century under consideration here. To put it more briefly, one speaks of the change from a "calendric" to a "festal" conception of the liturgical year. Recall that the Ember Days were originally thought of as the fasts of the first, third, seventh and tenth months. Recall also that the Veronensis was organized on a monthly basis. For another obvious example of the calendric conception, there is the Rule of St. Benedict, where the principal division of the year is into winter and summer, with winter defined as 1 November to Easter.[33] Easter, of course, is the central landmark of the church year. One should picture it and the seasons that gradually accumulate around it, first the quinquagesima of Paschaltime followed by the quadragesima of Lent, as something that is imposed upon the grid of the months. The festal occasions have a spiritual and emotional force that is bound to make the more neutral calendric year eventually obsolete, but one must be alert to its lingering presence.

An area where we are able to witness the change from the calendric to festal year with particular clarity is in the readings for matins, thanks to a series of *ordines romani* that provide these for the seventh- and eighth-century Roman Office.[34] All these documents begin the year with the Lenten season, no doubt an antique feature that reflects the notion of March as the first month, but even here the earlier *ordines* differ from the later. *Ordo XIV*, the oldest preserved type, which according to Andrieu provides the practice of St. Peter's from about 650 to 700,[35] has the reading of the Heptateuch begin "in the time of spring, that is seven days before quadragesima,"[36] whereas *Ordo XIIIA*, providing the practice of the Lateran from about 700 to 750,[37] begins the Heptateuch on Septuagesima Sunday.[38] The two *ordines* provide altogether more striking differences than this. *Ordo XIV*, an extremely brief document, has virtually no Proper readings for specific feasts, but only entire biblical books assigned to broad stretches of the year: "the epistles of the Apostles, the Acts of the Apostles and the Apocalypse in the days of the Pasch until Pentecost," and then "Kings and Chronicles in the time of summer to the middle of autumn, that is 15 October." Next are read "the books of Solomon, of the Women, of the Maccabees and the Book of Tobit until 1 December," and "before the birth of our Lord Jesus Christ, Isaiah, Jeremiah and Daniel until the Epiphany."[39] Leaving aside for the moment the question of Advent, one notes how no specific readings are assigned to Christmas day by *Ordo XIV*; this is in sharp contrast to *Ordo XIIIA*, where we find: "On the vigil of the birth of the Lord they first read three lections from Isaiah, that is, the first lection has at its beginning *Primo tempore adleviata est terra Zabulon*. The second lection," etc.[40] *Ordo XIIIA*, obviously a document several times the length of *Ordo XIV*, continues with similar detail for the feasts of St. Stephen, St. John the Evangelist, the Holy Innocents, the octave of Christmas, and others.

Again, what one observes in these two *ordines* is the transition from a calendric to a festal conception of the church year, a "properization" of the year, to use an ungainly but apposite locution,[41] and one notes, incidentally, that this development takes place in the Lateran, the home of the schola cantorum. But what of Advent? We noted above that the season was not explicitly mentioned in *Ordo XIV*, which simply assigns the Prophets Isaiah, Jeremiah and Daniel to the period extending from 1 December to the Epiphany. *Ordo XIIIA*, with its accustomed specificity, has the following: "On the first Sunday of the month of December, that is, on the first Sunday of the Advent of the Lord, they read (*ponunt*) Isaiah the Prophet until the birth of the Lord."[42] Thus, as late as the earlier eighth century, and in the progressive liturgical milieu of the Lateran, the monks responsible for the singing of the Office there continue to speak as if Advent were confined to the month of December.

ADVENT: THE CHANT BOOKS

It is in the chant books—the three Roman graduals and the six Frankish manuscripts of the *Sextuplex*—that we finally witness Advent as a season of four Sundays, without regard to the beginning of December. And of even greater significance, it is in the chant books that we finally see Advent at the beginning of the church year, in contrast to all seventh-century Roman sacramentaries and lectionaries. There is, moreover, a third difference in the manner that Advent appears in the chant books, a point of telling evidentiary detail: only they give the Roman stational indications with any degree of frequency (see table 9). These are lacking in the sacramentaries and lectionaries, with the sole exception of the third Sunday in Gregorian sacramentaries. Even the chant books, however, while providing the rubrics altogether more often than the other liturgical books, are not always consistent in this regard. These circumstances lead to a pair of related conclusions: (1) the relative inconsistency of the stational rubrics in the chant books themselves suggests that the Advent Sundays became stational only at a comparatively late date; and (2) the fact that it is the chant books nonetheless that display these indications suggests that the establishment of the Advent Sundays as stational was associated with the creation of the Advent chant Propers.

This linking of the Advent stations with the chant books, along with the unequivocal numbering of the Advent Sundays as four and especially the placement of Advent at the beginning of the church year, where it serves as an elegantly crafted prelude to Christmas—all this makes an overwhelming case for the proposition that the Roman singers were the ones who created Advent as we understand it today. To state it more concretely, the composition of the Advent Mass Propers and the creation of Advent as a fully

Table 9. Advent Sunday Stations in Chant Books

	Vat lat 5319	Bod 74	SPtr F22	Rheinau	Blandin	Compiègne	Corbie	Senlis
Advent I	...	...	...	...	...	Andream[a]	Mariam	...
Advent II	...	Hierslm	...	...	Hierslm	Hierslm	Hierslm	Hierslm
Advent III	...	Petrum	...	...	Petrum	Petrum	Petrum	Petrum

[a] Apparently correct; see René-Jean Hesbert, *Antiphonale Missarum Sextuplex* (Brussels: Vromant, 1935), xxxvi–xxxvii.

articulated liturgical season are one and the same thing. Extravagant as such a claim might seem, it is entirely plausible upon reflection. As suggested in the preceding chapter, there is nothing quite as proper as a Proper chant; it has a concreteness about it that grants it a degree of fixity beyond that of the more malleable prayer sets and more easily reassigned readings. Consider an introit like the first Sunday of Advent's *Ad te levavi*; it stands out in the imagination like a sculptured object, causing us to identify the entire liturgy of Sunday with it. Indeed eventually the Sundays of the year come to be referred to by their introits. And remember that already in the eighth century the Franks referred to the entire Roman liturgy as simply the *cantus romanus*. It is not surprising, then, that sets of Proper chants designed especially for the first, second and third Sundays of Advent—chants, moreover, of special musical beauty set to warmly evocative prophetic poetry—should serve to give these Sundays a status that would override the relatively meaningless detail of whether a Sunday fell within the month of November or December.

And then, too, one should not look upon the Roman schola cantorum as a peripheral group, like the parish choir of our time that fills in the musical slots of a clerically determined order of service. It would be more accurate to think of the organization as a kind of Lateran department of liturgy. Its members were learned and distinguished Roman priests who instructed the most talented young aspirants to the clerical state in chant and the other ecclesiastical disciplines. The schola numbered among its alumni, in fact, no less a figure than Sergius I (687–701).

DATING THE ADVENT CHANTS

If, then, the schola cantorum created Advent with the composition of the Advent Mass Propers, the first step in the execution of the Advent Project, can we assign a date to their activity? The first consideration in attempting to do so is the matter of fixing the number of Advent Sundays at four. *Ordo XIIIA*, as we have seen, which Andrieu dates to between 700 and 750, still specifies the first Sunday of December as the first Sunday of Advent. A literal reading of this evidence would place the beginning of the Advent Project at a very late date indeed. But one must make allowances for obsolete language in any liturgical book, redacted as they often are with exemplars of earlier ones open before those responsible for their revision. And one must keep in mind, also, that *Ordo XIIIA*, as a document recording Office usage, is a guide for the Lateran monks rather than their clerical colleagues of the schola cantorum. No doubt these organizations were in close contact with each other, yet they are not one and the same. Still, the general tendency of all seventh- and earlier eighth-century liturgical books, other than the Mass antiphonary, to waver on the number of Advent Sundays suggests a relatively late date for the schola cantorum's innovation, perhaps one toward the end of the seventh century.

But the key chronological indication is the unique placement of Advent in the chant books at the beginning of the church year. It is difficult to imagine that so compelling and appropriate a conception would have been realized already in chant Propers as early as, say, the first decades of the seventh century and fail to exercise any influence upon the placement of Advent in the other liturgical books, whether it be the mid-seventh-century lectionaries or the later seventh-century sacramentaries, such as the Hadrianum.

These chronological considerations can do no more than suggest an approximate date for the commencement of the Advent Project, let us say sometime in the later decades of the seventh century. But this is significant enough for present purposes. Can we not think of the later seventh century, then, as a terminus a quo for the final revision of the Mass Proper, to go along with the terminus ad quem of Gregory II's establishment of the Lenten Thursdays as liturgical in about 720?

CHAPTER 7
Dating the Mass Proper II
The Sanctorale

This chapter on the sanctorale is the longest and most complex of the present volume; there is in fact an attempt here to compress a monograph-length topic into a more suitable dimension. Such compression, however, must allow a substantial amount of highly detailed discussion to stand. Only in this way can the chronological argument involved be creditably worked out. It is, as remarked in the introduction, an argument pivotal to dating the creation of the Roman Mass Proper, confirming my long-standing conviction that it must have taken place considerably later than the time of Gregory I, but not nearly as late as I once thought to be the case.

BISHOP FRERE'S PRINCIPLE

Walter Howard Frere (1863–1938), Anglican bishop of Truro in Cornwall, was a particularly creative historian of liturgy and chant. And, as remarked above, he coined the famous axiom that "fixity means antiquity": a chant (and a reading or prayer for that matter) that enjoys stable assignment throughout the sources is quite likely to be a relatively ancient item. He, too, developed the principle that will figure prominently in the present chapter—uniquely assigned chants are more likely to be earlier than those shared by a number of liturgical occasions.[1] The principle is applied by chant scholars especially to those sanctoral festivals that were added to the Roman calendar in the course of the seventh and eighth centuries. Frere and most other chant and liturgical scholars of his time assumed that the bulk of the Roman Mass was given its definitive shape under the supervision of Gregory I (590–604). Gregory's reign, then, was considered the climax of the creative phase of chant development. After his time new festivals would be assigned Proper chants from those already in the repertory; or, if a new festival called for special texts, these would be adapted to existing melodies.

What most liturgical scholars take to be the earliest post-Gregorian festival, however, the 13 May *dedicatio ecclesiae Sanctae Mariae ad martyres*, has a uniquely assigned set of Proper chants beginning with the well-known introit *Terribilis est locus iste*. The festival is thought to have been established by Pope Boniface IV (608–15), when, according to the *Liber pontificalis*, "he asked the emperor Phocas for the temple called the Pantheon, in which he made the church of the blessed Mary, ever a virgin, and of all the martyrs."[2] The occasion's Mass Proper, then, is looked upon as bringing to an end the creative phase of Roman chant creation, the age of Gregory the Great. In Frere's words: "Proper music was provided for the day. It is therefore in origin slightly later than the Gregorian revision of the chant, but written before the decay of the musical art set in."[3]

I made an attempt to come to grips with this question of the Proper for the Dedication of Sancta Maria ad Martyres (hereafter simply the "Dedication" festival) in "The Emergence of Gregorian Chant in the Carolingian Era."[4] This essay, written in 1988, was my first venture into chant scholarship, and I read it now with some embarrassment, particularly for my awkward handling of the liturgical evidence when treating the issue in question. I argued that the notion of a creative phase of chant creation coming to an end with the Dedication Proper was plausible enough, but that the conventional dating of the festival to the time of Boniface IV was much too early. I noted that the *Liber pontificalis* did not say that Boniface IV established the Dedication festival, but only that he transformed the Pantheon into a church of Mary and all the martyrs. And, importantly, I observed that certain liturgical books failed to list the date. I was right about the earliest of these, the mid-seventh-century lectionaries, but failed to discriminate among the various redactions of the Gregorian sacramentary and to assign them proper dates. As a result, while being on the right track, I went too far and suggested an overly late date for the establishment of the festival, the reign of Gregory III (731–41), when the roof of Sancta Maria ad Martyres, which had suffered from long neglect, was elaborately restored.[5] More on this particular festival later in the chapter; for now I turn to the most recent treatment in the musicological literature not just of it but of the more general question of seventh- and eighth-century additions to the Roman calendar.

Peter Jeffery, in his "Rome and Jerusalem: From Oral Tradition to Written Repertory," handles the subject in greater detail and with considerably more sophistication than I did.[6] He revisits the key point of the Dedication festival but also discusses several other late additions to the Roman calendar, including the four great Marian festivals and a number of other sanctoral dates. He recapitulates the essence of Frere's position, noting that these later feasts "rarely have chant texts of their own, but rather tend simply to re-use texts and melodies that were already in the repertory assigned to older feasts," concluding that these observations suggest the existence of "a core repertory that to some degree was regarded as 'closed.'" He is not altogether explicit about the time at which the Mass Proper was substantially complete but implies strongly that it was the early seventh century, this, because even some of the chants of the Dedication festival "show signs of dependence on earlier ones."

In reading Jeffery's essay, as preparation to writing the present chapter, I must confess to having been momentarily shaken in my conviction that the date for the final revision of the Roman Mass Proper, my Advent Project, was sometime toward the end of the seventh century. But certainly many of the nonpsalmic communions, particularly the responsory-communions, were so obviously late that they at least could not be thought of as creations of the Gregorian period. I had noted that for two cases of the later dates, the feasts of St. Apollinaris and of the Purification, Jeffery singled out their communions as exceptional instances of original chants in otherwise borrowed Propers. I seriously entertained the possibility, then, that the bulk of the repertory might date to the early seventh century, while a large proportion of the communions (and certainly the alleluias) might be the product of a final burst of creative effort that came several generations later.

Nothing would do, then, but an entirely new start, one involving a systematic study of the entire sanctorale that would first establish the relative date of every festival and then move on to compare their chant assignments in both the Roman and early Frankish graduals. I had done comparable studies of the temporal cycle for each genre of the Mass Proper over the past decade but stopped short of doing the same for the sanctorale. To state it more concretely, I had always arranged the chants of the temporale in liturgical order, separating them into the four major portions of the church year—Advent-Christmas, Lent, Paschaltime and the post-Pentecostal season—but had usually arranged the sanctoral chants alphabetically rather than calendrically. My central concern was with compositional patterns and plans that are more likely to emerge from the liturgical structures that are inherent in the temporale but are absent from the sanctorale.

A systematic survey of the sanctorale would necessarily differ in method from one of the temporale. It would follow through on the start provided by Jeffery and seek to determine for every date in the calendar the proportion of uniquely assigned chants as opposed to shared chants. It would not be enough, however, to study only the relatively small number of more recent dates; every sanctoral festival would have to be examined in order to compare the distribution of unique chants between the earlier and later dates. And the broad distinction between earlier and later dates would not be fine enough. The calendars of all liturgical books—lectionaries, sacramentaries and chant books—would have to be compared with a view to discerning as many chronological layers as possible. A comparison of the Roman and Frankish graduals would enter into the equation also; the Roman graduals, late as they are, proved to be indispensable witnesses to the seventh- and eighth-century Roman sanctorale once their calendar and chant assignments were checked against those of the early northern sources.

THE SEVENTH- AND EIGHTH-CENTURY ROMAN SANCTORALE: THE LITURGICAL BOOKS

One observes the growth of the Roman sanctorale in the seventh and eighth centuries by comparing the calendars of a series of liturgical books—the Würzburg epistolary, the Old Gelasian sacramentary, the PI evangeliary, the Paduensis and Hadrianum recensions of the Gregorian sacramentary, the Roman graduals and the Frankish unnotated graduals of Hesbert's perennially useful *Sextuplex*. It may seem a formidable array at first mention, but the first two items, the Würzburg epistle list and the Old Gelasian sacramentary, will be treated only with a view to showing their irrelevance to the work at hand. At the other end of the series, the Frankish graduals will be used only to demonstrate the validity of using the Old Roman graduals to define the Roman sanctorale in the first half of the eighth century. There is implicit in this last consideration, by the way, a modest contribution to general liturgical history. Liturgiologists work without benefit of the Roman graduals. I hope to show that these books, particularly Vat lat 5319, can be used as a link between the Hadrianum sacramentary and the Frankish liturgical books in tracing the development of the Roman sanctorale.

THE WÜRZBURG EPISTLE LIST

We saw in chapter five that this book has an extraordinarily limited sanctorale, only a dozen dates (if one excludes vigils from the count), mostly of particularly important saints like Peter, Paul, Lawrence and Andrew.[7] We should not take this small group of festivals to represent the extent of the Roman sanctorale in the earlier seventh century. We should see in it rather an indication that only a fraction of the sanctorale was assigned Proper epistles at the time. Most festivals, we must assume, made use of the Common epistles that appeared in the book under rubrics such as IN NATALE SANCTORUM and IN NATALE PAPE [abbreviations realized]. More broadly stated, it appears that the earlier seventh-century Roman sanctorale lagged behind the temporale in the degree of its properization, a point to be taken up again in the course of this chapter. At issue for now is the circumstance that the Würzburg epistle list, the only surviving seventh-century Roman epistle list, can be omitted from our efforts to reconstruct the seventh-century Roman sanctorale.

THE OLD GELASIAN SACRAMENTARY

This mid-seventh-century book can be omitted from consideration for entirely different reasons. It has a full sanctorale of some sixty-one dates (again, not counting vigils), but it is the sanctorale of the *tituli*, quasi-parish churches of Rome, not the sanctorale of the papal liturgy as conducted at the Lateran basilica and in the pope's stational peregrinations. This should be clear from the Paschaltime portion of the Roman sanctorale (see table 10). The first column on the left after the calendric date gives the sanctorale of the Old Gelasian; the four other columns give the papal sanctorale—the PI-type evangeliary of about 645; the Gregorian sacramentary of the later seventh century ("Pad and Had" indicating that the Paduensis and Hadrianum recensions of the type are combined here); Vat lat 5319 as representative of mid-eighth-century Rome; and the Blandin gradual as representative of about 800 in Carolingian Francia. The name of a saint within a column indicates the first appearance of the festival within the books included in the table or, in a few rare cases such as the 3 May Finding of the Cross, the reappearance of the festival after a period of absence. An ellipsis within the first column, that of the Old Gelasian, indicates the omission of a festival from the book (within subsequent columns ellipses indicate the absence of a festival that appeared in the immediately previous column). Dashes indicate continuity with the preceding column, continuity of either exclusion or inclusion. Table 10 is designed, then, not just to indicate inclusion or exclusion of a festival but, more immediately, to present a visualization of continuity or the lack thereof.

Thus at 13 April Euphemia's name appears in the Old Gelasian column, indicating her presence in that book's sanctorale, but an ellipsis appears in the next column, that of the PI evangeliary, indicating the festival's absence in that book; dashes in subsequent columns indicate its continued absence. The feast of Euphemia, then, is observed in the Roman presbyteral liturgy

Table 10. Roman Paschaltime Sanctorale (comparison of liturgical books)

	Old Gelasian	PI Evangeliary	Pad and Had	Vat lat 5319	Blandin
13 Apr	Euphemia	. . .	—	—	—
14 Apr	. . .	Tiburtius & Valerian	—	—	—
23 Apr	. . .	—	George	—	—
27 Apr	. . .	Vitalis	—	—	—
1 May	Philip & James	—	—	—	—
3 May	Juvenalis	. . .	—	—	—
	. . .	Alex & Event	—	—	—
	Inventio	. . .	—	Inventio	. . .
10 May	. . .	Gordianus	—	—	—
12 May	Ner, Ach & Pan	—	—	—	—
13 May	. . .	—	Dedication	—	—
19 May	. . .	Pudentiana	. . .	Pudentiana	—

but not in the papal sanctorale. At 23 April there is an ellipsis in the Old Gelasian column, indicating absence from that book of a date that will appear eventually, the relatively late feast of St. George; there is a dash in the PI Evangeliary column, indicating the continued absence of the feast, and finally the name of George under "Pad and Had," indicating that its first Roman appearance is in the later seventh-century Gregorian sacramentaries. The dashes in the next two columns indicate the maintenance of the feast in the chant books. At 1 May the names of the Apostles Philip and James appear already in the Old Gelasian column, and the dashes in the subsequent columns indicate that the feast appears in all subsequent liturgical books. At 3 May the word *Inventio* (finding of the Cross) within the Old Gelasian column indicates the appearance of the feast in that book, but the ellipsis in the PI Evangeliary column and the dashes in the Pad and Had column tell us that the feast does not find a place in the papal liturgy until its appearance in the eighth-century Roman gradual as represented by Vat lat 5319. (The seemingly contradictory presence of this feast in the Old Gelasian and its absence in the immediately following papal books could be explained as one of the many Frankish additions to the lost Roman prototype of the earlier book).

If one studies the entire range of sanctoral dates represented in the five columns of the extended (and necessarily complex) table 11, two fundamental conclusions are demonstrable: (1) the sanctorale of the Old Gelasian

Table 11. The Roman Sanctorale

	Old Gelasian	Pl Evangeliary	Pad and Had	Vat lat 5319	Blandin
13 Dec	…	Lucy	—	—	—
31 Dec	…	Sylvester	—	—	—
14 Jan	Felix in Pincus	—	—	—	—
16 Jan	Marcellus	—	—	—	—
18 Jan	…	Prisca	—	—	—
20 Jan	Sebastian, etc.	—	—	—	—
	Fabian	—	—	—	—
21 Jan	Agnes I	—	—	—	—
22 Jan	…	Vincent (& Anastasius)	—	—	—
28 Jan	Agnes II	—	—	—	—
2 Feb	Purification	…	Purification	—	—
5 Feb	Agatha	—	—	—	—
10 Feb	Soter	…	—	—	—
14 Feb	Valentine	—	—	—	—
16 Feb	Juliana	…	—	—	—
9 Mar	Perpet & Felicitas	…	—	—	—
12 Mar	…	—	Gregory (Had)	—	—
25 Mar	Annunciation	…	Annunciation	—	—
13 Apr	Euphemia	…	—	—	—
14 Apr	…	Tib & Valerian	—	—	—
23 Apr	…	—	George	—	—
27 Apr	…	Vitalis	—	—	—

Date				
1 May	Philip & James	—		—
3 May	Juvenalis	⋯		—
	Inventio	Alex & Event		—
10 May	*Inventio*	⋯	(*Inventio*)	—
12 May	Ner, Ach & Pan	Gordianus		—
13 May	⋯	—		—
19 May	Pudentiana	—	Dedication	—
25 May	⋯	Pudentiana	Urban	Pudentiana
1 June	⋯	—	Ded Nicomedes	—
2 June	Peter & Marcellus	—		⋯
	Cyrinus, Nab & Naz	—		—
9 June	⋯	⋯		Primus & Felicianus
12 June	⋯	—		Basilidis
15 June	Vitus	⋯		—
18 June	Marcus & Marcellinus	—		—
	Vigil Ger & Prot	⋯		—
19 June	Gervasius & Protasius	—		—
23 June	Vigil John Bapt	—		—
24 June	John Baptist	⋯		—
25 June	Vigil John & Paul	—		—
26 June	John & Paul	⋯		—
28 June	Vigil Peter & Paul	—		—
29 June	Peter	—		—
	Peter & Paul	—		—

(*continued*)

Table 11. (*continued*)

	Old Gelasian	Pl Evangeliary	Pad and Had	Vat lat 5319	Blandin
30 June	Paul	—		—	—
2 July	...	Processus & Martinianus	—	—	—
6 July	Octave Peter & Paul	—	—	—	—
10 July	...	Seven Brothers	—	—	—
21 July	...	—	—	Praxedis	—
23 July	...	Apollinaris	...	Apollinaris	—
29 July	Felix, Faustinus, etc.	—	—	—	—
30 July	Abdon & Sennon	—	—	—	—
1 Aug	Macchabees	...	—	—	—
2 Aug	...	Stephen (pope)	—	—	—
6 Aug	Sixtus	—	—	—	—
8 Aug	Donatus	Felicissimus & Agapitus	—	—	—
9 Aug	...	Cyriacus	—	—	—
9 Aug	Vigil Lawrence	—	—	—	—
10 Aug	Lawrence	—	—	—	—
11 Aug	Tiburtius (& Susanna)	—	—	—	—
13 Aug	Hyppolitus	—	—	—	—
14 Aug	...	Eusebius	Vigil Assumption (Had)	—	—
15 Aug	Assumption	...	Assumption	...	...
17 Aug	Octave Lawrence	—	—	—	Octave Lawrence

Date						
18 Aug	Agapitus	—	—	—	—	—
19 Aug	Magnus	—	—	—	—	—
22 Aug	…	Timothy & Hyp	—	—	—	—
25 Aug	…	—	—	…	(Genesius)	—
27 Aug	Ruffus	—	—	—	—	—
28 Aug	Hermes	Sabina	—	—	—	—
29 Aug	…	—	—	—	—	—
30 Aug	…	Felix & Audactus	—	—	—	—
1 Sept	*Coll* John Baptist	—	(in Pad only)	…	(*Coll* John Bapt)	… (1 Jan)
8 Sept	Prisca	…	Nativity Mary	—	—	—
8 Sept	Nativity Mary	Nativity Mary	…	—	—	—
9 Sept	Gorgonus	Hadrian	…	—	Hadrian	—
11 Sept	…	Protus & Hyac	—	—	—	—
14 Sept	Cornelius & Cyprian	—	Exaltation	—	—	—
15 Sept	Exaltation	Nicomedes	…	—	—	—
17 Sept	…	Lucy & Euphem	Lucy & Geminiana (Had)	—	—	—
18 Sept	…	—	—	—	Vigil Matthew	—
27 Sept	Cosmas & Damian	…	—	—	Matthew	—
29 Sept	Michael	—	—	—	—	—
7 Oct	…	Mark (pope)	—	—	—	—
9 Oct	Marcel & Apol	…	—	—	—	—

(continued)

Table 11. (continued)

	Old Gelasian	Pl Evangeliary	Pad and Had	Vat lat 5319	Blandin
14 Oct	...	Callistus	—	—	...
27 Oct	...	—	—	Vigil Simon & Jude	—
28 Oct	...	—	—	Simon & Jude	—
1 Nov	...	Caesarius	—	(All Saints)	...
7 Nov	Quatuor Coronati	—	—	—	—
9 Nov	...	Theodore	—	(Ded Salvatoris)	—
11 Nov	...	Mennas	—	—	...
12 Nov	...	Martin	—	...	—
22 Nov	Cecilia	—	—	—	—
23 Nov	Clement	Clement & Felicitas	Clement	—	—
	Felicitas	...	Felicitas	...	—
	...	Chrysogonos	—	...	—
29 Nov	Saturninus, etc.	—	—	...	—
	Vigil Andrew	—	—	—	—
30 Nov	Andrew	—	—	—	—
7 Dec	Octave Andrew	...	—	—	—
21 Dec	Thomas	...	—	—	—

sacramentary is strikingly different from all other documents represented; and (2) the other documents—a series that (as will be shown here momentarily) provides the fullest picture of the papal sacramentary of the seventh and eighth centuries available to us—present a remarkably homogeneous sanctorale.

It is the first of these conclusions that is at issue for the moment, the anomalous character of the Old Gelasian's sanctorale. To compare it with that of the roughly contemporary PI evangeliary, there are 66 sanctoral occasions in the Old Gelasian (counting vigils), 39 of which appear in the PI evangeliary and 27 of which do not. There are 70 sanctoral occasions in the PI evangeliary, 39 of which appear in the Old Gelasian and 31 of which do not. Or to state it somewhat more succinctly, of the 66 sanctoral occasions in the Old Gelasian and the 70 in the PI evangeliary, only 39, less than 60 percent in each case, are shared. The sanctorale of the Old Gelasian, then, representing as it does the liturgy of the Roman *tituli* rather than the papacy, is substantially different from that of the PI evangeliary and must be omitted from any survey of the papal sanctorale's development in the seventh and eighth centuries.

THE PI-TYPE EVANGELIARY

Just as clearly does the PI evangeliary of 645 represent the papal sanctorale of the mid-seventh century. There are two reasons in particular for which we can be confident of this. The first is the obvious one that the evangeliary (in contrast to the Old Gelasian sacramentary) provides the papal stational indications. The second is that the evangeliary (again, in contrast to the Old Gelasian) represents a virtually identical sanctorale to that of the Gregorian sacramentaries, books that are by definition papal in character. There are, of course, additions to the Gregorian sacramentaries, some ten in number, which are to be expected in books several decades later than the evangeliary. But there are only four dates in the evangeliary of 645 (19 May's Pudentiana, 23 July's Apollinaris, 30 August's *Decollatio* [beheading] of John the Baptist and 8 September's Hadrian) that do not appear in the Gregorian sacramentaries. And all four of these are reinstated in the Roman graduals.

The evangeliary of 645, moreover, is our earliest witness to the seventh-century papal sanctorale and as such must be used here to define an "early" as opposed to a "later" festival. Its relatively late date should not be considered a cause for regret because it would appear to represent a period not far removed from that when the Roman sanctorale finally achieved a fully properized list of gospels. We have just seen evidence that only the most important sanctoral dates had epistles assigned to them in the earlier seventh century, and in the previous chapter we saw evidence pointing to a similar situation for the sanctoral gospels. In a comparison of the gospels cited in Gregory I's homilies with those given in the PI evangeliary, it will be recalled, only four of the thirteen Gregorian sanctoral gospels matched those of the PI evangeliary. We concluded that the gospels of the sanctorale were for the most part not yet assigned in Gregory's day, and that they achieved this state only sometime between then and the finalization of the PI evangeliary in about 645. The bulk of the temporale gospels, however, at least those of the more important dates, were fixed already in Gregory's time. This lag between the properization of the temporale and the sanctorale is of considerable significance and will be referred to again in the course of the present chapter.

Some might see in the papal biographies of the *Liber pontificalis* a source that fills in the gap in our knowledge of the sanctorale's development between the time of Gregory and the PI evangeliary of 645. It is commonly assumed that one can date the adoption of a new festival by observing which pope it is who builds or restores a church in honor of the saint in question. One recalls, indeed, that it is just such a reference on which the famous case of the Dedication of Sancta Maria ad Martyres is built. The biography of Boniface IV tells us that he transformed the ancient Pantheon into a church dedicated to Mary and all the martyrs, and one assumes, then, that he established the 13 May Dedication festival at the same time. The *Liber pontificalis* gives some twelve references of this sort from the death of Gregory I in 604 to that of John IV in 642, with the majority of them, no less than nine, appearing in the biography of Honorius (625–38). A review of these references, however, produces results of only limited value.

Take, for example, the case of St. Cyriacus; Pope Honorius is said to have "built from the ground up the church of blessed Cyriacus the martyr."[8] Cyriacus, it turns out, is mentioned already in the Philocalian Calendar of 345 as a martyr whose death was commemorated annually at Rome, and one would hardly wish to claim that he was introduced into the Roman sanctorale under Honorius. Similar references to churches of Agnes, Marcellinus and Peter, the Quattuor Coronati and Lucy of Syracuse involve cases of the same sort, that is, of saints commemorated already in the Philocalian Calendar, the sixth-century Martyrology[9] or the Canon of the Mass.

Then there are references in the *Liber pontificalis* to saints who have churches built in their honor but whose feast days fail to appear in the evangeliary of 645. For example, Honorius built a church dedicated to St. Severinus,[10] but his festival is totally absent from the Roman calendar—it does not appear in the evangeliary, the Gregorian sacramentaries or the chant books. Probably this is because the church was situated outside the city limits of Rome, indeed, some twenty miles distant near the town of Tibur. But this is not the case with St. Apollinaris. Pope Honorius built a basilica in his honor and decreed that there would be a procession from this church to nearby St. Peter's every Saturday. Yet the feast of Apollinaris also is missing from both the evangeliary and the Gregorian sacramentaries; it makes its first Roman appearance in the chant books, signaling an adoption into the papal calendar the better part of a century later. Something of the same is true for the Dedication of Sancta Maria ad Martyres. Boniface IV, as we have seen, transformed the Pantheon into a church in honor of Mary and all the martyrs; he did this sometime during his reign from 608 to 613, yet the 13 May festival commemorating the event does not appear in the PI evangeliary of several decades later. We must await the Gregorian sacramentaries from the last quarter of the century for evidence of the feast's celebration. The situation with this occasion is more complex than that, however, and just as I begin this chapter with a reference to it, so too will the chapter close.

The point at issue now is that we must rely upon the evangeliary for our definition of the papal sanctorale in 645. That being said, there are a few events recorded in the *Liber pontificalis* from the period in question that do make a contribution, slight though it might be, to our knowledge of the earlier seventh-century development of the sanctorale. Take the case of St. Hadrian, one of the many saints in whose honor Pope Honorius dedicated a church.[11] Hadrian does not appear in ancient sources like the Philocalian Calendar, but he does find a place in the PI evangeliary. We are led to believe, then, by the reference in Honorius's biography, that Hadrian's 8 September festival may very well have been added to the Roman calendar on the occasion of his church's dedication sometime during the twelve-year reign of Honorius. There are two other festivals meeting these criteria of absence from the ancient documents and presence in the PI evangeliary: the 15 September feast of St. Nicomedes, to whom Boniface V (619–25) dedicated a cemetery;[12] and the 13 December feast of St. Lucy of Syracuse, to whom the tireless Honorius dedicated a church.[13]

The evidence of the *Liber pontificalis*, then, adds something, however limited, to our knowledge of the earlier seventh-century Roman sanctorale: we probably know the occasion on which the last three dates cited here were added to the calendar. It is liturgical books, however, which define that calendar for us, and we are fortunate enough to have it so defined for the mid-seventh century by the gospel list of 645.

THE GREGORIAN SACRAMENTARIES:
PADUENSIS AND HADRIANUM

This nearly identical pair of books provides us, as was seen in chapter five, with the Roman papal liturgy of the later seventh century.[14] The Paduensis manuscript represents a papal sacramentary that was brought from the Lateran to St. Peter's sometime before 680 and was adopted there for basilican use. The Hadrianum, the form of sacramentary sent by Pope Hadrian to Charlemagne in the late eighth century, distinguishes itself by a small number of additions to the sanctorale of the Paduensis, changes made between 682 and the close of Sergius I's reign in 701. The feast of St. George appears to have been added during the reign of Leo II (682–83), and the feast of St. Peter in Chains during the reign of Leo's successor, Benedict II (684–85).[15] More significantly, Sergius added the 12 February feast of St. Gregory the Great and the 14 September Exaltation of the Cross; he also made important changes to the four Marian feasts, instituting a procession that assembled at St. Hadrian's for the *collecta* prayer and moved from there to Santa Maria Maggiore for Mass. The *collecta* prayers that appear in the Hadrianum for each of these four feasts date to the reign of Sergius, who established the pre-Mass processions. The Hadrianum also has new prayer sets for three of the four feasts (Annunciation, Assumption and Nativity), formularies that differ from those of the Paduensis. This suggests the possibility that the new Proper chants for these three Marian feasts might also date to Sergius's reign, a hypothesis to be pursued toward the close of this chapter.

The Paduensis and Hadrianum sanctorales, in any event, are virtually identical and can appear in the same column of table 11, with "Had" appearing in parentheses after those few dates that the Hadrianum adds to the Paduensis.

Jean Deshusses makes an observation about the character of their sanctoral prayer sets that is of considerable relevance to present purposes.[16] We saw evidence above that both the epistle and gospel lists of the sanctorale were not yet fully properized in earlier seventh-century Rome. Only the most important feast days had permanently assigned epistles and gospels; most dates, we must assume, took their readings on an ad hoc basis from a list of Common pericopes. Deshusses shows that a similar situation must have existed for the sanctoral prayer sets. He finds that all three of the Mass prayers are unique and appropriate for dates of the temporale, but only within the collect for the sanctorale. Some four-fifths of sanctoral secrets and post-communions are shared, and not only that, they appear to be assigned with little care to their coordination with the Proper collects, leaving, for example, conflicts between plural and singular persons. This evidence clearly suggests, then, a situation in the earlier seventh century when the sanctoral secrets and post-communions, like epistles and gospels, were not yet permanently assigned. As for collects, there are two possibilities. Either they were all created and assigned earlier in the seventh century, or, more likely, perhaps, they were the result of an effort undertaken later in the century (a kind of Advent Project for prayer sets) that was too large a task to extend in systematic fashion to all the orations of the Mass. In any case Proper sanctoral Mass prayers are still imperfectly provided for even later in the seventh century, just as we saw in chapter five that sanctoral readings also became fixed only at a relatively late date. Both circumstances suggest that something of the same might be true for the third element of the sanctoral Proper, the chants—a hypothesis to be considered toward the close of the present chapter.

There is a final point to be made about the Gregorian sacramentaries, one having to do with the Hadrianum in particular: it appears to have been essentially completed during the reign of Sergius I (687–701), indeed probably fairly early during his tenure. This should cause some surprise because we know that this book, taking its name from Pope Hadrian I (772–95), is the type of Gregorian sacramentary sent to Charlemagne by that pope sometime between 784 and 791. Deshusses says that the copy sent to Charlemagne was probably made at the time of Sergius's liturgical innovations and deposited then in the papal archives (the *bibliothecae cubiculum* cited in the preface of its Carolingian exemplars), there to remain until Hadrian found it and sent it to Charlemagne.[17] It is true that the Carolingian manuscripts of the Hadrianum have the Thursdays in Lent, which were added to the Roman liturgy under Gregory II in about 720, but these do not appear to be well integrated with the surrounding text.[18] They were, in Deshusses's view, derived from the Old Gelasian, copied out in a confusing manner and inserted into the finished Hadrianum in a single leaf or *bifolium*.

More to present purposes, the festivals added during the eighth century do not appear in the Hadrianum's sanctorale. There are about ten of these, including, for example, 9 June's Primus and Felicianus and 12 June's Basilidis. In table 11 there are dashes for such dates in the Pad and Had column, indicating that just as they failed to appear in the earlier Pl evangeliary, they fail to appear in the Gregorian sacramentaries. They do appear, however, in the Roman graduals, as is indicated by their names in the column Vat lat 5319. They appear, moreover, in the early Frankish graduals as indicated by the dashes in the Blandin column. The conclusion to be drawn from this is that these ten festivals came into the Roman liturgy in the first half of the eighth century, between the time of the redaction of the Hadrianum under Sergius I (d.701) and the redaction of the manuscripts used in the transmission of the *cantus romanus* to the north, a process begun with Pope Stephen's visit to King Pépin III in 754.

The Roman graduals, and in particular Vat lat 5319, thus serve as our evidentiary link between the Hadrianum and the Frankish liturgical books. This finding is the modest contribution to general liturgical history referred to above; I will make the case for it in what follows.

VATICANA LATINA 5319

First it must be shown that Vat lat 5319 can be taken as representative of the three extant Roman graduals. One would hope to be able to use a single manuscript for the practical reason of maintaining already complex tables at a manageable state, and the late-eleventh- or early-twelfth-century Vat lat 5319 is the obvious candidate for this since the Bodmer 74 gradual of 1071 is incomplete (breaking off after the 26 June feast of John and Paul), and the thirteenth-century San Pietro F22 has the occasional northern addition to its Roman church year. But the case for using Vat lat 5319 as representative of the Roman tradition goes beyond such practical considerations: a comparison of the three graduals shows virtually identical sanctoral cycles.

If one compares the sanctoral cycles for the three manuscripts up to the point where Bodmer 74 breaks off, the following remarkably stable picture results. Vat lat 5319 has thirty-four sanctoral dates between 13 December's Lucy and 26 June's John and Paul (I spare the reader a table). Every one of these thirty-four appears in Bodmer 74, which adds only one feast outright, 15 June's Vitus, a date appearing in the Old Gelasian but in none of the papal liturgical books. In addition, Bodmer 74 has an early morning Mass between the Vigil of John the Baptist and the Mass of the day. San Pietro F22's sanctorale is only slightly more divergent from Vat lat 5319's than is Bodmer 74's: it adds the 22 February *Cathedra Sancti Petri* and omits the 10 May Gordianus and Epimachus and the 25 May Urban.

Even more telling is the striking stability of the chant formularies. Of the thirty-four dates shared between Vat lat 5319 and Bodmer 74 there are only two chants with differing assignments, the offertories of 20 January's Fabian and 5 February's Agatha. One would expect more discrepancies than this between Vat lat 5319 and San Pietro F22 because of the Gregorian influence on the latter, but even here the commonality of assignment is remarkable, with only two graduals, one offertory and two communions differing.

Thus we should have no qualms about using Vat lat 5319 for the broad purposes of the present chapter.

That point aside, the more fundamental consideration is the manifest continuity of the papal sanctorale observed in the PI evangeliary and the Gregorian sacramentaries with that of Vat lat 5319. Of the seventy-eight sanctoral occasions in the Hadrianum, only five fail to appear in Vat lat 5319. At least two of these, 23 November's Chrysogonos and 29 November's Saturninus, can be explained because they coincide with other sanctoral dates, namely with 23 November's Clement and 29 November's vigil of Andrew. It is one thing for a sacramentary to give redundant prayer sets on the same day, but another to provide for the singing of competing masses.

There are, of course, additions in Vat lat 5319 to the sanctorale of the Hadrianum, reflecting for the most part additions to the Roman sanctorale after the time of Sergius I. Among these fifteen occasions—or thirteen, should one wish to subsume the vigils of Matthew and of Simon and Jude to the festivals in question—an important distinction remains: one must separate the ten that appear to have been added before the mid-eighth-century transmission of the *cantus romanus* to the north, and the five (in parentheses in table 11) that were probably added later. The distinction is made on the basis of whether a festival appears also in the Blandin gradual or not. This point is of crucial methodological significance and will be argued immediately below.[19]

THE CAROLINGIAN GRADUAL: BLANDIN

This unnotated manuscript, dating from about 800, is our earliest complete witness to the *cantus romanus* as it appears within the Carolingian milieu. It stands, I believe, beyond controversy as a representative of the early Frankish Mass Proper, at least for the broad purposes of the present chapter. The authenticity of its calendar and chant assignments is corroborated by the graduals of the later ninth and earlier tenth centuries.

The use I make of it here is as the fourth and final link in a chain of liturgical continuity—a chain that begins with the PI evangeliary, continues with the Hadrianum, then with the Roman gradual as represented by Vat lat 5319, and ends with the early Carolingian gradual as represented by Blandin. Blandin serves to corroborate the status of Vat lat 5319, albeit a manuscript copied centuries later, as representative of what would have been copied in mid-eighth-century Rome. We saw in chapter six that this is an entirely legitimate position to take as far as the repertory of the Mass temporale is concerned, and now table 11 demonstrates that the same is true for the annual cycle of feasts in the eighth-century Roman sanctorale. A glance at the Blandin column in table 11, with its consistent use of dashes, should be sufficient for one to appreciate the extraordinary continuity between its sanctorale and that of Vat lat 5319.

There are just ten discrepancies between the sanctoral calendar of Vat lat 5319 and the Blandin. Half of these constitute the group of five late additions to the Roman sanctorale mentioned above (those within parentheses in the Vat lat 5319 column in table 11); these are dates so late, apparently, that they were not yet included in the first Roman Mass antiphoners sent to the Franks in the second half of the eighth century. Their failure to appear in Blandinensis is, of course, what we should expect. An obvious example of such a date is the 1 November feast of All Saints, not promulgated for universal observance until the reign of Gregory IV (827–44). Another of the five, the 9 November feast of the Dedication of Our Savior, may date to the time of Hadrian I, who, according to the *Liber pontificalis*, "freshly renewed the Savior's basilica also called Constantinian, close to the Lateran patriarchate, which was in ruins."[20] The 25 August feast of Genesius could date to the reign of Gregory III; the *Liber pontificalis* says of him that "in the church of St. Genesius the martyr he freshly restored the roof; there too he set up an altar in the name of the Savior our Lord God."[21] Gregory III reigned, of course, before Stephen's journey north in 753–54, but it could very well be that the copying of the Roman gradual involved in the initial transmission of the Mass Proper was redacted somewhat earlier.[22] For the two remaining dates of this group of five late additions to the Roman Sanctorale—14 September's Exaltation of the Cross and 30 August's *Decollatio* of John the Baptist—we are lacking external evidence for the probable date of their entry into the calendar and must rely simply upon our basic premise in dealing with the entire group, that is, that their absence from the Hadrianum and Blandin and presence in Vat lat 5319 is best explained by the adoption of the feast into the Roman calendar after the redaction of the Roman gradual that was sent north in the mid-eighth century.

What of the other five discrepancies between the sanctorale of Vat lat 5319 and the Blandinensis, cases where the Frankish gradual appears not to maintain continuity with its Roman exemplar? The five, a small enough number as it is, are for the most part easily understood. For one, the Franks responsible for the Blandin combine the two 20 January celebrations of St. Sebastian and St. Fabian into a single mass of SS. Sebastian and Fabian. They lack the recently added Roman vigil of the Assumption and add the octave of St. Lawrence, which the Roman graduals fail to observe for some unknown reason in spite of its early establishment in the papal liturgy. They celebrate the Nativity of Mary not on the more recent date of 8 September but on the 1 January date of the original Roman feast of Mary. Finally they drop the 14 October feast of St. Callistus, the only outright omission from the sanctorale of Vat lat 5319.

In sum, the continuity between the sanctorales of Vat lat 5319 and the Blandinensis is little short of absolute; it is closer than that of any other books representing the papal liturgy. Once we witness this demonstration, however, and reflect upon it, the extraordinary continuity should cease to cause surprise. It is what one might expect from an exemplar of the Frankish gradual carefully copied from a nearly contemporary exemplar of the Roman Mass antiphoner. We gain some real sense of this when we reread that remarkable rubric that the copyist of the Blandin felt compelled to add before the new Frankish mass of the seventh Sunday after Pentecost: ISTA HEBDOMATA NON EST IN ANTEFONARIOS ROMANOS.

To step back for the moment and survey this series of liturgical books, we can be confident now that we have a substantially accurate picture of the seventh- and eighth-century development of the Roman sanctorale. The PI evangeliary represents it for around 645; the Gregorian sacramentaries do so for the later decades of the seventh century; Vat lat 5319 does so for the immediately following period, showing us some ten feast days added after the redaction of the Hadrianum but before the redaction of the Mass antiphoners used in the transmission (perhaps in the earlier eighth century). Finally, Vat lat 5319 provides another five dates (absent from Blandin) that were added at some undetermined later time. None of the numbers involved can be given as absolutes; we must always assume that unknown circumstances surround one or another festival's entry or omission from a particular document. But certainly we have a sound enough chronology of the Roman sanctorale to serve as context for our survey of the chant Propers.

ROMAN SANCTORAL CHANTS: UNIQUE AND SHARED

Once the groundwork of establishing the seventh- and eighth-century history of the papal sanctoral calendar is firm, it is a comparatively straightforward exercise to test Frere's principle against it, that is, to observe the chronological distribution of the unique and shared chants. The task does, unfortunately, require a table of ungainly proportions (table 12), but one that furnishes appropriate results at a glance. The table lists the ninety sanctoral dates of Vat lat 5319 on the left and gives the incipits of the unique

Table 12. Unique Sanctoral Chants in Vat lat 5319

Group I: Early Festivals (before 645)

13 Dec	Lucy		
31 Dec	Sylvester		
14 Jan	Felix in Pincus		
16 Jan	Marcellus	Intr *Statuit ei dominus* (Sir 45.30)	
18 Jan	Prisca	Comm *Feci judicium*	
20 Jan	Sebastian	Grad *Pretiosa in conspectu*	
20 Jan	Fabian		
21 Jan	Agnes I	Intr *Me expectaverunt*	
		Comm *Quinque prudentes* (Mt 25.4–6)	resp-comm
22 Jan	Anastasius (Vincent)		
27 Jan	Agnes II		
5 Feb	Agatha	Intr *Gaudeamus*	
		Grad *Adiuvavit eum deus*	
		Tract *Qui seminant*	
		Comm *Qui me dignatus est* (nonbibl)	resp-comm
14 Feb	Valentine	Tract *Desiderium anime*	
14 Apr	Tiburtius & Valerian		
27 Apr	Vitalis	Comm *Ego sum vitis vera* (Jn 15.5)	resp-comm
1 May	Philip & James	Intr *Exclamaverunt ad te* (Neh 9.27)	
		Off *Repleti sumus*	
		Comm *Tanto tempore* (Jn 14.1–13)	resp-comm
3 May	Alexander & Theodulus		
10 May	Gordianus & Epimachus		
12 May	Pancratius & Nereus	Intr *Ecce oculi dei*	
18 May	Marcus & Marcellinus		
2 June	Marcellus & Peter		
19 June	Gervasius & Protasius	Intr *Loquetur dominus*	
23 June	Vigil of John the Baptist	Intr *Ne timeas Zacharia* (Lk 1.13)	
		Grad *Fuit homo missus* (Jn 1.6–7)	

(continued)

Table 12. (*continued*)

Group I: Early Festivals (before 645)

Date	Feast	Chants	
24 June	John the Baptist	Intr *De ventre matris* (Is 49.1–2)	
		Grad *Priusquam te formarem* (Jer 1.5–9)	
		Comm *Tu puer propheta* (Lk 1.74)	resp-comm
26 June	John & Paul	Intr *Multe tribulationes*	
		Comm *Et si coram hom* (Wis 3.4–6)	
28 June	Vigil of Peter & Paul	Intr *Dicit dominus Petro* (Jn 21.18–19)	
		Comm *Tu es Petrus* (Mt 16.18)	
29 June	Peter & Paul	Off (*Constitues eos*)	
		Comm *Symon iohannes* (Jn 21.15–17)	resp-comm
30 June	Paul	Intr *Scio cui credidi* (2 Tm 1.12)	
		Grad *Qui operatus es* (Gal 2; 1 Cor 15)	
		All *Magnus sanctus Paulus* (nonbibl)	
		Comm *Amen dico . . . quod vos* (Mt 19.28–29)	
2 July	Processus & Martinianus	Comm *Beati mundo corde* (Mt 5.8–10)	
6 July	Octave of Peter & Paul	Intr *Nunc scio vere* (Acts 12.11)	
		All *Tu es Petrus* (Mt 16.18)	
		Off *Beatus es symon* (Mt 16.17)	
		Comm *Domine si tu es* (Mt 14.28–31)	resp-comm
10 July	Seven Brothers	Intr *Laudate pueri*	
		Comm *Quicumque fecerit* (Mt 14.50)	
28 July	Felix		
30 July	Abdon & Sennen	Grad *Gloriosus deus* (Ex 15.11, 6)	
2 Aug	Stephen (pope)		
6 Aug	Sixtus		
	Felicissimus & Agapitus		

(*continued*)

Table 12. (*continued*)

Group I: Early Festivals (before 645)

8 Aug	Cyriacus	Intr (*Timete dominum*)
		Grad (*Timete dominum*)
		Comm *Signa eos* (Mk 16.17–18)
9 Aug	Vigil of Lawrence	Intr *Dispersit dedit*
		Grad *Dispersit dedit*
		Off *Oratio mea* (Jb 16.18–21)
10 Aug	Lawrence	Grad *Probasti domine*
		Off *Confessio et pulchritudo*
		Comm *Qui mihi ministrat* (Jn 17.26)
11 Aug	Tyburtius & Susanna	Intr (*Justus ut palma*)
13 Aug	Hippolytus	Intr *Justi epulentur*
		Comm *Dico autem vobis* (Lk 12.4)
14 Aug	Eusebius	
18 Aug	Agapitus	
22 Aug	Timothy & Hippolytus	
28 Aug	Hermes	Intr *Justus non conturbabitur*
29 Aug	Sabina	Comm *Principes persecuti*
30 Aug	Felix & Audactus	Comm *Quod dico vobis* (Mt 10.27)
11 Sept	Protus & Hyacinth	
14 Sept	Cornelius & Cyprian	
15 Sept	Nicomedes	
27 Sept	Comas & Damian	All *Cantate domino . . . laudatio*
29 Sept	Michael the Archangel	Intr *Benedicite dominum*
		Grad *Benedicite dominum*
		Off *In conspectu angelorum*
		Comm *Benedicite omnes* (Dn 3.58)
7 Oct	Mark (pope)	
14 Oct	Callistus	
1 Nov	Caesarius	
7 Nov	Quatuor Coronati	Grad *Vindica domine*
9 Nov	Theodore	
11 Nov	Mennas	
22 Nov	Cecilia	Comm *Confundantur superbi*
23 Nov	Clement	Intr *Dicit dominus . . . sermones* (Is 59.21, 5–7)

(*continued*)

Table 12. (continued)

Group I: Early Festivals (before 645)

24 Nov	Chrysogonos		
29 Nov	Vigil of Andrew	Intr *Dominus secus* (Mt 4.18–19)	
		Comm *Venite post me* (Jn 1.41–42)	resp-comm
30 Nov	Andrew	Comm *Dicit Andreas* (Jn 1.41–42)	

Group IIA: Later Festivals (645–680)

2 Feb	Purification	Grad *Suscepimus deus*	
		Off *Diffusa est*	
		Comm *Responsum* (Lk 1.26)	resp-comm
13 May	Dedication Maria ad Martyres	Intr *Terribilis est* (Gn 28.17, 22)	
		Grad *Locus iste* (nonbibl)	
		Off *Domine deus* (1 Chr 29.17–18)	
		Comm *Domus mea* (Mt 21.13)	
25 May	Urban	All *Memento domine*	
14 Sept	Exaltation of the Cross		

Group IIB: Later Festivals (680–701)

25 Mar	Annunciation	Intr (*Vultum tuum*)
		Grad (*Diffusa est*)
		Off *Ave Maria* (Lk 1.28)
23 Apr	George	Comm *Laetabitur justus*
15 Aug	Assumption	Intr (*Vultum tuum*)
		Grad (*Diffusa est*)
		Off (*Diffusa est*)
8 Sept	Nativity of Mary	Intr (*Vultum tuum*)
		Grad (*Diffusa est*)
		Off (*Diffusa est*)

Group IIC: Later Festivals (687–701)

12 Mar	Gregory	Tract *Beatus vir*
14 Aug	Vigil of the Assumption	
17 Sept	Lucy & Geminiana	

(continued)

Table 12. *(continued)*

Group III: Very Late Festivals (after 701?)		
19 May	Pudentiana	
9 June	Primus & Felicianus	
12 June	Basilidis	
21 July	Praxedis	
23 July	Apollinaris	Intr *Sacerdotes tui*
	Felix, Faustinus & Beatrice	Comm *Sint lumbi vestri* (Lk 12.35–36)
8 Sept	Hadrian	
17 Sept	Vigil of Matthew	
18 Sept	Matthew	
27 Oct	Vigil of Simon & Jude	
28 Oct	Simon & Jude	
31 Oct	Vigil of All Saints	
Group IV: Still Later Festivals (?)		
3 May	Finding of Cross	
25 Aug	Genesius	
30 Aug	*Decollatio* of John Baptist	
1 Nov	All Saints	
9 Nov	*Dedicatio Salvatoris*	

chants (as they appear in Vat lat 5319) on the right. The dates for which no such incipits are provided are, of course, festivals lacking in unique chants.

The left-hand column begins with the sixty-two "early festivals" of Group I, that is, sanctoral dates appearing already in the PI evangeliary of 645. The eleven feast days of Group II's "later festivals" are subdivided into three groups: the four dates of Group IIA enter the calendar sometime between the 645 redaction of the PI evangeliary and the 680 redaction of the Paduensis; to pass over Group IIB, for the moment, the three dates of Group IIC are additions from the reign of Sergius I (687–701). Of the four dates in Group IIB, there are grounds for placing the three Marian festivals in Group IIC, although I tentatively assign them to Group IIB purely as a cautionary gesture. My own view is that they are additions of Sergius I, adopted at the same time he established pre-Mass processions for them, and hence do in fact belong in Group IIC. The point will be discussed below in a separate section devoted to the four Marian festivals. Finally Group III and Group IV provide considerably later dates, twelve after the reign of Sergius but before the redaction of the Roman antiphoners used in the transmission (they appear in Vat lat 5319 and the Blandin), and five after the transmission (they appear in Vat lat 5319, but not in the Blandin).

The right-hand column, as just stated, provides incipits of uniquely assigned chants. In addition to these it provides incipits (given in parentheses) that are not unique in the literal sense but must be considered so for present purposes. Take the offertory *Constitues eos* for the 29 June feast of Peter and Paul; it appears a second time in the Roman calendar, for the post-701 feast of Simon and Jude, on 27 October. Obviously it was a unique chant at the time of its initial assignment to the earlier feast of Peter and Paul and was subsequently borrowed for the later feast of Simon and Jude. Consequently it is classified as a unique chant for the former date, but not for the latter (hence its failure to appear on the table at 1 November). Similarly the introit *Vultum tuum* appears four times in the Roman calendar, but three of these are for the group of three contemporaneous Marian festivals: the Annunciation, the Assumption and the Nativity. The fourth appearance is for a later festival, 17 September's Lucy and Geminiana, which borrows the chant from the Marian group. Again, the three presumably original appearances are classified as unique and the fourth is not.

I arrive, finally, at the central point of the chapter, the test of Frere's principle—are unique chants more characteristic of earlier or later Roman sanctoral dates? Table 12 shows that they are most certainly not more characteristic of pre-645 festivals than those added between 645 and the time of Sergius I. If anything, there is something of an increase in unique chants in the Group IIA and IIB categories. I am not inclined to make too much of this marginal increase, however, and would rest content with the observation that the information in table 12 most decidedly does not support the notion of a creative phase of chant production that comes to a close shortly after the time of Gregory I (d.604).

Must we reject Frere's principle, then? Not the principle but only its chronological application. There is a stark cutoff in the incidence of unique sanctoral chants after the time of Sergius I; surely this suggests an end to the creative phase of Roman Mass Proper chant production even if it comes close to a century after Gregory's reign.

As for Sergius's reign, I am inclined to see the cutoff as taking place relatively early within it, a point to be taken up below. Thus the conclusion anticipated already in the introduction to this volume. My late turn to take up work on the sanctorale, while confirming my long-held view that the final revision of the Mass Proper was considerably later than the time of Gregory I, inclines me to believe that it was not quite as late as the earlier decades of the eighth century.

THE SANCTORAL PROJECT

There is a second major observation resulting from an analysis of table 12—the absence of calendric patterns in the sanctorale chants similar to those encountered in the Advent Project. There we observed work on the temporale beginning with Advent and proceeding systematically through the church year, but nothing of the sort is present in the sanctorale. There is, however, a pattern of an entirely different sort—festivals are allotted unique chants more or less according to their importance. Not one date is given a full complement of five, that is, an introit, gradual, alleluia, offertory and communion. Five, however, have four: the feasts of Agatha, Paul and Michael, the octave of Peter and Paul and the Dedication festival. Another nine have three: the feasts of Philip and James, John the Baptist and Cyriacus, both vigil and feast of Lawrence, and the four Marian festivals, Annunciation, Assumption, Purification and Nativity. To complete the count, eight dates have two unique chants, twenty-three have one, and forty-five (approximately half of the sanctorale) have none.

The pattern is clear enough: the thirteen feast days that are favored with four or three unique chants (Cyriacus excepted?) include the majority of the principal dates in the annual Roman sanctoral cycle. Given the absence of any calendric pattern here, and the obvious intention to allot unique chants according to a festival's status, the best explanation for the distribution of such chants is that at a certain point there was a decision taken to embark upon a kind of limited sanctoral project. It would have been hopelessly impractical to furnish every date with a full set of four or five chants, as in the case of the temporale's Advent Project, and so the eminently sensible plan of a distribution of unique chants by and large in keeping with an occasion's eminence. The plan will be formally recognized in what follows by referring to it as the Sanctoral Project.

There is a pair of further considerations that adds credence to the notion of a concerted effort to provide a worthy sanctoral Proper and that helps to begin the task of assigning a date to it. These are the parts played in the project by nonpsalmic chants and by responsory-communions. Nonpsalmic chants reveal no chronological pattern in their distribution among the unique sanctoral items; table 12 shows no marked preponderance of them among either the earlier or later festivals. This suggests that the unique sanctoral chants, or at least the nonpsalmic ones, were created at approximately the same time. Moreover, since nonpsalmic chants represent, in a broad sense, a later layer of Mass Proper chants, the time of their creation should be considered a relatively late one.

Responsory-communions most certainly constitute one of the very latest layers of the entire Mass Proper, shared as they are by Office and Mass in an attempt by the Roman singers to complete the annual cycle of responsories and communions in a fitting manner.[23] Fifteen of the responsory-communions are sanctoral, and nine of these (see table 12) are unique chants. As was the case with the nonpsalmic chants, they are distributed more or less proportionately among the earlier and later feast days, eight of them among the sixty-two earlier dates and one among the eleven later dates, thus suggesting a contemporary creation of the repertory of unique sanctoral chants. And again, the presence of chants from such a late layer of the Mass Proper in the formularies of earlier feast days speaks for a generally late date for the repertory of those earlier occasions. Toward the close of this chapter there will be an attempt to be somewhat more precise about what that date might be.

BEFORE THE SANCTORAL PROJECT

Obviously the schola cantorum sang regularly at sanctoral Masses before their undertaking of the Sanctoral Project, just as they sang at temporal Masses before the Advent Project, and inevitably it must be asked what it is that they might have sung. If the temporal chants at this stage in the history of the Mass Proper consisted primarily in lists of psalmic chants for general use, the sanctoral chants might have consisted in a kind of proto-Common, that is, sets of psalmic chants comprising an introit, gradual, (alleluia?), offertory and communion for a particular category of saint such as martyr, virgin or pope. It might be tempting to look at the final sanctoral repertory and to speculate about which chants might have been utilized in this manner. Included, perhaps, were some of the most widely used psalmic chants: the introit *Os justi* (Ps 36.30), for example, the gradual *Beatus vir* (Ps 111.1), the offertory *Inveni David* (Ps 88.21–22) and the communion *Magna est gloria* (Ps 20.6). Still, we can only guess about this entire subject; it is entirely possible that even some of the most regularly shared psalmic chants might have originated at the time of the sanctorale's final revision.

Table 13. The Four Seventh-Century Marian Feasts

2 Feb, Purification	Intr	*Suscepimus*	2
	Grad	*Suscepimus*	1
	Off	*Diffusa est*	3
	Comm	*Responsum*	1
25 Mar, Annunciation	Intr	*Vultum tuum*	4
	Grad	*Diffusa est*	3
	Off	*Ave Maria*	1
	Comm	*Ecce virgo concipiet*	2
15 Aug, Assumption	Intr	*Vultum tuum*	4
	Grad	*Diffusa est*	3
	Off	*Diffusa est*	3
	Comm	*In salutare tuo*	3
8 Sept, Nativity	Intr	*Vultum tuum*	4
	Grad	*Diffusa est*	3
	Off	*Diffusa est*	3
	Comm	*In salutare tuo*	3

THE MARIAN FESTIVALS

At an earlier stage in this chapter it was found necessary, for the sake of presentational continuity, to postpone discussion of the four Marian feasts. There are two distinctly different aspects of the subject to be treated: the question of precisely which chants should be classified as unique or shared and the question of when the feasts might have been established in the Roman sanctoral calendar.

The first of these is introduced by table 13, which gives the incipits of the introit, gradual, offertory and communion for each date (but not alleluias because, as will be shown in the chapter on that genre, they are not yet assigned in seventh-century Rome to most liturgical occasions). Underlined incipits are considered unique—a view that might seem to be contradicted by the numbers in the last column after each incipit; these numbers refer to occurrences of the chant in question in Vat lat 5319.

To take the chants in order of their appearance on the table, the Purification's introit, *Suscepimus*, is used twice, by both the Marian date and one of the post-Pentecost Sundays, the third after the feast of the Apostles. Here it must be admitted that the Purification's use of *Suscepimus* cannot be considered unique; it appears to have been borrowed from the preexisting temporal chant. Consider the comparative likelihood of two alternative scenarios. For one, we begin with *Suscepimus deus misericordiam tuam in medio templi tui* (Ps 47.10–11), a psalmic introit that figures simply as an item within a series of numerically ordered psalmic post-Pentecostal introits. The bulk of the series is already in existence at the time that the Marian festivals are being provided with Proper chants, and the appropriateness of the *Suscepimus* text to the feast of the Purification catches the attention of those responsible for the task. The Roman singers can well imagine the words of the chant in the mouth of the saintly priest Simeon as he takes the child Jesus in his arms on the occasion of Mary's purification in the temple: "We receive, O God, thy mercy in thy temple." The text is an obvious complement to that of the feast's communion, *Responsum* (Lk 1.26), which is taken directly from Luke's narration of the event: "Simeon received a response [to his prayer] from the Holy Spirit that he would not see death before he had seen the Lord's anointed." So nice a fit were the words of the introit *Suscepimus* that not only did the members of the schola borrow the chant from the post-Pentecost Sunday, but they went on to create an entirely new gradual using the same text.

Consider briefly the alternate scenario, that of borrowing the preexisting Purification introit, *Suscepimus*, to help fill out the post-Pentecostal series of psalmic introits. Once the text *Suscepimus* has been invested with the sort of Purification associations just discussed, would it not be unseemly to remove it from its proper context and relegate it to the role of indistinguishable member within a series of psalmic texts without thematic content? And why that particular introit from literally dozens of other psalmic possibilities? One must conclude that the Purification's introit was, in all probability, borrowed from the preexisting post-Pentecostal chant; it cannot be considered unique in its Marian usage.

Next in order is the gradual *Suscepimus*, obviously a unique chant, inspired perhaps, as just suggested, by the borrowed introit of the same text. The Purification offertory, *Diffusa est*, appears three times among the Roman sanctoral chants, but a glance at the table shows that the other two occasions are the Marian feasts of the Assumption and Nativity. The obvious conclusion is that the chant was created with the Marian feasts in mind and simultaneously assigned to them; it must be categorized here as unique. The communion *Responsum* obviously is a unique chant, so that three of the Purification's four chants, its gradual, offertory and communion, are indicated on table 13 (underlined) as unique.

To turn now to the Annunciation (its introit, *Vultum tuum*, was discussed above), the chant has four appearances: three are on Marian dates and a fourth on the obviously later feast of Lucy and Geminiana; it is thus classified in its Marian assignments as unique. So too is the gradual *Diffusa est* (precisely parallel case to the offertory *Diffusa est*) and the offertory *Ave Maria*.[24]

The Annunciation's *Ecce virgo concipiet,* which appears twice in the Roman calendar, here and on the Wednesday Ember Day of Advent, is a case of considerable complexity—and one of sufficient interest to warrant extended discussion. One can, to begin with, easily assume that it is a parallel case to the Purification's introit, *Suscepimus,* that is, a preexisting temporal chant borrowed for the presumably more recent festival of the Annunciation. Its text, *Ecce virgo concipiet et pariet filium et vocabitur nomen ejus Emanuel,* appearing originally in Isaiah (7.14), is paraphrased in the gospel's narration of the Angel Gabriel's announcement to Mary: "And behold, you will conceive in your womb and bear a son and call his name Jesus" (Lk 1.31). Isaiah's verse is the ne plus ultra of Annunciation texts. If the communion that set it did in fact preexist in the temporale, its adoption into the Annunciation's Proper would have been irresistible.

But unlike the case of the Purification's introit, *Suscepimus,* the alternate scenario is not entirely implausible. The difference is that whereas *Suscepimus* lacked any measure of specific liturgical appropriateness within its original context of a numerically ordered post-Pentecostal psalmic sequence, *Ecce virgo concipiet* does have precisely that sort of meaning as a chant of the Ember Wednesday in Advent Proper. That date itself has an Annunciation theme. Its gospel, Luke 1.26–38, is the same as that of the Annunciation and its introit, *Rorate caeli,* has great poetic aptness for the Annunciation: "Drop down dew from above, ye heavens, and let the clouds rain the just one; let the earth be opened and generate a savior" (Is 45.8). Augustine already, in commenting on Psalm 84.12, *Veritas de terra orta est,* saw Mary as the Earth from which Christ, the Truth, was arisen.[25] Thus the two occasions, the Annunciation and Ember Wednesday in Advent, share an Annunciation theme; one might say the Annunciation is celebrated twice in the Roman liturgy, in Advent and again on 25 March. It could be argued in the abstract that either one or the other of the dates could have been borrower or lender of their shared communion, *Ecce virgo concipiet.*

There is one historical circumstance, however, that suggests Ember Wednesday rather than the Annunciation as the original home of *Ecce virgo concipiet.* The date appears in the Roman evangeliary of 645, with Luke's Annunciation narrative as gospel, whereas the Annunciation was introduced into the papal calendar at a later date. Thus it could be said the "first Annunciation," Ember Wednesday in Advent, was already there providing Proper chants to be borrowed when the eastern festival of the Annunciation was taken into the Roman liturgy. But festival and Proper chant formulary, as we observed in chapter five, are not contemporaneous in the period before the Roman Mass Proper received its final revision. My own view that the Proper chants of Advent date from the time of this final revision, the period of my purported Advent Project, leads me to believe that the chant Propers of Ember Wednesday in Advent and the Annunciation are roughly contemporary. I find myself indeed going so far as to entertain the thought that the Annunciation Proper might have been created just prior to those of Advent; otherwise the Ember Wednesday introit, *Rorate caeli*, would have been assigned to the Annunciation rather the less thematically appropriate *Vultum tuum* ("the wealthy among thy people shall entreat thy countenance"). Caution, however, requires that the Annunciation's use of *Ecce virgo* be classified here as shared rather than unique.

The only chant remaining to be considered is the curious case of *In salutare tuo*, the communion for three occasions, the two Marian feasts of the Assumption and Nativity and the post-Pentecostal date of the fifth Sunday after the dedication of St. Michael the Archangel. *In salutare tuo* can hardly be imagined as originally assigned to a Marian festival. It lacks any reference to a Marian theme; it belongs rather, along with *Tu mandasti domine* and *Memento verbi tui*, to a group of three communions that I have dubbed elsewhere the "justice postscript" to the post-Pentecostal series, three chants deriving their texts from Psalm 118 that express the theme of God's coming eventually to the aid of the beleaguered just man.[26] Without hesitation I classify it as a shared chant in its Marian context; indeed I am at a loss to explain its adoption for the Assumption and Nativity.[27]

In summary, it seems fair to maintain what was indicated on table 12 and again on table 13—that all four of the Marian festivals have at least three chants each that are unique in the sense that they were originally created for use on these occasions.

DATING THE MARIAN FESTIVALS

The Purification is the first of the four originally eastern feasts to be adopted into the Roman calendar. It appears in the Paduensis with its pre-Mass *ad collectam* prayer (processional oration) and its three Mass prayers, all four of which are identical to those of the Hadrianum. The festival was represented, then, in the sacramentary that came from the Lateran to St. Peter's sometime before 680. How much earlier we do not know, but some liturgical historians are inclined to place the Roman adoption of the festival as early as the reign of Pope Theodore I (642–49).[28] But, again, the point at issue here is that if the Purification has the same orations in the Paduensis and the Hadrianum, these constitute a genuine papal formulary that demonstrates papal celebration of the feast before 680.

As for the other three feasts we have two sources of information. There is the much quoted passage from the *Liber pontificalis* biography of Sergius I: "He decreed that on the day of Annunciation of the Lord, the Dormitian [Assumption] and Nativity of the Holy Mother of God, ever a virgin, and on the feast of St. Simon, which the Greeks call Hypopanti [purification], a litany would go forth from St. Hadrian's, and the people would congregate at St. Mary's."[29] And we have the prayers of the Hadrianum: an *ad collectam* prayer for each of the four feasts and Mass prayer sets for the three at issue (Annunciation, Assumption and Nativity). All of these prayers are different from those of the Paduensis; they are new ones universally acknowledged to be the work of Sergius I.[30] What bearing does all this have on the date of the three feasts? That the passage from the *Liber pontificalis* mentions only the institution of processions, and not the introduction of the feasts as such, leaves open two possibilities. For one, the prayer sets of the three that appear in the Paduensis could in fact be authentic papal creations, that is, they were in the sacramentary that was sent from the Lateran to St. Peter's sometime before 680 to form the basis of the Paduensis. This, even if they were replaced by new ones at the time that Sergius instituted the processions. Thus the Annunciation, Assumption and Nativity would already have been part of the papal sanctorale before 680.

The second possibility is that the three feasts were not yet part of the papal liturgy when the pre-680 papal sacramentary was adopted at St. Peter's and that the prayer sets of the Paduensis are not genuinely papal but were added later, perhaps by the Franks who compiled the Paduensis. If this is the case, then, the report in the *Liber pontificalis* that Sergius ordered a procession for the four feasts should be taken to imply more than it says, namely, the adoption by Sergius of the three later Marian feasts.

There is much to recommend this second possibility. Why, for example, should Sergius have found the Paduensis formulary for the Purification satisfactory but deemed it necessary to produce fresh ones for the other three feasts if those in the Paduensis were already authentically papal? It is true that he had to produce new *ad collectam* prayers for the three dates, but nevertheless the abandonment of traditional papal Mass prayers does not seem likely.

And then there is the general character of the notice in the *Liber pontificalis*. For those who would take it literally, rather than as a laconic reference to a larger liturgical innovation, there is the inconsistency of its having Sergius order a procession for a feast, the Purification, which already enjoyed one well before his time.[31] There is another inconsistency as well. We know that Sergius instituted a vigil of the Assumption on this same occasion, but it, too, is passed over in silence by the *Liber pontificalis*.[32] Thus it is not at all unlikely that Sergius introduced not just processions for the Annunciation, Assumption and Nativity but the festivals themselves.

But even if the festivals were already part of the papal sanctorale before his time, the fact that he saw fit to have new prayer sets composed for them suggests that the chant formularies might also date to the same time. Just as the addition of the Marian prayer sets, then, brought work on the Hadrianum to a close, it could be that work on the Marian chant formularies (and that of the Dedication festival, as will be seen presently) similarly came toward the completion of the Mass Proper's musical component. Perhaps a date of around 690 for both events is a plausible approximation.

THE DEDICATION FESTIVAL

The Dedication festival, it will be recalled, was the starting point for this entire chapter. The occasion, purportedly established by Boniface IV (608–615), has a set of unique Proper chants, the celebrated *Terribilis est* formulary, and has been considered by many to mark the end of the creative phase of Roman chant development that took place under Gregory I. I have shown already in this chapter that whatever the extent of Boniface's activity—he did, as the *Liber pontificalis* tells us, transform the Pantheon into a church in honor of Mary and all the martyrs—he appears not to have instituted a permanent annual commemoration of the event on 13 May. It is not recorded in the Roman evangeliary of 645; its first appearance in liturgical books is in the later seventh-century Gregorian sacramentaries.

But the question of the Dedication festival is more complex than that, and indeed considerably more interesting. The first observation to be made about it is the anomaly of dedicating the former Pantheon to Mary and all the martyrs; the transfer of honor from all the pagan gods to all the Christian martyrs is obviously appropriate, but why Mary? Theodor Klauser has an explanation for this that is both ingenious and plausible.[33] He searched through Christian liturgies West and East for a precedent that Boniface might have wished to emulate. There exists nothing of the sort in the various western liturgies, but he found a strikingly close fit in the east Syrian city of Nisibis. The great fourth-century Christian poet Ephraem speaks of a dual festival of Christ's Ascension and of all the martyrs, celebrated, moreover, on the very date of 13 May. Klauser concludes that the Syrian community of Rome brought this to the attention of a sympathetic Boniface. The substitution of Mary for the Ascension was a natural one because the Ascension was already represented in the Roman calendar, but there was no Marian festival, in contrast to several Marian dates in the eastern liturgies. The Pantheon, moreover, was centrally located as opposed to the rather remote basilica of Santa Maria Maggiore.

The second observation to make about the festival is by way of expansion on what has already been said concerning its appearance or lack thereof in liturgical books. We have noted its absence from the Roman evangeliary of 645 but not yet remarked upon the peculiar nature of its entry in the later Roman evangeliaries. Unlike every other date in these books it lacks its own gospel and has instead the following indication: *legitur lectio cuius concurrerit* [or *cuiuscumque occurrerit*] *ebdomadae eo quod semper in die dominico celebratur ipsa sollemnitas* (the gospel of the concurrent week is read since this festival is always celebrated on a Sunday). The festival thus lacks a Proper gospel and borrows instead the gospel of the Sunday on which it is celebrated. But why was it always celebrated on a Sunday, rather than on whatever day of the week 13 May happened to fall, surely a peculiar condition to place upon any sanctoral date?

The answer to this question lies, I think, in the third and decisive observation to be made about the festival: its Proper chants, and in fact its prayers and readings (when they are finally assigned) have no allusion whatsoever to Mary. They are instead focused almost exclusively on the theme of dedication. This is especially true of the magnificent chants: the introit *Terribilis est locus iste;* the gradual *Locus iste;* the alleluia *Adorabo ad templum;* the offertory *Domine deus* with its first verse, *Majestas domini aedificant templum;* and the communion *Domus mea.* This is a Mass Proper about temples and churches, a dedication formulary; it is totally lacking in reference to Mary (or for that matter to martyrs). The same is true of the epistle, a reading from the Apocalypse (21.2–5) beginning *Vidi sanctam civitatem Jerusalem novam descendentem de caelo.* . . . *Ecce tabernaculum dei cum hominibus.* This epistle, by the way, first attested to in the early Frankish "Epistolary of Alcuin," is no longer assigned to a specific 13 May festival but to a Common mass, *In dedicatione ecclesiae.* The gospel, a reading from Luke 19.1–10, tells the story of the tax collector Zacchaeus to whom Jesus says, *hodie salus domui* [!] *huic facta est;* it does not yet appear in the early Frankish sources and thus serves simply as a late confirmation of the non-Marian character of the Dedication mass formularies.

Clearly what we are witnessing here is the transformation of an occasion from the specific commemoration of the Pantheon to Mary and all the martyrs to a Common mass for the dedication of a church. The prayers of the Hadrianum represent something of a transitional stage. They have no reference to Mary, but one of them, the secret, does allude to the *martyrum . . . solemnitate*, and another, the collect, mentions the *gaudia aeterna* of those being commemorated on that day.

What it all adds up to, I believe, is that the *Terribilis est* Mass Proper may indeed represent the end of the creative phase of Roman chant production but cannot have originated at the time that Boniface IV (d.615) dedicated the Pantheon to Mary and all the martyrs. Rather it was composed when it was no longer necessary to honor Mary with a 13 May festival because the four great Marian festivals were already in place. Its history might have been something like the following. It had an early celebration on 13 May, but perhaps only a local one at the Pantheon, which accounts for the fact that the 13 May date is unrecorded in the later liturgical books. There was from the beginning something anomalous, as we have seen, about honoring Mary on this particular date, and the absence of the feast from the Roman evangeliary of 645 suggests that it no longer enjoyed an annual observance in the papal liturgy of the time. The indication of the later evangeliaries that it was always observed on a Sunday offers a hint as to the evolving nature of the date: the dedication of a new church in Rome was generally celebrated on a Sunday,[34] and this must be the explanation for the liturgical peculiarity that the festival was celebrated only on a Sunday. The prayers of the Hadrianum, as we have seen, give some indication of the changing nature of the feast: they make no mention of Mary, nor do they yet invoke the theme of dedication but retain instead a measure of reference to the martyrs.

If the evidence of the evangeliaries and sacramentaries offers only hints as to the changing character of the occasion, the chants are clear and unambiguous: they make no reference to Mary or to martyrs whatsoever but offer instead a marvelous evocation of the theme of a sacred edifice. Clearly they were created not as the Proper of a particular date but as the Common for the dedication of a church. And, again, the absence of reference to Mary surely indicates their creation at a time when it was no longer necessary to maintain a provisional Marian festival; it is easy to imagine this taking place under Sergius contemporaneously with the provisioning of the four genuine Marian days with thoroughly Marian Mass Propers.[35] Finally, the Common nature of the entire Dedication formulary—its chants, readings and prayers—is confirmed by its move in the liturgical books from its 13 May placement to a position toward the end of these documents along with the other Common Masses; one observes this already in the early Frankish epistolaries and the Roman graduals.

DATING THE SANCTORAL PROJECT

In the previous chapter the Advent Project was dated no more precisely than sometime in the later seventh century; this was done on the basis of approximately when the season of Advent might have been given its definitive form at the hands of the schola cantorum. The Sanctoral Project would seem to add a measure of refinement to the date. This would stand to reason: the Sanctoral Project, though probably begun later than the Advent Project, might have been completed at about the same time. The later chants of each project share general characteristics—a large proportion of nonpsalmic chants, for example, and the innovation of the responsory-communion— while a handful of spectacular sanctoral and post-Pentecostal offertories, which will be discussed in the chapter on that genre, appear to be among the very last chants added to the Mass Proper.

That the Sanctoral Project is late in a general sense is indicated by the circumstance that it was indeed an enterprise carried out over a limited span of time rather than something executed in separate chronological stages, and that it was characterized, as just mentioned, by later categories of chant such as nonpsalmic pieces and responsory-communions. But something approaching precision of dating is supplied by the likely proposition that the Sanctoral Project was in the process of completion in the early years of Sergius I's reign (after 687), the period when he was engaged in bringing to perfection the full cycle of four Marian feasts.

To put the argument more explicitly, much appears to converge at this very time—much liturgical activity followed by its abrupt cessation. There is the composition of the Marian prayer sets, the last to be added to the Hadrianum; similarly there are the unique chant Propers of the Marian feasts and the Dedication festival, after which there is a virtually total cutoff in sanctoral chant production. There is, moreover, the most striking affinity between the final sanctoral and temporal offertories to be added to the repertory, extraordinary chants, as we shall see, that surely represent the climax of Mass Proper creation.

And finally considerable plausibility is added to our claim when one recalls that there are only three seventh-century popes associated with ecclesiastical song in the *Liber pontificalis*, and that all three reigned during this very period. Leo II was "distinguished for his chanting and psalmody, which he interpreted elegantly and with the most sensitive and subtle touches."[36] Leo's successor Benedict II "showed himself as befitted a man worthy of his name ... in divine scripture and chant while he was still a boy."[37] And finally Sergius himself, perhaps the most liturgically active of all seventh-century popes, "because he was studious and competent in the task of chanting, was handed over to the precentor [of the schola cantorum] for education."[38] What more likely then that work on the Roman Mass Proper, both temporale and sanctorale, was brought to a climax under the leadership of these musical popes, an enterprise capped off by the creation of the splendid Dedication chants in around the year 690?

III

THE ADVENT PROJECT

CHAPTER 8

The Introit

The earliest unequivocal reference to the Roman introit is from the turn-of-the-eighth-century *Ordo romanus I,* where the chant is described in its fully developed early medieval form.[1] Consisting of an antiphon and psalm, it is sung during the entrance of the pope at the beginning of Mass. The pope, who had arrived with his retinue at the stational church of the day, vested in the *secretarium,* a kind of sacristy near the church's entrance. Meanwhile the members of the schola cantorum took their places in the nave near the sanctuary, forming two double rows of singers that faced each other, boys in front and adults behind. By the time of *Ordo I,* many Roman churches would have been equipped with the eastern architectural arrangement of the *dromos* (racecourse), an extension of the chancel barriers into the nave, which art historians are wont to call the schola cantorum. When the pope was ready, he had a signal to begin the introit relayed to the schola by way of a member of the group, the *quartus scholae,* who stood just outside the *secretarium.* The pope and attendant clergy then moved down the nave, passing between the singers. After he arrived in the sanctuary and greeted his assistants with the kiss of peace, he nodded to the schola; they, in turn, broke off the singing of the psalm and went to the *Gloria patri* and concluding repetition of the antiphon. We do not know how often the antiphon was sung at this time, whether only at the beginning and end of the psalm, or also in some alternating pattern between the verses. In any case, the singing of the introit and the procession it accompanied in early-eighth-century Rome was an elaborately developed ritual event that must have enjoyed a considerable prehistory.

ORIGINS

One can only speculate about the origins of the Roman introit.[2] We saw in chapter two that it was not yet in place during the later fourth- and earlier fifth-century period of abundant patristic liturgical reference and must therefore have been introduced sometime during the centuries of relative silence preceding *Ordo I*. There is no mention of an entrance psalm in the writings of western Church Fathers like Ambrose and Augustine, and we were, in fact, introduced above to a passage from Augustine that speaks positively against its existence. He describes a crowded church before Easter Mass at Hippo in the year 426: he enters the church from the sacristy, greets the congregation (with *Pax sit vobiscum*, or the like), and the readings begin immediately. "I greeted the people," he writes, "and when all had become silent there was the accustomed reading from the Holy Scriptures."[3]

There is no mention, similarly, of an entrance chant in the writings of eastern patristic authors such as Basil and John Chrysostom, and while there is no passage from their works quite as clear on the subject as that just quoted from Augustine, there are some that seem to imply the absence of any ritual activity before the opening greeting of the celebrant.[4] The earliest evidence of an eastern entrance chant involves the late-fifth- or early-sixth-century introduction of the Trisagion at Constantinople.[5] The Trisagion, of course, is not a variable antiphonal psalm like the Roman introit but an invariable hymn—an Ordinary item, one might say, rather than a Proper one. In subsequent centuries the Trisagion comes to be preceded by three Ordinary antiphons (and to be replaced on feasts of the Savior by Ὅσοι εἰς χριστόν and on feasts of the Holy Cross by Τόν σταυρόν), but the Byzantine entrance chants remain, nonetheless, essentially different from the contemporary Roman introit, which has some 145 variable antiphons and psalms. It is the character of the Roman introit as variable antiphonal psalmody that prompts us to seek its origin in the cradle of that genre, the monastic Office: those clerics responsible for the psalmody of the Roman Mass were daily witnesses to, perhaps even occasional participants in, the Office as sung by the monastic cadres attached to the great Roman basilicas.

In chapter five I explored the possibility that the introit's origin owed much to the Office psalmody of the basilican monks. That the monastic format of antiphonal psalmody was a model for the shape that the introit adopted remains a strong likelihood, but a search for actual repertorial concordances between the two genres was singularly disappointing.

Surely the stational system had something to do with the origins of the introit. It was probably sometime in the sixth century that the papal practice of visiting a different church on dates of special liturgical significance began, and it seems only appropriate that a musical accompaniment of some sort would have been provided for the procession of the pope and his retinue down the nave and into the sanctuary; the visit of a pope to a neighborhood church would, after all, have been an event worthy of celebration. The existence, in fact, of the elaborate introit ritual described in *Ordo I* is evidence in itself for linking the origins of the introit psalm to the papal entrance at the stational churches.

In the later sixth and earlier seventh centuries, before the schola cantorum came into existence, there must have been different practices in different churches. There might have been silence in some or, more likely, an enthusiastic response from the faithful to the repeated greeting of "peace" from the pope as he moved through the crowded church to the sanctuary. In those basilicas with a monastery attached, it could very well have been customary from the beginning for the monks to sing an antiphonal psalm during the pope's entrance. These are, in fact, the great churches like St. Peter's and St. Mary Major, where the principal feasts were celebrated by the pope, and festive musical activity might be expected within their spacious confines. And perhaps the example of the monastic choirs would have prompted the Lateran clergy who accompanied the pope to imitate the monastic practice at the many smaller churches where there were no monks in residence. We have no way of knowing how close any of these speculations approach what actually happened, but two covering generalizations are plausible enough: (1) the singing of a psalm was probably an increasingly normal practice during the later sixth and earlier seventh centuries; and (2) the development of the usage would have followed the long-term liturgical tendency, described above in chapter one, of moving from the ritually free and spontaneous to the unified and regularized.

If it is disappointing, as remarked above, that there is virtually no repertorial continuity between the antiphonal psalmody of the monastic office and the introit, this conclusion is not without its own merit. It supports the broader claim put forth in this volume that the creation of the Roman Mass Proper was more a matter of concerted effort over a relatively confined span of time than a matter of centuries-long evolution. And there are in fact indications that this claim applies to the introit with particular appropriateness. For one thing, there is the music of the introit, characterized by the complementary traits of stylistic homogeneity and melodic individuality, and, for another, the seeming perfection of the annual cycle with a unique chant assigned to virtually every date in the temporale and an even-handed apportionment of unique chants over the sanctorale. We search the genre in vain for some chink in the armor, some seam in the garment, that might betray its creators at work and thus provide evidence of chronological layering. At least this is one's initial impression.

INTROITS: MELODICALLY HOMOGENEOUS AND INDIVIDUAL

The 144 introits of the core repertory (those shared by the Roman and Frankish sources) are notably uniform in style, never starkly syllabic nor extravagantly melismatic, but rather consistently neumatic with only the occasional melisma or brief syllabic passage.[6] The same sort of moderation is evident in their length; they are rarely as short as the first Mass of Christmas' *Dominus dixit,* and not very often as long as the feast of John the Baptist's *De ventre matris,* which is exceeded in this respect, curiously enough, only by the vigil of that same day's *Ne timeas Zachariae.* Nor do they manifest extremes in their ambitus; they are typically an octave or a seventh in range, less often a sixth, and only occasionally less than a sixth or more than an octave. These characteristics are shared by the Gregorian and Old Roman versions, so that it seems safe to attribute them to the original Roman melodies as well.

What is truly remarkable in view of this stylistic homogeneity is the fact that virtually every introit has an individual (hereafter "unique") melody. There are no model melodies like the alleluia's *Dies sanctificatus,* nor are there closely related melodic groups like the A-mode and F-mode graduals and the G-mode tracts. Neither are there extended melodic formulas that reappear from introit to introit (not in the Gregorian versions, that is; the question of formulaicism in the Roman versions will be taken up below in a "digression" on the subject). It is true that there are brief cadential figures that are shared by many introits; these, however, are not melodic formulas in the accepted sense, that is, distinctive passages that are clearly recognized as such when transferred from one chant to the next, but simply idiomatic fragments of the respective tonal languages of Roman and Frankish chant. Something of the same might be said of certain opening gestures like the characteristic mode-1 motif of the introit *Factus est* (example 1), given here in its corresponding Gregorian and Roman forms; while it appears in several introits, it is also very common in Office antiphons and is occasionally met with in offertories.[7]

The melodic uniqueness of the Gregorian introits is so extraordinarily consistent that those slight deviations from it that do exist invite comment. I have observed but two myself (I exclude from consideration, of course, late Gregorian contrafacta like the appropriation of the Epiphany's *Ecce ad-*

Example 1. Introit *Factus est*

venit for the Marian *Salve sancta parens*). The first of these involves *Eduxit eos dominus* and *Eduxit dominus*, the introits, respectively, of the Friday and Saturday in Easter week; their openings are nearly identical except for the extra notes required to set the word *eos* in the first of the pair (example 2). The melodies go their own way after their common start and in the process give us a brief glimpse of the schola cantorum at work on the introit cycle. The singers choose texts that begin similarly for successive days in Easter week and decide upon a common opening motif for the two, but after doing so they return to their policy of creating unique melodies for each and every introit. (One should not, incidentally, fail to be struck by the fact that the Roman and Gregorian versions, while different, maintain their respective formulas in precisely the same way; I shall comment on this frequently encountered phenomenon—what I call formulaic "analogy"—in the promised digression on the subject of formulas in Roman introits.)

In the second example, involving the introits *Da pacem domine* and *Statuit ei dominus* (example 2), nearly the entire first half of each chant is melodically identical. The remainder of each, however, bears no relationship to the other, thus providing an example parallel to that of *Eduxit eos* and *Eduxit dominus*, except for the circumstance that the common portions of this second example are so much longer. But does the example afford us a similar glimpse of the schola cantorum at work? The first is unmistakably the result of deliberate action on the part of the singers, involving, as it does, closely related texts on successive days of the church year, but the second involves dissimilar texts and different segments of the church year—*Da pacem* is from the second Sunday after the Dedication of St. Michael and *Statuit* from the 16 January feast of Pope Marcellus. I am content to look upon the case of these two chants as an interesting anomaly, or at least something beyond my own powers of explanation.

To summarize, the stylistic homogeneity and melodic uniqueness of the

Example 2. Introits with similar openings

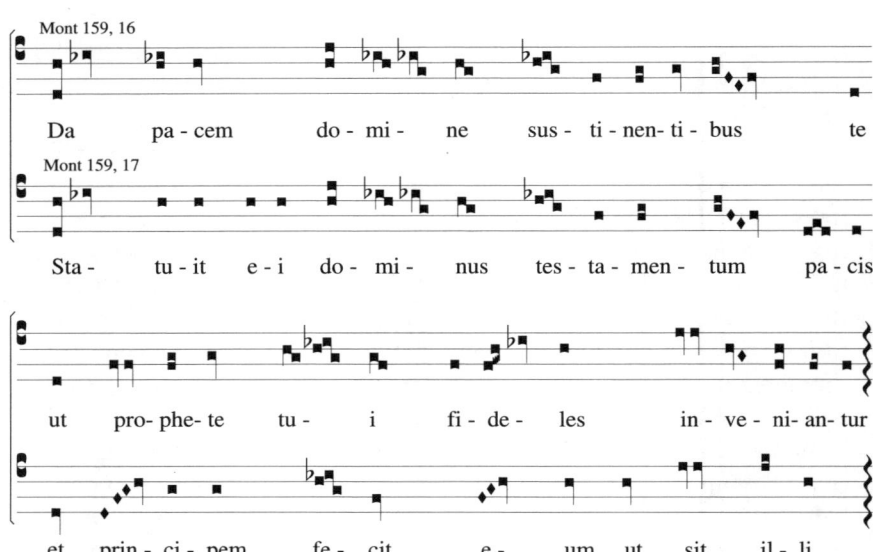

introit repertory (at least as manifested in the Gregorian versions) frustrate any attempt on the part of a scholar to detect chronological layering within the genre. This, in contrast to a genre like the gradual, for example, where we see the A-mode and F-mode chants laid out in a liturgically significant sequence, or the communion, where we see antiphon-like and responsory-like chants that are, in fact, Office antiphons and responsories borrowed to bring the annual cycle to completion. But, again, the seamless garment of the introit repertory might point to the equally significant chronological conclusion that it is the work of a single generation of singers. A similar line of thought will be pursued for the second major aspect of the introit's

The Introit / 201

repertory—the manner of its liturgical assignment throughout the liturgical year. But first a digression on the subject of formulaic usage in the Roman versions of the genre.

A DIGRESSION: FORMULAIC USAGE IN THE ROMAN INTROIT

The melodic uniqueness, or individuality, of introits is not absolute; there are just enough exceptions to the trait to require serious attention to the subject. There are, in fact, two quite distinct topics to discuss: that referred to above as formulaic, or figural, "analogy" between the Gregorian and Roman versions; and the larger matter of formulaic usage that is confined to the Roman versions. Both are questions more appropriate to our epilogue on the musical aftermath of the Advent Project, yet they must be dealt with here to the extent that they qualify the purported melodic uniqueness of the introit.

Formulaic analogy is a fascinating phenomenon. It was present in all three musical examples so far provided in this chapter. Take the first, the opening gesture of the mode-1 Gregorian *Factus est* (example 1), with its distinctive leap of a fifth from D to a. It is utterly different from the Roman oscillation on a-b, yet the Roman figure typically appears whenever the Gregorian one does.[8] There is a variation on the pair of figures that makes their analogous behavior all the more striking (example 3). When the Gregorian figure has the leap of a fifth preceded by a CD, as in *Gaudeamus*, the corresponding Roman chants typically begin themselves with the opening fifth, but not the preceding CD.[9] There is a certain logic to the difference between the two pairs of figures, having to do with word accents.[10] The group of chants represented by example 3 begins with an unaccented syllable followed immediately by an accented one. Thus the opening Gregorian D to a and the corresponding Roman a-b regularly fall on an accented syllable, and the opening Gregorian CD and Roman D regularly fall on an unaccented syllable. Thus the analogous usage between the two versions is even more remarkable than at first thought to be the case.

The phenomenon would seem to defy the common sense of oral transmission. It is almost as if we have Roman and Frankish cantors conferring with each other and deciding that when one group uses one figure the other will use their own version of it, whereas we would expect the two bodies of singers to go their own way and to develop the contrasting melodic surfaces of their chant in a free and unpredictable fashion. But just how consistent is the phenomenon? Consistent enough, as we shall see in the coming chapters, particularly in a heavily formulaic genre like the gradual, to

Example 3. Introit *Gaudeamus*

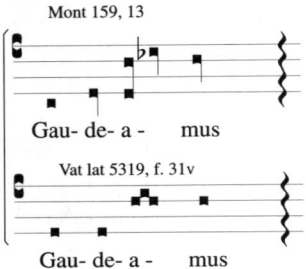

arouse a full measure of wonder and curiosity, at least on the part of the present author.

ROMAN INTROIT FORMULAICISM: PASCHALTIME

A more serious threat to the claim of the introit's melodic uniqueness is posed by the larger matter of melodic formulas that appear exclusively in the Roman versions. It can, after all, be argued that these were present in the original Roman melodies and subsequently purged from them by the Frankish cantors.[11] Such Roman formulaicism is considerably more common in Paschaltime, in both the temporale and the sanctorale, than at any other time in the church year; table 14 provides the most important instances of the trait in that season.[12] The second column gives the incipits of those chants that open with a formulaic passage; an ellipsis indicates a lack of formulaicism. The next column refers to the alleluia inserted in the middle of a Paschaltime introit, with the number after the alleluia designating one of seven different Roman formulas. The text that follows gives the words that are set formulaically in the second half of the chant. Finally, there is the concluding alleluia and the Roman final and Gregorian mode.

The formulaicism of the Roman Paschaltime introits boasts a number of interesting tendencies. The most prominent of these is that the more important liturgical occasions such as Easter, the feast of Philip and James, Ascension and Pentecost are relatively free of melodic formulas, whereas ferias, ordinary Sundays and lesser sanctoral dates employ them regularly. Noteworthy also, indeed remarkable, is the thorough integration of the sanctoral introits into the overall picture presented by the temporal chants.[13] The presence of alleluias in the introit texts of Paschaltime is an added factor in the quantity of formulaicism in the season; they are clearly an invitation to employ formulas. Finally, the overwhelming prevalence of the same

Table 14. Melodic Formulas in Roman Paschaltime Introits

Easter	...	...	...	...	E-4
Monday	...	...	...	...	G-8
Tuesday	...	...	...	all 4	E-7
Wednesday	...	...	...	all 4	E-7
Thursday	...	all 1	...	all 4	E-8
Friday	Eduxit eos—	all 2	inimicus eorum	all 4	B-4
Saturday	Eduxit dns—	all 2	in laetitie	all 5	C-7
Low Sunday	...	...	...	all 6	C-6
Easter II	...	...	...	all 4	B-4
Easter III	Jubilate deo	...	...	all 4	E-8
Easter IV	Vocem ioc	all 1	...	all 4	E-3
Easter V	Cantate dno—	all 2	fecit dominus	all 4	B-6
14 Apr—Tiburtius & Valerian	Sancti tui	all 1	...	all 4	E-3
15 Apr—Litany	Exaudivit	all 1	...	all 7	E-4
23 Apr—George	Protexisti	all 3	...	all 4	E-7
1 May—Philip & James	...	...	...	all 6	G-1
3 May—Alexander & Theodulus	Clamaverunt	all 3	...	all 7	E-2
12 May—Pancratius & Nereus	Ecce oculi	all 3	...	all 4	E-3
Ascension	...	...	...	all 6	G-7
Sunday	...	...	...	all 7	C-1
Pentecost	...	...	...	all 6	C-8
Monday	Cibavit eos—	all 2	saturavit eos	all 5	C-2
Tuesday	Accipite	all 1	...	all 7	E-4
Wednesday	Deus dum	all 1	iter facientes ei all	all 7	E-3
Friday	Repleatur	all 1	ut possim cantare all	all 4	E-3
Saturday	...	all 1	per inhabitantem	all 4	E-3

final, E, in these chants is surely related to their formulaic propensity; fifteen of the twenty-six have their final on E and three more on the other deuterus final, b.

Perhaps the most interesting of the more particular observations involves *Eduxit eos* and *Eduxit dominus*, the chants that we singled out above

204 / The Advent Project

Example 4. Introits *Deus dum egredereris* and *Jubilate deo*

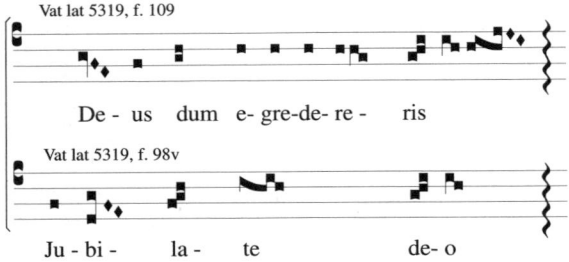

as a case of formulaic analogy in Roman and Gregorian chant. In the Gregorian versions only the opening melodic gesture is shared by the two chants, and only the two chants are involved, but in the Roman versions there is a particularly thoroughgoing application of formulaic treatment. To start with, there are no less than five chants with the shared opening (indicated in table 14 by underlining), and four of the five continue with a few words on a common recitation formula (indicated in the table by dashes), followed by a common inserted alleluia ("all 2"); and then in the latter half of the chant there appear a few words on a common figure (underlined on the table). Curiously, two of the four chants have the very common concluding alleluia "all 4," rather than the expected "all 5," which is unique to the type.[14]

Even more common than the opening gesture of the two *Eduxit*'s is one indicated in table 14 by those incipits that are not underlined (see example 4); there are nine instances of it in Paschaltime, ranging from the third Sunday after Easter's *Jubilate deo* to Pentecost Friday's *Repleatur os meum*. The figure furnishes another illustration of the point made above about how the Roman versions adapt to differing word accents. Example 4 provides an example of a chant beginning on an accented syllable, *Deus dum egredereris*, and one where the accent seems to fall most strongly on the third syllable, *Jubilate deo*;[15] in the latter circumstance the distinctive three-note descending neume is always preceded by a single note, thus rendering the entire group of four into a kind of "upbeat." Even more strikingly consistent about this figure is that the version beginning on an accented syllable always continues with the syllabic material illustrated here, while the version beginning with the upbeat group continues with the corresponding neumatic material.

The *Eduxit* figure and the one just discussed (let us call it the *Jubilate* figure) account for a large proportion of the Paschaltime introits, well over half of those assigned to ferias, ordinary Sundays and lesser sanctoral dates.

Are they equally well represented outside of Paschaltime? The *Eduxit* figure, appearing five times during the Easter season, is used only once outside the period, for *Exultate deo*, the introit for Wednesday in the September Ember Days; and the *Jubilate* figure, used eight times during the Easter season, is used only three times outside the period, for three weekday Lenten chants, *Sicut oculi*, *Reminiscere* and *Deus in nomine tuo*. This last group illustrates a peculiarity of the Roman use of opening figures, something observed already with the *Eduxit* pair—the tendency, not surprising, to use the same figure for chants that open with similar words. Thus *Ecce oculi* of Paschaltime is matched by the Lenten *Sicut oculi* and *Deus dum egredereris* of Paschaltime is matched by the Lenten *Deus in nomine*.

The relative absence of the *Eduxit* and *Jubilate* figures outside of Paschaltime provides further evidence of that season's special propensity for formulaic usage, and so too does what is perhaps the most striking instance of the practice indicated in table 14. I refer to the last three introits of the season, which share their melodic material for a significant portion of the second half of each chant.

The season of Lent provides a challenge, if a minor one, to Paschaltime's monopoly on introit formulaicism. There is one group of five chants with a common beginning that extends beyond the incipit,[16] and a similarly endowed group of three that, interestingly enough, has the same opening word, *Ego*.[17] As far as quantities are concerned, one observes, then, eight formulaic Lenten introits from a total of thirty-seven chants (see below for this latter figure) and fourteen Paschaltime introits from a total of twenty-six. More significant than such figures, however, is the liturgical placement of the formulaic chants. The eight Lenten examples are scattered unsystematically throughout the season, whereas the Paschaltime ones, as observed above, are used for ordinary Sundays and ferias as opposed to more festive dates.

PASCHALTIME FORMULAICISM: ROMAN VERSUS GREGORIAN

Gregorian Paschaltime introits are totally free from formulaic usage except for a handful of shared opening figures and shared alleluias. The *Eduxit* pair has been mentioned above more than once; its special significance is that it is the only case where a Gregorian opening figure extends to a third word, whereas Roman opening formulas regularly extend to three or four. The Gregorian *Vocem iocunditatis* and *Ecce oculi* utilize a fairly common mode-3 opening figure that, needless to say, is not followed by additional formulaic material. The alleluias are of special interest. One would expect them—the single one inserted in the middle of the chant and the group of two or three added at the end—to employ stock tunes. As someone who sang Gregorian introits every Sunday for much of my youth and early adulthood, I find many of the alleluia melodies to be familiar and had always assumed that they consisted in a set of standard formulas, one for each mode. In the preparation of this chapter, however, I was surprised by their virtually endless melodic variety. Take, for example, just the single inserted alleluias of the mode-3 introits; there are six such introits in Paschaltime and six distinct alleluia tunes. For all the chants in all the modes there are a total of over sixty melodies for the inserted and added alleluias. A certain amount of repetition with these tuneful exclamations is of course inevitable; yet it remains remarkable to what extent they partake of the overall melodic uniqueness and variety of the Gregorian introit.

Roman introits themselves, to put the matter in larger perspective, are comparatively unformulaic when compared to a genuinely formulaic genre like the gradual or tract; it is only when matched against the Gregorian introits that they can be said to manifest the trait to any significant extent. But it is introits that concern us at present, not graduals or tracts, and what is one to make of the difference between the Roman and Gregorian versions in this respect? What historical conclusions does the contrast suggest?

There are two equally plausible positions that one might adopt. For one, it could be argued that the formulaic character of the Roman versions was present in the original Roman chants transmitted to Francia, and that the Frankish cantors purged it from the chants, rendering each introit a unique and individual melody. For the other, it could be maintained that the original Roman introits were free of formulaic usage and that they acquired this trait in the course of their centuries-long history of oral transmission.

There are at least three reasons why the latter view is more likely. The first has to do with the Roman Paschaltime introit texts. There is, as we shall see below, nothing in them to parallel the sort of expedients undertaken in the Roman Paschaltime music in an apparent effort to have the season completed expeditiously. They manifest, rather, the same obvious care to provide each date of the season with the same sort of individually suitable texts as there are in the other festal season of the introit cycle, Advent-Christmas. And when we turn to the music of the Gregorian Paschaltime introits we witness a total lack of musical patterns and tendencies. In a word, the extant Roman musical versions of the Paschaltime introits are a bad fit with the entire festal layer of the introit. They fail to match the compositional approach of the Paschaltime texts, the Gregorian Paschaltime melodies, the Advent-Christmas texts and the Gregorian and Roman Advent-Christmas melodies. Their formulaic tendency, then, would seem to be anomalous in every respect and to have been the product of a different period from that of the original Roman introit temporale.

The Paschaltime sanctorale contributes to this impression. The Roman sanctoral melodies share the temporal chants' tendencies. They manifest them, in fact, in the most extreme manner: every sanctoral introit (except that for the major feast of Philip and James) is in E-mode; every introit has the same opening figure and has formulaic alleluias. When the body of Roman Paschaltime introits, both temporal and sanctoral, are viewed in liturgical succession (in the order of Vat lat 5319), it is obvious that their melodies are the product of a single continuous effort. But we saw in the previous chapter that the sanctorale, when examined in its entirety over the annual cycle, is altogether lacking in indications of different compositional policies for different times of the year. I do not believe that one could find another instance in the entire Mass Proper, within any of its chant genres, of the sort of fit that there is between the sanctoral and temporal melodies of the Roman Paschaltime introits. Again, these melodies appear foreign to what we should expect of the original Roman introit cycle.

The third and final point of this series has to do with the transmission of the Roman chant to the Carolingian north. Does it not seem improbable that the Frankish cantors, in their strenuous efforts to capture the Roman melodic idiom, would have ignored an entire system of modal economy and formulaic usage in the Paschaltime chants? Surely it is more likely that they would have used it as an aid to their formidable task. And one must keep in mind that those chant genres with undeniably formulaic origins—graduals and tracts—are comparably formulaic in both the Roman and Gregorian versions. Perhaps there is no more compelling argument than this for the anomalous status of the Roman Paschaltime melodic versions.

The contrast between the formulaicism of the Roman Paschaltime introits and the Gregorian lack thereof obviously involves the central question of Gregorian chant and will be taken up again in our epilogue. For now the issue at hand is the apparently seamless garment of the annual introit cycle.

INTROITS: THE FLAWLESS ANNUAL CYCLE

There were 102 dates with assigned introits in the Roman temporal cycle of the later seventh century, and there were 101 temporal introits in existence at the time. The single shared chant is not surprising: the vigil of the Epiphany borrows *Lux fulgebit* from the second mass of Christmas.[18] This record of unique assignment stands in contrast to the deficiencies of graduals, offertories and alleluias in this respect. I count 74 graduals for 99 assignments, and 92 offertories for 103 assignments. Roman alleluias, of course, in the neighborhood of just 50, are assigned for only a small minority of liturgical occasions.

Communions, as has been pointed out several times in these pages, share this trait of fully unique assignment with the introit; there are, according to my reckoning, 102 temporal communions for 103 assignments (the first Sunday after Pentecost borrows *Narrabo* from Lent). But there is a fundamental difference between the two cycles. That of the communion is remarkable throughout for evidence of compositional planning, not just in the numerical series of weekday Lenten communions, a matter of general knowledge among chant scholars, but also in the less obvious sets and sequences of related chants that characterize the Christmas and Easter seasons and even the post-Pentecostal period. Nothing of the sort is apparent in the introit temporale; each date in the cycle is provided with a unique and appropriate chant in a seemingly isolated act of liturgical assignment. There are, for example, no sets of prophetic chants laid out in contrast to sets of gospel chants, no modally ordered series of chants and no numerically ordered sequences of psalmic chants (the seeming exception of the numerically ordered post-Pentecostal introits will be dealt with below).

That this trait of the introit—the unique homogeneity of its annual cycle —is suggestive of particularly concentrated work on the genre is a hypothesis to be considered at the close of this chapter. For now a few more general remarks about the character of the introit temporale.

ADVENT, CHRISTMAS, LENT, AND PASCHALTIME

The Advent-Christmas introits are presented in table 15; their incipits are given along with the scriptural derivation of the texts; an asterisk after an incipit indicates an instance of substantial textual adjustment. The chants have the characteristics one expects from an Advent-Christmas sequence that was assembled during the period of the Advent Project. All the temporal chants are uniquely assigned except for the above mentioned *Lux fulgebit* (in square brackets) of the Epiphany's vigil mass. The feasts of Stephen, John the Evangelist and the Innocents are given the conventional classification of temporal dates, a status confirmed both by traditional placement in the liturgical books and by their uniquely assigned introits. The vigil of John the Evangelist's *Ego autem* and Sylvester's *Sacerdotes eius* (in parentheses) are better considered sanctoral items; the former appears twice in the Roman Mass antiphoner and the latter five times.

Table 15. Roman Advent-Christmas Introits

Advent I	*Ad te levavi*	Ps 24.1–4
Advent II	*Populus sion**	Is 30.19–20
Advent III	*Gaudete in domino**	Phil 4.4–7
Ember Wednesday	*Rorate caeli*	Is 45.8
Ember Friday	*Prope esto*	Ps 118.151
Ember Saturday	*Veni et ostende**	Ps 79.4
Vigil Xmas	*Hodie scietis**	Ex 16.6–7
Xmas I	*Dominus dixit*	Ps 2.7
Xmas II	*Lux fulgebit**	Is 9.2, Lk 1.33
Xmas III	*Puer natus est**	Is 9.6
Stephen	*Etenim sederunt**	Ps 118.23, 86
Vigil John	*(Ego autem)*	(Ps 51.10–11)
John Evangelist	*In medio ecclesiae*	Sir 15.5
Innocents	*Ex ore infantium*	Ps 8.3
Sylvester	*(Sacerdotes eius)*	(Ps 131.16)
Sunday	*Dum medium*	Wis 18.14–15
Vigil Eph	*[Lux fulgebit]*	
Epiphany	*Ecce advenit**	Mal 3.1
Eph I	*Omnis terra*	Ps 65.4
Eph II	*In excelso throno**	Dn 7.9, Is 6.1
Eph III	*Adorate deum*	Ps 96.7–8

Every one of the temporal chants (with the obvious exception of the three Sundays after the Epiphany) has the most explicit thematic suitability to its liturgical occasion, whether it be Advent's *Veni et ostende,* Christmas' *Puer natus est* or Epiphany's *Ecce advenit.* Such appropriateness is greatly aided by the high instance of nonpsalmic texts (ten from nineteen of the temporal dates), but the Roman singers found any number of just as obviously fitting texts in the psalms as well—Ember Friday's *Prope esto* (Ps 118.151), for example, and the Innocents' *Ex ore infantium* (Ps 8.3). The thematic appropriateness of the texts is further enhanced by an extraordinary application of textual adjustment. Nine of the eighteen uniquely assigned chants are examples of the practice, with a number of them, such as *Populus sion, Hodie scietis* and *Lux fulgebit,* being instances of the most extreme form of scriptural paraphrase.

Lent, of course, as a nonfestal portion of the church year, presents little opportunity for thematically appropriate chants and must utilize for the most part psalmic chants of a general nature.[19] Still there are six non-psalmic Lenten introits, which are used to good advantage in helping to define the character of their assigned dates. There is, for example, Laetare Sunday's *Laetare Hierusalem* (Is 66.10–11) and Wednesday and Saturday of the fourth week's *Dum sanctificatus* (Ex 36.23–26) and *Sitientes venite* (Is 55.1), chants related to the baptismal Scrutinies (Latin *Scrutinium*).[20]

More significant, perhaps, is the near absolute incidence of uniquely assigned chants. Aside from Holy Thursday's *Nos autem*, every Lenten introit appears to have been originally intended for its place in the final sequence. (This excludes, of course, the six introits borrowed in about 720 to supply the Thursdays with chants.) There are, in sum, thirty-seven different Lenten introits at the time of the Advent Project, thirty-two psalmic and five nonpsalmic (*Salus populi*, the nonscriptural chant, it will be remembered, is a late borrowing). One wonders how many of the nonpsalmic thirty-two were part of the fund of pre-Advent Project chants. We can only guess, of course, but the rather high proportion of Lenten introits specifically targeted for particular dates suggests that there might have been a fairly large number of new introits created at the time of the Advent Project to provide an individual chant for each day. Perhaps about twenty chants in the earlier general list is a plausible surmise.

The incipits of the Paschaltime temporal introits are given in table 16, along with their textual derivations (inside square brackets); examples of substantial textual adjustment have an asterisk after the incipit. There are twenty-one chants in the series, uniquely assigned without exception. Ten of the twenty-one are nonpsalmic, attesting to the effort to achieve texts that are liturgically appropriate to each date. The effort is aided by the considerable use of textual adjustment, even if its application is not quite as extreme as it is for the Advent-Christmas season. Several of the texts are especially apt, particularly when the character of the feast day lends itself to thematically suitable texts. Thus, for example, there is Easter's *Resurrexi*, Ascension's *Viri Galilei*, and Pentecost's *Spiritus domini*. All in all, however, Paschaltime is not quite as rich in such occasions as the Advent-Christmas season, so that the reference of text and the date is not always as direct. None of the texts, however, is ever inappropriate to the joyous nature of the season, and one cannot but admire the truly splendid choice of Pentecost Saturday, bringing Paschaltime and indeed the entire festal portion of the year to a fitting close: *Karitas dei diffusa est in cordibus vestris, alleluia; per inhabitantem spiritum eius in vobis, alleluia alleluia* (Rom 5.5).

The case for the "seamless" quality of the introit cycle is manifest in the three portions of the church year just presented; there is no evidence of the

Table 16. Roman Temporal Paschaltime Introits

Easter	*Resurrexi**	Ps 138.18 [5–6]
Monday	*Introduxit**	Ex 13.5 [9]
Tuesday	*Aqua sapientiae**	Sir 15.3–4
Wednesday	*Venite benedicti*	Mt 25.34
Thursday	*Vitricem*	Wis 10.20–21
Friday	*Eduxit eos*	Ps 77.53
Saturday	*Eduxit dominus*	Ps 104.43
Low Sunday	*Sicut modo*	1 Pt 2.2
Easter II	*Misericordia*	Ps 32.5–6
Easter III	*Jubilate deo*	Ps 65.1–2
Easter IV	*Vocem iocunditatis*	Is 48.20
Easter V	*Cantate domino**	Ps 97.1
Litany	*Exaudivit de templo*	Ps 17.7
Ascension	*Viri Galilei**	Acts 1.11
Sunday	*Exaudi domine**	Ps 26.7–9
Pentecost	*Spiritus domini*	Wis 1.7
Monday	*Cibavit eos*	Ps 80.17
Tuesday	*Accipite iocunditatem*	4 Esdr 2.36–37
Wednesday	*Deus dum egredereris**	Ps 67.8–9 [20]
Friday	*Repleatur os meum**	Ps 70.8 [23]
Saturday	*Karitas dei*	Rom 5.5

sort of prearranged strategies that characterize the communions in particular. But do not the numerically arranged psalmic introits of the post-Pentecostal series introduce this trait into the introit temporale?

THE POST-PENTECOSTAL SERIES

Table 17 represents the combined Roman and Frankish post-Pentecostal sequence plus the September Ember Days (after Lawrence VI). There are twenty-three chants in the post-Pentecostal set, twenty-two in the original Roman series and the added *Omnes gentes* of the Frankish seventh Sunday after Pentecost. The traditional style of Roman numbering is indicated in the column on the left: four Sundays after Pentecost (more precisely four Sundays after the octave of Pentecost, itself a DOMINICA VACANS);[21] five Sundays after the 29 June feast of the Apostles Peter and Paul; six after the 10 August feast of St. Lawrence and seven after the 29 September feast of the Dedication of the Basilica of St. Michael the Archangel. The Franks

Table 17. Post-Pentecostal Introits, Roman and Gregorian

Pentecost I	I	*Domine in tua*	Ps 12.6
Pent II	II	*Factus est dominus*	Ps 17.19–20
Pent III	III	*Respice in me**	Ps 24.16, 18
Pent IV	IV	*Dominus illuminatio**	Ps 26.1–2
Apostles I	V	*Exaudi domine**	Ps 26.7, 9
Apost II	VI	*Dominus fortitudo*	Ps 27.8–9
	[VII	*Omnes gentes*	Ps 46.2]
Apost III	VIII	*Suscepimus*	Ps 47.10–11
Apost IV	IX	*Ecce deus**	Ps 53.6–7
Apost V	X	*Dum clamarem**	Ps 54.17–23
Lawrence I	XI	*Deus in loco**	Ps 67.6, 36
Lawr II	XII	*Deus in adj*	Ps 69.2–3
Lawr III	XIII	*Respice domine**	Ps 73.19–23
Lawr IV	XIV	*Protector noster*	Ps 83.10–11
Lawr V	XV	*Inclina domine**	Ps 85.1–3
Lawr VI	XVI	*Miserere, ad te**	Ps 85.3–5
Sept Wednesday		*Exultate deo**	Ps 80.2–5
Sept Friday		*Laetetur cor*	Ps 104.3–4
Sept Saturday		*Venite adoremus**	Ps 94.6–7
Angel I	XVII	*Justus es domine**	Ps 118.137, 34
Angel II	XVIII	*Da pacem domine**	Eccl 36.18
Angel III	XIX	[*Salus populi*]	nonbibl
Angel IV	XX	*Omnia que fecisti**	Dn 3.29–42
Angel V	XXI	*In voluntate**	Est 13.9–11
Angel VI	XXII	*Si iniquitates*	Ps 129.3–4
Angel VII	XXIII	*Dicit dominus**	Jer 29.11–14

substituted the consecutively numbered series of twenty-three Sundays (indicated by the column of Roman numerals); to bring the number to twenty-three, they added a complete liturgy, inserting it after the sixth formulary of the Roman series.

Twenty-three is the minimum number of Sundays that occur in a given year, and twenty-six the maximum, depending upon the date of Easter. The Frankish system accommodates these requirements in a less complex manner than the Roman. The twenty-three formularies are run through consecutively and then the twenty-third is repeated as often as necessary. In the Roman system such adjustments are made within the four segments of the season; a formulary might have to be repeated in a given year in one or the other of the three later divisions, while the one following immediately after Pentecost would be subject to change virtually every year. Three is the minimum number of Sundays in the period and six the maximum, and since the first of these is a DOMINICA VACANS, anywhere from two to five chant formularies are needed each year. With four available, one would have to be duplicated occasionally (about six times a century), and more often one or the other would not be sung.

In any event it is the series of numerically ordered psalmic introits at the beginning of the season that concerns us at present. If one eliminates from consideration the added Frankish *Omnes gentes,* there is a series of sixteen such chants, followed by a group of six with mixed textual derivation. Extravagant claims have been made for the significance of the set of sixteen. For one, it is regularly compared to the numerical sequence of the weekday Lenten communions. The two are thought to reflect a particular manner of chant creation and hence to belong to the same chronological period—an especially early period in keeping with the common assumption that the weekday Lenten communions represent a particularly early layer of chant. What is wrong with the comparison is the notion that the two series are of essentially the same kind. There is a fundamental difference between items numbered consecutively from 1 to 26, as are the Lenten communions, and those numbered, for example, 12, 17, 24, 26, etc., as are the post-Pentecostal introits (see tables 17, 34). Clearly the former is the product of an a priori plan, while the latter is more likely to be the result of a numerical ordering of previously existing items (or in an exceptional instance of more or less new material). In the case at hand, that of the post-Pentecostal introits, it is true that this could very plausibly be a matter of separating sixteen older psalmic chants from a smaller set of later nonpsalmic chants and ordering the former group numerically. Such an arrangement, however, would constitute a violation of the previously claimed "seamless garment" for the introit's temporal cycle. And, as we shall see, the surprisingly high proportion of textual adjustment in the post-Pentecostal psalmic introits speaks strongly against their preexistence as a body of ancient psalmic chants for general use. The separation involved, then, could be merely one of roughly contemporaneous psalmic from nonpsalmic material—this, to conform to the general practice of utilizing numerically ordered psalmic sequences for all post-Pentecostal items of the Mass Proper. A gesture of this sort would conform well to the dictates of the Advent Project.

More on the idea of textual adjustment presently, but to return to the notion of an ancient (indeed pre-Gregorian) numerically ordered group of sixteen psalmic introits, Antoine Chavasse is its chief protagonist.[22] He paired the sixteen introits with the sixteen prayer sets for ordinary Sundays of the Old Gelasian sacramentary and went on to find supposedly analogous sequences of sixteen chants at the beginning of the post-Pentecostal series of the other items of the Mass Proper. Finally, by claiming that the resultant set of sixteen prayer and chant formularies was repeated each year, he was able to match it with sequences of thirty-two epistles and gospels that he managed to reconstruct from the lectionaries. Thus the precise number of liturgies necessary to cover the ordinary Sundays of the year was achieved (a total of twenty-nine for the post-Epiphany and post-Pentecost Sundays, four for Advent and one subtracted for the DOMINICA VACANS following the September Ember Days). There are many problems with this ingenious scheme, of which I will mention but two here. For one, the purported groups of sixteen chants in the Mass Proper items other than the introit are simply not there to be found. And more important, the notion that the Old Gelasian's sixteen generic prayer sets were permanently assigned to specific Sundays is anachronistic; they were rather a fund of formularies that were simply available for use on ordinary Sundays at a time before the Sundays after Pentecost and after the Epiphany had been assigned Proper orations. In all probability what one has in the sixteen prayer sets of the Old Gelasian and the sixteen numerically ordered psalmic chants of the Roman post-Pentecostal introit cycle is a coincidence—an intriguing coincidence, to be sure, but nothing more.

What are we, then, to make of the Roman post-Pentecostal introit series with its structure of sixteen numerically ordered psalmic chants followed by a miscellaneous block of six (which includes, it should be noted, the psalmic *Si iniquitates*)? First off, the most noteworthy feature of the sequence as a whole is that it comprises a set of twenty-two uniquely assigned chants (indeed twenty-five including those of the Ember Days), a further testimony to the extraordinary completeness of the introit's annual cycle.

As for the significance of the number of sixteen numerically ordered psalmic chants, it appears to be merely coincidental because it is not duplicated in the other chant genres. There are numerically ordered series of post-Pentecostal offertories and communions, but not of precisely sixteen chants, and the sequences are interspersed with nonpsalmic chants. Still one might imagine, in the case of the introit, that there did exist a stage in the history of the post-Pentecostal series when there simply happened to be a list of only sixteen psalmic chants that came to be ordered numerically at the time of the Advent Project, when six more chants were added to bring the total to the required twenty-two. Such a stage would have succeeded an earlier one when the post-Pentecostal season shared its list of psalmic introits with the Lenten fund of pre-Advent Project chants spoken of above. The steps leading from this purported common list to the final shape of the Lenten and post-Pentecostal series would of course be hidden from us, but one assumes that Lent would be given first attention as a time of stational observance. The structuring of Lent, moreover, is different in that it consists of a scaffolding of Sundays with interspersed weekdays, whereas the latter consists in a straight series, inviting a numerically ordered sequence.

As plausible as might be the idea of a shared Lenten and post-Pentecostal list of early psalmic introits, it happens that there is serious reason to doubt that such an arrangement did in fact exist. One must take into consideration the practice of textual adjustment. We have observed already the presence of much textual adjustment in both the Advent-Christmas and Paschal-time introits. Table 17 indicates textual adjustment for the post-Pentecostal introits in the usual way with an asterisk after the incipit (only substantial adjustment is identified; minor adjustment is ignored). The incidence of the practice is extraordinarily high: fourteen of the twenty-one biblically derived Sunday introits are involved (*Salus populi* is nonbiblical), and two of the three Ember Day chants. There are, moreover, several examples of the most extreme form of scriptural paraphrase in chants such as *Respice domine, Da pacem* and *Omnia que fecisti*. What significance ought we to attach to this—to both the extraordinary prevalence of the practice within the introit, especially in its post-Pentecostal series, and to the phenomenon of textual adjustment in general?

TEXTUAL ADJUSTMENT

The subject of chant texts as quasi librettos was introduced above, at the beginning of chapter five. It was shown there that a Mass Proper text is frequently not just a literal segment of Scripture but rather the product of adjustments to the original wording that are undertaken with a view to providing a suitable vehicle for an independent musical creation. These adjustments can be slight, the insertion of the vocative *domine,* for example, in a chant addressed to the Lord, or the omission of some logical connective like *autem,* rendered unnecessary when the passage is removed from its context. But just as often they are substantial, the omission of large segments of the original text, for example, or even its radical paraphrase.

A survey of the entire Mass Proper results in the surprising conclusion that this practice extends to at least half the total repertory. And it is rather surprising, too, that it is employed more frequently in introits than in any other item of the Mass Proper. I count 90 of the 144 introits to be involved. It is not immediately apparent why introits are so extreme in this respect; I assumed before undertaking my survey that communions would lead the way, to be followed by introits. Communions are the most eccentric of all Mass Proper items. Among other things they have the highest proportion of nonpsalmic chants, and nonpsalmic chants, typically later than psalmic chants, might then be expected to have a higher proportion of textual adjustment, a practice that one assumes to be itself relatively late in appearance. Yet communions, with 61 of their repertory of 141 chants nonpsalmic (43 percent) as opposed to 43 of 144 introits (30 percent), have fewer adjusted texts than introits, 78 of 141 chants (55 percent) compared to 90 of 144 introits (63 percent). These percentages take into account both substantial and minor adjustment;[23] more significant is the practice of substantial adjustment, and the figures here are comparable to those just given. There are 56 of 151 communions that employ substantial adjustment (39 percent) and 67 of 144 introits (47 percent). Meanwhile the other genres of chant run true to expectation: the predominantly psalmic graduals, alleluias and offertories have markedly less textual adjustment than either introits or communions.

In any event the present concern is not to compare the textual adjustment of introits with other items of the Mass Proper but rather to make comparisons within the annual introit cycle itself. Two areas are of particular interest: one involves the psalmic chants of Lent and the post-Pentecostal season, the other the psalmic chants of the sanctorale. As for the first of these, it turns out that there is a considerably higher proportion of adjusted texts in the post-Pentecostal season than in Lent; indeed the post-Pentecostal season has the highest incidence of textual adjustment in the entire introit cycle, more even than the festal seasons of Advent-Christmas and Paschaltime with their many nonpsalmic chants. Remarkably the prevalence of textual adjustment in the post-Pentecostal introits extends also to the psalmic chants: it may not be surprising that all five of the nonpsalmic chants of the season are substantially adjusted, but it is that no less than twelve of the twenty psalmic chants are. As for the Lenten introits, their textual adjustment has an interesting pattern that is simple enough to be made clear without benefit of a table—the early and late portions of the season are consistently characterized by substantial adjustment, while the larger middle part is almost entirely free of it. The introits of Septuagesima Sunday, Sexagesima, Ash Wednesday, Quadragesima and the first three ferias of Quadragesima week have extreme adjustments to their texts, as do the last five chants of the season (including all those of Holy Week). Throughout the interior weeks, that is, from Monday of the second week to Wednesday of the fifth, there are just three instances of the practice, two of which are for dates of special liturgical significance, associated as they are with the baptismal Scrutinies: the introits for Wednesday and Saturday of the fourth week, *Dum sanctificatus,* which has three large omissions in its text, derived from Ezekiel 36.23–26, and *Sitientes,* which paraphrases its Isaiah 55.1 source.[24]

It is an altogether plausible assumption that Lenten and post-Pentecostal chants of whatever Mass Proper item share a common fund of psalmic chants that predate the Advent Project, but the observations just recorded about textual adjustment in the introit cast considerable doubt on the validity of applying the assumption to this particular genre. The extraordinary amount of adjustment among the post-Pentecostal introits as well as its radical nature create the impression that the bulk of these chants may be among the last introits to be created. Taking the two seasons together, then, it would appear that something like the following succession of events might have taken place. The bulk of the pre-Advent Project list of psalmic chants for general use (numbering, to guess freely, some twenty or so pieces) were situated in the central portion of Lent. At the time of the Advent Project a substantial number of new introits were added to fill out the season with a complete set of uniquely assigned Propers; these included the Septuagesima-Sexagesima-Quinquagesima trio, the first several days of Lent itself, Holy Week and a few special dates between. The composition of the post-Pentecostal season followed sometime later, probably after the completion of Paschaltime. Textual adjustment of introits was already a common practice, and the members of the schola indulged their creative urge in this respect to an unprecedented degree.

The sanctorale is the second area requiring comment. There is less textual adjustment within the sanctoral introits than in any other segment of the repertory, even than in Lent. It is true that the sanctorale has a high proportion of psalmic chants, which, of course, tend generally to be less subject to textual adjustment, but Lent has an even higher, indeed much higher, proportion of psalmic chants. My count is as follows: for Lent, of 37 chants, 15 are substantially adjusted, 6 are slightly adjusted and 16 remain integral; for the sanctorale, of 43 chants, 15 substantially, 5 slightly and 23 integral. The figures tell us little until we make the distinction between nonpsalmic and psalmic sanctoral introits. Here there is a dramatic difference: of 12 nonpsalmic sanctoral chants, a significant majority, 8, are substantially adjusted, with 1 slightly adjusted and 3 remaining integral. The remarkable number comes in the psalmic chants: of the total of 31, only 7 are substantially adjusted and 4 slightly, while no less than 20 remain integral. These 20 integral texts from a total of 31 are by far the highest proportion of any area of the introit repertory. What is the significance of the number?

The answer lies in the distinction between sanctoral introits that are *uniquely assigned* and those that are *shared*. In the previous chapter I proposed the existence of a fund of Common psalmic chant sets—a kind of proto-Common of the Saints—that were used until the undertaking of the effort I choose to call the Sanctoral Project. Thus the uniquely assigned sanctoral chants would be the product of this final revision, and coming as late as the revision does, we should expect to see a good measure of textual adjustment among the unique sanctoral introits, even among the psalmic ones. This is in fact the case: whereas unique sanctoral introits, whether psalmic or not, are greatly subject to textual adjustment, this is not true of shared sanctoral introits. There are just three examples of nonpsalmic texts among the shared sanctoral introits, two of which are substantially adjusted (*Sacerdotes dei* and *Sapientia sancti*), but of the 18 psalmic chants that are shared, only 2 are substantially adjusted and 2 slightly adjusted, while an overwhelming majority of 14 utilize their scriptural derivation with its integral text. The numbers are strikingly congruous with those of the psalmic introits from the interior Lenten weekdays: there, of 16 chants, we have one substantially adjusted (*Ego clamavi*), 2 slightly and 14 integral.

We have, thus, an overwhelming preponderance of integral texts for only two portions of the entire introit repertory: the shared psalmic chants of the sanctorale and the psalmic chants of the interior Lenten weekdays. These are precisely the two segments of the repertory where we would expect to find the bulk of the introits created by the schola cantorum before the onset of the Advent and Sanctoral Projects.[25] The analysis of chants, then, by recourse to their degree of textual manipulation might seem at first a fragile enough chronological determinant, but the results obtained from its use with other chronological indications boost confidence in it as a tool capable of corroborating our conclusions.

TEXTUAL ADJUSTMENTS: FURTHER REFLECTIONS

The presence of textual adjustment, not just in introits but in all genres of the Mass Proper, tells us that the Roman singers took great care with their chant texts. If a scriptural passage were an appropriate text just as it stood, it would of course be used as such, but if it were not, it would be altered, radically if need be, to be rendered a fit vehicle for the music. The result was a carefully crafted quasi libretto.

This has implications for that splendid debate on the nature of chant transmission that graced the pages of our musicological journals in recent years.[26] To simplify the positions of the participants, their concern was primarily with the chant as sung by the ninth-century Franks, and they tended to look upon its melodies as either fixed or in a state of year-to-year quasi-improvisational reconstruction. They had very little to say about the condition of the chant in seventh- and eighth-century Rome, but most seemed to assume it to have been somehow subject to annual change.

But should we assume that improvisation was the original Roman model? Does not the practice of textual adjustment suggest that it never was— never with the members of the Roman schola, that is, as opposed to the lectors and cantors who had chanted the responsorial psalm at Mass since patristic times? The singers of the schola did not declaim psalms; they produced carefully crafted chant texts that they then set to music. It may be conceivable that they would have so composed a text with the set purpose of improvising upon it from year to year, but it is much more likely that their intention, at least, was the corresponding crafting of a particular melody. Certainly the 144 individual melodies of the introit repertory (even assuming a limited measure of formulaicism) give credence to the existence of such an approach. Now I must emphasize that I am not now claiming the original Roman melodies to be precisely the same as the Frankish ones that we call Gregorian chant. Rather I am only proposing that the original *aim* of the Roman singers was to create unique melodies; the question of how permanent the results of their efforts might have been I leave open until the epilogue to this volume.

For a final reflection of immediate relevance, however, there is a particular difficulty with the idea of seventh-century Roman singers retaining individual and fixed melodies to match their carefully crafted texts. It is one thing to maintain, as does David Hughes, that the Franks could preserve much of an already fixed Mass Proper in memory from year to year[27]—a position to which I am firmly attached myself—but quite another to claim that the Roman singers could so reproduce melodies during the very period that they were being created. Those of us who have been privileged to memorize a large quantity of Gregorian melodies managed to do so by singing them annually over a period of several years; but how does one reproduce melodies created only a year before and, presumably, not sung in the intervening time? I have an altogether plausible answer to this question from a conversation with Edward Nowacki in which he suggested that new chants remained the particular responsibility of those who originally created them. Thus, for example, the composer of the group of ten prophetic Advent–

Christmas Day communions, my so-called Master of the *Re-Fa* Advent Lyrics, would be sure to remember these chants and be sure to refresh the memory of his colleagues for as many years as was necessary. One should keep in mind that the stational liturgy occupied the members of the schola only in the morning, and then not for every day, leaving them many hours free for musical production and rehearsal. This system of shared memory would not be an absolutely sure one—even members of the schola cantorum would die or move on to other positions—but it could account for a substantially stable retention of a large and expanding repertory.

THE INTROIT AND COMMUNION CYCLES COMPARED

The introduction to this volume made it clear that the annual communion cycle furnished the impetus for undertaking a study on the creation of the Roman Mass Proper. More particularly, the discovery of evidence for compositional planning in the temporal cycle, a phenomenon rich in chronological suggestion, sparked my enthusiasm as an historian. Historical enthusiasm, in turn, gave way to aesthetic enthusiasm and caused me to call the communion temporale "a creation of epic proportions, like some great symphony, characterized on the one hand by the most patent symmetry and organization, and on the other by a consistent programmatic tendency that would have each episode within the whole thematically appropriate to the liturgical occasion."[28] I have no reason now to retract that rather extravagant statement. The prophetic lyricism of the Advent–Christmas Day group, for example, set in sharp contrast to the colorful narrative character of the post-Christmas New Testament group, is undeniably a thing of beauty. And the ingenuity and resourcefulness that went into sustaining a series of divergent strategies throughout the entire cycle—even if it involved compromises such as borrowing Office antiphons and responsories—are altogether praiseworthy.

In contrast, I was initially disappointed when, after turning to introits, I found none of the compositional planning that characterizes the communion temporale. But the more time one spends with introits the more one should come to appreciate their remarkable achievement—unique within the Mass Proper. The very lack of reliance upon the compositional aid and impetus accorded by prearranged sets and strategies (with their attendant compromises) renders the accomplishment all the more admirable.

At the same time historians need not be entirely disappointed in their search for chronological indications within the introit's annual cycle. The very stylistic homogeneity of the genre, and its lack of recourse to model melodies and formulaicism (whether absolute or relative), creates the impression of its creation within a more or less confined span of time, itself a chronological conclusion of considerable value. And a closer look at the genre's repertory, especially through the lens of textual adjustment, very likely allows one to discern at least some measure of chronological layering within that limited time span. There is good reason, in particular, to see in those psalmic chants of the Lenten weekdays and shared sanctorale, with their integral texts, the bulk of the pre-Advent Project introit repertory.

CHAPTER 9

The Gradual

Ordo romanus I, the source of our first unambiguous reference to the singing of the early medieval gradual, is more laconic than one would have thought in reporting on so important a liturgical event. It tells us: "The cantor ascends and sings the *responsum.*"[1] From the context, however, and various other eighth- and ninth-century documents, albeit Frankish ones, we are able to reconstruct a fairly complete description of the chant.

The cantor had been designated before Mass while the pope and clergy were gathered in the *secretarium.*[2] After the subdeacon finished his reading of the epistle on the second highest step of the ambo (the highest was reserved for the deacon's reading of the gospel), the cantor assumed the same place for his performance. This circumstance accounts for the name of the chant, *responsum gradale,* and eventually simply *graduale,* an adjectival form of the Latin word for step, *gradus. Ordo I* cites the singer's *cantatorium,* certainly a songbook (or more precisely, *libellus*) of some sort, although it would be anachronistic to think of it as a *cantatorium* in the sense of the early preserved exemplars like the famous St. Gall 359, that is, a book with all the cantatorial Mass chants—graduals, alleluias and tracts—of the year.

The singing probably proceeded according to a fourfold format: the cantor's singing of the response, the schola's choral repetition of it; the cantor's singing of the verse and the final choral singing of the response. The scheme has plausibility in view of the gradual's prehistory as a responsorial chant, and there is a measure of concrete evidence for it, albeit Frankish. Amalarius tells us the gradual is called a response because "when one sings, others respond";[3] and the fact that the oldest manuscripts of the *cantatorium* notate the full response rather than only the incipit suggests that it is the entire response the soloist sings rather than just an intonation. Amalarius goes on to specify: "that very soloist sings the verse."[4] The final repetition of the verse is not mentioned in any of the sources but seems a likely enough way to complete the procedure. Dom Hesbert, however, holds that a decision to repeat the response or not is made for each gradual on an individual basis, depending upon the sense of the text.[5] For a gradual like St. John the Evangelist's *Exiit sermo* (Jn 21.22–23), for example, "This saying went abroad among the brethren that that disciple should not die; 'but I wish [said Jesus], only that he remain until I come—follow thou me,'" the repetition of the opening respond would defy all logic. Hesbert offers other plausible examples that speak either for or against repetition of responds, but one could argue nevertheless that early medieval cantors would be more liable to conform to a conventional practice than to change it from day to day because of textual considerations. In any event the overall format of the gradual was abbreviated in later centuries to the familiar twofold form of a choral respond intoned by the cantor, followed by a solo verse of which the chorus sings the final phrase.

ORIGINS

Much has been written in previous chapters of this volume about the origins of the gradual. It began, according to the view put forth here, as a psalm that figured occasionally among the Old Testament readings of the Fore-Mass. By the late fourth century it had become a regular liturgical item in its own right, still spoken of as a reading but described at the same time as a distinctly musical event, a psalm chanted by a lector and responded to with a tuneful congregational refrain. It is quite possible that the psalm was sometimes sung without responses, particularly on less festive occasions, but the evidence suggests that responsorial performance was more typical. An alleluia might be sung as the response if the psalm was one of those twenty that have the exclamation appended to them in the Book of Psalms. This would more likely have been the case during Paschaltime. It seems historically appropriate to refer to such instances as the singing of the gradual psalm with an alleluia response rather than the singing of a proto-alleluia. The latter would require the regular presence of two responsorial psalms, the second of which always had alleluia as its refrain—precisely the set of circumstances attested to in early-fifth-century Jerusalem but not duplicated anywhere in the contemporary West.

By the end of the fourth century the singing of the gradual psalm was well established in eastern centers such as Antioch, Constantinople and Caesarea of Cappadocia, and in western centers such as Milan, Carthage and Hippo. Rome appears to have lagged behind somewhat in its adoption of the practice but certainly had joined the other regions in this respect well before the end of the fifth century. In later sixth-century Gaul and Rome we hear less of the responsorial psalm being recited by youthful lectors, as had been the case in Augustine's Hippo, and more of its being sung by deacons, and sung, too, in an overtly musical fashion. Gregory I found it necessary to complain of deacons being chosen on the basis of their fine voices, and he ordered that the psalmody of the Mass be sung by subdeacons and other lesser clergy.

Despite such vocal display we continue to observe at this time what is essentially lector chant and not schola chant, that is, the quasi-improvisational chanting of a psalm by a soloist with traditional choral responses, rather than set pieces performed by a rehearsed cantor and schola. The latter style of ecclesiastical song would come into existence with the founding of the Roman schola cantorum sometime in the earlier or mid-seventh century. There is, then, an essential musical difference between the responsorial psalmody sung by deacons (and lesser clergy) in Gregory's time and the gradual sung by the members of the schola cantorum a few decades later. I have, moreover, been at pains throughout this work to emphasize the repertorial difference between early Christian psalmody and early medieval ecclesiastical chant, what I refer to as "discontinuity of liturgical assignment." But still there must certainly be elements of continuity in the history of the changeover from gradual psalm to gradual as such—continuity, that is, beyond the obvious circumstances that the two musical genres perform the same liturgical function and have the same responsorial format.

The measure of discontinuity and continuity between the two is best discussed in the context of that hypothetical model invoked above—that of the responsorial psalm, having grown so long and elaborate in the course of time that it had all but its initial verse lopped off, leaving only the melismatic response and verse of the gradual. Such a model, a caricature perhaps, represents the idea of continuity in its crudest form. There is evidence against its historical validity in the existence of nonpsalmic graduals, in the use of textual adjustment for graduals and in the fact that the majority of gradual verses are derived from others than the first of the psalm. All three of these traits are incompatible with that hypothetical single psalm verse remaining after the rest of the psalm had been cut. But, again, the strongest argument against repertorial continuity that has been advanced in these pages is that of discontinuity of liturgical assignment. The evidence is overwhelming that the particular psalm sung on a specific liturgical date in the early Christian period is seldom the same psalm from which the early medieval gradual for the same occasion derives its text. Indeed it can be shown that the very concept of fixed liturgical assignments for the early responsorial psalm is an anachronism. Only in exceptional cases is the traditional association of a certain psalm with a particular festival maintained from the fourth to the seventh century.

But, necessary as it is thus to make the case for discontinuity, both repertorial and musical, there is also a brief to be made for continuity—a historiographically more gratifying cause. If the beginnings of repertorial continuity are admittedly meager (precious examples such as *Haec dies, In omnem terram* and *Pretiosa in conspectu*), surely similar associations must have accumulated in Rome by Gregory I's time. We have no sources to assure us of this, but a glance at the gradual repertory itself allows us to single out psalms that it would have been all but impossible for the cantors of the late sixth century to miss. This is true especially of psalms that figure prominently in the shared sanctoral graduals, most notably Psalms 44 and 20, the sanctoral psalms par excellence, female and male, respectively. Psalm 44, in particular, with lines like *concupivit rex speciem tuam* (verse 12), is used for no less than four different graduals, each of which is shared by a number of female saints. One can only assume that it was frequently sung as the responsorial psalm for various female saints' days in Gregory's time. There are good possibilities among the temporal feasts as well: Christmas' Psalm 109, for example, with its verse 2, *Notum fecit dominus,* and Advent's Psalm 79 with its verse 3, *Excita domine et veni.* If on balance the argument for discontinuity of liturgical assignment remains stronger than that for continuity, it is probably not nearly so much the case as suggested by the patristic evidence alone.

The musical aspect of the subject would appear to have still more to offer for the cause of continuity than the repertorial. There is, to begin with, much to recommend the general notion of a responsorial psalm that had grown too long and elaborate and that stood thus in need of radical curtailment. What is wrong with the idea, as generally understood, is the assumption that a particular psalm assigned to a specific feast day undergoes in place the full historical process of elaboration and abbreviation. It is the element of fixed liturgical assignment that runs afoul of the evidence. There are no such objections to the simple thought that the responsorial psalm could have been drawn out in rhapsodic fashion at the hands of certain exuberant deacons. One could well imagine the pope nodding to such singers that the time had come to curtail their display (not unlike the documented nod to the schola to cut short the introit psalm), and one could further imagine the decision on the part of the schola to retain a melismatic style for the singing of the gradual, but to confine it to fixed pieces of a single verse and response.

It is entirely possible in such a set of historical circumstances—in fact quite likely—that there would be a fair measure of melodic continuity between the responsorial psalms of the deacons (and lesser clergy) and the graduals of the schola. In all probability some of these clerical singers were among the first members of the schola. They would have brought their manner of performing the responsorial psalm into the new organization, where, with the leisure of full-time dedication to ecclesiastical chant, they could effect the change from their quasi-improvisational psalmody to the creation of a large repertory of set pieces. Certainly some of the more successful melodic ventures of their previous musical experience would be incorporated into the new compositions. It could very well be that we have here the answer to the mystery of why a chant like the gradual is generally formulaic and a chant like the introit is not. We can assume that individual singers had developed a variety of recurring melodic groupings that they integrated into their psalmodic declamations, and it is not unlikely that some of these would have been shared with other singers. We can imagine in the newly founded schola further such sharing on the one hand, and a discriminating selectivity on the other. The result, not surprisingly, would be a chant genre like the gradual, typified by a number of formulaic melodies.

At the same time we must not think that the entire gradual repertory came into being in this way. When, in the section of this chapter devoted to an overview of the gradual's annual cycle, I attempt to uncover indications of chronological layering, it will be seen that most of the repertory, even when utilizing traditional formulaic types, probably originated as set pieces rather than "frozen" improvisations. But before we turn to that task, a few remarks about the general musical attributes of the gradual are in order.

THE GRADUAL: MUSICAL CHARACTERISTICS

Both the respond and verse of the gradual are generally described as melismatic. To put it more precisely, each sense unit of the text, a phrase or short clause of some three, four or five words, interjects one melisma (occasionally two) of some twenty, thirty or forty notes into its typically neumatic texture. The trait is common to both Roman and Gregorian versions, although the distinction between neumatic and melismatic passages is somewhat less sharp in the Roman, where the neumatic sections are on average

Example 5. Gradual verse *Sed sic eum*

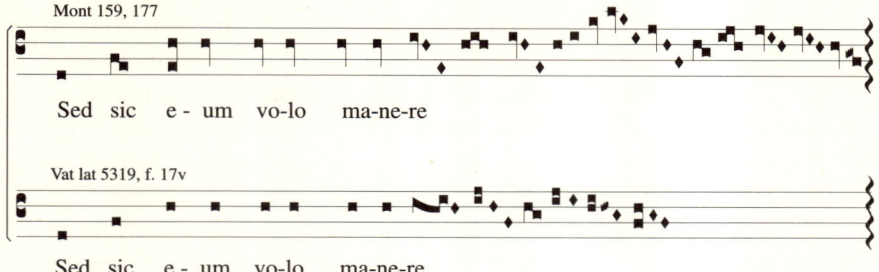

slightly more florid and the melismas not quite as long as their Gregorian counterparts. Usually the melismas happen at the corresponding places in the two versions, a feature one would expect in view of their historical relationship.

The verse is marginally more melismatic than the respond and, moreover, has a somewhat higher tessitura, both traits in keeping with its soloistic nature. Again, both Roman and Gregorian versions share these characteristics, although the Gregorian manifests them in rather sharper relief. I recall the sensation I had as a seminarian in my early teens when I heard the senior cantors soar into the tonal stratosphere (such it seemed to me) of a verse like that of John the Evangelist's *Exiit sermo: Sed sic eum* (example 5). I do not think it is just because of my youthful experience that I find a passage like that on the word *manere* no less than thrilling, nor do I think it is just because of my greater familiarity with Gregorian chant that I find the Roman version rather bland in comparison. One must go a long way toward suppressing all natural musical reaction to deny that either the Roman version lost something in its centuries of oral transmission, or that the Gregorian version gained something at the hands of late-eighth-century Frankish musicians of genius.[6]

Graduals are, apart from tracts, the most formulaic of Mass chants. The trait can be detected in virtually all 105 chants of the core repertory (those transmitted from Rome to the north), but it is most pronounced in two melodic types: those mode-2 Gregorian graduals that share an A-final with the Roman version ("A-2" graduals here) and mode-5 chants that share an F-final with the Roman ("F-5" here). (The A-2 graduals are conventionally referred to as the *Justus ut palma* type, a singularly infelicitous choice because *Justus ut palma* is a Frankish adaptation of the type; the chant is absent from the Roman repertory.) The two types account for well over half of the core repertory; there are twenty-one examples of the A-2 type in the Roman versions and no less than forty-four of the F-5.[7]

One must qualify these figures, however, by noting that the Roman type is not always matched in the Gregorian. Of the twenty-one Roman examples of the A-2 gradual, only sixteen of the corresponding Gregorian graduals maintain the type.[8] The F-5 type, however, is much more consistent in this respect; forty of forty-four potential Gregorian chants utilize it. This is surprising in view of the circumstance that A-2 graduals are usually more consistently formulaic than F-5 chants; several of them appear almost to employ a genuine model melody in the manner of the alleluias of the *Dies sanctificatus* type. One would expect ease of transmission between Rome and Francia in direct proportion to the degree of adherence to a melodic model; it seems only natural that it would be easier to transmit orally a melody that is sung several times a year than one sung only once. A likely explanation for the anomaly of the A-2 type's seeming lapses in transmission lies in Nowacki's use of the concept of "thrift" that was invoked in the previous chapter. This is to say that examples of the A-2 type in the Roman versions that are not matched in the Gregorian might be instances where the Roman cantors of the tenth or eleventh centuries resorted to using a melody that was more easily produced than a less formulaic one. This possibility will be pursued with respect to a particular trio of post-Pentecostal A-2 chants later in the chapter.

A noteworthy characteristic of the gradual's formulaicism is that "analogy" between Roman and Gregorian formulaic usage mentioned in the previous chapter. It is nothing short of remarkable in the more formulaic examples of the genre. One can take Apel's system of formulas for the Gregorian melodies and construct a precisely corresponding set for the Roman melodies: whenever a certain formula appears in a Gregorian gradual, its counterpart will appear in the same place in the Roman version. Take, for example, Apel's formula A_{10} (that is, his tenth formula to cadence on a), which appears regularly as the second phrase of Gregorian A-2 graduals. It is given in example 6 as it appears in the verse of *A summo caelo* along with its Roman counterpart. Of the sixteen examples of A-2 graduals that are shared by the Roman and Gregorian sources, fifteen have the A_{10} formula in the expected place in the Gregorian versions and all fifteen are matched with the Roman version of the formula.

Easter's *Haec dies; Confitemini* is the only one of the sixteen A-2 graduals shared by the Gregorian and Roman sources that does not have the full A_{10} formula.[9] In its place, on the words *quoniam bonus* (example 7), it has melodic material classified by Apel as formula A_{11}, which might be looked

Example 6. Gradual verse *Caeli enarrant*

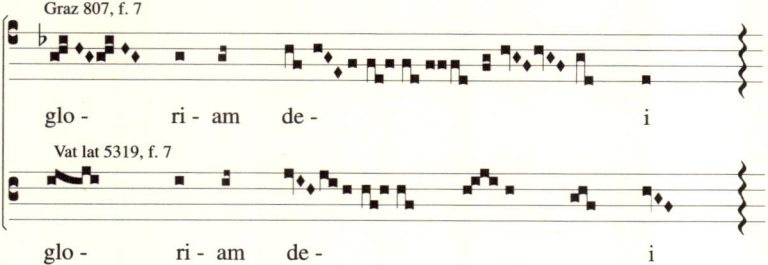

Example 7. Gradual *Haec dies; Confitemini*

upon as a variant of A_{10}, differing as it does in its opening portion (on the word *quoniam*) but remaining the same in its closing portion (*bonus*). What is remarkable is that the Roman and Gregorian versions are completely analogous in the treatment of the phrase: the opening portion is irregular in both, while the closing is formulaic in both. This is a condition maintained throughout the entire repertory of graduals with a sufficiently high degree of consistency to raise the most intriguing questions about the process of oral transmission. How can one explain it? Should we think that the Frankish cantors, rather than struggling to learn the Roman graduals as they were, decided instead to systematically replace each Roman formula with a version of their own invention? Or should we think that the Roman cantors of the eleventh century, with similar efficiency, systematically replaced the older Roman formulas with newer ones? I find neither possibility to be very plausible—in each case it is what appears to be the self-consciously consistent nature of the process that is puzzling—and must admit to having no satisfactory explanation for it.

Less mysterious but equally interesting is a final musical trait of the gradual: the Roman and Gregorian versions are more closely related melodically than most other items of the Mass Proper, certainly the introit.

Example 8. Gradual *Adjutor in opportunitatibus; Quoniam*

Example 9. Gradual *Miserere mei; Misit*

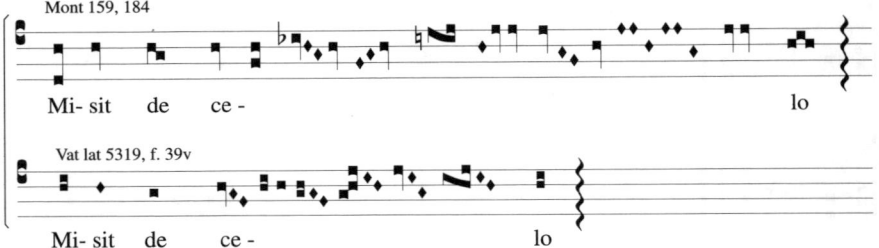

The sort of similarity one observes in a phrase like that of *pacientia pauperum* (example 8) from the mode E-3 *Adjutor in opportunitatibus; Quoniam* is not altogether atypical with its sharing of overall contour and of key pitches such as the final note. It is worth observing also that graduals are almost entirely lacking in that trill-like oscillation that is so characteristic of much Roman chant and so dissimilar to the more melodically varied Gregorian. A distinctive trait of Gregorian graduals—but absent from the Roman—is what Apel calls the "reiterative style,"[10] consisting in series of repeated notes in the form of repercussive neumes, such as the *bistropha* and *tristropha*, usually appearing on the pitch c and less often F. Example 9, from Ash Wednesday's mode D-1 *Miserere mei; Misit*, gives the first phrase of the verse. While the Roman version does not have the repeated notes on c, however, it does manage to stress the pitch in a similar, if somewhat less emphatic, manner; this, again, is not atypical of Roman graduals. The musical function of the reiterative style in graduals is that of heightened tonal focus (it has nothing to do with generation from psalm tones, occurring as it does only in melismas and not on all of the so-called Gregorian tenors, but only on the two pitches F and c). Thus the Roman graduals manage to salvage in this respect a measure of the characteristic Gregorian tonal focus.

THE TEMPORAL CYCLE: ADVENT-CHRISTMAS

Table 18 presents an overview of the Christmastime graduals, providing the incipits of responds and verses, their textual derivation and their Roman and Gregorian modal designations (with substantial textual adjustment indicated by asterisks after the incipits). The season is separated by spaces into four liturgical subsets: the three Advent Sundays (the fourth is a *dominica vacat* in Rome); the three Ember Days with their multiple graduals; the Christmas through Epiphany festival sequence; and the three Sundays after the Epiphany. Included in the festival group, of course, are the three saints' days after Christmas, the feasts of Stephen, John the Evangelist and the Innocents, and also the feast of Sylvester, for reasons to be given below.

The graduals of the Christmas season have been cited several times already in this study as exemplifying the meticulous work of those responsible for the Advent Project. The qualities of specific liturgical appropriateness and unique liturgical assignment are consistently present in them, with only a handful of easily explained exceptions. As for the former of these traits, all ten of the Advent graduals make explicit reference to the coming of the Savior, and all ten of the festal group make explicit reference to the date on which they are sung. Several nonpsalmic sources are called upon for this latter group, providing poetically apt texts like the Epiphany's Isaiah-derived *Omnes de Saba* ("All they shall come from Saba, bearing gold and frankincense, and proclaiming praise to the Lord"), a passage as colorful as it is theologically appropriate. Four of these ten texts are nonpsalmic, a high proportion in view of the fact that only eleven of the total of 105 graduals are nonpsalmic. The proportion of those with substantial textual adjustment is relatively high also, four responds and one verse; textual adjustment is generally rare in graduals.[11]

The only graduals from the season that do not make explicit textual reference to their festival are those of the three post-Epiphany Sundays. This is obviously the case because ordinary Sundays lack themselves the sort of specific liturgical themes enjoyed by feasts like Christmas and Epiphany. For this reason it is not surprising that two of the graduals from this group, *Misit dominus* and *Timebunt gentes*, are borrowed for use on other occasions. The only other shared Christmastime gradual is Sylvester's *Ecce sacerdos*, which is assigned to three other sanctoral dates. There are reasons, however, that make *Ecce sacerdos* appear to be both an integral part of the Christmastime group and a genuinely Proper chant created originally for Sylvester's feast and subsequently assigned to the others. It is an F-5 gradual

Table 18. Roman Advent-Christmas Graduals

			Mode	
			Rom	Greg
Advent I	Universi qui; Vias	Ps 24.3; 4	D	1
Advent II	Ex sion; Congr	Ps 49.2–3; 5	F	5
Advent III	Qui sedes*; Qui regis	Ps 79.2–3; 2	G	7
Ember Wednesday	Tollite portas; Quis asc	Ps 23.7; 3–4	A	2
	Prope est; Laudem	Ps 144.18; 21	F	5
Ember Friday	Ostende nobis; Benedixisti	Ps 84.8; 2	A	2
Ember Saturday	A summo caelo; Caeli	Ps 18.7; 2	A	2
	In sole posuit; A summo	Ps 18.6; 7	A	2
	Domine deus virtutum; Excita	Ps 79.8; 3	A	2
	Excita domine; Fiat	Ps 79.3; 18	A	2
Vigil Xmas	Hodie scietis*; Qui regis	Ex 16.6 & Is 35.4; Ps 79.2–3	A	2
Xmas I	Tecum principium; Dicit dominus	Ps 109.3; 1	A	2
Xmas II	Benedictus qui*; A domino	Ps 117.26–27; 23	F	5
Xmas III	Viderunt omnes; Notum fec	Ps 97.3–4; 2	F	5
Stephen	Sederunt principes*; Adiuva	Ps 118.23; 86; Ps 108.2–6	F	5
John Evangelist	Exiit sermo; Sed sic*	Jn 21.22–23	F	5
Innocents	Anima nostra; Laqueus	Ps 123.7; 7–8	F	5
Sylvester	Ecce sacerdos; Non est	Sir 44.16; 20	F	5
Sunday	Speciosus forma; Eructavit	Ps 44.3; 2	D	3
Epiphany	Omnes de Saba; Surge	Is 60.6; 1	F	5
Eph I	Benedictus dominus; Suscipiant	Ps 71.18; 3	G	7
Eph II	Misit dominus; Confiteantur	Ps 106.20; 21	F	5
Eph III	Timebunt gentes; Quoniam	Ps 101.16; 17	F	5

and as such an apparent link in the chain of these chants in the season. And more than that, it is a very special member of the F-5 family: it is one of three F-5 graduals (the nearby *Sederunt principes* of St. Stephen and *Christus factus* of Holy Thursday are the other two) that are so similar melodically that they form a genuine model melody. All three are, moreover, representatives of the small minority of nonpsalmic graduals. They give the appearance of a simultaneously created group figuring in the final revision of the gradual cycle. Sylvester's *Ecce sacerdos* thus shares the status of the other two as a genuinely Proper chant rather than a Common one from the fund of early sanctoral graduals.

Not only are the graduals of the season characterized by thematic appropriateness and unique liturgical assignment, but they display one of the most obvious cases of compositional planning in the entire Mass Proper. I refer, of course, to the series of A-2 graduals assigned to the Ember Days and early Masses of Christmas Day, and the series of F-5 graduals assigned to the later Christmas Day Masses and the following feast days up to and including Epiphany. There is clearly reason to believe in the existence of some sort of preconceived strategy at work here. Still, each modal sequence is broken once by a chant of disparate tonality: the A-2 series by *Prope est* (F-5) and the F-5 series by *Speciosus forma* (D-3). This circumstance requires an explanation, and one will be attempted in the imagined scenario that follows. But first a methodological note about the chronology of modal types like the A-2 and F-5 graduals.

It was mentioned above that the A-2 type is much more melodically homogeneous than the F-5. True as that is, there are also degrees of melodic similarity *within* each type, and this raises the question of whether we should consider the more stereotypically formulaic chants to be later or earlier representatives of their category. It would seem more likely that a group of chants that are at once extremely similar melodically and closely related liturgically—the four A-2 graduals of Advent's Saturday Ember Day, for example, or the four mode-8 Gregorian canticle-tracts of Holy Saturday—are in all probability relatively late in the history of a melodic type; they give the appearance of resulting from an expeditious use of a melodic type already well established. At the same time, if a singularly unstereotypical example of a type appears on a major festival such as Christmas or Easter, we have reason to suspect that it might be an early representative of its kind. These ideas—by no means absolute principles—will be made use of in the following attempt to spell out a plausible scenario for the creation of the Christmastime graduals.

The graduals for Christmas Day and Epiphany were in place already before the Advent Project began in earnest. The first mass of Christmas' *Tecum principium* and, significantly, Easter's *Haec dies* are two of the least formulaic examples of the A-2 type, while the third mass of Christmas' *Viderunt omnes* and Epiphany's *Omnes de Saba* are two of the least formulaic examples of the F-5 type. The correspondence between major feast days and particularly atypical applications of the formulaic melodies is too consistent to be coincidental.

In considering the rest of the chants one separates out the three post-Epiphany chants; they have more in common with the Lenten and post-Pentecostal graduals. It is quite possible that they were already in existence before the Advent Project but not yet permanently assigned to the three Sundays. Rather, they would have been simply three of a fund of psalmic graduals available for use on the ordinary Sundays and during Lent.

Within the Advent Project itself, texts are carefully chosen for the three Advent Sundays. The primary concern is that they explicitly invoke Advent themes, but special circumstances help guide the choice for individual dates; Advent I's *Universi qui*, for example, shares its derivation from Psalm 24 with *Ad te levavi*, the introit of the day, and Advent II's *Ex sion* invokes the date's stational theme of Jerusalem. Melodies are chosen for the three using three different tonal types: D, G and the more common F. As work on the Ember Day chants begins, texts and melodies for the pair of graduals for Wednesday are selected with similar care as those for the three Sundays, while Friday is assigned a chant that might very well have already been in existence, *Ostende nobis domine* (Ps 84.8; 2). Its melody shares with Christmas' *Tecum principium* and Easter's *Haec dies* the distinction of being one of the three least formulaic of the A-2 type, and its text is one of those most frequently associated with Advent in all the liturgy. Perhaps it was a Common Advent chant in use before the season was given its definitive form of four Sundays in the Advent Project. At this point the decision is made to finish the Advent graduals, that is, the four of Saturday, as expeditiously as possible. The most likely choice is the A-2 type, in use already at the first mass of Christmas and on both Wednesday and Friday of the Ember Days. The four texts are taken from just two Psalms, 18 and 79, and the melody is used in a radically formulaic manner.

The choice of the A-2 type for the vigil of Christmas' gradual is an obvious one: it is simply a matter of filling in the remaining slot in the A-2 sequence since the first mass of Christmas' A-2 *Tecum principium* is already in place. The melody is typical even if the text, *Hodie scietis*, in keeping with the solemnity of the occasion, is a truly radical case of textual adjustment, consisting in a mélange of two paraphrased passages from Exodus and Isaiah.

The switch from the A-2 type to the more festive F-5 is an equally obvious choice when one takes into account that the third mass of Christmas' F-5 *Viderunt omnes* and Epiphany's F-5 *Omnes de Saba* are already in place. Thus the remainder of the season is filled in with chants of the F-5 type. But what of the seemingly anomalous D-3 *Speciosus forma* (Ps 44.3; 2) on the Sunday within the octave of Christmas? The explanation for it lies in the dual circumstances that it is derived from Psalm 44, the psalm cited above as that traditionally associated with female saints, and that the liturgy for the Sunday after Christmas is typically conflated with that of 1 January, the date of the ancient feast of Mary's Nativity. The celebration of the festival was made obsolete when the four great Marian feasts (including the 8 September observance of the Nativity) were adopted in the later seventh century, but the memory of the older occasion probably remained fresh at the time of the Advent Project (the date is still observed in the Blandin, Monza and Compiègne graduals).[12] *Speciosus forma*, then, might have been either a preexisting Common gradual for female saints that was assigned its place during work on the Advent Project, or it might have been one of those exceptional chants like the Christmas Day and Epiphany graduals already assigned before the Project began. In any event it must predate the decision to fill out the Christmas festal sequence with F-5 graduals.[13]

LENT

It was remarked above that the three graduals of the Sundays after the Epiphany have more in common with the graduals of Lent and the Sundays after Pentecost than with those of the rest of the Christmas season. This is true of all Mass Proper chants for the liturgical occasions in question. The distinction involved is the general one, cited several times in this study, between chants for the two festal portions of the year—the Christmas and Easter seasons—and the two others, Lent and the post-Pentecostal period. The former invite the creation of chants with specific liturgical themes; the latter do so only exceptionally. Among the Lenten exceptions are the fourth Sunday's Laetare Sunday, with its motif of joy amidst penitence, and the gradual accordingly is *Laetatus sum; Fiat pax* (Ps 121.1; 7). There are also the two days of the baptismal Scrutinies, the Wednesday and Saturday of the fourth week; Wednesday's pair of graduals, *Venite filii* (Ps 33.12; 1) and *Beata gens* (Ps 32.12; 6), have clear references to baptism. And finally there is Holy Thursday with its obviously appropriate nonpsalmic gradual *Chris-*

tus factus est (Phlm 2.8–9). One might have thought that Palm Sunday, with its triumphal entry into Jerusalem, would have inspired colorful chants evoking processional motifs, but its entire Mass Proper harks back to the more ancient association of the date with the Passion; if the chants of the day, including the gradual *Tenuisti manum* (Ps 72.23–24; 1–3), have a theme, it is that of the suffering Jesus seeking consolation from God the Father. The communion of the day, in fact, *Pater si non potest hic calix transire nisi bibam illum* (Mt 26.43), is nonpsalmic and expresses this theme with exceptional explicitness.

Not every one of this small group of festal graduals is necessarily a contribution of the Advent Project. The most obvious possibility is Holy Thursday's *Christus factus*, the only nonpsalmic gradual of Lent, and one of that set of three chants (Stephen's *Sederunt principes* and Sylvester's *Ecce sacerdos* are the others) that share identical F-5 melodies. Laetare Sunday's *Laetatus sum* is a better possibility than the graduals of Palm Sunday or the days of baptismal Scrutiny on the grounds of its more recent liturgical association. The Scrutinies chants, while no doubt permanently assigned from the time of their composition, could very well figure among that minority of permanently assigned graduals such as those of Christmas Day and the Epiphany that predate the Advent Project.

Aside from the minority of chants with specifically appropriate liturgical assignments, the graduals of Lent—numbering more than forty and by and large lacking in indices such as nonpsalmic chants and textual adjustment—would appear to offer little scope for speculation on their chronological breakdown.[14] There is, however, an intriguing source of information that might help to identify some of those that constituted its pre-Advent Project repertory, the Psalter of St-Germain-des-Prés.

Of the seventy-one psalm verses in the manuscript that are indicated as responds by an *R* in the margin, seventeen correspond to Roman graduals; the seventeen are given in table 19 with their Roman liturgical assignments. A strikingly large number of them appear in Lent, nine of the seventeen (underlined in the table). It is true that we cannot take the Psalter of St-Germain, a later sixth-century document of unknown provenance, as anything approaching a precise index of the early- to mid-seventh-century Roman repertory of responsorial psalms. But we can take it as a guide to the sort of psalm verses that were probably in general favor as psalm responses throughout Italy and Gaul at the time. The majority of the psalter's indicated responses do not figure in the Roman gradual repertory, but as for those that do (these seventeen), their presence in the psalter gives us reason to suspect that they might be among the earliest representatives of Roman

Table 19. The Gradual Responds of the Psalter of St-Germain-des-Prés

Ps 16.8	*Custodi me*	Lent I Thursday; Sunday I after Lawrence
Ps 18.9	*Ab occultis*	Lent III Tuesday
Ps 33.12	*Venite filii*	Lent IV Wednesday
Ps 34.13	*Ego autem*	Holy Week Tuesday
Ps 34.23	*Exsurge dne et int*	Holy Week Monday
Ps 44.3	Speciosus forma	Sunday after Xmas
Ps 44.11–12	Audi filia	St. Agnes II; St. Cecilia
Ps 49.14	Immola deo	Ordination of bishop
Ps 56.2	*Miserere mei*	Ash Wednesday
Ps 71.18	Benedictus dns	Sunday I after Epiphany
Ps 72.23–24	*Tenuisti manum*	Palm Sunday
Ps 79.8	Domine deus virtutum	Advent Ember Saturday
Ps 91.2	*Bonum est confit*	Lent II Saturday; Sunday II after Lawrence
Ps 109.3	Tecum principium	Xmas first mass
Ps 109.4	Juravit dominus	Sanctoral Common
Ps 117.24	Haec dies	Easter
Ps 140.2	*Dirigatur*	Lent I Tuesday; Ember Days

graduals. We have, then, this large proportion of Lenten gradual responses, a circumstance that matches our hypothesis that many of the Lenten graduals were in existence before the Advent Project. And we have, moreover, a similar match for no less than four chants already singled out here on other grounds as possibly of similarly early vintage: the above-discussed Sunday after Christmas *Speciosus forma*, Palm Sunday's *Tenuisti manum*, Christmas' *Tecum principium* and Easter's *Haec dies*. The numbers involved here are simply too remarkable to be ignored—no less than thirteen of the psalter's seventeen response verses give some evidence of appearing in the gradual's pre-Advent Project repertory.

DUM CLAMAREM AND TOLLITE HOSTIAS

There are two particular Lenten graduals that draw attention to themselves by highly singular circumstances: Tuesday in the second week's *Jacta cogitatum* (Ps 54.23; 17–19) and Thursday in the fifth week's *Tollite hostias* (Ps 95.8–9; Ps 28.9). *Jacta cogitatum*'s verse, *Dum clamarem*, is one of only two psalmic gradual verses (from a total of some 110) that are the product of substantial textual adjustment;[15] it was fashioned by freely paraphrasing portions of three verses from Psalm 54. But what is more remarkable about the verse is that it shares its text with *Dum clamarem,* the introit for the fifth Sunday after the feast of the Apostles. For which chant might this extraordinary text have been originally crafted? In all probability it was the introit. The Roman cantors routinely applied the technique of substantial textual adjustment to introits but did so for gradual verses, apparently, with great reluctance. The preexistence of a particularly apt text in the introit repertory, however, might very well have overcome their inhibitions in this respect. There are chronological implications involved with this extraordinary text that will be explored when the introit and gradual cycles are compared in the final chapter of this volume.

Tollite hostias, gradual for Thursday of the fifth week of Lent, is one of the most mysterious chants in the entire Mass Proper. As a chant on a Lenten Thursday we expect that it, like all other such chants, would have been borrowed from somewhere else in the Mass Proper when Gregory II established the Lenten Thursdays as liturgical in about 720, some two decades after the conclusion of the Advent Project. But *Tollite hostias* is uniquely assigned to this Lenten Thursday! Are we to believe, then, that it was composed for the occasion at the time of Gregory II's late liturgical intervention? All circumstances point to that conclusion, but it remains altogether implausible that a single chant would be composed for a mere Lenten feria twenty years or more after the creation of new Mass Proper chants had come to a halt. I find this notion simply too unlikely to accept, but I have nothing to substitute in its place. The alternate solution, that *Tollite* was originally a member of the post-Pentecostal sequence and was dropped from that group of chants in about 720, is equally implausible. Its presence as the sole chant of any genre uniquely assigned to the Lenten Thursdays remains a mystery, something that I, for one, find historiographically comforting; we should not expect to understand everything about the creation of the Roman Mass Proper.

To close now with a more general consideration of the Lenten gradual sequence, its most remarkable feature may be that virtually every one of its chants seems to be uniquely assigned. This is not immediately apparent because nine of its forty-four are shared with the Sundays after Pentecost (I spare the reader a table). But once the probable direction of borrowing is sorted out (three of the nine are late borrowings from the post-Pentecostal season for the Thursdays in Lent, and the other six more likely earlier borrowings in the other direction), there remain forty-one properly Lenten graduals at the conclusion of the Advent Project, an impressive number by any standard.[16]

I would imagine that a fairly large proportion of these chants existed already before the Advent Project, as part of that fund of psalmic chants used on an ad hoc basis for all but a number of exceptional dates in the temporal cycle. With the Advent Project these chants were given fixed assignments, and their number was supplemented with a substantial number of new chants. We cannot discern compositional patterns that tell us how this distribution of chants was carried out, nor can we tell precisely the proportion of preexisting and newly created chants. The best we can do is suggest that the number of preexisting graduals might have been substantially higher than the figure of about twenty proposed for introits. This, because of the larger number of Lenten introits with the presumably advanced traits of nonpsalmic texts and substantial textual adjustment, and the large number of Lenten gradual response verses corresponding with those of the Psalter of St-Germain-des-Prés. As for identifying individual chants that might have belonged either to the original fund or to the additions of the Advent Project, the nine graduals with responses concordant with those of the just-mentioned psalter are plausible candidates for earlier chants, and a number of individual graduals such as *Christus factus, Jacta cogitatum* and *Laetatus sum* are equally plausible candidates for additions of the Advent Project. To the latter group we might add all those graduals with substantial textual adjustment (another seven beyond *Christus factus* and *Jacta cogitatum*); surely it is of some significance that not a single gradual with substantial textual adjustment figures among the seventeen represented in the Psalter of St-Germain. All in all, then, one has grounds to at least venture a guess about the broad chronology of the Lenten gradual repertory; it is not unlikely that it contains the largest fund of pre-Advent Project chants of any portion of the completed Roman Mass Proper.

PASCHALTIME

There is, of course, but one Paschaltime gradual, *Haec dies,* or to put it more precisely, there is but one gradual respond, *Haec dies,* which is sung on Easter with the verse *Confitemini* (Ps 117.1) and repeated on the five subsequent days of Easter week with different verses, most of them drawn from Psalm 117. This is an extraordinary circumstance, one that requires immediate explanation. A second extraordinary circumstance is the absence of graduals from the remainder of Paschaltime, that is, from the Saturday of Easter week to the Saturday of Pentecost week, when two alleluias are sung at each Mass rather than the accustomed gradual and alleluia. This, too, calls for at least introductory observations in this chapter and a more thorough examination in the chapter on the alleluia.

The singing of *Haec dies* throughout Easter week, the subject of diverse ingenious theories, has, I believe, a simple enough explanation. We saw in chapter two that Psalm 117 was sung in the early Church with its response verse 117 (*Haec dies*) throughout Easter week. It is not unlikely, therefore, that in the earlier seventh century at Rome, before the schola's development of the gradual, the responsorial psalm for Easter week continued to be Psalm 117, with *Haec dies* as refrain. With the creation of the gradual, then, *Haec dies* was continued as the respond for Easter week, and individual verses, mostly from Psalm 117, were chosen for each day.

This explanation fits the evidence far better than the conventional notion that the Easter week graduals are the result of distributing the Easter responsorial psalm throughout the week. The most obvious difficulty with that notion is the fact that only a handful of verses are chosen for service in the graduals, including, moreover, one derived from a different psalm, Tuesday's *Dicant nunc qui* (Ps 106.2). The music as well speaks against the idea of distribution from a single chant. The five Easter week verses are among the least formulaic examples of the A-2 type, differing substantially from one another, whereas, if they were genuine representatives of a single chant, we should expect them to be melodically homogenous, like the A-2 graduals of the Advent Saturday Ember Day. They are, in a word, individual chants, united by their traditional use of the same respond.

As for the time of the *Haec dies* group's creation, the circumstance that they share with Christmas' *Tecum principium* the distinction of being among the least formulaic examples of the A-2 type suggests that they might be examples of those graduals that were permanently assigned before the Advent Project.

The second major question about the Paschaltime graduals—why they are absent from the season outside of Easter week—is related to the first. If the early Christian tradition of singing Psalm 117 throughout Easter week continued into the earlier seventh century, so too might have the early Christian tradition, suggested above on more than one occasion, of singing responsorial psalms with alleluia as response throughout the rest of Paschaltime. This raises the question of a proto-alleluia of the Mass, a genre in existence before the Advent Project; its consideration is better left to the chapter on the alleluia.

THE SUNDAYS AFTER PENTECOST

The Roman post-Pentecostal series of graduals, unlike that of introits, corresponds well to the simile spelled out in the opening pages of this volume, where the post-Pentecostal season is likened to the unfinished rear portion of a house. It is given here in tabular form (table 20) along with the two post-Pentecostal series of the early Frankish Blandin gradual (c.800). The Roman incipits are given as they appear in Vat lat 5319, after the traditional Roman manner of indicating the Sundays. The underlined incipits are those either unique to the season or (indicated by added asterisks) originally unique to the season and borrowed for Thursdays in Lent. The remainder of the chants are all borrowed from Lent except for *Timebunt gentes*, which is borrowed from the third Sunday after Epiphany.

The column of Roman numerals before the two columns of incipits from the Blandin manuscript provides the Frankish numbering of the twenty-three Sundays after Pentecost. The primary reason for including the graduals of the Blandin manuscript is to confirm the existence of the Roman series at the time of the mid-eighth-century transmission of the *cantus romanus* to the Franks (the first Blandin series is almost identical to the Roman). The graduals of the second Blandin series (arranged by psalm number) appear in the manuscript after those of the first: for each Sunday the first gradual is given with the rubric RESP. GRAD. and the second with the rubric ITEM RESP. GRAD. Five Sundays have only one gradual. The Rheinau manuscript, however, the other Frankish gradual copied in around 800, has the identical series, with the five missing graduals in place. The five are the same as those for the corresponding Sunday from the Blandin's first series, which explains why the scribe of the Blandin manuscript did not include them—it would have made little sense to indicate the same gradual twice on these dates.

The presence of the two series in the Blandin gradual tells us that there were two such series in circulation at the time of the manuscript's copying, the original Roman series and another that could have been a second Roman series or, more likely perhaps, a Frankish substitute that was numerically ordered after the manner of post-Pentecostal introits, offertories and communions. This numerically ordered series is encountered only in the Rheinau and Blandin manuscripts; the standard Frankish and later Gregorian series is substantially the same as the first Blandin and original Roman one.

With this basic information established, what might one conclude about the origins of the Roman series? It can be assumed that it was put together only after the Lenten series was completed. The Lenten dates are stational and would no doubt have required the attention of the schola before the nonstational Sundays after Pentecost. This consideration, incidentally, raises the intriguing question of the schola's day-to-day activity during this long period, some five months of the summer and fall, when the Sundays

Table 20. Post-Pentecostal Graduals

	Vat lat 5319		Blandin I	Blandin II	Psalm
Pentecost I	Ego dixi domine	I	Ego dixi domine	Miserere mihi	6
Pent II	Ad dominum	II	Ad dominum	Domine deus noster	8
Pent III	Jacta cogitatum	III	Jacta cog	Adjutor	9
Pent IV	Propitius esto	IV	Propitius esto	Exsurge domine	9
Apostles I	Protector noster	V	Protector noster	Ab occultis	18
Apost II	Convertere	VI	Convertere	Unam petii	26
		VII	Venite filii	—	33
Apost III	Liberasti nos	VIII	Liberasti nos	—	43
Apost IV	Esto mihi	IX	Esto mihi	Speciosus	44
Apost V	Domine deus noster	X	Dne deus noster	Benedictus dns	71
Lawrence I	*Custodi me	XI	Custodi me	Sciant gentes	82
Lawr II	Benedicam dnm	XII	In deo speravit	Protector noster	83
Lawr III	Bonum est confit	XIII	Benedicam dnm	Convertere	89
Lawr IV	*Respice domine	XIV	Respice domine	Domine exaudi	101
Lawr V	Bonum est confid	XV	Bonum est confit	Timebunt gentes	101
Lawr VI	Benedicam dnm	XVI	Bonum est confid	Misit dominus	106
Angel I	Timebunt gentes	XVII	Timebunt gentes	Bonum est confid	117
Angel II	Quis sicut dominus	XVIII	Quis sicut	Laetatus sum	121
Angel III	Laetatus sum	XIX	Laetatus sum	Dirigatur	140
Angel IV	*Oculi omnium	XX	Oculi omnium	Eripe me	142
Angel V	Domine refugium	XXI	Domine refugium	—	89
Angel VI	Ecce quam bonum	XXII	Ecce quam bonum	—	132
Angel VII	Timebunt gentes	XXIII	Timebunt gentes	—	101

are not stational. We should not imagine that the time was a period of extended summer vacation, even if the singers might have been allowed to escape the heat of the city for limited periods of time. There are a number of sanctoral festivals during the period that are stational along with dates like the September Ember Days.[17] It was suggested in the previous chapter that this time of relative inactivity could have been used during the later seventh century for both the creation of new chants and maintenance of the growing repertory. The summertime visit of Guido d'Arezzo, who came to Rome in around 1028 to display the pedagogical efficacy of his notated antiphoner to Pope John XIX and his singers, suggests that even at this late date the Roman singers were present in the city and seriously occupied with musical pursuits.[18] And surely, to return our attention to the seventh century, the schola would have sung Mass regularly for the pope at the Lateran on nonstational dates of the summer and fall. Thus some sort of musical provision for the Sundays after Pentecost was necessary.

There are twenty-two assignments in the series, using twenty different graduals (*Benedicam dominum* and *Timebunt gentes* each appear twice). Nine of the chants appear to be original to the series (those underlined in table 20); ten are borrowed from Lent and one from the third Sunday after the Epiphany. The large proportion of borrowed chants and the repetition of two chants within the series creates the impression of something better described as cobbled together than something carefully crafted. The uniquely assigned chants themselves may be said to contribute to this impression with their high incidence of the more common modal types: three A-2 and four F-5 from a total of nine.

The three A-2 graduals (*Ego dixi domine, Liberasti nos* and *Benedicam dominum*) are chants of special interest. They are very typical examples of the Roman formulaic melody yet are set differently in the Gregorian versions: the first of the three is in mode-5 and the latter two in mode-7. This is surprising because one would think that these chants would have been particularly easy to match. It is all the more surprising when one considers that every other chant in the series is matched at least in regard to its final. Helmut Hucke brought attention to the anomalous trio already in 1955, concluding that the Roman singers at some late date abandoned the original melodies of the chants and resorted to the expedient of replacing them with a common formula.[19] Students of oral transmission in chant might refer to this as an exercise of "thrift" on the part of the Romans; the example will be brought up again in the epilogue to this volume.

Finally, a brief note is in order on the numerically ordered series of Frankish graduals, that finding place in the Rheinau manuscript and as doublets in Blandin. Could it also be a Roman series transmitted toward the end of one of the Roman Mass Proper *libelli* brought to the Franks in the mid-eighth century? Some like to look upon the Rheinau gradual as one reflecting a more ancient Roman tradition than the other Frankish books. One must agree with Dom Hesbert, however, who finds the manuscript more eccentric than archaic: it has as many innovative features as obsolete ones and is characterized above all by inexplicable omissions.[20] The presence of the numerical gradual series in this manuscript, then, speaks neither for nor against the possibility of the series' Roman origins. What does speak strongly for the negative side is the inclusion of two graduals, *Unam petii* and *Domine exaudi*, that are originally Frankish chants, entirely absent from the Roman repertory. On the positive side is the presence of five concordances with the Psalter of St-Germain, as opposed to only two in the Vat lat 5319 series, as well as an even higher incidence of borrowing from Lent and the post-Epiphany season, fourteen and three chants respectively.

It remains, I believe, a fascinating possibility, if not a probability, that the Rheinau numerical series is derived from a Roman post-Pentecostal series, one that predated the Advent Project. It would have been a numerically ordered list of psalmic graduals used on an ad hoc basis throughout the season. To reconstruct it one must remove from the Rheinau series the graduals that the Franks added to bring its number to twenty-three. These include the two Frankish chants (*Sciant gentes* and *Domine exaudi*); the three chants in the series that are uniquely assigned in the Vat lat 5319 series (*Domine deus, Liberasti* and *Ecce quam bonum*) and hence products of the Advent Project; and finally the one of the non-numerically ordered cluster of three at the end (*Domine refugium*) that is not already excluded for other reasons.[21] Dare we to think that the resulting numerically ordered list of sixteen psalmic chants is the first Roman post-Pentecostal gradual series? The number sixteen, incidentally, should raise eyebrows in view of what was said in the previous chapter about Antoine Chavasse's adventures with that number.

THE GRADUAL SANCTORAL CYCLE

An analysis of the sanctoral graduals for chronological indications is similar to that undertaken with the Lenten graduals; it is a matter of trying to separate graduals belonging to an earlier fund of Common chants from those added in the project to provide an adequate sanctoral Proper. The task might be marginally more rewarding with the sanctoral graduals because of a somewhat higher incidence of chronologically suggestive factors: the presence of slightly more nonpsalmic chants and chants with substantially adjusted texts as well as the distinction between uniquely assigned chants and shared ones.

Within the early fund one would certainly want to place at least some of the graduals derived from Psalms 44 and 20. There are five of the former and two of the latter, accounting for a total of no less than twenty annual assignments.[22] Another obvious candidate for inclusion in this group would be *Beatus vir* (Ps 111.1; 2) with its seven assignments. And surely a gradual for festivals celebrating two or more saints would have been necessary; *Clamaverunt justi* (Ps 33.18; 19) with its five assignments is a good possibility, as is *Exultabunt sancti* (Ps 149.5; 1) with its five. Altogether these ten graduals account for well over half of the shared sanctoral assignments. These are, of course, assignments made permanent only at the time of the final revision of the sanctorale, but the probability remains that they roughly reflect earlier practice.

It seems likely that all nonpsalmic graduals would be later additions, this, in view of the essentially psalmic prehistory of the gradual; there are just six of these chants among the thirty-two sanctoral graduals. Virtually every one of the nonpsalmic graduals is uniquely assigned,[23] and thus a product of the attempt to provide a Proper sanctorale. And every one without exception of the nonpsalmic graduals that is biblically derived (*Locus iste* is nonbiblical) is the subject of substantial textual adjustment, a trait that is, as noted above, comparatively rare in graduals.[24] Obvious cases, then, of late graduals would be chants like the Vigil of John the Baptist's *Fuit homo; Ut testim* (Jn 1.6; 7) and Paul's *Qui operatus; Gratia* (Gal 2.8–9, 1; 1 Cor 15.10), both having uniquely assigned nonpsalmic texts that are substantially adjusted, and both, moreover, in the festive F-5 mode. Among the less obvious cases I would add the five psalmic graduals that are uniquely assigned to the six nonpsalmic ones, for a total of eleven. Thus—keeping in mind that one is dealing here only in varying degrees of probability—we have succeeded in a tentative categorization of eleven sanctoral graduals as products of the final sanctoral revision and ten as members of the earlier list, accounting for about two-thirds of the thirty-two sanctoral chants.

A final observation about the Roman sanctoral graduals involves the next stage in their history—their transmission to the Franks. The Roman liturgical assignments are only imperfectly maintained in the early Frankish sources. I count twenty-five of forty-two cases of continuity between Vat lat 5319 and the early-ninth-century Blandin and twenty-two of thirty-five between Vat lat 5319 and the mid-ninth-century Monza.[25] Thus the early Frankish graduals have the same sanctoral gradual somewhat less than two-thirds of the time, whereas Christmastime and Lenten graduals (and sanctoral introits, for that matter) are almost perfectly maintained. How to explain the difference?

It could be a matter of deficiencies in the Roman Mass antiphoners used in the transmission or fallibility on the part of the Frankish cantors. The former seems more likely because the lapses in continuity involved are almost exclusively a matter of liturgical assignment, whereas there is exceptionally good musical continuity between the Roman and Gregorian versions; almost all thirty-two sanctoral graduals have the same finals and clearly related melodies in both versions.[26]

There is a factor that allows us to come closer to identifying what the difficulty with these sources might be. Ten of the eleven uniquely assigned sanctoral graduals have continuity of assignment between the Roman and Frankish sources;[27] it is in graduals that are shared where the large proportion of discrepancies are to be found. It could be, then, that the Roman Mass antiphoners, while assigning unique sanctoral graduals, frequently left the choice of shared chants up to the cantors on an annual basis. Lending credence to this possibility is the circumstance that the Blandin gradual, while invariably assigning a sanctoral introit, fails to provide a gradual for about a dozen dates.[28] This early Frankish source, then, might be mirroring a Roman source in this respect. We shall see that the Roman graduals failed to provide fixed assignments of alleluias (the latest addition to the Mass Proper) for the overwhelming majority of dates in the calendar; sanctoral graduals (themselves a relatively late subject of attention on the part of the Roman singers) might very well share this condition, even if to a considerably lesser extent.

THE SEVENTH-CENTURY ROMAN GRADUAL

The changeover from the responsorial psalm to the gradual (one might say the move from lector chant to schola chant) as such was the work of the newly founded schola cantorum sometime in the mid-seventh century. Its members established the format of a melismatic choral respond and a somewhat more overtly virtuosic solo verse, reworking a selection of traditional melodic material from the responsorial psalmody of the Roman churches into a variety of more firmly fixed melodic types. They maintained a kind of repertorial continuity also, retaining a number of psalmic associations with certain important festivals and preserving a larger number of favored response verses for more general usage. Thus, at an early stage of the new schola chant's history, there existed already a number of permanently assigned graduals such as Christmas' *Tecum principium* and Easter week's *Haec dies* group, as well as a larger fund of chants available for day-to-day temporal and sanctoral usage. The liturgical tendency to properization led to an increase in the number of specific calendric associations and eventually to the decision to undertake the great work of providing an appropriate and permanently fixed set of Mass Proper chants for each date in the calendar—the ambitious enterprise referred to here as the Advent Project.

A number of graduals for the Advent-Christmas season were already in place as work on the project began, among them no doubt Christmas' *Tecum principium* and *Viderunt omnes*, the following Sunday's *Speciosus forma* and Epiphany's *Omnes de Saba*. The open dates, previously served from the lists of temporal and sanctoral chants, were filled in with new chants, all of them with explicit thematic reference to their liturgical occasion, a number of them using the innovative features of nonpsalmic texts and textual adjustment, and most of them arranged in two sets of chants with homogeneous melodies. The result was the attractive finished product that came to be maintained in use for over a millennium. The project moved on, within a year or two for all we know, taking the substantial fund of perhaps thirty or so previously existing temporal psalmic chants, permanently assigning them to the Sundays after the Epiphany and to the Sundays and weekdays of the Lenten season (beginning with Septuagesima Sunday) and adding enough new psalmic graduals to provide unique chants for every day of Lent except the Saturday Ember Day, where three of five graduals were borrowed from earlier in the same week. The gradual for Holy Thursday, *Christus factus est,* is the only nonpsalmic gradual of Lent; it may have been added after the rest of the season was completed, taking its melody literally from *Sederunt principes* and *Ecce sacerdos,* Christmas week sanctoral chants.[29]

The Easter *Haec dies* set was in place before the Advent Project, but the post-Pentecostal series, with its makeshift aspect, was the last portion of the temporale to be given a set of permanently assigned graduals. Work on it may have been contemporary with the completion of the sanctorale. The post-Pentecostal graduals and the shared sanctoral graduals manifest the same trait of less than perfect continuity of liturgical assignment between the Roman and Frankish sources.

To compare the two chants that have been treated individually so far— the introit and the gradual—I would guess that there was a considerable fund of graduals for general use before the introit repertory achieved a comparable state. This is suggested by the archaic features of the gradual: predominantly psalmic texts, relatively rare use of textual adjustment and reliance upon traditional melodic formulas. The comparatively adequate condition of the early gradual repertory, then, might have allowed work on it to be delayed and greater attention to be paid the introit during the period of the Advent Project. As events turned out, the gradual was never completed perfectly in accord with the ideals of the Advent Project, whereas the introit most certainly was. There is, moreover, one item of hard evidence supporting the claim that the entire introit cycle was finished before that of the gradual; the radically paraphrased text of the Lenten gradual verse *Dum clamarem* was borrowed in all likelihood from a post-Pentecostal introit, the *Dum clamarem* of the fifth Sunday after the feast of the apostles.

CHAPTER 10

The Alleluia

It is *Ordo romanus I*, as was the case with the introit and the gradual, that gives us our first unequivocal reference to the alleluia of the Mass. The passage that cites the gradual, "the cantor with *cantatorium* goes up and sings the *responsum*," continues, "if it be the time to sing the alleluia, then good, if not, however, the tract."[1] One manuscript of *Ordo I* assures us that it is not the same cantor who is responsible for both chants: "Then another [sings] the alleluia."[2] The musical format of the alleluia, like that of the gradual, is responsorial, consisting in the alleluia, the verse and a repetition of the alleluia. We do not know precisely how this was rendered in seventh- and eighth-century Rome. Throughout much of the Middle Ages the standard practice was for a cantor to begin by intoning a neumatic alleluia melody, which was repeated by the chorus, who extended the final syllable *a* with a melismatic "jubilus" (to be discussed below); one or two cantors then sang a moderately melismatic verse, which the chorus completed by singing the final melismatic syllable; the chant was concluded with the singing of alleluia by the chorus.

The alleluia is sung after the gradual on most festive occasions of both the temporal and sanctoral cycles. It is omitted on penitential dates, most notably during Lent, and on occasions of sorrow such as the Requiem Mass. At such times, for example the Sundays of Lent, it might be replaced by the tract. During Paschaltime, beginning with Low Sunday (the Saturday of Easter week in the Old Roman rite) the gradual is omitted and two alleluias are sung.

ORIGINS

Alleluia is a Hebrew exclamation meaning "praise God."[3] It was appended to twenty psalms in the Hebrew Bible and was no doubt sung as a response

249

to these psalms in the Temple of Jerusalem.[4] The early Christians adopted the use of the word (much as they did "Amen"), employing it both as an independent exclamation and as a psalm response. The former usage might be fairly described as informal rather than liturgical. We observe it, for example, in Jerome's description of the Roman child Paula, who leaps upon the chest of her grandfather as she sings alleluia,[5] and, while it is undocumented, we can well imagine the faithful, during those earliest centuries of more charismatic liturgical gatherings, uttering spontaneous cries of alleluia.

As liturgical procedures begin to crystallize toward the end of Christian antiquity, it is the use of alleluia as psalm response that comes more to the fore. This is particularly the case in monastic offices. Cassian of Marseilles (d.435), describing the practice of Palestine, says that monks there are careful not to sing alleluia as a response unless the word is inscribed in the psalm's biblical title, thus appearing to imply the existence of a common tendency to the contrary. The impression is confirmed a century later by St. Benedict, who gives detailed instructions for the use of the alleluia response in his description of the early Monte Cassino Office. And a Roman clerical contemporary of Benedict goes so far as to advocate that, in the singing of the Office, "alleluia should always be affixed to all psalms, so that there be a common response in every place."

The same sixth-century Roman cleric, however, calls for a much more limited use of the practice at Mass; there he advocates that the addition of alleluia to psalms "be confined to a period of fifty days from the holy Resurrection to the sacred Pentecost." The same restraint is evident in Augustine's references to the subject. He, too, defines Paschaltime as the period "when we sing alleluia," and in the numerous passages where he speaks of responsorial psalmody at Mass he specifies the response alleluia only for those psalms that have the word affixed to them in the biblical text. Thus in preaching on Psalm 113, he cites "this psalm to which we just now responded by chanting ... alleluia."

If Augustine, then, speaks of the singing of alleluia as response to certain psalms during the Fore-Mass of Paschaltime, can we look upon this as the origin of the alleluia of the Mass? Only in a limited sense; this is a subject that I have written on at length, both already in this volume and elsewhere, and I will summarize my position on it here as briefly as possible.[6]

A psalm came to be sung regularly in the Fore-Mass during the later decades of the fourth century. It was typically a single psalm, especially in the West, and it was generally sung responsorially. Declaimed for centuries to come by youthful lectors and eventually deacons and subdeacons, it performed the same function and occupied the same position in the liturgy as the gradual, the fixed chant created by the Roman schola cantorum in the mid-seventh century. It seems fair to refer, then, to the later fourth-century responsorial psalm as the gradual psalm. In doing so, however, one must keep in mind two important qualifications: the psalm might very well have been sung occasionally without refrains, especially during Lent, hence serving as a kind of proto-tract, and we know that it was sung sometimes, especially during the Easter season, with alleluia as response, hence serving as a sort of proto-alleluia. One might thus say that the gradual psalm was occasionally a tract psalm and occasionally an alleluia-psalm. The central factor that legitimizes this way of thinking is the norm of a single psalm in the ancient Fore-Mass, a chant that can be shown to have a direct historical relationship, in its format and in its liturgical placement, with the early medieval gradual.

To warrant the claim that the alleluia-psalm existed in the same full sense as the gradual psalm, it would be necessary to show the regular presence of a second responsorial psalm in the ancient Fore-Mass, one with alleluia as its refrain. This is not the case in the western liturgical centers at the turn of the fifth century. For early-fifth-century Jerusalem, however, we have the testimony of the Armenian Lectionary that two responsorial psalms, the second with alleluia refrain, were regularly sung in the Fore-Mass. The practice appears to have become widespread throughout the East in the succeeding centuries.

I think it explains an important passage in the psalm commentary of Cassiodorus (d.580), where he speaks of "ever-varying melodies" (*tropis semper variantibus*).[7] This matches precisely Christian Thodberg's description of the sixth-century Byzantine alleluia with its six distinct alleluia melodies (*without* jubili!), two for each of the three modes (the tritus has no alleluias).[8] Peter Wagner misinterprets the passage to read "ever-varying *melismata.*" That is, ever-varying jubili, and Roman ones at that,[9] whereas it is surely Byzantine alleluia melodies of which Cassiodorus speaks, not western alleluia jubili. Cassiodorus wrote his psalm commentary, one must remember, during his long stay in Constantinople.[10]

In any event we have no compelling evidence for the existence of the alleluia of the Mass in the principal western liturgical centers, including Rome, during the fifth and sixth centuries. There is, of course, the much discussed letter of Gregory the Great (d.604) in which he admits to allowing "alleluia to be said at Masses outside the Pentecost period [the fifty days of Paschaltime]," but the most plausible interpretation of the passage is that it refers not to the Mass Proper genre we know as the alleluia, but to the common practice of affixing alleluia to psalms.[11] The probability remains that the Fore-Mass psalmody of Gregory's time was essentially the same as that of Augustine's; that is, a single psalm was typically sung, generally the responsorial psalm soon to be transformed into the gradual, even if it may have been sung without refrains on some penitential occasions and was very likely sung with alleluia refrains throughout much of Paschaltime.

It was necessary, then, that a fundamental structural change take place in the Roman Fore-Mass for the alleluia as such to come into existence. The norm of a single psalm must be replaced by the norm of two consecutively sung psalms. This is the sort of liturgical change more likely motivated by some specific reason, such as a memorable event or a compelling external influence. In this particular case it would appear to be the latter kind of motivation, the influence of the Byzantine liturgy, with its dual responsorial psalms, the second of which is the *alleluia-alleluiarion*, a splendid prelude to the gospel.

THE BYZANTINE INFLUENCE

The evidence for the Byzantine influence on the origins of the Roman alleluia (or at least on its early development) could hardly be more telling; Thodberg has shown that three Byzantine *alleluia-alleluiaria* were taken over en bloc, both their texts and music, as Roman alleluias.[12] *Alleluia-alleluiarion* (henceforth simply alleluia) is the term for the alleluia and verse of the Byzantine eucharistic liturgy. The chant appears precisely at that place in the liturgy where its apparent ancestor, the alleluia-psalm of the early-fifth-century Jerusalem liturgy, was sung, that is, after the first responsorial psalm and before the gospel. Its format is that of an abbreviated psalm with alleluia response, consisting in the intonation of alleluia by the *psaltes* (cantor), a choral repetition of the alleluia, the singing of the *alleluiarion* (usually two or three psalm verses) by the cantor and the concluding choral repetition of the alleluia. The form is identical to that of the Roman alleluia except for the absence of a jubilus after the alleluia and the usual presence of two or three verses as opposed to the typical single verse of the Roman chant.

A substantial portion of *O kyrios,* one of the three Byzantine adoptees (*Epi sy kyrios* and *Oty theos* are the other two), is given in example 10; the upper staff provides the text and melody of the Byzantine version (labeled "Byz"), and the lower the Roman melodic version (labeled "Rom"), with its transliteration of the Greek text into Latin characters.[13] The relationship between the two is undeniable. Among the more obvious points of similarity are the close resemblance of the alleluia melodies themselves; the con-

Example 10. *Alleluia; O kyrios*

sistent correspondence between the syllables of the original Greek verse text and those of the Roman transliteration; the maintenance of virtually identical melodic contours by the two versions; and the precise duplication of pitches at key points in each phrase, such as beginnings and endings. These similarities clearly go well beyond the possibility of coincidence.

It is, by the way, remarkable that so much of the original melodic identity survived centuries of divergent oral transmission in the two versions. The extant Roman version dates from the later eleventh century and the Byzantine from the twelfth, while the Roman adaptation of the Byzantine chant took place toward the end of the seventh century at the latest.

If the Roman borrowing of these three Greek alleluias—a phenomenon not observed in any other genre of the Mass Proper—is the central item of evidence for Byzantine influence on the origin of the Roman alleluia, there is a comparably significant additional indication in the high proportion of textual concordances between the Roman and Byzantine alleluia repertories.

Table 21 provides the entire Roman alleluia repertory as it appears in Vat lat 5319. Given first are the nineteen chants that have independent melodies,[14] followed by the thirty-five that utilize the three melody types (the D-mode *Dies sanctificatus* type, the G-mode *Ostende* type and E-mode *Excita* type). The table (which will be used for other purposes in this chapter beyond the present one) provides first the textual incipit, then the textual derivation and finally the textual concordance or lack thereof with the Byzantine repertory. The presence of a letter and number (taken from Thodberg's catalogue of the Byzantine repertory)[15] indicates the presence of a concordance, ellipses the absence.

One notes at a glance the comparatively high proportion of textual concordances within the group of chants not using the melody types (hereafter chants with "individual" melodies) as opposed to those using them. It is the chants with individual melodies that concern us especially at this point because, as we shall argue more fully presently, they constitute by and large an earlier layer of the Roman repertory. (This is not to say that *all* chants using the model melodies are later, but that a large proportion of them were added to the original fund of chants in an effort to fill out an obviously meager repertory as expeditiously as possible.) There are eight textual concordances (including the three Greek chants with melodic concordances) from a total of nineteen alleluias with individual melodies. It is a proportion that in itself would appear to exceed the possibility of coincidence, but one that proves altogether more significant when compared with that of the two other Mass Proper chants with Byzantine cognates, the gradual and the communion. Of the 105 Roman graduals, only five have textual concordances with the Byzantine *prokeimenon*, and of the 141 Roman communions, only three have concordances with the Byzantine communion song (the koinonicon).[16] And to dwell for a moment on the relationship of the gradual and the *prokeimenon*, there are two points to be observed, both suggesting for these chants the absence of the sort of direct influence we

Table 21. Roman Alleluia Repertory (with Byzantine textual concordances)

Vat lat 5319		Byz Concord
Other than melody type		
Adorabo ad templum	Ps 137.2	. . .
Beatus vir	Ps 111.1–3	A 46
Confitebor	Ps 137.1	. . .
Confitemini . . . quon	Ps 117.1	. . .
Dominus regnavit	Ps 92.1	A 39
Epi si kyrie	Ps 30.2	A 15a
Gaudete justi	Ps 32.1	. . .
Haec dies	Ps 117.24	. . .
Jubilate deo	Ps 99.2	. . .
O kyrios	Ps 92.1	A 39a
Oty theos	Ps 94.3	A 27b
Pascha nostrum	1 Cor 5.7–8	. . .
Preoccupemus	Ps 94.2	A 50b
Qui confidunt	Ps 124.1–2	. . .
Qui sanat contritos	Ps 146.3	. . .
Quoniam confirmata	Ps 116.2	. . .
Spiritus domini	Wis 1.7	. . .
Te decet hymnus	Ps 64.2	A 32
Venite exultemus	Ps 94.1	A 27
Ostende melody type		
Diffusa est	Ps 44.3	A 48b
Dominus dixit	Ps 2.7	. . .
Dominus in Sina	Ps 67.18–19	. . .
Lauda anima mea	Ps 145.2	. . .
Lauda Hierusalem	Ps 147.12	. . .
Mittat tibi	Ps 19.3	. . .
Nimis honorati	Ps 138.17	. . .
Ostende nobis domine	Ps 84.8	. . .
Paratum cor meum	Ps 107.2	. . .
Specie tua	Ps 44.5	. . .

(continued)

Table 21. (continued)

Vat lat 5319		Byz Concord
Dies sanctificatus *melody type*		
Dies sanctificatus	nonbibl	...
Disposui testamentum	Ps 88.4	...
Hic est discipulus	Jn 21.24	...
Hi sunt qui	Rv 14.4	...
Inveni David	Ps 88.21	[A 7a?]
Justus non conturbabitur	Ps 36.24	...
Magnus sanctus Paulus	nonbibl	...
Quoniam deus magnus	Ps 94.3	A 27
Sancti tui	Ps 144.10	...
Tu es Petrus	Mt 16.18	...
Video caelos	Acts 7.56–60	...
Vidimus stellam	Mt 2.2	...
Excita *melody type*		
Ascendit deus	Ps 46.6	A 14b
Cantate domino ... cantate	Ps 95.1	...
Cantate domino ... laudatio	Ps 149.1	...
Cantate domino ... quia	Ps 97.1	...
Confitebuntur	Ps 88.6	...
Emitte spiritum tuum	Ps 103.30	...
Excita domine	Ps 79.3	A 52b
Exultabunt sancti	Ps 149.5	...
Laetatus sum	Ps 121.1	...
Laudate dominum ... omnes gentes	Ps 116.1	...
Laudate dominum ... quoniam	Ps 134.3	...
Laudate pueri	Ps 112.1	...
Qui posuit fines	Ps 147.14	...

note for the *alleluia-alleluiarion* and alleluia. For one, at least two of the *prokeimenon*-gradual pairs, *Haec dies* and *In omnem terram*, may very well reflect not seventh-century sharing of repertory, but a common liturgical association with Easter and the Apostles' feasts, respectively, which goes back to the fourth century. And for another, there is no apparent melodic relationship between any one of the five Byzantine *prokeimena* and its

Roman textual counterpart, at least nothing approaching that manifested by the three Greek Roman alleluias.[17] And to add a final point, there are no Roman graduals, or communions for that matter, with Greek texts.

On the matter of Greek texts, in fact, I have mentioned only the three alleluias of the Mass with Greek texts; there are four others that appear in the celebrated Roman vespers of Easter week. If this Office, the so-called *gloriosum officium*, might seem at first to lie outside the subject of the alleluia of the Mass, it has in fact an important relationship with the Mass chant; vespers and Mass share a significant number of alleluias, both Greek and Latin. It is necessary, then, to enter into a digression on the Easter week vespers before summarizing the case for Byzantine influence on the origins of the Roman alleluia of the Mass.

THE ALLELUIAS OF THE ROMAN EASTER WEEK VESPERS

During Easter week at Rome the principal clergy of the city gathered at the Lateran for a vesper service of particular splendor.[18] From two to four alleluias were sung on each day with multiple verses. Some of the alleluias were borrowed from the Mass repertory, while others were unique to the vesper service, utilizing a relatively simple common "vesper tone." Table 22 gives the alleluias as they were distributed over the week.[19] An "M" indicates that a verse is sung with the melody of its respective Mass alleluia, a "v" that it is sung to the vesper tone. The five underlined texts are transliterations from the Greek; *O kyrios*, as we have seen, is a Mass alleluia, while the other four are unique to vespers. Byzantine textual concordances are added in the final column. If a Mass verse such as *Pascha nostrum* is used, its own alleluia melody is sung. If the verse is one of those using the vesper tone, the alleluia of *Dominus regnavit decorem* is sung; Thodberg, in fact, makes the plausible claim that the vesper tone is derived from the verse melody of that chant.[20]

There is sufficient information summarized in the table to suggest a possible sequence of events in the development of the vesper rite, a process that, I would imagine, took place within a relatively short space of time. The introduction of the alleluia into the Mass, itself an event of dramatic impact, inspired the Roman clergy to transform Easter Sunday vespers, hitherto a vesper service of the standard format, into one of special splendor. The four alleluias sung during the ceremony, at various stations throughout the Lateran complex, are a group of particularly important chants. *O kyrios* is one of the three borrowed from Byzantium, while *Dominus regnavit decorem*, its Latin cognate, can lay claim to being a kind of Roman ur-alleluia: not only

Table 22. Roman Easter Week Vesper Alleluias

		Verse 1		Verse 2		Verse 3	Byz Concord
Easter	Dominus regnavit	M	—	v	—	v	A 39
	Pascha nostrum	M	—	M			...
	<u>O kyrios</u>	M	—	M			A 39a
	Venite exultemus	M	—	M			A 27
Monday	Domine refugium	v	—	v			...
	<u>O pimenon</u>	v	—	v	—	v	A 52a
	In exitu Israel	v	—	v	—	v	...
Tuesday	Paratum cor meum	v	—	v	—	v	...
	<u>Prosechete laos</u>	v	—	v			A 21a
	Confitebor	M	—	M	—	v	...
Wednesday	Te decet hymnus	M	—v	v	—	v	A 32
	Confitemini . . . et inv	v	—	v			...
Friday	Laetatus sum	v	—	v	—	v	...
	Qui confidunt	M	—	v	—	v	...
Saturday	Cantate . . . quia	v	—	v			A 11
	<u>Y urani</u>	v	—	v			A 1a
Sunday	<u>Deute galliasometha</u>	v	—	v			A 27a
	Omnes gentes	v	—	v	—	v	A 14

does it come at the head of this group and contribute its alleluia melody to the rest of the week, but it appears no less than five times in the Roman temporale, including important occasions such as the second Mass of Christmas and Easter Monday. Philippe Bernard has good reason to suspect that it was the original Easter Sunday alleluia, replaced by the nonpsalmic *Pascha nostrum*, another member of this group.[21] *Venite exultemus*, finally, is assigned to three masses in the Roman calendar, including Easter Tuesday. It shares, by the way, the melody of its alleluia and the first half of its verse with *Te decet hymnus*, another Mass alleluia, borrowed for use at Easter week vespers. There were not enough similarly appropriate Mass alleluias to provide alleluias for the entire week and hence the decision to abstract the vesper tone from *Dominus regnavit decorem* and to stamp out a considerable variety of new verses. In doing so the Roman singers made generous use of Byzantine *alleluiarion* verse texts, including no less than four transliterated from the Greek.

I cannot, of course, be certain that all this took place just as described here, but there are a number of indications that it could not have been very much different. On the matter of Easter Sunday's chronological priority, for example, we have the circumstance that the subsequent days do not use the normal sequence of vesper psalms (Monday's Psalms 114–17 and 119–20; Tuesday's Psalms 121–25, etc.) but repeat Sunday's Psalms 109–13 each day. On the priority of the establishment of the Mass alleluia over the vesper ceremony, we have—in addition to the general difficulty of imagining scenarios to the contrary—the fact that the vesper tone is not borrowed for the Mass alleluia; if this tone had been in use before the creation of the Mass alleluia, it would have afforded an expeditious way to furnish repertory for the newer genre. Finally, that the four vesper tone Greek alleluias do in fact adopt their texts from the Byzantine alleluia repertory is self-evident: all four are transliterations of texts that appear in the *alleluiarion* repertory.

At the close of this chapter I will attempt to create a plausible chronology of the Mass alleluia's development, and in doing so to say more precisely what part the obviously central Byzantine influence might have played in it. For now just one question needs to be answered: what form should we imagine the Byzantine influence to have taken? Was it, for example, a matter of written or oral transmission? Certainly it was nothing comparable to the transmission of the *cantus romanus* to the Carolingian north. There, written Mass antiphoners were involved, and to compensate for the lack of notation in these documents, Roman cantors took up residence in Frankish centers to teach the melodies and Frankish cantors went to Rome for instruction. In the case of Byzantine influence on the Roman alleluia, something like the following might have happened.

To start with, certain seventh-century Roman clerics must have been familiar with the liturgical phenomenon of the Byzantine alleluia from their visits to Constantinople; certainly they would have been duly impressed with the splendor of the chant as Cassiodorus had been before them. At some time after the schola cantorum had embarked upon their efforts to complete the Mass Proper, the decision was made to incorporate the new chant into the Mass. It would be, for one thing, an excellent musical fit, almost identical in form as it was to the gradual. At a very early point in the development of the new genre one or the other Byzantine cantor exiled in Rome was called upon to aid in the process. The teaching involved was purely oral, or at the very most was accompanied by a list of *alleluiarion* texts. The evidence for this is that although there is a high incidence of textual concordance between the Roman and Byzantine alleluia, there is almost no concordance of liturgical assignment. Of the total of twelve or thirteen textual concordances of Mass alleluias (there are an additional six for vespers), only two are assigned to the same date in both liturgies: *Oty theos* to the Easter octave and *Ascendit deus* to the Ascension (this second case being so obvious a choice that it might just as likely have come about independently rather than as a matter of influence). A written document other than a mere list would have had on it liturgical assignments that the Romans would surely have been inclined to duplicate to a substantial extent.

One can imagine, then, a Byzantine cantor managing to teach three important Greek alleluias from his own memory to the Roman singers. The Romans learned the melodies after considerable effort and recorded their texts, by ear again, in rather clumsy transliterations into Latin script. They did not succeed in gaining complete control over additional melodies—either from a failure of memory on the part of the Byzantine provider, lack of time and patience on the part of the Roman recipients or, an option I favor, a feeling on their part that they were fully capable of providing their own melodies. Still, many additional *alleluiarion* texts were adopted, either from conversation with a Byzantine cantor or from a list of some sort. Whatever actually did take place, there are a number of general considerations that are virtually beyond dispute: the Byzantine influence on the Roman alleluia was of central importance; it did not, however, involve a document providing Byzantine liturgical assignments; it worked its effect within the context of a highly developed Roman musical culture; and it took place, as will be argued in the remainder of this chapter, at an early stage in the development of the alleluia, but a late stage in the development of the Mass Proper as a whole. A central factor in establishing the comparatively late development of the alleluia is its much-discussed instability of liturgical assignment.

THE PLACE OF THE ALLELUIA IN THE LITURGY

The alleluia is characterized by a great lack of fixity in its liturgical assignments, a phenomenon made much of already by Apel.[22] Not only are post-Pentecostal alleluias completely unassigned in many early manuscripts and provided instead in lists, but even Paschaltime alleluias, which one would expect to be more ancient and hence firmly fixed in place, vary significantly from manuscript to manuscript. Only alleluias of the Christmas season show an appreciable degree of stable assignment. In coming to this conclusion, Apel and other scholars compared only Frankish and Gregorian manuscripts; it will be observed here that if the Roman manuscripts are taken into account the unstable assignment of the alleluia is even greater than had been thought to be the case.

Apel rightly looked upon this trait as evidence that the alleluia, as we know it from the chant books, is a late-developing chant. At the same time he was confronted with what were for him indications of the chant's ancient establishment, namely, the patristic talk of a wordless jubilus and Gregory I's comments on the alleluia mentioned above. He resolved his dilemma with the ingenious, not to say bizarre, solution that the alleluia of the Mass must have existed for centuries as no more than the melismatic chanting of that single word, to which verses were added as late as the eighth and ninth centuries. He described the ancient alleluia, moreover, as a chant that, unlike most Mass Proper chants, was not a true psalmic chant.[23]

I hope that I have succeeded in showing elsewhere that the patristic jubilus has absolutely nothing to do with the alleluia of the Mass (nor with any other liturgical chant, for that matter),[24] and that the exclamation alleluia is essentially linked to the chanting of psalms (so much so that the Byzantine cantor introduces the alleluia with the announcement, "Alleluia: a psalm of David").[25] And I hope I succeeded in establishing at least the probability that Gregory, in speaking of saying alleluia at Mass, was referring to the liturgical practice of affixing alleluia to psalms rather than to the fully developed genre of the Mass alleluia. In short, there is no indisputable evidence for the early existence of the alleluia, and we are free to assess the phenomenon of the alleluia's unstable liturgical assignment for what it is worth.

Table 23 provides the Roman and Frankish alleluia assignments for the Advent-Christmas season. Those of Rome can be given under one column because the three Roman graduals have essentially the same assignments. Following the Roman assignments are those of the six early Frankish manuscripts of Dom Hesbert's *Sextuplex*. An incipit entered in one of the six *Sextuplex* columns indicates an assignment different from the Roman; an ellipsis indicates that there is no alleluia, either because the date fails to appear in the manuscript or because the Franks omitted the chant for some reason, and dashes indicate the continuation of the Roman assignment.

One observes at first glance that there is a large measure of change from the Roman to Frankish assignments, unlike the near perfect continuity observed above in chapter six for the introit. Still there is a very clear pattern involved: the Sundays of Advent and the Sundays after the Epiphany manifest a total lack of continuity, whereas the festal time from the first Mass of Christmas to the Epiphany boasts near perfect continuity. Indeed the two blemishes during the latter period, the lack of Frankish alleluias for the vigil of John the Evangelist and for the feast of the Holy Innocents, are easily explained: the Franks routinely omitted alleluias from sanctoral vigils, and

Table 23. Roman and Frankish Christmastime Alleluias

	Rome	Monza	Rheinau	Blandin	Compiègne	Corbie	Senlis
Advent I	Excita	Ostende	Ostende	Ostende	...	Ostende	Ostende
Advent II	Ostende	Laetatus	Laetatus	Laetatus	...	Laetatus	Laetatus
Advent III	Excita	Excita	Excita	Excita	Excita	Excita	Excita
Advent IV	[VACAT]	...	...	...	Veni dne	...	Veni dne
Xmas I	Dominus dixit	—	—	—	—	—	—
Xmas II	Dominus regnavit	—	—	—	—	—	—
Xmas III	Dies sanctificatus	—	—	—	—	—	—
Stephen	Video caelos	—	—	—	—	—	—
John Evg	Hic est discipulus	—	—	—	—	—	—
Innocents	Hi sunt qui	...	...	...	...	...	...
Sunday	Dominus regnavit	—	—	—	—	—	—
Epiphany	Vidimus stellam	—	—	—	—	—	—
Eph I	Te decet	Jubilate	Jubilate	Jubilate	Jubilate	Jubilate	Jubilate
Eph II	Adorabo	Laudate	Laudate	Laudate	Laudate	Laudate	Laudate
Eph III	Dominus regnavit	Dns ... exu	Dns ... exu	Dns ... exu	Dns ... exu	Dns ... exu	Dns ... exu

they dropped the alleluia *Hi sunt qui* from the feast of the Innocents because, as Amalarius tells us, they considered the occasion to be one of sadness.[26] A final observation to be made about the alleluias of the Christmas season is that, whereas those of the Advent and post-Epiphany Sundays lack continuity between Rome and Francia, the Frankish alleluias manifest virtually complete stability of assignment within themselves. There are thus three fundamental observations to be explained: (1) internal Roman stability; (2) internal Frankish stability; and (3) continuity between Rome and Francia only for the seven of the festive masses from Christmas to Epiphany. But first a presentation of the second festal season, Paschaltime.

Table 24 is arranged in the same manner as table 23.[27] The one addition is the abbreviation QL VL in the *Sextuplex* columns, which stands for QUALE VOLUERIS (whatever you might wish), the rubric used when the choice of a chant is left up to those responsible for a particular service. Examination of the table shows precisely the same broad pattern as in the previous one: ordinary Sundays and (in this case) ferias do not maintain continuity of assignment from Rome to Francia but major festivals do—the Easter vigil, Easter Sunday, Easter Monday, Easter Saturday (the last day of the baptismal celebration), the Major Litany, the Ascension, the Pentecost vigil and Pentecost Sunday. There is a difference, however, on the Frankish side of the table: the stability of assignment present in the Advent-Christmas season is absent from Paschaltime. The three factors to be explained here, then, are (1) internal Roman stability; (2) internal Frankish lack thereof; and (3) continuity of assignment from Rome to Francia only for the eight major dates of the season (involving a total of eleven alleluia assignments).

The explanation for internal Roman stability of assignment for both the Christmas and Easter seasons must be that the Romans succeeded in completing the liturgical assignment of alleluias at some time after the redaction of the Mass antiphoners that were used in the transmission of the *cantus romanus* to the Franks. We will see below that they did so even for the Sundays after Pentecost. The explanation for the Frankish stability of assignment for the Advent-Christmas season and the lack thereof for Paschaltime would appear to lie in a kind of small-scale Advent Project on the part of the Frankish cantors: in their efforts to assimilate the *cantus romanus* they managed to bring the Roman Advent-Christmas alleluia cycle to completion but failed to sustain the effort upon reaching the Paschaltime chants. One detail of their work on the Advent alleluias is, in any event, admirable. The second Sunday of Advent, with its station at "Jerusalem" (the church of Santa Croce in Gerusalemme), has a number of Roman chants that cite the Holy City—the introit *Populus sion,* the gradual *Ex sion* and

Table 24. Roman and Frankish Paschaltime Alleluias

	Rome	Monza	Rheinau	Blandin	Compiègne	Corbie	Senlis
Vigil Easter	Confitemini	—	—	—	—	—	—
Easter	Pascha nostrum	—	—	—	—	—	—
Monday	O kyrios	—	—	—	—	—	—
Tuesday	Venite exultemus	In te dne	...	QL VL	Redempt	Redempt	Redempt
Wednesday	Adorabo	Quoniam deus magnus	Redempt	QL VL	Dns...exul	Jubilate	Jubilate
Thursday	Qui confidunt	Lauda Hier	...	Lauda Hier	Quon deus	Lauda Hier	Lauda Hier
Friday	Epy si kyrie	Surrexit	...	QL VL	Lauda Hier	Quon deus	Quon deus
Saturday	Haec dies	—	—	—	—	—	—
	Laudate pueri	...	Haec dies	QL VL	Haec dies	...	Exultate
Sunday	Laudate pueri	QL VL	Pascha no	QL VL	Pascha no	...	Pascha no
	Oty theos	QL VL		QL VL			

Easter II	Quoniam confirmata	QL VL	Confit in	QL VL	Surrexit	...	Qui posuit
	Oty theos	QL VL	Confit qu	QL VL	Dns ... dec	...	Quon deus
Easter III	Preoccupemus	QL VL	Redempt	QL VL	Laudate pueri	...	Jubilate
	Epy si kyrie	QL VL	Eduxit	QL VL	In te dne	...	Te decet
Easter IV	Paratum cor meum	QL VL	Surrexit	QL VL	Venite benedicti	...	Dns ... exul
	Confitebor	QL VL	...	QL VL	Quon deus	...	Venite exultemus
Easter V	Te decet	QL VL	Confitntr	QL VL	Redempt	...	Laudate d
	Jubilate deo	QL VL	Cantate	QL VL	Qui sanat	...	Confit in
Litany	Confitemini	—	—	—	—	—	—
Ascension	Dominus in sina	—	—	—	—	—	—
	Ascendit deus	—	—	—	—	—	—
Sunday	Lauda anima	...	Ascendit	...	Regnavit	...	Lauda anima
	Qui confidunt	...	Confitntr	...	Dns ... dec	...	Paratum
Vigil Pent	Confitemini	—	—	—	—	—	—
Pentecost	Emitte spiritum	—	—	—	—	—	—
	Spiritus domini	—	Haec dies	—	—	—	—

the communion *Hierusalem surge*;[23] for their alleluia the Franks selected the text *Laetatus sum*, the first verse of a psalm that celebrates the city from beginning to end, and they composed an entirely new melody for it.

The central conclusion to be drawn from these observations about the comparison of Roman and Frankish alleluia assignments is that alleluias were assigned to only fifteen temporal festivals in the Roman Mass antiphoners used in the mid-eighth-century transmission of the chant to the Franks. The remainder of the chants must have been indicated in a list, not unlike those lists of post-Pentecostal alleluias in the early Frankish sources. There is a distinct pattern to which dates had alleluias assigned and which did not: festivals like Christmas, Epiphany and Easter had them assigned; ordinary Sundays and ferias did not. One notes, too, that the originally assigned alleluias have explicit reference to their liturgical dates, *Vidimus stellam* to the Epiphany, for example, and *Emitte spiritum* to Pentecost, whereas those on our purported list do not. *Adorabo ad templum*, for example, appears in the Roman graduals on Wednesday in Easter week, even though it lacks seasonal reference (it appears also at the second Sunday after Epiphany). In contrast the Roman introit for Easter Wednesday, *Venite benedicti*, refers to the newly baptized, and the communion for the same date, *Christus resurgens*, obviously refers to the Resurrection. This suggests that the originally assigned Roman alleluias (like the introits and communions) were created with their assigned dates in mind, while those assigned after the redaction of the Mass antiphoner used in the transmission were assigned from those that happened to be available in the existing repertory.

The broader chronological conclusion to be drawn from the small proportion of originally assigned alleluias is the conventional one maintained already by Wagner and Apel, that is, that alleluias are "late." One evokes again Bishop Frere's maxim that "fixity means antiquity," and its obverse, that instability of assignment points to a relatively late date. Sound as Frere's principle is, I believe it should be qualified by saying that instability of assignment allows us to *suspect* a more recent date, but that we must justify our suspicion in each instance by particular reasons. As for the present case, it seems altogether unlikely that such a small group of permanent assignments would exist already at an early date, say, the time of Gregory I, and be allowed to stand thus for nearly a century while the majority of temporal dates from the same seasons of Christmas and Easter are allowed to remain without assigned chants. This, in the face of the other genres of the Mass Proper that have permanently assigned chants for their entire temporal cycles.

There is a second broad indication for the late date of the Roman alleluia: its strikingly small repertory. One might, in fact, see this as related to the genre's paucity of fixed assignments; there were simply not enough alleluias to provide fixed, unique and appropriate assignments for every date in the Roman temporale. But the central point is that so small a repertory suggests that the alleluia developed at too late a stage in the creative period of Roman chant composition to have its full range of chants completed. The character of the repertory further supports this view. We saw in table 21 that the majority of Roman alleluias are set to the three model melodies, no less than thirty-five from a total of fifty-four. The most plausible explanation for so large a proportion of chants set to model melodies within so small a repertory is an attempt on the part of the Roman singers to provide a more or less adequate number of chants within a limited period of time—to catch up, so to speak, with the other genres of the Mass Proper. This generalization can be exemplified in the particular (indeed peculiar) case of the Roman post-Pentecostal alleluia series.

THE ROMAN POST-PENTECOSTAL ALLELUIAS

The Roman post-Pentecostal alleluias are an extraordinary story in themselves. It seems almost a contradiction in terms to speak of such a series in view of the notorious instability of assignment that prevails in that season throughout the entire history of the alleluia. There is, nevertheless, a Roman series of a sort, one, however, that was apparently put in place after the redaction of the Mass antiphoners involved in the mid-eighth-century transmission to the north. The series is stable in the two Roman graduals for which the relevant portion of the manuscript survives (Vat lat 5319 and San Pietro F22) but fails to leave a trace in any Frankish or early Gregorian gradual. And more than that, it will be seen that no less than eight of the chants in the series fail to make an appearance anywhere in the Frankish repertory.

Table 25 provides the Roman series as arranged in Vat lat 5319, that is, in the standard Roman four groups rather than in a single numerical set. After the verse incipit the Roman melody type, if applicable, is given. There follow four columns providing melodic comparisons with four representative Gregorian manuscripts.[29] This part of the table will be explained presently; first a word about the Roman series itself. The underlined chants, eight of twenty-two, are unique to the series; they appear nowhere else in the Roman calendar. This is truly surprising. It would seem an unwarranted

Table 25. Post-Pentecostal Alleluias—Melodic Continuity with Gregorian

Sunday	Verse	Melody	Graz 807	Paris 903	Bene 34	Mont 159
Pentecost I	<u>Qui sanat contritos</u>		?	=	...	?
Pent II	Lauda Hierusalem		...	diff	...	...
Pent III	<u>Qui posuit fines</u>	Excita	...	...	...	...
Pent IV	Jubilate deo		—	—	—	—
Apostles I	Venite exultemus		diff	=	diff	diff
Apost II	<u>Laudate dominum quon</u>	Excita	...	=	...	...
Apost III	Lauda anima	Ostende	—	—	—	—
Apost IV	Dominus regnavit		—	—	—	—
Apost V	Te decet hymnus		?	=	?	?
Lawrence I	Preoccupemus		...	...	...	...
Lawr II	Confitebor		...	...	diff	...
Lawr III	Adorabo		...	...	—	—
Lawr IV	Paratum cor meum		diff	=	diff	diff
Lawr V	<u>Cantate dno ... cantate</u>	Excita	diff	...	...	...
Lawr VI	<u>Cantate dno ... quia</u>	Excita	...	...	...	...
Angel I	Laudate pueri	Excita	—ᵃ	—	—	—
Angel II	<u>Laetatus sum</u>	Excita	diff	=	diff	diff
Angel III	Qui confidunt		diff	diff	diff	diff
Angel IV	Quoniam confirmata	Ostende	...	...	...	...
Angel V	<u>Laudate dominum omnes gentes</u>	Excita	diff	=	diff	diff
Angel VI	<u>Quoniam deus magnus</u>	(Dies)	diff	diff	diff	diff
Angel VII	Dominus regnavit		—	—	—	—

ᵃ The Gregorian *Laudate pueri* has the same verse melody but a different alleluia.

luxury—in view of the very limited alleluia repertory and the resultant indiscriminate borrowing during Paschaltime—to provide so much as a single unique chant for the post-Pentecostal series.

A further look at the eight unique chants reveals that nearly all, seven of eight, are set to melody types, six of them indeed to the one type, *Excita*. If this suggests haste on the part of the Roman singers in providing repertory, so too does the pairing of similar texts, a *Laudate dominum* pair and a *Cantate domino* pair, both set, moreover, to the *Excita* melody. It was mentioned above that the Roman post-Pentecostal alleluia series appears to be a particularly late arrangement. This seemingly hasty provision of similar chants corroborates that view, but there is another circumstance that makes it a virtual certainty; it is precisely this group of eight unique chants that fails to find a place in the Gregorian repertory. This is not the same thing as the failure of the Roman post-Pentecostal series, qua series, to appear in the Frankish graduals, but something altogether more extreme. The eight chants, taken individually, are absent from the Gregorian sources; some of the texts appear, it is true, but with entirely unrelated melodies.

To return to table 25 and the first of the unique (underlined) chants, *Qui sanat contritos*, this is the only one of the eight that is not a melody-type chant and the only one that might possibly have been transmitted to the north with its melody. The question mark under Graz 807 indicates that the manuscript has an alleluia with the text *Qui sanat contritos*, one that has a melody I can neither confidently identify with the Roman melody nor say for certain that it is not related. The equals sign indicates that the same dubious melody of Graz 807 appears in Paris 903 and again in Montpellier 159, while the ellipses under Benevento 34 tell us that neither text nor melody appears in that manuscript.

The second unique chant, *Qui posuit fines*, set to the *Excita* melody in Rome, is entirely absent from the Gregorian sources. The same is true of the third chant, *Laudate dominum quoniam*, while the text of the fourth, *Cantate domino . . . cantate*, appears in Graz 807, but with a different melody, and fails to appear at all in the other three manuscripts. All in all, not one of the eight chants finds a place in the Gregorian sources (surely the same text with a different melody is not the same chant), with the possible exception of *Qui sanat contritos*, the one chant among the eight not set to a melody type.[30]

There is a final striking circumstance that lends considerable support to the view that the eight were added late to the Roman repertory: without these eight there simply are not enough Roman alleluias to provide a series of twenty-two post-Pentecostal chants. If one takes the fourteen borrowed chants of the series (those not underlined in table 25) and views them in the context of the entire Roman repertory (as it appears in table 21), it will be seen that they are the only chants available for reuse in the post-Pentecostal series. That is to say, if one eliminates from the total repertory the sanctoral chants and the chants with explicit seasonal or festal reference, the remaining chants suitable for general liturgical use (and hence for borrowing for the post-Pentecostal series) are the precise group of fourteen so borrowed. Hence the absolute necessity to produce in an expeditious fashion an additional eight chants to make up a sequence of twenty-two.

While this set of eight was apparently added to the Roman repertory after the redaction of the *libelli* used in the transmission, I would imagine that this was done only shortly thereafter. The chants represent a continuation, if with somewhat diminished originality, of the creative phase of Roman chant production. We have seen evidence that that period came to a close sometime in the reign of Sergius I (687–701), and if the gap between then and the visit of Stephen with Pépin in 754 seems a long time for liturgical books to lie about unrevised, we have the above-discussed precedent of the Hadrianum sacramentary remaining essentially untouched from the time of Sergius to that of Pope Hadrian I (772–95). My own guess is that the addition of the eight chants took place around the end of the seventh or beginning of the eighth century.

If the addition of the eight represents the last phase in the history of the early Roman alleluia, it would seem time now to attempt a summary of that history. There are, however, two important questions that must first be made explicit, it not answered definitively; these involve the status of the alleluia sung by the priest at the Easter vigil Mass, and the existence of the Roman alleluia jubilus (absent both in the Easter vigil alleluia and the Byzantine alleluia).

THE EASTER VIGIL ALLELUIA

It is universally acknowledged that the Roman Easter vigil ceremony bears the mark of great antiquity. Cited in this respect especially are the omitted chants (the offertory, *Agnus dei* and communion), which had become regular items of the Roman Mass by the end of the seventh century, whereas items of undoubtedly ancient inclusion (the *Gloria in excelsis* [at festive episcopal celebrations], the epistle, the Fore-Mass psalmody and the gospel) are present. The psalmody consists in an alleluia with the verse *Confitemini domino quoniam bonus* (Ps 117.1), followed by the tract *Laudate dominum*.

There is much that is anomalous about the alleluia. It is sung, for one

Example 11. *Alleluia; Confitemini domino quoniam bonus*

thing, before the tract, whereas we should expect a typical Mass alleluia to be sung immediately before the gospel. And it is traditionally sung not by the cantors, but by the officiating priest—three times, in fact, with each repetition on a higher pitch. This, however, I think can be discounted as a later medieval custom. There is no indication whatsoever in the early sources—not in the sacramentaries, the liturgical commentaries, the *ordines romani*; not in the Roman or Frankish chant books—that this alleluia is to be treated differently than are others. On the contrary the presence of its notated melody in the graduals and especially in early *cantatoria* such as St. Gall 359 points to its singing by the cantor. Perhaps it is the relative simplicity of the melody that prompted its eventual arrogation by the celebrating priest. The character of the alleluia melody, in any case, is another of the exceptional traits of the chant. It is given in example 11 in both its Roman and Gregorian versions. They are very similar, incidentally, and offer a particularly apt case for speculating on our central question: did the early Franks pare down the original ornamentation slightly or did the eleventh-century Romans add a measure of their characteristic whole tone oscillation? The final anomaly of the chant, and perhaps the most serious, is the absence of its repetition after the verse *Confitemini*.

I think the best explanation for this exceptional chant is the most obvious: it is simply the seventh-century remnant of the ancient alleluia-psalm, Psalm 117, *Confitemini domino*, that was probably sung on the Easter vigil in the early Church. It is thus at one with the other ancient features of the seventh-century Roman ceremony. We have in support of this view the fact that Augustine in Sermon 29A, a homily preached on Easter, speaks of Psalm 117, "to which we responded with one mouth and one heart Alleluia."[31] He does not say explicitly that this took place at the vigil itself, and he is not, of course, preaching at Rome, but he tells us that Psalm 117 was sung at Easter with alleluia as response in a later fourth-century venue that we know to be closely related to Rome. In doing so he lends an added measure of likelihood to the basic probability of the view expressed here: there is no reason to deny the antiquity of this alleluia while admitting the antiquity of every other item of the vigil Mass.

But what of the failure of the alleluia to reappear as a response after the verse *Confitemini*? At first examination this is troubling, but surely the reason for it lies in the circumstance that the immediately following tract, *Laudate dominum,* is a setting of an alleluia-psalm, the brief Psalm 116, and furthermore that *Laudate dominum* is Latin for "alleluia." Thus the tract serves as concluding alleluia response. Appropriately enough the passage quoted above from Augustine's Sermon 29A continues: "to which we responded with one mouth and one heart Alleluia—which means praise the Lord (*Laudate dominum*) in Latin." We may not be sure of the precise nature of the early Christian arrangement, but that it must have consisted in the responsorial psalm *Confitemini*, followed by the psalm *Laudate* sung *in directum*, is strongly suggested by the seventh-century format—the ancient alleluia melody, the schola-style verse *Confitemini*, and the concluding schola-style tract *Laudate* serving as alleluia response. The three chants are in the same G-mode and are sung in succession without interruption.[32]

Finally, the simple melody, so unlike the typical alleluia of the Mass with its extended jubilus, is certainly another indication of the ancient character of this chant. I see no reason, in fact, to deny that it is very similar in its early medieval form to what might have been sung in the fourth century. Certainly it would seem very strange indeed for the Roman singers to deliberately fashion an eccentrically simple tune for this solemn occasion after the typical melismatic alleluia had become the norm for all other festivals, minor and major. The character of this presumably ancient melody, however, bereft as it is of extended jubilus, raises the question of the origins of that distinctive feature of the Roman alleluia.

THE JUBILUS

I allow myself to use the conventional term "jubilus" in referring to the melismatic extension of the alleluia on its final syllable, not because the word as invoked by Church Fathers such as Augustine had reference to any form of ecclesiastical song, but because medieval ecclesiastical writers such as Amalarius made the connection. Amalarius, familiar with the commonplace of the psalm commentaries that spoke of a wordless agrarian chant, and familiar with the presence of wordless passages in the chant, applied the word to the latter. He did not confine the application to the alleluia, however, as do modern music historians, but used it also to describe melismatic passages in the gradual and on one occasion the famous triple *neuma* of the responsory *In medio ecclesiae*.[33] As the later Hugh of St. Victor (d.1141) puts it: "Neumata, which take place in the alleluia and other chants of a few words, signify the jubilus."[34] Thus, while a seventh-century ecclesiastical savant would not yet have made the connection between the term and the musical phenomenon (Gregory I and Isidore of Seville failed to do so),[35] the notion has a goodly measure of later medieval justification.

But my concern here is not with the term but the musical phenomenon. The question of the latter's origin would hardly require attention were it not for two seemingly contrary musical indications: the absence of a jubilus in the Easter vigil alleluia and the absence of a jubilus in the Byzantine alleluia, the chant genre that played such a key role in the early history of the Roman alleluia. Were we not faced with these two musical manifestations, we would be free simply to say that the melismatic extension on the final syllable of the alleluia is perfectly in accord with the melismatic style that was codified by the schola cantorum for use in all the cantatorial Fore-Mass chants—the gradual, the alleluia verse and the tract. Extended final cadences are common in these chants, and what could be more appropriate than such an extension of the ecstatic acclamation alleluia?

One has, too, in aid of such thinking the view of Dom Claire, who sees the origins of many particular alleluia melodies to lie in the alleluias of the Office, short syllabic acclamations that are melismatically extended in the schola's Mass style.[36] I for one find this to be an attractive hypothesis (even if I am not convinced by the specific examples Claire adduces). It accords well with the ancient and pervasive custom of affixing alleluia acclamations to Office psalmody as well as with the fundamental musical duality that characterizes the Mass alleluia—the neumatic acclamation strikes one as a thing apart, a musical event independent of its jubilus.

Whatever the explanation for the addition of the jubilus to the Roman alleluia of the Mass, I think that the context in which this musical development took place was that of the alleluia-psalms sung during Paschaltime after Easter week's Psalm 117 with its *Haec dies* refrain had run its course. More than once before in this study I have claimed the likelihood that the responsorial psalm of the season was frequently drawn from the psalms with alleluia refrain. And it turns out that a high proportion of these psalms furnish the alleluia verse of the Paschaltime assignments. Three verses—*Lauda anima* (Ps 145.2), *Lauda Hierusalem* (Ps 147.12) and *Laudate pueri* (Ps 112.1) —appear for a total of ten times on Paschaltime Sundays and ferias, fairly dominating Pentecost week assignments in particular.[37] These are late assignments, it is true, but could it be that such alleluias for general usage were used even more frequently before being replaced by newer ones during the period of Byzantine influence?

The musical setting of the three is of special interest as well. *Lauda anima* and *Lauda Hierusalem* use the *Ostende* melody type and *Laudate pueri* the *Excita* type. These melodies may be the very shortest of the entire alleluia repertory. Perhaps they are among the first alleluia melodies devised by the newly formed schola in the mid-seventh century—or better, the first to achieve a fixed form at the time. Just as might be the case with the responsorial psalms that became formulaic graduals, they might very well have had a long history at the hands of clerical lectors and cantors as quasi-improvisatory melody types.

The existence of such alleluias and their jubilus is easily reconciled with the lack thereof in the Easter vigil's *Confitemini* and in the Byzantine alleluia. The ancient Easter vigil alleluia would quite naturally retain its traditional shape without jubilus, while the Romans would just as naturally add a jubilus to any Byzantine alleluia they adopted and, of course, to all new alleluias created during the period of Byzantine influence. What may not appear to be so easily reconciled is the existence of such proto-alleluias with my previous insistence on the essential part played by the Byzantine influence in the origins of the alleluia. This seeming contradiction is best explained in an attempt to narrate an overview of the genre's early history.

THE EARLY ROMAN ALLELUIA

When the singing of a responsorial psalm during the Fore-Mass became a regular feature of the Roman liturgy, presumably during the earlier fifth century, the Paschaltime practice was probably similar to that observed a few decades earlier in Augustine's North African church. Psalm 117, *Confitemini domino*, was sung at the Easter vigil, preceded by the acclamation alleluia and followed by the brief *Laudate dominum*, and the same psalm was sung Easter Sunday morning and throughout the week with the response *Haec dies*. For the remainder of Paschaltime alleluia was the frequent response, sung as refrain to psalms from that group of twenty with alleluia superscribed in the biblical texts, our so-called alleluia-psalms. By a century or two later in the East the regular practice, first observed in early-fifth-century Jerusalem, was to sing two responsorial psalms in the Fore-Mass, the second of which always employed alleluia as response, even if the psalm was not one of the twenty alleluia-psalms. The custom failed to make its way immediately to the West, owing no doubt to the breakdown of communications attendant upon the collapse of the western empire.

In the course of time at Rome, while the original melody of the Easter vigil alleluia was retained, a number of others were developed for use during the time extending from the octave of Easter to the end of Pentecost week. These melodies, which may have their roots in antiquity, eventually acquired melismatic extensions, either at the hands of the schola or, just as likely, already as sung by the pre-schola clergy. The *Ostende* and *Excita* melodies are likely candidates to be numbered among these early Roman alleluias, sung as they are with the three chants—*Lauda anima, Lauda Hierusalem* and *Laudate pueri*—that utilize alleluia-psalms for their verses and that figure prominently among the alleluias sung on ordinary Sundays and ferias of Paschaltime.

But what of the alleluias of major festivals during Paschaltime, such as Ascension Thursday and Pentecost Sunday, a consideration not yet taken up in this chapter? If the single responsorial psalm of the Roman Easter season is sung with alleluia response, would not these dates eventually command a psalm with explicit liturgical reference, a requirement not met by the two *Laudas* and *Laudate*? The alleluias eventually assigned to Ascension are *Dominus in Sina* (Ps 67.18–19) and *Ascendit deus* (Ps 46.4), *Ostende* and *Excita* chants, respectively. Quite possibly, then, one of the two psalms was the original Ascension responsorial psalm, sung with the original form of either the *Ostende* or *Excita* melody. The Pentecost alleluias are *Emitte spiritum* (Ps 103.30) and *Spiritus domini* (Wis 1.7). Here the choice seems to fall on the former, with its psalmic text and *excita* melody, whereas the latter has both a nonpsalmic text and a melody not derived from either of the two melody types in question. There is an additional circumstance that contributes to the probability of this claim for the early use of the *Ostende* and *Excita* melodies in Paschaltime: the third melody type, *Dies sanctificatus*, is not used for a single alleluia of the Roman Paschaltime temporale.

Thus there was very likely a musically developed alleluia, even if one of limited usage, at the time of the Byzantine influence, the period I would characterize as the second phase in the early history of the Roman alleluia. The essential feature of that influence, which was overwhelming and all-pervasive, was the adoption of the Byzantine format of two responsorial chants in the Fore-Mass, the second of which was an alleluia; in effect it meant the addition of an alleluia to virtually every festal date in the calendar. Outside of Paschaltime this resulted in the standard pattern of gradual and alleluia, while during Paschaltime it resulted in the pattern of the gradual *Haec dies* plus alleluia for Easter week and of two alleluias for the remainder of the season. A massive increase in repertory was immediately required, a challenge that could be met only with limited success by the Romans, coming as late as it did in the development of the Mass Proper. Judging by the condition of the repertory, I would imagine it to have taken place after much of the work on both the Advent Project and Sanctorale Project was completed, perhaps in the 680s, the time of musician popes, Leo II, Benedict II and Sergius I.

In any event there was outright adoption of at least three Byzantine alleluias, both melody and text (with only an added jubilus), and the adoption of a considerable number of Byzantine texts. *O kyrios* gives some insight into the centrality of the Byzantine role: not only did the original Greek version come to serve as both Mass alleluia for Easter Monday and as one of the four alleluias of Easter vespers, but its Latin cognate *Dominus regnavit decorem* is the most frequently encountered alleluia in the Roman temporale, appearing five times, including even Christmas Day. It contributed, moreover, the melody for the alleluia used with the Easter vesper tone, and quite probably the vesper tone melody itself is derived from its verse. The virtual omnipresence of this single chant, all other considerations aside, is enough to demonstrate that the Byzantine alleluia was present at the beginning of this second and most decisive phase in the history of the Roman alleluia (that is, the move to dual responsorial chants). I find much plausibility, indeed, in Bernard's contention that *Dominus regnavit* was the original Easter Sunday alleluia, later replaced with the nonpsalmic *Pascha nostrum* (1 Cor 5.7–8).

Nonpsalmic alleluia verses, in fact, might be taken as one of the characteristics of a third phase of Roman alleluia production, the Roman effort to complete an adequate repertory for annual temporal and sanctoral cycles after the phase of Byzantine absorption was exhausted. Byzantine *alleluiarion* texts are exclusively psalmic (with the exception of three derived from the Christmastime canticles of Luke's gospel), and we must assume that Roman alleluias from the phase of Byzantine absorption also utilized psalmic verses, several of them, indeed, inspired by Byzantine texts. *Te decet hymnus* (Ps 64.2) and *Venite exultemus* (Ps 94.1) are among prime candidates for inclusion in this group. They stand out for their partially shared melodies, their Byzantine textual concordances, their use in Easter week vespers and their prominence in the Roman temporale. *Preoccupemus* (Ps 94.2), *Adorabo* (Ps 137.2), *Jubilate deo* (Ps 65.1) and *Confitebor tibi* (Ps 137.1) are among other temporal chants that share at least some of these traits.[38]

When I speak of a third phase in the history of the early Roman alleluia,

I do not mean to imply a chronological gap between it and the phase of Byzantine absorption. The two take place within a relatively narrow span of time and within the context of a Roman Mass Proper already in an advanced stage of development. The need was felt from the beginning of the Byzantine phase to produce an annual cycle of alleluias that was at least roughly comparable to that which had been achieved already for the other items of the Mass Proper. The third phase, then, was simply the extension of this effort to the production of alleluia repertory that no longer owed anything to direct Byzantine influence. The inclusion of nonpsalmic verses, as mentioned above, is a trait of this purely Roman activity, as is the free use of the three melody types.

There are just two nonpsalmic chants in Paschaltime, both already mentioned, Easter's *Pascha nostrum* (1 Cor 5.7–8) and Pentecost's *Spiritus domini* (Wis 1.7). Neither chant appears to owe anything to Byzantine influence, and, in fact, it was suggested above that *Pascha nostrum* might have replaced the Byzantine derivative *Dominus regnavit* as the Easter Sunday alleluia. If this happened, however, it must, for reasons given above, have taken place relatively soon after the phase of Byzantine influence, and *Spiritus domini* would have joined the psalmic *Excita* chant *Emitte spiritum* (Ps 103.30) as second Pentecost alleluia at about the same time.

As for expansion of the *Ostende* and *Excita* repertories, we saw that these two melody types were possibly in use during Paschaltime before the Byzantine adoption. It is worth mentioning now that the three chants singled out above as likely candidates for early Paschaltime use—*Lauda anima*, *Lauda Hierusalem* and *Laudate pueri*—are without Byzantine textual concordances. I have just cited the *Excita* chant *Emitte spiritum* as the probable original Pentecost alleluia, while either the *Excita* type *Ascendit deus* (Ps 46.4) or the *Ostende* type *Dominus in Sina* (Ps 67.18–19) was the original Ascension alleluia, with the other added in the phase of expansion. The expansion extended to the Christmas season with the provision of a pair of Advent alleluias, the namesake chants *Excita domine potentiam tuam* (Ps 79.3) and *Ostende nobis domine* (Ps 84.8), and the *Ostende* chant sung at the first Mass of Christmas, *Dominus dixit* (Ps 2.7).

The Christmas season melody par excellence, however, is the incomparably beautiful *Dies sanctificatus* type. It is used in series for all five festive alleluias from the third Mass of Christmas' *Dies sanctificatus* itself (nonbiblical) to the Epiphany's *Vidimus stellam* (Mt 2.2). All five, moreover, are nonpsalmic chants, for the most part from the New Testament, reminding us of the narrative communions of the same liturgical period. These five join Easter's *Pascha nostrum* (1 Cor 5.7–8), Pentecost's *Spiritus domini*

(Wis 1.7) and the *Dies* chant sung on the octave of Peter and Paul, *Tu es Petrus* (Mt 16.18), as the only nonpsalmic alleluia verses in the entire core repertory.[39] *Dies sanctificatus*, incidentally, figures prominently in the literature on the alleluia;[40] the origins of both its melody and nonbiblical text are much discussed, with claims being made for its Byzantine provenance. None of the evidence adduced for the various positions evinced is sufficiently convincing to warrant its summary here, and I leave the question of the chant's remote origins open. What is clear is the systematic usage of the melody type in the Christmas season and its large proportion of nonpsalmic texts (seven of its twelve). This latter trait, along with the way in which the *Ostende* and *Excita* types are distributed throughout the liturgical year, suggests that the Paschaltime alleluias were completed first, followed (immediately) by the Christmas season chants, a reversal of the process observed in all other items of the Mass Proper and still another indication that the development of the alleluia took place well after the Advent Project had commenced.

The *Dies* type figures prominently also in the sanctorale. The four Common sanctoral alleluias using the melody—*Disposui testamentum, Inveni David, Justus non conturbabitur* and *Sancti tui*—account themselves for nearly half the sanctoral assignments of Vat lat 5319. We can take this, however, as only an approximation of what might have been the state of sanctoral alleluia assignment at the end of the seventh century. There is so little continuity between the Roman and Frankish sources in this respect that we must assume most Roman sanctoral alleluias had not yet been permanently fixed at the time of the redaction of the Roman graduals used in the transmission north. And there is another trait of Roman sanctoral alleluias that indicates a late date for the alleluia in general: the extraordinarily small number of uniquely assigned sanctoral alleluias. There are only two—the *Dies* chants *Tu es Petrus* and *Magnus sanctus Paulus*.

That most of the alleluia sanctorale was assigned after the transmission raises the subject of a fourth and final phase in the early history of the Roman alleluia, one undertaken to complete work on the genre after the redaction of the Mass antiphoners involved in the transmission. The demonstrable portion of this activity is that remarkable creation of a post-Pentecostal sequence, a project requiring the addition of eight (or at least seven) new chants to the existing repertory, all but two of them using the *Excita* melody. I would guess that the remainder of the Christmas and Easter season alleluias (those beyond the chants assigned to the fifteen favored dates discussed above) were given fixed assignments at the same time, and perhaps the sanctoral alleluias as well (they are, as will be recalled from chapter seven, stable *within* the three Roman graduals).

Much of what is written in this attempted survey is highly speculative, particularly the remarks about specific chants, but several general points enjoy considerable probability. There was very likely a small repertory of Roman alleluias before the period of Byzantine influence, including the Easter vigil alleluia and a number of chants with melodies consisting of the standard acclamation and jubilus, sung with verses taken from alleluia-psalms. The Byzantine influence, when it made itself felt, was massive, bringing with it both a fundamental change in the structure of the Roman Fore-Mass (the adoption of a second responsorial chant) and the supplying of a substantial repertory of melodies and especially texts. The Roman response to this influence involved the provision of many additional chants, making full use of the three melody types and introducing nonpsalmic verses into the repertory. The period of Byzantine influence and Roman response was short-lived and came late in the development of the Roman Mass Proper, overlapping apparently with the later stages of the Advent Project and the project to create an adequate sanctorale. Work on the Roman alleluia, in fact, was not completed before the redaction of the Mass antiphoners used in the transmission of the *cantus romanus* to the north. The final result was a repertory much smaller than that of other genres of the Mass Proper, about half that of the gradual and offertory and a third that of the introit and communion.

CHAPTER 11

The Tract

It is all too easy to adopt the revisionist view of the tract as simply the other side of the coin from the alleluia. It makes its first documented appearance in history, after all, in the same brief passage from *Ordo romanus I* that introduces the alleluia: "After the subdeacon has finished reading [the epistle], a cantor holding a cantatorium ascends [the ambo] and sings the gradual (*responsum*). If it be the season to sing the alleluia, then yes; if not, however, then the tract; if neither, then only the gradual." One can be forgiven for reading into the passage that its author looked upon the alleluia and tract pair as no more than an afterthought to the more essential gradual. This is true especially in view of the late introduction of the alleluia into the Roman Mass and its correspondingly meager repertory. We can well imagine that the tract, with its even more limited repertory, was introduced as a penitential season counterpart to the festive alleluia, and that this took place at so late a time in the creative period of Roman chant production that plans for the chant's deployment throughout the liturgical year were never fully implemented. It was apparently this trait of the tract, its skeletal assignment, that caused Helmut Hucke to counter the conventional view that the chant was of ancient vintage with the claim that it was an especially late item of the Mass Proper.[1]

The conventional wisdom—that the tract is a chant of great antiquity—was well expressed already by Peter Wagner: "The length of the Tract is a proof of its great antiquity. . . . Its present melodic form must be that which belonged to all Responsorial psalms before their abbreviation. It is then probable that the Tract melodies are extremely old and venerable monuments of the chant of the Latin Church, and that they preserve *the melodic forms of the solo-psalmody of the Mass* in the shape in which they were used *up to the 4th and 5th centuries in Italy*, when the solo-singers began to deck them out with richer *melismata* than before, and by this innovation brought on the abbreviation of the psalm [emphasis is Wagner's]."[2]

I think now that both Wagner and Hucke were right, not entirely right of course, but both right in their central insights: Wagner's recognition of a vestige of early Christian psalmodic practice in the length of certain tracts, and Hucke's identification of the tract's meager and scattered repertory as the mark of an unfinished product. When I say that I find merit in both positions, I mean this in a serious historical sense; that is, that a full examination of the available evidence finds indications of both great antiquity and late manipulation in the tract's history. It is true that if one ignores the evidence and deals only in abstractions, Hucke's position can be explained away and subsumed within that of Wagner. Indeed one might say that Wagner, writing the better part of a century before Hucke, anticipated the latter scholar's point of the tract's limited repertory. He claimed that in the beginning all Fore-Mass chants took the form of the tract, that is, psalmody *in directum*, and that in the course of the centuries they were transformed into graduals, that is, into responsorial chants as they became increasingly melismatic. Hence the small number of remaining tracts.

The difficulty with such a position should be clear to one who has read the early chapters of the present volume. While Wagner's scheme may be plausible in the abstract, it runs counter to the evidence: our earliest evidence that speaks directly to the psalmody of the Fore-Mass—descriptions from the pens of later fourth-century Church Fathers such as Basil, John Chrysostom, Ambrose and Augustine—creates the overwhelming impression that the typical manner of Fore-Mass psalmody was responsorial. A lector, frequently an adolescent boy, declaimed the psalm in its entirety, and the congregation responded with a chosen verse (or with alleluia) set to a memorable tune. It is indisputable that Fore-Mass psalmody was commonly performed responsorially centuries before the abbreviated form of the medieval gradual appeared.

I dwell on Wagner's position now because a number of younger French scholars have come to advocate one that is very similar.[3] They also claim that the tract came first and was transformed into a gradual, but they differ from Wagner in that they acknowledge the existence of responsorial psalmody in the later fourth-century Fore-Mass. For them, however, fourth-century responsorial psalmody is an innovation, following upon an earlier period, the third century, of ecclesiastical psalmody without refrains, or psalmody *in directum*. This particular point, that responsorial psalmody follows historically upon psalmody *in directum*, while lacking supporting evidence, is not without a certain plausibility; I will return to it presently but must first complete my summary of the position in question.

If third-century psalmody *in directum* came before fourth-century responsorial psalmody, it follows, so the argument goes, that graduals developed from tracts. Perhaps there is a kind of logic to this proposition when considered in the abstract, but just how it is supposed to play out in history I find baffling. Take the gradual *Haec dies*, which, it is claimed, shows its origins as a tract because it has multiple verses. We know, however, that Psalm 117, *Confitemini quoniam bonus*, was sung in the fourth century as a responsorial psalm with verse 24, *Haec dies*, serving as response. But let us concede, even if there is no evidence for the point,[4] that Psalm 117 was sung *in directum* in the third century and that the response verse *Haec dies* was not yet singled out for special treatment. We would then have a three-stage historical succession: third-century psalm *in directum*; fourth-century responsorial psalm; and early medieval gradual. And where does the tract enter into the historical process? That third-century Psalm 117 sung *in directum* must have already been a tract before becoming a fourth-century responsorial psalm.[5] Now how a tract can evolve into a responsorial psalm is beyond my comprehension; perhaps I am missing something in the argument. In any case I leave the question to the consideration of the reader and move on to an alternate theory of the origins of the tract. For me, in a word, the tract does not evolve into the gradual, but the two genres pursue their respective histories side by side.

ORIGINS

If psalmody *in directum* preceded responsorial psalmody, it probably did so only in the sense that the psalm sung regularly in the Fore-Mass of the later fourth century owes its origins to the occasional reading of a psalm in the earlier Fore-Mass as an Old Testament reading, a reading that very well might, even if declaimed somehow in a quasi-musical fashion, have been performed without congregational responses. It is nonetheless possible that this early psalm as reading, even when recited in a manner close to the modern sense of reading rather than singing, would have frequently prompted congregational responses. Indeed we might expect this to be the case for alleluia-psalms at least. But we have no evidence one way or the other before the later fourth-century profusion of patristic liturgical reference. We know only, from that late-fourth-century evidence, that the psalm of the Fore-Mass was still spoken of as a reading, thus revealing its origins.

We know also from that later fourth-century evidence (and here I summarize what was spelled out in detail in chapter two) that the psalm of the Fore-Mass, although a reading in name, was looked upon at the same time as a genuinely musical event. And we know from numerous citations to that effect that responsorial performance of that psalm was extremely common. We assume, moreover, that the psalm was sometimes, probably on penitential occasions, sung without refrains. There is no positive evidence for this because of the nature of the phraseology involved: if a psalm response is mentioned in a passage describing the singing of a psalm, we know that the psalm is sung responsorially, but if the passage simply states that a psalm is sung, with no mention of responses, we do not know if it is sung with responses or without.

The best evidence for the assumption that the fourth-century Fore-Mass psalm is sometimes sung without responses is the very existence of the early medieval Roman tract. It seems highly unlikely that the schola cantorum would simply invent an entirely new genre in the seventh century, one that has no roots in the traditional psalmody of the Fore-Mass, and especially one that is musically at variance with the predominantly responsorial mode of performing Fore-Mass psalmody. We have seen the evidence for this predominance in the abundant patristic references to Fore-Mass psalmody and in the scattered western literary evidence of the fifth, sixth and seventh centuries; and we see it above all in the predominance of responsorial chants in the Roman Mass Proper, particularly in its 105 graduals as opposed to its only sixteen (more probably fifteen) tracts. It is this very minority status of the tract that renders its seventh-century origin unlikely. But at the same time, one must take this minority status at face value and assume that it by and large reflects the status of Fore-Mass psalmody *in directum* as opposed to responsorial psalmody in the centuries before the seventh-century emergence of the Roman Mass Proper genres.

That being said, one turns to the seventh-century Roman tract in an attempt to determine which particular chants might boast links with antiquity, and which might be part of the general seventh-century Roman expansion of the Mass Proper.

THE SEVENTH-CENTURY ROMAN TRACT: THE D-2 CHANTS

Table 26 presents the Roman tracts with their liturgical assignments; omitted are only the assignments of the Pentecost vigil, which are identical to those of the Easter vigil. In point of fact, the four so-called canticle-tracts

Table 26. Roman Tracts

Advent Ember Saturday	Qui regis	Ps 79.2–3	G-8
5 Feb, Agatha	Qui seminant	Ps 125.5–6	G-8
14 Feb, Valentine	Desiderium anime	Ps 20.3–4	G-8
12 Mar, Gregory	Beatus vir	Ps 111.1–3	G-8
25 Mar, Annunciation	(Laudate dominum)		
Septuagesima	De profundis	Ps 129.1–4	G-8
Sexagesima	Commovisti domine	Ps 59.4–6	G-8
Quinquagesima	Jubilate domino	Ps 99.2–3	G-8
Quadragesima	Qui habitat	Ps 90.1–7, 11–16	D-2
[Ember Wednesday	De necessitatibus	Ps 24.17–18, 1–3	D-2]
Ember Saturday	(Laudate dominum)		
Quad III	Ad te levavi	Ps 122.1–3	G-8
Quad IV	Qui confidunt	Ps 124.1–2	G-8
Quad V	Saepe expugnaverunt	Ps 128.1–4	G-8
Palm Sunday	Deus deus meus	Ps 21.2–9, 18–19, 22, 24, 32	D-2
Maj Wednesday	Domine exaudi	Ps 101.2–5 & 14	D-2
Good Friday	Domine audivi	Hb 3.2–3	D-2
	(Qui habitat)		
Vigil Easter	[Cantemus domino	Ex 15.1–2	G-8]
	[Vinea domini	Is 5.1–2	G-8]
	[Attende caelum	Dt 32.1–4	G-8]
	[Sicut cervus	Ps 41.2–4	G-8]
	Laudate dominum	Ps 116	G-8
Pentecost Ember Saturday	(Laudate dominum)		

of the Easter vigil (enclosed here in square brackets) were not Roman tracts but rather lector chants, fashioned into tracts by the Franks, a point to be developed here later. When these four are removed from the Roman repertory, there remain sixteen tracts. Two of them, *Qui habitat* and *Laudate dominum*, are assigned more than once; the original assignment for the former is probably Quadragesima Sunday and for the latter, the Easter vigil (secondary assignments are given in parentheses and lack the scriptural derivation and modal designation). Ember Wednesday's *De necessitatibus* (in square brackets) might very well have originally been a gradual, as will be seen below; if this is true, its removal would reduce the number of genuine tracts to fifteen.

The modal designations of the tracts are of central importance, offering the best possibility of a glimpse into the prehistory of the genre. If their distribution seems somewhat scattered at first glance, there is a clear and significant pattern to it—D-2 tracts occur only during the first week of Lent and Holy Week. More particularly, the two tracts that appear on the two most important Sundays of Lent, *Qui habitat* on Quadragesima Sunday and *Deus deus meus* on Palm Sunday, are the very chants that have attracted attention because of their great length. I think Wagner is right in seeing this characteristic to be an indication of antiquity. Why should the schola cantorum create two entirely new melismatic chants of such exceptional dimension at a time when they otherwise create chants of only one verse, or less often of just two or three? There seems little reason to doubt that the multiple verses of these chants reflect the fourth-century practice of singing an entire psalm. I use the word "reflect" advisedly because neither chant uses the entire psalm (as is frequently claimed): *Qui habitat* (Ps 90.1–7; 11–16) uses thirteen of the psalm's sixteen verses and *Deus deus meus* (Ps 21.2–9; 18–19; 22; 24; 31) uses thirteen of thirty-one. We are reminded thereby that this is the period of "schola chant" and not the early Christian period of "lector chant." Still the point stands: these are chants of inordinate length that the schola allows to retain much of their ancient text (choosing no doubt those verses they consider to be most liturgically appropriate).

I would imagine, then, that these two chants existed in continuity with ancient psalmic assignments, that is to say, that Psalm 90, *Qui habitat,* was chanted by the lector or deacon without congregational refrains on Quadragesima Sunday as early as the fifth century, and Psalm 21, *Deus deus meus,* was similarly recited on Palm Sunday. Psalm 90, which I lean to as originally assigned to Quadragesima Sunday rather than to Good Friday, has very explicit appropriateness to the occasion. The psalm is cited in the gospel of the day (Mt 4.1–11), surely an extremely ancient assignment itself, telling as it does of the forty-day fast of Jesus in the desert. Satan, in tempting Jesus, paraphrases the words of verse 11, *Quoniam angelis suis mandavit de te,* and in fact those angels administer to Jesus after the departure of Satan. Psalm 21, likewise, is particularly suited to Palm Sunday, to its original theme, that is, which has to do with the Passion of Christ rather than his triumphal entry into Jerusalem. The psalm, with verses like its second, *Deus deus meus . . . quare me dereliquisti,* and its seventh, *Ego autem sum vermis, et non homo,* is the Passion psalm par excellence.

If Psalm 90, then, was the ancient psalm *in directum* of the Quadragesima Sunday Fore-Mass and Psalm 21 the original psalm of Palm Sunday, I would think that the graduals appearing on these dates were added in the schola period as part of the program to provide every date in the liturgical year (outside of Paschaltime) with a gradual. The gradual *Angelis suis* (Ps 90.11–12) has every appearance of being a later chant: it is set to a particularly routine example of the A-2 melody type, and its text is identical to two verses of the tract, presumably borrowed in an attempt to invoke the motif of the ministering angels. The texts, moreover, of the introit *Invocabit* (Ps 90.15–16), offertory *Scapulis suis* (Ps 90.4–5) and communion *Scapulis suis* (Ps 90.15–16), certainly later chants than the tract, would seem similarly to be borrowed from it. The introit, gradual, offertory and communion, then, give every appearance of being products of the Advent Project and constitute, incidentally, one of those exceptional Mass Propers created horizontally rather than vertically.

Hesbert also sees the gradual *Angelis suis* as a late addition to the Quadragesima Mass.[6] His suspicions were aroused by the fact that the Blandin manuscript has *Tenuisti* rather than *Angelis suis* as gradual for the date, and his subsequent investigations uncovered considerable melodic instability for *Angelis suis* in the sources: the A-2 melody type is the most common setting, but there are many manuscripts, including the very early Laon 239, that give the mode-3 melody of *Benedicite* (from the feast of St. Michael). Hesbert takes this melodic instability as a sign of a more recent chant, and I would endorse his position by adding that such tenuousness of transmission is characteristic of the very latest products of the Roman creative period.

While I accept Hesbert's position that the gradual *Angelis suis* is a late addition and that the tract *Qui habitat* is the original chant of the Quadragesima Fore-Mass, I cannot agree with him on the nature of *Qui habitat*. For him *Qui habitat* must be in reality a gradual because the responsorial psalm is one of the most essential and most ancient elements of the primitive Mass.[7] For me *Qui habitat* is a prime example of a chant that owes its origins to one of those exceptional psalms *in directum* of the early Fore-Mass. Hesbert goes on to conclude that all D-2 tracts are in fact graduals, a point to be taken up presently.

If the gradual *Angelis suis* is a late addition to the Quadragesima Mass, one suspects the same of the gradual *Tenuisti manum*, which occupies a precisely analogous liturgical placement before the long D-2 tract *Deus deus meus* of the Palm Sunday Mass. *Tenuisti* is a curious chant, with the longest of all gradual texts, set as it is to a virtually unique melody. If not as obviously late a piece as *Angelis suis*, its uncertain musical transmission points in that direction; it has a mode-4 melody in the Gregorian sources that is only remotely, if at all, related to its D-final Roman counterpart.[8] Its text, moreover, is out of step with the Passion theme of the other items of the Mass Proper; the words *et cum gloria assumpsisti me* would appear to be more appropriate to the later theme of the triumphal entry into Jerusalem. In any event, whatever the history of the graduals *Tenuisti* and *Angelis suis*, I see no reason to doubt that the tracts *Qui habitat* and *Deus deus meus* are not true tracts, and descendants, moreover, of ancient psalms *in directum*.

The other three D-2 tracts are united by the curious circumstance that the early Frankish manuscripts refer to them as graduals (*resp. grad.*) rather than tracts. In view of this fact it is hardly surprising that scholars such as Hesbert conclude that all five D-2 tracts are in fact graduals. I am impressed, however, by Hucke's singling out of *De necessitatibus* as the one likely possibility of the sort.[9] Aside from the chant's opening intonation and closing cadential formula it has little in common with the other four D-2 tracts, and more than that its second and third verses partake to some extent of the typical melodic characteristics of gradual verses. They display a measure, in both Roman and Gregorian versions, of the higher tessitura of gradual verses, and in the Gregorian version the characteristic use of bistropha and tristropha neumes. Even more telling is the succession of verses in the text (Ps 24.17–18, 1–3). This is typical of a gradual, a response selected for its special significance from the interior of the psalm, and a verse (or verses) from the beginning, whereas tracts move in order through the psalm text because they lack a chosen response verse. The liturgical placement of *De necessitatibus* is suggestive also of its status as a gradual; it appears on a Wednesday Ember Day, and Wednesday Ember Days have as a matter of course two responsorial psalms. But why did the Romans designate this gradual-like chant as a tract? I can only guess that it has something to do with the striking intonation it shares with the D-2 tracts and with the example of the parallel assignment of a tract to Wednesday of Holy Week.

On the more general question of whether the other four chants are in reality tracts or graduals, I have already expressed my views on the prehistory of *Qui habitat* and *Deus deus meus* as psalms *in directum*. I would add now that they and *Domine exaudi* and *Domine audivi* are musically homogeneous and, moreover, that all the verses of the four chants are musically homogeneous with respect to one another—there is no sign of the musical differentiation that exists between gradual responses and verses. Nor is there any instance of a verse taken out of psalmic order, as is the case with a large proportion of graduals (approximately 50 percent).

But how to explain the rubric RESP. GRAD. that is used in the early Frankish manuscripts to introduce the D-2 tracts on the three occasions of Ember Day Wednesday, Wednesday in Holy Week and Good Friday? The Roman graduals are consistent in designating them as tracts, and the presumption must be, then, that the Frankish copyists are somehow mistaken. The presumption is confirmed by the *ordines romani*. We do not have descriptions in these books of the Wednesday Ember Day, but we do have them for the two dates of Holy Week, and it turns out that the documents of more purely Roman content refer to our chants as either tracts or canticles, whereas those of Frankish taint tend to call them graduals. To cite, for example, the authentically Roman *Ordo XXVII* for Good Friday: "The subdeacon goes up to read and after the lection the canticle *Domine audivi* is sung with its verses. . . . There follows then the second lection after which follows the tract *Qui habitat*."[10] *Ordo XXXB*, however, described by Andrieu as the work of a Frankish monk writing in the later ninth century, has: "Then the archdeacon signals the subdeacon to read the first lection. There follows the responsorium *Domine audivi*. Then another reading and there follows the tract *Qui habitat*."[11] Curiously the Frankish documents continue to refer to *Qui habitat* and *Deus deus meus* as tracts. Could it be that the length of these two chants makes them stand out in the minds of Franks, while the majority status of the gradual somehow allows them to refer loosely to most other Fore-Mass chants as graduals (*resp. grad., gradale* or *responsorium*), even in the case of a canticle like *Domine audivi*?

To return to commenting on individual D-2 tracts, I have little to say on *Domine exaudi* (Ps 101.2–5, 14) other than that I see no reason to doubt that it is a genuine tract, and one existing in continuity with a psalm *in directum* of some antiquity. Wednesday in Holy Week is a day of considerable liturgical significance with its two Old Testament readings and its Passion of St. Luke; the chanting of both a responsorial psalm (Psalm 68, *Ne avertas*) and a psalm *in directum* (Psalm 101, *Domine exaudi*) would not appear to be an extravagance.

Finally, Good Friday's canticle-tract *Domine audivi* (Hb 3.2–3) is a curious piece, bordering on the enigmatic. Its first two verses begin by adhering rather closely to the Habakkuk text, but its latter three verses lack even a remote relationship to it. Is the text, then, a product of the textual adjustment of the Advent Project or is it an ancient composition of unknown origin? Suggestive of antiquity is the circumstance that the chant serves as a canticle at Friday Office lauds. Speaking against a late date, moreover, is the use of the D-2 melody, since late tracts invariably employ the G-8 one. The chant deserves a more thorough investigation than I am able to grant it here.

D-2 TRACTS: THE MUSIC

The characteristic of tracts in general that has prompted the most discussion in the literature is their employment of melodic formulas. This has been so with good reason, but still there is a tendency to exaggerate the trait, perhaps because of its inclusion within the various systems of analysis of later Gregorian tracts, which tend to be more formulaic than the chants of the original repertory. The particular feature of the D-2 chants that has attracted the most attention is a succession of phrases within each verse cadencing on D, C, F and D. This quadripartite structure has been likened to a latent psalm tone with its intonation, flex, mediation and termination.[12] The D-C-F-D pattern, however, is far from omnipresent. It is true that it does occur in twenty-six of the thirty-eight verses of the four authentic D-2 tracts (*De necessitatibus* is excluded from the count), but intervening cadences frequently obscure the pattern so that it exists in its pure four-phrase form in only fifteen verses of the thirty-eight. What is, however, nearly invariably present (thirty-seven of thirty-eight verses) is the central C-cadence. I am normally skeptical about claims for latent psalm tones in fully developed chant forms, but this persistent C-cadence, appearing about halfway through the tract verses, in tandem, of course, with the always present final cadence on D, would seem to me to be a vestige of the D-2 tract's prehistory as a psalm *in directum*. And it can be added that a similar observation is in order for the G-8 tracts, where an F-cadence is consistently present in each verse at a likely point of mediation.

THE G-8 TRACTS

Table 27 shows the G-8 tracts of the temporal cycle; one examines it for indications that might reveal some aspect of these chants' early history. But the absence of chants of great length along with the elimination of four utterly central dates in the Lenten liturgy—Quadragesima Sunday, Palm Sunday, Wednesday in Holy Week and Good Friday—lends the G-8 tracts a general aura of less authentic antiquity. Yet there is an occasion of more than comparable significance to the four just cited, the Easter vigil, and one looks to its G-8 tract, *Laudate dominum*, for signs of antiquity.

We saw already in the previous chapter that *Laudate dominum* formed a fitting conclusion to the presumably ancient alleluia-psalm of the Easter vigil Mass, *Confitemini quoniam bonus*; *Laudate dominum*, Latin for the Hebrew *alleluia*, could stand in for the alleluia response otherwise missing

Table 27. Roman Temporal G-8 Tracts

Advent Ember Saturday	*Qui regis*	Ps 79.2–3	G-8
Septuagesima	*De profundis*	Ps 129.1–4	G-8
Sexagesima	*Commovisti domine*	Ps 59.4–6	G-8
Quinquagesima	*Jubilate domino*	Ps 99.2–3	G-8
Lent Ember Saturday	(*Laudate dominum*)		
[Quadragesima II	VACAT]		
Quad III	*Ad te levavi*	Ps 122.1–3	G-8
Quad IV	*Qui confidunt*	Ps 124.1–2	G-8
Quad V	*Saepe expugnaverunt*	Ps 128.1–4	G-8
Vigil Easter	*Laudate dominum*	Ps 116	G-8
Vigil Pentecost	(*Laudate dominum*)		
Pent Ember Saturday	(*Laudate dominum*)		

from the end of Psalm 117. The tract *Laudate dominum*, moreover, is a complete psalm, even if a short one, the only such text in the entire Roman Mass Proper. Then there is the joyful character of the text, an exception among tracts, and surely such in the minds of seventh-century Roman liturgists, who assigned new tracts only to penitential occasions. Finally there is the wide distribution of the chant, assigned as it is to the four temporal dates in table 27 (and also to the 25 March feast of the Annunciation). There is a pattern to the four temporal assignments: all are to vigil ceremonies. One suspects that one occasion served as model for the others, and the Easter vigil is the obvious candidate for the honor, not just because of the antiquity of its liturgy, but because the joyful nature of *Laudate dominum*'s text (and its quality as synonym for *alleluia*) makes it explicitly appropriate for the Easter vigil.

Laudate dominum is not assigned to the Saturday vigil of the Advent Ember Days; rather *Qui regis* is, with its text of obvious Advent reference (including the words *Excita, domine, potentiam tuam et veni*). *Qui regis*, certainly, can have no claim to great antiquity, since Advent texts were entirely absent from any aspect of the Roman liturgy before the later sixth century. It is not unlikely that *Laudate dominum* was originally sung on this Saturday in the centuries before the December Ember Days acquired Advent content and was later replaced by *Qui regis*. The date for this would quite probably be the time of the Advent Project, not just for the general reasons given above in chapter six, but because *Qui regis* seems to be of a piece with that particularly factitious set of four A-2 graduals assigned to the date. It will be recalled that the four derived their texts from just two psalms, a pair of them from Psalm 18 and a second pair from *Qui regis*'s Psalm 79. Indeed the two graduals and the tract all use verse 3, *Excita domine, potentiam tuam et veni*.

The Sunday series has a trait of special interest; once Quadragesima and Palm Sunday are removed from it, there exists a numerically ordered set of five chants extending from Sexagesima Sunday to the fifth Sunday of Lent (utilizing texts from Psalms 59, 99, 122, 124 and 128). I would assume that the final arrangement is deliberate on the part of the Roman singers, and it resembles, of course, one of those cases of numerical rearrangement such as those of the introits, offertories and communions of the Sundays after Pentecost, rather than an instance of preconceived planning such as the weekday communions of Lent. This being said, there are various possible explanations for the history of the series. The most obvious, perhaps, if not the most likely, is that both the creation of the chants and their assignment are very late, from the time of the Advent Project.

An objection to this, however—the fact that Septuagesima Sunday's *De profundis* (Ps 129.1–4) violates the order of the series—suggests a second possibility. It could be that the series was established after the introduction of Sexagesima Sunday into the liturgy but before that of Septuagesima Sunday, thus at some point in the middle to late sixth century. Quinquagesima, Sexagesima and Septuagesima Sundays were introduced into the Roman liturgy in a gradual extension of the Lenten fast. Sexagesima is attested to already at the Council of Orléans (541), but Septuagesima probably dates to later in the century.[13] If this second possibility is the correct one, it must be borne in mind, however, that not the tracts as such but their predecessors are involved, full psalms sung *in directum*.

A third possibility, and one that I lean to even if not with total conviction, is that the group of three psalms assigned to the Lenten Sundays (the third, fourth and fifth) is very early (pre-sixth century), but later than the assignment of *Qui habitat* and *Deus deus meus* to Quadragesima and Palm Sundays. I single out the three not just because they complete the Lenten season and because it seems plausible that a set of nonresponsorial psalms would be appropriate for the five Sundays of Lent, but because their close numerical proximity (Psalms 122, 124 and 128) is suggestive of contemporaneity, as is the circumstance that the first verse of each is retained in the final version of the tract. If this possibility is the correct one, the three Sundays of the Septuagesima season could either have had psalms *in directum*

Table 28. Roman Sanctoral Tracts

5 Feb, Agatha	*Qui seminant*	Ps 125.5–6	G-8
14 Feb, Valentine	*Desiderium anime*	Ps 20.3–4	G-8
12 Mar, Gregory	*Beatus vir*	Ps 111.1–3	G-8
25 Mar, Annunciation	(*Laudate dominum*)		

assigned as they entered the liturgy or, perhaps more likely, had tracts created for them at the time of the Advent Project in the currently favored G-8 manner.

The point involving the G-8 melody is important. Surely it is significant that the D-2 repertory is confined to only four chants of undoubtedly ancient lineage, and that all other chants, including some of indisputably late date, use the G-8 type. This is not to deny, of course, that *Laudate dominum* is a chant with roots in antiquity, and that its seventh-century G-8 melody is the final form of its fourth-century psalm tone, but only to suggest that the G-8 melody was the only one in use during the later seventh century when there was need of adding tracts to the repertory. The sanctoral tracts (table 28) would seem to confirm this. Everything learned in chapter seven about uniquely assigned sanctoral chants would seem to point to the later seventh-century creation of the tracts for the feasts of Agatha, Valentine and Gregory; indeed, regarding Gregory's tract, his feast itself was not created until that period. Finally, the assignment of *Laudate dominum* to the feast of the Annunciation may be an action not taken until the passing of the creative period of Roman Mass Proper creation (sometime around 690, as suggested above).

The latest of all Roman tracts, however, are the four G-8 canticle-tracts of the Easter vigil, making their appearance in Roman liturgy, it could be said, only in the eleventh century.

THE FOUR G-8 CANTICLE-TRACTS OF THE EASTER VIGIL

I am not the first to voice the suspicion that the canticle-tracts of the Easter vigil were a Frankish addition to the tract repertory, introduced at Rome only in the eleventh (or possibly tenth) century. The suspicion stems from the puzzling circumstance that the four appear in the Roman graduals with the Gregorian version of the G-8 melody rather than the Roman version. Some have sought to explain this by claiming that the original Roman melody was lost by the time the Roman manuscripts were copied but, as John

Boe points out, the melody was obviously present in the other G-8 Roman tracts, in particular *Laudate dominum,* sung at the very Easter vigil service.[14] It was Boe's remarks on the subject that prompted me to explore the issue at length in a recent essay, the main points of which I will summarize briefly here.[15]

There are references to the celebration of the Easter vigil, Augustine's *mater omnium vigiliarum,* already in the second century, and by the later fourth century it had acquired its classic shape—a ceremony of light, followed by a series of Old Testament readings preceding the baptism of the catechumens. The choice of readings varied from place to place and from time to time, but several of them were regular in their appearance. Exodus 14–15 was one of these; its narration of Moses' triumphal leading of the Israelites from Egypt was too fraught with baptismal symbolism for omission. The reading concludes with the canticle of Moses, *Cantemus domino,* and we saw in chapter two a passage from Augustine telling us that it was sung at the Easter vigil in his church. The same is true of Psalm 41, *Sicut cervus,* providing us with precious early Christian references to the ancestors of two of the four chants eventually sung at the Easter vigil.

The earliest explicit Roman evidence comes in the Old Gelasian sacramentary, listing the prayers that are said after the Easter vigil readings of the later sixth or earlier seventh-century Roman urban liturgy. A series of ten readings are cited, followed by Psalm 41, *Sicut cervus.* Among the ten are the three that conclude with the canticles *Cantemus domino* (Ex 15.1–18), *Vinea domini* (Is 5.1–8; 54.17; 55.1–5) and *Attende caelum* (Dt 32.1–43). It is important to bear in mind that the three canticle-tracts (although not the psalm *Sicut cervus*) were originally the concluding portion of readings rather than set pieces of chant. One assumes that they were chanted by the lector, even if somewhat more lyrically than the preceding portion of the reading, and that they were recited in their entirety. The question, therefore, is *when* did they come to be radically shortened and sung as elaborate chants by trained singers. *Sicut cervus* also appears to figure as no more than the final reading of the series; we know of its existence only by the rubric, ORATIO POST PSALMUM XLI. It was not, by the way, chanted during the procession to the baptismal font, as is regularly reported in the musicological literature; this is a development that took place several centuries later than the time in question here—it was the litany that was recited during the procession.

The Gregorian sacramentaries, recording the papal liturgy of the later seventh century, provide prayers for just four readings plus *Sicut cervus.*

Omitted from the four is the reading concluding with *Attende caelum,* a clear indication that *Attende* figured not at all in the papal liturgy of the time, neither as lector canticle nor as schola tract.

The absence of *Attende* aside, the central question is whether the existing canticles (including *Sicut cervus,* frequently called a canticle in the early sources) still existed essentially as readings or as set pieces using the G-8 tract melody. The sacramentaries give the impression that the former is the case: they simply provide prayers after the list of readings, whether the readings end with a canticle or not. Much more telling is the witness of the *ordines romani*. Not once does an earlier example of the genre cite one of the four canticle-tracts by name, whereas they consistently cite every Fore-Mass chant of Holy Week and every chant of the Easter vigil itself. At Good Friday, for example, they mention the canticle *Domine audivi* and the tract *Qui habitat,* and for the Easter vigil, the litany, the *Gloria in excelsis,* the alleluia *Confitemini* and the tract *Laudate*.[16] They even specify which chants are omitted from the vigil Mass—the offertory, *Agnus Dei* and communion—but there is no mention of the canticles, only a general reference to the lector's ascending the ambo and beginning each reading immediately without the customary prefatory phrase: "Et ascendit lector in ambone. Non pronunciat: 'Lectio libri Genesis,' sed incoat: 'In principio,' plane. Similiter et illas alias lectiones omnes."[17]

In sharp contrast to this, the early unnotated Frankish graduals give the four chants with their complete (albeit abbreviated) texts and the early notated graduals give them with the G-8 tract melody. The melodies of the four, by the way, represent a particularly stereotypical use of the G-8 melody, one, moreover, that is closely related to that of *Laudate dominum*. It would appear, then, that the Franks shortened the canticles and provided them with the G-8 melody, modeling it after the Easter vigil tract, *Laudate*.[18]

There are various additional indications of this spelled out in the above-cited publication: the absence, for example, of the canticles from the eighth-century Sárospatac leaf described by Peter Jeffery,[19] and their appearance as fully texted readings in a ninth-century document from Wales described by Bonifatius Fischer.[20] But the central argument consists in these three factors: (1) the absence of the canticle-tracts from the seventh- and eighth-century Roman sources; (2) their presence in the ninth- and tenth-century Frankish sources; and (3) their final appearance in eleventh-century Roman manuscripts as Gregorian rather than Old Roman chants.

We do not know precisely how they were sung in the later seventh-century papal liturgy, that is, how the three were sung (*Attende* we must exclude). They may have been sung *in directum* to a traditional psalm tone, and they may even have been sung in an elaborate fashion requiring occasional abbreviation of the text, but their absence from the Roman graduals in the G-8 Roman melody would seem to eliminate the possibility that they were sung as G-8 tracts.

OVERVIEW

The psalm in the later fourth-century Fore-Mass was apparently sung responsorially throughout most of the year but was probably sung *in directum* on some penitential occasions. In all likelihood the distribution of graduals versus tracts in the seventh-century Roman Mass Proper roughly matched the distribution of responsorial psalms and psalms *in directum* of the earlier period. This is not to say that the same psalms were sung on the same liturgical occasions over this span of about three centuries; we have seen that this is certainly not the case for graduals. But it is possible that a higher proportion of the limited tract repertory may have ancient roots, not fourth-century in most cases, but perhaps fifth-century.

Laudate dominum could be the earliest of all tracts, sung in conjunction with the alleluia-psalm *Confitemini* already in the fourth century. Quadragesima Sunday's *Qui habitat* and Palm Sunday's *Deus deus meus* may be nearly as ancient, dating perhaps to the time of the establishment of regular Fore-Mass psalmody at Rome, that is, the early to mid-fifth century (I speculate here with even more than accustomed abandon). The Holy Week chants, Wednesday's *Domine exaudi* and Friday's *Domine audivi,* might date to roughly the same period. We should hardly need reminding that these are not tracts in the mature sense but psalms sung *in directum,* sung, presumably, in a tonality that crystallized eventually into either the G-8 or D-2 tract melody. If my speculations on the chronology of the earliest tracts are correct, then, the ur-tract *Laudate dominum* was sung in the G-tonality, but the four fifth-century Roman chants were sung in the D-tonality. The latter tonality was not used again for permanently assigned psalms *in directum,* although a D-2 responsorial psalm, *De necessitatibus; Ad te domine,* was given the form of a tract in seventh-century Rome.

The next three psalms *in directum* to receive permanent assignments are *Ad te levavi, Qui confidunt* and *Saepe expugnaverunt* (Psalms 122, 124 and 128, respectively), sung on the remaining Sundays of Lent. A chronological gap of some time is likely between these and the previously assigned psalms. This, for two reasons: because the process of properization (before the wholesale effort of the Advent Project) proceeds naturally from important festivals to more ordinary occasions, and because there is a marked and permanent shift in the favored tonality for psalms *in directum,* from D to G.

This chronological gap might have been no more than a matter of decades, thus placing the three psalmic assignments in the later fifth century (the possibility favored above), or it might have been a matter of centuries, placing the creation of the three in the seventh-century schola period. In the latter case the three would have originated as mature tracts modeled on *Laudate dominum,* the sole example of a G-8 tract existing at the time; they would then have been contemporary with the Septuagesima-Sexagesima-Quinquagesima set, which would also have originated as mature tracts. The strongest argument against this possibility is that it so diminishes the entire phenomenon of psalmody *in directum* at fifth- and sixth-century Rome as to eliminate any need of the seventh-century schola to provide tracts for the six Sundays in question. And if they nevertheless were so moved to create these chants, they would have more likely employed the D-2 melody that was used for those two Sundays already having tracts, Quadragesima and Palm Sundays, rather than turning to the G-8 melody of the Easter vigil. I continue to lean to the belief, then, that the psalms of the three Lenten Sundays were sung *in directum* to the ancestor of the G-8 melody at an early date, perhaps the later fifth century, and that the Septuagesimal three were added in a different period altogether—either before the end of the sixth century (when Septuagesima Sunday itself entered the liturgy) or still later, with the Advent Project.

The three sanctoral G-8 tracts, however, and the G-8 Advent tract *Qui regis,* for reasons given above, must have lacked a prehistory as psalms *in directum* and almost certainly originated during the time of the Advent Project.

This brings us full circle to Hucke's view of the tract as a late genre of incomplete repertory, a repertory, moreover, that was assigned as the penitential counterpart of the equally late alleluia. There is surely something to the idea. The Saturday of the Advent Ember Days was given a Proper tract, *Qui regis,* but *Laudate dominum* was called into service for use at the Saturdays of the Pentecost week and of the Lenten Ember Days, the latter assignment not appearing to be a particularly appropriate one (just as *Laudate dominum* is not an especially felicitous choice for the Annunciation, either). The Saturday of the September Ember Days, moreover, lacks a tract altogether. And then there is the confinement of the Lenten tracts to Sundays. The Franks saw fit to expand the use of the tract to Lenten Mondays and Wednesdays, and one wonders whether the Romans would have done the same if their creative period of Mass Proper creation had not come to such an abrupt end in the late seventh century.

Even if there is some validity to Hucke's position, in that a number of tracts are clearly late, Wagner's view of the tract as a chant with ancient roots is ultimately one of deeper significance. In the end what is impressive about the history of the tract is that the most limited of all Mass Proper genres may have the largest number of individual chants that can lay claim to continuity with the psalmody of the early Church.

CHAPTER 12

The Offertory

The offertory is a world unto itself, a world I cannot claim to have conquered (even if I am not alone in this).[1] There is simply too great a quantity of music: the ninety-two offertories of the core repertory,[2] when one includes the verses, are roughly twice the length of any other item of the Mass Proper. And then there is the special problem of the Gregorian verses. Ranging in number from one to four for each offertory, they gradually fell into disuse during the eleventh, twelfth and thirteenth centuries. They were by and large ignored during the chant revival of the nineteenth century and failed to find a place in the modern chant books, resulting in their neglect by students of chant. Caspar Ott's edition of 1935,[3] designed to fill this void, is now recognized as occasionally unreliable,[4] and the single corrective to it, Finn Egeland Hansen's 1974 transcription of the Montpellier 159 tonary, must itself be used with discretion.[5] It is not Hansen's transcriptions that are questionable, but the manuscript itself, with its sometimes eccentric readings that go against the majority of contemporary sources.

The offertory is bedeviled also by conceptual difficulties, in particular uncertainty over whether it should be considered a responsorial or antiphonal chant. The conventional view long favored the latter alternative. Encouraged by the rubric that appears in some late manuscripts, ANTIPHONA AD OFFERTORIUM, liturgical and musical historians alike argued from analogy with the indisputably antiphonal introit and communion. Joseph Dyer, however, has pointed out that *Ordo romanus I*, which describes the introit and communion as antiphonal chants, does not do so with the offertory and, moreover, refutes the view that the offertory, like the introit, was a processional chant.[6] *Ordo I* is especially clear on this point: the gifts of bread and wine are not brought in procession to the sanctuary, but rather the pope himself goes down to the *senatorium* (where the male nobility are gathered) and the corresponding *pars feminarum* to receive them.

But if the offertory is a responsorial chant, I hope to show that it is not one in the same sense that the gradual is. Actually I am not alone in my reluctance to refer to the offertory (the chant minus the verses) as either a respond or an antiphon,[7] but I may be the first to claim, as I will presently, that an offertory verse is not in fact a genuine verse.

I hope, in any event, by following the same approach employed in this volume for the other items of the Mass Proper, to help in some small way to deal with both the conceptual and the quantitative difficulties that the offertory poses for the music historian.

ORIGINS

I have already expressed my view in chapter two that the frequently quoted passage from Augustine, conventionally taken to refer to the ancient offertory psalm, does not in fact do so. Augustine speaks of a certain Hilary who vehemently objects to the "custom which had begun then in Carthage . . . of singing at the altar hymns from the Book of Psalms both before the oblation and while what had been offered was distributed to the people."[8] The second place cited in the passage for singing psalms in the service, during the distribution of communion, is not disputed by modern scholars; the first of these, "before the oblation" (*ante oblationem*), is in question.[9] The obvious reading to me of "before the oblation" is during the Fore-Mass, when the gradual psalm was sung. We know from numerous sources that a psalm was sung then in Augustine's church, and in many other ecclesiastical centers as well, just as we know that a communion psalm was also sung. But there is not another passage in all of patristic literature that has been proposed as evidence that an offertory psalm was sung in the later fourth and earlier fifth centuries. Hence, again, the obvious reading of the passage is that Augustine refers to the gradual and communion psalms.

The objection that one might make to this is that the gradual psalm was a practice of such long standing that a figure like Hilary would not find it controversial. But this is simply not so. There is no indisputable evidence for the existence of the gradual psalm before it is mentioned by later fourth-century figures like Basil, John Chrysostom, Ambrose and Augustine. Augustine's very language of still referring to the gradual psalm as a reading suggests that its transformation into a discrete musical event was still in a state of transition. He found it necessary, moreover, as did his contemporary Niceta of Remesiana, to defend the singing of psalms at any time by Christian congregations; indeed he found it necessary to defend the custom against his own scruples, as is well known from his famous ruminations about the pleasure he experienced in hearing the psalmody of the Milanese church.

It seems all the more reasonable to look upon the gradual psalm of Augustine's church as an innovation in the later fourth century when we consider that the practice appears not to have been established in Rome until the time of Pope Celestine I (422–32). The passage from the *Liber pontificalis* that bears witness to the event, moreover, sheds considerable interpretive light on the passage of Augustine presently at issue. The two texts have much in common. The Roman one tells us that Celestine ordered that "the 150 psalms of David be sung before the sacrifice," whereas previously "only the epistle of blessed Paul was recited and the holy gospel." This is a clear reference, as shown in chapter four, to the early content of the Fore-Mass, with its three events of epistle, psalm and gospel. And note when the passage has them take place—"before the sacrifice" (*ante sacrificium*)—that is, before the sacrificial rite of the Eucharist, during the Fore-Mass or Mass of the Catechumens as opposed to the Mass of the Faithful. As for the Augustinian passage, *oblatio* is an obvious synonym for *sacrificium*, so that the more plausible meaning of *ante oblationem* would seem also to be before the sacrificial rite of the Eucharist taken as a whole rather than before the offertory portion of it in particular.

But let us assume, for the sake of argument, that *oblatio* is to be taken in the restricted sense of the offering of the gifts of bread and wine, a meaning that finds support in early medieval documents especially.[10] The psalmody in question, then, takes place *before* the offering of gifts, not *during* it, as would be the case for an offertory psalm. There is nothing ambiguous about Augustine's language with respect to the timing of the two psalmodic events: the first takes place before the oblation, whether taken in the narrow or wide sense, and the second during the distribution of communion. The passage, then, by its seeming inclusion of all places where psalmody was employed in the service and its failure to mention offertory psalmody is in effect an implicit denial of the singing of psalms during the offering of the gifts.

So, if we must cease to rely on the testimony of Augustine for the introduction of the offertory psalm, when did it come to be sung at Mass? We are placed in a very similar situation to that involving the Roman introit. In each case our first indisputable evidence for the existence of the chant is *Ordo romanus I*, which describes a pontifical Mass of about 700. Again, in both instances we assume that the papal ceremonies accompanying the chant, the entrance of the pope into the stational church and his reception and preparation of the offerings, are long-established rites that might very well have been accompanied by psalmody for generations and even centuries before the time of *Ordo I*. We have, too, the analogy with the Byzantine liturgy, which introduced the singing of the Cheroubikon as its offertory chant in the late fifth century, and the Gallican liturgy described by Pseudo-Germanus (late-sixth-century Paris?) with its alleluiatic *sonus*. But still there is no Roman evidence as such before that of *Ordo I*.

The reference in *Ordo I* itself, in fact, raises further questions about the origins of the offertory. It is laconic in the extreme, not describing the chant and not mentioning when it begins, but only when it ends. The offertory rites themselves are very elaborate and described in great detail. We assume that they are accompanied by singing because at the conclusion of the description we read: "The pope bows slightly to the altar, then looks to the schola and signals that they be silent."[11] Not only is the reference brief but it is troubling in that it shares with *Ordo I*'s references to the introit and communion the indication that the pope cut off the chanting with a mere nod. In the case of the introit and communion we know that the bulk of the chanting involves psalm verses, hence the appropriateness of an arbitrary stop to the singing when the accompanied action is at an end. But are not the offertory and its verses set pieces of elaborate chant that it would be disruptive to cut off in full flight?

The *Ordo I* reference is one Willi Apel ought to have invoked in his notorious argument that offertory verses before that time were sung to psalmodic formulas of some sort because their musical style was so advanced that they could not have been composed until the later ninth century.[12] His position would have remained untenable nevertheless (it is soundly refuted by scholars such as Dyer and Steiner),[13] and I would add myself only that the elaborate verses that gave Apel pause are present already in the Roman manuscripts and are clearly related to the Gregorian versions, textually and musically. They must therefore, as is the case with the rest of the Mass Proper, have been in existence at the time the Roman manuscripts used in the transmission to the north were redacted.

The pope's nod to the schola, then, appearing in a document describing the pontifical Mass of about 700, remains puzzling. I suspect it to be an instance of obsolete language, dating from a time when the offertory might still have been a psalm. In around 700, I would imagine, the pope and the schola would be inclined to coordinate their timing, and the pope would be willing to accommodate a minute or so of singing beyond the completion of the offertory rites. This was the very period of Roman history, after all, when a pope, such as our Sergius I (687–701), was a graduate of the schola cantorum. We would expect popes of the time to have an insider's appreciation of the offertory in all its musical splendor.

THE OFFERTORY CHANT DESCRIBED

What is the nature of the offertory chant? Apel, as mentioned above, found its characteristics, both musical and textual, to be so extraordinary that he placed its creation in the later ninth century. I, too, will argue eventually for a late date for the chant, although certainly not one as late as the ninth century. But first an attempt to describe it, an attempt complicated by the circumstance that when dealing with the music, I must take both Roman and Gregorian versions into account, distinguishing between those traits that the two versions hold in common and those that are peculiar to the one or the other.

The chant has already been referred to here as one consisting in the offertory as such with from one to four added verses (two or, less often, three being the norm). Chant scholars writing after Dyer's initial publications on the subject avoid the term "antiphon" in referring to the initial segment of the chant; they might use the alternate "respond," if this, too, only with reluctance. I share their reluctance but use the term for presentational convenience, keeping in mind that the portion of the chant that it refers to is not a respond in the same strict sense as the gradual respond. The gradual respond is an integral unit, sung in its entirety by either cantor or chorus, whereas the offertory respond, typically longer than that of the gradual, is divided into two sections, the first of which is usually about twice the length of the second. It is only the shorter second section of the respond that is treated as a refrain in offertory performance. A number of offertories, in fact, musically highlight this function by having the verses end with the same cadential formula as immediately precedes the refrain portion of the respond.

The essential difference between the two types of respond has historical implications. That of the gradual is a genuine respond; its text has the same length and general character as the response verse of ancient responsorial psalmody. It is true that only a small minority of gradual responds exist in direct historical continuity with specific early Christian congregational responses, but even most of those that are clearly the products of late invention, for example nonpsalmic gradual responds, share the formal attributes of their more venerable partners. A single significant verse, or portion thereof, is sung as a unit, just as was done spontaneously by the Christian congregations of antiquity. The offertory respond, by contrast, has the appearance of formal contrivance. Its text is generally longer than would be suitable for use as a refrain and is frequently stitched together, as we shall see, from separated fragments of a scriptural passage, with its responsorial character being salvaged only by the shorter refrain portion at its conclusion. Such a format clearly suggests compositional artifice rather than the character of a spontaneous response.

THE OFFERTORY "VERSE"

The so-called verses contribute to the same impression of formal invention. They are not genuine verses like those of the gradual, nor those of the tract and alleluia, for that matter. Gradual verses have both a musical and a textual integrity lacking in offertory verses. They manifest, with considerable consistency, a slightly more melismatic texture and a slightly higher tessitura than the respond that marks them as solo chants. Gradual texts, moreover, consist generally in a single psalm verse in its unaltered biblical form —thus a verse in the strict sense of the word. Offertory verses, however, are not as a rule musically distinct from the responds: the same "moderately florid style, punctuated by occasionally lengthy melismas," to borrow Kenneth Levy's formulation, is shared by verses and responds.[14] If it is true that from time to time extravagant intervals, extreme ranges, abnormally high or low tessituras and inordinately long melismas are to be met with in the verses, there is no consistency in the appearance of these traits. And, in fact, many of the more exceptional musical features of offertories pointed out by Apel have been shown to be the product of Ott's editorial practices,[15] whereas the genuinely extravagant feature of several offertory verses, the greatly extended melismas,[16] do not have their parallels in the Roman versions. They are, apparently, Frankish insertions.

If the verses generally have no consistently employed musical traits that define them as solo verses distinct in style from the responds, the texts, as often as not, are verses in name only. Gradual, alleluia and tract verses are just that, typically single and integral verses of a psalm, unchanged from their biblical original except for the occasional insertion of the vocative *domine*. By contrast, take *Ego autem*, the second verse of *Exaudi deus*, the offertory for Monday in the third week of Lent. Its text (the left-hand column in table 29) is derived from Psalm 54.17–21 (the right-hand column). The offertory verse selects three portions of the biblical original, stitching them together into a new creation. The first portion is allowed to remain in-

Table 29. The Text of the Offertory Verse *Ego autem*

Chant Text	Psalm 54.17–21 (Psalterium Romanum)
Ego autem ad deum clamavi	17. <u>ego autem ad dominum clamavi</u> et dominus exaudivit me
	18. vespere mane et meridie narrabo et adnuntiabo et exaudiet vocem meam
libera animam meam	19. <u>liberabit</u> in pace <u>animam meam</u> ab his qui adpropiant mihi quoniam intermultos erant mecum
	20. exaudiet deus et humiliabit eos qui est ante saecula et manet in aeternum
	non est enim illis commutatio et non timuerunt deum
et extende manum tuam in retribuendo illis.	21. <u>extendit manum suam in retribuendo illis</u> contaminaverunt testamentum eius

tegral (the *deum* as opposed to *dominum* is a common variant in the manuscripts of the Psalterium Romanum). But the second two portions change the verb from third person to imperative, thus making of them a prayer addressed to the Lord. The two invocations of the prayer are united by *et* (a common addition in offertory textual creation), and the *in pace* of the first is simply dropped. What we have here, then, is not a verse in the biblical sense, but a "libretto" in the sense described by Levy. It is something that is utterly incompatible with the notion of evolution from the verse of an ancient offertory psalm. And, needless to say, no music historian should be tempted to examine it for traces of the medial cadence of an ancient psalm tone, as one does legitimately in the case of a tract verse.

The nature of both respond and verse, then, dubiously named as they are, casts doubt on the notion that the offertory is the final stage in a centuries-long evolution of musical form; it appears more like a carefully crafted genre, the creation of quasi-professional liturgical musicians. The element of textual adjustment is crucial to this impression and one must ask whether *Ego autem* is typical in this respect or exceptional. Much of what follows in this chapter will be devoted to an examination of this question, but before turning to that task I take the opportunity of dealing with a number of issues much discussed in the literature of the offertory, which, fortuitously, are well illustrated by the verse *Ego autem*.

EGO AUTEM: A MUSICAL INTERLUDE

Ego autem provides a good example of the point made above about the doubtful authenticity of certain purported musical extravagancies of the offertory verses. At issue is the setting of its final words, *in retribuendo illis*. Example 12 presents it in a number of readings. The first, labeled "Gai" (for reasons that will be clear presently), is that of Ott's collection; it provides a virtually stratospheric ending for the verse. The chant as a whole, that is to say the respond and the first of its two verses, is an example of typical mode-8 melody in range, centering within the tetrachord G-c while moving occasionally lower or higher by one or two pitches. The verse *Ego autem*, however, lies generally in the higher c-f tetrachord, and, in this version, as we see, eventually moves into a still higher region, adding a third to the range of the chant and bringing it to a close on c, rather than the final G. One cannot help suspecting the reading, even if it gains support from its appearance in Montpellier 159.

Indeed, it appears also in other manuscripts, including the Aquitanian gradual Paris 776, the gradual of Gaillac (hence "Gai" in the music example). This provides the opportunity to compare it within a controlled sample, the three most prominent Aquitanian graduals: that of Gaillac; that of St-Yrieix (Paris 903, here "Yri"), and that of Toulouse (London, Harley 5341, here "Tou"). Tou begins the verse as does Gai, in the relatively high tessitura, but drops the extraordinarily high ending of Gai by a fourth, a solution that maintains the verse within both previous tessitura and mode. Yri, finally, copies the entire verse a third lower, bringing it to a close on *a*, providing a more plausible tessitura for the entire verse, but requiring the addition of several b-flats and changing the modal quality at times to protus and at times to deuterus. It is not my intention here to suggest a preferred reading; that could come only, if at all, from an exhaustive comparison of Gregorian sources. I use the example simply to illustrate the oft-made point that one must look carefully at each instance of purported musical extravagance in a Gregorian offertory.

The fourth version given in example 12 (that of Vat lat 5319, labeled "Rom") serves other purposes here, primarily that of bringing us back to the seventh and eighth centuries and reminding us once more of the central question of Gregorian chant, that is, what can a comparison of later notated Roman and Gregorian versions tell us about the character of the original Roman music?

The Roman and Gregorian versions of the offertory *Exaudi deus* (the

Example 12. Offertory *Exaudi deus*

Example 13. Offertory *Exaudi deus*

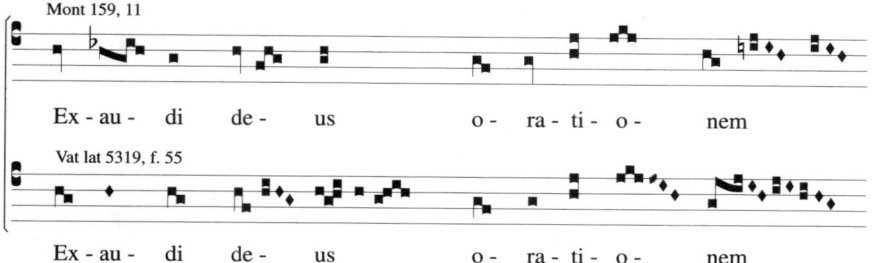

parent chant of *Ego autem*) are in the same tonality, that of G-final, whether authentic or plagal, and show undeniable evidence of melodic relationship. The beginning of the respond, one of the more obviously related places, is given in example 13. The respond and the first verse continue in roughly similar fashion, pursuing the same overall contour for the most part, placing melismas on the same syllables, remaining oriented to the same G-c tetrachord with its tonal focus upon the c, even if this last feature is usually more prominent in the Gregorian version with its repeated notes on c. We are obviously dealing, then, with a chant that is part of the mid-eighth-century transmission from Rome to the north. We might take the occasion, also, to formulate for the first time in this volume a general principal that should be involved in any attempted solution to the central question. Common features of the later Roman and Gregorian versions are in most cases genuine features of the Roman original. Thus we can add to our knowledge of the original *Exaudi deus* text and liturgical assignment the musical traits of the sort just cited: its tonality, its approximate dispensation of syllabic and melismatic styles, its general melodic contour, its tessitura and many of its key pitches.

The Roman version of the verse *Ego autem* provides still more specific suggestion of its original state. It begins similarly to the Gregorian melody,

Example 14. Offertory verse *Ego autem*

in its more frequently encountered version, that is, it begins on d and dwells in the higher c-f tetrachord (example 14). The verse continues in this range throughout most of its length, thus giving credence to the high tessitura of the Gregorian version. And what of the verse's conclusion? If we return to example 12 we see that most of the setting of *in retribuendo illis* is rather closely related to the more common Gregorian version (Gai), sharing with it many key pitches, its general contour and tessitura and, most strikingly, the sharp ascent to a' at the end of the melisma. A change comes finally on the syllable *do*, which prepares for the lower ending on the word *illis*, an ending with the same melodic contour as the Gregorian version but one that is set a fourth lower and comes to rest on the proper final G rather than the c above.

One could argue from this comparison with the Roman version that the original Gregorian melody (sung, let us say, as it was at Metz in the late eighth century) had an ending more like that of Tou than Gai. But more interesting than this is the light that the comparison of the entire offertory throws on the Roman version of the later seventh century. *Exaudi domine* appears to have had a respond and first verse confined to a typical G-plagal tessitura centered about the tetrachord G-c. Its second verse, however, *Ego autem*, was set in a considerably higher tessitura and made a surprising abrupt ascent to a' toward its close. If many of the musical eccentricities of the Gregorian offertory verses pointed out by Apel have turned out to be of dubious authenticity, here is one that is verified by reference to the Roman version and, more than that, appears to have originated in Rome. How frequently do such extravagances occur in Roman offertories? What chronological significance might they have? Here I must remind the reader of my admission at the beginning of this chapter that the vast musical world of the offertory is not one that I can claim to have conquered. I would only make the point that such extraordinary musical events, however often they might occur, do not constitute a consistent musical style employed in the verses as opposed to the responds; note that in this very chant the first verse shares the musical characteristics of the respond.

Time and space are best spent in this chapter not by continuing to engage in exhaustive musical analysis, but by applying to the offertory the same approach used in dealing with the other items of the Mass Proper, that is, the examination of the genre in the context of its liturgical assignments. In the case of the offertory the question of textual adjustment is especially pertinent to such examination.

THE OFFERTORIES OF THE ADVENT-CHRISTMAS SEASON

The liturgical assignments of the Roman Christmastime offertories are given in table 30 under the rubric "textual adjustment."[17] Before we discuss that particular subject, however, it is necessary first to attend to the more basic task of establishing the original repertory of the season. Of the eighteen Advent-Christmas assignments, probably sixteen (at the very least thirteen) can be looked upon as original. Twelve (those underlined in the table) are unique to Advent-Christmas and hence most certainly are origi-

Table 30. Roman Christmastime Offertories—Textual Adjustment

		Respond	Verse 1	Verse 2	Verse 3
Advent I	*Ad te domine levavi*	—	—	gap!	
Advent II	*Deus tu convertens*	—	—	gap!	
Advent III	*Benedixisti domine*	—	—	—	
Ember Wednesday	*Confortamini & jam*	—	—		
[Ember Friday	*Ad te domine levavi*]				
Ember Saturday	*Exulta satis filia*	—	—	—	
Vigil Xmas	*Tollite portas*	—	—	—	
Xmas I	*Laetentur caeli*	gap!	—	—	
Xmas II	*Deus enim firmavit*	—	—	gap	
Xmas III	*Tui sunt caeli*	gap!	gap!	gap!	gap!
Stephen	*In virtute tua*	—	—		
John	*Justus ut palma*	—	—	—	—
Innocents	*Anima nostra*	—	—	—	
[Sunday	*Deus enim firmavit*]				
Epiphany	*Reges Tharsis*	—	—	—	—
Eph I	*Jubilate deo omnis*	rep, gap	rep	rep	
Eph II	*Jubilate deo universa*	—	—	—	
Eph III	*Dextera domini*	—	—	gap	

nal to that season. To this number *Ad te domine* must be added (bringing the preliminary total to thirteen); it is widely shared throughout the year, appearing even in Lent and after Pentecost, but it is clearly an Advent chant with the refrain portion of its respond reading *et enim universi qui te expectant non confundentur*. Less certainly *Jubilate deo universa* and *Jubilate deo omnis* can be added as well. The former appears also on the fourth Sunday after Easter and the latter on the Monday after Laetare Sunday; these secondary dates have no special claim to these offertories, and the earlier appearance of the chants in the year when the aims of the Advent Project were fresh suggests that their proper place is in fact the first two Sundays after the Epiphany (thus a probable total of fifteen original chants). The sixteenth is John the Evangelist's *Justus ut palma*; it is shared with the equally prestigious festival of John the Baptist. I tend, however, to categorize it as an original Advent-Christmas chant for somewhat the same reason as for the pair of *Jubilate*, that is, because of its liturgical placement well within the early stages of the Advent Project. Finally the second appearance of

Deus enim firmavit and *Ad te domine* (marked with square brackets) within the same season obviously require their subtraction from the overall total of eighteen possibilities.

In summary we have a certain thirteen and a probable fifteen or sixteen offertories created for a season with eighteen slots to fill. It is a respectable number, showing the general care exercised for chants of Christmastime during the Advent Project. On the other hand, the outright reuse of two chants within the series, *Ad te domine* and *Deus enim firmavit*, speaks to the difficulty the schola cantorum must have experienced in attempting to realize perfectly the ideals of the Advent Project for this lengthy genre of chant.

Another basic point, this one not indicated in the table, is that of continuity of liturgical assignment between Rome and Francia. There is a high degree of such continuity. The only real lapse is on Ember Friday, where the Franks borrowed *Deus tu convertens* for Ember Friday rather than *Ad te domine*. They also made the same curious switch of chants between the first two Sundays after the Epiphany as they did for the introit, although in the case of the offertory the seeming lapse is more understandable since both chants begin with the words *Jubilate deo*. (There are several instances of such verbal confusion scattered throughout the early Frankish Mass Proper.) This substantial continuity of assignment has important chronological implications. We have spoken frequently here of "late" traits in the offertory, but its continuity of assignment with Francia is strong evidence that its repertory was in liturgical place before the redaction of the Mass antiphoners used in the transmission to the north. This, in contrast to the alleluia, which, as we have seen, had only eight Christmastime chants (including the Innocents' *Anima nostra*) so assigned. Late the offertory may be, then, but not quite as late as the alleluia.

Musical continuity is also in evidence. Every chant maintains the same final except the third Mass of Christmas' *Tui sunt caeli*, a protus chant in the Roman version and a deuterus one in the Gregorian. (It is frequently observed, by the way, that offertories are difficult to classify as authentic or plagal because of the variable tessituras in some verses.) More important, there is an undeniable musical relationship between the Roman and Gregorian versions, albeit not quite as consistently close as in other chant genres. Even *Tui sunt caeli*, the lone offertory that has differing finals in the two versions, is clearly related throughout the bulk of its respond and its lengthy verses.[18] The Frankish cantors, then, managed to come to terms with these melodies also, even if not reproducing them precisely, surely the most difficult task they faced as far as Mass chants are concerned.[19]

THE CHRISTMASTIME OFFERTORIES: TEXTUAL ADJUSTMENT

To turn finally to the question of textual adjustment, my findings are provided in the four right-hand columns of table 30. A series of dashes means that the biblical text of a respond or verse (in most cases from the Psalterium Romanum) is used by and large intact. To simplify the table, I do not indicate minor adjustments such as the insertion of the vocative *domine* or the omission of a connective like *autem*, but include only substantial ones. The most common of these, indicated by the word "gap," consists in a considerable omission of text. When such omissions are especially extensive, I place an exclamation point after the word "gap." For example *Respice in me*, the second verse of *Ad te domine*, derived from Psalm 24.16–20, begins with a few words from the beginning of verse 16 and then skips the remainder of the verse and all of verses 17, 18 and 19, to conclude with verse 20.

Appearing also on the table is the abbreviation "rep" (see *Jubilate deo omnis*), standing for "repetition"; this indicates a repeated portion of the biblical text, usually at the beginning of a respond or verse. This frequently discussed device is unique to offertories and deserves a word of comment. To me the most likely explanation for it is the commonsense one that the offertory is the longest Mass Proper chant because the ceremonies it accompanies are the longest of the papal Mass, and that the repetition of texts is part of the general expansiveness of the genre. It should be noted also that it is another indication of sophisticated formal contrivance as opposed to evolutionary adaptation of an ancient psalmodic format.[20]

To summarize the information represented in the table, of the fifty responds and verses of the Advent-Christmas season, twelve, or about one-fourth, utilize the device of substantial textual adjustment. Nine of the twelve items are verses, supporting the view proposed above that offertory verses are not verses in the same sense as gradual, alleluia and tract verses, which very seldom change the biblical original. Moreover, even in cases where the biblical text is used integrally, offertory verses sometimes begin or end at a place in the text that violates the integrity of the dualism of a psalm verse. *Orietur in diebus* (Ps 71.7–8), for example, the third verse of *Reges Tharsis*, uses all of the psalm's verse 7 and continues with verse 8 but cuts off its second half, as indicated here by a slash: *Et dominabitur a mari usque ad mare / et a flumine usque ad terminos orbis terrae*.

The particular type of adjustment employed in the offertories of Christmastime is that of creating large gaps in a biblical text that is otherwise left intact. This device is different in kind from that of free paraphrase; the latter is obviously a matter of taking greater liberty with a text and quite possibly an indication of more recent composition. It need be asked if there is any difference in this respect between the offertories of Christmastime and those of the other segments of the church year.

THE LENTEN OFFERTORIES

The Lenten offertory cycle, with its forty-five assignments, is more than twice the length of the Christmastime cycle; still, I would hope to be able to describe its principal characteristics without benefit of ungainly tables. It shares several of these traits with the Christmas cycle.

The Lenten cycle also is reasonably well supplied with originally assigned chants. Of the forty-five assignments, seven are obviously late borrowings: those for the six Thursdays and the second Sunday. These are dates added to the liturgy after the substantial completion of the Roman Mass Proper and hence are not at issue when dealing with the original chants of any item of the Mass Proper. Of the remaining thirty-eight dates, twenty have chants that are unique to Lent and another eighteen are shared with other seasons. Fourteen of the latter group are shared with the post-Pentecostal season and thus would seem to be originally assigned Lenten chants that were borrowed for the post-Pentecostal cycle, a safe assumption for reasons already established in this volume. There remain just four offertories, then, that appear to be outright borrowings, that is, chants taken from elsewhere in the church year at the time the Lenten cycle took its final form: these are Wednesday in the second week's *Ad te domine*, borrowed from the first Sunday of Advent, Monday in the fourth week's *Jubilate deo omnis*, from the second Sunday after the Epiphany; Tuesday in the third week's *Dextera domini*, from the third Sunday after the Epiphany and Holy Thursday's *Dextera domini*, borrowed also from that same date. This borrowing of a chant, incidentally, by so solemn an occasion as Holy Thursday, is one more indication of that date's surprisingly late Proper chants. The larger point at issue here is the proportion of originally assigned offertories for the season, and we see that it is substantial (thirty-four from thirty-eight), as was the case with the Christmas season, but lacking in the absoluteness seen in introits, communions and even graduals.

The second fundamental point to be considered is that of continuity of assignment between Rome and Francia. We saw that this was impressive, but not perfect for Christmastime, and might expect the same for Lent, with possibly a few more discrepancies because of the sheer scope of the effort

314 / *The Advent Project*

needed by the Frankish cantors in this case. Surprisingly, the continuity, save for a few lapses in the eccentric Rheinau gradual, is virtually perfect, comparable to that of a more manageable genre like the introit.[21]

THE LENTEN OFFERTORIES: MUSICAL CONTINUITY

Musical continuity is, however, a different matter; it is substantially present, but not nearly to the degree that it is in the offertories of Christmastime. The burden of capturing so great a quantity of music in oral transmission, apparently, was almost too much for the Frankish cantors.[22] Of the thirty-four chants I consider to be original to the Lenten cycle, no less than eleven, almost a third, have different finals in the Roman and Gregorian versions. This, of course, does not in itself preclude a musical relationship. It was pointed out above that *Tui sunt caeli*, the one chant from the Christmas cycle with divergent finals, displayed a fairly close relationship in the two versions. Of the eleven such offertory responds (I leave the examination of the verses to specialists) in the Lenten cycle, however, not one (except perhaps Tuesday in Holy Week's *Custodi me domine*) is as closely related as *Tui sunt caeli*. What is present in most of these chants are just enough instances of similarity—the same placement of melismas, for example, or the distinctive shape of certain neumatic groupings—to be beyond coincidence, even if dissimilarities far outweigh similarities. I would summarize my impressions by saying that I think one could make a case for a musical relationship for the majority of these chants, but not for some, such as Tuesday in the fifth week's *Sperent in te* and Saturday in the fourth week's *Factus est dominus* (this chant, by the way, is a rare instance of substantially different texts in the Roman and Gregorian versions).[23]

The twenty-three offertories with common finals are, not surprisingly, more obviously related but still not nearly as closely as, for example, the typical introit or formulaic gradual. I found only about four of the twenty-three to achieve that status: Wednesday in the third week's *Domine fac mecum*, Wednesday in the fourth week's *Benedicite gentes*, the fifth Sunday's *Confitebor tibi* and Wednesday in the fifth week's *Eripe me*. Again, I define such a relationship as possessing melismas on the same syllables, manifesting a similar overall melodic contour, hovering about the key pitches F and c in the same portions of the chant and displaying occasional instances of identical key pitches and pitch groupings. To provide one example of a particularly obvious sort, I offer the opening of the verse *Ego autem* of *Confitebor tibi* (example 14). Keeping in mind the exceptional nature of this example, it serves to illustrate two more points of more or less general validity: (1) the melodic relationship of the two versions tends to be more obvious in the earlier rather than in the later portion of offertory responds; and (2) the Roman versions tend to have a consistently greater degree of figuration.

What is one to conclude from this survey of continuity between the Roman and Gregorian versions of the Lenten offertories—both the continuity of liturgical assignment and the musical continuity (or the lack thereof)? On the positive side there *is* continuity. The Franks accurately copied the offertories of the unnotated Roman Mass antiphoners and made a valiant effort to master the music as well. The latter project, however, was simply too much for them. Assuming, as I do, that musical mastery of the Roman melodies was their overall intention, the sheer quantity of offertory music caused them to stray from what they heard the Roman cantors sing.[24] I do not mean to imply by saying this that, in spite of a formal commitment to reproduce the Roman melodies, some enterprising and talented Frankish cantors did not occasionally take it upon themselves to "improve" the Roman melodies.

Nor do I mean to imply, certainly, that the extant Roman versions are precisely the same as the eighth-century Roman versions with which the Frankish cantors had to work. Rather I revert to the point made above that shared characteristics between extant Gregorian and Roman versions point to probably authentic characteristics of the Roman original. Sharply divergent versions can be interpreted in various ways: one version, for example, could be closer to the original and the other all the more distant. In the present case my guess is that the extant Gregorian versions are very different from those of the eighth-century Roman Mass antiphoners for the reasons suggested above, that is, those having to do with the quantity of music involved. I would imagine at the same time, though, that for the very same reasons the Romans would have had difficulty in maintaining the eighth-century versions for more than three centuries of oral transmission. Unfortunately, the overall probability is that, just as shared characteristics of the extant Roman and Gregorian versions bring us blessedly close to the original Roman chants, greatly divergent versions present us with a nearly impenetrable barrier to visualizing anything like the original melodies.

But these are concerns that have more to do with the epilogue to this volume than the present chapter; of more relevance at present is the question of textual adjustment in the Lenten offertories. The basic information can be summarized without the aid of a table. The most obvious point is that substantial textual adjustment is far more common in Lenten offertories than in those of the Christmas season. To cite the overall numbers, of the total of 112 Lenten offertory responds and verses, forty-nine (close to half) employ substantial textual adjustment. This is altogether beyond what we encountered in the psalmic graduals of Lent (six from thirty-nine responds and two from thirty-nine verses) and even in psalmic introits (six from thirty-one), the genre where textual adjustment is generally the most common. The typical sort of adjustment continues to be that of the insertion of large gaps between integrally reproduced portions of text, while there are occasional instances of more radical procedures, as when a verse like *Confitebor tibi*'s lengthy *Viam veritatis* (Ps 118.30, 34, 36–37 and 39) is stitched together from multiple fragments, or when a verse like *Ego autem*, given above in table 29, actually makes changes in the biblical text.

THE PASCHALTIME CYCLE

The observation of genuine significance that emerges from an examination of the Paschaltime offertories (see table 31) involves the liturgical placement of its borrowed, as opposed to its unique, chants. Before turning to that subject one can briefly survey a number of other considerations (not indicated in the table). The continuity of liturgical assignment between Rome and Francia is substantial, if not nearly as close to absolute as was the case with the Lenten offertories.[25] The substantial continuity is in contrast to the lack of this trait for the Paschaltime alleluias and is one more in a series of indications placing the completion of the Roman offertory cycle prior in time, if only slightly, to that of the alleluia. Musical continuity, while still observable, moves another step in the negative direction. The Paschaltime offertory melodies are clearly less closely related than those of Lent: six of the thirteen chants unique to the season have different finals, and even the seven that share finals are only vaguely related. It appears that as the Franks work through the church year, they have increasing difficulty in controlling the Roman melodies.

A point of some interest in the area of textual adjustment is that non-psalmic chants such as *Angelus domini* (Mt 28) and *In die sollempnitatis* (Ex 13) go beyond the technique of allowing large gaps to occur in the biblical original, to that of freely paraphrasing the text and thereby producing an entirely new composition.

The matter of greatest significance in the Easter offertory cycle is, as mentioned above, that of borrowed versus original chants. Table 31 gives the incipits of the thirteen chants unique to their liturgical assignments (underlined and followed by their scriptural derivations) and gives those of the nine borrowed chants without the scriptural derivations and with an

Table 31. Roman Paschaltime Offertories

Easter	*Terra tremuit*	Ps 75.9–10
Monday	*Angelus domini*	Mt 28.2, 5–6
Tuesday	*Intonuit de caelo*	Ps 17.14–16
Wednesday	*Portas caeli*	Ps 27.23–15
Thursday	*In die sollempnitatis*	Ex 13.5
Friday	*Erit nobis hic*	Ex 12.14
Saturday	*Benedictus qui*	Ps 117.26–27
Easter I	*Benedictus qui	
Easter II	*Deus deus meus*	Ps 62.2–5
Easter III	*Lauda anima mea*	Ps 145.2
Easter IV	**Jubilate deo universa*	
Easter V	**Benedicite gentes*	
Litanies	*Confitebor*	Ps 108.30–31
Ascension	*Ascendit deus*	Ps 46.6
Sunday	*Lauda animam	
Vigil Pent	*Emitte spiritum*	Ps 103.30–31
Pentecost	*Confirma hoc*	Ps 67.29–30
Monday	**Intonuit de caelo*	
Tuesday	*Portas caeli	
Wednesday	*Meditabar	
Friday	*Populum humilem	
Saturday	**Domine deus salutis*	

asterisk. The early chants in the series (whether psalmic or nonpsalmic) not only are unique to their assigned dates but tend to enjoy texts that are explicitly related to their liturgical date or season. The same is generally true of the four uniquely assigned chants that fall later in the season, those for the feasts of the Litany, Ascension and Pentecost. Once those four are eliminated from consideration, a clear pattern emerges: beginning with the fourth Sunday after Easter, every ordinary Sunday and every feria has a borrowed chant.[26] To place this observation in perspective, one recalls that all of the eight dates in question have uniquely assigned introits and communions. Surely the most plausible explanation for the abrupt change in policy that takes place about halfway through the offertory set is that this is the point of breakdown in adherence to the aims of the Advent Project. These aims are simply too ambitious in the case of the lengthy offertories, and here the members of the schola make the prudent decision to borrow chants for the lesser dates remaining in the season and to provide new ones only for the principal festivals.

THE POST-PENTECOSTAL OFFERTORIES

With the post-Pentecostal offertories we follow the progress of the schola cantorum into what is without doubt the most interesting portion of the offertory's annual cycle. Table 32 provides the incipits of the twenty-two chants of the series in the typical Roman arrangement. The incipits of borrowed chants (nearly all from Lent) are preceded by an asterisk and lack scriptural derivations. The four incipits followed by an asterisk appear also on Lenten Thursdays, so we can assume them to be chants originally created for the post-Pentecostal series and assigned to Lent when Pope Gregory II established the Lenten Thursdays as liturgical in about 720. The remaining five chants are unique to the post-Pentecostal series; thus they, together with the four borrowed by Lenten Thursdays, constitute a group (underlined in the table and followed by their scriptural derivations) of nine original post-Pentecostal offertories.

The pattern—obvious enough with its borrowed chants followed by originally assigned ones—presents a striking, indeed, surprising, contrast to the Paschaltime series with its original chants followed by borrowed ones. How do we account for this in view of the explanation for the pattern of the Paschaltime series as an act of withdrawing from the rigors of the Advent Project? Why this outbreak of creative activity at the very end of what we assume to be the least important segment of the liturgical year? Several of the chants involved, moreover, are among the most extraordinary in the entire Mass Proper.

In truth, this seemingly anomalous burst of creative activity well matches one's expectations both for the overall workings of the Advent Project and also for typical human behavior. As far as the Advent Project is concerned, we must keep in mind that the majority of offertories in the post-Pentecostal series are in fact borrowed, thirteen as opposed to only nine original chants, a far greater proportion than for any other segment of the annual offertory cycle. The post-Pentecostal offertory series is very similar in this respect to the post-Pentecostal gradual series with its own nine original chants and thirteen borrowed ones. And one might well suspect, incidentally, that several of the borrowed offertories, like the borrowed graduals, belong to a repertory of common psalmic offertories in existence before the Advent Project, to be used on an ad hoc basis, especially for ordinary Sundays and ferias. Such a repertory of offertories, however, would probably

Table 32. Roman Post-Pentecostal Offertories

Pentecost I	*Intende vocis	
Pent II	*Domine convertere	
Pent III	*Sperent in te	
Pent IV	*Illumina oculos	
Apostles I	*Benedicam dominum	
Apost II	*Perfice gressus	
Apost III	*Populum humilem	
Apost IV	*Justitie domini	
Apost V	*Ad te levavi	
Lawrence I	*Exaltabo te	
Lawr II	Precatus est moyses*	Ex 32.11–15
Lawr III	*In te speravi	
Lawr IV	Inmittet*	Ps 33.8–9
Lawr V	*Expectans expectavi	
Lawr VI	*Domine in auxilium	
Angel I	Oravi deum meum	Dn 9.4–19
Angel II	Sanctificavit moyses	Ex 24.4–5
Angel III	Si ambulavero*	Ps 137.7
Angel IV	Super flumina*	Ps 136.1
Angel V	Vir erat	Jb 1.2, 7
Angel VI	De profundis	Ps 129.1–4
Angel VII	Recordare mei	Est 14.12–13

be more recent, by a decade or so perhaps, than the common fund of graduals and would also lack the latter's prehistory as Roman responsorial psalms.

Differing, too, from the gradual sequence is the concentration of original offertories at the very end of the series and, more than that, the extraordinary character of these chants. Five of the nine are nonpsalmic chants, accounting for more than a third of the fourteen offertories of the sort in the entire Roman repertory. These five, moreover, are great sprawling creations, in some cases the product of freely paraphrasing their scriptural derivations rather than merely stitching them together from separate portions of the integral text. *Sanctificavit moyses*, in fact, is a free composition of enormous length that portrays Moses in his role of intermediary between God and the people of Israel; it is inspired by biblical events, particularly those narrated in chapters 24, 33 and 34 of the Book of Exodus, but it goes altogether beyond paraphrase.

Vir erat, to cite just one more example, while remaining closer to the biblical language of its extracts from chapters 1, 6 and 7 of the Book of Job, employs the device of textual repetition in such extreme and consistent fashion that commentators from Amalarius to Apel have seen it as an attempt to depict the halting speech of the sick and grief-stricken Job. And Apel adds on the subject of the chant's music: "The dramatic character of the text is paralleled and even surpassed by the music which transforms these outcries into a most stirring crescendo of expressiveness. Certainly, we are here in the presence of a composition which, for its subjective and dramatic character, is without parallel in the Gregorian repertory."[27] In point of fact, the most extraordinary single feature of the music, in addition to its great length, is its sudden brief movement to a higher range on several of the repeated words, namely, the second *ultimam* and second *calamitas* of verse 1, the second *quae* of verse 2 and the third *quoniam* and third *videat* of verse 4. All but the first of these five passages are matched in the Roman version by a corresponding elevation of pitch, thus attesting to the Roman origin of these gestures.

Should we be surprised that the most extraordinary concentration of chants comes where it does in the efforts of the schola cantorum to produce an ideal Mass Proper? If my reconstruction of their work is at all valid, the Roman singers had struggled mightily (and with considerable success) to provide original offertories and verses for the Christmas season, Lent and Paschaltime. Their aims proved simply too ambitious, however, and about halfway through work on the Paschaltime series they resorted to the prudent compromise of borrowing previously created chants for the ordinary Sundays and ferias of the season. Arriving finally at the post-Pentecostal season they took a somewhat similar route to the one they followed with graduals. With both genres there was sufficient preexisting repertory to supply a series of twenty-two chants lacking in seasonal liturgical reference, and hence appropriate for the seemingly faceless post-Pentecostal period. Yet in each case the Roman singers chose to supply at least a representative amount of new chants.

This seems natural enough behavior for a high-spirited community of talented liturgical musicians. They were, after all, providing completely unique series of twenty-two post-Pentecostal introits and communions (plus an additional three chants each for the September Ember Days). It would appear unseemly to renounce all creative activity at the end of the gradual and offertory annual cycles. This would be true especially in the case with offertories, already established as the most extraordinary of chant genres. From a musical point of view there is no more exceptional a creation than the second Sunday after the Epiphany's *Jubilate deo universa*, and the radical paraphrase approach to the text had already been employed with Easter Monday's *Angelus domini* and Thursday's *In die sollempnitatis*, another of those free compositions inspired by the Book of Exodus. So why not pull out all the stops, so to speak, when fashioning the last group of offertories for the annual cycle? That such spectacular chants find a place here rather than on major festivals has puzzled music historians, and for good reason, but the explanation for the seeming extravagance would seem to lie in the chronology of the Advent Project and in satisfying the creative impulses of those realizing the project.

There is an intriguing correspondence between the creative behavior of the Roman singers in dealing with the last phase of the offertory cycle and the musical reaction of the Frankish cantors. Of the nine original post-Pentecostal offertories, only two have different finals in the two versions: *Vir erat* (G-2) and *De profundis* (F-2), whereas the proportion of such chants for the combined Lenten and Paschal seasons is much higher, seventeen of forty-six. More important, the melodic relationship between the Roman and Gregorian versions of the nine post-Pentecostal offertories is considerably closer than that of the Lenten and Paschaltime chants. At least this is my impression, with only *De profundis* and *Recordare mei* appearing to be barely related, if at all. If my observations are sound, it would appear that the Frankish cantors, themselves nearing the end of a long and demanding project, and recognizing the extraordinary character of these chants, made a special effort to master them.

TWO THEMES: SACRIFICE AND JUSTICE

To return now to the Roman singers, if they seem to indulge their zest for creation in these post-Pentecostal offertories, they are by no means unmindful of liturgical propriety. There is nothing arbitrary about the choice of texts for these nine chants, and in this consideration, perhaps, lies the most fascinating aspect of the group. The texts must be understood in the light of the texts for the post-Pentecostal communions. At the core of those chants, as we shall see in the following chapter, lies a rich theme made up of the related motifs of Old Testament sacrifice, the Temple of Jerusalem, harvest and communion.[28] The first six of the original post-Pentecostal offertories partake of this same theme, omitting only reference to the harvest motif. There is, for example, Moses' sacrifice in *Sanctificavit moyses*, the verse *Adorabo ad templum* of *Si ambulavero* and, most strikingly, the communion text par excellence, the verse *Gustate et videte* of *Inmittet angelus*.

But what of the last three chants of the group? There is no hint of the sacrifice theme in these. But herein rests surely the most remarkable similarity with the communion series. Several years ago, when first examining the post-Pentecostal communion texts, I found myself at the end of what I took to be the original cycle with a group of three chants left over, so to speak, from the sacrifice-communion set.[29] I labeled the three the "justice set" because they had texts that spoke of the just man seeking aid and solace from the Lord in the midst of his tribulations. Only in the very writing of the present chapter did I discover the striking similarity of theme with the last three chants of the offertory cycle: *Vir erat*, of course, depicting the ultimate example of the just man, Job, crying to the Lord in his misery; *De profundis*, where the just man cries out from the depths of his travail; and *Recordare mei*, where he asks the Lord to remember him and to grant him the strength to withstand the enmity of the powerful. The relationship is altogether beyond coincidence; both the offertory and communion post-Pentecostal sequences close with a three-chant just man set.

THE SANCTORAL OFFERTORIES

If these nine offertories are the last to be added to the genre's temporal cycle, their character well matches the chants that appear to be the last added to the sanctoral cycle. There are twenty-two sanctoral offertories in the Roman core repertory, of which eight are uniquely assigned and fourteen are shared. One assumes that several of the shared chants joined similarly functioning introits, graduals and communions to form a sort of proto-Common of the saints. These chants are by and large unremarkable examples of the offertory genre, all psalmic in derivation and almost entirely lacking in textual adjustment. Even the eight uniquely assigned offertories are not so extraordinary as a group, but three of their number do stand out. These are the only three nonpsalmic sanctoral offertories: the Annunciation's *Ave Maria* (Lk 1.28), the vigil of Lawrence's *Oratio mea* (Jb 16.18–21) and the feast of the Dedication's *Domine deus in simplicitate* (1 Chr 29.17–18).

Musically, *Oratio mea*, with its soaring range, and especially *Ave Maria*, with its internal melodic rhyming, its surging climaxes and its sheer sensuous beauty, can stand with any other offertory as particularly splendid examples of the genre. But it is their textually adjusted nonpsalmic texts that are of special interest here. *Ave Maria* is the least radical of the three, not surprisingly, because so much of Gabriel's message to Mary is perfectly suitable in its integral biblical form as a chant text (it is used also for a gradual and communion). *Domine deus*, however, is an altogether free paraphrase of several passages from chapter 29 of 1 Chronicles to chapter 7 of 2 Chronicles, telling of David's sacrifice that presages the building of the temple and Solomon's sacrifice that serves to dedicate it. *Oratio mea*, finally, is a free composition inspired by Job as he appeals to God to judge him in the midst of his troubles.

Not only do these three sanctoral chants, then, match the post-Pentecostal offertories in musical and textual aesthetic, but two of them invoke the same liturgical themes in the most explicit fashion: *Domine deus*, the sacrifice and temple motifs, and *Oratio mea*, the theme of the just man as exemplified in Job. Their extraordinary affinity of subject matter, even more than their stylistic characteristics, locks in this pair of sanctoral chants as the work of the same individual or group who produced the much admired temporal chants such as *Sanctificavit moyses* and *Vir erat*. This should occasion no surprise from a chronological point of view since we have every reason to expect the last stages of temporale and sanctorale offertory creation to be roughly contemporaneous. And what more fitting than just as *Domine deus* represents the Dedication festival, the third chant of the nonpsalmic sanctoral trio, *Ave Maria*, represents one of the three late Marian feasts.

THE ROMAN OFFERTORY IN PERSPECTIVE

We have no indisputable evidence of the existence of a Roman offertory chant before its brief mention in *Ordo romanus I*. We know, however, of a Byzantine offertory chant, the Cheroubikon hymn that was introduced in the earlier sixth century, and a Gallican offertory chant, probably the Cheroubikon also, is mentioned by Pseudo-Germanus, writing apparently toward the end of the sixth century. It is not unlikely, then, that Rome, too, would have introduced an offertory chant considerably earlier than the time of *Ordo I*. The origins of the Roman chant would no doubt have been associated with the development of the offertory rites of the papal stational liturgy. These rites are very elaborate as described in *Ordo I*, and although we assume that they were somewhat less so in the sixth century, when the custom of papal visitation to the various churches of the city began, we can well imagine the appropriateness of accompanying them with song at a relatively early date.

The character of the chant, in the most general sense, is not difficult to guess. It was no doubt that of variable psalmody, just as was that of the Roman introit, gradual and communion. The chants of the Roman Mass Proper, inspired no doubt by the Office psalmody of the basilican monasteries, all but inevitably copied this mode of ecclesiastical song. It would have been altogether appropriate that the Roman clergy also adopt the celebrated Byzantine Cheroubikon, but it is unlikely that they would have done so and then dropped it without a trace. There are, moreover, no signs of other Byzantine offertory ceremonies in their Roman counterpart, the use of the *turris* of the Great Entrance, for example, which we observed above in the Gallican rite of Pseudo-Germanus.

But if the original Roman offertory chant was a variable psalm, we know no more than that bare fact. To see through its final form to an earlier type of psalmody is difficult, if not impossible, since it follows neither the gradual's pattern of responsorial psalmody, the introit and communion's pattern of antiphonal psalmody, nor the tract's pattern of direct psalmody. The thought that it takes as its starting point the Office responsory, with its own bifurcated respond, must also be rejected because the respond of the Roman responsory was not so split into opening portion and closing refrain portion but was sung as a response in its entirety.[30]

What makes it truly difficult to discern some original pattern of respond and verse in the offertory is that so many of the responds and verses we know have so little in common with a genuine psalmic respond or verse. An offertory verse like *Ego autem*, for example, stitched together from widely separated fragments of different psalm verses, which are altered in the process, could never have been sung in any manner of psalmody; *Ego autem*, rather, is a text contrived as it is in order to be suitable for a set musical piece. Perhaps the route to go is to separate out those psalmic offertories with plausible responds and verses and to examine just them with a view to seeing in them traces, textual and musical, of an original psalmodic format, one unique to the offertory psalm. This is a task, however, far beyond the scope of the present chapter.

The offertory chant we actually have, in any event, is the most splendid of all Roman chants, whether for Mass or Office. This splendor is one that matches the elaboration of the papal offertory rites themselves, nor should it surprise students of western music history that such a display of music takes place at this point in the service, which will see in the course of the centuries similar musical largesse in the form of offertory motets, organ voluntaries and the like.

Most chant scholars view the offertory as a "late" member of the Mass Proper, and I see no reason to disagree. For my own part the most compelling evidence in this respect is the frequency with which the device of textual adjustment is employed in the genre: it is very common throughout the entire offertory repertory except in the shared sanctoral chants and those of the Advent-Christmas season. The offertory, moreover, often employs a type of textual adjustment unique to itself, the repetition of short phrases of the original biblical text. Yet as late as the Roman offertory appears to be, its nearly absolute continuity of liturgical assignment in the Roman and Frankish manuscripts shows that it was in place before the later seventh-century redaction of the Mass antiphoners used in the transmission.

The offertory's annual cycle corresponds to our expectations of how the schola cantorum proceeded in realizing the goals of the Advent Project for the chant. The Christmas and Lenten seasons have mostly uniquely assigned offertories, but the Easter and especially post-Pentecostal seasons do not provide the same complete repertory that we see in the introit and communion. Unique to the offertory, however, is a startling outburst of creativity at the very end of the post-Pentecostal series, manifested especially in a group of nonpsalmic chants such as *Sanctificavit moyses* and *Vir erat*, equally daring in their approach to text and music. These extraordinary chants are, apparently, the last to be added to the offertory's temporal cycle, and they have a striking kinship with offertories that would seem to be the last added to the sanctoral cycle—the Annunciation's *Ave Maria*, for example, and the Dedication's *Domine deus in simplicitate*.

A fascinating chapter in the history of the offertory, even if one that takes us beyond the scope of the present volume, is the creative reaction of the Franks to the Roman offertory. They added no less than twelve chants to the Roman repertory, six of which are nonpsalmic. It would be instructive to see to what extent their additions match the textual and musical traits of the more extravagant Roman offertories. Can there be any doubt, by the way, that the chants we refer to here as Roman are in fact just that? It has been suggested that all nonpsalmic offertories are Gallican in origin yet this simply cannot be unless everything said in this volume about liturgical and musical continuity between Rome and Francia is altogether invalid.[31] The core of the argument for the Gallican origin of the nonpsalmic offertories lies in their use of textual adjustment. But this is a practice regularly employed in most genres of Roman chant, especially the introit and communion. We turn now to that last mentioned item of the Mass Proper, the communion, a chant vignette compared to the epic offertory, but a genre matching it in its capacity to stir surprise and admiration.

CHAPTER 13

The Communion

The introduction to this volume told how my adventure with the Mass Proper began in that fall 1989 seminar on the communion. The discovery that sent me on my way was that the entire temporal cycle of the communion was characterized by compositional planning. It had long been recognized that the weekday Lenten communions with their numerical series of psalmic derivations were an example of such planning, but it became clear to me that a program of one sort or another was also used to organize the three other major divisions of the church year—the Christmas and Easter seasons and the post-Pentecostal period. In the enthusiasm of the moment I leapt to two conclusions: the first, that similar programmatic design was to be found in all genres of the Mass Proper, and the second, that the chronological indications emerging from an analysis of such design would place the completion of the Roman Mass Proper at a very late date, well into the first half of the eighth century.

The reader of the previous chapters will have observed that both these expectations have had to be modified. Programmatic design, while frequently present in other genres of the Mass Proper, is seldom as overt as it is in the case of the communion, and my date for the completion of the Mass Proper, although still late by the standards of many other chant scholars, has been moved forward a generation or so, from the time of Gregory II (715–31) or Gregory III (731–41) to that of Sergius I (687–701).

The present chapter will revisit the annual cycle of the communion, reexamining each segment of it in the light of what has been learned from the other items of the Mass Proper. But first a brief speculation on how the communion came to be established in the Roman Mass.

ORIGINS

As is the case with most items of the Roman Mass Proper, our first unequivocal evidence for the existence of a communion chant is from *Ordo romanus I*. The communion is described there as an antiphon and psalm accompanying the distribution of the eucharistic elements, the singing of which is broken off after a signal from the presiding pope to the schola cantorum. Unlike the case of introit and offertory, however, there is already considerable evidence for the singing of a psalm at communion time from early Christian documents. At least in the East.[1] Several eastern sources, all from the second half of the fourth century,[2] testify to the singing of a communion psalm, typically Psalm 33 with its appropriate verse 9, "Taste and see that the Lord is good." There is only one contemporary western reference, the passage from Augustine (discussed above in reference to the offertory), where he cites Hilary's objection to the innovation at Carthage of singing psalms at two places in the Mass, the second of which is during the distribution of communion.

What does the evidence suggest for the early history of the communion at Rome? If we know that the singing of Psalm 33 was a regular occurrence at several principal liturgical centers of the East—an Ordinary item, in effect, rather than variable psalmody—Augustine's wording ("singing . . . of hymns from the Book of Psalms") could very well be taken to refer to variable psalmody. The circumstance, moreover, that this singing was an innovation at Carthage leads us to suspect that Rome (generally slow to adopt psalmody at Mass) took up the regular singing of psalms during communion at a somewhat later date than did the North African church.

The more important consideration here, however, is the character of the Roman communion psalm rather than the date of its introduction. If the patristic evidence merely suggests that it was a variable psalm as opposed to the Ordinary psalm of the East, the subsequent histories of both Byzantine and Roman communion chants emphatically endorse the point. The key factor is the fundamentally different role played by the response verse "Taste and see" in each liturgy. Γεύσασθε καὶ ἴδετε never relinquishes its privileged status in the repertory of the Byzantine koinonicon.[3] Even as other koinonica came to be added, it retained its place as the invariable communion antiphon of the ancient liturgy of the Pre-Sanctified. The second koinonicon to come into regular usage was Αἰνεῖτε τὸν κύριον ("Praise the Lord" [Ps 148.1]), sung on several dates of Paschaltime and on Sundays throughout the year, while another pair, functioning as Common chants, were the next additions: Ποτήριον σωτηρίου ("Cup of salvation" [Ps 115.4]), sung on feasts of the Theotoktos (Mary), and Ἀγαλλιᾶσθε δίκαιοι ("Rejoice ye righteous" [Ps 32.1]), sung on other sanctoral dates. In succeeding centuries these four were joined, and on some liturgical occasions replaced, by chants of a more Proper character, for example, Τὸ πνεῦμά σου ("Thy spirit" [Ps 142.10]), taking the place of the original Αἰνεῖτε on Pentecost Sunday. Among the later koinonica were a number of nonpsalmic and even non-biblical chants, created in order to achieve a more explicit reference to the festival on which they were to be sung. Still, by the tenth century the repertory of the Great Church consisted in only twenty-two koinonica (Dimitri Conomos lists twenty-six by the twelfth century);[4] and Γεύσασθε καὶ ἴδετε (Ps 33.9) retained its central position as the koinonicon of the Mass of the Pre-Sanctified.

Gustate et videte, the Latin equivalent of the venerable Byzantine Γεύσασθε καὶ ἴδετε, occupies no such privileged position in the Roman Mass Proper; it figures simply as one of the numerically ordered psalmic communions of the post-Pentecostal cycle—indeed as just one of no less than 141 seventh-century Roman communions. The Roman communion is of an entirely different character from the Byzantine koinonicon, providing as it does a Proper chant for virtually every day of the temporale and for a substantial portion of the sanctorale. And if there are chronological indications within the Roman series, they are of a different character from those of the Byzantine koinonicon. It is true that I have made much of the annual communion cycle's potential to reveal such indications, but the history of the Roman communion remains one that works itself out in decades or at most generations, rather than in centuries, as does the Byzantine koinonicon.

It would appear that by the mid-seventh century the schola cantorum had created a fund of psalmic communions for general use, many of which survive in the weekday Lenten series of numerically ordered psalmic chants, and a lesser amount within the post-Pentecostal sequence. Close in time to these, roughly contemporaneous probably, followed a group of Common psalmic communions for sanctoral occasions. Soon the penchant for providing thematically appropriate communions for important festivals gave way to the ambitious plan of the Advent Project, with its aim of providing a unique and fitting chant for every date of the temporale. At an early point in this process the device of the gospel-communion was developed, and not long after that the device of the responsory-communion, the latter partly from the urgent need to provide a repertory but just as much to make a virtue of necessity, resulting in several of the most extraordinary examples of the communion genre. Only the earliest communions fail to display some eccentric trait or another—syllabic antiphon-like melodic styles, dramatic dialogue texts, and radical forms of textual adjustment to the biblically derived texts. All this is best viewed season by season. I attempted to do so at considerable length in my 1992 article, "The Eighth-Century Frankish-Roman Communion Cycle"; what follows will at times contract and at other times expand upon what appears there.[5]

THE ADVENT-CHRISTMAS SERIES

From a purely aesthetic point of view the Advent-Christmas sequence must claim pride of place. It takes the form of two distinct groups of greatly contrasting character, separated accordingly by a space in table 33. The first group, consisting of the ten communions for the three Sundays of Advent (the fourth was of course a *dominica vacat* at the time), the three Ember Days and the vigil and three Masses of Christmas, form a homogeneous set of short lyric chants, all with texts from the Prophets in the more conventional sense or from David. The texts tell us either that the Lord is nigh or (on Christmas day) already at hand.

The second group could hardly be more different: all nine texts are from the New Testament; indeed all are derived from the gospel of the day, except for Stephen's *Video caelos*, from the Acts of the Apostles, a book serving generally as a sort of fifth gospel, and in this case as the only source of the story of Stephen's martyrdom. The nine communions are colorful narrative chants, several examples of which employ a flamboyant dramatic style that plays fast and loose with the biblical original. The second Sunday after the Epiphany's *Dicit dominus*, in particular, might be called a liturgical play in the shape of a communion antiphon. It is stitched together from five fragments of John 2.7–11, changing the language when necessary to produce a nicely coherent dramatic vignette of the marriage feast of Cana, employing even musical characterization with the solemn tones of Jesus, the excited exclamations of the chief steward and the matter-of-fact summing up of the narrator at the end of the piece.[6]

That striking dualism between the lyric prophetic chants and colorful narrative ones remains the overarching truth of the Advent-Christmas communion sequence, but there is much other information encoded in table 33. An underlined incipit in the table indicates a responsory-communion (an antiphon-communion in the case of *Puer Jesus*). There appears to be no particular significance to the distribution of the six; *Video caelos* is a flamboyant chant of the type one might expect from responsory-communions, but similarly dramatic communions like *Fili quid* and *Dicit dominus* are not

Table 33. Roman Advent-Christmas Communions

Advent I	*Dominus dabit*	Ps 84.13	
Advent II	*Hierusalem surge**	Bar 5.5, 4, 36	
Advent III	*Dicite pusillanimis**	Is 35.4	
Ember Wednesday	*Ecce virgo*	Is 7.14	
Ember Friday	*Ecce dominus**	Zec 14.5–7	prophetic group
Ember Saturday	*Exultavit*	Ps 18.6–7	
Vigil Xmas	*Revelabitur*	Is 40.5	
Xmas I	*In splendoribus*	Ps 109.3	
Xmas II	*Exulta satis filia sion*	Zec 9.9	
Xmas III	*Viderunt omnes*	Ps 97.3	
Stephen	*Video caelos**	Acts 7.56–60	
John Evangelist	*Exiit sermo*	Jn 21.22–23	
Innocents	*Vox in rama*	Mt 2.18	
Sylvester	*Beatus servus*	Mt 24.46–47	gospel group
Sunday	*Tolle puerum*	Mt 2.20	
Epiphany	*Vidimus stellam*	Mt 2.2	
Eph I	*Fili quid**	Lk 2.48–49	
Eph II	*Dicit dominus**	Jn 2.7–11	
Eph III	*Puer Jesus*	Lk 2.52	

responsory-communions. An asterisk after an incipit indicates substantial textual adjustment. Again there is no obvious pattern present, whereas one might expect textual adjustment to predominate in the post-Christmas group and to be associated with the more extravagant chants.

Continuity of liturgical assignment between Rome and Francia for the Advent-Christmas communions is nearly absolute and requires no comment.[7] Musical continuity appears to be consistently present also—at least on the surface. Only *Vox in rama* (E-7) fails to share the same final in the Roman and Gregorian versions, and this pair of chants may be the only one from the season that is not obviously related melodically. But I, at one time, expected much more than this in the way of musical relationship from several of these chants, and it is essential that I record my disappointment in this respect.

Beginning, as I did a decade ago, with my extremely late date for the bulk of the communion repertory (as late as the second quarter of the eighth century), it seemed to me that there could be very little difference between the eighth-century Roman and Gregorian versions of certain chants, especially those that were both comparatively simple and, more important than that, engagingly tuneful. How could these talented Roman and Frankish cantors fail to come to a musical meeting of the minds on such melodies? Take the Gregorian version of *Ecce virgo concipiet,* one of the seven melodies by the *re-fa* Advent Master.[8] I recall tapping it out on the piano in a seminar at Chapel Hill several years ago, and one of the graduate students was so moved as to call it one of the most beautiful melodies he had heard in his entire life.

It will be reproduced in both Gregorian and Roman versions in the epilogue to this volume (examples 25 and 27) and will be the subject there of detailed analysis. For now I simply note my surprise that the two are so different. The Roman one may have a certain beauty of its own, but the distinctive melodic traits of the Gregorian version are absent from it, replaced by and large by that sort of oscillating figuration that reduces the individuality of so many Roman chants. As I came to know *Ecce virgo* some ten years ago, along with the other communions of the Advent Master, I assumed that such simple and memorable tunes would appear closely related in their Roman and Gregorian versions. Eighth-century Roman and Frankish cantors involved in the transmission could hardly fail to make a smooth exchange of the original melodies, and the melodies were such that they could survive whatever vicissitudes of oral transmission awaited them in both Rome and Francia.

Having noted my chagrin on this point, I can only promise that some measure of historical benefit will be salvaged from it in our epilogue. For now the relevant subject is the annual communion sequence, and I continue my survey of it with the weekday Lenten communions, one of the most intriguing segments of the entire Mass Proper.

THE WEEKDAY LENTEN COMMUNIONS

The weekday Lenten communion series (see table 34), with its famous set of five gospel communions, makes for a good story and, although told elsewhere,[9] merits repetition here. To begin with, of course, there are the presumably original twenty-six psalmic communions derived in numerical order from Psalm 1 for Ash Wednesday to Psalm 26 for the Friday before Palm Sunday (the Saturday before Palm Sunday being a *sabbato vacat,* a day on which the pope dispensed with his normal stational liturgy to distribute alms).[10] Basic to our understanding of the series is the obvious circumstance that it long predates Pope Gregory II's establishment of the

Table 34. Lenten Weekday Communions

	Numerical Series	Thursdays	Gospel Series
Ash Wednesday	*Qui meditabitur* (Ps 1.2–3)		
Thursday		*Acceptabis* (Ps 50.21)	
Friday	*Servite* (Ps 2.11–12)		
Monday	*Voce mea* (Ps 3.5–7)		
Tuesday	*Cum invocarem* (Ps 4.2)		
Wednesday	*Intellege* (Ps 5.2–4)		
Thursday		*Panis quem* (Jn 6.52)	
Friday	*Erubescant* (Ps 6.11)		
Saturday	*Domine deus* (Ps 7.2)		
Monday	*Domine deus* (Ps 8.2)		
Tuesday	*Narrabo omnia* (Ps 9.2–3)		
Wednesday	*Justus dominus* (Ps 10.7)		
Thursday		*Qui manducat* (Jn 6.5–7)	
Friday	*Tu domine* (Ps 11.8)		
Saturday	[Ps 12]		*Oportet te* (Lk 15.32)

Monday	Quis dabit (Ps 13.7)		
Tuesday	Dominus quis (Ps 14.1–2)		
Wednesday	Notas mihi (Ps 15.11)		
Thursday		Tu mandasti (Ps 118.4–5)	
Friday	[Ps 16]		Qui biberit (Jn 4.13–14)
Saturday	[Ps 17]		Nemo te (Jn 8.10–11)
Monday	Ab occultis (Ps 18.13–14)		
Tuesday	Laetabimur (Ps 19.6)		
Wednesday	[Ps 20]		Lutum fecit (Jn 9.6–38)
Thursday		Domine memorabor (Ps 70.16–18)	
Friday	[Ps 21]		Videns dominus (Jn 11.33–44)
Saturday	Dominus regit (Ps 22.1–2)		
Monday	Dominus virtutum (Ps 23.10)		
Tuesday	Redime me (Ps 24.22)		
Wednesday	Lavabo (Ps 25.6–7)		
Thursday		Memento (Ps 118.49–50)	
Friday	Ne tradideris (Ps 26.12)		

Lenten Thursdays as liturgical in about 720; the series simply makes no provision for these days in its numerical ordering, supplying instead a seemingly arbitrary selection of six post-Pentecostal communions.

Within the other interruption in the numerical series lies our tale of liturgical intrigue. The basic mechanics of what happened are clear enough from table 34. At some point in Roman liturgical history—obviously prior to the just-mentioned adjustments of about 720—five of the numerically ordered psalmic communions were dropped from the series and replaced by communions with gospel-derived texts. The five discarded communions are represented in the table by numbers in square brackets (Pss 12, 16, 17, 20 and 21); their less prosaic replacements (*Oportet te* [Lk 15.32], etc.) are given in the far-right-hand column. Why the abandonment of the five psalmic communions and their replacement by gospel communions?

The traditional view, recounted regularly in the liturgical and musicological literature alike, has to do with the Roman Lenten prebaptismal Scrutinies.[11] There is more than a little sound liturgical history underlying the view. The Scrutinies were a peculiarly Roman institution: on three Sundays of Lent, the third, fourth and fifth, the baptizands were thoroughly quizzed about their new faith. In the course of the fifth and sixth centuries, however, as the population of Rome became more exclusively Christian, the frequency of adult baptism gave way to that of infant baptism, and the Scrutinies lost much of their original importance. They were relegated from their position of special distinction on three Sundays to the lesser one of three weekdays, Friday in the third week of Lent, and Wednesday and Friday of the fourth week. With this change, apparently, the gospels of the three Sundays were transferred to the three weekdays. We do not have direct knowledge of what the three original Roman Sunday gospels were, but we have good reason to assume what they were because the Mozarabic, Beneventan and Ambrosian liturgies have identical gospels on the three Sundays in question. Indeed they name the Sundays after the gospels: there is the Sunday *De Samaritana,* after its gospel, John 4.6–42, which narrates the conversation of Jesus with the Samaritan woman at the well; the Sunday *De caeco,* after John 9.1–38, which tells of the man blind from birth; and the Sunday *De Lazaro,* after John 11.1–45, which tells of the raising of Lazarus from the dead. That the three appear on the Sundays in question in the other Latin liturgies gives us good reason to suspect that they were likewise placed originally on the same three days in Rome and subsequently moved to the three weekdays on which they appear in our earliest redaction of the Roman evangeliary, the PI-type of about 645.

The connection of these three presumably moved *Scrutinium* gospels to our five celebrated Lenten gospel communions is that the three weekdays where the gospels make their final resting place in the Roman evangeliary are three of the five dates on which that group of five communions are to be found. According to the conventionally accepted course of events, at the time of the gospel transfer, five psalmic communions of the original series of twenty-six were discarded and in their place five new gospel communions were composed, each of the five being nicely fashioned so as to narrate in a brief and colorful manner the gist of the day's gospel. Thus, for example, *Nemo te condemnavit* (Jn 8.10–11), "Does no one condemn thee, woman," the communion of Saturday in the third week of Lent (and usurper of the original communion of the day derived from Psalm 17) is inspired by the gospel of the day, John 8.1–11, which tells the famous story of the woman taken in adultery.[12]

Again, there is much to recommend the conventional explanation. The three gospels *De Samaritana*, *De caeco* and *De Lazaro* were in all probability moved from Lenten Sundays to weekdays when the Roman Scrutinies were transferred to weekdays (sometime before 645), and three of our five gospel communions grace the three weekdays in question. But it fails to convince ultimately for at least two reasons, the first of which I would classify as something casting serious doubt on it, the second as something all but disqualifying it.

The first, a simple enough point, has to do with chronology. Those advocating the conventional view have always assumed that the five gospel communions were composed at the very moment the Sunday Scrutinies gospels were transferred to weekdays. But even if it is true that the composition of the gospel communions was somehow meant to celebrate the *Scrutinium* (why, for another point, celebrate something that is being downgraded?), it does not follow that this had to be done at the time of the transfer. Indeed it would more likely have been done considerably later in the seventh century, when the creation of gospel communions had become very much a popular liturgical practice. One reason, by the way, given for the early date of the gospel communions is that the five displaced psalmic communions "are no longer to be found anywhere in the manuscript tradition."[13] I hope to show presently, however, that at least three of them are very much a part of the communion core repertory.

But the more serious objection to the conventional view, and surely one that the attentive reader must by now have observed independently of any prodding from the present author, is this: there are only three Scrutiny dates and gospels involved, but there are five gospel communions (a point, surprisingly enough, never mentioned in the voluminous literature on the subject). The explanation that the group of Lenten gospel communions was somehow related to the shift from Sunday to weekday observation of the *Scrutinium* should surely cover all five of the communions in question, not just three. Yet two of the communions have no relationship whatsoever to the Scrutinies: *Oportet te,* inspired by the greatly loved parable of the Prodigal Son (Lk 15.11–32), and *Nemo te,* inspired by the comparably popular story of the woman taken in adultery (Jn 8.1–11).

If these two chants, then, have nothing to do with the Scrutinies, what do they share with the other three, for which such a relationship can be claimed? Just what is it that the five have in common? It turns out that the five do in fact have an utterly fascinating bond; they are inspired, quite simply, by the five single most attractive stories in the entire Lenten weekday evangeliary. There are the two unrelated to the Scrutinies, *Oportet te* and *Nemo te.* And then there are the three that may (or may not) be related to the Scrutinies: *Qui biberit,* inspired by the story of Jesus' fascinating conversation with the Samaritan woman; *Lutum fecit,* by the story of the man blind from birth; and *Videns dominus,* by the story of the resurrection of Lazarus. I defy anyone to go through the entire seventh-century weekday Lenten evangeliary and find another gospel of comparable narrative power to these five. The post–Vatican II Catholic Church apparently shares my opinion: they have moved the five gospels in question from Lenten weekdays back to Lenten Sundays. And let me add finally that it is difficult to imagine a modern film on the life of Jesus that could omit any one of the five stories.

The explanation for the five Lenten gospel communions, then, would seem to be this. At a fairly late point in the history of the Roman communion, the members of the schola cantorum, by this time much taken with the practice of creating colorful gospel communions, found the tabula rasa of the twenty-six numerically ordered Lenten psalmic communions an irresistible area in which to exercise their cherished art. Irresistible, too, were these five Lenten gospels; it was surely their very special character that prompted the late addition of five more gospel communions to the already extensive repertory of the type, even if it remains possible that the connection of the *Scrutinium* could have played a partial role in the selection process.

THE MUSIC OF THE FIVE LENTEN GOSPEL COMMUNIONS

The musical aspects of the story just told are possibly better known to music historians than even the liturgical aspects. I can be very brief in dealing

Example 15. Communion *Oportet te*

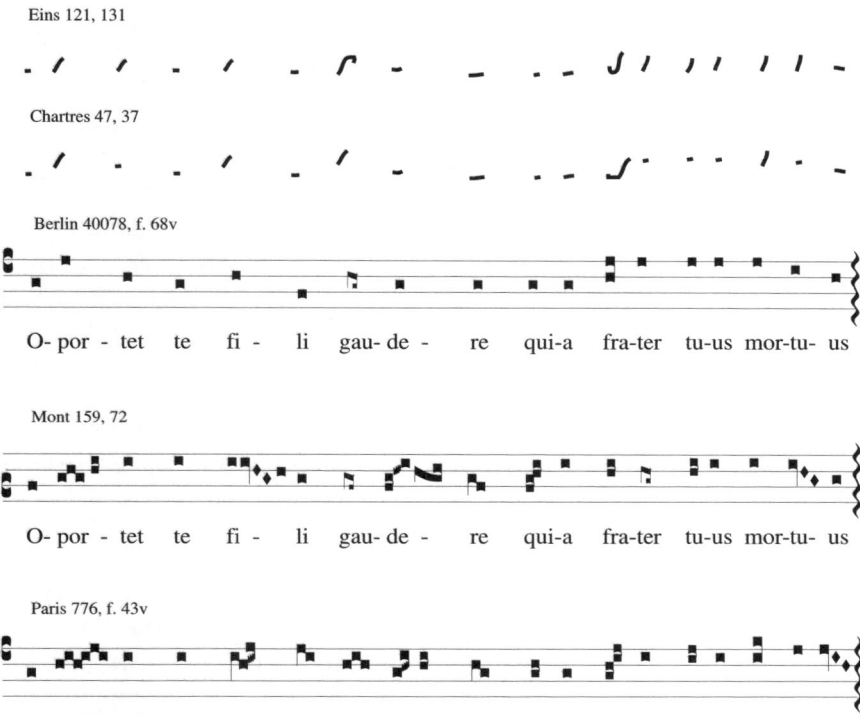

with them, therefore, although I cannot omit them altogether because they involve a key discovery in the early history of the Roman communion—the existence of what I call the "antiphon-communion." The five Lenten gospel communions are frequently cited for their simple syllabic style, a trait that gives them more the appearance of Office antiphons than of the typically neumatic communion antiphons. And not only are the five remarkable for their antiphon-like style, but they tend to appear in later Gregorian sources with a profusion of different melodies, typically much more elaborate than their original syllabic versions. I offer a limited sample of the phenomenon in example 15 with a segment of the original *Oportet te* and the corresponding segment from two later melodies of the more elaborate type.

It should be pointed out also that the five Lenten gospel communions are not the only representatives of the type; there are some eleven or twelve of them all told.[14] The peculiar behavior of these communions has greatly intrigued musicologists, and I believe Helmut Hucke and Michel Huglo were on the right track to explaining the phenomenon when they wrote of the chants that they "resemble simple Office antiphons" and that "the editors of the Gregorian gradual were concerned to make clear distinctions between liturgical genres, and they therefore replaced some of the original melodies by others, more elaborate in style, and closer to the other communions of the repertory."[15]

But in point of fact these original syllabic communions do not just resemble Office antiphons; they *are* Office antiphons, borrowed, apparently, to fill out the communion repertory as expeditiously as possible at a point in the history of the Advent Project when—whether haste was an important consideration or not—the Office antiphons in question very nicely fulfilled the aesthetic and devotional aims of those members of the schola cantorum responsible for the communion cycle. The eleventh- and twelfth-century cantors who produced the new melodies, then, were anxious to do so, presumably, in order to avoid repeating a communion antiphon melody sung earlier that very morning at matins.

That antiphon-like communions were in fact "antiphon-communions" first became clear to me not in my study of the five Lenten gospel communions but while I worked with the Paschaltime portion of the communion cycle. In this segment of the church year they reveal their true significance, along with that of their sibling genre, the "responsory-communion." I turn to this phase of the communion cycle after the briefest of remarks about the communions of the Lenten season not yet treated, those of the Sundays and of Holy Week.

About these chants I have nothing to add beyond what was said in my article of 1992. I would simply confirm what remains my general impression about them and mention only a handful of the more interesting individual pieces. My general impression is hardly one of great originality: the Sunday and Holy Week communions appear by and large to be a somewhat later layer of chant than the weekday numerically ordered psalmic series, later in the sense, that is, that they are products of the Advent Project, whereas the weekday psalmic chants make up the bulk of the pre-Advent Project fund of generic communions available for use on an ad hoc basis.

Three of the later additions that deserve special mention (all three nonpsalmic chants) are the fifth Sunday's *Hoc corpus;* Palm Sunday's *Pater si non potest* and Holy Thursday's *Dominus Jesus*. The first of these, *Hoc corpus* (1 Cor 11.24–25), the first communion so far encountered in these pages that is derived from a Pauline epistle (even if with a considerably adjusted text), celebrates the sacrament of communion in a melody of impressive dramatic scope, particularly in the soaring notes that set the words of Jesus: *Hoc facite, quotiescumque sumitis in meam commemorationem. Hoc corpus* is, moreover, a responsory-communion and, more than that, has a verse in its Roman version. Palm Sunday's antiphon-communion, *Pater si non potest* ("Father if it is not possible that this chalice pass from me . . ." [Mt 26.42]), has musical relationships among its various versions that bear attention in our epilogue. Finally, Holy Thursday's *Dominus Jesus* (Jn 13.12–15), telling the story of Jesus' washing of his disciples' feet on the evening of the Last Supper, must be mentioned for purely aesthetic reasons if for none other. I think it is not necessary to be a believer (of whatever religious persuasion) to be touched with both the text and melody of this exquisite musical composition. *Pater si* may share text with Bach's St. Matthew Passion, but *Dominus Jesus* comes closer to conveying the aesthetic impact of that work.

THE ROMAN PASCHALTIME COMMUNIONS

As much as I shall try to compress my remarks on this important segment of the communion cycle, I am forced nonetheless to focus them upon a particularly detail-laden table (table 35). One begins an examination of the season with very much the impression that the policies of the post-Christmas communions are being continued. Communions are derived from the New Testament rather than the Book of Psalms, and they express the exuberance of the post-Christmas narrative chants rather than the reflective spirit of the Advent prophetic lyrics. An enhancing element is introduced, moreover, in the inclusion of several communions with texts from the New Testament Epistles, the main contributor to the complication of the table. The table begins typically with the festal date followed by its incipit (underlined incipits are either responsory-communions or antiphon-communions) and scriptural derivation; there follows the gospel of each date and the epistle also, but the latter only if the communion in question derives its text from an epistle. To be observed about these communions with epistle texts is that they do not, with the exception of Easter's and that of Pentecost, derive their text from the epistle of the day—something of a disappointment, after being accustomed to observing the derivation of gospel communions from the gospel of the day. As for the gospel communions themselves, the expected policy of so deriving their texts is in fact maintained here until the

Table 35. Roman Paschaltime Communions

		Gospels	Epistles
Easter	*Pascha nostrum* (1 Cor 5.7–8)	Mk 16.1–7	1 Cor 5.7–8
Monday	*Surrexit dominus* (Lk 24.34)	Lk 24.13–35	
Tuesday	*Si consurrexistis* (Col 3.1–2)	Lk 24.36–47	Acts 13.26–33
Wednesday	*Christus resurgens* (Rom 6.9)	Jn 21.1–14	Acts 3.13–19
Thursday	*Populus acq* (1 Pt 2.9)	Jn 20.11–18	Acts 8.26–40
Friday	*Data est mihi* (Mt 28.18–19)	Mt 28.16–20	
Saturday	*Omnes qui* (Gal 3.27)	Jn 20.19–31	1 Pt 2.1–10
Sunday	*Mitte manum* (Jn 20.27)	Jn 20.24–31	
Easter II	*Ego sum pastor* (Jn 10.14)	Jn 10.11–16	
Easter III	*Modicum* (Jn 16.16)	Jn 16.16–22	
Easter IV	*Dum venerit par* (Jn 16.8)	Jn 16.5–14	
Easter V	*Pater cum essem* (Jn 17.12–15)	Jn 16.23–30	
Litany	*Petite et accipietis* (Lk 11.5–11)	Lk 11.5–11	
Ascension	*Psallite domino* (Ps 67.33–34)	Mk 16.14–20	
Sunday	*Tristitia vestra* (Jn 16.20)	Jn 15.26–16.4	
Pentecost	*Factus est* (Acts 2.2–4)	Jn 14.23–31	Acts 2.1–12
Monday	*Spiritus sanctus* (Jn 14.26)	Jn 3.15–21	
Tuesday	*Spiritus qui* (Jn 15.16–17)	Jn 10.1–10	
Wednesday	*Pacem meam* (Jn 14.27)	Jn 6.44–51	
Friday	*Spiritus ubi* (Jn 3.8)	Lk 5.17–26	
Saturday	*Non vos relinquam* (Jn 14.18)	Mt 20.29–34	

Greater Litany's *Petite et accipietis* (Lk 11.5–11)—but only until that point in the season.

It is at this juncture in the Eastertime communion cycle that a truly striking change of policy in the derivation of texts takes place. Up until now in the annual communion cycle, communions with a gospel text routinely derived it not just from any passage in the Gospels, but from the gospel of the day. Here in the Paschaltime communion cycle, however, that is, after the feast of the Greater Litany, not a single communion—although nearly all have gospel texts—derives its text from the gospel of the day. Why might this be? There does appear to be an element of expediency involved—the demands of fulfilling the aims of the Advent Project cannot be perfectly realized and the Roman singers find themselves resorting to a compromise. Interestingly enough they do so in the latter portion of the Paschaltime sequence, the precise place in the liturgical year where we observed in just the last chapter a similar compromise with offertories. There, it will be recalled, the provision of original offertories for ordinary Sundays and ferias ceased abruptly with the third Sunday after Easter's *Lauda anima mea*.

Generally similar as this pair of compromises may appear, however, the one employed by the communion is altogether unique. This set of eight communions is simply borrowed from the Office (primarily matins) of Ascension Thursday and Pentecost Sunday.[16] Six of the underlined chants are responsories, not particularly surprising, but what is remarkable is that the three beginning with the word *Spiritus* are Office antiphons: two of them are most certainly matins antiphons (*Spiritus sanctus* and *Spiritus qui*), while the somewhat longer *Spiritus ubi vult* is in all probability a Magnificat antiphon.[17] The existence of responsory-communions was well known before the appearance of my 1992 article on the communion, but it was the emergence of antiphon-communions that surprised me as I worked on that piece. There are, as stated above, some ten of them all told, and I leave the subject of them now with the simple remark that they are one more device employed by the seventh-century cantors to provide a polished and elegant communion cycle, even if the awareness of the source of these chants leaves us now with the knowledge that only the introit can lay claim to having achieved the ideals of the Advent Project without compromise.

But to return to the context of the Paschaltime communion cycle as a whole, my view of precisely what happened at the point in question of the cycle must be placed in a somewhat different perspective from that of the time of the 1992 article. Since then, thanks to the dissertation of Brad Maiani, we know of the existence of many more responsory-communions than previously suspected.[18] There are some forty altogether, or well more than a quarter of all communions, and, what is more relevant to present purposes, the responsory-communions tend to cluster together during Paschaltime (as the underlined incipits of table 35 show).

It is true that the essential point remains: the unique expedient of turning to the Offices of Ascension and Pentecost to search out appropriate responsories and antiphons with which to complete the final ten days of the Easter season communion cycle. And it should be added, incidentally, that even if the compromising nature of the overall gesture is clear, there is nothing lax or arbitrary about the individual choices made by the members of the schola who were responsible for them. How more deftly, for example, could one close out the Easter cycle than with the text of Pentecost Saturday's *Non vos relinquam* (Jn 14.18): "I will not leave you orphans, I will come to you again and your heart shall rejoice"?

But what is the significance of the greater number of responsory-communions revealed by Maiani's work, especially those of Paschaltime? To begin with, one must retain the distinction between the group of post– Greater Litany chants I have singled out and the many that come earlier in the Paschaltime cycle. The distinction is this: the responsory-communions with gospel texts from the earlier part of the season do in fact derive some texts from the gospel of the day, whereas those from the later part of the season do not. The implications of this are quite important. The later group, that is, those of Ascension Thursday to Pentecost Saturday, must surely have been borrowed from the Office, but there are various possibilities for the others. Take, for example, *Ego sum pastor bonus* (Jn 10.14), communion for the second Sunday after Easter, with a text borrowed from the gospel of the day, John 10.11–16, the familiar story of the Good Shepherd. Surely this chant originated as the communion of the day and was borrowed subsequently for use also as an Office responsory. But it is not necessary that a responsory-communion was initially intended as either a communion or a responsory. Maiani has shown that the Paschaltime responsory repertory itself (like that of the Paschaltime communions) was inadequate to meet full liturgical requirements.[19] Thus the possibility that the composition of certain responsory-communions was intended for simultaneous use in both Office and Mass. This, incidentally, raises the fascinating question of what might have been the relationship between the schola, whose primary responsibility was the papal Mass, and the basilican monastic choirs, who were chiefly responsible for the Office.

But such considerations cannot be explored here, and the point to retain in mind as we turn now to the post-Pentecostal communion cycle, is that the schola cantorum found itself resorting to the sort of compromise in completing the Paschaltime communions that we might have been more inclined to associate with a genre like the alleluia or the offertory.

THE POST-PENTECOSTAL COMMUNIONS

If the communion's Paschaltime cycle is probably the most seriously revealing about the nature of the genre, the post-Pentecostal cycle is perhaps the most diverting (see table 36). In 1990 I wrote a highly speculative essay on the purported history of the twenty-two chants that make up the cycle.[20] This was both my first venture into historical reconstruction of the sort, and a bolder and more complex speculation than anything similar that I have tried since. As I reconsider the results of my efforts now, however, I find they have grown to seem more plausible and less venturesome than they did when I originally proposed them. This, if for no other reason than that the central point of my conception—the presence of two distinct subject matter groupings in the cycle, one that might be called the "sacrifice-eucharist" set and another, the "justice" set—was confirmed, as we have seen in the previous chapter, by a strikingly precise parallel in the post-Pentecostal offertory sequence.

The "sacrifice-eucharist" set (the twelve chants bracketed with the rubric "sacrifice-harvest set" in table 36)[21] is the more important of the two subject matter groupings. The theme is also much richer than the shorthand term "sacrifice-eucharist" suggests. There are actually four motifs rather than two involved: sacrifice, temple, harvest and eucharist. The four are clearly, indeed beautifully, related. It is in the Old Testament temple that sacrifice is performed; it is the first fruits of the harvest that are sacrificed; and it is in the "sacrifice" of the eucharist that a medieval Christian sees the fulfillment of these ancient religious practices and conceptions.[22]

An attempted reconstruction of the entire post-Pentecostal sequence will be a central concern in our treatment of it. As for the twelve of the sacrifice-eucharist set, one asks at the moment only whether they came together in stages or simultaneously. Most obviously the psalmic communions (along with *Honora dominum* from the Old Testament Book of Proverbs) can be thought of as separate from the nonpsalmic (chiefly gospel) chants—thus producing a relatively consistent divide between a presumably earlier Old Testament theme of temple-sacrifice-harvest and a later one expressing the eucharistic motif. Just as plausible, perhaps, is a nearly contemporaneous creation of all twelve communions. A detail supporting this possibility is the

Table 36. Roman Post-Pentecostal Communions

Pentecost I	*Narrabo omnia*	Ps 9.2–3	from Lent
Pent II	*Cantabo domino*	Ps 12.6	
Pent III	*Ego clamavi*	Ps 16.6–8	
Pent IV	*Domine firmamentum*	Ps 17.3	
Apostles I	<u>*Unam petii*</u>	Ps 26.4	sacrifice-harvest set
Apost II	*Circuibo et immolabo*	Ps 26.6	
Apost III	*Gustate et videte*	Ps 33.9	
Apost IV	*Primum quaerite*	Mt 6.33	
Apost V	*Acceptabis*	Ps 50.21	
Lawrence I	*Honora dominum*	Prv 3.9–10	
Lawr II	*De fructu*	Ps 103.13–15	
Lawr III	*Panem de caelo*	Wis 16.20	
Lawr IV	*Panis quem ego*	Jn 6.52	
Lawr V	*Qui manducat*	Jn 6.57	
[Lawr VI	*Domine memorabor*	Ps 70.16–18]	
Angel I	*Vovete et reddite*	Ps 75.12–13	
Angel II	*Tollite hostias*	Ps 95.8–9	
Angel III	*Tu mandasti domine*	Ps 118.4–5	justice set
Angel IV	*Memento verbi tui*	Ps 118.49–50	
Angel V	*In salutari tuo*	Ps 118.81–86	
Angel VI	*Dico vobis*	Lk 15.10	gospel addition
Angel VII	*Amen dico vobis*	Mk 11.24	
Sept Wednesday	*Comedite pinguia*	Neh 8.10	September Ember Days
Sept Friday	*Aufer a me*	Ps 118.22–24	
Sept Saturday	*Mense septimo*	Lv 23.41–43	

presence of *Unam petii* (Ps 26.4) at the beginning of the group. While both a psalmic chant and one confined to the Old Testament aspects of the theme, it is also a responsory-communion (the only one of the post-Pentecostal sequence), and as such suggestive of a relatively late date of creation.

Questions of chronology aside for the moment, the sequence of twelve appears to form the core of the post-Pentecostal communion series, and the just-mentioned *Unam petii* serves as a good introduction to the poetic richness of the group's multifaceted theme. The text, "One thing I have asked of the Lord, this I seek, that I may dwell in the house of the Lord all the days of my life" (Ps 26.4), is a passage of rare poignancy, speaking as it does of the dedication of youth to a life of sacrifice and service within the sacred precincts of the Lord. Its immediate context as a psalm is the anointment of the boy David by Samuel (1 Sm 16), but surely it brought to the mind of medieval ecclesiastics other events of the same sort: for example, the touching story of the barren Anna, future mother of Samuel, promising the dedication of her son to a life of divine service should the Lord grant her a male child. Indeed they would think, too, of the presentations of both Mary and her son Jesus in what was to them the same house of the Lord where Samuel lived out his days.[23] And to move into the Christian era, is there any liturgical ceremony so wrought with sweet sadness as that of the investiture of a young nun or clerical aspirant? *Unam petii* must have meant all of this to the members of the schola cantorum, and we must not forget that they, too, as hardly more than boys, had dedicated their own lives to a life of communal service at the Lateran, and at a time in the early history of a religious institution that is typically characterized by fervor and purity of intention.

The motif of sacrifice is made explicit already in the second communion of the series, *Circuibo* (Ps 26.6), the text of which follows almost immediately upon that of *Unam petii* in the original psalm: "I shall go round about and immolate a victim of jubilation in his tabernacle; I shall sing and declaim a psalm to the Lord" (this second clause, no doubt, of added significance to the members of a musical organization). I do not mean to imply here that the four motifs of the theme follow in logical order throughout the sequence. The third text of the series, *Gustate et videte* (Ps 33.9), is of course a eucharistic text, and others of the same kind, such as *Panis quem ego* (Jn 6.52) and *Qui manducat* (Jn 6.57), intervene before the final communion of the set, *Tollite hostias* (Ps 95.8–9; "Take up victims and enter into his courts"), obviously referring to sacrifice in the temple. Intervening also are the texts that have to do with the harvest motif, for example, that of *Honora dominum* (Prv 3.9–10; "Honor the Lord with your substance and give to him the first of your fruits"). I have done no more here than touch the surface of the theme with these examples; if, as proposed above, the Advent-Christmas chants make the greatest overall aesthetic impact of the annual communion cycle with their coordinated textual and musical duality, the sacrifice-eucharist chants of the post-Pentecostal sequence are their equal on the purely poetic level.

To return to the point that the four motifs of the theme are not run through in logical order, the obvious reason for this would seem to be the desire on the part of the Roman singers to create still another of their post-Pentecostal numerical sequences (sequences, that is, of the subsequently arranged type with gaps in the numerical order, as opposed to the less common a priori planned type without such gaps). One chant violates the order, and I think its anomalous position contributes to our understanding of the vital importance of the sacrifice-eucharist theme to its creators. The chant *De fructu* (Ps 103.13–15), while obviously out of numerical order, finds itself immediately between two other representatives of the harvest motif, *Honora dominum* and *Panem de caelo*. Here thematic (actually motivic) relevance overrides numerical symmetrization.

THE JUSTICE SET

There is one other anomaly in the series, the position of *Domine memorabor* (Ps 70.16–18). It finds proper place in the numerical order but belongs thematically with the three other chants of the justice set: *Tu mandasti, Memento verbi tui* and *In salutari tuo*, all three derived from Psalm 118. The theme, totally free from the motifs of its sacrifice-eucharist counterpart, is that of the soul striving after righteousness while appealing to the justice of God in the face of tribulation and persecution. The existence of the theme is explicit enough in these four communions to stand on its own but is strikingly corroborated, as we have seen in the previous chapter, by the analogous set of three offertories, centering on the figure of Job in *Vir erat*. But why was not the numerical order violated in this case (as it was for *De fructu*) by placing *Domini memorabor* with its three companion chants of the justice set? Granted that this might have been the more strictly logical thing to do, one can think nonetheless of several reasons to support the minor anomaly involved: the wish, for example, to avoid still another compromise with the numerical order; the circumstance that *Domine memorabor* stands alone as the only chant of the justice group not from Psalm 118; and the presumably lesser importance of the justice theme compared to the sacrifice-eucharist theme.

THE RECONSTRUCTION

This last cited point, the lesser importance of the justice set, raises a more important question: why create this brief justice group at all, when surely there must have been enough scriptural material available to expand the sacrifice-eucharist theme almost indefinitely? My answer to the question comes in the form of an admittedly speculative reconstruction of the entire post-Pentecostal communion series. Imagine, to begin with, an original group of about ten psalmic communions. Either by design or, more likely, by accident, the subject matter of the chants consists in a slightly larger group expressing the motifs of sacrifice, temple and harvest, and another group expressing the ideas of the justice theme. At the time of the Advent Project several steps are taken. The presence of the two themes is recognized by the singers and given formal acknowledgment; the first of them is favored by the addition of several chants, mostly nonpsalmic, expanding it into the finished sacrifice-eucharist set. The whole is then given a slightly compromised numerical psalmic order and the chants are assigned to fixed liturgical dates, beginning with the first Sunday after the feast of the Apostles Peter and Paul.

There remain two gaps to be filled before the standard Roman post-Pentecostal series of twenty-two chants is achieved: two are needed at the end and four at the beginning. The two at the end are supplied by two gospel chants—*Dico vobis* (Lk 15.10) and *Amen dico vobis* (Mk 11.24)—neither of them corresponding to the gospel of the day, but each at least expressing frequently quoted sayings of Jesus (and vaguely related, perhaps, to the justice set). It is a rather easy solution, and so is that of filling in the gap of four at the beginning of the series by borrowing four psalmic chants from Lent and placing them in numerical order. But a fascinating circumstance lies behind this group of four, especially in its three latter chants. The first of the four, *Narrabo omnia* (Ps 9.2–3), is interesting enough in itself: it is the perfect choice for a group of chants designed as a coordinated sequence of musical praise: "I will tell of all thy marvelous deeds," it reads. "I shall rejoice and exult in thee; I shall sing a psalm to thee, O Most High." The next three will be recognized as nothing less than the first three of the five Lenten psalmic communions displaced by the five gospel chants. The displaced communions, it will be recalled, were derived from Psalms 12, 16, 17, 20 and 21; and here we have *Cantabo domino* (Ps 12.6), *Ego clamavi* (Ps 16.6–8) and *Domine firmamentum* (Ps 17.3). The mathematical possibilities of pure coincidence here are too remote for serious consideration; these three must surely be the first three of the missing five.[24] The five were, it will be recalled, supposed to have been displaced at a very early date because of their total disappearance from the sources, but the reappearance of three of them here suggests that both the act of displacement and that of borrowing to complete the post-Pentecostal cycle might have taken place quite close in time. All the related events, in any case, conform very well with the typical procedures of the Advent Project.[25]

THE SEPTEMBER EMBER DAYS

Before leaving this segment of the communion cycle, there remains only the addition of a postscript on the three communions of the September Ember Days: Wednesday's *Comedite pinguia* (Neh 8.10), Friday's *Aufer a me* (Ps 118.22–24) and Saturday's *Mense septimo* (Lv 23.41–43).[26] Even prior to undertaking any investigation of the set, one's curiosity ought to be piqued by scriptural sources used so rarely in the Mass Proper as Nehemiah and Leviticus. The theme invoked by the texts is, in fact, rare in Mass chants to the point of eccentricity, but more than that attractively ingenious.

Mense septimo is the key to understanding it—an allusion to September, our ninth month, but the seventh month of the ancient liturgical calendar (a circumstance betrayed by its obvious etymology). The typical medieval term for the September Ember Days was *jejunium mensis septimi* (fast of the seventh month). But the choice of these texts goes beyond the mere invocation of September. Leviticus 23.41–43 is, of course, an Old Testament text, and it refers to the seventh month of the Hebrew calendar, Tishri, and the celebration of Sukkoth ("booths" or "tabernacles"), the third of the three great Jewish pilgrimage festivals. In translation the text of the communion (an example, incidentally, of substantial textual adjustment) reads: "In the seventh month, celebrate feasts, since I, I your Lord God, have caused the sons of Israel to dwell in tabernacles, and have led them out of the land of Egypt."

Comedite pinguia et bibite mulsum makes another direct allusion to Sukkoth. The text is taken (with virtually no adjustment) from the eighth chapter of Nehemiah, which is devoted to a description of the feast in post-exilic Jerusalem; at one point in the narration Nehemiah addresses the people with the words of the communion: "Eat fat meats and drink sweet wine, and send portions thereof to those who have made no preparations for themselves, for this is a holy day to the Lord; be not sad, for the joy of the Lord is our strength."

Friday's communion, disappointingly, the psalmic *Aufer a me* (Ps 118.22–24), does not share in the Sukkoth theme; it would fit, in fact, quite nicely within the justice group. This chant aside, what are we to make of the Sukkoth pair? One thing to be observed, certainly, is the obvious contradiction between the Old Testament feast and the New Testament fast. Is there nothing more, then, in the choice of these texts than the coincidence of two religious events taking place each year in the seventh month? We did observe something of the same fascination with Old Testament events (without any attempt at explicit Christian interpretation of them) in post-Pentecostal offertories such as *Precatus est moyses* (Ex 32.11–15) and *Sanctificavit moyses* (Ex 24.4–5). An obvious source of such fascination might be the calendric conjunction of the Old Testament readings at matins with such chants. This solution, however, has the difficulty that, while historical books such as Chronicles and Nehemiah furnish the inspiration of several of these chants and are read during the summer and early fall—the very time that these chants appear in the Mass Proper—equally important sources such as Exodus and Leviticus are read in the late winter and early spring.[27] I leave the subject with the simple remark that there must have been some clerics of lively poetic imagination in the schola cantorum of the later seventh century, individuals who were particularly attracted to colorful Old Testament themes.

THE SANCTORAL COMMUNIONS

I have said before that treating the sanctorale is an inexact science, and I am reminded now of that remark as I work on the sanctoral communions. The more time I spend on this group of forty-two chants,[28] and the more detailed information I amass, the less able I am to fashion any overriding hypothesis about them. I will therefore confine myself, for the most part, to a few unsystematic observations, some of them quite narrow in focus, indeed of a kind of closely detailed character that I generally try to avoid in this volume.

The most obvious consideration of a broader nature is the large proportion of gospel communions. Twenty-eight of the forty-two sanctoral communions have gospel texts (ten have texts from the psalms, three from other books of the Bible, while one chant, *Qui me dignatus*, is nonbiblical). The communions with gospel texts, moreover, are mostly gospel communions in the narrow sense; that is, the texts are taken from the gospel of the day. One must distinguish here, however, communions that are uniquely assigned from those that are shared. A communion shared by several sanctoral feasts can be a gospel communion of this sort—in relation to all of these dates—only if every one of the dates has the same gospel. If that formulation sounds abstract, I will illustrate it presently with examples that make it clear, but for now a few words on the uniquely assigned gospel communions.

There are some eighteen of these in the repertory and the overwhelming majority of them are gospel communions in the strict sense.[29] There are only two outright exceptions: *Beati mundo corde* (with a text from Matthew 5.8–10) for a feast, 2 July's Processus and Martinianus (with a gospel from Matthew 24.3–13), and *Signa eos* (with a text from Mark 16.17–18)

Table 37. The Assignments of *Domine quinque talenta*

		Festival	Gospel
Domine quinque talenta (Mt 25.20–21)	<u>16 Jan</u>	<u>Marcellus</u>	<u>Mt 25.14–23</u>
	6 Aug	Sixtus	Mt 10.16–22
	14 Sept	Cornelius & Cyprian	Lk 11.47–54
	<u>23 Nov</u>	<u>Clement</u>	<u>Mt 25.14–23</u>

for a feast, 8 August's Cyriacus (with a gospel from Matthew 10.26–32). There are, moreover, two pairs of quasi exceptions involving the vigil and feast of the apostles Peter and Paul (28–29 June) and the vigil and feast of the apostle Andrew (29–30 November). In each of these cases the expected relationships are reversed, that is, the communion of the vigil corresponds with the gospel of the feast, and vice versa.[30]

In any event, the practice of providing gospel communions in the strict sense is quite consistent in the uniquely assigned sanctoral communions, but what about the complications that are created by shared gospel communions? Take the example of *Domine quinque talenta* (Mt 25.20–21); it is, as we see in table 37, assigned to four feasts. The communion matches the gospel of two of the feasts (those underlined in the table) but fails to match the other two. This latter circumstance is hardly surprising. Gospels, of course, were assigned to these dates before the communions were provided for them—in the evangeliary of 645—and the schola cantorum had to work with this fact. It is true that if the schola had provided uniquely assigned communions for all sanctoral dates, they could have devised a gospel communion in the strict sense for every one of them, but we know, of course, that shared chants were a necessary compromise in the economy of the sanctorale. Gospel-communions in the strict sense must be the subject of compromise also, and we see in the case of *Domine quinque talenta* that two of the four festivals to which the chant is assigned are awarded such a communion, whereas the other two are not. Some gospel-communions manage to achieve perfect congruency with the gospels of the feast to which they are assigned because all of the feasts involved happen to share the same gospels. There are two such chants: *Multitudo languentium* (Lk 6.17–19) and *Simile est* (Mt 13.45–46)—even if the former is assigned to only two feasts and the latter to three.

One final episode of close detail must be aired before the subject of sanctoral gospel communions can be put behind us. I have included three communions in the core repertory (*Beati mundo corde, Domine si tu es* and

Sint lumbi vestri) even though they fail to appear in the early Frankish graduals. This is an apparent violation of my general policy, which is based on the proposition that chants found in Vat lat 5319 but not in the *Sextuplex* sources (only a very small number in each genre) were added to the Roman repertory after the transmission to Francia in order to accommodate later Roman liturgical occasions such as the nuptial mass and Mass for the Dead. These three communions, however, are gospel communions uniquely assigned to dates firmly established in the Roman sanctoral cycle well before the later seventh-century completion of the Mass Proper. Why, then, do they not appear in the *Sextuplex* sources? There are two possibilities: the Roman singers, at some time well after the end of the creative period of Mass Proper production, singled out just three sanctoral occasions (relatively obscure ones, as we shall see) and created new gospel communions for them; or the three chants were in the core Roman repertory but for some reason failed to be included in the early Frankish repertory.

The latter is obviously the more likely alternative, and there are specific reasons to opt for it. In the case of *Sint lumbi vestri* it could be a matter of confusion about the festival itself. Vat lat 5319 assigns the chant to 23 July's Felix, Faustinus and Beatrice (on the same day as Apollinaris), and in another place to 28 July's Felix; while the Roman evangeliaries and sacramentaries have a 29 July Felix, Simplicius, Faustinus and Beatrice. The *Sextuplex* graduals, in turn, while maintaining the 29 July date, have curious variations on the saints involved, such as Blandin's Simplicius, Faustinus and Viatoris (the last possibly a corruption of the Roman Beatrice at the *via Portuense*). Perhaps, then, the absence of *Sint lumbi vestri* from the early Frankish graduals is best explained by the colloquialism that it was "lost in the shuffle."

As for the other two communions, they are for feasts that follow immediately one upon the other in the graduals, both Roman and Frankish. *Beati mundo corde* appears in Vat lat 5319 on folio 116v for the 2 July feast of Processus and Martianus, and *Domine si tu es* on folio 117v for the 6 July octave of Peter and Paul. If one turns to the *Sextuplex* manuscripts, there it will be observed that it is not only these two Roman communions that fail to appear, but rather a consecutive series of six chants beginning with 2 July's communion *Beati mundo corde*, continuing through 6 July's introit, gradual, alleluia and offertory, and closing with its communion *Domine si tu es*. It seems clear enough that there was a defect at this point in the Roman Mass antiphoner that established the central Frankish repertory, one that covered just these six consecutive chants. *Beati mundo corde*, therefore, and *Domine si tu es*, along with *Sint lumbi vestri*, would appear

352 / *The Advent Project*

to belong to the Roman core repertory despite their absence from the early Frankish graduals.

So much for sanctoral gospel communions. To turn to psalmic communions, the obvious question to ask is whether there is evidence of a fund of original psalmic chants (as we have observed in other genres of the Mass Proper), serving within a proto-Common of the Saints before the time of the Sanctoral Project. There are, it will be recalled, only ten sanctoral psalmic communions, and one of these, *Unguentum* (Ps 132.2–4), belongs to that curious category of chants involved in the Commons of popes and bishops. There may be something useful, nonetheless, to be concluded from an examination of the nine from the aspect of textual adjustment. It will be recalled that in the case of sanctoral introits and offertories, psalmic chants that were shared were significantly less subject to substantial textual adjustment than were uniquely assigned psalmic chants.[31] This suggested to us in each case that shared sanctoral psalmic chants might represent an earlier layer of the repertory. An examination of communion texts yields precisely the same results. Although only nine in total, the difference between the shared chants (six in number) and the uniquely assigned (three) may be sharp enough to be statistically significant. Only one of the six shared chants, *Posuerunt* (Ps 78.2–11), has a substantially adjusted text, while all three of the uniquely assigned communions do. Thus it may be that shared sanctoral chants with texts derived literally from the psalms—*Posuisti* (Ps 20.4), for example, and *Magna est gloria* (Ps 20.6)—belong to the earliest layer of sanctoral communions. It should be added that the numerically ordered psalmic communions of the Lenten weekdays, a group of chants thought to be early for any number of reasons, also have a very low proportion of substantially adjusted texts.

THE TRANSMISSION OF SANCTORAL COMMUNIONS

A final observation about sanctoral communions as a whole is in order: how do they fare in the transmission to the north, that is to say, what is their degree of continuity from Rome to Francia, with respect to both liturgical assignment and music?

As for liturgical assignment, while temporal communions, not surprisingly, maintain close to absolute continuity,[32] there is an appreciable instance of discontinuity in sanctoral communions. It is not random, however, and there are two significant distinctions to be observed. For one, there are virtually no instances of discontinuity in uniquely assigned communions. Indeed, the only three that I observe are the very three (*Beati mundo corde*,

Domine si tu es and *Sint lumbi vestri*) described above as chants of the Roman core repertory that failed to appear in the early Frankish manuscripts. That they are, by the way, the only exceptions in this matter of discontinuity offers a striking additional confirmation of the previous claim made for them.

It is within the shared sanctoral communions, then, that discontinuity of assignment exists to any appreciable degree, and the second of our two distinctions has to do with where within the church year the chants in question are to be found. They are found only in the post-Pentecostal season; here I count some nine examples of discontinuity,[33] while I find not a single one in the sanctoral communions of the Advent-Christmas and Easter seasons. The nine instances of discontinuity appear in a total of some twenty-eight post-Pentecostal sanctoral dates with shared communions—approximately a third of the whole. This is, to start with, an exceptionally large proportion of discontinuity for any phase of the Mass Proper. The point at issue here, however, is the striking difference between the Advent through Pentecost portion of the church year and the post-Pentecostal portion. What does it mean?

It cannot mean that sanctoral communions, like alleluias, are not yet permanently assigned and exist rather on a list for ad hoc use. The facts of the matter are, again, that uniquely assigned communions display near-perfect continuity of assignment over the entire year and shared communions of the Advent to Pentecost portion of the church year display a similar degree of continuity, whereas only shared communions of the post-Pentecostal period display any appreciable proportion of discontinuity (and then only in a minority of cases, about one in three). It would appear, therefore, not to be a matter of policy but another instance of that phenomenon observed in some liturgical enterprises of manifesting less exactitude in their later stages. There is, in a word, some kind of haste involved here, some lack of attention to detail toward the end of a large project—whether on the part of Romans or Franks, cantors or copyists, I will not hazard a guess.

On the question of musical continuity between Rome and Francia for the sanctoral communions, I will be very brief, reserving any more detailed musical discussion for the epilogue of this volume. In general the degree of continuity is fairly high, perhaps somewhat more so than expected. There are only six cases of different finals between the Roman and Gregorian versions, and in the majority of these the chants are at least arguably related. Overall the sanctoral communions are nearly as closely related as the Advent-Christmas communions and certainly more closely related than sanctoral offertories. Perhaps the two sanctoral communions that stand out the most in this respect are *Posuisti* and *Tu es Petrus*. I single them out because they are the two chants that are clear examples of the style of our purported Advent Master, and while they may be the most closely related of the sanctoral communions, the Roman and Gregorian versions are different enough to produce the same disappointment to my expectations expressed above in connection with the seven Advent and Christmas day communions of the same type.

THE ANNUAL COMMUNION CYCLE AS SYMPHONY?

At the close of my 1992 article on the communion I expressed my admiration for the genre's temporal cycle with these words:

> What is not a matter of speculation is the splendor of the communion temporale. It is a remarkable creation of epic proportions, like some great symphony, characterized on the one hand by the most patent symmetry and organization, and on the other by a consistent programmatic tendency that would have each episode within the whole thematically appropriate to the liturgical occasion.[34]

I invoked these same words at the close of the chapter on the introit, endorsing the symphonic figure then. And now after surveying the entire Mass Proper, I see no reason to temper my original enthusiasm for the final shape of the annual communion cycle. This, even if I see a somewhat higher degree of compromise and expediency in the way the schola cantorum realized their plans for certain portions of it.

My reason for bringing up the symphonic figure here, then, is not to abandon it, but in fact to pursue it further as I prepare to attempt an overview of the entire Mass Proper in the next chapter. What I have in mind is the "four-movement plan" of the communion's temporal cycle. The cycle is clearly divided into four discrete portions: Advent-Christmas, Lent, Paschaltime and the post-Pentecostal period. There is no "through-composition," no instances of transition from one season to the next. The schola cantorum eliminated these from the church year. The decisive step in making this so was their establishment of Advent at the beginning of the church year with the result that the Advent-Christmas chants form a coherent group. Before the singers took this step the Advent Sundays simply rounded off the post-Pentecost Sundays in the Roman liturgical books. And then there are the three Sundays of the Septuagesima, Sexagesima and Quinquagesima set. They are not, strictly speaking, part of Lent, which begins, of course, on the Wednesday after Quinquagesima, Ash Wednesday; they are rather a transition between the Christmas season and Lent. But they are not treated as such in the communion cycle; structurally they are part of Lent. There is an unmistakable break between the gospel-communions of the Sundays after Epiphany and the psalmic communions that begin with Septuagesima. Opening then with Septuagesima Sunday, Lent forms a self-contained segment in the annual communion cycle, just as Paschaltime and the post-Pentecostal period constitute obviously independent third and fourth units. And not only are the divisions between the four clear, but each of them is a coherent whole in itself that is fashioned, as we have seen, according to its own formal procedure.

If we are to exhaust the symphonic metaphor completely, it must be asked finally if we should see "cyclic treatment" in the communion temporale. The obvious candidate for identification with this device is the gospel-communion, which recurs throughout the four seasons, sometimes in unexpected places, as with the Lenten five. The content of the gospel-communions, however, differs with each usage, and I would say that the better analogy for their employment throughout the year is with some stylistic or technical trait rather than a repeated motif.

The serious consideration in all of this is the existence of the quadripartite structure of the communion temporale. And while clearest and most explicit in the communion, it is, as we have seen, undeniably present in the other items of the Mass Proper. I emphasize the point now before embarking upon an attempt to create an overall picture of the Mass Proper's development. The four-movement plan of the sung Mass Proper is the most promising analytic framework in which to carry out such a task.

CHAPTER 14

The Creation of the Roman Mass Proper

It can be said that Mass psalmody originated at the Last Supper, but not the sung Mass Proper. The positive portion of this twofold proposition is not without significance for our subject. When Jesus and his disciples sang a "hymn" at the close of the Last Supper—quite possibly the Hallel—they were singing at the first "Mass." They set the tone, moreover, for early Christian gatherings, eucharistic and otherwise, of a warm appreciation for religious song.

THE PRECONDITIONS FOR A SUNG MASS PROPER

But preconditions for the creation of a sung Mass Proper are not in evidence until the later decades of the fourth century. These are chiefly two: the existence of a stable order of worship with set places for singing; and the existence of an annual cycle of festivals. As for the first of these, the patristic literature of the period, East and West, reveals the formalization of a two-part eucharistic service: a Fore-Mass or Mass of the Catechumens, consisting of scriptural reading and instruction; and the eucharistic rite as such, or Mass of the Faithful. Psalmody comes to be regularly employed at the time in two places of the service: during the distribution of communion and during the Fore-Mass. The existence of communion psalmody speaks for itself, but the psalmody of the Fore-Mass is a more complex matter.

The typical western Fore-Mass of the later fourth century consists of just three items before the homily: the epistle, the psalm and the gospel, all three of which (including the psalm) are referred to as "readings." That the psalm is still thought of as a reading at this time suggests much about its previous history, but of more relevance for present purposes is that it is also looked upon as a set musical piece. Typically it was sung in the responsorial manner: a lector would declaim the psalm and the people would respond with a chosen verse sung to a traditional tune. By reason of liturgical placement and psalmodic format it seems legitimate to see in this psalm the ancestor of the early medieval gradual and thus to refer to it as the "gradual psalm."

This is not to deny that the Fore-Mass psalm was sometimes chanted without refrains, particularly on penitential occasions. We have no positive evidence for this, but it seems a safe assumption, and it seems, moreover, fair to look upon this type of psalmody as the ancestor of the tract. The prehistory of the alleluia is not as simple. Those twenty psalms that have the exclamation alleluia affixed to them in the Psalter were sung, we trust, with alleluia as congregational refrain. Quite possibly this was done as the norm during Paschaltime. It might be tempting to look upon the custom, then, as the origins of the early medieval alleluia, but in a formal sense it seems better to think of it as singing the gradual psalm with alleluia refrains. Doubtless the practice played a preparatory role in the development of the alleluia as a discrete liturgical genre, but the establishment of that item of the Mass Proper required the existence of two responsorial psalms, the second of which has alleluia as its regular refrain. Precisely this arrangement was in evidence already in fifth-century Jerusalem; it spread rapidly throughout the East but does not seem to have made its appearance in Rome until sometime in the seventh century.

Thus by the end of the fourth century a gradual psalm (occasionally sung without refrains) and a communion psalm were established items in the western Mass. (There were as yet no indications of entrance or offertory psalms.) The contemporary evidence for this comes to us from important western centers such as Carthage, Hippo and Milan but not from Rome. Later evidence, however, gives us good reason to presume that similar psalmodic arrangements were in place there at least by the first half of the fifth century. Present in Rome also were the monastic communities attached to the great basilicas. They were primarily responsible for the singing of the Office rather than the Mass, but their Office psalmody doubtless had a profound impact upon the eventual shape of the Roman Mass Proper, particularly its penchant for variable psalmody at the expense of attractive Ordinary items such as the Cheroubikon and Trisagion.

The second precondition for the development of a Mass Proper is an annual cycle of feasts. It is in the later fourth century also that this begins to take shape, even if it is still far removed from the quadripartite structure produced by the Advent Project. The emerging liturgical year is rather one of two foci—centering upon the feasts of Christmas and Easter. The second of these develops much earlier than the first. The quinquagesima of

Easter and Pentecost is virtually apostolic in origin, owing much to the quinquagesimal framework of the three great Jewish pilgrimage festivals—Passover, Weeks and Tabernacles—each separated by fifty days. By the later fourth century Ascension Thursday is in place (forty days after Easter), and the pre-Easter Lenten fast is observed for forty days, beginning with Quadragesima Sunday (the extension to Ash Wednesday is much later). The Christmas cycle is in its infancy, consisting only of Christmas day and the recently adopted eastern celebration of Christ's birth, the Epiphany. There is no Advent, unless Rome also practices the three-day pre-Christmas fast for which we have Gallican evidence at the time.

Sundays outside of Lent and Paschaltime are observed but not defined. The post–Vatican II preference for referring to these days as Sundays in "Ordinary Time" is, by the way, based on an attempt to restore early Christian conceptions and to undo the work of early medieval liturgists. These Sundays, in any event, came to be named eventually and assigned their own prayers, readings and, finally, chants. By the early seventh century the Roman sacramentaries and lectionaries had Sundays after the Epiphany (in varying numbers), the Septuagesima trio, groups of Sundays named after the principal summer sanctoral feasts such as that of the apostles Peter and Paul and Sundays of Advent (again, in varying numbers and placed at the end of the post-Pentecostal series). The result was not yet the quadripartite format of the Advent Project, but much of that structure was implicit in the early-seventh-century state of the annual cycle.

The most decisive step taken by the Roman singers to achieve the final form of the year was to stabilize the number of the Advent Sundays at four, and to place them at the beginning of the church year as a lyric prelude to Christmas. Chants of the various genres were provided (most of them new) so as to create a coherent unit beginning with the first Sunday of Advent and ending with the third Sunday after the Epiphany. The Septuagesima trio was given psalmic chants resembling those of Lent, creating a second homogeneous unit. The third unit, Paschaltime, was extended with Proper chants (including dual alleluias), to the Saturday after Pentecost. This was in effect a violation of the traditional quinquagesima, making of it a period of fifty-six rather than just fifty days, but the new quadripartite annual structure was given precedence over the underlying ancient one. And finally the post-Pentecostal period, while retaining the somewhat ungainly signposts of the key Roman sanctoral dates, was unified with continuous sequences of twenty-two chants for each genre, made up largely of numerically ordered psalmic chants. Interestingly enough, the Franks were the ones who completed the rationalization of this last segment of the year by adding a Sunday and numbering the sequence from one to twenty-three (the required minimum between Pentecost and Advent).

But to return to the later fourth century, that period saw the establishment of the two most essential preconditions for a sung Mass Proper—a stable order of the Mass with set places for psalmody, and an annual cycle of feasts—even if neither of these was nearly as developed as it would be by the seventh century. The circumstances were then present to draw up a calendar of permanently assigned gradual psalms for the existing festal portions of the year, and to provide an accompanying list of favored psalms and response verses for the ordinary Sundays of the year. But this was not done. Instead, gradual psalms appear to have been chosen on an ad hoc basis from year to year, with only certain exceptions, such as Easter's Psalm 117 and its response verse, *Haec dies* (*Hic est dies* at the time). Surely traditional psalmic associations of the sort accumulated in succeeding centuries, but the majority of textual assignments, both psalmic and especially nonpsalmic, were certainly the work of the seventh-century schola cantorum.

The two preconditions described above were adequate for the establishment of an annual cycle of psalmic assignments (even if the opportunity was not exploited), but this still would not have been the sort of Mass Proper we think of today. A calendar of psalmic assignments is not the same thing as an annual cycle of several hundred set pieces, composed to fit the differing formal requirements and stylistic norms of each liturgical genre, and composed, moreover, to match texts that are as often as not freely adapted from their biblical sources so as to provide appropriate vehicles for their musical settings. I refer here to what must be looked upon as a third precondition for a sung Mass Proper in the full sense—the move from lector chant to schola chant. Such a change did in fact come about in Rome before the creation of the Advent Project; it is a "paradigmatic shift" in the sense that Karol Berger uses the term, arguably as important as any other such development in the history of western music.[1]

That shift required the establishment of the Roman schola cantorum, an event that both evidence and probability place in the seventh century. The documentary evidence shows that the organization was not in existence at the time of Gregory I (590–604), but that it was in the time of Sergius I's mentor Adeodatus (672–76), while the historical background suggests that the overall conditions for its founding had also become more favorable as the seventh century progressed. It is no small thing to set up a group like the schola cantorum; it requires a goodly measure of economic prosperity, spiritual commitment and common psychological well-being to release valuable clergy from their other duties, and to provide a residence for them and support them generously while they devote themselves exclusively to the development of ecclesiastical music. One is reminded of the lavish fifteenth-century court chapels and their noble patrons. Rome in Gregory's time, still suffering from the unspeakable ravages of the Gothic war and the Lombard incursion, was hardly able to sustain such an enterprise, let alone initiate it. But Gregory, even if not the founder of the schola as was once thought to be the case, deserves much credit for restoring civil and ecclesiastical order to Rome and setting it on a course that would eventually provide a favorable environment for the organization. The city, in fact, did recover and prosper in the course of the century: it enjoyed relative peace and a dramatic influx of pilgrims, and it increasingly asserted itself against its nominal Byzantine rulers, both theologically and politically, as it came to look upon itself as a world ecclesiastical center. The time was ripe for the establishment of the schola, which must have taken place sometime during the middle third of the seventh century.

THE IMMEDIATE LITURGICAL BACKGROUND

There were other liturgical forces at work in seventh-century Rome besides the schola. Earlier in the century, before its founding, the prayers and readings of the Mass were being subjected to the same process of properization that the chants were later to undergo. It is greatly instructive to observe this happening in the sacramentaries and lectionaries and to compare it with what one observes in the Mass antiphoner. The difference is striking. The sacramentaries and lectionaries show a centuries-long development in stages, a movement from choice of prayers and readings to their permanent assignment even for ordinary Sundays and minor saints. The different redactions of these books, as they make their way in the eighth century to the Carolingian realm, cause confusion among the Frankish ecclesiastics ("liturgical anarchy," in Gerald Ellard's phrase), who strive mightily to create coherent liturgical books. The Mass antiphoner by contrast is unified from the start. There are no apparent stages in its development, and the Franks experience none of the confusion with it that they do with sacramentaries and lectionaries. This is not so much a matter of chants versus other liturgical items, but a matter of the uniqueness of the Mass Proper. The Office antiphonary manifests the same sort of instability as do the sacramentary and lectionary. The Carolingian liturgical scholar Helisachar, writing in about 820, nicely summarizes the situation:

> I first gathered from here and there antiphoners and cantors, and also an abundance of books and skilled readers, and then carefully set about

to test the concordance of the antiphoners. Now, while they differed among themselves very little with respect to the chants of the Mass ... few were found to manifest unity with respect to the chants of the Office.[2]

The unity of which Helisachar speaks is that which was imposed on the Mass Proper by what I call the Advent Project (and Sanctoral Project). The creation of the Roman Mass Proper was more a single concerted act than one that took place in stages. To say this is clearly to oversimplify, but it is a necessary corrective to the notion that the Mass Proper was the result of a centuries-long evolution, in which more or less the same texts were reworked in changing musical styles from generation to generation. It is true that much had to happen before that final revision of the Mass Proper that takes the form of Advent and Sanctoral Projects. I speak here not of the liturgical and institutional preconditions summarized in the opening portion of this chapter, but developments of a musical nature. There is the long prehistory of clerical responsorial psalmody and monastic antiphonal psalmody, and, more immediately, the activity of the schola cantorum itself before the decision to create the ideal Mass Proper. Certainly the formal stylistic distinctions between the different genres of chant were established, and no doubt substantial repertories of psalmic chants were produced for general usage. And a goodly number of pieces individually assigned to principal feasts—graduals, for example, such as Christmas' *Tecum principium* and Easter's *Haec dies*—were no doubt already in existence prior to the period of the Advent Project. Indeed it was probably the increasing number of such chants that inspired the decision to do the job right once and for all by providing unique Proper chants for the entire temporale and much of the sanctorale.

When the decision was made to undertake that ambitious enterprise, it cannot be assumed that everything went quickly and smoothly. There may have been fits and starts, disagreements, disappointments, lulls in the activity. Perhaps the project took as long as twenty or thirty years to complete. I am more inclined, however, to think that the schola, driven by the need to complete a house in which they were living, encouraged by a series of musical popes and buoyed by their own creative enthusiasm, completed the task in a matter of years rather than decades. While we can only guess just how long the enterprise took to complete, we have the final product, and it offers us much material with which to surmise over its relative internal chronology. Throughout this volume there has been considerable discussion about the possible chronology within an individual item of the Mass Proper, but very little about a comparative chronology between the different items. To achieve anything of the sort with even reasonable plausibility will not be easy, but it is surely a task worth trying.

TOWARD A CHRONOLOGY OF THE ADVENT PROJECT

There are a number of factors, observations accumulated in the course of this study, that aid in such an attempt. The first did not originate here: Peter Wagner spoke of it, even if this volume abundantly corroborates it. It is that the chants of the Mass Proper were created more genre by genre than festival by festival. There are of course exceptions to this, particularly the formularies of major festivals, and certainly singers working on one genre were not unaware of what was happening with another. But nevertheless each genre of the Mass Proper took shape according to its own plan and procedure.

Yet not continuously for *the entire church year*, but rather for one at a time of the four portions of the quadripartite annual chant cycle. This is the second of the observations that should aid in our attempt at reconstruction, and one every bit as basic as the first. I could in fact oversimplify the task by saying that it amounts to arranging sixteen units in chronological order, that is, the four segments of the church year (our four movements) for each of the four genres in question—the introit, gradual, offertory and communion (the alleluia and tract are subject to different principles of composition). While clearly an oversimplification of what is involved, this general approach seems to be the single route that offers any hope of success in our speculations.

A more particular factor that should aid in the development of a chronology is the nature of the chant texts, specifically whether they are psalmic or nonpsalmic, and whether they use the biblical original more or less intact or substantially adjusted. Generally speaking nonpsalmic texts and texts that have been substantially changed from their biblical originals are later than chants with psalmic texts and those that retain the integral biblical original. These distinctions are particularly helpful with certain chant genres and in certain circumstances. Nonpsalmic graduals, for example, appear to be conspicuously late in the context of a genre whose repertory is overwhelmingly psalmic, in accord with its psalmic origins. And post-Pentecostal offertories, for another example, with freely paraphrased nonpsalmic texts, have every appearance of being later than the psalmic chants that constitute the bulk of the season's cycle.

In addition to these three factors that are almost exclusively helpful to our efforts, there are a number of others that serve as much to complicate as to facilitate the task. For one, we can never forget that need to build a house while living in it. It is next to inconceivable, to continue the metaphor, that the Roman singers would continue to live in their old home while the new one was under construction elsewhere, awaiting completion before being moved into. Rather we must imagine an incomplete Mass Proper, one made up principally of psalmic chants for general usage with a limited number of permanently assigned festival chants, which was added to segment by segment over a number of years. Surely groups of new chants would be introduced into the annual cycle as created, not kept in storage, so to speak, until the Mass Proper was completed. Not only would such a policy be contrary to all reasonable human behavior, but it would increase the burden upon the musical memory of the schola to a point straining all credibility.

This reference to musical memory serves to introduce another factor, one equally helpful and complicating; this is the distinct possibility, indeed probability, that different individuals and groups of the schola were simultaneously at work on different genres or on different portions of the same genre. The idea was invoked above as an explanation of how a body such as the schola could remember *new* chants in subsequent years after their creation. We know that it took several years (Guido d'Arezzo says ten) for a novice singer to master the traditional chant repertory within a community that had retained it for centuries within group memory. But apparently the only way to keep new chants in memory was to assign them to particular individuals, who were responsible for their retention for as many years as it took for all to learn them. And obviously the most likely individuals assigned to remember certain new chants would be their creators. I would say, then, that this division of labor in both the maintenance and the composition of the Mass Proper was not only a possibility but a necessity. It is a factor that, while rendering more plausible the view that the Mass Proper was created within a limited period of time, presents difficulties as we try to envision a single step-by-step chronology for the process.

Another complicating factor is nothing less than the most basic premise behind the idea of the Advent Project—that work on the Mass Proper began with the chants of Advent and proceeded subsequently through the remainder of the church year. Should we imagine, then, that work began simultaneously with the introit, gradual, offertory and communion? Was it a kind of race, beginning with the four genres lined up on the starting line of the first Sunday of Advent, and continuing thereafter at their own pace? I think, in fact, that something of the sort actually happened, but how is one to reconcile this with the fact that certain items of the Mass Proper, offertories for example, are said to be "late"? If one genre is later than another, how can we say that the Advent chants of each were planned and created at about the same time?

I hope that a full answer to that question will emerge in the course of my attempt to reconstruct the internal chronology of the Advent Project. But a tentative answer would appear to be in order now. It is a matter of how fully developed a particular genre was at the time the Advent Project commenced. Take graduals, for example: in our chapter on them we concluded that a particularly large repertory of psalmic chants for general use and a considerable number of festal chants were already in existence before the Advent Project began, thus accounting for a more generally ancient cast to the genre as a whole—so we speak of it as an "early" genre. Still certain individual graduals have all the hallmarks of late chants, indeed several of them appearing in the Advent-Christmas portion of that chant's annual cycle. Thus the late chants of an early genre can be created contemporaneously with the early chants of a late genre.

Our final complicating factor is also a matter of "early" and "late" chants—how does the alleluia, the latest of Mass Proper items, figure into the chronology of the Advent Project? If it is so obviously late, should we imagine that the four central items of the Mass Proper were first completed, and that the alleluia was hastily added afterward, thus accounting for its clearly unfinished state? This is not an acceptable alternative because the alleluia, finished or not, is an integral part of the Mass Proper's structure. Its analogous positioning with the tract and its replacement of the gradual during Paschaltime make it part of the plan. To put it another way, the move to dual Fore-Mass chants could not have taken place after the completion of the Mass Proper: dual Fore-Mass chants are an integral feature of the Proper's format, not present necessarily at the inception of the Advent Project, but present certainly before its completion.

So much for preliminary considerations. Can we now create a passably credible scenario for the inner history of the Advent Project (while not entirely neglecting the Sanctoral Project)?

RECONSTRUCTING THE ADVENT PROJECT

To start with, I assume the simultaneous beginning of work on introit, gradual, offertory and communion with the chants of the Advent-Christmas season. By simultaneous I do not mean necessarily the same day or even the same year, but I mean that the intention, the plan, to provide an ideal annual cycle for the four genres was a single conception, and that work began on all four without unreasonable delay. "Contemporaneous" is perhaps a better word than "simultaneous." A noncontemporaneous start does not seem very likely. Should we imagine that there was a decision to provide, for example, a perfect annual cycle of introits, and that it occurred to the members of the schola, only after coming to admire their handiwork on that genre, to extend the project to the others? Certainly the overarching truth that the plan for all four genres was realized with near perfection for the Advent-Christmas season and more than adequately for Lent, but only with serious compromises for Paschaltime, suggests an approximately contemporaneous start by the four.

But if work began on their annual cycles at about the same time, this is not to say that they enjoyed equal repertories of pre-Advent Project chants. The gradual, as mentioned above, stands out in this respect with not only a particularly large original fund of psalmic chants for general use, but also a considerable number of specifically assigned ones, especially for important liturgical occasions; Easter's *Haec dies*, for example, accounting for the entire Easter season, and at least three chants of the Advent-Christmas period —Christmas day's *Tecum principium*, the Sunday after Christmas' *Speciosus* and Advent's *Ostende nobis*. For the Advent-Christmas season it was a comparatively easy task to add to these a few suitable ones from the common fund, and to fill out the remainder of the series with new chants utilizing *Tecum principium*'s A-2 melody type for Advent and the more festive F-5 type for the remainder of the time. Several of the new chants display the same advanced characteristics as the so-called later items of the Mass Proper. Four graduals of the period have nonpsalmic texts, a high proportion for the genre, and a number have substantially adjusted texts, the vigil of Christmas' *Hodie scietis*, for example, consisting of a scarcely traceable mélange of material from the Books of Exodus and Isaiah.

One might expect the gradual to have been the first of the four items to have its entire annual cycle completed; it had a large fund of original material available for use in Lent, its Advent-Christmas season was readily fashioned, and its single Paschaltime chant had long since been in place. But this seems not to have been the case; it is the introit that appears to have been first finished. For one thing the introit gives this general impression. It is the only chant that appears to have followed its initial plan to perfection. The reader will recall the striking homogeneity of the genre: every introit is an individual melody of generally uniform style. And then there is the equally remarkable circumstance that of the 101 dates in the temporale there are no less than 100 uniquely assigned chants (the single exception, *Nos autem*, proving the rule, as we shall see). There were, then, no fits and starts in the realization of the plan for the introit, no breakdowns and no compromises. One has the impression that the schola—dealing here with the first item of the Mass Proper, and one comparatively manageable because of its relative brevity—got on with the job and completed it quickly and efficiently. The burden on the memory of creating some 145 chants over a period of perhaps only a few years, and retaining them in memory, would no doubt have required a division of labor, but certainly the different individuals and groups involved would have worked in close concert.

That the introit was completed before the other items of the Mass, or at least the gradual, is not just a matter of impression; there is evidence for the proposition in the form of two specific introits and the corresponding graduals assigned to the same liturgical occasions. The first of these is that single shared introit of the temporale, Holy Thursday's *Nos autem*, borrowed from Tuesday in Holy Week. We have noted above the surprising tendency of this solemn occasion to borrow chants, surely an indication of a very late adoption of its Mass Proper (something I remain unable to explain). There is, in any event, no other explanation for the borrowing of *Nos autem*, the only instance of borrowing in the entire introit temporale, than that the cycle was already completed at the time Holy Thursday was provided with a sung Mass Proper. But not so for the gradual of the feast. Holy Thursday has a uniquely assigned gradual, *Christus factus est* (Gal 6.14), an obviously late example of the genre, with its nonpsalmic text (freely paraphrased moreover), which is set to the most stereotypical form of the F-5 melody along with its two Christmastime counterparts, Stephen's *Sederunt principes* and Sylvester's *Ecce sacerdos*. The best explanation for all this is that only after the annual cycle of the introit was completed did the schola turn to the graduals of Lent, giving fixed assignments to the large fund of existing psalmic graduals and adding however many were necessary to complete the season, including Holy Thursday's *Christus factus est*.

The case of the second introit in question, *Dum clamarem*, of the fifth Sunday after the feast of Peter and Paul, is even more telling. The text of *Dum clamarem* (Ps 54.17–23) is an example of the most radical type of textual adjustment, stitched together from bits and pieces of seven verses of the psalm and changed from the original when necessary to achieve the desired result. It is, then, a unique creation, one that can be repeated only if intentionally borrowed, as it is in fact for the verse of *Jacta cogitatum*, the gradual for Tuesday in the second week of Lent. But are we certain that the borrowing is by the Lenten gradual from the post-Pentecostal introit, and not the reverse? Virtually certain, because while substantial textual adjustment is typical of introits, *Dum clamarem* is the single example of a substantially adjusted psalmic gradual verse text in the entire temporale.³ Thus the temporal cycle of the introit, including the post-Pentecostal sequence, appears to have been completed before the schola turned to the Lenten graduals. This seeming lag in work on the graduals is not ultimately surprising. Once the Advent-Christmas graduals were in place, there was little need for haste in completing the annual cycle; Paschaltime was taken care of with *Haec dies*, and there was a sufficient list of older psalmic graduals (and a number of tracts) to cover Lent, even if with some repetition, and the same can be said for the post-Pentecostal period.

If we can assume, then, that the Advent-Christmas season of all four genres and the entire temporale of the introit were first completed, what followed? The Lenten chants of the gradual, offertory and communion are the most likely candidates. But as for the order in which they were undertaken, there are no clear indications, so that one can only surmise. Let us say that the gradual came next, simply because this would seem to follow the most orderly procedure, and say also that the communion was undertaken at about the same time as the offertory, perhaps just before it, because its numerically ordered psalmic series cried out for being put in proper placement. Indeed one could imagine work undertaken on the Lenten communions even before the completion of the introit cycle, but there is no way of knowing this, and for reasons of maintaining a manageable exposition I will proceed with what amounts to little more than pure assumption that the Lenten graduals, communions and offertories were worked on in that order.

The Lenten graduals, in their final revision, adopted a momentous change in liturgical format, one involving the tract. I concluded earlier in this volume that the lengthy D-2 tracts of Quadragesima and Palm Sundays (or more precisely the psalms *in directum* from which the tracts developed), as well as the D-2 chants of Wednesday in Holy Week and Good Friday, were in place at Rome from a very early date, and that the G-8 chants for the three other Lenten Sundays were added not much later. These psalms *in directum* would have stood in the same liturgical position as the more typical responsorial psalm, and in the period immediately preceding the Advent Project, the corresponding tracts would have been sung on these dates *rather than* graduals from the list for general use. But with the Advent Project a gradual is assigned to every day of Lent, with the result that both a gradual and a tract are sung in succession on the dates in question. It is something of an anomalous arrangement, and I would think therefore that it was adopted at the same time as the analogous practice of adding an alleluia to the gradual outside of Lent (a second alleluia in Paschaltime), a point to be taken up below.

When the Lenten communion cycle was undertaken, the numerically ordered psalmic chants were assigned to the weekdays beginning with Ash Wednesday, and mostly new chants were added for the Sundays and for Holy Week, a number of these being of the most advanced type, such as the fifth Sunday's flamboyant responsory-communion, *Hoc corpus* (1 Cor 11.24–25). Holy Thursday is provided with its own communion, the affecting nonpsalmic chant *Dominus Jesus* (Jn 13.12–15), suggesting, by the way, that the Lenten communions, like the graduals, were also worked on after the completion of the entire introit cycle. The weekday psalmic series consists in twenty-six chants, precisely the required number for each feria from Ash Wednesday to the Friday before Palm Sunday (the Saturday is nonliturgical). Now it is clearly too much of a coincidence that this exact number of twenty-six chants was available for general use on weekdays and Sundays of Lent before the Advent Project, thus matching perfectly the twenty-six ferias of Lent when the time came to assign them permanently to these dates. More likely would have been a somewhat shorter list of original chants, say, twenty or so, requiring the addition of five or six to cover the twenty-six dates; and, in fact, Brad Maiani sees more advanced stylistic traits in about that number of chants at the end of the series, suggesting their later composition.[4]

The Lenten offertories are an impressive accomplishment: there are only four dates with shared chants (including Holy Thursday), requiring a total of 121 responses and verses (thirty-four responses and eighty-seven verses). A striking feature of these chants is that, while they are entirely psalmic, substantial textual adjustment is practiced here far in excess of that for any other segment of the offertory repertory. The technique used, moreover, is quite consistent for both responses and verses, nearly always involving the omission of substantial portions of the biblical original (what I refer to above as leaving "gaps"), which is otherwise used in literal form. The homogeneous character of the effort creates the impression that this was done with set purpose by the particular individuals assigned to complete the Lenten offertories. It suggests, moreover, the availability of a considerably lesser fund of pre-Advent Project offertories than for some of the other items of the Mass Proper. If nothing else it remains a curiosity, with only eight of thirty-four Lenten offertories entirely free of substantial textual adjustment, whereas this is true of eleven of the fourteen shared psalmic sanctoral chants, the group generally producing the same results in this respect as the psalmic chants of Lent.

There remain only the Paschaltime offertories and communions and the post-Pentecostal graduals, offertories and communions to consider. I will assume here that the Paschaltime communions were worked on prior to the offertories of the season on the admittedly fragile grounds that the Lenten communions and also post-Pentecostal communions appear to have been finished before the respective offertories. In any event both the communions and offertories of Paschaltime show definite signs of compromise in an effort to complete the festal portion of the church year. Both begin the season with uniquely assigned and liturgically apt chants that continue the policies of the Advent-Christmas season, but both, each in its own way, surrender to expediency toward the end of the season. The last nine communions are borrowed from the responsories and antiphons of the Ascension and Pentecost Offices. This fact at least preserves the appearance of the original plan with chants that are altogether liturgically appropriate. The offertory series, on the other hand, is brought to a close by simply borrowing the chants for the last eight ferias and ordinary Sundays from elsewhere in the liturgical year (chiefly Lent), without much regard for seasonal suitability.

To turn, finally, to the post-Pentecostal graduals, offertories and communions, it seems only natural that the graduals would be attended to first, perhaps even at the same time the Lenten sequence is being completed. In so doing the schola would be simply preserving the obvious order of things after completing the introit, and they would be performing a task with little to differentiate it from fixing the Lenten chants in place. Of the twenty graduals that make up the post-Pentecostal sequence (two are repeated to achieve the required twenty-two), eleven are borrowed from Lent, and the nine others have largely nondescript texts that appear somewhat hastily produced, with all but two employing either the A- or F-final formula.

Communions and offertories are quite different in this respect; here there are groups of chants that sharply contrast with each other by way of their expedient assignment or their striking originality. The communions appear to predate the offertories for two reasons. For one, as we observed in our reconstruction of the communion set, there are signs of different chronological stages in the development of its sets for sacrifice-eucharist and justice. This is not the case with the offertories, where their remarkably related pair of thematic groupings (sets for sacrifice and the just man) are both so tightly controlled and homogeneous in content that they appear to be fashioned at one time, according to plan. They give the impression thus of being modeled on the less artificially developed communion sets. And for a second reason, the offertories in question are such utterly extraordinary pieces, coming as they do, moreover, after a long run of indiscriminately borrowed chants, that they appear to function as a final burst of creative exuberance on the part of the schola, rescuing the very last days of work on the Advent Project from the routine into which the singers had of necessity fallen.

A brief word about the Sanctoral Project before we turn to the alleluia. It was shown to be a "late" effort in the chapter on the sanctorale, but how late? In a word, was it taken up only after the completion of the Advent Project or did work on it overlap with the later stages of the Advent Project? The first alternative is possible, but the second is much more likely. Nothing new in the way of compositional style or technique is introduced in the sanctoral chants; rather the same practices, such as an increasing use of nonpsalmic texts, textual adjustment, and, in the case of the communion, responsory-communions, are employed. In addition to general considerations of this sort there is the particular case of the three nonpsalmic sanctoral offertories, *Ave Maria* (Lk 1.28), *Dominus deus in simplicitate* (1 Chr 29.17–18) and *Recordare mei* (Est 14.12–13). The three are extraordinary chants that have much in common with the offertories that close out the post-Pentecostal sequence. But more than that, *Dominus deus* belongs in every respect to the sacrifice group and *Recordare* to the just man group. The two chants give every appearance of being created at the same time and by the same musicians as these post-Pentecostal offertories, and thus of bringing work on the Sanctoral Project to a closely contemporaneous close with that of the Advent Project.

THE ALLELUIA

In the chapter on the alleluia I spoke of stages in the history of the genre, three in number, with a kind of fourth coming after the redaction of the Mass antiphoners used in the transmission to the north. The first stage is the pre-Advent Project one, which developed from the practice of singing alleluia-psalms during Paschaltime. Psalm 117, with the response verse *Haec dies*, it will be recalled, was sung in ancient times as the gradual psalm of Easter week, and certain of the twenty psalms with an alleluia affixed in the biblical text were probably sung with alleluia as response for the remainder of the season. By the time immediately preceding the Advent Project, the schola was singing the fully developed gradual *Haec dies* during Easter week, and for the rest of the season a limited repertory of alleluias rather than graduals. This repertory included alleluias for general use that were developed from alleluia-psalms, chants such as *Laudate pueri* (Ps 112.1), *Ascendit deus* (Ps 46.4) and Pentecost's *Emitte spiritum* (Ps 103.30). Most of these alleluias—*Lauda anima* (Ps 145.2) and *Lauda Hierusalem* (Ps 147.12), and eventually festal alleluias such as the Ascension's—were sung to either the *Excita* or *Ostende* model melody.

The second stage in the alleluia's history came after work on the Advent Project was well under way. It was the result of the decision to adopt the Byzantine practice of paired responsorial chants in the Fore-Mass, the second of which was an alleluia. We know the step was taken after the completion of the Advent-Christmas portion of the Mass Proper because the Advent-Christmas alleluias (aside from the second Mass of Christmas day's *Dominus regnavit decorem*) show no evidence of Byzantine influence. This influence manifests itself almost exclusively during Paschaltime; it consists in the outright adoption of at least three Byzantine alleluias, preserving even their Greek language, and the use of several Byzantine texts, even if in Latin versions with new Roman melodies. The time of this activity was near to that of work on the Lenten graduals, because the decision to preface each Lenten tract with a gradual appears to be of a piece with the decision to follow each gradual (or alleluia) outside of Lent with a second responsorial chant, invariably an alleluia.

The third stage in the history of the Roman alleluia, following immediately upon, and probably overlapping with, the phase of Byzantine influence, involves the Roman musical response to that influence. A considerable repertory was needed to provide even a roughly adequate covering of liturgical needs, and the Roman singers, while producing ten or so entirely original chants, resorted primarily to the use of the three model melodies. The need was greatest in Paschaltime, with its dual alleluias, but it was necessary to turn also to the Advent-Christmas season as soon as possible. Here the *Excita* and *Ostende* melodies of the original Roman Eastertime alleluias were used to provide two Advent chants for general use, *Excita domine* and *Ostende nobis*, but it was the *Dies sanctificatus*-type (not once used during Paschaltime and presumably a later creation) that was the Advent-Christmas melody of choice, being employed continuously from the third Mass of Christmas to the Epiphany. The *Dies*-type, it should be noted, was also the preferred melody for sanctoral alleluias, another need that had to be met with in all haste. The comparative lateness of the type's repertorial expansion, moreover, is attested to by the fact that the overwhelming majority of nonpsalmic alleluias are set to it.

That the alleluia is generally a latecomer in the development of the Roman Mass Proper is abundantly clear from at least three circumstances: (1) the extremely limited repertory of approximately fifty chants; (2) the need to resort to the use of the three model melodies for the majority of these chants; and (3) the fact that the alleluias for only fifteen key dates of the church year were permanently assigned at the time the Mass antiphoners used in the transmission were redacted. The alleluia, then, came late and never really caught up with the other items of the Roman Mass Proper. Compare it to the offertory, another late genre, with its ninety-two chants of great length and its permanent assignment to every date of the temporale.

AFTER THE ADVENT PROJECT

The Advent Project and the Sanctoral Project (including the alleluia) appear to have been completed during the reign of Sergius I (687–701) and recorded in a Mass antiphoner, roughly at the same time as the sacramentary we call the Hadrianum. These books remained virtually untouched for much of the eighth century—the only significant change resulting from Gregory II's addition of the Lenten Thursdays in about 720—and were passed on as such to the Franks. And not only were the books untouched but, remarkably, the Mass liturgy, at least as far as the chants are concerned, was itself frozen in time, as it were.

There is just one notable addition to the Roman sung Mass (other than the borrowing of chants to accommodate the Thursdays in Lent):[5] the permanent assignment of alleluias to those dates, temporal and sanctoral, beyond the original fifteen principal festivals, and the intriguing creation of eight new alleluias (all but two set to the *Excita* melody) to complete a post-Pentecostal cycle. This activity appears to be of a piece with the Advent Project, a kind of postscript to it, but apparently one that took place after the redaction of the Mass antiphoners used in the transmission. Its results are clearly and uniformly present in the later Roman graduals but leave not a trace in the early Frankish books.

The central fact remains that work on the Roman Mass Proper ended with startling, indeed almost mysterious, abruptness, something not adequately explained by the common formulation that the "creative phase" of Roman Mass Proper production was at an end. Why was it at an end? Why should not the schola have continued to make adjustments on a year-to-year basis with the Mass Proper, improving it and adding to it, particularly by replacing shared chants with uniquely assigned ones? I find, in fact, what happened not to be surprising but rather to be what one ought to expect; there are at least three reasons for this conclusion.

The central one is that the Mass Proper *was* completed (once the alleluia was stabilized). Take the offertory. It is true that there is a run of about twenty shared chants extending from the latter portion of Paschaltime through much of the post-Pentecostal period, but this is not an intolerable situation, particularly when the annual cycle is brought to a dramatic conclusion with that group of extraordinary chants such as *Sanctificavit moyses* and *Vir erat*.

The second reason is the enormity of the task of maintaining the Mass Proper once completed. We have seen numerous indications that, while by and large successfully accomplished, the task strained the common musical memory of the Roman singers almost to the breaking point. The fragility of musical transmission to the Franks, for example, of certain portions of the repertory such as the Lenten and Paschaltime offertories could very likely be as much a matter of melodic instability on the Roman side as of too much music to be absorbed on the Frankish side. Thus there was work enough in maintaining what they had accomplished without adding to it.

A final reason involves the Office; circumstances suggest that the schola might have become engaged in work on the Office in the earlier decades of the eighth century. We are accustomed to think in stark categories about the musical and institutional distinctions of early medieval Rome: the schola worked exclusively out of its Lateran residence and was responsible only for the papal stational Mass, while the monastic cadres attached to the city's basilicas were solely responsible for the Office. But these distinctions would eventually be obliterated—as basilican monks became secular canons like their counterparts at the Lateran, and churches such as Santa Cecilia in Trastevere (Bodmer 74) would sing the same chant that was sung at St. Peter's (Vat lat 5319)—and there are signs of them becoming blurred at a considerably earlier date. We observe already in the Advent Project that Office responsories were adopted for service as communions, and communions, in turn, as responsories. Pope Gregory III (731–41) rebuilt a monastery, which had long been abandoned, adjacent to the Lateran basilica and "established an abbot and congregation of monks there to perform the holy offices of divine praise . . . as ordained for day and night, according to the model of the services of Blessed Peter the Apostle."[6] The possibility of substantial interaction by schola and basilican monks is suggested by this passage, especially when read in conjunction with John the Deacon's claim that Gregory the Great had established residences for the schola, "one near the steps of the basilica of St. Peter the Apostle, and another near the lodgings of the Lateran palace . . . for the sake of the daily convenience of the ministry at both places."[7] John, of course, writing in about 880, is guilty of anachronism in attributing these foundations to Gregory I, but they must have existed for a considerable period before John's time in order to have acquired a reputation for antiquity in his. There may be no concrete evidence that the schola became involved in work on the Office during the first half of the eighth century, but at the very least the physical contiguity between monks and schola at St. Peter's and the Lateran is suggestive of musical cooperation between the different groups.

The invocation of the Office here serves as a reminder of one of the most basic truths of the Roman Mass Proper. The Roman Office represents a more typical mode of liturgical development than does the Mass Proper. This development was at first far in advance of the sung Mass, but it was never completed in the same way. We read Helisachar's complaint that the books of the Office which he gathered on Frankish soil (unlike those of the Mass) were manifestly lacking in uniformity, and we observe the same ourselves when studying the Office manuscripts of succeeding centuries. This is true even of the Roman Office antiphoners, with their numerous discrepancies of repertory and assignment. Today most chant scholars do not share Helisachar's hankering after uniformity; indeed they tend to revel in the differences among the many local Office traditions, not to speak of the marvelously rich diversity of trope and sequence repertories as well as regional alleluia production. I have no brief for liturgical and musical uniformity myself; I simply report the unique phenomenon of the Roman Mass Proper's creation as something undertaken with set purpose and brought to closure within a limited span of time. But if I have no brief for such activities, neither am I inclined to apologize for this particular one; it was an enterprise of daunting proportions, accomplished with both profound dedication and consummate artistry. It is one of the outstanding legacies of medieval civilization.

Epilogue
The Central Question of Gregorian Chant

What is one to make of the difference between the extant Roman and Frankish versions of the chant? They share virtually identical texts and liturgical assignments, but while their melodies are in most cases undeniably related, they manifest substantially different stylistic traits. Several decades ago, when this question first became the subject of serious debate, a number of scholars settled on the theory that there were two distinct chant dialects existing contemporaneously in the city of Rome. The most representative variant of this theory, shared by no less than Bruno Stäblein and Stephen van Dijk,[1] held that the extant Roman version (commonly called Old Roman chant) was the original Roman chant, sung in the basilicas of the city from the time of Gregory I (590–604), until finally notated toward the end of the eleventh century. The version that we call Gregorian chant was developed by the schola cantorum under Pope Vitalian (657–72). It was conceived as a style of ecclesiastical chant worthy of the prestige of the papacy during the period when it increasingly asserted itself against Byzantium; it was to be a chant of universal musical appeal as opposed to the parochial urban chant. And it was, of course, the chant that Pope Stephen's singers conveyed to the Carolingian realm, where it was notated around 900 in the familiar Gregorian version. The unspoken assumption about both versions is that they remained melodically intact through their period of oral transmission, the Roman for more than four centuries, the Gregorian for some two and a half.

Present-day scholars retain great respect for figures like Stäblein and van Dijk, but they are virtually unanimous, after sharing the benefit of long reflection on the question at hand, that any sort of "two-chant" theory is utterly implausible for numerous reasons. There is first and foremost the overall improbability of co-religionists within the same city singing, without aid of notation, two sharply contrasting musical settings of a Mass

Proper consisting in several hundred chants with identical texts.[2] Try to imagine the schola visiting a church on several stational dates each year and singing the Gregorian versions, while on the very day after such visits the local cantors would sing the Roman versions. And how is it that each of the thirty or so stational churches could manage to reproduce the same Roman version note for note, again, without the aid of musical notation? It is possible to go on multiplying such improbabilities or, indeed, absurdities: to mention just one more, the apparent disappearance of the Gregorian version from Rome after the schola transmitted it to the north—did the schola lose it somewhere up north after teaching it to the Franks?

It is not surprising, then, that chant scholars have come to accept the general framework proposed by Helmut Hucke as a young man during the very period that two-chant theories were in vogue. He maintained, with obvious good sense, that there was only one original Roman chant and that this body of music underwent certain changes, both in the course of its assimilation by the Franks and at home in Rome during its long period of oral transmission.[3] The central question of Gregorian chant, then, involves the attempt to assess precisely what these changes within the two versions might have been, or, to put it in the terms I prefer, to determine which of the extant versions is closer to the Roman original.

I will offer my thoughts on that presently, but first there is a question to be answered about Roman chant in the seventh century, one that was in fact addressed by the advocates of two-chant theories, but has not as yet been addressed by the proponents of the presently maintained majority view. What did the urban churches sing during the period in which the schola cantorum was developing the Mass Proper? The former scholars, recognizing certain differences between urban and papal liturgies in the earlier seventh century, concluded that the urban singers had their own body of chant, a view just now found untenable. In the present volume I have attempted to portray how enormous a task it was for the schola to produce an ideal Mass Proper, one nearly as exacting in its textual aspects as its musical. I, for one, cannot imagine that such an enterprise could have been successfully completed decades before in the urban churches with the results somehow maintained simultaneously by numerous bodies of local singers. But if this is so obviously unlikely, what was it, again, that was sung in these churches during the earlier decades of the schola's existence? We know that eventually the same chant was sung by all in Rome—the schola had residences at both the Lateran and St. Peter's, and the same chant was sung by the canons of Santa Cecilia in Trastevere and by the schola at St. Peter's.

I would imagine that the urban churches continued to sing throughout much of the seventh century as they had for centuries; that is, they performed the same sort of antiphonal and responsorial psalmody that the papal entourage itself had sung before the establishment of the schola, in a word, "lector" rather than "schola" chant. This kind of singing might have differed considerably from church to church depending upon the abilities of the lower clergy assigned to cantorial duties, and it might just as well have shared a goodly measure of pan-Roman melodic substance—popular antiphons, for example, traditional responses and related psalmic formulas. But essentially it would have remained lector chant until the circumstances prevailed whereby the new schola chant could spread to the various churches. Joseph Dyer has furnished the key to how this might have come about with his observation that many, perhaps most, graduates of the schola did not go on to high ecclesiastical office, as did the future Sergius I, but rather went to serve as singers in the urban churches.[4] They would thus have been well placed to teach the new chants to their colleagues in these establishments. There is here, incidentally, an interesting analogy between this transmission of the Roman chant to the churches of the city and its transmission to the various ecclesiastical centers of the Carolingian realm. But surely it was a considerably easier task in Rome as former schola members took up permanent residence in the urban churches and enjoyed, moreover, the benefit of periodic visits from the schola on stational dates.

To turn now to direct consideration of the central question, all my prejudices incline me toward looking upon the Frankish or Gregorian version as closer to the Roman original than the extant Roman version. Since taking up the study of Roman chant about a decade ago, I have come to admire the achievement of the schola cantorum in composing the Mass Proper and to think that the admirable musicians of that organization must surely have played an essential part in creating the sublime melodic ductus of the Gregorian version. The Franks no doubt had a hand in this, but certainly, it seemed to me, they could not have made fundamental changes in the style of the chant. Two findings of chronological import contributed to my beliefs. There was, for one, my own position on the period in which the Roman Mass Proper was completed. At the time of my 1992 article on the communion I believed it to be as late as the earlier eighth century, and even if I have now adjusted the date forward by a generation or so, this, too, is a time considerably later than once thought to be the case by most scholars. And then there was the publication in 1987 of David Hughes's work, which convinced me that the Gregorian versions of about 900 revealed the chant as it existed in Charlemagne's time, this, whether or not aided by notation, as Kenneth Levy has so forcefully argued.[5] Thus there was a chronological gap of less than a century between the Roman creation of the chant and its permanent fixation by the Franks, whereas there was a gap of some four centuries before the Roman versions were so stabilized. There existed, to be sure, the potential for disjunction in transmitting the chant from the Roman to the Frankish cantors, but there were opportunities of the same sort in the troubled history of Rome during the ninth, tenth and eleventh centuries.

Thus my prejudices. But prejudice is not the same thing as evidence, and it must be asked if there is, in fact, enough of the latter historiographic coin to arrive at conclusions of any degree of persuasiveness on the matter at hand.

THE TRANSMISSION OF MODEL MELODIES

Edward Nowacki can be credited with a powerful argument for Frankish fidelity to the original Roman chant in at least one area of the repertory, Office antiphons with model melodies.[6] The argument, while confined to Office antiphons, is not, as will be seen presently, without application to the Mass Proper.

There are many more antiphons with model melodies in the extant Roman antiphoners than in their Gregorian counterparts; that is to say, there are numerous instances where a particular antiphon text will appear at its Roman liturgical assignment with a model melody, while its Gregorian counterpart will have a unique melody. The question is, then, did the Romans, in the course of time, substitute model melodies for the original unique melodies, or did the Franks take it upon themselves to create new melodies in place of the Roman types? Nowacki presents three cases where clusters of model melodies appearing at certain junctures in the Roman liturgical year are matched mostly by unique melodies in the Gregorian sources and maintains with considerable persuasiveness that the change must have taken place in Rome itself. The fundamental argument is that it seems unlikely that the Franks, struggling to assimilate the vast Roman repertory, would have passed up the opportunity to ease their task by accepting the model melodies as they were, rather than increasing their burden by devising numerous new melodies. The Roman penchant, therefore, for model melodies must be a manifestation of the principle of "thrift," which frequently characterizes musical repertories subject to long periods of oral transmission.

I greatly simplify Nowacki's more nuanced presentation and will add just one additional point that he makes. The melodic correspondence between the Roman and Gregorian sources is much higher for Roman antiphons with unique melodies than for those with model melodies. This shows the Franks succeeding in the more difficult task of assimilating numerous divergent melodies, but supposedly failing in the easier one of assimilating the model melodies. This seems unlikely enough for the reasons just given.

What bearing does this example of Office antiphons have on chants of the Mass Proper? It has both a direct and an indirect application. As for the former, the very same phenomenon can be observed in the Mass Proper, even if to a lesser extent. There are at least two places in the extant Roman Mass Proper where chants with highly formulaic melodies (if not precisely model melodies) would seem to have replaced ones that were originally unique. The two were discussed above in the respective chapters dealing with the genres in question: the post-Pentecostal graduals and the Paschaltime introits. There are three post-Pentecostal graduals—*Ego dixi domine, Liberasti nos* and *Benedicam dominum*—that are particularly stereotyped examples of the Roman A-2 type but have totally unrelated melodies in the Gregorian versions.[7] One applies precisely the same argument here as in the case of Office antiphons: there was no reason for the Frankish cantors to pass up the opportunity to match the Roman type at this juncture of their labors, when they had consistently done so before in the earlier portions of the church year. As for the Paschaltime introits (a group of several highly formulaic temporal and sanctoral E-final chants, appearing in sequence in the Roman graduals but not matched in the Gregorian sources), I argued at some length that this was an instance of expediency, haste or economy on the part of the later Roman singers rather than creative excess on the part of the Franks.

Indirectly, the example of the Office antiphons—by showing a particular instance of "thrift" in Roman chant—leads us to suspect that this might be a general tendency in Roman chant. That is to say, that the overall greater individuality that one observes in Gregorian melodies might very well reflect a corresponding individuality in the Roman melodies at the time of the transmission, and that the general stylistic homogeneity of the extant Roman melodies might reflect a blurring of distinctions from melody to melody in the course of centuries of oral transmission. I must, however, repeat what I said above in expressing my skepticism about the notion of incremental evolutionary change in any melodic style: I favor the view that when substantial melodic change takes place in a body of liturgical chant over time, it is more likely to be a matter of disruption than gradual change. Just as some degree of change was all but inevitable in the disruption of transmitting the Roman chant to Francia, there was certainly the possibility of seriously disruptive events in the history of early medieval Rome as well. One can well imagine, for example, a period when the schola was silenced by warlike conditions in the city and forced subsequently to attempt a restoration of its imperfectly remembered chant.

The example, in any event, of unmatched model melodies, while by no means insignificant, is still somewhat peripheral to the central question, which is more a matter of the fundamentally differing styles of the two versions. I have just now said, without amplification, that Gregorian melodies are more "individual" in character and Roman more homogeneous and claimed further that the "thrift" manifested in the penchant of Roman chant for model melodies suggests that the same thrift plays a part in the homogeneity of the Roman style. But this hardly addresses the central question with the required directness. First we must reflect further on the nature of the stylistic difference between the two versions and then ask if there is any evidence that points to the one or the other being closer to the Roman original.

GREGORIAN AND ROMAN STYLES DEFINED

The claimed "individuality" of the Gregorian melodies can serve as a starting point. We may take this trait as a given since chant scholars tend not to dispute it, even if they describe it in different terms and derive from it different historical ramifications. Thomas Connolly, for example, emphasizes the less formulaic nature of Gregorian chant as opposed to the Roman.[8] Having in mind the psalmic origins of chant, and the indisputably formulaic character of psalmody, he concludes that the more formulaic Roman chant must be closer to the original chant than the less formulaic Gregorian. Robert Snow sees the Roman chant as "monotonous" and "verbose" and the Gregorian as "precise and definitive," interpreting this as an indication of the former's greater antiquity. To quote him more fully: "Its [the Roman chant's] formulae are less well balanced than those of the Gregorian and are often monotonous as a result of the use of an almost continual stepwise motion . . . [and] are more verbose, as it were, and frequently lack the precise and definitive character of those of the Gregorian tradition. In comparison with Gregorian chant, the Old-Roman clearly gives the impression of being an earlier, tentative version of the same body of traditional liturgical chant."[9]

Richard Crocker says of *In splendoribus,* the communion for the first Mass of Christmas, that it "is a compact, intense expression of a tonal plan from Office antiphons. . . . The Urban-Roman version uses the same plan but overlays it with a fuller, redundant kind of ornament characterized by turning figures (a-b-a) combined with descending scalar figures; all of this is typical not just of Urban-Roman Communions but of the whole Mass repertory, when compared with the Gregorian."[10] Helmut Hucke, finally, sees the essential stylistic difference between the two versions as follows: "generally," he says, "the melodic line in the Old Roman tradition is less purposeful . . . than in Gregorian chant," and again, "it is the continuation of the melodic flow that is apparent rather than the melodic structure."[11]

There is a commonality of aesthetic reaction and stylistic observation in all of these remarks. Old Roman chant, while not explicitly denigrated by any of these scholars, is described as having an overlay of formula and consistently stepwise ornament that is "monotonous," "verbose," "redundant" and "less purposeful" than Gregorian melody, which is more "compact," more "definitive," more "purposeful" and, to expand upon that last word, more characterized by the "intense expression of a tonal plan."

It is this last feature of the Gregorian style that I find to be the central one, that is, its purposeful tonal plan—in a word, and a very dangerous one, its "tonality." It, I believe, principally accounts for our aesthetic affinity with Gregorian chant. We are conditioned by western music of the eighteenth and nineteenth centuries, with its extreme manner of tonal focus, to look for this trait in all music, and perhaps we sense the tonality of Gregorian chant to be somewhat more "purposeful" than as felt by singers in the early Middle Ages, but the quality is surely there in comparison with Roman chant. It is not present equally in all Gregorian chants, and for this reason, I think, we instinctively favor some chants over others. I first observed this when I directed a choir of boys and men at a church in New York City. The men met on Thursday evenings; they were a group of about a dozen fine singers, a few professional but most amateur, all with some experience in singing Gregorian chant. We began our session by rehearsing the introit for the following Sunday, a chant that we continued to sing in Latin even after Vatican Council II (the period in question is 1957–66). When the first reading of the introit was concluded, one or the other singer might remark, "Now that's a good one," or something to that effect. The favorable response was generally elicited by chants with a particularly strong tonal plan. Such chants "clicked" on first reading. They had structure, purpose, gestalt; they were "tunes" you might find yourself humming the next day. Yes they were "individual," but their melodic variety was sustained by something more than a unique succession of pitches.

That something—that purposefulness—is a kind of tonality. Now the last thing I wish to do here is to speak of proto-dominant and tonic, or incipient major and minor or anything of that anachronistic sort. I wish simply to note certain musical qualities we frequently sense in the Gregorian versions to a much greater degree than in the Roman.

To begin with, while it is true that Gregorian finals (with the possible exception of F, as we shall see) do not generally function as tonics, that is, as "key tones" to which all others in a scale gravitate, there is, nevertheless, a kind of tonic in Gregorian chant. There are in fact two of them, not the tonics of individual chants, but two pitches that persist throughout the entire repertory independent of the four finals. They are the notes F and c above it, existing in the manner of two tonal horizons, the lower one frequently stronger and more marked, the upper existing as a goal to be reached upon occasion, subsequently to be departed from as the melody settles back to the fundamental area of the F.

There is, I believe, strikingly concrete evidence confirming our musical sense of these two pitches. Look at a manuscript of the eleventh-century "Guidonian" type with its bold red line extending across the page at each F, a firmly drawn "horizon," and note further the somewhat lighter green or yellow line of the c's. We have, moreover, theoretical confirmation of this visual image in the choice of the only two notes that are favored with clefs in the Gregorian system, F and c. But even more telling is the observation of David Hughes, that in the entire vast Gregorian repertory, these two pitches alone are singled out as the carriers of the repeated note neumes, the bistropha and tristropha.[12]

But if we refer to these two notes as tonics, they are not such in the sense of finals (except sometimes in chants of mode-5 and mode-6). They are rather the ever-present framing notes of a tonal grid upon which are placed the essential tonal elements of the system, tonal clusters more often than individual notes. The most frequently encountered of these clusters, or pitch sets, is the one anchored in the interval *re-fa* or D-F, given here in example 16. It extends downward to C to make up the most fundamental of all tetrachords in musical systems the world over, one used by two- and three-year-old children in their playtime chants. It is frequently extended, moreover, to the major third above. The first phrase of the communion *Qui manducat* (example 17) is an obvious example of this tonal grouping. (*Qui manducat* is, by the way, a mode-6 chant, and as such one in the hearing of which we might be forgiven for sensing the final F as a tonic in the modern sense.) But this consideration should not distract us from the more basic one of the cluster as a functioning tonal unit, and the primacy of the *re-fa* interval in the group. Take the first two phrases of the brief mode-2 introit *Dominus*

Example 16. *Re-fa* pitch sets

Example 17. Communion *Qui manducat*

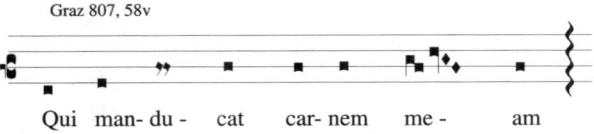

Example 18. Introit *Dominus dixit*

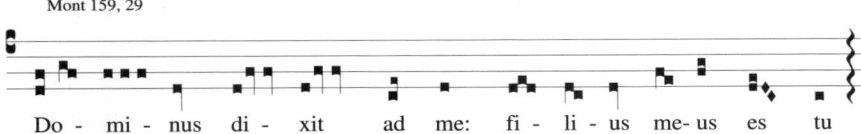

Example 19. Communion *In splendoribus*

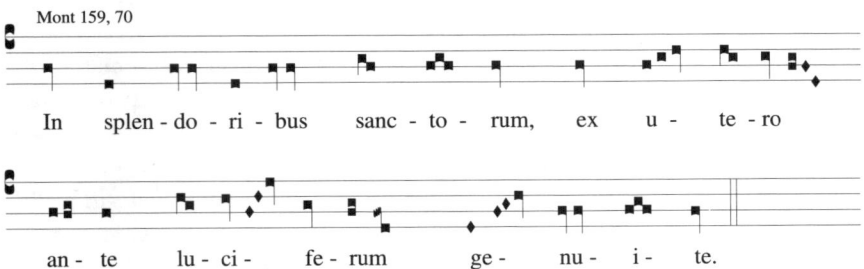

dixit (example 18), where the upper extension is touched upon only once with a sort of neighboring G, while the fundamental *re-fa* brings the C below into strong play, particularly at the end of the second phrase (*es tu*), where the note, given this emphatic placement, cries out for resolution.

I think it fair to say that these two communions, while using the *re-fa* interval as a kind of tonal center, give themselves away as F-final and D-final chants respectively well before their endings. But take the first two phrases of the communion *In splendoribus* (example 19); while in fact an F-final chant, equally plausible final cadences could be fashioned for it on either D or F. Indeed it is a well-known phenomenon that many chants (the introit

Example 20. *La-ut* pitch sets

Misericordia, for example), which spend much of their existence in this same tonal sphere, surprise one with a sudden move to E-final at their close.

Rivaling the *re-fa* pitch set in importance is the analogous one centered above on *la-ut* or a-c. It can be given in the same abstract form as its lower counterpart (example 20), but it functions differently in different types of chants. In D- and E-final chants it serves as an upper region to be explored briefly, creating a sense of elevation and tension that gives the return to the *re-fa* region a feeling of satisfactory release. This is well illustrated in *In splendoribus*. The phrase *ante luciferum* is masterful, taxiing, so to speak, before takeoff on *ante*, gathering propulsive tension on the a-G-a of *luci-* and flinging itself aloft on the F-a-c, to settle back to *re-fa* at the end of the phrase (using, incidentally, the identical figure that brought the previous phrase to a close). I will not continue with my inadequate attempt to express in words what one experiences in the singing of this petite masterpiece. It can be sung hundreds of times and continue to satisfy, and surely its ultimate rightness has much to do with its structure, that is, its perfectly balanced play of tonally contrasting units. It is not, however, just a matter of formula. One can say precisely the same things about the structure of the equally beautiful *Qui manducat*, but each chant, while following a similar plan, has an altogether individual melody of which every note counts.

Before returning to *Qui manducat*, a further word about the *la-ut* pitch set. *In splendoribus* utilized the a-c nucleus of the set to good advantage but did not move up into the c-d-e extension. This limitation is typical of chants that dwell principally in the *re-fa* region, but there are a comparable number of Gregorian chants that exist primarily in the upper *la-ut* area: most mode-3, mode-7 and mode-8 chants, and many in mode-5. These will utilize the c-d-e extension in the same manner that the chants we have been examining (D- and F-final pieces) utilize the F-G-a one. Indeed, they will sometimes reach up to f, and they might even employ the occasional bistropha or tristropha neume on this note. But I am beginning to venture here into a book-length subject; I can make no pretense at comprehensives and will complete my exemplification of Gregorian tonality by retreating to our engaging brief chants that find their home in the *re-fa* area.

Example 21. Mode-5 pitch clusters

Example 22. Communion *Ultimo festivitatis*

Qui in me cre - dunt

Qui manducat is, as stated above, very similar in tonal plan to its somewhat briefer cousin *In splendoribus,* with its initial establishment of the *re-fa* set, its intensifying movement to the *la-ut* group, and its subsequent return to *re-fa.* It ends quite differently, however. For one thing it prepares the final phrase by cadencing on G, thus creating a strong need for resolution, but the point I wish to make here is the melodic variety introduced by the final phrase, *dicit dominus,* with its b-flat and movement downward from that note to the final F. There is a tonal region employed here that is entirely absent from *In splendoribus.* As lovely as that piece is, its restrictive tonality would not suffice for an entire repertory: *varietas* is required.

In this case *varietas* is furnished by what might be construed as a borrowing of tonal material encountered regularly in mode-5. Mode-5 chants are characterized by particularly complex material, merely suggested in example 21 by four of the more typical pitch clusters (the one involving *Qui manducat* is the last of the four, introducing the b-flat). To dwell for the moment on the general character of mode-5 tonality, the anomalous nature of the pitch F (and f) serves as a salutary reminder of the difference between a tonic and a functioning Gregorian final. The lengthy communion *Ultimo festivitatis,* for example, has not a single F until the final cadence before the concluding alleluias. More characteristic of the piece is melodic material such as that setting the words *qui in me credunt* (example 22), which would be typical of a mode-7 chant. The final alleluias (example 23), however, have what one is accustomed to think of as mode-5 material in its familiar form. It would be dogmatic to insist that the final phrase of *Qui manducat* (example 24) borrows this material from mode-5. The point is that whatever the relationship with this mode-5 material, the last phrase of *Qui manducat* introduces distinctive tonal color, absent in the chant up to that

Example 23. Communion *Ultimo festivitatis*

Example 24. Communion *Qui manducat*

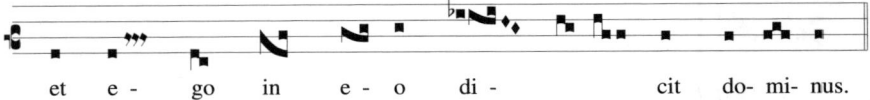

point, and entirely absent from *In splendoribus*. The melodic individuality of the melisma on the word *dicit*, by the way, deserves mention. There is no redundancy or verbosity here; every note is exquisitely tailored to produce a melodic gesture of rare beauty.

ECCE VIRGO CONCIPIET

The incomparable *Ecce virgo concipiet* (example 25) can serve as a final example of a brief chant anchored in the *re-fa* cluster.[13] It has a melody altogether more complex than that of *In splendoribus* and *Qui manducat* and boasts a particularly rich mixture of tonal contrasts. The opening words, *Ecce virgo*, are set to a brief evocation of the *re-fa* motif; seemingly simple, it is nonetheless unique and memorable. It is immediately balanced by a second phrase, *concipiet*, which comes to rest on D (with a three-note neume E-F-D that mirrors the three-note D-F-E at the beginning of the chant). What is most noteworthy about the second phrase is its opening C-E-G-a on the syllables *conci-*. This is made up of different tonal material from the *re-fa* set; the singer experiences it as a tonally foreign area requiring resolution back to the familiar *re-fa* material. Through the years I have noticed that students experience difficulty in sight-singing the interval E-g in chants of mode-1 and mode-2, and I am reminded of the observation of Alejandro Planchart that the G in the mode-2 gradual *Haec dies* is a "dissonance."[14] One further notes that as the chant makes its move up to the *la-ut* region, a gesture familiar to us now from its use in *Qui manducat* and *In splendoribus*, it does so the hard way, using the interval E-G.

What follows prevents *Ecce virgo* still more sharply from being a tonally homogeneous exemplar of the *re-fa* type. The pitch set G-a-b-flat in the

Example 25. Communion *Ecce virgo concipiet*

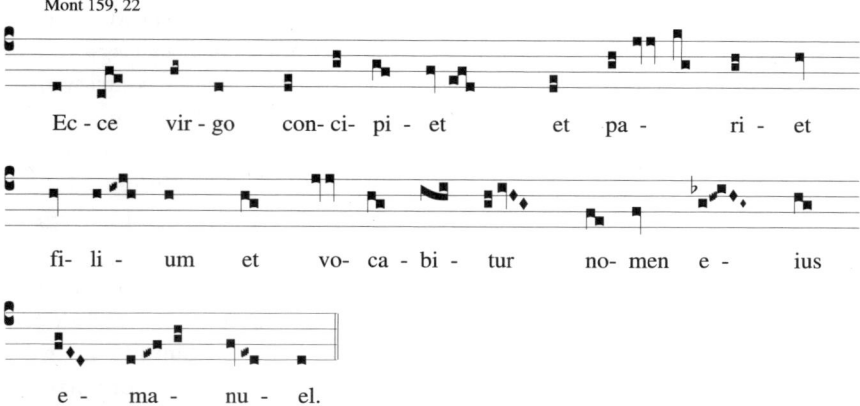

Example 26. Communion *Scapulis suis*

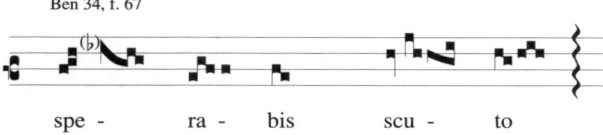

second half of the two phrases *et vocabitur* and *nomen ejus* takes us into a sweetly piquant tonal sphere that bridges the *la-ut* area with the concluding cadence on D. Defining the area is not easy. It reminds one of material frequently encountered in mode-3 and mode-4 chants, that can be exemplified by the passage in the mode-3 communion *Scapulis suis*, at the words *sperabis scuto* (example 26). I am not claiming that the two kinds of material are identical, or that we have here a "modulation" from the protus to the deuterus. This would be to indulge in the sort of reification I wish most studiously to avoid. But neither do I wish to underestimate what is taking place in *Ecce virgo concipiet*. We have a sense of the tonally "other" in the passage *et vocabitur nomen ejus* and a sense of return with the closing phrase, *Emanuel;* and that "other" is undeniably closer to typical deuterus material than to protus material.

And it is this sort of "tonality" that I claim to be the chief defining trait of Gregorian chant. It is not a tonality of tonal centers, nor a tonality of four finals and four tenors or reciting tones. Individual tones play a part in it, especially the dual horizons of F and c, but these pervade the whole system more than they function as finals and tenors in specific modes. The tonality, rather, is more one of tonal clusters, a term perhaps preferable to pitch sets, which might connote too strict a definition of the notes involved. These clusters are marked out within an individual piece by a careful crafting of melodic gestures, as in the two opening phrases of *Ecce virgo concipiet;* but just as important, they are defined also by the tonal contrast afforded by the use of different tonal groupings. Thus the "dissonance" of the E-G interval heightens the sense of a goal achieved both in the *Ecce virgo concipiet* passage and in its upper counterpart *et pariet filium,* and the tonal coloring of *et vocabitur nomen eius* provides an episode of *varietas* before the final reassuring cadence on *Emanuel.*

Ecce virgo concipiet is an extraordinarily lovely piece. It is, one recalls, the chant that elicited the enthusiastic response from a graduate student when tapped out on the piano during a seminar. I am not claiming, in any case, that the tonal play in it is what makes it so beautiful, any more than I would claim that the tonic-dominant formulation of a Mozart melody, nor even its chromatic piquancy, is what makes it beautiful. Nor is it the structure of *Ecce virgo*, its careful balance of contrasting phrases, that achieves such a result, any more than the period form of a Mozart theme does so. There is something far more complex and indefinable that goes into choosing from the myriad possibilities that create a memorable tune. What I am trying to define is a style, musical prerequisites that if once removed render impossible the melodic achievement that we observe in these chants.

These stylistic qualities are absent from the Roman version of *Ecce virgo* (example 27). There is the most patent melodic relationship between the two versions. Still, the strongly felt tonal areas of the Gregorian one, with its carefully sculptured melodic segments, in which each note counts, whether occurring in syllabic or neumatic passages—all this is obscured in the Roman version by its continuous, virtually minimalist, figuration. My point is not that the Roman lacks positive musical qualities of its own. Sensitively sung, with a fine ensemble, in one of the exquisite Roman collegiate churches of the eleventh and twelfth centuries such as San Clemente or Santa Maria in Cosmedin, it would no doubt have created its own aura of ghostly beauty. But this is not the same thing as the timeless miracle of the Gregorian *Ecce virgo*. Many of the particular characteristics that my New York choir, my graduate students, myself and (I trust) most chant scholars would judge to be good traits are absent from the Roman *Ecce virgo*. And it is these very qualities that define the Gregorian versus the Roman style.

The central question can therefore be stated as follows: are these qualities that were added by the Franks or ones that were lost by the Romans? I have already stated my prejudices in the matter—that much was in fact

Example 27. Communion *Ecce virgo concipiet*

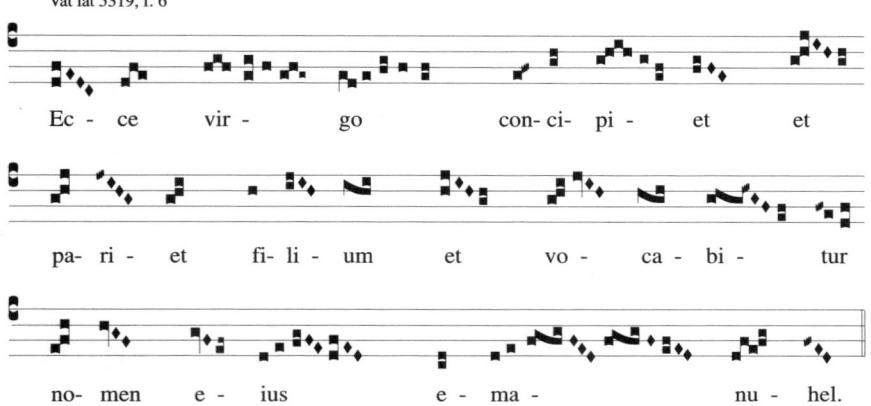

forgotten by the Romans—and have also outlined the argument for this position from the admittedly limited area of model melodies. Is there also a case to make for it by a direct consideration of the essential stylistic differences between the two versions?

THE ARGUMENT FROM STYLE

If there is such an argument, it must go more or less as follows. The Roman and Gregorian versions of certain melodies are not just related but virtually identical. We can assume, then, that this is their original state. Now it happens that such melodies conform more to Gregorian than to Roman style, and that therefore the Gregorian style must be closer to the original Roman than is the style of the extant Roman versions.

But are there such chants? There are at least some. Compare, for example, the alleluia sung at the Easter vigil in the two versions (example 28). They are almost identical; the Roman could be said to be the same as the Gregorian with but one small decorative element added at each of the three places at which the melody has an ascending gesture. At the first such place it fills in the descending third, and at the second and third places it does the same, but in such a way that it manages to incorporate a brief oscillating figure. These figures are typically Roman melodic events, perhaps the single most characteristic feature of the Roman style. Here, however, they are employed with great restraint, requiring only a few notes more than the Gregorian version. The overall impression of the Roman version is that it is closer to Gregorian than to Roman style, allowing one to argue that the

Example 28. *Alleluia; Confitemini domino quoniam bonus*

Example 29. Communion *Pater si non potest*

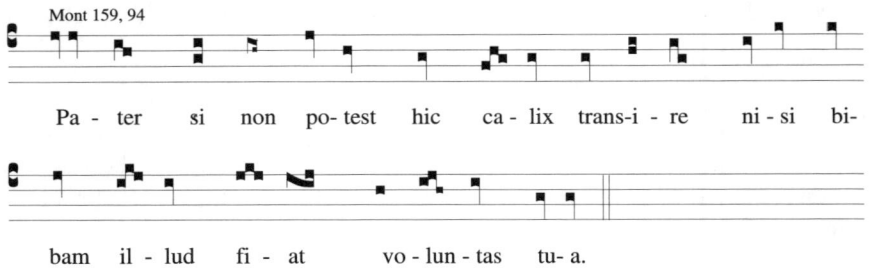

chant was a very spare one originally, one that the Romans allowed to remain close to its original state because of the great respect they had for its privileged place in the ancient rites of the Easter vigil.

More interesting perhaps is *Pater si non potest,* the communion for Palm Sunday. If one compares only the communion in its Gregorian and Roman versions, there is nothing new to be learned (examples 29 and 30). The two, while clearly related, retain their typical styles, so that we are left with the perennial question of whether the Franks "streamlined" the original Roman or the Romans rendered it more florid in the course of time. A Roman Magnificat antiphon on the same text, however, adds an entirely new dimension to the question (example 31). It is melodically related to both versions of the communion (departing substantially from them only in its middle portion, at the words *hic calix transire,* where it moves in a lower tessitura than the two communions). It is the melodic relationship with the Gregorian communion, however, that is at issue here, and one must conclude from it an original identity of Roman Magnificat antiphon and Gregorian communion. Now it happens that the style of the Roman antiphon is clearly closer to what is typically Gregorian than Roman; indeed one is hard put to find any slightest detail of the antiphon (such as is found in the

Example 30. Communion *Pater si non potest*

Example 31. Magnificat antiphon *Pater si non potest*

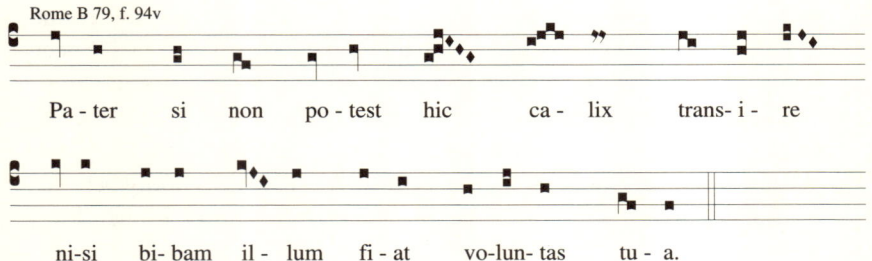

alleluia just discussed) that distinguishes it from a Gregorian chant. There are, moreover, places of near melodic identity between the Roman antiphon and the Gregorian communion; note, for example, the two settings of *fiat voluntas tua*.

There is a case to be made here, then, that the Roman antiphon and the Gregorian communion represent a style closer to the original Roman style and, moreover, that they allow us to come very close (at least for about two-thirds of its extent) to the original seventh-century melodic substance of the Roman communion *Pater si non potest*.

Can the argument be extended beyond this one chant? It can be if we continue to focus for the moment on chants in the style of the Roman Office antiphons. Nowacki has transcribed all the Roman antiphons, well over a thousand of them, and one can see at a glance that they employ a generally syllabic style, laced with frequent neumatic and occasional melismatic passages, but seldom with the oscillating figuration that is so typical of Roman Mass chants.[15] They are much like the Gregorian communion *Pater si*, and thus much like comparable Gregorian chants. Could it be, then, that the original Roman Mass Proper as a whole was set in styles similar to the Gregorian Mass Proper, but that the Roman singers at some considerably later point in history, for reasons unknown to us, began to sing it in the ornate oscillating style?

But what of entire categories of Mass Proper chants, introits, for example, and offertories, that appear in the Roman graduals, not in an antiphon-like style, but with the more typical oscillating figuration? Could it be that the simpler, Gregorian-like manner of the extant Roman antiphons reflects a style in use by the monastic communities, while the more ornate style of the extant Roman Mass chants reflects a style developed by the early members of the schola cantorum? Let it be emphasized, by the way, that this is not a "two-chant" theory in the sense described above; there we were talking about the same texts and the same liturgical genres, but here about different texts and different genres. In any case, if there were these two different styles in existence at the time of the transmission, then the Franks would have had to choose between them for their version of the Mass Proper. They would have had to reject the figurated style of the introits and offertories and decide instead to adapt the entire repertory to a style more like that of the neumatic Roman antiphons. That such a choice was available seems most unlikely; did there really exist such a sharp dichotomy between two available styles within the seventh- and eighth-century Roman Mass Proper?

But again, are there Roman chants beyond the Easter vigil alleluia and antiphon-communions like *Pater si* that betray Gregorian-like traits? Not many, perhaps, but more than can be ignored. *Christus qui natus est* (example 32), the communion of the Roman Mass for the Dead, is a remarkable instance; it has altogether more the appearance of a Gregorian than a Roman Mass chant (and it is not an antiphon-communion). If *Christus qui* is exceptional, there are more than a few others that are comparable,[16] and also occasional brief passages that are nearly identical in the Roman and Gregorian versions, such as *nisi videret* in the communion *Responsum* (example 33). This is admittedly a minority phenomenon, but its significance is that while there is a far from negligible quantity of Gregorian-like melody in the Roman sources, there are, to my knowledge, no instances of the Roman oscillating style in the Gregorian versions. Surely if the oscillating style was typical of Roman chant at the time of the transmission, one would expect to see at least isolated traces of it in the Gregorian corpus.

Example 32. Commmunion *Christus qui natus est*

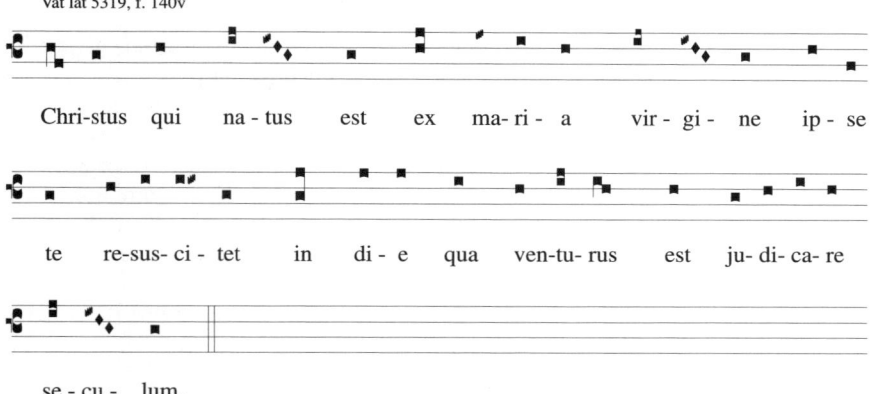

Example 33. Communion *Responsum*

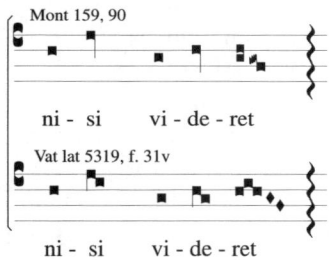

INTENTION VERSUS REALIZATION

In comparing Roman and Gregorian versions, one inevitably thinks of the Roman chant as it existed at the time of the transmission (the mid-eighth century) and the Frankish reception of it at that time. But what of the intervening period of several decades between the era of the chant's creation and its transmission? It may appear that so far in this chapter the tacit assumption has been maintained that the chant remained stable. This question was briefly addressed toward the close of the chapter on the introit. There I offered the opinion that the *intention* of the Roman singers was to create fixed and stable chants, but that whether they were able to realize this intention was open to question. A more thorough treatment of the issue is now in order.

Richard Crocker provides an imaginative recreation of Roman singers engaged in creating "pre-arranged and stabilized melodies"; it merits being quoted in full.

> I can identify three essential moments in the production of a new piece of chant, that is, a way of singing a new set of words not previously provided with a melody. First, the materials to be used were indeed generated by improvising—in private. Second, and most important, the results of improvising were scrutinized, selected, and refined; for it is surprisingly difficult to produce results that sound truly random, given the closure of the pitch set on one hand, and the needs of stylistic consistency on the other. Only some of the results of improvising are acceptable. This process leads inescapably, I feel, to the third essential moment, fixation, on the spot, of the results so achieved, so that they will not have to be re-invented next time.[17]

Crocker goes on to summarize this description by saying that the "Roman cantor pre-arranged and stabilized . . . melodies inside himself, so that he could faithfully reproduce them, then teach them to the chorus. These pre-arranged and stabilized melodies, one for each set of words, are, I believe, faithfully preserved in the written records prepared some time later."[18]

Crocker is alone both in so explicitly addressing the issue of original Roman chant creation and in coming down so forcibly on the side of chants that were fixed from the beginning. Most scholars who were involved in the celebrated debate over oral transmission, even those who took issue with the Treitler-Hucke position of year-to-year reconstruction,[19] were willing to concede that the chant was melodically unstable before its Carolingian fixation. No less than David Hughes writes, "Since the evidence shows the chant to have been fixed well before the conventionally accepted time for the origin of notation—at least by the time of the Carolingian diffusion—the improvisational era must have antedated that. In that earlier time, it is easy and attractive to imagine that the chant repertoire—or perhaps repertoires—was still in a fluid state, improvised at least in part, no doubt in ways similar to those described by Professors Treitler and Hucke."[20]

I agree with both Crocker and Hughes; that is, I agree that Roman cantors intended to create stable chants and I agree also that there was, at one time, a Roman "improvisational era." It is a matter of chronology and, more than that, a matter of different categories of chant. Let me attempt to express a number of distinctions. For one I would place "the improvisational era" before the Advent Project, indeed, before the establishment of the schola cantorum. To employ, again, the terms of this study, I would place it in the period of lector chant as opposed to schola chant. Thus the adolescent lector of Augustine's church might sing one or more locally known psalm tones in his own individual manner, and a Roman deacon at the time of Gregory I might do something essentially the same, even if more expertly, more elaborately, and more informed by accumulated melodic tradition. The schola, then, would fix these fluid melody types into individual chants, and—to borrow Treitler's words—"the oral origin" of such chants (formulaic graduals and tracts) would eventually be "visible through the written surfaces that are its progeny."[21]

It should be added, though, that fixed melodies as well must have existed already in the era of lector chant. One can enumerate various possibilities: tuneful congregational responses in the time of Augustine, the ancient Sanctus described by Levy,[22] the alleluia of the Easter vigil, venerable chants such as the Trisagion and Cheroubikon (even if not sung in the Roman Mass), and probably many of the Office antiphons that were frequently repeated throughout the church year. It is barely conceivable that such melodies would be remembered as structures or tonal outlines to be filled in each year with appropriate material. That is not the way a tune is remembered.

Then there is the obvious factor of choral song. It may not have been the majority mode of performance in the seventh-century Roman Mass, but it certainly formed a substantial portion of that ceremony's singing. The testimony of *Ordo romanus I* is difficult to refute: if the gradual, tract and alleluia were sung by solo cantors, the introit, offertory and communion (and *Sanctus* and *Agnus* as well) were sung by the schola. Now year-to-year reconstruction by a cantor is an entirely plausible notion, but an unlikely one for a chorus. One can only imagine it taking place in rehearsals, to be followed at the subsequent service by a literal reproduction of what had been agreed upon.

To return to the issue of intention versus realization, I continue to find it unlikely that the members of the schola did not *wish* to create fixed melodies; I can well imagine that they composed their chants in some way similar to Crocker's model. We know that the texts were fashioned as carefully crafted individual sets of words rather than casually borrowed segments of Scripture, and it seems only likely that the same attitude would have prevailed in the task of setting the texts to suitable melodies. Somehow the notion of planning a year-to-year reconstruction of the melodies according to a set of consciously adopted rules and procedures strikes me as foreign to the thinking of early medieval clerics. And my thoughts on the matter aside, there is the evidence of the extant melodies. Take Roman introits, for example, where no matter how one interprets the formulaicism of a minority of the Roman repertory, there remains a large majority of individual melodies. I do not know how one can reconcile that result with an original intention to re-create introits each year as melody types. Altogether more plausible is the idea expressed above of a repertory of 145 original introits with individual melodies, into which a certain measure of formulaicism, the working of "thrift," was introduced at Rome in the course of the centuries.

We have, of course, no documentary evidence of the intentions of seventh- and eighth-century Roman singers, but we have a wealth of such evidence that the Franks strove to recapture the Roman melodies. We also have evidence that the Frankish intentions in this respect were far from perfectly realized. We have documentary evidence to that effect, for example, in the frequently quoted accounts of John the Deacon and Nokter of St. Gall, and we have seen confirming musical evidence in this volume, for example, in the poorly assimilated Lenten and Paschaltime offertories as opposed to those at the beginning and end of the church year. But if the intentions of the Franks were imperfectly realized in their efforts to reproduce the Roman melodies, their intentions to maintain their own version of these melodies, once stabilized in the later decades of the eighth century (I refer to the Hughes position), were marvelously successful.

And we wonder if the purported Roman attempt to maintain its seventh-century Mass Proper melodies intact might have anticipated to some degree this Frankish success. In each case the melodies were originally crafted with great care by a body of expert singers devoting years of full-time labor to the task. The Frankish versions, by the way, could only have been created at one place. We know that several ecclesiastical centers were active in attempting to assimilate the Roman chant, but only one version prevailed, and the evidence is overwhelming that this was the work of the schola established under Chrodegang of Metz (742–66) and fostered by his successor Angilram (768–91). There must have been musicians of great talent there to start with, and numerous circumstances conspired to make their work secure for the future. There was the general medieval penchant for memorization; there was the factor of youth (at least some of the Metz choristers would have been adolescents with their ability to absorb large quantities of music in a spontaneous, anoetic manner); there was the keen desire of the Carolingians for authenticity (Treitler makes felicitous reference to their effort at "musicology"),[23] an impulse aided by their theoretical bent, first manifested in tonaries; and finally they probably (as Crocker points out in commenting on Angilram's payments to the individual singers of certain lengthy chants) relieved much of the burden on the common memory by permanently assigning various chants, the longer tracts, for example, to particular cantors.[24]

Many of these factors were also present in the Roman schola cantorum of the later seventh century. The absent one might be the very particular Carolingian penchant for authenticity, system and theory, but surely the Roman singers were not entirely lacking in such tendencies. They were, after all, a group set apart and commissioned to create a very special body of ecclesiastical music, and more particularly they must have shared a body of music theory, even if only orally transmitted. They were full-time quasi-professional singers, some of them surely with absolute pitch; they would have been aware of a kind of tonal space made up of a succession of whole and half steps, and certainly their acquaintances among the Byzantine cantors would have told them about the four finals. And even if not so informed on this last point, they themselves would have observed that there are only four possible configurations of whole and half steps by which one approaches a final pitch. We have striking confirmation of Roman theoretical knowledge in the circumstance that the Roman manuscripts notate the A-2 graduals, just as do the Gregorian, on a, in an apparent expedient to avoid the E-flat that would result from employing the typical protus plagalis D-final. If the eleventh-century Romans notated this class of chants on a because of Gregorian influence, then how account for the numerous E-final Gregorian chants with Roman b-finals and F-final Gregorian chants with Roman c-finals? The seventh-century Roman singers would have had to be tone-deaf not to understand finals.

In summary, I will proceed in what follows with the assumption that the intention of the schola cantorum members (both during the Advent Project and immediately before it) was to create stable melodies. How much success they might have had in realizing this intention will figure to some extent in my final musings on the central question, although the basic style of the original Roman chant will be my chief concern.

THE LAST WORD: INTENTION REVISITED

I begin my final task with two disclaimers. Although I will maintain a position here roughly in keeping with my previously announced prejudices, I must admit that I do not *know* the answer to the central question. Far from it; I cannot even claim a high degree of probability for my speculations. And more specifically, I must admit that I continue to be troubled by the fact that the Roman versions fail to reproduce those brief and memorable communions of great beauty such as *In splendoribus, Qui manducat* and *Ecce virgo concipiet*.[25]

I start the positive phase of my argument with a final invocation of the claim that it was the intention of the mid-seventh-century Roman singers to create individual and fixed melodies. They approached different portions of the repertory, however, in different ways. For one thing they distinguished stylistically between the different genres of chant—introits being more neumatic, for example, and graduals interspersing a basically neumatic style with strategically placed melismas. Introits differed from graduals also in that every introit was an individual melody, whereas graduals, in continuity with their history of improvised psalmic types, retained stylized versions of their ancient melodic formulas while integrating them organically into carefully planned compositions. Model melodies were resorted to especially in the alleluia, where, in the effort to supply an adequate repertory in an expeditious fashion, three such melodies were used to supply well over half of this repertory. With communions, like introits, virtually the entire repertory consists in unique melodies, although fully a third of them are shared with Office responsories and antiphons. Offertories received an immense amount of attention from the Roman singers. They were chants of great length, amounting to a vast expanse of musical material (even if many of them are shared by different liturgical occasions). But they are usually, and I would say astonishingly, nonformulaic.

Now all of this suggests to me (particularly in view of the fact that texts were carefully crafted as unique vehicles for particular chants) that the Roman singers looked upon themselves as creating individual chants. To express it negatively, the activity in question seems to be incompatible with the notion that the singers intended to reconstruct the chants from year to year according to certain rules and conventions. How to explain the distinction between totally individual melodies, formulaic melodies and model melodies within such a scheme of things? How to explain the very existence of literally hundreds of individual melodies? How to explain the need to resort to sharing graduals and offertories and the need to borrow Office antiphons and responsories to complete the annual communion cycle? None of this would be necessary if it was only a matter of *re*-improvising chants from year to year.

If the intention, then, was to create set pieces, chants that would be repeated from year to year, how successful might the Romans have been in maintaining their Mass Proper in a melodically stable form until the time of the transmission, a time span of some fifty or sixty years? Were they able to achieve the nearly miraculous stability that the Frankish version of the chant enjoyed for the first century of its existence? Here we are reduced to little more than guessing, and I would say that it is probably too much to expect a perfect duplication of the Frankish miracle. Still, the Roman circumstances, as described above, are not all that different from the Frankish circumstances, and I would imagine a limited success, after taking into account the myriad possibilities of failure on the part of certain individuals responsible for certain portions of the repertory, and the inherent difficulty in managing vast expanses of chant such as the offertory verses.

THE LAST WORD: STYLE

And what of the crucial question, the nature of the Roman musical style? Was it more characterized by the quasi-minimalist Old Roman ornamented ductus, or was it closer to the leaner, more sharply chiseled Gregorian manner? The key point to keep in mind in responding to this question is the stylistic differentiation among the different items of the Mass Proper that exists in the Gregorian versions. This trait is much less apparent in the extant Roman versions, which tend to blur stylistic distinctions among the chant genres. Is it a Frankish innovation, then, or an original Roman trait? What was said above about the different compositional approaches taken by the seventh-century Romans to the different items of the Mass Proper would seem to suggest a concomitant stylistic differentiation, but do we have any evidence for this?

Perhaps so, especially in the graduals. In our chapter on the genre we observed that the Roman and Gregorian versions of this chant manifested striking similarities. They were "analogous" melodically; that is, each Roman formula was matched by a Gregorian formula of similar makeup. Wherever a particular Roman formula appeared in a chant, its Gregorian counterpart would appear in the same place, and wherever there was a nonformulaic passage in the Roman there would also be a nonformulaic passage in the Gregorian. The formulas, moreover, were quite similar, having the same finals, the same tessiturae, many identical pitches and the same placement of melismas. Graduals, then, in their extant Roman and Gregorian versions may be closer to each other melodically than with any other genre of the Mass Proper. What is relevant about this observation for present purposes is that they are *stylistically* quite similar: the Roman graduals are not as laden with the persistent oscillating figures that characterize the Roman style in general and hence allow for more clearly defined melodic contours and even more firmly etched tonal patterns. Such similarity speaks for similarity of the Roman versions at the time of transmission and probably similarity at the time of original composition. In a word, there is a fairly high degree of likelihood that the original Roman graduals were at least superficially similar to the extant Gregorian versions.

But what of the other genres (introits, offertories and most communions), which all share, in the extant Roman versions, a similar style, in which the ever-present figuration threatens to submerge the melodic individuality of the chants? Is this the original Roman style or a later one adopted as a kind of improvised overlay upon the earlier melodies? Or to ask the same question from the Frankish perspective, do the Gregorian versions of introits, offertories and communions by and large correspond to the mid-eighth-century Roman chants in the matter of syllabic, neumatic and melismatic textures, as do the Gregorian graduals, or do they represent melodies that substantially reduce the Roman figuration? Is this last possibility to be explained by a Frankish need to simplify the more complex Roman melodies in order to capture them in a more easily retained form?

There are a number of indications that render it more plausible that the Frankish melodies had a general overall resemblance to the mid-eighth-century Roman. The point has already been made that Gregorian and Roman graduals are substantially similar in overall style. And this should remind us that the Franks were perfectly capable of maintaining a large repertory of melismatic chants; they had no need to render elaborate Roman chants into simpler versions. It should remind us, too, that while they were perfectly capable of handling elaborate chants, there are no instances in the entire Gregorian repertory of the characteristic oscillating Roman figuration—neither in the gradual nor in the other items of the Mass Proper. Surely if this feature had been consistently present in mid-eighth-century Roman chant, there would be at least occasional examples of it in the Gregorian Mass Proper.

And conversely there are, as noted earlier in this chapter, examples in the extant Roman versions of chants that are closer to Gregorian style than what we think of as Roman. We saw exceptional examples such as the Easter vigil alleluia and the communions *Pater si* and *Christus qui* and noted cases of less consistently Gregorian-like chants as well as instances of Gregorian-like passages within otherwise typically Roman chants. While admitting this is a minority phenomenon, we noted that the opposite circumstance is never met with, that is, the presence of the Roman oscillating figuration in Gregorian versions.

A final indication speaking against the antiquity of the Roman oscillating ornamentation is the improbability that pieces in this style could retain their individuality over centuries of oral transmission. Brad Maiani, a daily singer of chant, makes the point that while it is relatively easy to memorize Gregorian chants, it is extremely difficult to memorize Roman chants.[26] One *can* memorize a Roman chant but it is a task differing in kind from memorizing a Gregorian chant; it is primarily noetic rather than anoetic memorizing. The repetitious figuration makes necessary the intellectual task of "seeing" the chant and remembering how many notes in each figure, how many whole or half-tone oscillations, in which direction the chant moves for its next flourish, and so on, whereas Gregorian chants can be memorized as tunes, with the singer being instinctively propelled from one sharply sculptured and tonally etched phrase to the next. The Gregorian memorization is not quite as unthinking a process as remembering a metrical hymn tune, but it is considerably closer to it than is trying to memorize a Roman chant.

Maiani believes that it is virtually impossible that the extant Roman melodies could have been reproduced by memory for centuries; he sees the style involved as an improvisational one and concludes that when the Roman chant was notated in the eleventh century it was a matter of capturing improvisations in writing, much as Treitler and Hucke claimed for the Gregorian. How to account, then, for the relative melodic stability of the three Roman graduals? The crucial difference between the stability of the Roman graduals and the stability of the earliest preserved notated Gregorian graduals is that the former are from the same city, whereas the Gregorian manuscripts are from different regions. That the canons of Santa Cecilia in Trastevere and their associates at St. Peter's share their written tradition is only to be expected.

One might acknowledge all this and still claim that the Roman style was always of the same general nature, that is, that precise pitches would change each year, but that the style of florid, oscillating figuration would have been maintained since the seventh century. What speaks against this is that underneath the ornamental surface of the Roman chants individual melodies are present, that is, the general contour of these melodies, along with numerous key pitches and distinctive melodic gestures. This is what strikes me as the ultimate implausibility, that the essential individuality of literally hundreds of discrete melodies would have endured for four centuries if these melodies were never free to assert themselves in easily graspable form but had always been overlaid with a style of profuse ornamentation. What is plausible is that they enjoyed much sharper melodic profiles originally but acquired the improvisational style at some period in their long history of oral transmission, perhaps as a new style adopted with set purpose during a time when it was necessary to restore the city's chant after some severe disruption in its ecclesiastical life (a thought suggested more than once in the course of this volume).

If the original Roman Mass Proper, then, was not so far removed in style from the Gregorian, what changes did the Franks introduce in their efforts to assimilate it? We know that there were changes from the frequently quoted reports of John the Deacon and Nokter Balbulus, just as we know it from the detailed reports given in previous chapters of this book on the lack of melodic continuity existing between the Roman and Frankish chants for certain portions of the liturgical year for the differing items of the Mass Proper. Here, finally, I will attempt a guess (I use the word advisedly) at what might have been the single most essential point of difference between the Frankish chants and their mid-eighth-century Roman models.

I imagine that the Roman and Frankish versions of a chant were superficially similar but that the Franks, in their efforts to absorb the Roman melodies, recognized the existing Roman tonality and brought it into sharper focus. They did so in their effort to render the melodies more memorable, more tuneful, more easily taught, and they succeeded thereby in creating a repertory of singular melodic beauty. In doing so they were aided by their overt theoretical aims and their profound desire to create something that was permanent and authentic. But such attitudes were not enough; there had to have been the fortuitous historical circumstance that musicians of genius were present. No one remotely familiar with the marvelous result can doubt this.

And these individuals, as emphasized already, needed to have worked in *one place*. It would have had to be somewhere that they could enjoy the leisure of devoting themselves tirelessly to the project for years, in an environment within which the fruits of their labor could be made to last, and at an ecclesiastical center that enjoyed sufficient prestige, by its connection to the Carolingian court, to make its version of the chant authoritative. Metz was such a center. The full story of Metz and its implications for the origins of Gregorian chant has yet to be told. The implications of the rule of Chrodegang (Pépin's cousin, one notes), and of his successor Angilram's extraordinary document listing payment for singers, have been no more than touched upon in the musicological literature. And to cite just one of many supporting evidentiary items, the remarkable story of Aldric, who left the court of Louis the Pious to live a saintly life at Metz, there to learn the "Roman chant" and eventually become "senior cantor," has, as far as I know, never even been cited.[27] There is much more of the same, detailing the history of a schola cantorum that was preeminent in the Carolingian realm for generations.

I offer, then, as a final claim that two cities and two scholas can take credit for the creation of the Gregorian Mass Proper. There was Rome and its schola, which performed the first miracle, the fundamental one of creating the Mass Proper in its original guise, with its marvelous set of texts for the temporal and sanctoral cycles, and its melodies that we can dimly discern in their Frankish manifestation. And there was Metz with its schola, which adjusted the Roman melodies into the form that we know and love, creating that marvelously balanced tonal interplay between subtly contrasting pitch clusters, working the magic of *varietas* within the space defined by the twin horizons of F and c.

Notes

Works often cited (q.v. inf.: ch., n.) have been identified by the following abbreviations:

Andrieu	Andrieu, ed., *Les ordines romani du haut moyen âge* (ch. 4, n. 32)
Apel	Apel, *Gregorian Chant* (ch. 5, n. 1)
CCL	*Corpus christianorum, series latina* (ch. 2, n. 8)
Deshusses	Deshusses, *Le sacramentaire grégorien* (intro., n. 6)
Duchesne	Duchesne, *Le liber pontificalis: texte, introduction* (intro., n. 10)
"Frankish-Roman"	McKinnon, "Eighth-Century Frankish-Roman Communion Cycle" (intro., n. 8)
"Gregorian Chant"	McKinnon, "Emergence of Gregorian Chant" (intro., n. 11)
Hanssens	Hanssens, ed., *Amalarii Episcopi opera liturgica* (ch. 5, n. 21)
Hiley	Hiley, *Western Plainchant: A Handbook* (ch. 4, n. 51)
MECL	McKinnon, *Music in Early Christian Literature* (intro., n. 4)
PL	*Patrologiae latina* (ch. 2, n. 24)
"Post-Pentecostal"	McKinnon, "Roman Post-Pentecostal Communion Series" (ch. 7, n. 26)
"Preface"	McKinnon, "Preface to the Study of the Alleluia" (ch. 4, n. 19)
Sextuplex	Hesbert, *Antiphonale Missarum Sextuplex* (intro., n. 1)
Vogel	Vogel, *Medieval Liturgy* (ch. 5, n. 3)
Wagner	Wagner, *Gregorian Melodies* (intro., n. 1)

INTRODUCTION

1. See Peter Wagner, *Introduction to the Gregorian Melodies,* trans. Agnes Orme and E. G. P. Wyatt (London: Plainsong & Mediaeval Music Society, 1901), hereafter referred to as Wagner; and René-Jean Hesbert, *Antiphonale Missarum Sextuplex* (Brussels: Vromant, 1935), hereafter *Sextuplex*.

2. The idea of Gregory's revision is pervasive in the two works cited in the previous note; in spite of my different view on the Gregorian question, I find these two—Wagner's book and the introduction to Hesbert's indispensable edition—immensely valuable treatments of the Mass Proper.

3. See François-Auguste Gevaert, *Les origines du chant liturgique de l'église latine* (Ghent: A. Hoste, 1890).

4. James McKinnon, *Music in Early Christian Literature* (Cambridge: Cambridge University Press, 1987), hereafter *MECL*. [Editorial note: all citations from this work are by page numbers.]

5. See James McKinnon, "Liturgical Psalmody in the Sermons of St. Augustine," to appear in a volume of studies for Kenneth Levy, ed. Peter Jeffery (London: Boydell and Brewer).

6. For the Roman evangeliary of 645, see Theodor Klauser, *Das römische Capitulare Evangeliorum,* Liturgiegeschichtliche Quellen und Forschungen 28 (Münster: Aschendorff, 1935); for the sacramentary in question, the so-called Gregorian, in its various versions, see Jean Deshusses, *Le sacramentaire grégorien: ses principales formes d'après les plus anciens manuscrits,* 3d ed. (Fribourg: Éditions universitaires, 1992), hereafter Deshusses.

7. See David Hughes, "Evidence for the Traditional View of the Transmission of Gregorian Chant," *Journal of the American Musicological Society* [*JAMS*] 40 (1987): 378n. 3.

8. Much of what follows is covered in more detail in James McKinnon, "The Eighth-Century Frankish-Roman Communion Cycle," *JAMS* 45 (1992): 180–227 (hereafter "Frankish-Roman").

9. I use the terms "Old Testament" and "New Testament" from the viewpoint of an early Christian or medieval individual (and, needless to say, without modern theological bias). [Editorial note: all Latin spellings in verses cited have been regularized.]

10. See Louis Duchesne, *Le liber pontificalis: texte, introduction et commentaire,* with corrections and additions by Cyrille Vogel (Paris: E. De Boccard, 1957), 1:317; rather than the original 2-vol. work (Paris: Ernest Thorin, 1886–92); this 3-vol. ed. will be cited hereafter as Duchesne.

11. See James McKinnon, "The Emergence of Gregorian Chant in the Carolingian Era," in *Antiquity and the Middle Ages,* ed. James McKinnon (London: Macmillan, 1990), 106–9 (hereafter "Gregorian Chant").

12. See Wagner, 180–81, where the idea is at least implicit.

13. See especially Kenneth Levy, "Toledo, Rome and the Legacy of Gaul," *Early Music History* 4 (1984): 49–99.

14. I refer to Willi Apel, "The Central Problem of Gregorian Chant," *JAMS* 9 (1956): 118–127.

1. THE FIRST CENTURIES

1. The psalm numbers given here are those of the Hebrew Bible (followed in most modern Jewish and Protestant editions). Subsequently in this work these will be given only in contexts that are clearly Jewish; generally the numbering will be that of the Greek and Latin tradition (followed in most modern Catholic editions published before the Second Vatican Council).

2. The term "Mass" came into usage for the eucharistic celebration in the later fourth-century West; it will be used in this book beginning with the following chapter.

3. See James McKinnon, "Properization: The Roman Mass," in *Cantus Planus, Papers Read at the Sixth Meeting, Éger, Hungary, September 1993*, ed. László Dobszay (Budapest: Hungarian Academy of Sciences, 1995), 15–22.

4. I explored this point previously in "The Fourth-Century Origin of the Gradual," *Early Music History* 7 (1987): 93–95.

5. *Apologeticum* XXXIX, 16–18. The translation comes from my anthology (*MECL*, 43), where the reader will find full citations to modern editions.

6. *Paedagogus* II, iv (see *MECL*, 32–34, for a translation of the key portions of its discussion). There are issues raised by this passage that go beyond the concerns of the present book, most notably patristic attitudes toward musical instruments; these are dealt with briefly in the commentary that accompanies the translation of *MECL*.

7. Hippolytus, *Apostolic Tradition* 25 (*MECL*, 47; see commentary there on the problematic nature of this document's text). One must now add to the bibliography mentioned there the authoritative work of Paul Bradshaw, *The Canons of Hippolytus* (Bramcote: Grove Books, 1997).

8. They are, in the Latin and Greek numbering, Psalms 104–6, 110–18 (including the Hallel), 134–35 and 145–50.

9. *Ad Donatum* XVI (*MECL*, 49). In addition to the four passages quoted here, there is also Clement of Alexandria's description of the true Christian Gnostic, which reads in part: "His sacrifices are prayers and praise, converse with the Scriptures before the banquet, psalms and hymns at the banquet and before bed" (*Stromata* VII, vii, 49 [*MECL*, 36]).

10. John A. Smith and I both have emphasized the ceremonial meal as an important point of musical continuity between ancient Judaism and primitive Christianity; we have done so while calling into question the formerly conventional belief that the earliest Christian liturgical orders were derived from the synagogue. The essential difficulty in tracing early Christian liturgy to the synagogue is that certain of the purportedly relevant synagogue liturgical practices, most notably the daily singing of psalms, postdate the beginnings of Christianity. The usage of the ancient synagogue, however, which surely does in-

fluence early Christian liturgy, is the fundamentally important one of public reading from the Scriptures. See John A. Smith, "The Ancient Synagogue, The Early Church and Singing," *Music & Letters* 65 (1984): 1–16; and "First-Century Christian Singing and Its Relationship to Contemporary Jewish Religious Song," *Music & Letters* 75 (1994): 1–15. See James McKinnon, "On the Question of Psalmody in the Ancient Synagogue," *Early Music History* 6 (1986), 159–91. See also Paul Bradshaw, *The Search for the Origins of Christian Worship* (Oxford: Oxford University Press, 1992), 22–24.

11. *Apology* I, 67 (*MECL*, 20).

12. I will use the term Fore-Mass in this work as a presentational expedient, fully aware as I am of the discomfort it rightly causes some liturgical historians.

13. See Richard H. Connolly, *The De Sacramentis: A Work of Ambrose* (Downside: St. Gregory's Abbey, 1942).

14. This assumption will be examined in the following chapter.

15. *Apologeticum* XXXIX, 1–4 (*MECL*, 43).

16. *De anima* IX, 4 (*MECL*, 45).

17. This is the generally accepted conclusion of recent biblical scholarship. For a particularly valuable commentary on Corinthian liturgy, see Wayne A. Meeks, *The First Urban Christians* (New Haven: Yale University Press, 1983), 14–63.

18. For a thorough examination of the rich variety of early Christian lyric expression, see Edward Foley, *Foundations of Christian Music: The Music of Pre-Constantinian Christianity* (Bramcote: Grove Books, 1992).

19. *Adversus Marcionem* V, viii, 12 (*MECL*, 44).

20. My remarks about early Christian architecture are based especially on Richard Krautheimer, *Early Christian and Byzantine Architecture*, rev. Richard Krautheimer and Slobodan Curcic, 4th ed. (London: Penguin Books, 1986), 23–92.

21. Ibid., 27.

22. See Gregory Dix, *The Shape of the Liturgy* (Westminster [London]: Dacre Press, [1945]), 141.

23. To clarify this last point (which seems contradictory to my many pronouncements on the a cappella question), the distinction that must be made is between the earliest years of Christianity, when attitudes on such subjects were not yet fixed, and the fourth century, when ecclesiastical censure against the purported instrumental abuses of pagan society had become a commonplace. For a final summary of my views on the subject, see "A Cappella Doctrine versus Practice: A Necessary Distinction," in *La Musique et le rite sacre et profane*, Acts of the 13th Congress of the IMS, Strasbourg, 1982 (Strasbourg: Presses universitaires de Strasbourg, 1986), 238–42.

24. See the following chapter for references.

25. *Apology* I, 13 (*MECL*, 20).

26. *Stromata* VII, vii, 35 (*MECL*, 36).

27. *Epistula ad Marcellinum* 28 (*MECL*, 53).

28. See Balthasar Fischer, *Die Psalmenfrömmigkeit der Märtyrerkirche* (Freiburg: Herder, 1949).
29. *De carne Christi* XX, 3 (*MECL*, 45).
30. See *M. Tamid* 7, 4.
31. See *M. Pesahin* 5, 7.
32. See John A. Smith, "Which Psalms Were Sung in the Temple?," *Music & Letters* 71 (1990): 167–86.
33. *M. Sukkah* 5, 4.
34. See McKinnon, "Psalmody in the Ancient Synagogue," 183.
35. See, for example, Foley, *Foundations of Christian Music*, 58.
36. This objection applies even to a particularly cogent and responsible exposition of the position such as that of Ralph Martin, "Aspects of Worship in the New Testament Church," in *Vox Evangelica II*, ed. Ralph Martin (London: Epworth Press, 1963), 6–32.

2. THE LATER FOURTH CENTURY

1. What follows is mostly summarized from the superb monograph of Thomas J. Talley, *The Origins of the Liturgical Year* (Collegeville, Minn.: Liturgical Press, 1991).
2. See John F. Baldovin, *The Urban Character of Christian Worship*, Orientalia christiana analecta 228 (Rome: Pontifical Institute of Oriental Studies, 1987), 119–20.
3. I have attempted to describe the psalmodic movement in a number of recent publications; see especially "Desert Monasticism and the Later Fourth-Century Psalmodic Movement," *Music & Letters* 75 (1994): 505–521. The entire following section of this chapter is a summary of this work; full references to primary and secondary sources are to be found there.
4. *In I Timotheum*, Hom. XIV, 4 (*MECL*, 87).
5. Pseudo-Chrysostom, *De poenitentia* (*MECL*, 90).
6. *De psalmodiae bono* 5 (*MECL*, 136).
7. *In psalmum xli*, 1 (*MECL*, 80).
8. "Procedimus ad populum, plena erat ecclesia, personabat vocibus gaudiorum: Deo gratias, Deo laudes! nemine tacente hinc atque inde clamantium. Salutaui populum, et rursus eadem feruentiore uoce clamabant. Facto tandem silentio scripturarum diuinarum sunt lecta sollemnia" (*Corpus christianorum, series latina* 48 [Turnhout: Brepols, 1955], 826) (hereafter *CCL*).
9. *Sermo* CLXV, 1 (*MECL*, 161).
10. I apologize one last time for the use of the term "Fore-Mass," doing so particularly to Aimé Georges Martimort, my revered correspondent of recent years.
11. *Itinerarium Egeriae* XXV, 2 (*MECL*, 116).
12. *Liber retractationem* II, 37 (*MECL*, 166).
13. *Apostolic Constitutions* VIII, xii, 27 (*MECL*, 109).

14. See Kenneth Levy, "The Byzantine Sanctus and Its Modal Tradition in East and West," *Annales musicologiques* 6 (1958–63): 7–67.

15. *Mystagogical Catechesis* V, 20 (*MECL*, 77).

16. See *MECL*, 75; the weight of the evidence might very well point to the authorship of John over that of Cyril.

17. *Apostolic Constitutions* VIII, xiii, 16 (*MECL*, 109).

18. *In Isaiam* II, v, 20 (*MECL*, 144).

19. *Canons of Basil*, Canon 97 (*MECL*, 120). The precise date of the reference is difficult to determine; the *Canons of Basil* were begun in the later fourth century but reworked in subsequent years.

20. *In psalmum cxliv*, 1 (*MECL*, 82). There are obvious typographical difficulties with the *MECL* translation, which are corrected in the version given here in the text.

21. See the important article of Thomas H. Schattauer, "The Koinonicon of the Byzantine Liturgy: An Historical Study," *Orientalia christiana periodica* 49 (1983): 91–129.

22. James McKinnon, review of *Les lectures liturgiques et leurs livres*, by Aimé Georges Martimort, *Plainsong and Medieval Music* 5 (1996): 211–26. In the book (Turnhout: Brepols, 1992) Martimort summarizes the findings of a previous article, "A propos du nombre des lectures à la messe," *Revue des sciences religieuses* 58 (1984): 42–51.

23. See Louis Duchesne, *Christian Worship: Its Origin and Evolution*, trans. M. L. McClure, 5th ed. (London: Society for Promoting Christian Knowledge, 1931), 167–68.

24. *Sermo clxv* (*Patrologiae cursus completus, series latina*, ed. J. P. Migne [Paris, 1844–64], 38, col. 950 [hereafter *PL*]).

25. *Homilia nova in Matthaeum* IX, 37 (*MECL*, 85).

26. Cited in Martimort, "A propos du nombre des lectures," 47.

27. *De utilitate hymnorum* 5 (*MECL*, 136).

28. In the Martimort review (see note 22 above) I quote, following his lead, examples not only from Augustine but from contemporaries such as Ambrose (221).

29. *In psalmum cxix*, 1 (*MECL*, 159).

30. *In psalmum cxvii* (*MECL*, 82).

31. *Homilia habita in magnum hebdomadam* 2 (*MECL*, 83).

32. *In psalmum cxxxii*, 1 (*MECL*, 159).

33. See Philippe Bernard, "Les alléluia mélismatiques dans le chant romain: recherches sur la genèse de l'alléluia de la messe romaine," *Rivista internazionale di musica sacra* 12 (1991): 346n. 11.

34. *Explanatio psalmi xlv*, 15 (*MECL*, 127).

35. *Tractatus de psalmo ix* (*MECL*, 139).

36. The view has been developed especially by Olivier Cullin in his thesis, "Le trait dans les répertoires vieux-romain et grégorien: un témoin de la psalmodie sans refrain" (Université de Paris, Sorbonne, 1990), and in a series of several articles, for example, "De la psalmodie sans refrain à la psalmodie res-

ponsoriale," *Revue de musicologie* 77 (1991): 5–24. Perhaps the central argument of the view in question is that the reference to the singing of an entire psalm responsorially is evidence for an original direct performance. But surely the singing of an entire psalm is just as characteristic of responsorial psalmody in ancient times as it is of direct psalmody.

37. See Reinhard Flender, *Hebrew Psalmody: A Structural Investigation*, Yuval Monograph Series 9 (Jerusalem: Magnes Press, 1992), 57–60. The point is made at considerably more length in various studies of John A. Smith that have not yet appeared at the time of this writing.

38. See Terence Bailey, *Antiphon and Psalm in the Ambrosian Office* (Ottawa: Institute of Mediaeval Music, 1994), 60–65.

39. *De oratione XXVII* (*MECL*, 44).

40. McKinnon, "Liturgical Psalmody."

41. *Apostolic Constitutions* II, lvii, 6 (*MECL*, 109).

42. *In Matthaeum*, Hom. XI, 7 (*MECL*, 84).

43. The passage, as I argued in the review referred to earlier in this chapter, could also refer to the dismissal of the faithful after the entire Mass, in which case the multiple psalms could be taken to include also psalms at the communion.

44. Sermo CCCLII, *De utilitate agendae poenitentiae* II, 1 (*MECL*, 162; the *MECL* text's "song," as opposed to "sin," is obviously a typographical error).

45. *In psalmum cxiii*, 1 (*CCL* 40, 1635).

46. In Sermon 29A, alleluia is cited as the response for Easter itself, while Sermons 230 and 258, along with Guelferbytani 18, have *Hic est dies* (Augustine's psalter text) during Easter week. The distinction has profound consequences to be explored below. Fuller citations of the sermons involved can be found in my "Liturgical Psalmody."

47. *In psalmum cx*, 1 (*MECL*, 159).

48. See Sermo cclxvii, *In die Pentecostes I* (*PL* 38, col. 1231).

49. The Armenian Lectionary is edited by A. Renoux, *Le Codex arménien Jérusalem 121*, 2 vols., Patrologia orientalis, 35/1 and 36/2 (Turnhout: Brepols, 1969 and 1971). Renoux dates the original content to between 417 and 439; see 1:166–72.

50. For Milan see Helmut Leeb, *Die Psalmodie bei Ambrosius*, Wiener Beiträge zur Theologie 18 (Vienna: Herder, 1967). For Rome there is virtually nothing other than the sermons of Pope Leo the Great (440–61); they will be discussed in chapter four.

51. *Expositio in psalmum lxxx*, 4 (*MECL*, 54). I change *MECL*'s "into the whole world" to "in all the earth."

52. He does so three different years: Sermo ccxcv, 1 (*PL* 38, col. 1348); Sermo ccxcviii (*PL* 38, col. 1365); and Sermo ccxcix, 1 (*PL* 38, col. 1367).

53. *Protrepticus* XI, 116, 3 (*MECL*, 31).

54. Sermo cccvi, 1 (*PL* 38, col. 1400) and Sermo cccxxix, 1 (*PL* 38, col. 1454).

55. I explore the question of the Easter vigil canticles in "The Gregorian Canticle-Tracts of the Old Roman Easter Vigil," in *Festschrift Walter Wiora*

zum 90. Geburtstag, ed. Christoph-Hellmut Mahling and Ruth Seiberts (Tutzing: Hans Schneider, 1997), 254–69.

56. See Cyrille Lambot, "Les sermons de saint Augustin pour les fêtes de Paques," *Revue bénédictine* 79 (1969): 150.

57. "Quemadmodum desiderat cervus ad fontes aquarum, sic desiderat animae mea ad te, Deus. Et quidem non male intellegitur uox esse eorum qui, cum sint catechumeni, ad gratiam sancti lauacri festinant. Vnde et sollemniter cantatur his psalmus, ut ita desiderent fontem remissionis peccatorum" (*In psalmum xli,* 1 [CCL 38, 460]).

58. See Renoux, *Codex arménien,* 2:299.

59. See Bonifatius Fischer, "Die Lesungen der römischen Ostervigil unter Gregor d. Gr.," in *Colligere Fragmenta: Festschrift Alban Dold zum 70. Geburtstag,* ed. Bonifatius Fischer and Virgil Fiala (Beuron: Beuroner Kunstverlag, 1952), 151.

60. See R. Étaix, "Sermons ariens inédits," *Recherches augustiniennes* 26 (1992): 156.

61. See Philippe Bernard, "L'origine des chants de la messe selon la tradition musicale du chant romain ancien, improprement dit 'chant vieux-romain,'" in *L'eucharistie: célébrations, rites, piétés,* Conférences St-Serge, XLIe semaine d'études liturgiques, Paris 28 juin–1 juillet 1994, ed. A. M. Triacca and A. Pistoia (Rome: C.L.V., 1995), 19–97. On 28 Bernard writes, "mais il prouve . . . que les chants conservés dans les manuscrits du IXe siècle [remontent] au IVe siècle." There is one other reference in these sermons to the singing of a psalm: a sermon preached on the Epiphany (Étaix ["Sermons ariens," 158] has "sicut in presenti psalmo dictum est: 'Benedictus qui venit in nomen domini' [Ps 117.26]"). However, this text is not sung in the Roman Mass Proper on the feast of the Epiphany. Bernard compounds his error by assuming that several other psalms were in fact sung on the occasion of these sermons, when they are simply quoted without explicit mention of their having been sung, as is the case with *Dixit dominus* and *Benedictus qui venit.*

62. Sermo clxxxv, 1 (*PL* 38, col. 997); Sermo clxxxix, 2 (*PL* 38, col. 1005); Sermo cxcii, 2 (*PL* 38, col. 1011); and Sermo cxciii, 2 (*PL* 38, col. 1014).

63. *Homilia habita in magnam hebdomadam* 2 (MECL, 83).

64. Sermo CXCVIII, *De calendis Januariis* II, 1–2 (MECL, 162).

65. My attempt to summarize the evidence on this subject in "Liturgical Psalmody" has examples of discontinuity outweighing examples of continuity at about a six-to-one ratio.

66. The book is studied by Michel Huglo, "Le répons-graduel de la messe: évolution de la forme, permanence de la fonction," *Schweizer Jahrbuch für Musikwissenschaft,* n.s., 2 (1982): 53–77.

67. *In psalmum cxxxviii,* 1 (MECL, 160).

68. "Neque enim nos istum psalmum cantandum lectori imperavimus: sed quod ille censuit vobis esse utile ad audiendum, hoc cordi etiam puerili imperavit" (Sermo ccclii [*PL* 39, col. 1550]).

69. *Tractatus de psalmo vii* (MECL, 139).

70. *Tractatus de psalmo xvi* (ibid.).
71. See Sermo ccxxxii (*PL* 38, col. 1108).
72. See Anton Zwinggi, "Die Perikoppenordnungen der Osterwoche in Hippo und die Chronologie der Predigten des hl. Augustinus," *Augustiniana* 20 (1970): 5–34.
73. See Anton Zwinggi, "Die fortlauffende Schriftlesung im Gottesdienst bei Augustinus," *Archiv für Liturgiewissenschaft* 12 (1970): 85–129.

3. CENTURIES OF SILENCE: GAUL

1. The figures are taken from Richard Krautheimer, *Rome: Profile of a City, 312–1308* (Princeton: Princeton University Press, 1980), 65.
2. See Jean Claire, "L'évolution modale dans les répertoires liturgiques occidentaux," *Revue grégorienne* 40 (1962): 231–35. Much of the following section of this chapter is based on my own ruminations on Dom Claire's distinction; see James McKinnon, "Lector Chant Versus Schola Chant: A Question of Historical Plausibility," in *Laborare fratres in unum: Festschrift László Dobszay zum 60. Geburtstag*, ed. Janka Szendrei and David Hiley (Hildesheim: Weidmann, 1995), 201–11.
3. *De officiis* XLIV, 215 (*MECL*, 132).
4. *Apostolic Constitutions* VIII, xiii, 14 (*MECL*, 109).
5. See John the Deacon, *Life of Gregory the Great;* translation in *Strunk's Source Readings in Music History: The Early Christian Period and the Latin Middle Ages*, ed. James McKinnon, rev. ed. (New York: W. W. Norton, 1997), 69.
6. *De viris illustribus* 80 (*MECL*, 170).
7. The Georgian Lectionary is edited and translated by Michel Tarchnischvili, *Le grand lectionnaire de l'église de Jérusalem (Ve–VIIIe siècles)*, Corpus scriptorum christianorum orientalium 189 and 204 (Louvain, 1959–60). For a convenient summary of the ancient liturgical sources of Jerusalem, see Peter Jeffery, "The Lost Chant Tradition of Early Christian Jerusalem," *Early Music History* 11 (1992): 155–59.
8. "Sonat lector, sacerdos praedicat, diaconus disciplinae silentium clamat" (Sermo 20.2 [*CCL* 103, 92]).
9. "Haec igitur est dies, dilectissimi, quam fecit dominus, ut audistis" (Sermo 204.1, De pascha domini [*CCL* 104, 819]).
10. "Hodie, fratres carissimi, omnia quae nobis lecta sunt cum festivitate conveniunt. Psalmus enim: redde mihi, inquit, laetitiam salutaris tui, [et] spiritu principali confirma me [Ps 50.14]; evangelium autem: venit, inquid, spiritus veritatis [Jn 16.13]; scriptura vero apostolicorum Actuum: Repleti sunt, inquid, omnes spiritu sancto [Acts 2.4]. Completa sunt ergo omnia atque perfecta: psalmus adventum sancti Spriritus petiit, evangelium venturum esse promisit, scriptura apostolicorum Actuum iam venisse memoravit. Nihil itaque de rerum divinarum ordine in lectionibus deest: quia in propheta deprecatio est, in evangelio promissio, in Actibus plentitudo" (Sermo 209.1, De quinquagesimo [*CCL* 104, 841]).

11. "Interea iam medium prandii peractum, iubet rex, ut diaconem nostrum, qui ante diem ad missas psalmum responsorium dixerat, canere iuberem. Quo canente, iubet iterum mihi ut omnes sacerdotes qui aderant per meam commonicionem, datis ex officio suo singulis clericis, coram rege iuberentur cantare. Per me enim secundum regis imperium admoniti, quisque, ut potuit, in regis praesencia psalmum responsorium decantavit" (*Historia Francorum* VIII.3 [*PL* 71, col. 451]).

12. "et tam deformiter cecinit, ut ab omnibus irrideretur. Adveniente autem alia Dominica, dicente saepedicto Pontifice missas, jussit eum abire: Nunc, inquit, in nomine Domini quod volueris explicabis. Quod cum fecisset, in tantum vox eus praeclara facta est, ut ab omnibus laudaretur" (*Vitae patrum* VI.5 [*PL* 71, col. 1033]).

13. The manuscript, Paris, Bibliothèque nationale, ms latin 11947 (studied by Michel Huglo in "Le répons-graduel de la messe: évolution de la forme, permanence de la fonction," *Schweizer Jahrbuch für Musikwissenschaft*, n.s., 2 [1982]), came from the Benedictine abbey of St-Germain-des-Prés archives, which were absorbed into the national library after the French Revolution; hence its common title.

14. See Huglo, "Répons-graduel," 59.

15. See ibid., 66.

16. The twenty-one instances of possible continuity are not without their own significance, however; they will be discussed at length in the chapter on the gradual.

17. I use the edition of Edward Ratcliff, *Expositio antiquae liturgiae gallicanae* (London: [Henry Bradshaw Society], 1971).

18. See André Wilmart, "Germain de Paris (Lettres attribuées à saint)," *Dictionnaire d'archéologie chrétienne et de liturgie*, vol. 6, pt. 1 (Paris, 1924), cols. 1049–1102. The central argument in denying that the document is the work of Germanus, who died in 576, is its purported reliance upon the *Etymologiae* of Isidore of Seville, generally dated to about 620. A. van der Mensbrugghe, however, dissents with the conventional wisdom, claiming that Germanus is the genuine author and that Isidore depends upon him; see especially "Pseudo-Germanus Reconsidered," *Studia patristica* 5 (Texte und Arbeiten 80) (1962): 172–84.

19. Anders Ekenberg, "Germanus oder Pseudo-Germanus?," *Archiv für Liturgiewissenschaft* 35 (1993): 135–39. Central to Ekenberg's position are three points: (1) the document could not be the work of Germanus himself for the obvious reason that it cites him in the text; (2) but it is close in time to him because it refers to him simply as a bishop, whereas he was celebrated as a saint soon after his death; and (3) it is the source for the related remarks in Isidore's *Etymologiae*, rather than the opposite, just as van der Mensbrugghe claims.

20. "Secundum hoc etiam ecclesia seruat ordinem ut inter Benedictionem et Euangelium [Col]lectio [non] intercedat nisi tantum [m]odo Responsurium quod a paruolis canitur instar innocent[i]um qui perisse in euangelium consortes christi nativitatem leguntur vel eorum paruolorum [qui] properante ad

passione[m] domino clamabant in templum Osanna fili David, psalmista canente Ex ore infancium et lactantium perfecisti laudem" (Ratcliff, *Expositio*, 6).

21. See Caesarius of Arles, Sermo 69, 1 (*CCL* 103, 291).

22. See Ratcliff, *Expositio*, 7.

23. "Illud omnino studebat, ut omnes pueros qui in domo ejus nascebantur, ut primum vagitum infantiae relinquentes loqui coepissent, statim litteras doceret ac psalmis imbueret" (*Historia Francorum* VIII.2 [*PL* 71, col. 1042]).

24. "Hoc enim placit, ut omnes presbyteri, qui sunt in parochiis constituti, secundum consuetudinem, quam per totam Italiam satis salubriter teneri cognovimus, juniores lectores quantoscumque sine uxore habuerint, secum in domo, ubi ipsi habitare videntur, recipiant: et eos quomodo boni patres spiritaliter nutrientes, psalmos parare, divinis lectionibus insistere, et in lege domini erudire contendant" (*Concilium Vasense* 1 [*CCL* 148A, 78]).

25. On the Cheroubikon, see Hans-Joachim Schulz, *The Byzantine Liturgy*, trans. Matthew J. O'Connell (New York: Pueblo, 1986), 35–39.

26. See Johannes Quasten, "Oriental Influence in the Gallican Liturgy," *Traditio* 1 (1943): 70–71.

27. "Cum ... tempus ad sacrificium offerendum advenit, acceptuaque turre diaconus in qua mysterium dominici corporis habebatur" (*De gloria martyrum* 86 [*PL* 71, col. 781]).

28. On the Trisagion, see Schulz, *Byzantine Liturgy*, 22–25.

29. *Epistula* 3 (*PL* 59, cols. 210–11).

30. I take the opportunity to point to the near silence in this volume on the chant of early medieval Spain. If this is a genuine shortcoming, I take full responsibility for it and admit that my silence might possibly be traced primarily to a lack of competence in matters Iberian. In my defense I would say that, while I acknowledge there is a good argument to be made for a fully developed "schola chant" to have existed in Toledo at least as early as at Rome, I still fail to find (1) precisely the same sort of clearly relevant texts in the Spanish sources as are discussed in this chapter; and (2) a convincing argument that the Spanish Mass Proper influences that of Rome. I welcome correction on either point; the present volume cannot pretend to cover every aspect of so vast a topic.

31. It is first attested to in the mid-ninth-century gradual of Corbie; see *Sextuplex*, 97.

32. This is, I believe, the essential meaning of *antiphona* at this time; it does not, however, exclude the possibility that the singing is also conducted by alternating forces, a meaning of the term given already by Isidore of Seville, *Etymologiae* VI, 7.

33. "Mane autem facto, cum choris psallentium, apprehensum sarcophagum ante altar in absidam quam beatus episcopus aedificaverat, transtulerunt" (*Historia Francorum* VII.4 [*PL* 71, col. 1039]).

34. See, for example, Quasten, "Oriental Influence in the Gallican Liturgy," 77–78. Recently, however, Philippe Bernard has made the ingenious suggestion that the term "Trecanum" when spelled in Greek majuscules bears a striking resemblance to the term "Trisagion;" see "Le 'Trecanum': un fantôme dans

la liturgie gallicane?," *Francia: Forschungen zur westeuropäischen Geschichte* 23 (1996): 95–98. He notes further that the portion of the text citing the Trecanum is misplaced in the manuscript, concluding that there is no such entity as a Trecanum and that the reference is in reality to the Trisagion. I find Bernard's suggestion to be not just ingenious, but very plausible. I see, however, no evidence in the text for his further claim that the communion chant of the *Expositio* is the frequently encountered *Gustate et videte*.

35. See Ratcliff, *Expositio*, 17.

36. *Regula ad monachos* (*PL* 68, col. 396).

37. In point of fact the last Gallican council was held sixty-seven years before, that of Saint-Jean-de-Losne (673–75).

38. "Franci enim ut seniores dicunt plus quam per tempus octoginta annorum synodum non fecerunt nec archiepiscopum habuerunt nec Ecclesiae canonica jura alicui fundabant vel renovabant . . . per civitates episcopales sedes traditae sunt laicis cupidis ad possidendum . . . quidem inter eos episcopi, qui, licet dicant se fornicarios vel adulteros non esse, sed sunt ebriosi, et injuriosi, vel venatores, et qui pugnant in exercitu armati" (*PL* 89, col. 745).

39. For text and analysis of Chrodegang's rule, see William D. Carpe, "The Vita Canonica in the *Regula Canonicorum* of Chrodegang of Metz" (Ph.D. diss., University of Chicago, 1975). It is Carpe who establishes the composition of Chrodegang's rule in an earlier pre-Roman and later post-Roman stage. The rule, in its final stage, mentions the Roman clergy no less than three times.

40. The implications of Pope Stephen's visit for the transmission of Roman chant to the north will be treated at length in the epilogue to this book.

41. In fact he also mentions the *secundus, tertius* and *quartus scholae;* he does so in the remarkable document that lists the *stipendia* to be paid members of his clergy for the execution of various liturgical duties, including the singing of long chants; see Michel Andrieu, "Règlement d'Angilramne de Metz (768–791) fixant les honoraires de quelques fonctions liturgiques," *Revue des sciences religieuses* 10 (1930): 354.

4. CENTURIES OF SILENCE: ENGLAND AND ROME

1. "Unde et Dauiticum psalmum, dilectissimi, non ad nostram elationem, sed ad Christi Domini gloriam consona uoce cantauimus. Ipse est enim de quo prophetice scriptum est: Tu es sacerdos in aeternum secundum ordinem Melchisedech" (*Tractatus* III.1 [*CCL* 138, 10]).

2. "Non deest tamen Pontifex summus a suorum congregatione pontificum meritoque illi totius Ecclesiae et omnium sacerdotum ore cantatur: Iurauit Dominus et non paenitebit eum: Tu es sacerdos in aeternum secundum ordinem Melchisedech" (*Tractatus* V.3 [*CCL* 138, 23]).

3. "Hunc diem David canebat in psalmis dicens: Omnes gentes quas fecisti, uenient et adorabunt coram te, Domine, et honorificabunt nomen tuum. Et illud: Notum fecit Dominus salutare suum, ante conspectum gentium reuelauit iustitiam suam" (*Tractatus* XXXIII.10 [*CCL* 138, 176]).

4. *Tractatus* XXIV.10 (*CCL* 138, 112).
5. "Si autem Maria terra, agnoscamus quod cantamus, Veritas de terra orta est" (Sermo clxxxix, *In natali domini* VI [*PL* 38, col. 1005]).
6. "Hic fecit ut psalmi CL David ante sacrificium psalli [antephonatim ex omnibus], quod ante non fiebat, nisi tantum epistolae Pauli recitabatur et sanctum Evangelium" (Duchesne, 1:230).
7. Duchesne dated the second version slightly earlier; the modification is the conclusion of Cyrille Vogel, "Le 'Liber Pontificalis' dans l'édition de Louis Duchesne: état de la question," in *Monseigneur Duchesne et son temps: actes du colloque organisé par l'école française de Rome Palais Farnèse, 23–25 mai, 1973* (Rome: École française de Rome, 1975), 101–7.
8. Peter Jeffery does so in his important article "The Introduction of Psalmody into the Roman Mass by Pope Celestine I (422–432)," *Archiv für Liturgiewissenschaft* 26 (1984): 147–65.
9. Ibid., 154–56.
10. Ibid., 161.
11. I did so in a paper read at the annual meeting of the American Musicological Society, Denver, Colorado, 6 November 1980: "The Architectural Setting of Early Christian Psalmody."
12. For the text see Jeffery, "Introduction of Psalmody," 158.
13. Ibid., 157–59.
14. This is true even of the excellent recent translation of Raymond Davis, *The Book of Pontiffs* (*Liber pontificalis*) (Liverpool: Liverpool University Press, 1989), 34.
15. Jeffery, "Introduction of Psalmody," 163–65.
16. I think it essential to the historiography of this book's subject matter—its attempt to deal with the history of chant from apostolic times to the early Middle Ages—that I try to place in perspective the relationship of Jeffery's and my own approach to it. From the time I first met him some twenty years ago I have been struck how we have arrived independently at the same conclusions about most of the major issues involved in the subject, frequently in opposition to the received wisdom. This, I believe, is the larger truth of the matter. If differences have developed between us as we ponder this subject, I would characterize them as chiefly two: Jeffery tends to emphasize continuity between antiquity and the Middle Ages, while I tend to emphasize discontinuity, and he tends to place the maturity of Roman chant at a somewhat earlier date than I do.
17. Duchesne, 1:84.
18. "Introduction of Psalmody," 158.
19. See James McKinnon, "Preface to the Study of the Alleluia," *Early Music History* 15 (1996): 226–27 (hereafter "Preface").
20. Guy Ferrari, *Early Roman Monasteries, Notes for the History of the Monasteries and Convents at Rome from the V through the X Century* (Vatican City: Pontifical Institute of Christian Archeology, 1957).
21. *Epistula CVII*, 9 (*MECL*, 142).
22. "Fecit autem monasterium in Catacumbas" (see Duchesne, 1:234, 236).

23. "Hic constituit monasterium apud beatum Petrum apostolum" (ibid., 239).

24. "Hic fecit monasterium ad XII sanctum Laurentium. . . . Item monasterium intra urbe Roma ad Luna" (ibid., 245).

25. See Ferrari, *Early Roman Monasteries*, ix.

26. "Tertiam sextam et nonam vel matutinos in eadem ecclesia sanctae Dei genetricis cotidianis agerent diebus" (Duchesne, 1:308).

27. "Ubi et congregationem monachorum et abbatem constituit ad persolvenda cotidie sacra officia laudis divine [in basilica Salvatoris domini nostri Iesu Christi quae Constantiniana nuncupatur, iuxta Lateranis], diurnis nocturnisque temporibus ordinata, iuxta instar officiorum ecclesie beati Petri apostoli" (Duchesne, 1:419).

28. "Haec eo dicente, congregatis clericorum catervis, psallere jussit per triduum, ac deprecari Domini misericordiam. De hora quoque tertia veniebant utrique chori psallentium ad ecclesiam, clamantes per plateas urbis, Kyrie eleison . . . dum vocis plebs ad dominum supplicationis emisit, octoginta homines ad terram corruisse" (*Historia Francorum* X.1 [*PL* 71, col. 529]).

29. See John F. Baldovin, *The Urban Character of Christian Worship*, Orientalia christiana analecta 228 (Rome: Pontifical Institute of Oriental Studies, 1987), 114.

30. "Dudum consuetudo valde reprehensibilis exorta est, ut quidem ad sacri altaris ministerium cantores eligantur, et in diaconatus ordine constituti modulationi vocis inserviant, quos ad praedicationis officium et eleemosynarum studium vacare congruebat. Unde fit plerumque ut ad sacrum ministerium dum blanda vox quaeritur, quaeri congrua vita negligatur. Et cantor minister Deum moribus stimulet, cum populum vocibus delectat. Qua de re presenti decreto constituo, ut in sede hac sacri altaris ministri cantare non debeant, solumque evangelicae lectionis officium inter missarum solemnia exsolvant: psalmos vero ac reliquas lectiones censeo per subdiaconos, vel si necessitas exigit, per minores ordines exhiberi" (*Registrum epistolarum*, ed. Paul Ewald and Ludwig Hartmann, Monumenta Germaniae Historica, Epistolarum [Berlin, 1891], 1:363).

31. Joseph Dyer, "The Schola Cantorum and Its Roman Milieu in the Early Middle Ages," in *De Musica et Cantu: Studien zur Geschichte der Kirchenmusik und der Oper. Helmut Hucke zum 60. Geburtstag*, ed. Peter Cahn and Ann-Katrin Heimer (Hildesheim: Georg Olms, 1993), 32.

32. Michel Andrieu, ed., *Les ordines romani du haut moyen âge* (Louvain: Spicilegium sacrum Lovaniense, 1931), here *Ordo romanus I*, 52, 2:84 (hereafter Andrieu, for this 5-vol. ed., Spicilegium sacrum Lovaniense 11, 23–24, 28–29 [1931–60]).

33. *Ordo romanus I*, 42–43 (Andrieu, 2:81).

34. *Ordo romanus I*, 39 (ibid., 80).

35. Duchesne, 1:371.

36. *Ordo romanus I*, 105 (Andrieu, 2:101).

37. "Quia studiosus erat et capax in officio cantelenae, priori cantorum pro doctrina est traditus" (Duchesne, 1:376).

38. Ibid., 359.

39. Ibid., 363.

40. Among the secondary sources I find to be the most helpful in establishing the Roman background are Peter Llewellyn, *Rome in the Dark Ages* (London: Faber and Faber, 1971); Richard Krautheimer, *Rome: Profile of a City, 312–1308* (Princeton: Princeton University Press, 1980); and Thomas F. X. Noble, *The Republic of St. Peter* (Philadelphia: University of Pennsylvania Press, 1984).

41. The subject is discussed in Ferrari, *Early Roman Monasteries*, 389–91; and especially in Peter Llewellyn, "The Roman Church in the Seventh Century: the Legacy of Gregory I," *Journal of Ecclesiastical History* 25 (1974): 364–68.

42. "Hic domum suam monasterium fecit" (Duchesne, 1:317).

43. "Hic clerum multum dilexit, sacerdotes et clerum ad loca pristina revocavit" (ibid., 319).

44. "Misit servos Dei Mellitum, Augustinum et Iohannem et alios plures cum eis monachos timentis Deum; misit eos in praedicationem ad gentem Angulorum ut eos converteret ad dominum Iesum Christum" (ibid., 312).

45. "Reliquerat autem in ecclesia sua Eburacensi Iacobum diaconum, virum utique ecclesiasticum et sanctum, qui multo exhinc tempore in ecclesia manens. . . . Qui quoniam cantandi in ecclesia erat peritissimus, recuperata postmodum pace in provincia, et crescente numero fidelium, etiam magister ecclesiasticae cantionis iuxta morem Romanorum seu Cantuariorum" (*Historia ecclesiastica* II, 20 [ed. J. E. King, Loeb Classical Library (1979), 1:318–20]).

46. "Sed et sonos cantandi in ecclesia, quos eatenus in Cantia tantum noverant, ab hoc tempore per omnes Anglorum ecclesias discere coeperunt: primusque, excepto Iacobo de quo supra diximus, cantandi magister Nordanhymbrorum ecclesiis, Aeddi cognomento Stephans fuit, invitatus de Cantia a reverentissimo viro Vilfrido" (*Historia ecclesiastica* IV, 2 [ibid., 2:12]).

47. "Accepit et praefatum Iohannem abbatem Brittaniam perducendum; quatenus in monasterio suo cursum canendi annuum, sicut ad sanctum Petrum Romae agebatur, edoceret: egitque abba Iohannes ut iussionem acceperat pontificis, et ordinem videlicet, ritumque canendi ac legendi viva voce praefati monasteri cantores edocendo, et ea quae totius anni circulus in celebratione dierum festorum poscebat, etiam literis mandando: quae hactenus in eodem monasterio servata, et a multis iam sunt circumquaque transcripta. Non solum autem idem Iohannes ipsius monasterii fratres docebat, verum de omnibus pene eiusdem provinciae monasteriis ad audiendum eum, qui cantandi erant periti, confluebant. Sed et ipsum per loca in quibus doceret, multi invitare curabant" (*Historia ecclesiastica* IV, 18 [ibid., 2:98]).

48. I exclude from this series, regretfully, the attractive figure of Caedmon, to whom Bede devotes an entire chapter (*Historia ecclesiastica* IV, 24). Caedmon, an illiterate monk who is the earliest cited poet of the English language, is not described by Bede as a liturgical singer.

49. "Sed et historias passionis eorum, una cum ceteris ecclesiasticis voluminibus, summa industria congregans, amplissimam ibi ac nobilissimam bibliothecam fecit, necnon et vasa sancta et luminaria aliaque huiusmodi quae ad ornatum domus Dei pertinent, studiosissime paravit. Cantatorem quoque egregium, vocabula Maban, qui a successoribus discipulorum beati papae Gregorii in Cantia fuerat cantandi sonos edoctus, ad se suosque instituendos accersiit, ac per annos duodecim tenuit: quatenus et quae illi non noverant carmina ecclesiastica doceret; et ea quae quondam cognita longo usu vel negligentia inveterare coeperunt huius doctrina priscum renovarentur in statum" (*Historia ecclesiastica* V, 20 [Loeb ed., 2:322]).

50. *Councils and Ecclesiastical Documents Relating to Great Britain and Ireland*, ed. Arthur Haddan and William Stubbs (Oxford: Clarendon Press, 1869–73), 3:366–67.

51. For a summary of this development, see David Hiley, *Western Plainchant: A Handbook* (Oxford: Oxford University Press, 1993), 580–84 (hereafter Hiley).

52. See my "Gregorian Chant," 115–16; and my "*Gregorius presul composuit hunc libellum musicae artis*," in *The Liturgy of the Medieval Church*, ed. Thomas Heffernan and E. Ann Matter (Kalamazoo, Mich.: Medieval Institute Publications, 1999).

53. Edited by Bertram Colgrave, *The Earliest Life of Gregory the Great, by an Anonymous Monk of Whitby* (Lawrence: University of Kansas Press, 1968).

54. Only four times, according to Llewellyn, "Roman Church in the Seventh Century," 364n. 1.

55. Ibid.

56. I do not mean to imply for a moment here that I believe Gregory II is responsible for everything ascribed to Gregory I, but refer only to the way of thinking of the eighth-century Roman clerics who devised the *Gregorius presul* preface.

57. Bruno Stäblein, "'Gregorius Praesul,' der Prolog zum römischen Antiphonale," in *Musik und Verlag: Karl Vötterle zum 65. Geburtstag*, ed. Richard Baum and Wolfgang Rehm (Kassel: Bärenreiter, 1968), 537–61. What follows immediately relies heavily upon Stäblein's work.

58. On the central importance of Gregory II, see especially Noble, *Republic of St. Peter*.

59. See his biography in the *Liber pontificalis* (Duchesne, 1:417 and 418–19).

60. On the liturgical contribution of Alcuin see Gerald Ellard, *Master Alcuin, Liturgist* (Chicago: Loyola University Press, 1956). Ellard's masterful study is still valuable, even if the authorship of the famous *Hucusque* preface, here claimed for Alcuin, is now generally attributed to Benedict of Aniane.

61. See Strabo, *Liber de exordiis* (PL 113, cols. 946–48).

62. See Edward A. Syna, "John the Deacon," *Dictionary of the Middle Ages* (New York: Charles Scribner's Sons, 1986), 7:143.

63. The document is from the *Annales Laurissenses*, edited in Monumenta

Germaniae Historica, 1:170 –71; it is reproduced and discussed in Jean-Baptiste Pelt, *Études sur la cathédrale de Metz: la liturgie Ve–XIIIe siècles* (Metz: Journal le Lorrain, 1937), 117–18.

64. For a reproduction, see my *"Gregorius presul."*

5. SACRAMENTARY, LECTIONARY AND ANTIPHONER

1. Willi Apel, *Gregorian Chant* (Bloomington: Indiana University Press, 1958), 56 (hereafter Apel).

2. I treat the subject of textual adjustment in "Festival, Text and Melody: Chronological Stages in the Life of a Chant?," *Chant and Its Peripheries: Essays in Honour of Terence Bailey*, ed. Bryan Gillingham and Paul Merkley (Ottawa: Institute of Mediaeval Music, 1998), 1–11.

3. Verona, Biblioteca capitolare, codex 85 (olim 80) (Leo Cunibert Mohlberg et al., eds., *Sacramentarium Veronense, Rerum ecclesiasticarum documenta*, series major 1 [Rome: Herder, 1956]). In my discussion of sacramentaries, I follow, unless otherwise indicated, Cyrille Vogel, *Medieval Liturgy: An Introduction to the Sources*, trans. and rev. William Storey and Niels Rasmussen (Washington, D.C.: Pastoral Press, 1986), hereafter Vogel. By far the strongest portion of this work is its magisterial summary of the vast literature on sacramentaries. What follows, then, in the next several pages will be minimally documented.

4. The bulk of the manuscript is preserved in Codex Vaticanus Reginensis latinus 316, folios 3–245, and its conclusion in Bibliothèque nationale, codex latinus 7193, folios 41–56 (Leo Cunibert Mohlberg, et al., eds, *Liber sacramentorum romanae aecclesiae ordinis anni circuli, rerum ecclesiasticarum documenta*, series major 4 [Rome: Herder, 1968]).

5. The Paduensis (Padua, Biblioteca capitolare, codex D. 47) (in Deshusses) was copied in a scriptorium of the emperor Lothaire (840–55). On the possible date of 663, see Vogel, 94, for references to the speculations of Deshusses on the subject.

6. It is named for a single unnumbered manuscript at Trent, Museo nazionale, Castel del Buonconsiglio (olim Codex vindobonensis 700); unfortunately this important book, which has attracted the attention of liturgical historians only fairly recently, has not yet appeared in a published edition. It is treated, however, in an article by Jean Deshusses, "Le sacramentaire grégorien de Trente," *Revue bénédictine* 78 (1968): 261–82.

7. Gerard Ellard, *Master Alcuin, Liturgist* (Chicago: Loyola University Press, 1956), 1–30. This little-noticed work remains the best summary of the transmission of the Roman liturgy to the Carolingian north.

8. The original appearance of the remark, I believe, is in Walter Howard Frere, *The Sarum Gradual and the Gregorian Antiphonale Missarum: A Dissertation and an Historical Index* (London: Published for Members of the Plainsong and Mediaeval Music Society by B. Quaritch, 1895), x.

9. For a summary of the various positions on this question, see my "Gregorian Chant," 109–10.

10. For the Paschaltime readings in Augustine's church see Anton Zwinggi, "Die Perikopenordnungen der Osterwoche in Hippo und die Chronologie der Predigten des hl. Augustinus," *Augustiniana* 20 (1970): 5–34.

11. Gennadius, *De viris illustribus* 80 (*MECL*, 170).

12. "Solemnibus annuis paravit quae quo tempore lecta convenirent" (Sidonius Apollinaris, *Epistulae* 4, 11, 6 [*PL* 58, col. 616]).

13. See Vogel, 314–20; and Aimé Georges Martimort, *Les lectures liturgiques et leurs livres* (Turnhout: Brepols, 1992), 21–22.

14. For basic information on the book, see Vogel, 320–21.

15. I take the Gregorian gospels from Geoffrey Willis, *A History of Early Roman Liturgy to the Death of Pope Gregory the Great*, Henry Bradshaw Society Subsidial 1 (London: Boydell Press, 1994), 112–13; and Theodor Klauser, *Das römische Capitulare Evangeliorum*, Liturgiegeschichtliche Quellen und Forschungen 28 (Münster: Aschendorff, 1935). The three post-Pentecostal gospels (in square brackets in the table) not yet appearing in the PI-type are supplemented from later redactions of the Roman evangeliary (also from Klauser).

16. Nor do we have an adequate secondary source on the subject. The English language revision of Vogel's *Medieval Liturgy*, which is so reliable a guide to the history of the Roman sacramentary, disappoints with the contemporary lectionary. It accepts without question, for example, the chronology proposed by Antoine Chavasse in his earlier works after that scholar had abandoned it himself; see James McKinnon, "Antoine Chavasse and the Dating of Early Chant," *Plainsong and Medieval Music* 1 (1992): 135–36.

17. The manuscript Würzburg, Universitätsbibliothek, codex M.p.th.f.62, is thought to have been copied in England between 700 and 750; it is edited by Germain Morin, "Le plus ancien *Comes*, ou lectionnaire de l'église romaine," *Revue bénédictine* 27 (1910): 41–74. The same manuscript also has a somewhat later gospel list; see Vogel, 339–40, for a general description. The most recent detailed investigation is that of Antoine Chavasse, "L'épistolier romain du codex de Wurtzbourg. Son organization," *Revue bénédictine* 91 (1981): 280–331.

18. Martimort, *Lectures liturgiques*, 52, follows Chavasse on this.

19. The Roman Office antiphons are transcribed in Edward Nowacki, "Studies on the Office Antiphons of the Old Roman Manuscripts" (Ph.D. diss., Brandeis University, 1980), 2 vols.

20. I find only one example of such a relationship, the introit *Scio cui credidi* and the Office antiphon using the same text. These are, moreover, fairly elaborate chants, suggesting that the antiphon might be a later adaptation of the original introit. The entire phenomenon of the antiphon-communion, which will be treated in the chapter on the communion, is definitely a late development, irrelevant to present concerns.

21. Amalarius (d.c.850) tells us of the Roman custom of organizing books into separate collections of antiphons and responses. See John M. Hanssens, ed.,

Amalarii Episcopi opera liturgica omnia (Vatican City: Apostolic Library, 1947), 1:363 (hereafter Hanssens, for this 3-vol. ed., Studi e testi 138–40).

6. DATING THE MASS PROPER I:
ADVENT AND THE THURSDAYS IN LENT

1. In what follows I cover ground previously traveled in "Vaticana Latina 5319 as a Witness to the Eighth-Century Roman Proper of the Mass," in *Cantus Planus, Papers Read at the Seventh Meeting, Sopron Hungary, September 1995*, ed. László Dobszay (Budapest: Hungarian Academy of Sciences, 1998), 403–11; and my "Preface," 233–47.

2. See Kenneth Levy, "Toledo, Rome and the Legacy of Gaul," *Early Music History* 4 (1984): 98, where Gallican offertories are said to be "entrenched . . . firmly within the liturgy of Urban Rome."

3. The three Roman graduals are Vatican City, Biblioteca Apostolica Vaticana, Archivio di San Pietro, ms lat. 5319 (here Vat lat 5319); Vatican City, Biblioteca Apostolica Vaticana, Archivio di San Pietro, ms F. 22 (here San Pietro F22); and Cologny-Genève, Bibliotheca Bodmeriana, ms 74 (here Bodmer 74).

4. The material referred to in the following sentence is too well known and represented in too many secondary sources to require documentation.

5. See *Sextuplex*, 2–3.

6. Ibid., 86–87, given here in the wording of the Compiègne gradual.

7. Twenty-three is the minimum number of Sundays that intervene between Pentecost and the first Sunday of Advent. The Franks required the minimum number because they numbered the Sundays in one consecutive series. The Romans avoided the difficulty by numbering the Sundays in four groups after key summer festivals, and by repeating Sundays in the first and last of these to accommodate the length of the post-Pentecostal period in a given year.

8. See *Sextuplex*, 180.

9. Ibid., xix.

10. No seepage, that is, of the Frankish additions to the Mass Proper. There is, to be sure, the remarkable case of the *Veterem hominem* antiphons described by Edward Nowacki, "Constantinople-Aachen-Rome: The Transmission of *Veterem hominem*," in *De musica et cantu: Studien zur Geschichte der Kirchenmusik und der Oper. Helmut Hucke zum 60. Geburtstag*, ed. Peter Cahn and Ann-Katrin Heimer (Hildesheim: Georg Olms, 1993), 95–115.

11. See note 2 above. My disagreement with Kenneth Levy (a dedicatee of the present volume) on this particular point does nothing to lessen my overall admiration for the magisterial study where it is expressed.

12. "Hic quadragesimali tempore ut quintas ferias missarum celebritas fieret in ecclesias, quod non agebatur, instituit" (Duchesne, 1:402).

13. See Raymond Davis, *The Lives of the Eighth-Century Popes (Liber pontificalis)*, translated with an introduction and commentary (Liverpool: Liverpool University Press, 1992), 1–2.

14. "Nam sicut quorundam relatu didicimus, domnus apostolicus in eisdem diebus a stationibus paenitus vacat, eo quod ceteris septimanae feriis stationibus uacando fatigatus, eisdem requiescat diebus. Ob id scilicet ut tumultuatione populari carens, et aelemosinas pauperibus distribuere, et negotia exteriora liberius valeat disponere" (text from Deshusses, 351). The *Hucusque* preface, known as such from its first word, was long attributed to Alcuin of York. Deshusses's attribution of it to Benedict is now generally accepted; see Vogel, 85–86.

15. Liturgical scholarship on the subject is summarized in Irénée H. Dalmais, Pierre Jounel and Aimé Georges Martimort, *The Church at Prayer: The Liturgy and Time*, ed. and trans. Matthew J. O'Connell (Collegeville, Minn.: Liturgical Press, 1985), 67.

16. The Proper for Thursday in Holy Week has curiously late traits but surely was in place before 720.

17. Mention should be made here of the enigmatic gradual for the fifth Thursday in Lent, *Tollite hostias*, which is unique to the date. Could it have been created, then, as late as 720? The question will be taken up in the chapter on the gradual.

18. There is a single exception to uniqueness in Sylvester's *Beatus servus* (Mt 24.46–47); however, there is a good argument to be made for the proposition that the communion was originally created for this date because its text is derived from the gospel of the day, Matthew 24.42–47.

19. I am not sure that I find any unambiguous examples beyond *Diffusa est*, *Posuisti domine*, *Qui manducat* and *Qui me dignatus est*.

20. "Frankish-Roman," 181.

21. These traits are regretfully absent from the late Roman versions. The epilogue touches on the question of whether they were added by the Franks or somehow lost by the Romans in the long history of oral transmission.

22. There is a lesser manifestation of the same sort in the third Mass for Christmas; its gradual and communion are both derived from Psalm 97.

23. See Wagner, 81–82; and Apel, 378–81.

24. See my "Preface," 241–47.

25. Again, by a "fixed assignment" I mean one where the same chant appears at the same feast day in all three Roman graduals and all six of the *Sextuplex* manuscripts.

26. See my "Preface," 238 and 240.

27. Ibid., 248. In point of fact I claim more precise numbers for the alleluia in chapter ten, which is devoted to the genre. I count 54 on table 21, from which, however, I must subtract 8 as added after the time of Sergius I in order to provide a full post-Pentecostal sequence (see table 21).

28. And, as will emerge during the study of the individual items of the Mass Proper, they achieved relative success for Lent; it is in Paschaltime that the unmistakable breakdown will be seen to take place.

29. See Thomas J. Talley, *The Origins of the Liturgical Year* (Collegeville, Minn.: Liturgical Press, 1991), 148–49.

30. On the history of Advent, I find particularly useful Josef Jungmann,

"Advent und Voradvent," in *Gewordene Liturgie; Studien und Durchblicke* (Innsbruck: F. Rauch, 1941), 232–94 (originally published in *Zeitschrift für katholische Theologie* 61 [1937]: 341–90); Walter Croce, "Die Adventmessen des römischen Missale in ihrer geschichtlichen Entwicklung," *Zeitschrift für katholische Theologie* 74 (1952): 277–317; and T. Maertens, "L'avent: genèse historique de ses thèmes bibliques et doctrinaux," *Mélanges de science religieuse* 18 (1961): 47–110.

31. Actually a date identified as Feria IIII, with the gospel Mark 8.15–26, intervenes between St. Lucy and Ebdomada IIII.

32. Thus the Paduensis; the Hadrianum abbreviates *incipiunt orationes* to *ort*.

33. P. J. McCann, ed. and trans., *The Rule of Saint Benedict in Latin and English* (Westminster, Md., 1952), 8 and 10.

34. I am indebted to Brad Maiani for bringing to my attention this entire subject of matins readings in the *ordines romani;* see Maiani, "Readings and Responsories: The Eighth-Century Night Office Lectionary and the *Responsoria Prolixa,*" *The Journal of Musicology* 16 (1998): 245–81.

35. See Andrieu, 3:35.

36. "Tempore veris, hoc est VII dieb[us] ante initium quatragesimae" (ibid., 39).

37. Ibid., 3:35 and 2:478.

38. Ibid., 2:481.

39. "4. [in] diebus autem paschae epistulae apostolorum et actus apostolorum atque apocalypsin usque pentecosten; 5. in tempore autem aestatis, regum, paralipomenon usque ad medium autumni, hoc est XV kal. novembris; 6. deinde libri Salomonis et mulierum atque Macchabeorum et liber Tobi usque kal. decembris; 7. ante autem natalem domini nostri Iesu Christi, Isaiae, Hieremiae et Daniel usque ad epyfaniam" (ibid., 3:40).

40. "In vigilia natalis domini legunt primum de Esaia lectiones tres, id est, prima lectio sic continet in capite: Primo tempore adleviata est terra Zabulon. Secunda lectio" (ibid., 2:485).

41. See James McKinnon, "Properization: The Roman Mass," in *Cantus Planus . . . 1993*, ed. László Dobszay (Budapest: Hungarian Academy of Sciences, 1995).

42. "In dominica prima mensis decembris, id est in prima dominica de adventu domini ponunt Esaiam prophetam usque in natalem domini" (Andrieu, 2:485).

7. DATING THE MASS PROPER II: THE SANCTORALE

1. The principle underpins much of the reference to chant chronology in Walter Howard Frere, *Studies in Early Roman Liturgy: The Kalendar,* Alcuin Club Collections 28 (Oxford: Oxford University Press, 1930); this monograph remains the most valuable ever undertaken on the Roman sanctorale.

2. "Petiit a Focate principe templum qui appellatur Pantheum, in quo fecit

ecclesiam beatae mariae semper virginis et omnium martyrum" (Duchesne, 1:317).

3. Frere, *Kalendar*, 105.

4. See my "Gregorian Chant."

5. See Duchesne, 1:419.

6. Peter Jeffery, "Rome and Jerusalem: From Oral Tradition to Written Repertory," in *Essays on Medieval Music in Honor of David G. Hughes*, ed. Graeme Boone (Cambridge, Mass.: Harvard University Department of Music, 1995), 214–18.

7. I exclude from all my counts of the sanctorale the three post-Christmas feasts: December 26's St. Stephen; December 27's St. John the Evangelist and December 28's Holy Innocents. These three were always treated in liturgical books as dates of the temporale. I include, however, December 31's St. Sylvester; it did not boast quite the same status in the Christmas cycle as the other three. It should be noted further that the Old Gelasian, in addition to the twelve occasions cited here, includes a reading for St. Sabina—within its group of Common readings, not within its calendric sanctoral cycle.

8. "Fecit ecclesiam beato Cyriaco martyri a solo" (Duchesne, 1:324).

9. On the Martyrology see Frere, *Kalendar*, 8–10.

10. "Fecit ecclesiam beato Severino a solo, iuxta civitate Tiburina, miliario ab urbe Roma XX, quem ipse dedicavit, et dona multa optulit" (Duchesne, 1:324).

11. "Fecit ecclesiam beati Adriani in Tribus Fatis, quam et dedicavit, et dona multa optulit" (ibid.).

12. "Hic perfecit cymiterium sancti Nicodemi et dedicavit eum" (ibid., 321).

13. "Fecit ecclesiam beatae Luciae in urbe Roma, iuxta sanctum Silvestrum, quem et dedicavit, et dona multa obtulit" (ibid., 324).

14. What follows, as was the case in chapter five, continues to be based upon the standard edition, Deshusses.

15. The two dates appear in the Trent redaction (see chapter five), confirming that they are additions of the earlier 680s. Beyond this there is no need to involve Trent in the present chapter's discussion, thus allowing a measure of simplification in the tables.

16. See Deshusses, 52.

17. See Jean Deshusses, "Le sacramentaire grégorien de Trente," *Revue bénédictine* 78 (1968): 276–77.

18. See Deshusses, 55–56.

19. It should be pointed out that three of the ten earlier additions (19 May's Pudentiana, 23 July's Apollinaris and 8 September's Hadrian) appear in the PI evangeliary but not the Hadrianum sacramentary. The best explanation for this somewhat anomalous circumstance, perhaps, is that the three festivals were not part of the papal sanctorale in the second half of the seventh century, whatever their status before that time.

20. "Immo et basilicam Salvatoris quae et Constantiniana vocatur iuxta

Lateranense patriarchio in ruinis posita una cum quadriporticis suis atriisque et fontes, a noviter sicut ecclesias beatorum principum Petri et Pauli renovavit, in qua et mutavit trabes maiores numero XV" (Duchesne, 1:507).

21. "Item in ecclesia beati Genesii martyris tectum noviter restauravit, ubi et altare erexit in nomine Salvatoris domini Dei nostri" (Duchesne, 1:419).

22. Indeed, the copying occurred considerably earlier, a point of some significance to be established presently.

23. See Brad Maiani, "The Responsory-Communions: Toward a Chronology of Selected Proper Chants" (Ph.D. diss., University of North Carolina at Chapel Hill, 1996).

24. The Franks, of course, borrow *Ave Maria* for the fourth Sunday of Advent, a date they add to the calendar; see *Sextuplex*, 8 and 11.

25. See Sermo clxxxix, *In natali domini VI* (PL 38, col. 1005).

26. See James McKinnon, "The Roman Post-Pentecostal Communion Series," in *Cantus Planus, Papers Read at the Fourth Meeting, Pécs, Hungary, September 1990* (Budapest: Hungarian Academy of Sciences, 1992), 183 (hereafter "Post-Pentecostal").

27. The Franks, too, apparently found it inappropriate and substituted other chants for it; see *Sextuplex*, 22–23 and 150–51.

28. Thus Vogel, 95; although no reason is given for the date.

29. "Constituit autem ut diebus Adnuntiationis Domini, Dormitionis, et Nativitatis sanctae Dei Genetricis semperque virginis Mariae ac sancti Simeonis, quod Hypopanti Greci appellant, letaniae exeant a sancto Hadriano et ad sanctam Mariam populus occurrat" (Duchesne, 1:376).

30. See Deshusses, 54–55. It would be better perhaps if liturgical historians allowed for the possibility that the prayers were composed under the supervision of Sergius rather than by the pope himself.

31. See Frere, *Kalendar*, 93.

32. See Deshusses, 55.

33. See Theodor Klauser, "Rom und der Kult der Gottesmutter Maria," *Jahrbuch für Antike und Christentum* 15 (1972): 123–25.

34. Ibid., 123.

35. There is a remarkable circumstance offering further support for the late date of the Dedication chants. The offertory *Domine deus* —a free paraphrase from 2 Chronicles telling of David's sacrifice, which presages the building of the temple, and of Solomon's sacrifice, which serves to dedicate it—has the most striking similarity to those celebrated post-Pentecostal offertories such as *Sanctificavit moyses*. The point will be taken up again in the chapter on the offertory, where it will be argued that such offertories are among the very last chants to be added to the Roman Mass Proper.

36. "cantelena ac psalmodia praecipuus et in earum sensibus subtilissima exercitatione limatus" (Duchesne, 1:359).

37. "se in divinis Scripturis et cantilena a puerili etate ... exhibuit ut decem virum suo nomine dignum" (ibid., 363).

38. "quia studiosus erat et capax in officio cantelenae, priori cantorum pro doctrina est traditus" (ibid., 371).

8. THE INTROIT

1. See Andrieu, 2:81–83.
2. Its traditional association with the passage from Celestine I's *Liber pontificalis* biography was, of course, rejected here in chapter four.
3. See chapter 2, note 8.
4. See Frans van de Paverd, *Zur Geschichte der Messliturgie in Antiocheia und Konstantinopel gegen Ende des vierten Jahrhunderts,* Orientalia christiana analecta 187 (Rome: Pontifical Institute of Oriental Studies, 1970), 82–89 and 425–28. Liturgical historians are unanimous on the point; see, for example, Josef Jungmann, *The Mass of the Roman Rite,* trans. Francis A. Brunner (1951; reprint, Westminster, Md.: Christian Classics, 1986), 1:262.
5. On the introduction of the Trisagion see Johannes Quasten, "Oriental Influence in the Gallican Liturgy," *Traditio* 1 (1943): 58.
6. On the melodic homogeneity of the Gregorian introits, see Apel's comments (305–6).
7. There are three offertories of the sort (*Benedicam dominum, Confitebor tibi* and *Jubilate deo universa terra*), and one communion (*Amen dico vobis quidquid*).
8. In four out of five cases: *Factus est, Da pacem, Justus es* and *Statuit,* but not *Dicit dominus . . . sermones meos.*
9. In three out of four cases: *Gaudeamus, Rorate* and *Suscepimus,* but not *Inclina.*
10. Edward Nowacki is responsible for discovering the part that word accents play in the process; see his "Text Declamation as a Determinant of Melodic Form in the Old Roman Eighth-Mode Tracts," *Early Music History* 6 (1986): 193–226.
11. Precisely the position of Thomas Connolly, "Introits and Archetypes: Some Archaisms of the Old Roman Chant," *JAMS* 25 (1972): 157–74.
12. An essential methodological point—I do not define the mere presence of a common opening gesture in an introit as formulaicism in the full sense but require that the common melodic material continue for some distance beyond the incipit. I differ in this respect with the premises of Thomas Connolly's "The Introits of the Old Roman Chant" (Ph.D. diss., Harvard University, 1972), a work I have used with considerable profit.
13. Every sanctoral date of the season is given in the table—and in the order of its appearance in Vat lat 5319, except for two that have introits borrowed from earlier dates in the year.
14. The final alleluia of the Paschaltime introits, incidentally, is in fact a pair of alleluias as opposed to the single alleluia inserted in the middle of the chants. This concluding pair is not always so consistent in its formulaicism, especially the first of the pair, as is the single inserted alleluia.

15. I would guess that the cantors responsible for these figures made their choice more intuitively than theoretically, although those more schooled than I am in the subtlety of early medieval Latin scansion, accentual and durational, might be able to provide a more satisfactory explanation for the phenomenon in question.

16. They are *Domine refugium; In deo laudabo; In nomine domini; Meditatio cordis* and *Tibi dixit.*

17. They are *Ego clamavi; Ego autem cum justitia* and *Ego autem in domino.* One might be tempted to place *Ego autem sicut oliva* in the same category, but its common material fails to extend beyond the incipit.

18. There is another apparent exception: Holy Thursday borrows *Nos autem* from Tuesday in Holy Week. That such an important festival borrows a chant is surely testimony to a very late assignment, one probably falling outside the period in question. There are other anomalies associated with the chants of Holy Thursday, none of which I am able to explain adequately.

19. Lent was presented in tabular form early in chapter six (in connection with Vat lat 5319's use as witness to earlier Roman chant); the table, however, lacks scriptural derivations.

20. The other three nonpsalmic introits are Ash Wednesday's *Misereris omnium* (Wis 11.24–27), Tuesday in Holy Week's *Nos autem* (Gal 6.14) and Thursday in the third week's nonscriptural *Salus populi* (borrowed from the post-Pentecostal series).

21. Vat lat 5319 calls these Sundays after Pentecost but earlier on repeats the chants of Pentecost Saturday on the octave day. This, after a rubric that declares the date DOMINICA VACAT, surely an indication that the use of the Pentecost Saturday chants is a late adjustment.

22. See James McKinnon, "Antoine Chavasse and the Dating of Early Chant," *Plainsong and Medieval Music* 1 (1992): 123–47; what follows is summarized from 142–46.

23. Of the 144 introits, I count 67 with substantial adjustment, 23 with minor adjustment and 53 with integral biblical texts; for the 141 communions, 57 substantial, 21 minor and 62 integral. Note the presence of one nonbiblical introit, *Salus populi*, accounting for a more precisely relevant total of 143, and one nonbiblical communion, *Qui me dignatus*, accounting for 140. It should be further noted that the distinction between a slightly adjusted text and an integral one is not always clear, whereas the presence of substantial adjustment is always obvious.

24. The third is that of Tuesday in the third week's *Ego clamavi* (Ps 16.6–8), a day of no special liturgical significance to my knowledge.

25. A third area of the sort would appear to be the psalmic post-Pentecostal chants, but we have just seen this ruled out already at least in the case of introits.

26. I refer, of course, to the debate introduced by Leo Treitler's seminal article, "Homer and Gregory: The Transmission of Epic Poetry and Plainchant," *The Musical Quarterly* 60 (1974): 333–72. Closely allied with Treitler was Helmut Hucke, "Toward a New Historical View of Gregorian Chant," *JAMS* 33

(1980): 437–67. Taking opposing views to Treitler and Hucke were Kenneth Levy, "Charlemagne's Archetype of Gregorian Chant," *JAMS* 40 (1987): 1–30; and David Hughes, "Evidence for the Traditional View of the Transmission of Gregorian Chant," *JAMS* 40 (1987): 377–404.

27. See Hughes, "Evidence for the Traditional View."
28. "Frankish-Roman," 222.

9. THE GRADUAL

1. The most common reading has "Cantor cum cantatorio ascendit et dicit responsum" (Andrieu, 2:86). The "S" manuscript introduces the term "gradual": "Cantor cum cantatorio ascendens responsum gradale cantat" (ibid.).

2. "Deinde subdiaconus regionarius . . . dicit: Scola. Respondet: Adsum. Et ille: Quis psallit? Respondet: Ille et ille" (ibid., 79).

3. "Responsorium ideo dicitur, eo quod uno cantante, ceteri respondeant" (*Eclogae, De ordine romano*, 15 [Hanssens, 3:244]).

4. "Ipse idem solus versum cantat" (ibid.).

5. René-Jean Hesbert, "Le graduel, chant responsorial," *Ephemerides liturgicae* 95 (1981): 316–350.

6. I try my best in chant seminars to create an unprejudiced test of aesthetic reaction to the two versions. Early in the semester, before the students have had much experience with either the Gregorian or Roman repertory, I have them memorize and sing certain chants in both versions. Let me say only that their reactions seldom if ever occasion any surprise.

7. Discussion of the A-2 and F-5 graduals will suffice to prepare for the historical considerations that are the principal concern of this chapter. One may consult Apel, 345–62, for his still valuable formulaic analysis of the Gregorian versions of all graduals.

8. In these calculations I count *Haec dies* as only one chant in spite of its appearance throughout Easter week with different verses. I do so for the sake of presentational brevity.

9. For the sake of presentational brevity, here, too, I omit the five other appearances of *Haec dies* with different verses on the ferias of Easter week.

10. See Apel, 344–45.

11. Of 104 biblically derived responds (*Locus iste* is nonbiblical), I count just seventeen that are substantially adjusted; of verses, there are no more than a handful, and these are mostly nonpsalmic. The case of the only temporal psalmic verse that was substantially adjusted, *Dum clamarem*, is of special significance and will be treated at length below.

12. See *Sextuplex*, 22–23.

13. There is an additional reason to think of *Speciosus* as an older chant, its presence in the Psalter of St-Germain-des-Prés as one of the verses indicated with an R. The general significance of this psalter for the chronology of the Roman gradual repertory will be taken up at the close of the portion of this chapter dealing with the Lenten graduals.

14. One might, however, wish to consider the graduals of the fifth week as a possible exception. Three of the week's six gradual responds (*Eripe, Discerne* and *Pacifice*) are subject to substantial textual adjustment, a trait rare in graduals, and three of the six (*Discerne, Tollite* and *Pacifice*) are set in the F-5 melodic formula. The fifth week of Lent is, moreover, a period that liturgical historians speak of generally as being subject to later adjustments.

15. It is the only temporal verse and the only one to be so radically adjusted; the other example is the sanctoral verse *Audi* of *Specie tua* (Ps 44.5, 11–12), which simply has an omission of several words from the scriptural original.

16. Two of these (*Jacta cogitatum* and *Propitius*) are borrowed internally for Thursdays in Lent, and three (*Dirigatur, Protector* and *Salvum fac*) are borrowed to make up the complement of five graduals assigned to the Saturday of the Lenten Ember Days.

17. There is considerable inconsistency in the liturgical books about which sanctoral dates of the period were stational. To me this suggests a dual explanation: while certain major dates were understood to be celebrated at the church dedicated to the saint in question, and hence not indicated in the sources, there might at the same time have been a more informal attitude toward the observance of summer dates in particular.

18. Guido describes his innovative antiphoner in the "Prologue to His Antiphoner," translated in *Strunk's Source Readings in Music History: The Early Christian Period and the Latin Middle Ages*, ed. James McKinnon, rev. ed. (New York: W. W. Norton, 1997), 101–4.

19. See Helmut Hucke, "Gregorianischer Gesang in altrömischer und fränkischer Überlieferung," *Archiv für Musikwissenschaft* 12 (1955): 85–86. Edward Nowacki is publishing a partial translation and commentary on this seminal article in a forthcoming issue of *Plainsong and Medieval Music*.

20. See *Sextuplex*, xiii–xiv.

21. The other two are *Ecce quam bonum*, already excluded as unique to Vat lat 5319, and *Timebunt gentes*, which appears earlier in the series.

22. One of the graduals derived from Psalm 44, *Constitues eos*, is used for male saints, the Apostles Peter and Paul, and Andrew. It appears nonetheless ancient for this reason.

23. The sole exception is *Ecce sacerdos magnus* (Sir 44.16, 20), which, it was argued above, was originally uniquely assigned to the feast of St. Sylvester.

24. This consistent association of nonpsalmic chants with those that have substantially adjusted texts continues to boost confidence in the latter trait as a reliable chronological indication—a claim made in the previous chapter.

25. Once established, however, the stability of the Frankish assignments is virtually absolute; for the thirty-one times that both Blandin and Monza have graduals, they share a chant thirty times.

26. I note only two exceptions: *Posuisti domine* has both different finals (A-1) and unrelated melodies, while *Justorum animae*, although with different finals (F-1), still maintains related melodies.

27. The one exception is something of a curiosity, *Pretiosa*, a chant assigned

to 20 January's St. Sebastian in Vat lat 5319, and appearing in the *Sextuplex* sources only in the Senlis gradual for 22 August's St. Timothy. *Pretiosa*, a mode-E chant in the Roman versions, failed to become part of the Gregorian mainstream; I can locate only a handful of sources for it, all nondiastemmatic.

28. These dates appear in two clusters, one in June and the other in August.

29. The Holy Thursday gradual thus shares with the Holy Thursday introit, *Nos autem*, the only shared introit in Lent, an indication of its being a particularly late chant. For liturgical reasons that escape me, the Mass chants of Holy Thursday appear to have been added at an especially late date.

10. THE ALLELUIA

1. "Si fuerit tempus ut dicat Alleluia, bene; sin autem, tractum" (Andrieu, 2:86).

2. Ibid.

3. Most of what follows in this portion of the chapter is taken from my 1997 "Preface," 213–49; I refer the reader to that study for the documentary evidence cited here.

4. These psalms number, in the Hebrew (and Protestant) Bible: 105–7, 111–19, 135–36 and 145–50. The Greek and Latin (and Catholic) numbering, which is used in discussing Greek and Latin Christian chant in this volume, is slightly different: 104–6, 110–18, 134–35 and 145–50.

5. See *MECL*, 142. Citations for all references in the following two paragraphs can be found in my "Preface," 219–27.

6. Again, in addition to remarks made in previous chapters of this volume, it is especially my article "Preface" that I draw upon for what follows.

7. *In psalmum civ* (*CCL* 98, 942).

8. See Christian Thodberg, *Der byzantinische Alleluiarionzyklus: Studien im kurzen Psaltikonstil*, Monumenta musicae byzantinae subsidia 8 (Copenhagen: E. Munksgaard, 1966), 40–43.

9. See Wagner, 33.

10. See James J. O'Donnell, *Cassiodorus* (Berkeley: University of California Press, 1979), 131–36.

11. See "Preface," 229–31. In this I ally myself with the admirable study of Aimé Georges Martimort, "Origine et signification de l'alléluia de la messe romaine," in *Kyriakon: Festschrift Johannes Quasten*, ed. Patrick Granfield and Josef Jungmann (Münster: Aschendorff, 1970), 2:828. See also Hiley, 502 and 504.

12. Thodberg, *Alleluiarionzyklus*, 174–95.

13. Omitted from example 12 are the Roman Latin version of the chant, *Dominus regnavit decorem*, with its melody identical to that of the Roman *O kyrios*, and the Milanese and Gregorian *Dominus regnavit decorem*, with their related melodies. Omitted also are the manuscript sources for the two versions given in example 12, all of which is indicated in Thodberg, ibid., 175–76 and 179–80. Thodberg provides an additional example—a portion of *Oty theos* in

"Alleluia," *New Grove Dictionary of Music and Musicians*, ed. Stanley Sadie, 1:275.

14. In point of fact *Beatus vir* and *Haec dies* have nearly identical melodies throughout, and *Venite exultemus* and *Te decet hymnus* share the same melody for the alleluia and the first part of the verse.

15. Thodberg, *Alleluiarionzyklus*, 11–12.

16. On the *prokeimenon* see Gisa Hintze, *Das byzantinische Prokeimena-Repertoire: Untersuchungen und kritische Edition* (Hamburg: Karl Dieter Wagner, 1973), 17–19; on the *koinonicon* see Thomas H. Schattauer, "The Koinonicon of the Byzantine Liturgy: An Historical Study," *Orientalia christiana periodica* 49 (1983): 91–129.

17. Hintze, *Prokeimena-Repertoire*, compares the five chants and fails to find any musical relationship. Christian Troelsgaard, however (generously sharing an unpublished study with me), argues for such a relationship. I continue not to see it myself, but I acknowledge that he may be right in this respect. However, if there is in fact a musical relationship in the *prokeimenon*-gradual pairs, it is not remotely as close as that of the alleluia pairs and must be explained by other historical circumstances than a direct seventh-century transmission—for example, by fourth-century psalm tones common to both East and West.

18. For a thorough discussion of the ceremony, see Bruno Stäblein, *Die Gesänge des altrömischen Graduale Vat. lat. 5319*, Monumenta monodica medii aevi, 2 (Kassel: Bärenreiter, 1970), 84*–97*.

19. The table is based on *Ordo romanus XXVII* rather than the other source giving the complete sequence of chants, that is, Vat lat 5319. One notes the absence of Thursday from the table and the conclusion of the rite on the octave of Easter. Vat lat 5319, however, includes Thursday by simply moving the last four days forward. This is apparently a later arrangement.

20. Thodberg, *Alleluiarionzyklus*, 173.

21. See Philippe Bernard, "Les alléluia mélismatiques dans le chant romain: recherches sur la genèse de l'alléluia de la messe romaine," *Rivista internazionale di musica sacra* 12 (1991): 342–43.

22. And indeed Wagner before him; Apel follows Wagner on all major points of the alleluia's early history.

23. See Apel, 378. Apel follows Wagner in this also; see Wagner, 81–82.

24. See especially "Preface," 214–18; and James McKinnon, "The Patristic Jubilus and the Alleluia of the Mass," in *Cantus Planus: Papers Read at the Third Meeting, Tihany, Hungary, 19–24 September 1988*, ed. László Dobszay (Budapest: Hungarian Academy of Sciences, 1990), 61–70.

25. See Thodberg, *Alleluiarionzyklus*, 40.

26. *Liber officialis* I, 41 (Hanssens, 2:193).

27. Roman assignments, again, are sufficiently uniform to allow for the use of a single column; Bodmer 74's frequent additions of Gregorian alleluias and sequences (and substitution of Latin for Greek alleluias) are not indicated in the table.

28. Only the offertory *Deus tu convertus* makes no reference to Jerusalem; see Hesbert's attempt to explain this in *Sextuplex*, xxxvii–xxxviii.

29. The abbreviations given here stand for Graz, Universitätsbibliothek, ms 807; Paris, Bibliothèque nationale, fonds latin, ms 903; Benevento, Biblioteca capitolare VI, ms 34; and Montpellier, Bibliothèque de l'école de médecine, ms H159.

30. In fact, melody-type chants should be more easily transmitted, and while I spare the reader the details, comparisons similar to those indicated in table 25 demonstrate that melody-type alleluias are by and large faithfully transmitted to the Franks. Why the Romans seem to have provided a single original melody chant, *Qui sanat contritos*, for the post-Pentecostal series is another of those minor mysteries in the makeup of the Roman Mass Proper for which I have absolutely no explanation.

31. *MECL*, 161.

32. And might we not see in this G-tonality some affinity with the tonality of Kenneth Levy's fourth-century sanctus, described in his "The Byzantine Sanctus and Its Modal Tradition in East and West," *Annales musicologiques* 6 (1958–63): 7–67.

33. For the Amalarius citations see my "Preface," 218n. 19.

34. "Notandum autem quod Pneumata quae in Alleluia et caeteris cantibus in paucitate verborum fiunt jubilum significant" (*De officiis ecclesiasticis* II, 19 [*PL* 177, col. 422]).

35. See my "Patristic Jubilus and the Alleluia of the Mass," 69.

36. See Jean Claire, "Aux origines de l'alléluia," *Orbis musicae* 9 (1986–87): 17–57.

37. The Pentecost week assignments (including a total of seven for the three chants involved) are omitted from table 24 with a view toward making it less cumbersome; they appear in Vat lat 5319, folios 118 to 119v (see Stäblein, *Die Gesänge des altrömischen Graduale*, 658–59).

38. *Preoccupemus*, however, I find puzzling, as it fails to appear in the Frankish repertory.

39. *Magnus sanctus Paulus* (nonbiblical), a *Dies* chant also, fails to appear in the Frankish sources.

40. See Thodberg, *Alleluiarionzyklus*, 192–93, for a summary of the literature and the issues involved.

11. THE TRACT

1. See Helmut Hucke, "Tract," *New Grove*, 19:110, where Hucke writes: "It would appear, rather, that the tract is a more recently developed class of Gregorian chant and that its establishment in the liturgical order had not been completed by the end of the 8th century."

2. Wagner, 87–88.

3. See its Latin text in chapter two, note 8. And see too that chapter's note 36, which singles out Olivier Cullin, the foremost advocate of the view in question.

He is joined by (among others) Philippe Bernard; see "Les alléluia mélismatiques dans le chant romain: recherches sur la genèse de l'alléluia de la messe romaine," *Rivista internazionale di musica sacra* 12 (1991): 346n. 11 and 350n. 58.

4. I have reviewed all the available evidence in "The Fourth-Century Origin of the Gradual," *Early Music History* 7 (1987): 93–98, and failed to find a single indisputable example of a reference to *in directum* Fore-Mass psalmody. The one that comes closest is the passage from Tertullian where he speaks of a charismatic Montanist woman, the material for whose visions is supplied during Sunday liturgy, "as the scriptures are read, psalms are sung (*psalmi canuntur*), the homily delivered and prayers are offered" (*De anima* IX, 4 [*MECL*, 45]). The probability is that the "psalms" cited are not biblical but rather newly composed Montanist songs, but even if they are biblical psalms, there is nothing in the language that tells whether they are sung with responses or not. Cullin, nevertheless, relies heavily upon this single passage, speaking of "*le schéma de Tertullien*" (see "Le répertoire de la psalmodie *in directum* dans les traditions liturgiques latines: la tradition hispanique," *Études grégoriennes* 23 [1989]: 100 and 104). As for the passage from the *Didascalia* quoted by Cullin (ibid., 100), see the remarks in my *MECL*, 40.

5. On the supposed tract-like qualities of *Haec dies*, see Olivier Cullin, "De la psalmodie sans refrain à la psalmodie responsoriale," *Revue de musicologie* 77 (1991): 8–9.

6. See *Sextuplex*, l–li.

7. Ibid.

8. Hesbert (ibid., l) notes the striking coincidence that this very gradual, *Tenuisti*, replaces Quadragesima's *Angelis suis* in the Blandin manuscript. (See also his argument for the melodic uniqueness of *Tenuisti*, which he takes as a sign of late chant [ibid., n. 1 on lii].)

9. See Helmut Hucke, "Tractusstudien," in *Festschrift Bruno Stäblein zum 70. Geburtstag*, ed. Martin Ruhnke (Kassel: Bärenreiter, 1967), 116–120.

10. "subdiaconus ascendit ad legendum et post lectionem cantatur canticum Domine audivi, cum versibus suis. . . . Deinde sequitur altera lectio, post quam sequitur tractus Qui habitat" (Andrieu, 3:355).

11. "Deinde annuit archidiaconus subdiacono ut legatur lectio prima. Sequitur responsorium Domine audivi. Deinde alia leccio et sequitur tactus [*sic*] Qui habitat" (Andrieu, 3:471).

12. See Apel, 324.

13. See Jacques Froger, "Les anticipations du jeûne quadragésimal," *Mélanges de science religieuse* 3 (1946): 207–34; see also L. J. Crampton, "St. Gregory's Homily XIX and the Institution of Septuagesima Sunday," *Downside Review* 86 (1968): 162–66.

14. See John Boe, "Chant Notation in Eleventh-Century Roman Manuscripts," in *Essays on Medieval Music in Honor of David G. Hughes*, ed. Graeme Boone (Cambridge, Mass.: Harvard University Department of Music, 1995), 49–51. Boe discovered three of the chants notated in an eleventh-century Roman lectionary.

15. James McKinnon, "The Gregorian Canticle-Tracts of the Old Roman Easter Vigil," in *Festschrift Walter Wiora zum 90. Geburtstag*, ed. Christoph-Hellmut Mahling and Ruth Seiberts (Tutzing: Hans Schneider, 1997), 254–70. See this study for references cited in the immediately following pages.

16. See, for example, *Ordo romanus XXVII* (Andrieu, 3:355).

17. Ibid., 359–60.

18. *Attende*, by the way, is present in the Frankish sources in spite of the absence of the pertinent reading from the Hadrianum sacramentary. Frankish sacramentaries, it must be remembered, amalgamate in various ways the Gelasian and Gregorian sacramentaries, thus providing at least occasional examples of *Attende*'s reading. On the curious history of this chant in the ninth-century sources, see my "Gregorian Canticle-Tracts," 266–68.

19. The Sárospatac leaf was the subject of a paper at the annual meeting of the AMS, Chicago 1991, for which Jeffery prepared a useful transcription of the leaf.

20. See Bonifatius Fischer, "Die Lesungen der römischen Ostervigil unter Gregor d. Gr.," in *Colligere Fragmenta: Festschrift Alban Dold zum 70. Geburtstag*, ed. Bonifatius Fischer and Virgil Fiala (Beuron: Beuroner Kunstverlag, 1952), 144–59.

12. THE OFFERTORY

1. The scholar who has come closest to conquering it is Joseph Dyer in "The Offertories of Old-Roman Chant: A Musico-Liturgical Investigation" (Ph.D. diss., Boston University, 1971).

2. I define the core repertory here, as with other items of the Mass Proper, as those Roman chants included in the mid-eighth-century transmission to the north. The Romans added just two more offertories after the redaction of the manuscripts used in the transmission: *Domine Hiesu Christe* for the Mass for the Dead and *Beatus es Symon* for the octave of the feast of Peter and Paul. The eighth- and ninth-century Franks, for their part, added twelve offertories to the repertory, not nearly as many as for the alleluia but more than for any other genre of the Mass Proper.

3. Caspar Ott, *Offertoriale sive versus offertoriorum* (Tournai: Desclée, 1935). Ott's edition was republished by Rupert Fischer with neumes added by hand as *Offertoriale triplex cum versiculis* (Sablé-sur-Sarthe: Abbé de St-Pierre-de-Solesmes, 1985).

4. See especially the important article of Ruth Steiner, "Some Questions about the Gregorian Offertories and Their Verses," *JAMS* 19 (1966): 162–81.

5. *H 159 Montpellier: Tonary of St Bénigne of Dijon*, transcribed and annotated by Finn Egeland Hansen (Copenhagen: Dan Fog, 1974).

6. Dyer's views on this and related topics, developed initially in his dissertation, are further refined in "The Offertory Chant of the Roman Liturgy and Its Musical Form," *Studi musicali* 11 (1982): 3–30.

7. See Helmut Hucke, "Die Texte der Offertorien," in *Speculum musicae artis: Festgabe für Heinrich Husmann zum 60. Geburtstag am 16. Dez 1968*, ed. Heinz Becker and Reinhard Gerlach (Munich: W. Fink, 1970), 193–203.

8. "Morem qui tunc esse apud Carthaginem coeperat ut hymni ad altare dicerentur de psalmorum libro, sive ante oblationem, sive cum distribueretur populo quod fuisset oblatum" (*Liber retractationem* 2, 11 [CCL 36, 144]).

9. Much of what I will argue in the next several paragraphs has been expressed with considerably more detail and expertise by Joseph Dyer in "Augustine and the 'Hymni ante oblationem': The Earliest Offertory Chants?," *Revue des études augustiniennes* 27 (1981): 85–99. Indeed, in his concluding sentence Dyer can be said to be the first to cast doubt on the traditional interpretation of the Augustinian passage: "The 'traditional' interpretation of these *hymni* as the earliest offertory chants cannot be excluded, though henceforth it must not be considered a certitude."

10. See Dyer, "Offertories of Old-Roman Chant," 47–51.

11. "Et pontifex, inclinans se paululum ad altare, respicit scolam et annuit ut sileant" (Andrieu, 1:95).

12. See Apel, 512.

13. For Dyer, see "Offertory Chant of the Roman Liturgy," 16; for Steiner, see "Questions about the Gregorian Offertories," 177–79.

14. See Kenneth Levy, "Toledo, Rome and the Legacy of Gaul," *Early Music History* 4 (1984): 52.

15. See especially Steiner, "Questions about the Gregorian Offertories," 163–76.

16. David Hiley points out the most extraordinary examples (q.v. 129–30).

17. Scriptural derivations are omitted from the table in the interest of saving space; all derivations are psalmic except for *Confortamini* (Is 35.4) and *Exulta satis filia* (Zac 9.9).

18. The versions are compared in Richard Crocker, "Chants of the Roman Mass," in *New Oxford History of Music*, ed. Richard Crocker and David Hiley (Oxford: Oxford University Press, 1990), 2:191–93.

19. Liturgical and musical continuity between the Roman and Frankish Advent-Christmas offertory verses is perhaps the central finding of an excellent paper ("New Perspectives on the Transmission and Chronology of the Offertory Chant and Its Verses") given at the 1997 annual meeting of the AMS by Rebecca Malloy, a graduate student at the University of Cincinnati who works with Edward Nowacki.

20. The second verse of *Confortamini*, the lengthy *Audite itaque* (Is 7.13–14), is indicated on table 30 as an integral biblical text; this, in spite of the fact that it is so divergent from any extant reading as to appear to be a free paraphrase of the biblical original. I bow in this case to the expertise of Petrus Pietschmann, "Die nicht dem Psalter entnommenen Messgesangstücke auf ihre Textgestalt untersucht," *Jahrbuch für Liturgiewissenschaft* 12 (1932): 125–26, who sees the verse as probably quoting a lost ancient North African version.

21. Aside from the handful of discrepancies in Rheinau, Blandin has *Domine ad adjutorium* in place of Rome's *Domine in auxilium*, the same curious type of verbal confusion met with even in the occasional introit and communion.

22. This at least is the explanation (the enormity of the task facing the Frankish singers) I pursue in what follows for the lapses in musical continuity. Malloy, following upon her exhaustive examination of the offertory verses, is inclined to trace the problem to the circumstance "that the tradition of verse singing [by the Romans] in the later seasons was not yet stable at the time of the Frankish reception." I am in receipt of her paper at too late a stage to attempt a reevaluation of my position.

23. Dyer compared the texts of the Old Roman offertory responds and verses with the Psalterium Romanum and the Gregorian tradition; see his "Offertories of Old-Roman Chant," 134–47.

24. I refer the reader to note 22 above.

25. The Franks substitute *Angelus domini* for the octave of Easter's *Benedictus qui*, and *Lauda anima* for Pentecost Friday's *Populum humilem*. The creation, moreover, of a new Frankish Ascension offertory, *Viri Galilei*, causes a number of discrepancies on Ascension Thursday and the following Sunday.

26. The early borrowing in the series, that of the Easter octave from Easter Saturday, is simply one more indication of the complex liturgical relationship between these two dates, having to do with the moving of the baptismal octave from the Sunday to the Saturday.

27. Apel, 367. The reference to Amalarius is given on this same page.

28. See my "Post-Pentecostal," 180–85.

29. Ibid., 183. And, again, see the following chapter.

30. This is at least the case according to Amalarius—"quoniam altero ordine cantamus nostros responsorios quam Romani. Illi a capite incipiunt responsorium, finito versu, nos versum finitum informamus in responsorium per latera eius, ac si facimus de duobus corporibus unum corpus" (*Prologus antiphonarii* 12 [Hanssens, 1:362]).

31. I refer here, needless to say, to my single point of disagreement with Kenneth Levy; see chapter six, above, notes 2 and 11.

13. THE COMMUNION

1. See *MECL*, 76–77, 82, 109, 120, 144 and 166.

2. It is possible that the first item cited in the previous note is from the mid- rather than later fourth century, even if I favor the latter possibility.

3. What follows on the Byzantine koinonicon is summarized from Thomas H. Schattauer, "The Koinonicon of the Byzantine Liturgy: An Historical Study," *Orientalia christiana periodica* 49 (1983): 91–129. For further details, see Dimitri Conomos, *The Late Byzantine and Slavonic Communion Cycle: Liturgy and Music* (Washington, D.C.: Dumbarton Oaks Research Library and Collection, 1985), 1–51.

4. Ibid., 48–51.

5. See also my "Post-Pentecostal."

6. The text is the work of the Roman singers, but the musical characterization described here is, admittedly, apparent only in the extant Gregorian version.

7. Only the third Sunday after Epiphany's Gregorian *Mirabantur* is an exception in this respect. This involves a story, intriguing as it may be, that is simply too long in the telling; the curious reader must be referred to the pages of my "Frankish-Roman," where it forms a large proportion of the entire essay.

8. See ibid., 180–81.

9. My own telling of it appears principally in ibid., 183, 194 and 201–3.

10. It is more likely, in fact, that there were less than twenty-six communions in this group, perhaps about twenty, a point to be pursued in the following chapter.

11. See especially Camille Callewaert, "S. Grégoire, les scrutins et quelques messes quadragésimales," *Ephemerides liturgicae* 53 (1938): 191–203; René-Jean Hesbert, "Les dimanches de carême dans les manuscrits romano-bénéventains," *Ephemerides liturgicae* 48 (1934): 198–222; and Antoine Chavasse, "Le carême romain et les scrutins prébaptismaux avant le IXe siècle," *Recherches de science religieuse* 35 (1948): 325–81. See also Helmut Hucke and Michel Huglo, "Communion," *New Grove*, 4:592.

12. It is claimed that we even know the author of the five new gospels: none other than Gregory the Great; see Callewaert, "S. Grégoire, les scrutins," 198–202. Callewaert's argument rests on purported similarities of phraseology in the texts of the communions with passages in the works of Gregory. I find just one example of these convincing—that involving the communion *Videns dominus* and a place in Gregory's homily on Ezekiel—but see nothing to prevent Gregory's well-known homily from influencing the composer of the communion's text long after the pope's death.

13. See Hucke and Huglo, "Communion," 592.

14. Ten are identified in my "Frankish-Roman," 208–11, plus the possible *Cito euntes*, 213. More recently Palm Sunday's *Pater si non potest* has come to light.

15. Hucke and Huglo, "Communion," 592.

16. The Roman communion for the Sunday after the Ascension, *Tristitia vestra*, is replaced in the Frankish series by *Pater cum essem*, an action I cannot explain; see my "Frankish-Roman," 214–15.

17. See ibid., 190–92.

18. See Brad Maiani, "The Responsory-Communions: Toward a Chronology of Selected Proper Chants" (Ph.D. diss., University of North Carolina at Chapel Hill, 1996), 6.

19. Ibid., 220–22.

20. "Post-Pentecostal."

21. *Domine memorabor*, in square brackets on table 36, is not part of the group, a circumstance to be explained below.

22. Again, I use the terms "Old Testament" and "New Testament" without theological bias but rather as they relate historically to the conceptions of medieval Christian ecclesiastics.

23. I would hope it is not necessary to summarize here the complex history of ancient Judaism's various housings of the Ark of the Covenant, including the successive temples of Jerusalem, nor to explain the seemingly anachronistic way in which even the most sophisticated of medieval savants could bring all this into one synchronic entity.

24. I am not the first to have noticed this: R. Le Roux makes the same observation in "Les graduels des dimanches après la Pentecôte," *Études grégoriennes* 5 (1962): 125.

25. Why are only three of the five borrowed? That twenty-two is the required number of a Roman post-Pentecostal series of chants is of itself a sufficient explanation, but those wishing additional discussion of the issue may consult my "Post-Pentecostal," 185–86.

26. They were treated above briefly, in chapter six, along with all the chants of the Ember Days.

27. The annual readings cycles of matins for seventh- and eighth-century Rome are to be found in *Ordo romanus XIV* (Andrieu, 3:35); and *Ordo romanus XIIIA* (ibid., 2:478).

28. I include *Beatus servus,* already encountered in the Christmas cycle, because the feast of St. Sylvester shares it with three other dates. I include also, contrary to my general policy, three chants not transmitted to Francia (*Beati mundo corde, Domine si tu es* and *Sint lumbi vestri*); I do so because there are reasons, discussed below, to believe that they were in the Roman repertory before the time of transmission, even though they do not appear in early Frankish manuscripts.

29. I count among the eighteen Paul's (30 June) *Amen dico vobis quod uni;* it appears twice in Vat lat 5319, but the second appearance is for the obviously late feast of Simon and Jude (2 November).

30. In an earlier draft of the present chapter I subjected the four chants to an extended attempt at explaining the anomaly involved; there is enough such detail in the chapter as currently constituted.

31. Psalmic sanctoral graduals, not discussed from this aspect in the chapter on the genre, contribute little to the point; they are overwhelmingly nonadjusted, whether unique or shared (six of seven unique are nonadjusted, as are sixteen of seventeen shared).

32. The handful of exceptions (the communions for the third Sunday after the Epiphany, the fifth Sunday after Easter and the Sunday after the Ascension) are discussed in my "Frankish-Roman."

33. I exclude from the count, needless to say, the communions of feasts added to the Roman sanctorale after the transmission to the north, for example, that of the vigil and feast of Simon and Jude (1–2 November).

34. "Roman-Frankish," 222.

14. THE CREATION OF THE ROMAN MASS PROPER

1. See Karol Berger, "The Geneaology of Modern European Art Music," in *A Theory of Art* (Oxford: Oxford University Press, 1999).
2. Translation from *Strunk's Source Readings in Music History: The Early Christian Period and the Latin Middle Ages*, ed. James McKinnon, rev. ed. (New York: W. W. Norton, 1997), 66–67.
3. There is one example of a sanctoral verse that is not nearly as extreme: *Specie tua's* verse *Audi filia* (Ps 44.11–12) has an omission of eight words from the biblical text.
4. See Brad Maiani, "The Responsory-Communions: Toward a Chronology of Selected Proper Chants" (Ph.D. diss., University of North Carolina at Chapel Hill, 1996), 100–106.
5. And the later addition, needless to say, of a number of liturgical occasions such as the nuptial mass, the Mass for the Dead and a handful of sanctoral dates.
6. "Ubi et congregationem monachorum et abbatem constituit ad persolvenda cotidie sacra officia laudis divine [in basilica Salvatoris domini nostri Iesu Christi quae Constantiniana nuncupatur, iuxta Lateranis], diurnis nocturnisque temporibus ordinata, iuxta instar officiorum ecclesie beati Petri apostoli" (Duchesne, 1:419).
7. Translation from *Strunk's Source Readings: Early Christian Period*, 69.

EPILOGUE

1. For Bruno Stäblein, see especially the introduction to *Die Gesänge des altrömischen Graduale;* for Stephen van Dijk, "The Urban and Papal Rites in Seventh- and Eighth-Century Rome," *Sacris Erudire* 12 (1961): 411–87.
2. Perhaps the most cogent expression of the severe difficulties with two-chant theories is that of Edward Nowacki, "The Gregorian Office Antiphons and the Comparative Method," *Journal of Musicology* 4 (1985): 260–62.
3. See Helmut Hucke, "Gregorianischer Gesang in altrömischer und fränkischer Überlieferung," *Archiv für Musikwissenschaft* 12 (1955): 74–87, where this position is already implicit (Hucke was just twenty-seven at the time of the article's appearance).
4. See Joseph Dyer, "The Schola Cantorum and Its Roman Milieu in the Early Middle Ages," in *De Musica et Cantu: Studien zur Geschichte der Kirchenmusik und der Oper. Helmut Hucke zum 60. Geburtstag,* ed. Peter Cahn and Ann-Katrin Heimer (Hildesheim: Georg Olms, 1993), 37–38.
5. I refer, of course, to David Hughes, "Evidence for the Traditional View of the Transmission of Gregorian Chant," *JAMS* 40 (1987); and to Kenneth Levy, "Charlemagne's Archetype of Gregorian Chant," *JAMS* 40 (1987). As for the latter of these studies, I consider it unfortunate that we, the community of chant scholars, have failed to come to terms—either in agreement or disagreement—with the magnificent hypothesis expressed therein. Perhaps now with

the publication of Levy's *Gregorian Chant and the Carolingians* (Princeton: Princeton University Press, 1998), his notated Carolingian archetype will become the subject of the probing debate that it merits.

6. See Nowacki, "Gregorian Office Antiphons."

7. Helmut Hucke made the same observation many years ago, coming to conclusions very similar to mine; see his "Gregorianischer Gesang," 85–86.

8. See Thomas Connolly, "Introits and Archetypes: Some Archaisms of the Old Roman Chant," *JAMS* 25 (1972): 157–74.

9. Robert Snow, "The Old-Roman Chant," in Apel (q.v., 504); Snow's early essay on Old Roman chant is still valuable, an extraordinary achievement for its time.

10. See Richard Crocker, "Chants of the Roman Mass," in *New Oxford History of Music*, ed. Richard Crocker and David Hiley (Oxford: Oxford University Press, 1990), 2:186.

11. Helmut Hucke, "Gregorian and Old Roman Chant," *New Grove*, 7:696.

12. The observation was made in a paper read at the retirement gathering for Kenneth Levy.

13. "Incomparable" may not be quite the right word to characterize the chant; *Psallite domino*, the communion for the Ascension, has a striking similarity to it. Crocker says of *Psallite*, perhaps in calculated understatement: "In comparison to the very eloquent Gregorian version of 'Psallite Domino' (Ascension), the Urban-Roman can be described as less effective" ("Chants of the Roman Mass," 186).

14. Planchart made the remark in the discussion following the paper on Gregorian "tonality" read by David Hughes at the retirement gathering for Kenneth Levy.

15. The Nowacki transcriptions are to be found in his "Studies on the Office Antiphons of the Old Roman Manuscripts" (Ph.D. diss., Brandeis University, 1980).

16. There are, for example, three introits entirely free of oscillating figuration (*Sacerdotes dei*, *Me expectaverunt* and *Laetabitur justus*), assigned, interestingly enough, to successive sanctoral dates: 23, 24 and 25 January.

17. Richard Crocker, "Thoughts on Responsories," in *Essays on Medieval Music in Honor of David G. Hughes*, ed. Graeme Boone (Cambridge, Mass.: Harvard University Department of Music, 1995), 84.

18. Ibid., 85.

19. Regarding the term "reconstruction," it should be pointed out that Hendrik van der Werf prefers "re-improvisation" to "reconstruction"; see *The Emergence of Gregorian Chant* (Rochester, N.Y., 1983), 110, 158 and 164–65. Van der Werf's views, which anticipate to some extent those of Leo Treitler, went unnoticed in the early reaction to Treitler's article "Homer and Gregory: The Transmission of Epic Poetry and Plainchant," *The Musical Quarterly* 60 (1974): 333–72.

20. Hughes, "Evidence for the Traditional View," 401.

21. Treitler, "Homer and Gregory," 574.

22. Kenneth Levy, "The Byzantine Sanctus and Its Modal Tradition in East and West," *Annales musicologiques* 6 (1958–63).

23. Treitler, "Homer and Gregory," 342.

24. See Crocker, "Chants of the Roman Mass," 2:213.

25. The reader should also be aware of an eminently plausible suggestion of David Hiley that runs contrary to the general position taken in what follows; see Hiley, 562.

26. This, in discussion with me after Maiani read an early draft of the present chapter.

27. The story is given in Jean-Baptiste Pelt, *Études sur la cathédrale de Metz: La liturgie V$_e$–XIIIe siècles* (Metz: Journal le Lorrain, 1937), 133–35. Pelt's collection is a rich repository of material about Metz that has yet to be exploited by music historians.

Works Cited

Andrieu, Michel. "Règlement d'Angilramne de Metz (768–791) fixant les honoraires de quelques fonctions liturgiques." *Revue des sciences religieuses* 10 (1930).

———, ed. *Les Ordines romani du haut moyen âge.* Vols. 11, 23, 24, 28, 29. Spicilegium sacrum Lovaniense. Études et documents. Louvain: Spicilegium sacrum Lovaniense bureaux, 1931–60.

Annales Laurissenses et Einhardi. Monumenta Germaniae Historica. Scriptorum, 1. Hanover, 1826.

Apel, Willi. "The Central Problem of Gregorian Chant." *Journal of the American Musicological Society* 9 (1956): 118–27.

———. *Gregorian Chant.* Bloomington: Indiana University Press, 1958.

Augustine, Saint (bishop of Hippo). *Opera.* Corpus christianorum. Vol. 48. Series latina. Turnhout: Brepols, 1955.

Bailey, Terence W. *Antiphon and Psalm in the Ambrosian Office.* Bd. 50:3. Musikwissenschaftliche Abhandlungen. Ottawa: Institute of Mediaeval Music, 1994.

Baldovin, John F. *The Urban Character of Christian Worship: The Origins, Development, and Meaning of Stational Liturgy.* Vol. 228. Orientalia christiana analecta. Rome: Pontificium institutum studiorum orientalium, 1987.

Bede, "the Venerable." *Historia ecclesiastica.* Ed. J. E. King. 2 vols. Loeb Classical Library, 1979.

Berger, Karol. *A Theory of Art.* Oxford: Oxford University Press, 2000.

Bernard, Philippe. "Les Alléluia mélismatiques dans le chant romain: Recherches sur la genèse de l'alléluia de la messe romaine." *Rivista internazionale di musica sacra* 12 (1991): 286–362.

———. "L'Origine des chants de la messe selon la tradition musicale du chant romain ancien, improprement dit 'chant vieux-romain.'" In *L'Eucharistie: Célébrations, rites, piétés.* Conférences St-Serge, XLIe semaine d'études liturgiques, Paris, 28 juin–1 juillet 1994. Ed. A. M. Triacca, A. Pistoia and Constantin Andronikof. Rome: C.L.V.-Edizioni liturgiche, 1995.

———. "Le 'Trecanum': Un Fantôme dans la liturgie gallicane?" *Francia: Forschungen zur westeuropäischen Geschichte* 23 (1996): 95–98.
Boe, John. "Chant Notation in Eleventh-Century Roman Manuscripts." In *Essays on Medieval Music in Honor of David G. Hughes*, ed. Graeme M. Boone. Vol. 4. Isham Library Papers. Cambridge, Mass.: Harvard University Department of Music, 1995.
Bradshaw, Paul. *The Search for the Origins of Christian Worship*. Oxford: Oxford University Press, 1992.
———. *The Canons of Hippolytus*. Bramcote: Grove Books, 1997.
Callewaert, Camille. "S. Grégoire, les scrutins et quelques messes quadragésimales." *Ephemerides liturgicae* 53 (1938): 191–203.
Carpe, William D. "The Vita Canonica in the *Regula Canonicorum* of Chrodegang of Metz." Ph.D. diss., University of Chicago, 1975.
Chavasse, Antoine. "Le Carême romain et les scrutins prébaptismaux avant le IXe siècle." *Recherches de science religieuse* 35 (1948): 325–81.
———. "L'Épistolier romain du codex de Wurtzbourg. Son organization." *Revue bénédictine* 91 (1981): 280–331.
Claire, Jean. "L'Évolution modale dans les répertoires liturgiques occidentaux." *Revue grégorienne* 40 (1962): 231–35.
———. "Aux origines de l'alléluia." In *Essays in Honor of Edith Gerson-Kiwi. Orbis musicae* 9 (1986–87): 17–59.
Colgrave, Bertram. *The Earliest Life of Gregory the Great, by an Anonymous Monk of Whitby*. Lawrence: University of Kansas Press, 1968.
Connolly, Richard H. *The De Sacramentis: A Work of Ambrose*. Downside: St. Gregory's Abbey, 1942.
Connolly, Thomas Hugh. "The Introits of the Old Roman Chant." Ph.D. diss., Harvard University, 1972.
———. "Introits and Archetypes: Some Archaisms of the Old Roman Chant." *Journal of the American Musicological Society* 25 (1972): 157–74.
Conomos, Dimitri. *The Late Byzantine and Slavonic Communion Cycle: Liturgy and Music*. Vol. 21. Dumbarton Oaks Studies. Washington, D.C.: Dumbarton Oaks Research Library and Collection, 1985.
Crampton, L. J. "St. Gregory's Homily XIX and the Institution of Septuagesima Sunday." *Downside Review* 86 (1968): 162–66.
Croce, Walter. "Die Adventmessen des römischen Missale in ihrer geschichtlichen Entwicklung." *Zeitschrift für katholische Theologie* 74 (1952): 277–317.
Crocker, Richard L. "Chants of the Roman Mass." In *New Oxford History of Music, II: The Early Middle Ages to 1300*, ed. Richard Crocker and David Hiley. Oxford: Oxford University Press, 1990.
———. "Thoughts on Responsories." In *Essays on Medieval Music in Honor of David G. Hughes*, ed. Graeme M. Boone. Vol. 4. Isham Library Papers. Cambridge, Mass.: Harvard University Department of Music, 1995.
Cullin, Olivier. "Le Répertoire de la psalmodie *in directum* dans les traditions

liturgiques latines. La Tradition hispanique." *Études grégoriennes* 23 (1989): 99–139.

———. "Le Trait dans les répertoires vieux-romain et grégorien: Un Témoin de la psalmodie sans refrain." Thesis, Université de Paris IV, Sorbonne, 1990.

———. "De la psalmodie sans refrain à la psalmodie responsoriale: Transformation et conservation dans les repertoires liturgiques latins." *Revue de musicologie* 77 (1991): 5–24.

Dalmais, Irénée H., Pierre Jounel and Aimé Georges Martimort. *The Church at Prayer: The Liturgy and Time*. Ed. and trans. Matthew J. O'Connell. Collegeville, Minn.: Liturgical Press, 1985.

Davis, Raymond, trans. *The Book of Pontiffs (Liber pontificalis)*. Vol. 5. Translated Texts for Historians, Latin Series. Liverpool: Liverpool University Press, 1989.

———. *The Lives of the Eighth-Century Popes (Liber pontificalis): The Ancient Biographies of Nine Popes from A.D. 715 to 817*. Vol. 13. Translated Texts for Historians. Liverpool: Liverpool University Press, 1992.

Deshusses, Jean. "Le Sacramentaire grégorien de Trente." *Revue bénédictine* 78 (1968): 261–82.

———. *Le Sacramentaire grégorien: Ses Principales Formes d'après les plus anciens manuscrits*. 3d ed. Fribourg: Éditions universitaires, 1992.

Dix, Gregory. *The Shape of the Liturgy*. Westminster: Dacre Press, 1945.

Duchesne, Louis. *Christian Worship: Its Origin and Evolution*. Trans. M. L. McClure. 5th ed. London: Society for Promoting Christian Knowledge, 1931.

———. *Le Liber pontificalis: Texte, introduction et commentaire*. Corrections and additions by Cyrille Vogel. Paris: E. De Boccard, 1957.

Dyer, Joseph. "The Offertories of Old-Roman Chant: A Musico-Liturgical Investigation." Ph.D. diss., Boston University, 1971.

———. "Augustine and the 'Hymni ante oblationem': The Earliest Offertory Chants?" *Revue des études augustiniennes* 27 (1981): 85–99.

———. "The Offertory Chant of the Roman Liturgy and Its Musical Form." *Studi musicali* 11 (1982): 3–30.

———. "The Schola Cantorum and Its Roman Milieu in the Early Middle Ages." In *De Musica et Cantu: Studien zur Geschichte der Kirchenmusik und der Oper. Helmut Hucke zum 60. Geburtstag*. Ed. Peter Cahn and Ann-Katrin Heimer. Bd. 2. Musikwissenschaftliche Publikationen: Hochschule für Musik und Darstellende Kunst, Frankfurt am Main. Hildesheim: Georg Olms, 1993.

Ekenberg, Anders. "Germanus oder Pseudo-Germanus?" *Archiv für Liturgiewissenschaft* 35–36 (1993–94): 135–39.

Ellard, Gerald. *Master Alcuin, Liturgist*. Chicago: Loyola University Press, 1956.

Étaix, Raymond. "Sermons ariens inédits." *Recherches augustiniennes* 26 (1992): 143–79.

Ewald, Paul, and Ludwig Hartmann, eds. *Gregorii I papae Registrum epistolarum*. Monumenta Germaniae Historica. Epistolarum, I and II. Berlin: Weidmann, 1891–99.
Ferrari, Guy. *Early Roman Monasteries, Notes for the History of the Monasteries and Convents at Rome from the V through the X Century*. Vatican City: Pontificio Istituto di Archeologia Christiana, 1957.
Fischer, Balthasar. *Die Psalmenfrömmigkeit der Märtyrerkirche*. Freiburg: Herder, 1949.
Fischer, Bonifatius. "Die Lesungen der römischen Ostervigil unter Gregor d. Gr." In *Colligere Fragmenta: Festschrift Alban Dold zum 70. Geburtstag*. Ed. Bonifatius Fischer and Virgil Fiala. Beuron: Beuroner Kunstverlag, 1952.
Flender, Reinhard. *Hebrew Psalmody: A Structural Investigation*. Vol. 9. Yuval Monograph Series. Jerusalem: Magnes Press, 1992.
Foley, Edward. *Foundations of Christian Music: The Music of Pre-Constantinian Christianity*. Bramcote: Grove Books, 1992.
Frere, Walter Howard. *The Sarum Gradual and the Gregorian Antiphonale Missarum: A Dissertation and an Historical Index*. London: Published for Members of the Plainsong and Mediaeval Music Society by B. Quaritch, 1895.
———. *Studies in Early Roman Liturgy*. Vol. 1, *The Kalendar*. Alcuin Club Collections. Oxford: Oxford University Press, 1930.
Froger, Jacques. "Les Anticipations du jeûne quadragésimal." *Mélanges de science religieuse* 3 (1946): 207–34.
Gevaert, François-Auguste. *Les Origines du chant liturgique de l'église latine*. Ghent: A. Hoste, 1890.
Haddan, Arthur, and William Stubbs, eds. *Councils and Ecclesiastical Documents Relating to Great Britain and Ireland*. Oxford: Clarendon Press, 1869–73.
Hansen, Finn Egeland, ed. *H 159 Montpellier: Tonary of St Bénigne of Dijon*. Vol 2. Studier og Publikationer fra Musikvidenskabeligt Institut Aarhus Universitet. Copenhagen: Dan Fog, 1974.
Hanssens, Jean Michel, ed. *Amalarii Episcopi opera liturgica omnia*. Studi e testi, 138–40. Vatican City: Biblioteca Apostolica Vaticana, 1948–50.
Hesbert, René-Jean. "Les Dimanches de carême dans les manuscrits romano-bénéventains." *Ephemerides liturgicae* 48 (1934): 198–222.
———. *Antiphonale Missarum Sextuplex*. Brussels: Vromant, 1935.
———. "Le Graduel, chant responsorial." *Ephemerides liturgicae* 95 (1981): 316–50.
Hiley, David. *Western Plainchant: A Handbook*. Oxford: Oxford University Press, 1993.
Hintze, Gisa. *Das byzantinische Prokeimena-Repertoire: Untersuchungen und kritische Edition*. Vol. 9. Hamburger Beiträge zur Musikwissenschaft. Hamburg: Karl Dieter Wagner, 1973.
Hucke, Helmut. "Gregorianischer Gesang in altrömischer und fränkischer

Überlieferung." *Archiv für Musikwissenschaft* 12 (1955): 74–87.
———. "Tractusstudien." In *Festschrift Bruno Stäblein zum 70. Geburtstag.* Ed. Martin Ruhnke. Kassel: Bärenreiter, 1967.
———. "Die Texte der Offertorien." In *Speculum musicae artis: Festgabe für Heinrich Husmann zum 60. Geburtstag am 16. Dez 1968.* Ed. Heinz Becker and Reinhard Gerlach. Munich: W. Fink, 1970.
———. "Gregorian and Old Roman Chant." In *New Grove Dictionary of Music and Musicians,* ed. Stanley Sadie. Vol. 7. London: MacMillan, 1980.
———. "Toward a New Historical View of Gregorian Chant." *Journal of the American Musicological Society* 33 (1980): 437–67.
———. "Tract." In *New Grove Dictionary of Music and Musicians,* ed. Stanley Sadie. Vol. 19. London: MacMillan, 1980.
———, and Michel Huglo. "Communion." In *New Grove Dictionary of Music and Musicians,* ed. Stanley Sadie. Vol. 4. London: MacMillan, 1980.
Hughes, David. "Evidence for the Traditional View of the Transmission of Gregorian Chant." *Journal of the American Musicological Society* 40 (1987): 377–404.
Huglo, Michel. "Le Répons-graduel de la messe: Évolution de la forme, permanence de la fonction." *Schweizer Jahrbuch für Musikwissenschaft* (neue Folge) 2 (1982): 53–73.
Jeffery, Peter. "The Introduction of Psalmody into the Roman Mass by Pope Celestine I (422–432): Reinterpreting a Passage in the *Liber Pontificalis.*" *Archiv für Liturgiewissenschaft* 26 (1984): 147–65.
———. "The Lost Chant Tradition of Early Christian Jerusalem: Some Possible Melodic Survivals in the Byzantine and Latin Chant Repertories." *Early Music History* 11 (1992): 151–90.
———. "Rome and Jerusalem: From Oral Tradition to Written Repertory in Two Ancient Liturgical Centers." In *Essays on Medieval Music in Honor of David G. Hughes,* ed. Graeme M. Boone. Vol. 4. Isham Library Papers. Cambridge, Mass.: Harvard University Department of Music, 1995.
Jungmann, Josef. "Advent und Voradvent." In *Gewordene Liturgie: Studien und Durchblicke.* Innsbruck: F. Rauch, 1941.
———. *The Mass of the Roman Rite.* Trans. Francis A. Brunner. Westminster, Md.: Christian Classics, 1986.
Klauser, Theodor. *Das römische Capitulare Evangeliorum.* Vol. 28. Liturgiegeschichtliche Quellen und Forschungen. Münster: Aschendorff, 1935.
———. "Rom und der Kult der Gottesmutter Maria." *Jahrbuch für Antike und Christentum* 15 (1972): 120–35.
Krautheimer, Richard. *Rome: Profile of a City, 312–1308.* Princeton: Princeton University Press, 1980.
———. *Early Christian and Byzantine Architecture.* Rev. Richard Krautheimer and Slobodan Curcic. 4th ed. London: Penguin Books, 1986.
Lambot, Cyrille. "Les Sermons de saint Augustin pour les fêtes de Paques." In *Mémorial Dom Cyrille Lambot. Revue bénédictine* 79 (1969): 148–72.

Le Roux, R. "Les Graduels des dimanches après la Pentecôte." *Études grégoriennes* 5 (1962): 119–30.
Leeb, Helmut. *Die Psalmodie bei Ambrosius*. Vol. 18. Wiener Beiträge zur Theologie. Vienna: Herder, 1967.
Levy, Kenneth. "The Byzantine Sanctus and Its Modal Tradition in East and West." *Annales musicologiques* 6 (1958–63): 7–68.
———. "Toledo, Rome and the Legacy of Gaul." *Early Music History* 4 (1984): 51–101.
———. "Charlemagne's Archetype of Gregorian Chant." *Journal of the American Musicological Society* 40 (1987): 1–30.
———. *Gregorian Chant and the Carolingians*. Princeton: Princeton University Press, 1998.
Llewellyn, Peter. *Rome in the Dark Ages*. London: Faber and Faber, 1971.
———. "The Roman Church in the Seventh Century: The Legacy of Gregory I." *Journal of Ecclesiastical History* 25 (1974): 363–80.
Maertens, T. "L'Avent: Genèse historique de ses thèmes bibliques et doctrinaux." *Mélanges de science religieuse* 18 (1961): 47–110.
Maiani, Bradford C. "The Responsory-Communions: Toward a Chronology of Selected Proper Chants." Ph.D. diss., University of North Carolina at Chapel Hill, 1996.
———. "Readings and Responsories: The Eighth-Century Night Office Lectionary and the *Responsoria Prolixa*." *Journal of Musicology* 16 (1998): 254–82.
Martimort, Aimé Georges. "Origine et signification de l'alléluia de la messe romaine." In *Kyriakon: Festschrift Johannes Quasten*, ed. Patrick Granfield and Josef Jungmann. Vol. 2. Münster: Aschendorff, 1970.
———. "A propos du nombre des lectures à la messe." In *En hommage à Monsieur le Professeur Antoine Chavasse. Revue des sciences religieuses* 58 (1984): 42–51.
———. *Les Lectures liturgiques et leurs livres*. Turnhout: Brepols, 1992.
Martin, Ralph. "Aspects of Worship in the New Testament Church." In *Vox Evangelica II*, ed. Ralph Martin. London: Epworth Press, 1963.
McCann, P. J., ed. and trans. *The Rule of Saint Benedict in Latin and English*. Westminster, Md.: 1952.
McKinnon, James W. "On the Question of Psalmody in the Ancient Synagogue." *Early Music History* 6 (1986): 159–91.
———. "A Cappella Doctrine versus Practice: A Necessary Distinction." In *La Musique et le rite sacré et profane*. Actes du XIIIe Congrès de la Société Internationale de Musicologie, Strasbourg, 29 août–3 septembre (1982). Strasbourg: Presses universitaires de Strasbourg, 1986.
———. *Music in Early Christian Literature*. Cambridge: Cambridge University Press, 1987.
———. "The Fourth-Century Origin of the Gradual." *Early Music History* 7 (1987): 91–106.

———. "The Emergence of Gregorian Chant in the Carolingian Era." In *Antiquity and the Middle Ages: From Ancient Greece to the Fifteenth Century*, ed. James McKinnon. London: Macmillan, 1990.

———. "The Patristic Jubilus and the Alleluia of the Mass." In *Cantus Planus: Papers Read at the Third Meeting, Tihany, Hungary, 19–24 September 1988*, ed. László Dobszay. Budapest: Hungarian Academy of Sciences, 1990.

———. "The Roman Post-Pentecostal Communion Series." In *Cantus Planus: Papers Read at the Fourth Meeting, Pécs, Hungary, September 1990*, ed. László Dobszay. Budapest: Hungarian Academy of Sciences, 1992.

———. "Antoine Chavasse and the Dating of Early Chant." *Plainsong and Medieval Music* 1 (1992): 123–47.

———. "The Eighth-Century Frankish-Roman Communion Cycle." *Journal of the American Musicological Society* 45 (1992): 179–227.

———. "Desert Monasticism and the Later Fourth-Century Psalmodic Movement." *Music & Letters* 75 (1994): 505–21.

———. "Lector Chant versus Schola Chant: A Question of Historical Plausibility." In *Laborare fratres in unum: Festschrift László Dobszay zum 60. Geburtstag*. Ed. Janka Szendrei and David Hiley. Bd. 7. Spolia Berolinensia. Hildesheim: Weidmann, 1995.

———. "Properization: The Roman Mass." In *Cantus Planus: Papers Read at the Sixth Meeting, Éger, Hungary, September 1993*, ed. László Dobszay. Budapest: Hungarian Academy of Sciences, 1995.

———. "Preface to the Study of the Alleluia." *Early Music History* 15 (1996): 213–49.

———. Review of *Les Lectures liturgiques et leurs livres*, by Aimé Georges Martimort. *Plainsong and Medieval Music* 5 (1996): 211–26.

———. "The Gregorian Canticle-Tracts of the Old Roman Easter Vigil." In *Festschrift Walter Wiora zum 90. Geburtstag*. Ed. Christoph-Hellmut Mahling and Ruth Seiberts. Bd. 35. Mainzer Studien zur Musikwissenschaft. Tutzing: Hans Schneider, 1997.

———. "Festival, Text and Melody: Chronological Stages in the Life of a Chant?" In *Chant and Its Peripheries: Essays in Honour of Terence Bailey*, ed. Bryan Gillingham and Paul Merkley. Bd. 72. Musikwissenschaftliche Abhandlungen. Ottawa: Institute of Mediaeval Music, 1998.

———. "Vaticana Latina 5319 as a Witness to the Eighth-Century Roman Proper of the Mass." In *Cantus Planus: Papers Read at the Seventh Meeting, Sopron, Hungary, September 1995*, ed. László Dobszay. Budapest: Hungarian Academy of Sciences, 1998.

———, ed. *Strunk's Source Readings in Music History: The Early Christian Period and the Latin Middle Ages*. Rev. ed. New York: W. W. Norton, 1998.

———. *Gregorius presul composuit hunc libellum musicae arti*. In *The Liturgy of the Medieval Church*, ed. Thomas Heffernan and E. Ann Matter. Kalamazoo, Mich.: Medieval Institute Publications, 1999.

———. "Liturgical Psalmody in the Sermons of St. Augustine." To appear in

Tradition and Transmission in Mediaeval Chant: Comparative Studies of Greek, Latin, and Slavonic Liturgical Music for Kenneth Levy. Ed. Peter Jeffery. London: Boydell and Brewer.

Meeks, Wayne A. *The First Urban Christians.* New Haven: Yale University Press, 1983.

Mensbrugghe, A. van der. "Pseudo-Germanus Reconsidered." In *Papers Presented to the Third International Conference on Patristic Studies Held at Christchurch, Oxford, 1959. Part III: Liturgica, Monastica et Ascetica, Philosophica. Studia patristica* 5 (1962): 172–84.

Migne, J. P., ed. *Patrologiae cursus completus . . . Series latina.* Paris: Migne, 1844–65.

Mohlberg, Leo Cunibert, et al., eds. *Sacramentarium Veronense.* Rerum ecclesiasticarum documenta. Vol. 1. Series major. Rome: Herder, 1956.

———, eds. *Liber sacramentorum romanae aecclesiae ordinis anni circuli.* Rerum ecclesiasticarum documenta. Vol. 4. Series major. Rome: Herder, 1968.

Morin, Germain. "Le Plus Ancien *Comes,* ou lectionnaire de l'église romaine." *Revue bénédictine* 27 (1910): 41–74.

Noble, Thomas F. X. *The Republic of St. Peter.* Philadelphia: University of Pennsylvania Press, 1984.

Nowacki, Edward. "Studies on the Office Antiphons of the Old Roman Manuscripts." Ph.D. diss., Brandeis University, 1980.

———. "The Gregorian Office Antiphons and the Comparative Method." *Journal of Musicology* 4 (1985–86): 243–75.

———. "Text Declamation as a Determinant of Melodic Form in the Old Roman Eighth-Mode Tracts." *Early Music History* 6 (1986): 193–226.

———. "Constantinople-Aachen-Rome: The Transmission of *Veterem hominem.*" In *De musica et cantu: Studien zur Geschichte der Kirchenmusik und der Oper. Helmut Hucke zum 60. Geburtstag.* Ed. Peter Cahn and Ann-Katrin Heimer. Hildesheim: Georg Olms, 1993.

O'Donnell, James J. *Cassiodorus.* Berkeley: University of California Press, 1979.

Ott, Caspar. *Offertoriale sive versus offertoriorum.* Tournai: Desclée, 1935.

———. *Offertoriale triplex cum versiculis* (Ott's edition republished by Rupert Fischer, with neumes added by hand). Sablé-sur-Sarthe: Abbé de St-Pierre-de-Solesmes, 1985.

Paverd, Frans van de. *Zur Geschichte der Messliturgie in Antiocheia und Konstantinopel gegen Ende des vierten Jahrhunderts: Analyse der Quellen bei Johannes Chrysostomos.* Vol. 187. Orientalia christiana analecta. Rome: Pontificium institutum studiorum orientalium, 1970.

Pelt, Jean-Baptiste. *Études sur la cathédrale de Metz: La Liturgie Ve–XIIIe siècles.* Metz: Journal le Lorrain, 1937.

Pietschmann, Petrus. "Die nicht dem Psalter entnommenen Messgesangstücke auf ihre Textgestalt untersucht." *Jahrbuch für Liturgiewissenschaft* 12 (1932): 87–144.

Quasten, Johannes. "Oriental Influence in the Gallican Liturgy." *Traditio* 1 (1943).

Ratcliff, Edward. *Expositio antiquae liturgiae gallicanae*. London: Henry Bradshaw Society, 1971.
Renoux, Charles. *Le Codex arménien Jérusalem 121*. 2 vols. Patrologia orientalis, 35/1 and 36/2. Turnhout: Brepols, 1969 and 1971.
Schattauer, Thomas H. "The Koinonicon of the Byzantine Liturgy: An Historical Study." *Orientalia christiana periodica* 49 (1983): 91–129.
Schulz, Hans-Joachim. *The Byzantine Liturgy*. Trans. Matthew J. O'Connell. New York: Pueblo, 1986.
Smith, John A. "The Ancient Synagogue, The Early Church and Singing." *Music & Letters* 65 (1984): 1–16.
———. "Which Psalms Were Sung in the Temple?" *Music & Letters* 71 (1990): 167–86.
———. "First-Century Christian Singing and Its Relationship to Contemporary Jewish Religious Song." *Music & Letters* 75 (1994): 1–15.
Snow, Robert. "The Old-Roman Chant." In Willi Apel, *Gregorian Chant*. Bloomington: Indiana University Press, 1958.
Stäblein, Bruno. "'Gregorius Praesul,' der Prolog zum römischen Antiphonale." In *Musik und Verlag: Karl Vötterle zum 65. Geburtstag*. Ed. Richard Baum and Wolfgang Rehm. Kassel: Bärenreiter, 1968.
———, and Margareta Landwehr-Melnicki. *Die Gesänge des altrömischen Graduale Vat. lat. 5319*. Vol. 2. Monumenta monodica medii aevi. Kassel: Bärenreiter, 1970.
Steiner, Ruth. "Some Questions about the Gregorian Offertories and Their Verses." *Journal of the American Musicological Society* 19 (1966): 162–81.
Syna, Edward A. "John the Deacon." In *Dictionary of the Middle Ages*. Vol. 7. New York: Charles Scribner's Sons, 1986.
Talley, Thomas J. *The Origins of the Liturgical Year*. Collegeville, Minn.: Liturgical Press, 1991.
Tarchnischvili, Michel. *Le Grand Lectionnaire de l'église de Jérusalem (Ve–VIIIe siècles)*. Vols. 189, 204. Corpus scriptorum christianorum orientalium. Louvain: Secretariat du Corpus, 1959–60.
Thodberg, Christian. *Der byzantinische Alleluiarionzyklus: Studien im kurzen Psaltikonstil*. Vol. 8. Monumenta musicae byzantinae subsidia. Copenhagen: E. Munksgaard, 1966.
———, and Karlheinz Schlager. "Alleluia." In *New Grove Dictionary of Music and Musicians*, ed. Stanley Sadie. Vol. 1. London: MacMillan, 1980.
Treitler, Leo. "Homer and Gregory: The Transmission of Epic Poetry and Plainchant." *The Musical Quarterly* 60 (1974): 333–72.
Van der Werf, Hendrik. *The Emergence of Gregorian Chant: A Comparative Study of Ambrosian, Roman, and Gregorian Chant, I: A Study of Modes and Melodies*. Rochester, N.Y.: 1983.
Van Dijk, Stephen. "The Urban and Papal Rites in Seventh- and Eighth-Century Rome." *Sacris Erudire* 12 (1961): 411–87.
Vogel, Cyrille. "Le 'Liber Pontificalis' dans l'édition de Louis Duchesne: État de la question." In *Monseigneur Duchesne et son temps: Actes du colloque or-*

ganisé par l'école française de Rome, Palais Farnèse, 23–25 mai, 1973. Rome: École française de Rome, 1975.

———. *Medieval Liturgy: An Introduction to the Sources*. Trans. and rev. William Storey and Niels Rasmussen. Washington, D.C.: Pastoral Press, 1986.

Wagner, Peter. *Introduction to the Gregorian Melodies*. Trans. Agnes Orme and E. G. P. Wyatt. London: Plainsong & Mediaeval Music Society, 1901.

Willis, Geoffrey. *A History of Early Roman Liturgy to the Death of Pope Gregory the Great*. Henry Bradshaw Society Subsidial, 1. London: Boydell Press, 1994.

Wilmart, André. "Germain de Paris (Lettres attribuées à saint)." In *Dictionnaire d'archéologie chrétienne et de liturgie*. Vol. 6, pt. 1. Paris, 1924.

Zwinggi, Anton. "Die fortlauffende Schriftlesung im Gottesdienst bei Augustinus." *Archiv für Liturgiewissenschaft* 12 (1970): 85–129.

———. "Die Perikoppenordnungen der Osterwoche in Hippo und die Chronologie der Predigten des hl. Augustinus." *Augustiniana* 20 (1970): 5–34.

Index

Acca (bishop of Hexham), 92–93
Acceptabis (communion), *134*, 135
Adeodatus, 87, 359
Adjutor in opportunitatibus; Quoniam (gradual), *230*
Adorabo ad templum (alleluia), *264*, 266
Ad te domine levavi (offertory), 144, *145*, *310*, *310*, *311*, *312*, *313*
Ad te levavi (introit), 152, *209*
Advent-Christmas season: alleluia and, 144–46, *145*, 261–63, *262*, 277–78, 371; borrowed vs. original chants and, 231, 233, 247; chant books and, 151–52, *152*; chronology of Advent Project and, 365–67; communion and, 6, 137–40, *138*, 329–31; dating of Advent chants and, 152–53; early history of Advent and, 10–11, 146–49; establishment of annual cycle and, 149–51, 358; gradual and, 231–35, *232*, 247; introit and, 129–33, *130*, 208–9, *209*; liturgical assignments and, 261–63, *262*; offertory and, 309–13, *310*; in Roman Mass Proper, 137; in seventh-century Roman liturgical books, *148*; textual adjustment and, 312–13
Aeddi. *See* Stephen of Aeddi (singer)
agape feast, singing at, 21–24
Agiulf (deacon), 84
Alcuin of York, 97
Aldric (cantor at Metz), 402
alleluia: Advent-Christmas season and, 261–63, *262*, 277–78, 371; Byzantine influence and, 252–60, 274–79, 371; chronology of Advent Project and, 266–67, 364, 370–72; compositional planning and, 140, 141, 142; early Roman, 274–79; Easter Vigil and, 270–72, *271*, 274, *275*; Easter week vespers and, 257–60, *258*; Ember Days and, 144–46, *145*; Fore-Mass psalmody and, 51–52; formulaicism and, 428n14; jubilus, 270, 272–74; liturgical assignment and, 260–67, *262*; melody types and, 254–60, *255*–*56*, 267; nonpsalmic verses, 276; *Ordo romanus I* and, 249; origins of, 249–52; Paschaltime, 205–6, 263–66, *264*–*65*, 273–77, 371, 428n14; post-Pentecostal series and, 267–70, *268*; prehistory of, 357; Roman vs. Byzantine, 254–60, *255*–*56*; Roman vs. Gregorian, 267–70, *268*; stages in history of, 370–72; temporal assignment and, 208; in Vat lat 5319, 254–57, *255*–*56*
alleluia-alleluiarion, 252, 256, 258, 259, 260
Amalarius, 222, 263, 272–73, 438n30
Ambrose, 25, 48–49
Amen dico vobis (communion), *344*, *347*

455

Andrieu, Michel, 150, 288
Angelis suis (gradual), 286–87
Angelus domini (offertory), 316, 317
Angilram (Frankish leader), 15, 76, 396, 402
antiphonal psalmody, 73–74, 324. *See also* communion; introit; Office
antiphon-communion, 337–38, 341–43, 422n20
Antony (hermit), 36–37
Apel, Willi, 101–2, 301, 303, 309; alleluia and, 260–61, 266; gradual and, 228
Apollinaris (saint), 167
Apostolic Constitutions, 42, 43, 47, 50–51, 63
architecture, and the early Christian church, 27–28
Armenian Lectionary, 65–66, 117, 251
A summo caelo (gradual), 228, 229
Athanasius of Alexandria, 29, 37, 54–55
Attende caelum (canticle tract), 293–94, 436n18
Aufer a me (communion), 344, 348
Augustine (saint; d.430), 1, 4, 63; alleluia and, 250, 271–72; communion psalm and, 327; *Contra Hilarem*, 41, 43–44, 79, 80; *De civitate Dei*, 40, 60; Easter Vigil, 293; *Haec dies*, 54; introit and, 196; *Liber retractationem*, 41; offertory and, 299–300; other fourth- through sixth-century sources and, 78, 79, 80; psalmody and, 41, 43–44, 50, 51–52, 53, 55, 57–58
Augustine of Canterbury (saint), 89, 90
Aurelian of Arles, 61–62, 74
Ave Maria (offertory), 182, 184, 322–23, 325, 370
Avitus of Vienne, 72

Basil of Caesarea, 3, 47
Beati mundo corde (communion), 350–53
Beatus servus (communion), 440n28

Bede, "the Venerable," 62, 89–93, 96
Benedicam dominum (gradual), 242, 243
Benedic anima mea (offertory), 145, 146
Benedict (saint), 61, 250
Benedict II (pope), 87, 168, 191
Benedict Bishop (saint), 91
Benedict of Aniane, 107, 133–34, 420n60
Berger, Karol, 359
Bernard, Philippe, 48, 56, 258, 412n61, 415n34
biblical books, indication of chapters and verses in, 113
Blandin manuscript: comparison of liturgical books and, 158–65, 159–64; gradual and, 241–44, 242, 286; introit and, 129; offertory and, 438n21; sanctorale and, 158–65, 171–73; Vat lat 5319 and, 171–73
Bodmer 74 (gradual of 1071), 152, 17c
Boe, John, 292–93
Boniface (saint), 75
Boniface IV (pope), 11, 88, 155, 166, 167, 187–88
Byzantine influence: alleluia and, 252–60, 274–79, 371; communion and, 45, 327; Dedication festival and, 187–88; Gallican rites and, 71–73; koinonicon and, 327–28; offertory and, 323–24; transmission of, 259–60

Caedmon (monk), 419n48
Caeli enarrant (gradual), 228, 229
Caesarius of Arles, 61, 62, 66, 71, 74
Callewaert, Camille, 439n12
Canons of Basil, 43
Cantabo domino (communion), 344, 347
Cantate dominum cantate (alleluia), 268, 269
Cantate dominum quia (alleluia), 268, 269
cantatorium (libellus), 222, 249
Cantemus domino (tract), 55–56, 293

Index / 457

canticle tracts, 283–84, 292–95
capitulary, 113
Carolingian gradual. *See* Blandin manuscript
Carpe, William D., 416n39
Cassian of Marseilles, 250
Cassiodorus, 251
"cathedral office," 38
Celestine I (pope), 79–81, 300
Charles the Bald, 98
Chavasse, Antoine, 214
Cheroubikon (cherubic hymn), 71–73, 323–24
Christus factus est (gradual), 235–36, 239, 247, 366
Christus qui natus est (communion), 392, 393
Chrodegang of Metz, 15, 75–76, 94–95, 396, 402
Chrysostom, John (saint), 3, 37–38, 39, 43, 46–47, 48, 50–51, 54, 57
church year, 35–36; calendric vs. festal, 149–51; placement of Advent in, 146–49, 151, 153; quadripartite structure of, 13
Circuibo (communion), 345
Circuibo et immolabo (communion), 344
Claire, Jean, 62, 273
Claudianus Mamertus of Vienne, 112, 113
Clement of Alexandria, 22, 29, 55, 407n9
collecta prayers, 168
Comedite pinguia et bibite mulsum (communion), 143, 144, 344, 348
communion, 326; Advent-Christmas series, 137–40, 138, 329–31; annual cycle and, 220–21; antiphon-communion and, 337–38, 341–43, 422n20; Ember Days and, 142–44, 143, 184–85, 348–49; in fourth century, 42–45; gospel-communion and, 328, 334–39, 337, 349–52; Lent and, 6, 331–39, 337, 368; Lenten Thursday, 134–37, 134, 235–36; Lenten weekday chants, 331–36,

332–33; musical settings of, 7–8; origins of, 327–29; Paschaltime, 339–43, 340, 369–70; post-Pentecostal, 343–49, 344; psalmic, in fourth century, 42–45; responsory vs. antiphon and, 341–42; Roman vs. Byzantine, 327–28; Roman vs. Frankish, 350–52; sanctoral, 349–54; temporal assignment and, 208; texts and, 6–7, 8, 248–349, 339, 341; unique vs. shared assignment and, 143–44, 143, 349–50; variable psalmody and, 327
Confessio et pulchritudo (introit), 126, 136
Confitemini domino quoniam bonus (alleluia verse), 270–72, 271, 389–90, 390
Confortamini, deus noster . . . (offertory), 144, 145, 146
Connolly, Thomas, 380
Conomos, Dimitri, 328
Constantine the Great (Roman emperor), 4, 27–28
Constitues eos (offertory), 175, 179
continuity of liturgical assignment: Advent-Christmas communions and, 330; first chant books and, 69, 117–18; between fourth and seventh centuries, 53–58; gradual and, 224–26; offertory and, 311, 313–14; Paschaltime offertories and, 316; sanctoral communions and, 352–53
Corinthian church (first century), 26–27
Council of Clovesho, 94–96
Council of Vaison, 71
Crocker, Richard, 380–81, 393–94, 396
Cullin, Olivier, 49, 410n36, 434n3
Cyprian of Carthage, 23
Cyriacus (saint), 166
Cyril of Jerusalem, 42, 44

Damasus I (pope), 80, 81
Da pacem domine (introit), 199, 200, 212, 215

d'Arezzo, Guido. *See* Guido d'Arezzo
De caeco (communion), 334, 335
Dedication of Sancta Maria ad Martyres ("Dedication" festival), 155–56, 166, 167, 187–90, 427n35
De fructu (communion), 346
De Lazaro (communion), 334, 335
De necessitatibus (tract), 284, *284*, 287
Deo omnis (offertory), 310, 312, 313
De profundis (offertory), *319*, 321, 322
De profundis (tract), 291
De Samaritana (communion), 334, 335
Deshusses, Jean, 168–69
Deusdedit (pope), 88
Deus deus meus (tract), 285, 286, 287, 291, 295
Deus dum egredereris (introit), 204–5, *204*
Deus enim firmavit (offertory), 310–11, *310*
Deus tu convertens (offertory), *310*, *311*
Dextera domini (offertory), 313
Dicit dominus (communion), 7, 139, 140, 329, *330*
Dicit dominus implete (communion), *138*
Dico vobis (communion), 344, 347
Dies sanctificatus melody type, 5, 6, 254, 275, 277–78, 371
Diffusa est (gradual), 182, 184
Diffusa est (offertory), *182*, 183, 184
direct psalmody, 48–53, 324
Dix, Gregory, 28
Domine audivi (tract), 287, 288, 295
Domine deus (gradual), 242, 244
Domine deus (offertory), 322–23, 325, 370, 427n35
Domine exaudi (gradual), 242, 244
Domine exaudi (tract), 287, 288, 295
Domine firmamentum (communion), 344, 347
Domine memorabor (communion), 344, 346
Domine quinque talenta (communion), 350

Domine refugium (gradual), 242, 244
Domine si tu es (communion), 350–53
Domini memorabor (communion), 346
Dominus dixit (introit), 56, 382–83, *383*
Dominus Jesus (communion), 8, 338–39, 368
Dominus regnavit decorem (alleluia), 257–58, *258*, 276, 432n13
dromos (racecourse), 195
Duchesne, Louis, 45–46, 79
Dum clamarem (introit), 237–38, 366–67
Dyer, Joseph, 86, 298, 302, 377, 437n9

early Christian church: "directness" of, 27–29; fourth-century censures and, 408n23; morning Eucharist and, 24–27, 33; preconditions for liturgical proper and, 19–21, 32–33; psalmody and, 25–27; song at ritual meals and, 21–24, 33
Easter: alleluia and, 270–72, 274, *275*; borrowed vs. original chants and, 8, 316–18; canticle-tracts of, 283–84, 292–95; discontinuity of liturgical assignment and, 55–56; tract and, 283–84, 289–90; vesper alleluias and, 257
Ecce advenit (introit), 209
Ecce quam bonum, 63
Ecce quam bonum (gradual), 242, 244
Ecce sacerdos (gradual), 231, 232, 233
Ecce virgo concipiet (communion), 143, 144, 182, 184–85, 330, 331, 386–89, *387*, *389*
Ecclesiastical History of the English People (Venerable Bede), 89–93
Eduxit dominus (introit), 199, 200, 203–5
Eduxit eos dominus (introit), 199, 200, 203–5
Ego autem (introit), 208, 209
Ego autem (offertory verse), 303–4, *304*, 305–9, *308*, 314–15
Ego clamavi (communion), 344, 347

Ego dixi domine (gradual), 242, 243
Ego sum pastor bonus (communion), 340, 342
Ekenberg, Anders, 69
Ellard, Gerald, 109, 420n60
Ember Days (*quattuor tempora*), 142–46; alleluia and, 144–46, *145*; communion, 142–44, *143*, 184–85, 348–49; gradual and, 144–46, *145*; introit and, 142–44, *143*; offertory and, 144–46, *145*; tract and, 284, 287, 290, 296
Emitte spiritum (alleluia), *145*, 146
Ephraem Syrus, 32, 187
Eucharist, celebration of, 24–25
Eusebius of Caesarea, 113
evangeliary chronology, 113–16. *See also* lectionary, development of
evangeliary of 645. *See* PI-type evangeliary
Exaudi deus (offertory), 303–9, *306*, *307*
Exaudi domine (offertory), 309
Excita domine (alleluia), 371
Excita melody type, 254, 275, 277, 278, 371
Exiit sermo (gradual), 223, 227
Ex ore infantium (introit), 209
Expositio brevis antiquae liturgiae gallicanae (attributed to Pseudo-Germanus), 69–71
Ex sion (gradual), 232, 234
Exultate deo (introit), *143*, 144

Factus est (introit), 198, *199*, 201
Factus est dominus (offertory), 314
Factus est repente (communion), 7
Ferrari, Guy, 82
festivals, annual cycle of: institution of, 101–2; liturgical year and, 149–51; as precondition for sung Mass Proper, 356, 357–59
Fili, quid fecisti nobis sic (communion), 138, 140
Fili quid (communion), 329, *330*
Fischer, Balthasar, 30
Fischer, Bonifatius, 294

"fixity means antiquity" (axiom), 154, 266
Fore-Mass psalmody, 41, 45–58, 356–57; alleluia and, 250–52; evidence from *Liber pontificalis*, 79–80, 85; Gallican evidence and, 65–71; Gregory the Great and, 85–86; later fourth century and, 356–60; number of psalms, 45–47; origins of, 47–48; origins of the Mass Proper and, 24–25, 36, 40–42, 53–58, 356–57; as responsorial vs. direct, 48–53, 281–83, 295
formulaicism: gradual and, 227–29, 233; Gregorian chant and, 201–7, *203*; introit and, 201–7, *203*, 221, 428n12,14; tract and, 287, 289; transmission of chant and, 207, 228, 379
Frankish manuscripts: alleluia assignments and, 261–66, *262*, *264–65*; canticle tract and, 294; D-2 tracts and, 287–88; eighth-century Roman repertory and, 125–33; G-8 canticle-tracts and, 294–95; gradual and, 244, 246, 294; Mass antiphoner and, 110–11; stability of assignments and, 260, 261, 431n25. *See also Sextuplex*
Frere, Walter Howard, 110–11, 154–57, 179, 266

Gaillac manuscript, 305–9
Gaudeamus (introit), 201–2, *202*
G-8 tracts, 289–95, *290*, *296*, 367
Gelasian sacramentary, 105–6
Gelasius I (pope), 105
Gennadius (Gallican writer), 65
Georgian Lectionary, 66
Germanus of Paris (saint), 69, 414n18
Gevaert, François-Auguste, 2
gloriosum officium (office), 257–60
gospel-communion, 328, 334–39, *337*, 349–52
gradual: Advent-Christmas and, 231–35, *232*, 247; alleluia and, 250–51; antiphoner and, 73; canticle tract

gradual (continued)
and, 294–95; chronology of Advent Project and, 364, 365, 366–68, 369; compared with introit, 247–48; compositional planning and, 140, 141, 142, 233; Ember Days and, 144–46, 145; Fore-Mass psalmody and, 51, 357; formulaicism and, 227–29; Greek *prokeimenon* and, 254, 256–57; Hadrianum and, 169–70; Lent and, 235–39, 366, 367–68; musical characteristics of, 226–31; offertory and, 318–19; Old Roman vs. eighth-century repertory, 125–33; *Ordo romanus I*, 222; origins of, 223–26; Paschaltime and, 239–40; post-Epiphany chants and, 231, 233, 234, 235; post-Pentecostal series and, 240–44, 242, 318–19, 369, 379; Roman vs. Gregorian versions, 226–31; sanctoral, 244–46; schola cantorum and, 246–48; in seventh-century Rome, 246–48; style and, 399; temporal assignment and, 208, 231–44; unique vs. shared assignment and, 238–39, 245, 246; verses of, 303–9

Gregorian sacramentary, 106–7; Advent and, 149; canticle tract and, 293–94; Dedication festival and, 187, 188, 189; redactions in, 107–9; sanctorale and, 168–70, 173. *See also* Hadrianum sacramentary; Paduensis Gregorian sacramentary; Trent Gregorian sacramentary

Gregory I (Gregory the Great; pope), 2, 61, 62, 88, 105; alleluia and, 251–52, 261, 266; chant development and, 11, 84–86, 154–55; deacons and, 84–85, 224; evangeliary of, 114–15, 115–16; Gregorian legend and, 96–98; mission to England, 89, 93; monks and, 84, 88, 373–74; sanctorale and, 166; schola cantorum and, 86–89, 359–60; vocal display and, 85, 224

Gregory II (pope), 2, 8–9, 11, 96–98, 133, 134, 136, 326; communion series and, 331–32; variant in text on, 83

Gregory III (pope), 12, 83, 97, 326, 373–74

Gregory of Tours, 62, 67, 70–71, 72, 73, 74; *Historia Francorum*, 84

Gregory the Great. *See* Gregory I

Guido d'Arezzo, 243, 363

Gustate et videte (communion), 344, 345

Hadrian (pope), 107, 168
Hadrian (saint), 167
Hadrianum sacramentary, 107, 149, 372; Advent in, 148; comparison of liturgical books and, 158–65, 159–64; gradual and, 169–70; *Hucusque* preface to, 133–34; Marian festivals and, 186; prayer sets in, 107–8; sanctorale and, 158–65, 168–70, 189, 426n7
Haec dies (alleluia), 255, 256
Haec dies (gradual), 54, 57, 228–29, 237, 239–40, 256, 282, 365, 370, 386
Hallel, singing of, 19
Hansen, Finn Egeland, 298
Hartker antiphoner, 98
Helisachar (Carolingian scholar), 360–61, 374
Hesbert, René-Jean, 127, 223, 244, 261, 286, 287
Hierusalem surge (communion), 138, 141
Hilary (subject of lost Augustinian tract), 41, 43–44, 299
Hiley, David, 443n25
Hippolytus (Roman presbyter), 22–23, 77
Historia ecclesiastica (Venerable Bede), 62
Hi sunt qui (alleluia), 262
Hoc corpus (communion), 338–39
Hodie scietis (gradual), 232, 234, 365
Hodie scietis (introit), 209
Honora dominum (communion), 343, 344, 345, 346

Honorius (pope), 88, 166–67
Hormisdas (pope), 79
Hucke, Helmut, 243, 280, 281, 287, 296–97, 338, 376, 381
Hughes, David, 5, 219, 377, 382, 394
Hugh of St. Victor, 273
Huglo, Michel, 338

In die sollempnitatis (offertory), 316, 317
In excelso (introit), 130, 131
Inmittet angelus (offertory), 321
In omnem terram (gradual), 54–55, 256
In salutare tuo (communion), 182, 185, 344, 346
In splendoribus (communion), 138, 139–40, 380, 383–84, 383, 385
introit, 195–221; Advent-Christmas season, 129–33, 130, 208–9, 209; annual cycle and, 216–18, 220–21; chronology and, 9, 365–67, 368; compared with gradual, 247–48; compositional planning and, 220; Ember Days and, 142–44, 143; formulaicism and, 201–7, 203, 221; Lent and, 126–28, 126–27, 205, 209–10; melodic uniqueness and, 198–201; Office antiphons and, 120; *Ordo romanus I* and, 195; origins of, 196–98; Paschaltime, 203, 205–7, 211, 379; post-Pentecostal, 211–15, 212, 366–67; Roman and Frankish, 125–33, 126–27, 130; similar openings and, 199, 200; stational system and, 196–97; stylistic homogeneity and, 198–201, 220–21; textual adjustment and, 213, 215–20, 366–67, 429n23; uniqueness of assignment and, 141–42, 143, 207–8, 210–11, 218
Invocabit (introit), 286

Jacta cogitatum (gradual), 237
James the Deacon (singer), 89–90
Jeffery, Peter, 79–81, 155–56, 157, 294, 417n16

Jerome (saint), 3, 43, 49, 50, 58, 79, 81, 82
John (archicantor of St. Peter's), 91–92
John (bishop of Jerusalem), 42, 44
John Hymonides ("John the Deacon"), 15, 97–98, 373–74, 396, 402
John of Syracuse, 86
Jubilate deo (introit), 204–5, 204
Jubilate deo omnis (offertory), 310, 310, 312
Jubilate deo universa (offertory), 310, 310
jubilus: as musical phenomenon, 270, 273–74; as term, 272–73
Judaism: Ark of the Covenant and, 440n23; musical continuity with Christianity and, 407n10; psalmodic practices, 30–32
justice, as post-Pentecostal theme, 185, 321–22, 343, 344, 346–47, 370
Justinian I, 60, 61
Justin Martyr, 24–25, 26, 29, 33, 40, 112
Justus ut palma (gradual), 227
Justus ut palma (offertory), 310

Karitas dei diffusa (introit), 210, 211
Klauser, Theodor, 115, 116, 187–88

Laetetur cor (introit), 126, 136, 143, 144
Laetetur Hierusalem (introit), 210
Last Supper, 19, 21–24, 32, 356
Laudate dominum (tract), 272, 284, 284, 289–92, 293, 295, 296
Laudate dominum omnes gentes (alleluia), 268, 269
Laudate dominum quoniam (alleluia), 268, 269
la–ut pitch sets, 384
lectionary, development of, 65–66, 111–17, 360
lector vs. schola chant, 62–65, 224, 246, 284, 359, 376–77
Lent: chronology of Advent Project and, 367–69; communion and, 6, 331–39, 337, 368; gradual and,

Lent (*continued*)
235–39, 247, 366, 367–68; introit and, 126–28, *126–27*, 205, 209–10; offertory and, 313–16, 368–69; tract and, 285–88, 291, 295–96; weekday communion chants, 332–33; weekday psalmic series, 133, 368

Lenten Thursdays, 133–37, 235–36; borrowed vs. original chants and, 134–37, 238–39, 247, 429n18, 431n16; establishment of, 8–9, 333–34

Leo I (Leo the Great; pope), 62, 77–78, 105

Leo II (pope), 97, 168, 190–91

Leo III (pope), 83

Leonine sacramentary (Veronensis), 105, 106

Leo the Great. *See* Leo I

Levy, Kenneth, 42, 303, 304, 377, 441n5

Liberasti nos (gradual), 242, 243, 244

Liber pontificalis, 11, 12, 62; early Roman chant and, 79, 81, 87; Lenten Thursdays and, 133; Marian festivals and, 186–87; monasteries and, 82–84; offertory and, 300; sanctorale and, 166–67, 172, 190–91

Lowe, Bernard, 68

Lutum fecit (communion), *333*, 336

Lux fulgebit (introit), 209

Maban (singer), 92–93

Magnificat antiphon, 341

Maiani, Brad, 341, 342, 368

Malloy, Rebecca, 437n19, 438n22

Marian festivals, 182–87, *182*

Martimort, Aimé Georges, 45–46

Mass of the Faithful, and origins of the Mass Proper, 40–41

Memento nostri domine (introit), 130, 131

Memento verbi tui (communion), 344, 346

Mense septimo (communion), 344

Mense septimo festa celebratis (communion), *143*, 144, 348

Miserere mei; Misit (gradual), 230

Misit dominus (gradual), 231, 232

mode-5 pitch clusters, 385

monastic rules, 61–62

Monte Cassino Office, 119, 250

Morin, Germain, 142

Musaeus of Marseilles, 65, 112, 117–18

musical memory, 219–20, 363, 366, 373

Mystagogical Catechesis (Cyril of Jerusalem?), 42, 44

Narrabo omnia (communion), 344, 347

Nemo te (communion), *333*, 336

Nemo te condemnavit (communion), 335, 336

Niceta of Remesiana, 39, 47, 300

Non vos relinquam (alleluia), 5, 6

Nos autem (introit), 365, 366

Notker of St. Gall, 15, 98, 396, 402

Nowacki, Edward, 219, 378, 391

offertory, 298–325; Advent-Christmas season and, 309–13, *310*; annual cycle and, 325; characteristics of, 302–4, 323–24; chronology of Advent Project and, 368–70; compositional planning and, 141, 142; dating of, 324–25; Ember Days and, 144–46, *145*; Lent and, 313–16; origins of, 299–302, 323–24; Paschal-time, 316–18, *317*, 369–70; post-Pentecostal, 318–21, *319*; Roman vs. Gregorian versions of, 305–9; sanctoral cycle and, 322–23; variable psalmody and, 323–24; verses in, 303–9, 324

Office, 38, 81–84, 324; communion and, 338, 341, 342; introit of the Mass and, 119–20; Mass Proper and, 2, 373–74, 379–80; Roman vs. Gregorian versions and, 391–92; schola and, 373–74; transmission and, 378–80

O kyrios (alleluia), 252–53, *253*, 257–58, *258*, 276

Old Gelasian sacramentary: Advent and, 147–49, *148;* comparison of liturgical books and, 158–65, *159– 64;* sanctorale and, 158–65
Old Roman graduals, 125–33
Omnes de Saba (gradual), 231, 232, *234, 235*
Omnes gentes (introit), 129, 130, 131, *211, 212, 213*
Omnia que fecisti (introit), *212,* 215
Omnis terra (introit), *130,* 131
Oportet te (communion), *332,* 334, *336, 337*
Oratio mea (offertory), 322–23, *325*
Ordo XIIIA, 150–51, 153
Ordo XIV, 150–51
Ordo XXVII, 288
Ordo XXXB, 288
Ordo romanus I, 4, *41;* alleluia and, 249; choral song and, 395; communion and, 327; gradual and, 222; introit and, 195; offertory and, 298–99, 300–301, 323; schola and, 86–87; tract and, 280
Ostende melody type, 254, 275, 277, *278, 371*
Ostende nobis (alleluia), 371
Ostende nobis domine (gradual), *234,* 365
Ott, Caspar, 298, 303, 305

Pachomius (ascetic), 37
Paduensis Gregorian sacramentary, 107–8, 149; comparison of liturgical books and, 158–65, *159–64;* Marian festivals and, 186; sanctorale and, 158–65, 168–70
Panem de caelo (communion), *344, 346*
Panis quem ego, 344, 345
Pascha nostrum (alleluia), 257, *258*
Pascha nostrum (communion), 339, *340*
Pater si non potest (communion), 338–39, 390–91, *390, 391*
Paulinus (bishop), 89
Paul the Apostle (saint), 26–27, 29, 31–32

Petite et accipietis (communion), *340, 341*
Philo of Alexandria, 49
Pietschmann, Petrus, 437n20
PI-type evangeliary: Advent and, *148,* 149; communion and, 334; compared liturgical books and, 158–65, *159–64,* 173; Dedication festival and, 187, 188, *189;* Gregorian evangeliary and, *114–15, 115–* 16; sanctorale and, 158–67, 188, 426n19
Planchart, Alejandro, 386
Populus sion (introit), *209*
post-Pentecostal series: alleluia and, 267–70, *268,* 275; chronology of Advent Project and, 369; communion and, 7, 343–49, *344;* establishment of annual cycle and, 358; gradual and, 240–44, *242,* 318–19, 369, 379; introit and, 211–15, *212,* 366–67; offertory and, 318–21, *319, 323;* Sunday after Pentecost and, 135–37; themes in chants of, 321–22, 343–47, *344*
Posuerunt (communion), 352
Posuisti (communion), 354
Pretiosa (gradual), 431n27
prokeimenon, 254, 256–57, 433n17
Prope est (gradual), *232,* 233
Prope est dominus (gradual), *145, 146*
Prope esto (introit), *209*
Psalm 21, 285–86
Psalm 33, 44–45, 327
Psalm 90, 285–86
Psalm 117, 282, 370
psalmody: communion, in fourth century, 42–45; Fore-Mass and, 41, 45–58; late-fourth-century Rome and, 77–89; monastic, 36–39; at pre-Eucharistic service, 25–27. *See also* entries at Psalm; Fore-Mass psalmody; responsorial psalmody
psalmody *in directum:* responsorial psalmody and, 281–83, 295; tract and, 280–82, 294–96. *See also* tract

Psalter of St-Germain-des-Prés, 57, 68–69, 105, 430n13; first chant books and, 117–18; gradual and, 236–37, *237*, *239*, *244*
Pseudo-Germanus of Paris, 62, 69–71
Puer Jesus (communion), *138*, *139*, *329*, *330*
Puer natus est (introit), *209*

Quasten, Johannes, 71–72
quattuor tempora. *See* Ember Days
Qui biberit (communion), *333*, *336*
Qui habitat (tract), 284, *284*, 285, 286, 287, 288, 291, 295
Qui manducat (communion), *344*, *345*, *382*, *383*, 384–86, *386*
quinquagesima, 357–58
Qui posuit fines (alleluia), *268*, *269*
Qui regis (tract), 290–91, *290*, *296*
Qui sanat contritos (alleluia), *268*, *269*, 434n30

Ratcliff, Edward, 70
Recordare mei (offertory), *319*, *322*, *370*
re-fa pitch set, 382–84, *383*, *385*, 386–89
Reges Tharsis (offertory), 312
Respice domine (introit), *212*, *215*
responsorial psalmody, 117–18, 120–22, 324; alleluia and, 250–52; Fore-Mass and, 48–53, 85–86; Gallican evidence and, 65–71; gradual and, 121–22, 223–26; offertory and, 298–99, 302–4; psalmody *in directum* and, 280–83, 295; types of respond and, 302–3. *See also* Byzantine influence; lector vs. schola chant
responsory-communions, 180–81, 328, 341–43
Responsum (communion), *182*, *183*, *392*, *393*
responsum gradale. *See* gradual
Resurrexi (introit), *210*, *211*
Rorate caeli (introit), *129*, *130*, *185*

Sacerdotes eius (introit), *130*, *131*, *208*, *209*
Sacerdotes tui (introit), *130*, *131*
sacramentary: development of, 104–7, 360; lectionary and, 111–12; Roman vs. Frankish Gelasians and, 105–6; types of, 105; vs. stability of antiphoner, 109–11
sacrifice, as post-Pentecostal theme, 321–22, 343–47, *344*, *370*
"sacrifice-eucharist" communion set, 343–47
St. Martin's Fast, 147
St-Yrieix manuscript, 305–9
Salus populi (introit), *212*, *215*
Sanctificavit moyses (offertory), *319*, *319*, *321*, *323*, *325*
sanctorale: absence of calendric patterns and, 180–81; alleluia and, 278–79; communion and, 328, 349–54; comparison of liturgical books and, 158–65, *159–64*; dating principles and, 154–57; "Dedication" festival and, 155–56; *Dies* melody type and, 278; gospel communions and, 349–52; gradual and, 244–46; introit and, 218; liturgical books and, 157–73; Marian festivals and, 182–87; offertory and, 322–23; Paschaltime, 158–59, 207; post-Christmas feasts and, 426n7; psalmic communions and, 352; textual adjustment and, 217; tract and, 292, 296; transmission to the Franks and, 245–46; unique and shared chants in, 173–80, *174–78*, 182–85, 218, 244, 246, 278, 349–50; Vat lat 5319 and, 158–65, *170–71*, *173–80*, *174–78*
Sanctoral Project, 11–12; chronology of, 370; creation of Mass Proper and, 361; dating of, 190–91; eminence patterns and, 180
Sanctus, and later fourth-century Mass, 42
Scapulis suis (communion), *286*, *387*

Scapulis suis (offertory), 286
schola cantorum, 2, 64, 75–76, 76, 86–89, 195; Advent and, 10–11, 151–52; chant prior to establishment of, 376–77; communion and, 328; division of labor and, 364; establishment of, 86–89, 359–60; Fore-Mass psalmody and, 283; gradual and, 246–48; intentions of, 393–99; introit and, 366–67; lector vs. schola chant and, 62–65, 224, 246, 284, 359, 376–77; monastic choirs and, 122, 342; Office and, 373–74; popes and, 301–2; post-Pentecostal offertories and, 318–21; relationships among clerical groups and, 122, 342; responsorial psalmody and, 120–22; Sanctoral Project and, 181; textual adjustments and, 219; tract and, 285; transmission to the Franks and, 94–95; transmission within Rome and, 377
Sciant gentes (gradual), 242, 244
Scio cui credidi (introit), 422n20
Scrutinies, 236, 334–36
sectiones, 113
Sederunt principes (gradual), 232, 233
Sed sic eum (gradual verse), 227
Septuagesima Sunday, 291–92
Sergius I (pope), 2, 9, 11, 12, 108, 152, 302, 359; completion of the Mass Proper and, 326, 372; Hadrianum and, 169–70; Marian festivals and, 186; sanctorale and, 168, 179–80, 190, 191; schola cantorum and, 87, 359, 377
Severinus (saint), 166–67
Sextuplex, 261–63; alleluia assignments and, 261–66, 262, 264–65; Lenten introits and, 125–33; sanctoral gospel communions and, 350–51. *See also* Hesbert, René-Jean
Sicut cervus (canticle tract), 55–56, 293–94
Si iniquitates, 212, 214

Sint lumbi vestri (communion), 351–52, 353
Sitientes venite (introit), 210
Sixtus III (pope), 82
Smith, John A., 31, 407n10
Snow, Robert, 380
Speciosus forma (gradual), 232, 233, 235, 237, 365, 430n13
Spiritus domini (alleluia), 145, 146
Spiritus domini (introit), 210, 211
Spiritus qui (communion), 340, 341
Spiritus sanctus (communion), 340, 341
Spiritus ubi (communion), 143–44, 143
Spiritus ubi vult (communion), 340, 341
Stäblein, Bruno, 96–97, 111, 375
Statuit ei dominus (introit), 199, 200
Steiner, Ruth, 14
Stephen II (pope), 94–95, 375, 416n40
Stephen of Aeddi (singer), 90–91
Strabo, Walafrid, 97
Suscepimus (gradual), 182, 183
Suscepimus (introit), 182–83, 182, 184

Tecum principium (gradual), 232, 234, 237, 240, 365
Te decet humnus (alleluia), 258
Tenuisti manum (gradual), 237, 286–87
Tertullian of Carthage, 21, 25–27, 30, 34, 49, 435n4
textual adjustment, 13–14, 103–4; Christmastime offertories and, 310, 312–13; communion and, 330; gradual and, 237–38; introit and, 213, 215–20, 366–67, 429n23; offertory and, 315–16, 325, 368–69
Theodore I, 185
Theodore of Canterbury (saint), 90
Theodoric the Great, 61
Thodberg, Christian, 251, 252
Timebunt gentes (gradual), 231, 232, 241, 242, 243
Tollite hostias (communion), 344, 345

Tollite hostias (gradual), 237, 238–39, 424n17
"tonality" of Gregorian chant, 380–89
Toulouse manuscript, 305–9
tract, 280–97, *284*, *290*, *292*; canticle-tracts of Easter Vigil and, 292–95; conventional wisdom on, 280–82; D-2 modal designations, 283–88, 289; Fore-Mass psalmody and, 51; gradual and, 281–82, 286–88; G-8 tracts, 289–95, *290*; origins of, 282–83; sanctoral tracts, *292*, 296; Sunday series, 291–92, 295–96; transmission of Byzantine influence, 259–60
"Trecanum," 74
Treitler, Leo, 394, 396, 442n19
Trent Gregorian sacramentary, 108–9
Tribulationes (gradual), *145*, 146
Trisagion (hymn), 72–73, 196, 415n34
Troelsgaard, Christian, 433n17
"truncated psalm," 121
Tu es Petrus (communion), 354
Tui sunt caeli (offertory), *310*, 311, 314
Tu mandasti domine (communion), 344, 346
"two-chant" hypothesis, 111, 375–76, 392

Ultimo festivitatis (communion), 385, 386
Unam petii (communion), 344–45
Unam petii (gradual), 242, 244
Unguentum (communion), 352
Universi qui (gradual), 232, 234

van der Werf, Hendrik, 442n19
van Dijk, Stephen, 111, 375
Vaticana Latina 5319 (Vat lat 5319): alleluia and, 254–57, *255–56*, 267–70, *268*; Blandin and, 171–73; comparison of liturgical books and, 158–65, *159–64*; eighth-century Roman repertory and, 125–33; gradual and, 241, 242, 244; offertory and, 305–9; sanctorale and, 158–65, 170–71, 173–80, 351; unique sanctoral chants in, 173–80, *174–78*, *278*
Veni et ostende (introit), 129, *130*, 209
Venite exultemus (alleluia), 258
Venite filii (gradual), 235, 237
Veronensis. See Leonine sacramentary
Videns dominus (communion), 333, 336
Video caelos (communion), 7, *138*, 139, 140, 329, 330
Viderunt omnes (gradual), 232, 234, 235
Vidimus stellam (communion), *138*, 140
Vigilius (pope), 79
Vir erat (offertory), *319*, 320, 321, 322, 323, 325
Viri Galilei (introit), 210, 211
Vitalian (pope), 375
Vox in rama (communion), 330
Vultum tuum (introit), 177, 179, 182, 183–84, 185

Wagner, Peter, 1–2, 13, 251, 266, 280–81, 285, 297, 362
Wilfred (bishop), 90
Wilmart, André, 69
Würzburg epistolary, 116–17, 147–49, *148*, 157–58

Zachary (pope), 75
Zwinggi, Anton, 58

Text:	10/13 Aldus
Display:	Aldus
Composition:	G&S Typesetters, Inc.
Printing and binding:	Thomson-Shore, Inc.

ML
3088
.M35
2000